Planning Canadian Regions

Planning Canadian Regions

Gerald Hodge and Ira M. Robinson

UBCPress · Vancouver · Toronto

Printed in Canada on acid-free paper ∞

ISBN 0-7748-0850-0 (hardcover)
ISBN 0-7748-0851-9 (paperback)

National Library of Canada Cataloguing in Publication Data

Hodge, Gerald.
  Planning Canadian regions

  Includes bibliographical references and index.
   ISBN 0-7748-0850-0 (bound); ISBN 0-7748-0851-9 (pbk.)

  1. Regional planning – Canada. I. Robinson, Ira M. (Ira Miles), 1924- II. Title.

HT395.C3H62 2001   307.1′2′0971   C2001-911332-3

UBC Press acknowledges the financial support of the Government of Canada through the Book Publishing Industry Development Program (BPIDP) for our publishing activities.

Canadä

We also gratefully acknowledge the support of the Canada Council for the Arts for our publishing program, as well as the support of the British Columbia Arts Council.

UBC Press
The University of British Columbia
2029 West Mall, Vancouver, BC V6T 1Z2
(604) 822-5959
Fax: (604) 822-6083
E-mail: info@ubcpress.ca
www.ubcpress.ca

Dedicated to

Sharron Milstein
(G.H.)

and

Ruth Sarah MacDonald
(I.M.R.)

Contents

Figures and Tables

Figures

Tables

Preface

In this book we pursue an elusive, yet persistent, area of public policy in which Canadian planners have been practising and excelling for six decades. In rural and urban regions alike, this country's regional planning has been both innovative and diverse, tackling, among other problems, urban sprawl, regional economic disparities, and environmental conservation. Canadian regional planning has not always been effective nor has it always had the political support required to carry out its mandate. Yet, inconstant as its unfolding has been, regional planning has emerged time and again in Canada as the best perspective from which to approach extra-municipal problems as well as subprovincial and subnational dilemmas. Regional planning in Canada has evolved over the years in response to new spatial situations that now confront us, such as the emerging city-regions and the demand for sustainable development. Regional planning has been "irrepressible" in Canada, just as a British colleague, Urlan Wannop, found it to be in Europe.

Only a few countries have more experience with regional planning than does Canada, and these only by little more than a decade. Despite its persistence, regional planning experience in Canada has never been collated, much less evaluated. This field, in which both of us have practised and taught for most of our professional lives, needs to be examined, its essentials identified, and its directions (both past and present) illuminated, not least because of new cultural and political challenges already facing nations, regions, and communities. This is the task we set for ourselves.

Such a task, almost by definition, required more than our own personal resources and knowledge, and we want to acknowledge those who, often inadvertently and sometimes more extensively than they had anticipated, joined us in this task. They have enriched its outcome. We were helped immensely by regional planners across the country: Hugh Kellas of the Greater Vancouver Regional District, Richard Scott of the National Capital Commission in Ottawa, John Heseltine in Halifax, Hap Stelling in Fredericton, and Lynn Dale in Edmonton. Ben Hitchings, the senior planner with the Triangle J Council of

Governments in North Carolina, helped us understand some new trends in the United States, while Scott McAlpine at Grande Prairie Regional College and Professor Raphael Fischler of McGill University helped us with Canadian background. Peggy McBride of the University of British Columbia Planning Library, as usual, provided unstinting assistance, and the stellar help Mike Newman provided for computer problems cannot be underestimated.

We are indebted to anonymous reviewers for the care they took in reading the manuscript in its early and intermediate stages and for their observations and suggestions. We are especially grateful to Professor Ian Wight of the University of Manitoba, who, over the years between conception and completion of this text, provided us with many sharp and prescient comments. What he had to say was invaluable in producing the present version. Not least, we need to thank Peter Milroy, director of UBC Press, not only for his confidence in this project, but also his forbearance regarding its progress. At times, this story of regional planning must have seemed as elusive as the field it describes. We offer special thanks to our editors at UBC Press: Jean Wilson (our original acquisitions editor), Holly Keller-Brohman (who has managed and overseen the editing of the manuscript), and especially Randy Schmidt, who gave us valuable counsel during the development of the manuscript and kept us on track. There were others, too, whose names do not come easily to mind. To those overlooked here, as well as to those remembered, we extend thanks for their support, kindness, and help. Yet none of them is responsible for any errors of omission and commission that may have slipped in. That responsibility is totally ours.

Last, our families helped us on this journey in innumerable ways. Although there are insufficient means for us to show our gratitude, we wish it known nonetheless.

G.H., Denman Island, BC
I.M.R., Victoria, BC
February 2001

Acronyms

ACRA	Alberta Capital Region Alliance
ADA	Area Development Agency
ADB	Atlantic Development Board
ADF	Atlantic Development Fund
ALR	agricultural land reserve
ARDA	Agricultural Rehabilitation and Development Act; in 1966, the title was changed to Agricultural and Rural Development Act
BAEQ	Bureau d'aménagement de l'est du Québec
BCALC	British Columbia Agricultural Land Commission
BNA Act	British North America Act
CEA	cumulative effects assessment
CLI	Canada Land Inventory
CMA	census metropolitan area
CORE	Commission on Resources and Environment (British Columbia)
CUM	Communauté urbaine de Montréal
DREE	Department of Regional Economic Expansion
DRIE	Department of Regional and Industrial Expansion
EIA	environmental impact assessment
FBMP	Fraser Basin Management Program
FRED	Fund for Rural Economic Development
FREMP	Fraser River Estuary Management Program
GBI	Georgia Basin Initiative
GDA	general development agreement
GTA	Greater Toronto Area
GTB	Greater Toronto Bioregion
GTC	Greater Toronto Council
GTCC	Greater Toronto Coordinating Committee
GVRD	Greater Vancouver Regional District

GTSB	Greater Toronto Services Board
JBDC	James Bay Development Corporation
LMRPB	Lower Mainland Regional Planning Board
LRP	Livable Region Plan
LRSP	Livable Region Strategic Plan
MAPC	Metropolitan Area Planning Committee
MMC	Montreal Metropolitan Community
MMR	Montreal Metropolitan Region
MMRAA	Maritimes Marshland Rehabilitation Administration
MSERD	Ministry of State for Economic and Regional Development
MTAPB	Metropolitan Toronto Advisory Planning Board
MUC	Montreal Urban Community
MVA	Meewasin Valley Authority
NCC	National Capital Commission
NCR	National Capital Region
NDP	New Democratic Party
NRC	National Resources Committee
NRPB	National Resources Planning Board
OGTA	Office for the Greater Toronto Area
OPDQ	Office de planification et de développement du Québec
PAS	protected area strategy
PFRA	Prairie Farm Rehabilitation Act
PRRPC	Peace River Regional Planning Commission
RPA	Regional Plan Association
RPAA	Regional Planning Association of America
RPCs	regional planning commissions (Alberta)
STELCO	Steel Company of Canada
TCR	Toronto-Centred Region
TVA	Tennessee Valley Authority
WCS	World Conservation Strategy

Planning Canadian Regions

Introduction:
Regional Planning in Perspective

In the realm of Canadian public planning for spatial development, regional planning is only just reaching middle age, and, as with most public endeavours of the past half century, it has undergone significant change. Whereas six decades ago it was "drought assistance" and rehabilitation in the Prairies that challenged regional planners, as the new millennium begins we find concerns about resource use expressed in terms of "sustainable development," as, for example, in British Columbia's Fraser River Management Program. Another current perspective concerns the burgeoning, complex city-regions that already test planners' skills. They contrast with the more modest "metropolitan overspill" that, in 1940s Winnipeg, tested the skills of planners in Canada's first regional planning agency for metropolitan areas. And while regional planning for "conservation" sufficed as the goal for Ontario river basins in the 1940s, the operative concept by the 1990s was planning for "sustainability" and the more holistic "bioregion."

Many of the themes regional planners deal with today are new, but probably just as many have been recast over the past sixty years. Either way, the practice of regional planning has changed; indeed, it has had to change. On the one hand, it now has to deal with our expanded knowledge of the interrelations of social, economic, and natural elements of regions; on the other hand, our ideological needs and values have changed. Today, there is as much, if not more, concern for protecting a region's environment as there is for achieving its economic development. Further, the current milieu for making regional plans must now contend with situations that increasingly involve the participation of multiple stakeholders rather than only governments, public agencies, and planners.

Today's regional planning reflects the persistent need to employ the region as a platform in formulating and implementing public development strategies at the national, provincial, and subprovincial levels. This need has been evident since, at least, the national policies and programs for opening up the

Canadian West and linking it with railroads and a grain delivery system. With time, each decade brought its own spatial problems – drought, metropolitan overspill, river basin conservation, economic disparities, agricultural land loss, pressing energy needs, environmental degradation, vast urban growth – each with an insistent regional component in its resolution. And as regional problems have been tackled over the years, methods of regional planning and of regional governance have also changed. Yet a constant throughout has been something that Wannop (1995) also observed in Europe: the need to invoke the region as a planning stratagem has been, and remains, "an imperative" for public policy makers across Canada.

The persistent need for regional planning can be readily illustrated by arraying a selection of developmental situations that regional planning has dealt with in Canada, especially over the past half century. As well, its widespread use reflects the adoption of planning concepts and processes in the conduct of important aspects of public business. An appreciation of these basic planning concepts and how they are manifest in regional planning also needs to be lodged here; this will add to our understanding of the episodes of planning practice at the regional level that are reviewed in later chapters. Last, the need for regional planning is unlikely to diminish in this new century, but it is reasonable to expect that it will face new challenges. An outline of these challenges will provide a more complete perspective of how Canadian regional planning has developed and will likely develop in the future.

The Persistent Need for Regional Planning

The ongoing need for planning on a regional scale has manifested itself in two ways in Canada. The first was brought about by the vast and variegated terrain of this country, which demanded that we consider the interrelated desires and destinies of our regions while building a single, united nation in the northern half of North America (see Figure 1). The Confederation Bridge connecting Prince Edward Island to the mainland in the 1990s is among the most recent of such initiatives in Canadian history. It has counterparts in John Diefenbaker's vision of "roads to resources" in the North in the 1960s and, a century before that, in John A. Macdonald's "national dream" to link central Canada with the Maritimes and the West. These regional initiatives were, and continue to be, associated with the need for *nation building* – of embracing provinces, of fulfilling constitutional promises, of linking the industrial regions of Ontario and Quebec with the staples economies of the West and the Maritimes. In the regional planning terminology that was current in the 1960s, these initiatives represented efforts to make the "space economy" of Canada more "effective" (Isard 1960; Friedmann 1966a). Because nation building was the goal of these regional activities, the federal government took the lead role, as it did with its intense set of policies and programs aimed at erasing regional economic disparities between 1960 and 1980 (Brewis 1969; Savoie 1992). Suffice

Figure 1

Regions and selected urban areas of Canada

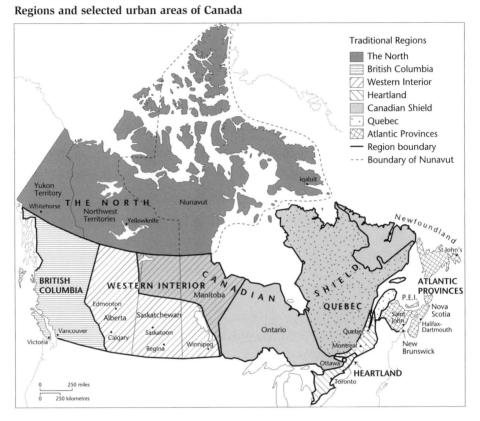

it to say that the planning invoked in these kinds of regional initiatives had a distinctive form, as later chapters will show.

The second manifestation of the regional planning imperative is the one most familiar in Canada today, and it is the one to which this text is mostly devoted. It derives primarily from the need for *province building*,[1] a need that arose most noticeably as the 1930s turned into the 1940s and the economic spatial organization of the country and its governance firmed up and population grew again, especially in cities. An urban industrial economy was developing strongly alongside a reinvigorated staples economy in many rural areas, and the regional issues that arose were mainly those concerned with the effective functioning of individual provinces – metropolitan growth, rural resources development, transportation links between regions, and the distribution of public services. Moreover, the jurisdiction over such issues lies primarily with the provinces. Regional planning today is, indeed, a product of the problems that were broached, the intergovernmental arrangements that were applied, and the style of practice that developed during this time of province building.

From a general perspective, the regional planning considered here is concerned with the interrelated fortunes of adjacent areas. It may come about because the growth in one area spreads its effects beyond its boundaries; or it may be the response to dealing with an environmental problem that affects many areas; or it may be to fulfil the goal of equally distributing the benefits of economic or social development. Or it may encompass all three of these broad purposes and more. However, regardless of its purpose, we need to recognize that regional planning efforts reflect responses to *publicly perceived* needs about problems of development, the spatial implications of which are extensive. As such, these efforts are public policy initiatives grounded in the milieu of government and political debate, and the form in which they are expressed is a reflection of the public mores of their time.

Expressions of the Need for Regional Planning

What we see in the overview of Canadian regional planning initiatives shown in Figure 2 is a confirmation of the repeated need, over the past sixty years, for regional planning in development situations. Significantly, these initiatives would not have come into effect without governmental sanction – in particular, provincial government sanction. When a province responds to a development need with a regional approach, this is tantamount to it revising its established allocations of authority (see Chapter 4). So a regional approach has to be of demonstrable benefit. Let us briefly examine some examples of this Canadian experience, for regional planning is not an abstract expression of need but, rather, a palpable response to real-world problems. Starting with one of the most recent examples, that of the regional Greenbelt around Ottawa, and working backward, we are able to see how different circumstances, along with different needs and settings, come together to reveal how regional planning operates.

National Capital Commission

In 1996, the National Capital Commission, which is mandated to plan for the 4,700-square-kilometre region around Ottawa, released its most recent plan for the well-known Ottawa Greenbelt, which encircles Ottawa about eight kilometres from Parliament Hill. The 20,000-hectare Greenbelt has been enhanced in the current plan to ensure a continuous natural environment. It will be increasingly ecologically oriented, with attention being paid to natural-area buffers around core natural areas and links between areas for maintaining the continuity of plant and animal life (see Chapter 8).

Peace River Regional Planning Commission

In the early to mid-1970s, the Regional Planning Commission for the Peace River Region, which covers 216,000 square kilometres in northwestern Alberta, began to prepare a plan for the development of the region's rich forest,

Figure 2

Major events in the evolution of regional planning in Canada

1. Early roots prior to institutionalization of regional planning
   - Parks development (1885-1920)
   - Commission of Conservation (1909-21)
   - Prairie Farm Rehabilitation Act (1935)
   - Rowell-Sirois Commission Report (1940)
   - Federal Advisory Committee on Reconstruction (1944)

2. Beginnings of formalized regional planning in the 1940s and 1950s
   - Metropolitan Planning Commission of Greater Winnipeg (1943)
   - Guelph Conference on the Conservation of Natural Resources of Ontario (1942)
   - Ontario's Conservation Authorities Act (1946)
   - Lower Mainland Regional Planning Board (1947), Capital (Victoria) Region Planning Board (1948), and four additional planning boards established in BC (1947-64)
   - Greber Plan (Plan for the National Capital)(1950)
   - District planning commissions in Edmonton (1950) and Calgary (1951)
   - Municipality of Metropolitan Toronto (1953)
   - National Capital Commission and National Capital Region (1958)

3. The 1960s and early 1970s: a period of intense activity

   (a) Federal economic development activities
   - Agricultural Rehabilitation and Development Act (ARDA) (1961)
   - Area Development Agency (1963), Atlantic Development Board (1962), Fund for Rural Economic Development (1966); ARDA expands its functions and title changed to Agricultural and Rural Development Act (1966)
   - Department of Regional Economic Expansion (1969)
   - General development agreements between the provinces and the federal government (1973)

   (b) Federal-provincial economic development initiatives
   - Mactaquac Regional Development Plan (New Brunswick)(1965)
   - Interlake Region Development Programme (Manitoba) (1966)
   - Lesser Slave Lake Program (Alberta) (1970)
   - Canada Land Inventory (1970)
   - South Saskatchewan River Development Project (1970)
   - Newfoundland Resettlement Program (1967-75)

   (c) Provincial activities in regional planning
   - Halifax-Dartmouth and County Regional Planning Commission (1964)
   - Regional districts established in BC (1965)
   - Ontario's Design for Development (1966), including Niagara Escarpment Plan and Toronto-Centred Region Concept
   - Nova Scotia and Alberta enact new planning acts (mid-1970s)

▶

- Agricultural Land Commission in BC (1973)
- Quebec establishes Commission de protection du territoire agricole (1978)
- Metropolitan-regional plans for Vancouver, Halifax-Dartmouth, St. John's (mid-1970s)
- Meewasin Valley Authority (Saskatchewan) (1979)

4. **The 1980s into the 1990s: Adjusting and retrenching**
- Demise of Ontario's Design for Development (1982)
- Department of Regional Industrial Expansion (DRIE) supersedes the Department of Regional Economic Expansion (1982)
- Regional planning function taken away from BC's regional districts (1983)
- Alberta regional planning commissions defunded (1993)

5. **Towards the new millennium: new mandates and partnerships**
- Community Futures organizations established in over 250 non-urban and First Nations regions (1989)
- Royal Commission on the Future of the Toronto Waterfront (Crombie Commission) formed (1989) and embraces the "bioregion" for planning purposes in its first report (1990)
- New Brunswick establishes Commission on Land Use and the Rural Environment to deal with rural sprawl and resource use (1992)
- Fraser Basin Management Program launched (including federal, provincial, regional, and First Nations governments (1992)
- British Columbia establishes the Commission on Resources and the Environment (CORE) to develop strategic regional land-use plans (1992)
- Regional Growth Strategies Act enacted in BC (1995)
- New Greenbelt Plan for Ottawa includes ecological components (1996)
- Mushuau Innu plan new community of Natuashish in Labrador (1998)
- Alberta Capital Regional Alliance (Edmonton) formed (1998)
- Montreal Metropolitan Community proclaimed (2000)

---

oil, gas, and mineral resources as well for the long-standing agricultural economy. The challenge the region's planners faced was to accommodate new resource development within environmental limits and without jeopardizing community life. The planners involved the people of the region in formulating key aspects of the plan, with the result that it came to embody strong policies to preserve good farmland and to minimize environmental degradation. In contrast to other plans of the time, it did not specify land-use allocations but, rather, provided a set of policies for development and a process by which the commission and its member municipalities could respond to proposals for development. In short, it was one of the earliest regional "strategic plans" in Canada (see Chapter 7).

Mactaquac Regional Development Plan

In 1964, the Mactaquac Regional Development Plan was prepared for a New Brunswick region subject to the province's electric power commission constructing a large hydroelectric power project on the Saint John River. This region's population had below-average incomes and education, farms that were often idle or non-productive, and forest resources that were held by absentee owners. The plan for this 4,000-square-kilometre region, stretching eighty kilometres along the river, was developed under the federal-provincial Agricultural and Rural Development Act (ARDA) and Fund for Rural Economic Development (FRED) programs. It provided for the relocation of 300 families from about 1,000 properties; shifting highways and bridges; establishing new industries and a new town; and instituting a development corporation to plan and manage land use, invest in infrastructure, and train workers for the new enterprises. Much of the plan was translated into action and represents a milestone in regional planning implementation in Canada (see Chapter 7).

Lower Mainland Regional Planning Board

In 1949, the Lower Mainland Regional Planning Board began to prepare a plan to cover a 3,500-square-kilometre region encompassing the Vancouver metropolitan area and its fringes. The prospects for rapid population growth in this region, as well as some of the unwelcome effects of that growth, were already evident. Valuable agricultural land was being built upon or set aside for future development, and new building in fringe areas was haphazard. The board was one of the first to use the term "urban sprawl" to describe what it saw in the expanding urban fringe. Over the next several years, the board's staff documented the problems of growth; projected the need for schools, industrial land, and highways; and assisted municipalities to plan for these changes. The regional plan they prepared envisioned a system of four regional town centres east and southeast of Vancouver that would concentrate development; they would be connected to the central city by rapid transit. The most recent plan for the region, prepared by the successor agency, the Greater Vancouver Regional District (GVRD) in 1996, has an additional four town centres to accommodate the continuing growth of what is now a city-region (see Chapter 9).

Two General Sources of Need

These four examples alone illustrate the point that the need for regional planning arises from two general sources. One is *the need to solve problems* associated with a particular project or ongoing development situation, as with the construction of the Mactaquac dam and the continuing encroachment of urban development on farmlands in the Lower Mainland. The other main need is *the desire to attain an improved regional situation*, as with the Ottawa Greenbelt Plan. Not uncommonly, the need may arise for regional planning to combine both the resolution of development problems and the achievement of a desired future, as in the Peace River Regional Plan.

Some Essential Characteristics of Regional Planning

Some of the main characteristics of regional planning are revealed by the four examples discussed above – the kinds of spatial settings where regional planning occurs, the types of problems it is called on to address, and the arrangements that are made for its operation. Thus, from Vancouver's fringes to New Brunswick's Saint John River Valley, regional planning involves areas of considerable size, from entire metropolitan areas to large resource regions. Although the actual size of what we call the "planning region" varies with the specific situation, as we see in these cases the area is larger than the boundaries of a single municipality but smaller than a province. Thus the first characteristic of regional planning is:

Regional planning is about responding to development needs that affect large areas for which no established governmental unit exists either locally or provincially. Regional planning is **large scale.**

The planning subject matter addressed in the four cases does not concern the design and regulation of the built environment (as is the case in city or community planning). Indeed, regional planning typically covers a wider array of concerns than single cities are usually able to deal with. For example, in the Mactaquac River Valley the needs ranged from dam construction and transportation relocations to providing new economic enterprises and training the residents to take advantage of them. In the Peace River Region economic matters were a concern but so were concerns about the environment and community life. Since large areas were under consideration, it mattered to the planners where various activities occurred in a region; it was important that everyone be able to enjoy their benefits and that their costs to all be minimized. Thus, the second characteristic of regional planning is:

Regional planning is concerned with the interrelated impacts of development on the location of social, physical, economic, and environmental facets of large areas. Regional planning is **interrelating.**

Not only does regional planning involve a full array of human concerns, social as well as physical and economic, but it also has a special concern with the relationship between human use and the natural landscape and environment. This characteristic of regional planning can be found in the earliest literature as well as in today's literature on bioregionalism and the stewardship of resources (see Chapter 1). In the past, this was often cited as achieving a "man/land harmony," an idea that is echoed in the contemporary notions of "bioregionalism" and "sustainable development." We see this in our examples of the Peace River and National Capital Regions. Thus, the third characteristic of regional planning is:

Regional planning incorporates a basic concern for the integrity of people and their place in the natural landscape. Regional planning requires **balance.**

But why should the residents of a region be concerned about the impacts of development? Why should it matter if agricultural land is lost to urban development on the Vancouver fringe? Or that there is adequate protection for the natural environment around Ottawa? Or that families relocated because of the Mactaquac Dam have a decent community environment to which to move? The broad answer to these questions is that regional planning intervention is what residents of these regions wanted. The decisions that were pursued in these cases represent deliberate choices about impending or actual problems and future conditions. Objectives had to be framed and debated before plans could be made in these regions; in other words, a *planning process* (i.e., a process to determine the best locations for various activities and projects) had to be conducted. In short, regional planning is about setting out the preferred order of priority for development. Thus the fourth characteristic of regional planning is:

Regional planning is about the preferred ordering of activities and facilities over large areas. Regional planning is **normative.**

But how do a region's priorities or objectives translate into such action as securing a greenbelt or protecting farmland? This is what we call the "implementation" of the regional plan and planning policies. And while it requires (usually provincial) authority to make a plan, implementation cannot be carried out without additional authority to make the needed decisions. Much of regional planning's successes and failures relate to the regional planning agency having sufficient governmental resources and authority to permit it to implement its plans, as we shall see in later chapters. Thus, the fifth characteristic of regional planning is:

Regional planning is made effective through the availability of sufficient resources and powers to implement planning priorities. Regional planning has ***implementation potential.***

These characteristics provide a useful threshold from which to begin considering the broader picture of regional planning, and they may be remembered by their respective keywords:

- large scale
- interrelating
- balance
- normative
- implementation potential

Now, we may usefully add a description of where and how regional planning has been used in Canada.

Types of Regional Planning in Canada

The spatial pattern of Canada's development is evident on almost any map (e.g., Figure 1). It consists of two broad components: first, a network of large cities stretching from coast to coast; and second, separating and bounding these cities, large areas that are predominantly rural. The large cities – twenty-five altogether – are designated as metropolitan areas, and at least one of these 100,000-plus population concentrations can be found in every province (except Prince Edward Island). Each is characterized by a core urban area surrounded by suburbs and, in the largest, by a further urbanizing fringe zone. The rest of Canada is primarily rural, or at least non-metropolitan, which means that it also contains small- and medium-sized cities and numerous towns and villages as well as low-density resource development areas. Regional planning in Canada has, thus, been used as a public strategy in these two distinctive spatial situations:

1 *Rural and non-metropolitan regions* of the country have seen regional planning used in various public efforts aimed at maintaining settlement systems, rejuvenating economies, and conserving resources. This is the focus of Part 2.
2 *Large urban and metropolitan regions* have seen regional planning employed in directing urban growth and development in viable, efficient, and harmonious patterns. This is the focus of Part 3.

The need for regional planning in both metropolitan and non-metropolitan regions arose concurrently, although for different reasons. These two approaches have often coexisted in adjacent regions and have sometimes overlapped, as in the case of planning for a city's countryside. While their paths and their practice developed quite distinctively, both metropolitan and non-metropolitan regions derive from the same roots and possess the same general characteristics: they are large scale, interrelating, balanced, normative, and have implementation potential. We shall briefly preview these two broad venues of regional planning in order to set the stage for descriptions of regional planning practice.

Regional Planning for Rural and Non-Metropolitan Regions

Regional planning for rural and non-metropolitan regions is quite diverse, no doubt because of the size of territory involved (about ten million square kilometres) and the inevitable diversity of regional situations within it. Nevertheless, three separate streams of rural-region planning practice emerged over the decades, which allows us to more readily grasp its diversity: first, there is practice aimed at maintaining and protecting rural regions and, especially, their communities; second, there is practice aimed at rural resource development and/or conservation; and third, there is practice aimed at rejuvenating rural economies. The term "rural" is used broadly in these descriptions to distinguish such regions and their regional planning practice from those that are largely urban and metropolitan. Rural regions may, and often do, include small- and medium-sized cities.

Rural-Region Planning and Community Maintenance

The rural areas that comprise the vast majority of Canada's space have a number of distinctive development problems, one of which focuses mainly on the future of the small communities we find throughout these regions. Decline in population, isolation, and a lack of housing services and transportation are often key concerns, as is the quality of the development that does occur. Local governments, where they exist in rural regions, are often too small and ill-equipped to confront such issues, and this has led to a wide array of responses across the country. Regional planning commissions in Alberta, district planning commissions in New Brunswick, county planning in Ontario, and regional districts in British Columbia are among the devices provinces have devised in response to the planning needs of these low-density regions. Important parts of this rural milieu are the regions that are home to Aboriginal peoples; here, special planning needs have increased efforts to develop appropriate planning approaches. The North is yet another special rural region requiring its own planning approach, partly due to Aboriginal land claims issues and partly due to the large scale and costs of development (see Chapter 5).

Economic Development Planning for Rural and Non-Metropolitan Regions

As any national economy develops it is inevitable that, given differences in resource endowments, population, and location, the various regions will develop at different rates and levels. So, as Canada's economy surged in the late 1950s and 1960s, disparities developed between regions, especially between urban and rural and non-metropolitan regions. With these disparities came strong political pressure for the federal government to redress regional imbalances. Thus, the federal government mounted a distinctive form of regional planning that was aimed mainly at the economic development of rural regions and their non-metropolitan urban centres – an effort that lasted for twenty-five years. It involved a wide array of federal programs, including aid to low-income agricultural and other resource regions (e.g., Newfoundland, Cape Breton Island, the Gaspé, Manitoba's Interlake region, and the Lesser Slave Lake region of Alberta). Growth pole strategies were employed to strengthen regional urban centres such as Moncton and Halifax. A plethora of acronyms emerged with these efforts – DREE (Department of Regional Economic Expansion), ARDA (Agricultural and Rural Development Act), FRED (Fund for Rural Economic Development), and so on. For a variety of essentially political reasons, this unusually vigorous period of federal involvement in regional planning came to an end in the 1980s (see Chapter 6), but it left behind a recognition of the importance of economic factors in regional planning (Economic Council 1977).

Rural-Region Planning for Resources Development, Conservation, and the Environment

Not surprisingly, in a country as rich in natural resources as Canada, foremost among instances of regional planning is a concern for resource development and use. Rural regions are, for the most part, natural resource-based regions, relying on the exploitation of timber, oil and gas, fish, minerals, scenic resources, or agricultural soils. Concern for resources in regional planning started formally with efforts to overcome drought in the Prairie region and continued with the planning and management of river basins in Ontario. Other instances include planning for the impacts of the Diefenbaker Dam in Saskatchewan in the 1960s and the recent sustainable development program mounted for the entire Fraser River Basin in British Columbia. Current analogies include programs to deal with the depleted fish stocks on both the east and west coasts and, especially, with the impacts on their resource communities. Through these efforts and dozens more, the essential feature has been the attempt to achieve a balance between resource development and human activities. More recently, such regional planning has incorporated strong concerns about both environmental degradation and the need to achieve a sustainable future for the regions involved (see Chapter 7).

Regional Planning for Metropolitan and City-Regions

The second general type of regional planning, and one in which Canada has been a world leader, deals with the seemingly inexorable tendency of large urban areas to increase in population and to extend their land needs into surrounding territories. This expansion contrasts with the regional planning for most rural regions, which has tended to deal with declines in population, the maintenance of existing balances of resources and population, or both. Herein lies a further reason for distinguishing these two broad types of regional planning.

The need for planning metropolitan regions and, more recently, for today's even larger city-regions, first made itself evident to Canadian regional planners in the early 1940s. The large cities in all provinces grew extensively in the wake of the resource development and industrial expansion occasioned by the Second World War. What began as the growth of a single city well within its municipal boundaries often became the growth of an urban area that was spreading beyond these legal confines to adjacent municipalities and beyond. The problems of one local government became the problems of several, and these governments began to involve the province in the search for solutions. In 1943, the Province of Manitoba established the first public metropolitan planning agency in Canada (perhaps in North America). Not long after, planning agencies would be established for the burgeoning metropolitan areas of Vancouver, Edmonton, and Calgary. The continent's first metropolitan planning agency within a formal metropolitan government, Metro Toronto, was established in 1953. Thus began the trend in metropolitan regions to "allow municipalities to do together what they cannot do alone," as a provincial minister in British Columbia said when establishing a new regional planning arrangement (Parr 1998). Today, the growth of several Canadian metropolitan regions is far exceeding previous expectations, so that we now need to think of each as a "city-region." This growth requires further adaptations of planning and governing strategies in order to deal with larger and much more complex urbanizing regions (see Chapters 8 and 9).

The Scope of Regional Planning Practice

So far we have conveyed the substantive scope of regional planning in Canada. Now, in order to more fully discuss the scope of regional planning, we must consider its milieu – where it fits within the realm of public planning, its relation to government and legislation, and the attributes of good practice.

Regional Planning as a Social Activity

Planning is an integral part of everyone's daily life: we are always in the process of choosing which activities to pursue and in which manner, but we are seldom aware of the process involved in making these daily choices. However, the larger the number of people impinged upon by the outcome of the choice, the more evident the process. This may be seen with regard to family decisions or those made by firms, communities, and governments. A great number of interests are affected by the outcome of government planning, and various preferences and needs must be accounted for. When public bodies plan, whether they are cities, provinces, regional planning commissions, or conservation authorities, their decisions reflect a composite of the preferences of the various interests involved (e.g., the state, citizens, corporations, and other political and social institutions) (Friedmann 1987).

Today, all levels of government and their subsidiary agencies undertake extensive planning processes in order to influence the outcome of development; but this was not always so. The tradition in Canada is, after all, based on a laissez-faire principle that assumes that decisions that households and firms make in their own interests will be in the best interests of all. All too often, however, the aggregate of these self-interests is not in the public interest but, rather, is unwittingly and systematically destructive. Garrett Hardin's (1977) well-known parable of the "tragedy of the commons" is a cogent example of such a failing within an open-ended social situation. Hardin discusses the destruction of the common grazing areas in medieval English villages. Typically, each herder, in an attempt to maximize his own self-interest and without regard for his/her neighbour's actions or the cumulative effect over time, grazed as many cattle on the common as was possible. The "common" land cost each herder nothing, so this was a reasonable decision to make. As a result, more and more cattle grazed on the common, thus destroying the pasture's regenerative capabilities and leaving all users poorer than before. A planned approach to this situation might have suggested a simple rationing system that would have redounded to the general benefit of all the herders. In today's terms, what occurred on the commons involved "externalities," or effects that spilled over from individual actions to adversely affect other people. This is what happens when what Snyder (1990) refers to as "common-pool resources" are abused because there is no clear rule for determining the use of shared resources. With this knowledge, today's regional planners increasingly have to expand the scope of community and individual involvement.

Contemporary analogies to the "tragedy of the commons" abound for regions and their common resource base. In a metropolitan region, for example, the individual actions of automobile users may cumulatively impair air quality. Or a new mining enterprise may discharge waste products into a region's streams, thus contaminating community drinking water. Or an industrial development initiative in an economically depressed region may attract workers only from outside the region, thereby causing housing shortages and not relieving local unemployment. Thus, a good deal of regional planning is as much about anticipating *potential* external effects as it is about responding to direct problems occasioned by externalities. Of course, many effects of development may not be known until well into the future, as we are coming to realize with regard to environmental impacts. Therefore, to a considerable extent, regional planning deals with *predicting* the problems, both anticipated and actual, associated with development proposals.

Regional Planning as Public Planning

Beyond solving real or anticipated problems, regional planning also addresses the goals of a region's residents. Thus, it fits within the general framework of most collective planning, and it involves four broad steps:

1 identify the desire to attain some goal (either to solve a problem and/or to achieve some ideal situation)
2 consider possible courses of action for attaining this goal or goals
3 identify and evaluate or predict the consequences that would follow from adopting various alternative courses of action
4 select the course of action that most nearly achieves the desired goal or goals.

This version of public planning (or, indeed, of more elaborate theoretical renderings) is, of course, highly simplified (Robinson 1972). However, at this point it is enough for us to know that these steps form the general basis for regional planning practice, which seeks to determine the implications and feasibility of achieving a region's goals and then selects the best course of action.

This orderly process was articulated a century ago by Patrick Geddes, often referred to as the "father of regional planning," who offered the following dictum to regional planners: "No Plan before Survey." He stressed the importance of first knowing a region's geography, history, economy, social conditions, and means of transportation and communications. He also advised planners that "survey and diagnosis must precede treatment" (Geddes 1968). Rather than considering these features individually, Geddes saw them as contributing to the whole of the region's functioning; as Gerecke (1988) put it in a review of Geddes' work, he understood their "integrative linking." (Chapters 1 and 2 provide a further context for Geddes' ideas.)

Regional planning is conducted either by governments or other public entities that are mandated to plan on behalf of the public. In the broad sense, then, regional planning is not different from other forms of public planning (e.g., that done by municipalities or by school districts). Both provincial and federal governments also engage in public planning, most notably in their annual budgets. These senior public entities have collateral governmental powers that permit them to plan, and they also have representative bodies (i.e., legislatures) that participate in and oversee the "planning" and have the requisite powers to carry out their plans. Subsidiary bodies such as municipalities and school districts, however, must receive or be delegated a mandate to carry out their planning. In constitutional terms, only the provincial and federal governments have the jurisdiction to make decisions about matters affecting their designated territories. This, as we shall see in later chapters, is a pivotal consideration in regional planning.

Regional Planning as a Public Normative Process

Besides being an orderly social process, regional planning is a normative process, meaning that it deals with establishing a course of action that takes into account many values and viewpoints. In any territorial unit with a complement of residents, firms, governments, and institutions, it is clear that each of these interests will have its own preferences and values and, therefore, that each will have a stake in the future of the region. It is primarily in the first and fourth steps of the so-called "synoptic" planning process (i.e., identifying goals and selecting the course of action) that planning is a public collective activity. This is when the various interests and stakeholders in the region are most explicitly involved in determining the goals to be sought and in selecting the means by which they are to be attained. These steps are among the most crucial and difficult in any planning endeavour. However, this collective input of preferences is what distinguishes public planning from private planning. Put another way, regional planning (or, for that matter, any public planning) intervenes in the value systems of all interests in a region and attempts to determine *norms* by which the various value orientations can be reconciled, whether they be economic, social, or environmental. In short, regional planning is a deliberate social activity that seeks to attain an array of goals through an orderly process of debate, analyses, and a set of proposals.

To accomplish its normative ends, regional planning must be conducted in the "public domain"; that is, as Friedmann (1987) says, in "a sphere of common discourse and concerns" supported by institutions and laws that regulate common conduct. It is through this "common discourse" that the competing values of the various participants in the region's planning can be resolved. Such a normative resolution in the public domain involves an inherently *political process*. The discourse that takes place allows the concerns of various interests to be blended into the region's plan, but the process by which this occurs can often be circuitous and protracted because of the diverse interests to be reconciled. Moreover, these interests do not, as regional planners once supposed, fit within a single rendering of the "public interest" (Meyerson and Banfield 1955; Friedrich 1962). Following Friedmann (1987; 1992), today's public domain for regional planning is more appropriately conceived of as comprising four overlapping domains – the state, civil society, the corporate economy, and the political community – in which the various regional interests array themselves according to their own core of formal and informal institutions.

Over the past decade, the normative scope of regional planning (and of all public planning) has been shifting to become more inclusive and to require planners to seek support and validation for policies and proposals from a network of interests inside and outside of the formal government. Every region has "multiple publics," to use Sandercock's (1999) phrase, each with its particular characteristics (including income, gender, age, ethnicity, and education as well as resource orientation, business links, workers, and owners) and the culture and values that accompany them (Tully 1995). Thus, in keeping with the postmodern idea that most concepts are usually "in flux" and have "blurred edges" (Wight 1999), regional planning has become more people-centred and collaborative. As will become evident in later chapters, various new modes of regional planning have been tried in recent years, including environmenteconomy roundtables, metropolitan forums, community facilitation, and resource co-management programs. Associated with the shift in the scope of participation, and in some ways responsible for it, has been a recognition that the substance of what regional planning deals with not only needs to be enlarged, but also better integrated; that is, a truly normative process must include all sectors (e.g., economic, physical, social, environmental, resources, and cultural) and, therefore, all participants in all sectors.

Regional Planning and Its Institutional Setting

When a province establishes a planning region, that region represents a division of that province's powers over its area of jurisdiction, as set out in Canada's Constitution. Of course the province does the same when it creates municipalities and school districts. This is sometimes called the "areal division of power" (see Chapter 4). As such, it reflects a strategic action by the province to accomplish some important end. In the case of municipalities and school districts the objectives are to provide considerable local autonomy in governance and education, respectively. Indeed, the traditional separation between these two local bodies reflects important differences between these two functions in the eyes of the province and, therefore, the need to legislatively distinguish them. In other words, each embodies different strategic aims for the province and the people in its communities. Thus, while all provinces now recognize the general need for such local governance and education, and have sanctioned their establishment, the province retains the power to establish them and control their operations (including terminating them). This power was evident in Ontario with the amalgamation of Metro Toronto municipalities into the single City of Toronto, and in several other provinces with the consolidation of many school boards.

The same considerations apply when there is seen to be a need to establish territorially based bodies to carry out the planning for a provincial region. Planning regions, if they are to be effective, require power from the province, and this, too, represents an areal division of provincial power. Accomplishing this division requires that a planning region, and any powers extended to a regional planning and governing body, be defined in legislation. This legislative sanction, in turn, places the planning region and its agencies within a formal structure, with all the obligations that go with being in the public domain (e.g., accountability and democracy). Thus we find regional bodies being given such formal names as "commissions," "boards," and "authorities" so as to denote their public stature. Despite their authoritative names, regional agencies are limited to operating within the mandate and powers the province allots to them. Further, a province never takes any such legislative move lightly.

On the one hand, there are long-term constraints on the province when powers are devolved to the regional agency; on the other hand, the province is obliged to provide support, often in financial terms, to the regional agency.

These concerns aside, there is an additional consideration when a planning region and agency are established, for there are (usually) already existing administrative and governing arrangements (e.g., municipalities and school districts, water boards, and conservation authorities) occupying all or part of the same area. Regional planning bodies, therefore, seldom have precedence in any given area; they begin by having to share power with other interests.[2] It must be remembered that both levels – the local and the regional – often have responsibilities to the same public. Both of them are engaged in planning in the public domain, even if they do so within different boundaries. And, since the regional-level body is presumed to have somewhat superior powers to the local-level bodies, there is an understandable tension between the two. We shall see in later chapters how this tension between levels persists in almost all regional situations and how it can thwart effective planning.

Regional Planning and Governance

The activity of public planning in and for a region and the activity of governing within that same territory are, thus, inherently connected. They are associated, on the one hand, with the generic connection between planning and action. All planning is premised on the desire to guide future action; that is, future action should fulfil the goals implicit in a plan or planning policy. On the other hand, there is the formal connection with a governing entity that is empowered to make decisions that will result in the actions needed to implement the plan's proposals. This second, more formal, connection is essential to bringing public planning to fruition. Beyond this formal side of governing, another increasingly important connection concerns the social context within which the governing, or what is known as the governance, of the region occurs. This third connection raises the question of who does the regional planning, and we shall return to it below.

Dealing first with formal, institutional planning arrangements, the history of regional planning in Canada is replete with instances of agencies being established to provide "advice" to other governing entities on how the development needs of the region as a whole might best be met. The regional planning commissions in Alberta, the county planning agencies in Ontario, and most metropolitan planning agencies are three examples among many. Their advice was intended to help local governments (below them) and provincial ministries (above them) determine the best way to make their individual efforts most effective for the entire region. Although this form of planning, in which local bodies (and, in some cases, even provincial ones) participate in decisions about the region, is not conceptually wrong, the fact is that it rarely works well. For a variety of basic political and human reasons, neither the local bodies nor the provincial ones had any initial loyalty to the regional agency and regional interests or, therefore, to their aims. Since there were seldom sanctions for not complying with regional plans and policies, much less incentives for promoting them, regional plans and policies often "sat on the shelf." This ambivalence is still known today, but signs of change are occurring, as we shall show in Parts 2 and 3.

One reason the formal aspect of regional planning has proved so troublesome is embedded in the distribution of "governmental resources" when the province chooses to establish a regional body and make it capable of planning and implementing plans for a region (see Chapter 4). The existing governments in a region already represent the province's previous distribution of planning powers. A new regional agency will need its own powers to plan for the entire region, which, almost by definition, will mean diminishing some of the planning powers of both existing governments and provincial agencies. It is no wonder that this is a politically sensitive action. Nor is it any wonder that provinces move cautiously and often end up providing insufficient planning powers, or what Healey (1997) refers to as the "hard infrastructure" of governing, to the regions they create.

More recently, added to the concern about the structure and powers of the regional agency is an equal concern about the extent and composition of the participation in the planning process. Thus, when the need for regional planning is considered important for a region, it is vital to design the "soft infrastructure" for governance. Regional planning involves all the domains of social practice, communication among cultural communities, consensus building, and mutual learning among all interests. If a regional plan is not only to be implemented, but also to be supported, then the *relational* aspects between and within both formal (governmental) participants and informal interests and communities must have an explicit place within the planning process (Innes 1995; Wight 1996; Healey 1997). Although much still needs to be done to determine the governing arrangements for a region that best complement its need to plan its future, *governance* is now the watchword in those efforts.

Future Challenges for Regional Planning

In Canada we have nearly six decades of regional planning experience upon which to reflect as we move into a new century. Only a few other countries have more years of experience with regional planning. We can learn from our experience, and a prime aim of this book is to identify the mistakes of the past as well as to illuminate what succeeded and, not least, to better perceive the challenges that regional planning faces as a new century and millennium unfold. In the future, regional planning will have new cultural and political ingredients to contend with in addition to having to overcome constraints from its past. To set the stage for the chapters in Parts 2, 3, and 4, we outline below the major challenges facing regional planning. First, there are the continuing challenges that have appeared and reappeared throughout the history of regional planning (these are elaborated in Chapter 10). These are followed by the challenges occasioned by conditions that began to emerge as the past century waned – conditions that are likely to continue to demand attention in this century (these are explored further in Chapter 11).

Continuing Challenges

As we have learned from past practice, certain challenges are an inherent part of the milieu of regional planning. We might say that they are endemic to regional planning practice. Unarguably, they will continue to recur. These challenges are outlined below.

Perennial Problem Settings

While the setting for regional problems may change in the twenty-first century, regional planning will continue to be called on to work within four broad regional settings:

1 natural resource development and its related concerns of conservation and environmental protection
2 metropolitan area (and now city-region) growth and expansion
3 countryside and rural settlement maintenance
4 regional economic imbalances.

Inherent Jurisdictional Tensions

The establishment of planning regions to tackle regional problems always impinges on already established jurisdictions (such as municipalities, counties, water districts, and even provincial and federal entities). Thus there must be a redivision of powers between the new planning region and its "neighbours," with consequent political tensions and constraints with regard to making and implementing regional plans. These jurisdictional tensions will continue to challenge regional planners and may be considered a natural part of regional planning's "turf."

Uncoordinated Planning Realms

Three substantive areas occur repeatedly in regional planning practice: (1) land use, (2) the environment, and (3) the economy. These are, of course, interrelated realms, and the solution to problems in any one area will have impacts on one or both of the others. For example, regional economic plans will, inevitably, have land-use and environmental repercussions. With rare exceptions, regional planning practice in Canada and elsewhere has separated these realms, and there has been little or no coordination among them. The resolution of these now-isolated efforts is a challenge to present and future regional planners.

Future Challenges

Some new elements have been introduced into the milieu within which Canadian regional planners will practise in the coming decades. They began to become evident a decade or two ago and show little sign of receding. We cannot be certain how they will shape future practice; however, we can identify two broad tendencies. On the one hand, there is the tendency that will *push* regions to act more in concert with external forces and factors; on the other hand, there is the tendency that will *pull* regions to favour their internal relations. Each of these tendencies is described briefly below.

External "Push" Factors

The recent globalization of so many of the world's activities has begun to affect regional planning through the effects of international marketing and corporate arrangements, which make a region's economy both more open to wider opportunities and less protected from global changes. A related aspect is the spatial reorganization of activities that is under way worldwide, especially reorganization that focuses on large cities as mega-centres of investment and distribution. The result is a new spatial form, the *city-region,* which is larger, more complex, more diverse, and more extensive than the metropolitan areas we have known. Another related factor is the concept of *sustainable development*, which has been universally embraced. This shift in perspective is opening regions to standards for resource development set by international agencies, corporations, and intergovernmental trade agreements.

Internal "Pull" Factors

A counter-tendency to global forces is also apparent in factors that demand an inward focus. *Bioregionalism* and *community economic development* are two such inward "pulls." Both initiatives insist on looking first at a region's needs as well as its environmental and social characteristics and then integrating them into a coherent whole. Closely related to this are the efforts at *ecosystem planning* and the pressures for greater *public participation* and involvement in a region's planning. Clearly, competing forces will not affect every region's planning in the same way. Yet there can be little doubt that they will condition and constrain regional planning well into the future.

Perspective of the Book

Regional planning is probably as widespread in Canada as it is in any other Western country. Nevertheless, there exists no comprehensive rendering of the origins and evolution of the approaches we use in regional planning. This book attempts to rectify that situation by providing a review of regional planning practice in Canada from the late 1930s to the present. It begins by identifying the intellectual and conceptual foundations of regional planning, following their development up to today, and it concludes by broaching the regional planning needs of the twenty-first century. It gives special attention to the distinctive planning needs of the latest kind of planning region in Canada – the city-region – which has emerged as a new challenge for regional planners.

Part 1: Regional Planning's Foundations

In regional planning a number of elements are fundamental to understanding the field in general and its practice in Canada in particular. Although the practice of planning Canadian regions as a conscious public strategy is a fairly recent activity, interest in achieving more sanguine regional conditions of living and working, getting around, and protecting the environment date back to the middle of the eighteenth century. The regional planning of today has its roots in the notions of an astonishing array of precursors, as is shown in Chapter 1; however, as a field of social practice, it is also founded on contemporary ideologies, theories, and concepts, as is shown in Chapter 2. Two other chapters round out this review of regional planning's foundations. First, Chapter 3 presents the importance of selecting boundaries as a basic building block for regional planning. Second, Chapter 4 examines the legislative foundations of regional planning in Canada's Constitution as well as the necessary role of senior governments in supporting the regional planning entities that they alone have the power to create.

Part 2: Regional Planning in Rural and Non-Metropolitan Canada

Regional planning in rural and in non-metropolitan regions in Canada has been practised longest and provides a wealth of experience – of both the successful and the less successful variety. Part 2 reviews the range of regional planning activities undertaken in response to the diversity that characterizes rural Canada (including the North) – regions that encompass by far the bulk of this country. Chapter 5 examines the many initiatives that have been taken to protect and maintain the rural countryside and its communities in the wake of urban expansion and economic and social transformations. Chapter 6 details the special features of regional economic development planning that flourished especially in the 1960s and 1970s and that occurred primarily in rural Canada. Regional planning was also widely practised in response to the conservation and development needs of natural resources that form the foundation of rural regions. More recently, as we also see in Chapter 7, this has encompassed planning for the environment. These chapters, and those that follow, illuminate the types of planning problems confronting planners as well as the practice that evolved to deal with them.

Part 3: Regional Planning for Urban-Based Regions

The planning of metropolitan areas and the recently emerging city-regions of Canada has given Canada a reputation as a leader in the field of metropolitan planning and governance in the western hemisphere. Experience in planning these urban-based regions showed, early on, the need for a commensurate level of government if such planning were to be effective. Thus, this becomes an integral part of the description in each of the chapters in this section. The planning (and governing) of metropolitan areas came first, and Chapter 8 describes the experience of Edmonton, Calgary, Winnipeg, and Ottawa–Hull, among others.

Since the mid-1980s, it has become evident that some metropolitan areas in Canada, and many abroad, in addition to being larger, have entered a phase of development that is more extensive and functionally more complex than was the preceding phase. We call these areas "city-regions." They are the result of global economic and social forces that, during the past two decades, have led to the extensive decentralization of people and jobs and that require new approaches both to planning and governance. We have identified three fairly advanced city-regions in Canada – Montreal, Toronto, and Vancouver – and Chapter 9 describes their planning problems and responses to them.

Part 4: The Future of Canadian Regional Planning

The prospects for regional planning after sixty years of practice indicate that there will be continued change in practice and theory to further test the essence of the field, which is all about dealing with change – both planned and unplanned. In a postmodern period we can expect to question past paradigms and contemplate new approaches. But, as with any epochal change, the roots of the new grow out of the soil of the old. We need, therefore, to take stock of what the past shows us about regional planning, and this is the thrust of Chapter 10. This review looks at a number of lessons from the past, thus offering an important perspective for forming the foundation blocks for regional planning in the future, whatever form it takes.

Building on this experience, and taking into account an array of new and emerging factors, the final chapter of the book proposes a paradigm for regional planning appropriate to the twenty-first century. It derives from, among other things, the contending forces noted above. Some will draw a region's perspective outward and some will draw it inward. As a result, regional planning's content, focus, method, administration, governance, and participants will all need to shift and adapt. For example, we envision shifts away from governmental *structures* that suited the past to regional governance *processes* that emphasize greater inclusiveness and that link physical planning to economic sustainability and natural ecosystems planning.

Part 1

Foundations of Regional Planning

1

Roots of Regional Planning

The regional planning we know today has roots extending back close to 200 years. As with many other twentieth-century public policy initiatives, including public health, city planning, and social work, regional planning emerged originally from intellectual and social ferment caused by the adverse conditions wrought by unrestrained industrialism, first in Europe and then in North America, in the late eighteenth and early nineteenth centuries. This is where we first find attempts to conceptualize planning on a scale broader than the individual city as people responded to the rapid urbanization associated with the Industrial Revolution and the enormous problems of health, sanitation, housing, water supply, and congestion it induced. At the same time, the movement for the conservation and proper development of our natural resources, as we have come to know it, began as a reaction to imprudent practices in resource development. The Industrial Revolution spawned some of the earliest public regional planning.

And, like these other policy initiatives, regional planning evolved slowly. First, those who wanted to create more humane settlements developed ideas (e.g., Charles Fourier) – and, indeed, in the mid-nineteenth century a number of them actually conducted social experiments that created new settings for human habitat (e.g., Robert Owen, Ebenezer Howard, and the British industrialists/philanthropists, George Cadbury, Titus Salt, and William Lever). Next came the beginnings of a science and profession, based on regional geography and sociology, that aimed to influence public policy concerning natural and human environments. In the first few decades of the twentieth century this blossomed into formalized regional planning on both sides of the Atlantic. By the 1930s, not only had regional planning become a tool of public policy, but the main conceptual positions had also been identified – positions that would inform the debate for years to come. Then, beginning in the 1960s, what has been referred to as "the modernist regional development paradigm" came under attack from many quarters, leading to many changes in the theory and practice of regional planning, which we shall document in Part 2.

In this chapter we chart the evolution of these building blocks over about a century and one-quarter until the early 1960s, about two decades after regional planning had gained a firm foothold in public policy. Although regional planning is a contemporary activity, whatever its manifestation – in the past, the present, or the future – it will always owe much to the ideas and experiences that came before it. Thus, the past half-century of Canadian regional planning is anchored in the ideas and activities of a number of influential people, movements, and conferences – what in total we refer to as regional planning's "precursors."[1] Though implicit in today's regional planning, our professional practice can only be enhanced by fully appreciating its roots.

Regional Planning's Precursors

Contemporary regional planning grew out of contrasting viewpoints about political and economic centralization, rural and urban poverty, class conflicts, the organization of human habitats, environmental degradation, and the lack of connection of people with nature – the Industrial Revolution having put all of these issues into high relief. The protagonists in these debates make up a seemingly curious melange of people, including utopians and anarchists, geographers and economists, planners and ecologists, activists, social scientists, and natural scientists (we refer to them as "seers," after Hall 1974), plus a set of important movements and conferences that existed until 1960.[2] To introduce the "precursors" and to indicate their diversity, we list the most important in chronological order, along with their main ideas (their interconnections are displayed in Figure 3):

- Utopian socialists, such as Charles Fourier (1772-1837), Robert Owen (1771-1858), and Ebenezer Howard (1850-1928), who described and, in a few instances, actually created new and humane settlements and societies.
- Anarchists such as Pierre Joseph Proudhon (1809-65), Peter Kropotkin (1842-1921), brothers Elie and Elisée Reclus (1827-1904, 1830-1905), and Jean Charles-Brun (1870-1946), who openly confronted forces of centralized political and economic control.
- Geographers, led by Vidal de la Blache (1845-1918) and Jean Brunhes (1869-1930), who championed stewardship of vital region-based cultures as the foundation of stable interrelations between human beings and nature.
- Followers of the new synthetic science of sociology, such as August Comte (1798-1857) and Frédéric Le Play (1806-82), which later, under Patrick Geddes (1854-1932), arguably the world's first regional planner, evolved into a potent applied human ecology.
- Thomas Adams (1871-1940) who, in the period between 1914 and 1930, was one of the outstanding planners in Britain, the United States, and Canada (where he was also considered the "father" of Canadian planning).

Figure 3

Regional planning precursors (pre-1960s)

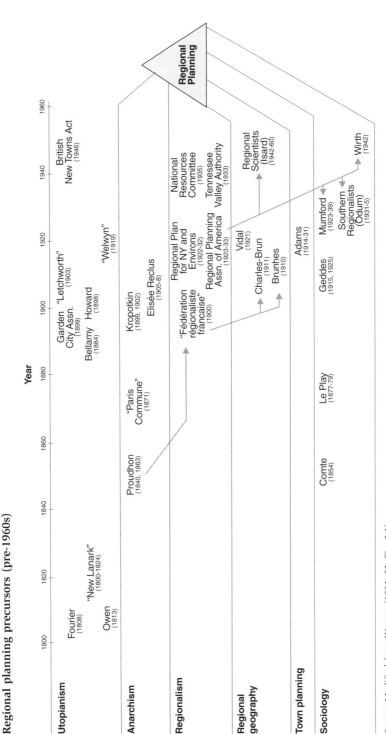

Source: Modified from Weaver (1984, 32, Fig. 3.1).

- Founders of the Regional Planning Association of America (1923-31), a remarkable non-governmental, "volunteer" organization based in New York City, composed of a small but outstanding group of architects, liberal-minded developers, conservationists, foresters, engineers, housing experts, planners, and urbanists who were led by Lewis Mumford (1895-1990), a sociologist-critic-writer-journalist.
- The Southern Regionalists, a group of southern academic-sociologists, led by Howard Odum (1884-1954), whose interest in regionalism was primarily political; they were rural-oriented (in contrast to the Regional Planning Association of America), wanted to keep northern industrialists and "metropolitan culture" from attacking southern rural values, and also wanted to alleviate poverty and racism.
- Conservationists and the Conservation Movement, in both the United States and Canada, whose beginnings go back to the late nineteenth and early twentieth centuries and who held important national conferences on the subject (e.g., the Canadian Resources for Tomorrow Conference held in Montreal in 1961).
- A group of New Deal economists and planners working for the United States National Resources Planning Board and the National Resources Committee under President Franklin Roosevelt (1935-43) who, among other things, developed and implemented the concept of the Tennessee Valley Authority (1933).
- Regional scientists and the regional science "movement," which began in the mid-1950s and flourishes today.

These seers and philosophers divide into two groups, according to their views on the following key issues:

A. The purposes of regional planning:
    - One group, as represented by, among others, the French geographers, Ebenezer Howard, the Southern Regionalists, and the planners and economists working for the United States National Resources Planning Board during the 1930s and early 1940s, held that regional planning was needed as a means of developing the *physical* resources of a region (especially its water resources) and for bettering the social and economic well-being of people in the region. This group also believed that regional life and culture in the "outlying" provinces and hinterlands must be restored and that this could be accomplished by mixing urban and rural occupations so as to overcome the increasing contradictions between town and countryside.
    - The other group of seers and philosophers, as represented by, for example, Thomas Adams, Louis Wirth (the University of Chicago sociologist), and most members of the Regional Planning Association of America

(especially Lewis Mumford), argued that planning should aim to preserve and protect local rural values and culture, as well as resources in hinterland regions, from supposedly chaotic economic and social forces emanating from the city. Underlying this view was a strong position, sometimes bordering on being anti-urban, that deplored the growing metropolis and advocated the planned decentralization of people and industry to smaller towns, including the building of new towns.

B. The nature and scale of the appropriate "planning region":
- For the first group, the proper planning region was the *natural* or *resource region,* as represented by the river valley basin or watershed. Some in this group envisioned enormous cultural or economic territories nearly as large as the nation-state itself (e.g., the Tennessee Valley, the Pacific Northwest, and the Sunbelt), while others postulated an "organic" region.
- The second group believed that it was the city that gave a region its cultural (and economic) vitality. It also functioned as the focal point of the flow of a region's energy, people, goods, and information. The city organizes this flow for the rest of the region and, thereby, controls its development. For this group, the logical unit for regional planning was the *city-centred* or *metropolitan region.*

C. The methodology to employ:
- The two groups do not necessarily align themselves in the same way on the issue of methodology: The first group tends to support urban design traditions, graphic methods, physical planning, qualitative research methods (e.g., observation and regional surveys), and the subjective experience of "place." It also tends to see the regional development "plan" as an expression of land use and physical infrastructure, as in City Beautiful and Garden City plans.
- The second group, coming from the social sciences, tends towards more abstract, quantitative research, quantifying and analyzing land use, housing, population, economic activity, and transportation demand, and building mathematical models of spatial structure. This group also tends to emphasize the goal of regional economic development and practises "strategic planning" rather than "comprehensive planning." Regional scientists epitomize this group.

These opposing views – "maps of the world" as it were – would come to influence much of the ideology and doctrine of regional planning practice (see Chapter 2). And, as we shall see in Part 2, they would also continue to be at odds with each other – whether through academics, professionals, and/or public officials – right up to the present day. Nevertheless, despite their opposing views, these seers and philosophers shared a belief in the need for a regional perspective in planning. Moreover, they held similar views on a number of substantive issues related to regional planning, several of which are of considerable relevance today. They all shared, for example, the following traits (see also Weaver 1984, 51):

- a basic revulsion towards the industrial city
- a strong negative reaction to economic and political centralization
- the need for a significant change in relations between industrial society and the natural environment
- the need for regional planning to establish a harmonious relationship between people and nature – one grounded in an ecological-ethics with a deep respect for the limits of human intervention in natural processes.

Interconnectedness among Seers and Philosophers

To begin this historical analysis, we should first note a remarkable fact: not only did many of the major seers and philosophers have ideas that often coincided, crossed, and in some instances actually duplicated one another (even when they worked in different disciplines), but they also wove a web of friendship and mutual aid that was not purely coincidental (Weaver 1984, ch. 3). Here we shall note but a few examples; later sections will note others.

One example is that Proudhon came from the same town as did Fourier, was his student, and later edited one of his books. Another example is that Patrick Geddes was intimately connected with the Reclus family. Elisée Reclus taught in Edinburgh with Geddes, while Elie, Elisée's sociologist brother, was also Geddes' guest in Edinburgh. And Paul Reclus (Elie's son) collaborated with Geddes in his final venture, le Collège des ecossais. Also, Paul became Geddes' executor in France. Other examples are recounted by Weaver (1984, ch. 3).

Utopians: Starting Anew

The despoliation of the towns and cities and the exploitation of the industrial labour force during the Industrial Revolution did not go unheeded. The nineteenth century was distinguished by a number of "utopian socialists," a term Karl Marx coined to describe a group of social thinkers whose attitude, he argued, was unscientific and idealistic and who hoped to improve working-class conditions by individual benevolence, philanthropy, and enterprise. These reformers believed that urban life could be transformed by building new, separate, planned industrial communities outside the large cities.

First and perhaps foremost among these utopian philosophers was Robert Owen, a rich English industrialist who proposed the creation of agricultural, cooperative villages of between 800 and 1,200 people, which would serve all the social, educational, and employment needs of the community (Hodge 1998,

87-8; see also Goodwin 1978). His proposal envisaged central heating, residents living near their place of employment, older children living communally, and only families with children under three years old living in private lodgings. He emphasized agriculture but included some industry on the outskirts of these villages. Owen's idea of the cooperative village was drawn from his own experience in New Lanark, a textile factory town near Glasgow that he purchased from his father-in-law. He managed it as an immensely successful private enterprise from 1800 until 1824, when he left for the United States to try (unsuccessfully) to develop a similar community, "New Harmony," in 1825. Nor was Owen successful in gaining support from authorities to build prototypes of his new town in Britain. Despite these disappointments, Owen's ideas were quite influential (Hodge 1998).

Owen's New Lanark and Saltaire, built by Titus Salt around his textile mill near Bradford (1853-63), date from the early years of the Industrial Revolution. Other powerful industrialists followed suit: the chocolate manufacturer George Cadbury built Bourneville outside Birmingham (1879-95), and the chemical magnate William Lever built Port Sunlight on the Mersey near Birkinhead (1889). In Germany, the engineering and armaments firm of Krupp built a number of similar settlements outside their works at Essen in the Ruhr district, of which the best preserved, Margaretenhöhe (1906), closely resembled Bourneville and Port Sunlight.[3]

The most well-known "contemporary" advocate of building new towns, and the person who probably had the most influence worldwide on new town building during the twentieth century, was Ebenezer Howard. Howard's importance as founder and contributor to the "Garden City" concept and movement is richly documented (see, for example, Cherry 1974; Creese 1966; Richert and Lapping 1998; and Hall and Ward 1998). Here we are mainly concerned with his influence on regional planning.

Howard was not an architect, town planner, or surveyor but, rather, a court reporter who, until middle age, "had never given any indication that he was capable of originality or leadership" (Fishman 1988). Nevertheless, as a result of his achievement in founding the Garden City movement, he ended up an English knight. Osborn (1946, 1965) referred to him as a "pragmatic inventor," and Mumford (1946, 1965) referred to him as "a practical idealist." He presented his ideas for new towns in the form of general diagrams rather than as specific plans for a particular community and location (see Figure 4).

Howard based a number of his ideas on the model towns the philanthropist-industrialists built. Certainly, his basic notion – to deliberately decentralize industry from the city, or at least from its inner sections, and to build a new town around a factory, thus combining working and living in a healthy environment – is similar to that of Owen and the other British philanthropists. These model communities were clearly forerunners of Howard's later garden cities. Howard, however, took the idea of a single company town and generalized it so that it involved a planned movement of people and industry away from the large, crowded, nineteenth-century urban centres.

There is no evidence of any direct link between Howard's work and the ideas of the utopians and anarchists (discussed in the next section) or of any relationship with his planning contemporary, Patrick Geddes. Howard himself attributed his ideas to Edward Bellamy's utopian vision of Boston in *Looking Backward* (1884). Bellamy had been heavily influenced by August Comte, as had Fourier, Proudhon, and Geddes. Howard, in his own work, *Garden Cities of To-morrow* (1898, 1902, 1946, 1965),[4] mentions both Owen and Fourier and also cites Kropotkin, but he never explicitly develops any of their ideas and several times denies any socialist intentions (Howard 1898, 131). It should be noted, however, that Howard's scheme for the Garden City definitely includes some "socialist"-type ideas, including community ownership of the land and a leasehold system, which would control physical planning and municipal finances; also, all increases in rateable value would accrue to the community, amortizing front-end capital investment.[5]

Howard argued that a new type of settlement – town-country, or Garden City – could uniquely combine all the advantages of the town by way of accessibility, and all the advantages of the country by way of environment, without any of the disadvantages of either. (He called these advantages "magnets.") This could be achieved by the planned decentralization of workers and their places of employment, thus transferring the advantages of urban agglomeration en bloc to the new settlement. The new town would be deliberately located outside normal commuter range of the old city. It would be fairly small (he suggested 30,000 people), and it would be surrounded by a large greenbelt, easily accessible to everyone.

Interestingly, Hall (who is an authority on Ebenezer Howard's work) notes that, in contrast to popular conception, Howard did not simply advocate the building of small, isolated garden cities or new towns (Hall 1974, 52; Hall and Ward 1998, 25); rather, he suggested that when any new garden city reached a population of 30,000, it should stop growing and its excess should be accommodated in another new town close by (then another and another). The result, over the course of time, would not be single, isolated garden cities but, rather, an entire cluster of such towns, each offering a range of jobs and services but each connected to all the others by a rapid transit system (or, as Howard referred to it, an "inter-municipal railway"). These clusters would, thus, possess all the economic and social benefits of a large city. Howard called this polycentric cluster of settlements the "Social City."[6]

The diagram of the Social City that Howard appended in the 1898 edition of his book showed it as having a population of 250,000, but he stressed that it could grow without limit. We have reproduced this diagram in Figure 4. His concept of the Social City has never been well understood, Hall says, because the diagram was omitted from later editions of his book, with only a truncated version shown. Consequently, Hall notes, most readers (including planners) have "failed to grasp the vital fact that social city, not the individual isolated garden city, was to be the physical realization of Howard's third magnet" (which shared the advantages of both town and countryside). Hall concludes his several analyses of Howard's work by stating (Hall and Ward 1998, 142) that his "message still has a startling, almost surreal relevance to us." Howard's influence on town and regional planning reached around the world. Perhaps the most direct instance of his influence in the twentieth century was the British new town policy of 1945, which clearly owed much of its purpose and concept to Howard's Garden City concept.

Figure 4

Ebenezer Howard's diagram of the Social City

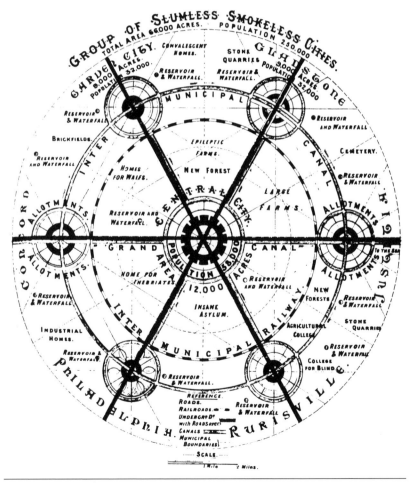

Source: Howard (1898)

Anarchists: Opponents of Centralized Control[7]

Among the precursors of regional planning, Weaver (1984, ch. 3) claims that the anarchists, led by P.J. Proudhon and including Kropotkin, Reclus, and Charles-Brun, were among the most important influences on early regional planning thought but rarely recognized for their contribution. While decentralization was part and parcel of the new town concept, Proudhon and his followers combined this with their own theory of society, the main elements of which included a decentralized social economy and regional federalism. Their social theories were a direct reaction to late eighteenth- and early nineteenth-century industrialization in France, which created a growing yet poverty-stricken urban working class and concentrated economic activities in a select number of urban locations. Consolidation of financial power in Paris only bolstered these tendencies towards centralization and, as a result, metropolitan and industrial cities monopolized national life, leaving the outlying provinces to suffer from a ruinous cycle of economic dislocation, out-migration, and underdevelopment.

According to Friedmann (1987), the major clue to understanding anarchism, what he terms "social anarchism," is its passionate denunciation of all forms of authority, especially the state's. It thus might be termed a movement dedicated to abolishing politics. In this and other respects, social anarchism bears similarities to the utopian movement; however, the differences are also clear. Friedmann distinguishes two branches of social anarchism: the first branch – its chief representatives being Proudhon and Kropotkin – advocates peaceful cooperation as the road to an anarchist social order. The second branch – its chief representatives being Bakunin and Sorel – defends physical violence in the destruction of all authority. Here we are concerned only with the influence on regional planning of the first branch of anarchists.

In place of what he called "industrial feudalism," Proudhon argued for *co-operation, mutualism,* and *federation* (Proudhon 1840; Woodcock 1962). For him, mutualism was a concept that could balance the eternal contradictions of economic life without loss of liberty. Under mutualism, individual workers would have the absolute right to the means of production (resources and technology) (Weaver 1984). Producers' associations would inherit the main branches of industry and then join together in freely contracted cooperative schemes for vertical and geographic cooperation and marketing. These "social contracts" would eliminate all need for central political authority, as the "natural" functional units of society worked out their own freely entered contractual agreements, and government would become the mere "administration of things."

Proudhon referred to the institutional framework of his social theory as a "social republic." This larger entity – a free federation – would be formed by a series of constantly re-negotiable social contracts. Starting at the level of the "natural unit" (the workplace/living group), contractual agreements would be developed between functional/territorial groupings, beginning with the production unit and the commune and working their way up to the regional and, finally, the European level. Thus, regional units defined by economic production and culture would be the largest building blocks of the social republic. These regions, Proudhon assumed, would provide all the prerequisites for a rounded development of human, social, economic, and cultural capacities within an environment free from political and economic coercion.

Proudhon's ideas found their way directly into regional planning ideas and practice through the work of Peter Kropotkin (1899, 1902), Elisée Reclus, and Jean Charles-Brun. Kropotkin and Reclus were geographers by profession and anarchists by political conviction. Charles-Brun was a leading latter-day Proudhonist and founder of the Fédération régionaliste française. Geddes is known to have warmly recommended Reclus' work to his own disciple, Lewis Mumford (Weaver 1984, 43). Reclus' contribution to regional planning was his argument that colonialism had destroyed or distorted the natural, collectivist small-scale societies of "primitive" peoples who were living in harmony with their physical environments.

Kropotkin further developed Reclus and Proudhon's ideas pertaining to small-scale communism, cooperation, and natural balance. His most important contributions to planning were his emphases on the idea of cooperation, or, as he called it, "mutual aid," and his elaboration of the idea of mixing rural and urban activities in order to overcome the contradictions created by capitalist urban-industrialization. Kropotkin's notion of mutual aid was that cooperation among members of a species was probably the most important force in natural evolution. His motivation was to refute what he considered to be Darwin and Huxley's over-emphasis on struggle, competition, and the "survival of the fittest." By contrast, he wanted to lay the empirical foundations for an anarchist interpretation of human society as a basically cooperative venture.

In his most famous work, *Field, Factories and Workshops: Or Agriculture Combined with Industry and Brain Work Combined with Manual Work* (1899), Kropotkin argued, as the title suggests, that this combination of agriculture and small-scale industry would overcome the contradictions between town and countryside and allow countries and regions to be virtually self-sufficient. Small-scale industrial villages, reminiscent of the new towns concept, were to be the vehicles of decentralization and would provide an environment combining the rural and the urban. New sources of power, hydraulic and especially electric, meant that newer industries tended to be small in scale, thus making big industrial concentrations outdated. These factors, he felt, could reinforce the trend towards decentralization and provide the necessary material basis for continued economic growth. This was one of the most crucial ideas that Geddes borrowed from Kropotkin, and, together with Howard's Garden City concept, it shaped Mumford's thinking on cities and city development, which he introduced to members of the Regional Planning Association of America, as we shall see later.

Regional Geographers: Beginnings of a Science

At the turn of the century, according to Weaver (1984, 46), regionalism was conceived as a mode of intellectual inquiry. And it was regional geography, in particular, and regional sociology (which developed as a response to political and economic centralization) that transformed the programs of regionalists such as Charles-Brun and anarchists such as Proudhon and Kropotkin into an academic paradigm that provided regionalism with study techniques and a classificatory system. Aberley (1985, 186) adds, perhaps not facetiously, that development of this academic discipline allowed the regional geographers (unlike their anarchist colleagues) to stay out of prison and to enshrine their discipline in conservative French universities.

In the field of regional geography, the French school, founded by Paul Vidal de la Blache, had a most important influence. Vidal not only held the chair of geography at the Sorbonne, where he founded the seminal organ of French academic geography, *Annales de géographie*, but he also trained the generation of scholars, including Jean Brunhes (1910), which was to establish geography as a subject of study throughout the French university system.

Regional geography is the study of culture in place, and the object of study for Vidal and his followers was the "geographic region," or *pays*, a complex locale – the creation of interaction among human culture, social institutions, technology, and the natural environment. Early on a debate began between the discipline's adherents: one school of thought, represented by Ratzel, a German, held that certain environments inevitably create a corresponding type of society. The Vidal and Brunhes school of thought took the opposite view. It argued that the physical environment provided the opportunity for a range of human responses, that humanity had a considerable number of choices, and that this "possibilistic" notion of regionalism puts people and nature on an equal footing, or, as one writer puts it, involves them in a "unique ecological unity" (Carpenter 1930, 130; cited by Aberley 1985, 187).

To save the regional habitat, it would be necessary, according to Vidal (1910), to study and understand it, and the way to understanding was through in-depth, holistic surveys of the regional environment. These would lead to a series of regional "monographs" that would, in turn, provide a fine-grained, detailed knowledge of all dimensions of regional life as well as a historical analysis of how a specific *genre de vie* had formed a particular *paysage*, or landscape. Systematic summaries of the French geographers' methods and findings were set out in textual form by Brunhes and Vidal and exercised considerable influence on planners in both Britain and the United States (Mumford 1938; Odum and Moore 1938). This regional survey methodology might seem absurdly simplistic now, but in its time it was one of the first efforts to conduct a "rational" observation of the physical and social world.

Patrick Geddes: The "First" Contemporary Regional Planner

Arguably, regional planning in the Western world began with Patrick Geddes. Originally trained in biology at the University of Dundee, where he also taught, Geddes has variously been described as a sociologist, planner, and geographer. He was a man of many interests and skills, and he came into contact with many of the leading social critics and reformers of his day.[8] From his contacts with French geographers, Geddes absorbed the creed of anarchistic communism based on free confederations of autonomous regions, and, presumably after reading Kropotkin's *Fields, Factories and Workshops,* he christened the new age of industrial decentralization the "neotechnic" era. In a display at the Paris Exposition, he used the terms "paleotechnic" and "neotechnic" (Hall 1988, 145) – terms he also borrowed from Kropotkin.

Geddes was perhaps the first among "contemporary" planners to sense the need for planning larger areas, especially around major urban centres. He was also one of the first to see the need for regional resource development and planning based on the river basin. He observed the spread of urban development in nineteenth-century England and roundly condemned "the dirty, sprawling industrial cities." He used the term "conurbation" to signify the consolidation and interdependence of these linked industrial cities, which formed a chaotic metropolitan development. This term would come into common usage among British geographers and planners to describe their major cities.

Drawing on his biological background, Geddes identified a number of evolutionary stages in the growth of cities. Working from the primitive to the more complex, the stages of evolution were from village to town, town to city, city to metropolis, metropolis to megalopolis, and megalopolis to necropolis. In the life cycle of cities, this was equivalent to human birth, life, and death. Geddes developed these evolutionary stages in his attempt to understand the modern city (Meller 1990, 117-18). Indeed, according to Meller (116), Geddes was the first to apply the term "megalopolis" to modern urban sprawl, and Mumford, his disciple, gave it widespread publicity in the 1930s.

Geddes, like so many of his critical compatriots, was looking for ways to make the earth more habitable and, especially, to achieve a balance between the human and natural environments. It is from his contacts with the founding fathers of French geography at the turn of the century (Reclus and Vidal) that Geddes gleaned his idea of the natural region, as exemplified by his well-known "valley section," or "valley plan of civilization." And, as Hall (1988, 140) notes, it is significant that, like them, he preferred to study the region in its purest form, far from the shadow of the giant metropolis. This led him to the "valley section" (see Figure 5), a hypothetical geographical unit that was his model for conducting regional surveys and understanding regional society (see Geddes 1915, 1925, 1968). The diagram was meant to represent a hypothetical

Figure 5

Diagram showing Patrick Geddes' model of the valley section

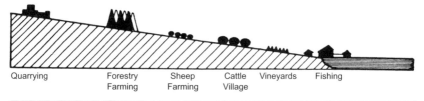

| Quarrying | Forestry | Sheep | Cattle | Vineyards | Fishing |
| | Farming | Farming | Village | | |

Source: Modified from Hodge (1998, 313).

river valley, running down from the mountains to the sea. Its dynamic force was the coastal city, located in the far right-hand corner of the drawing, and its purpose was to demonstrate the essential "unity in diversity" of the entire region.

Geddes used the hypothetical river valley to embody two basic principles of regional planning: first, the need to take a synoptic approach to regional problems in order to encompass the interrelations of areas and, second, the need to plan each area in coordination with adjoining areas. In this way the planner should see that, in a given region, different factors interact so that a change in one leads to changes in others. The use of the river basin to illustrate these principles made considerable sense, for much of human settlement began, and has continued to take place, in river valleys, and the various parts of river basins are clearly linked. Indeed, the idea of the river valley as the appropriate region for planning, although largely influenced by several unrelated historical factors in the United States, would play a significant role in the subsequent development of regional planning in that country.

Geddes was hostile to metropolitan cities as he felt they dominated their own countries and held a monopoly that was not necessarily in the interest of the people (Meller 1990, 119). The country was made up of regions and Geddes' major interest was to cultivate and sustain the balance in the region, which he defined in geographical terms. Large-scale urban growth into the megalopolis certainly did not fit *his* ideal of the valley section.

French geography lent academic legitimacy to the regionalist paradigm, but it was a French engineer and sociologist, Frédéric Le Play, as interpreted by Patrick Geddes, who presented planners with the clearest outline of the regional survey method. Geddes first learned of Le Play's work through a lecture given by one of Le Play's disciples at the 1879 Paris World's Fair. Le Play's notion of an empirical, regional sociology became one of the guiding concepts for Geddes' later social thought.

Le Play, a retired professor of metallurgy, believed that the social theories of Comte and the radical propagandists such as Proudhon were too grandiose.

His suggested strategy for achieving "social peace" involved a rejuvenation of regional life based on a thorough understanding of the reciprocal relationship between society and its local environment (Weaver 1984, 48). This goal could only be achieved by promoting the well-being of the family; furthermore, the family could be understood and rendered aid only through the application of the methods of empirical science, specifically of sociology. To this end he undertook a number of journeys across France, collecting huge amounts of empirical data pertaining to the country's thousands of working-class communities.

Folk-Work-Place Trilogy

Le Play analyzed this information through a three-part conceptual framework: *famille, travail, lieu* (folk, work, place). He argued that the well-being of the family was a product of the work in which it was engaged and that this, in turn, was affected by its place of residence, or geographical environment. He called the method of studying the interaction of all life within a region "sociography."

It was this trilogy of folk, work, and place that first attracted Geddes to Le Play's work. In it Geddes saw a parallel to the basic triad of biology – organism, function, and environment. He believed that it provided a framework not only for organizing, carrying out, and interpreting regional surveys, but that the interrelations among these factors signified the integrity of any region and the basis for organizing regional society. Geddes began by transposing Le Play's *famille, travail, lieu* into folk (the people of the region), work (the economy of the region), and place (the geographical dimensions of the region) – or sociology, economics, and geography – typically emphasizing the physical environment and how it relates to human occupations.[9] This formed the basis for the best known of Geddes' notorious "thinking machines." Folk, work, and place cut a diagonal across the diagram and thus provide a set of interrelated categories for the concrete study of human settlements.[10] Thus, in the words of Dickinson (1970, 25), Geddes' "sociology" rested on the interaction of community, work, and place.

Geddes argued that each area within the natural region, based on its natural environment and relationship with the city, would be the site of a particular "nature-occupation" (or place-work). The conditions of its residents, their culture, and their aptitudes would relate to this particular occupation. Conversely, the degree of development of all its various contributing localities would affect the regional city. Thus, to begin the task of replanning the industrial city, it was first necessary to have in-depth knowledge of the nuances and special attributes of not only the city itself, but also of its surrounding region. Based on the folk-work-place trilogy, planning must begin with a survey of the resources of a natural region, of the human responses to it, and of the resulting complexities of the cultural landscape (see Figure 7).

In all Geddes' teaching his most persistent emphasis was on the survey method. It is from this idea that, over the years, planners have preached and practised his no-plan-before-survey dictum.

Thomas Adams: The "Grand Seigneur" of Canadian Planning

In the first quarter of the twentieth century, Thomas Adams probably did more than anyone else to establish the substance and credibility of the professional and educational sides of planning in Canada and, to a large extent, in Britain and the United States. Adams came to Canada from England, where he was widely considered to be the leading member of the British planning "establishment." In 1900, he had been appointed the first secretary of the Garden City Association and then the manager of the first private Garden City Company, which constructed Letchworth – the first British new town built along the lines advocated by Ebenezer Howard and the Garden City Association. Later, the government placed him in charge of the new 1909 British Housing and Town Planning Act, and he also became the first president of the British Town Planning Institute, which was formed in 1914.

With such a dossier preceding him, it is not surprising that his appointment as town planning advisor to the Commission of Conservation was heralded in Canada. A petition from prominent Canadian institutions and leading individuals compelled the prime minister to request the British government to allow Adams to come to Canada to advise the Canadian government on planning matters. The British government at first refused, but after a second request from the Canadian prime minister, it acquiesced, and Adams was hired on a three-year contract to head the newly created Town Planning Branch of the Commission of Conservation (Gunton 1981, 103).

Contributions in Canada

In the comparatively brief period he was in Canada (between 1914 and 1923), Adams' contributions to Canadian planning, especially town planning, were enormous. He is considered the first professional planner in Canada and, arguably, the "father" of Canadian planning, or in Simpson's (1985, 102) words, its "Grand Seigneur." Under his guidance, the Commission of Conservation made a number of important and innovative contributions to the development of the planning movement in Canada. He (and the commission) set forth a body of planning theory, promoted the passage of planning legislation (most Canadian provinces adopted his proposed model Planning Act), promoted provincial departments of municipal affairs in a number of provinces, advised on the preparation of general plans, and generated public support for planning. As a private practitioner, Adams undertook plans for a number of new communities, including Corner Brook in Newfoundland, Témiscamingue in western Quebec, and most notably, the Richmond district of Halifax (Stein 1994b).

Adams was also a very active public speaker and consultant, and he was instrumental in publishing a new journal, *Conservation of Life*, to which he also contributed articles. He also helped set up the Civic Improvement League of Canada (made up of members of Canada's business elite, academics, professionals, and politicians) to promote interest in town planning. And in May 1919 Adams was instrumental in forming Canada's first planners' association, the Town Planning Institute of Canada.

While Adams' activities in town planning are both recognized and documented, especially those associated with his work on the Commission of Conservation (see a later section for a discussion of the commission's accomplishments), Adams also made some major (albeit much less well-known) contributions to *regional planning*. Paradoxically, his influence in this regard was far greater in the United States than it was in Canada. Adams' influence on American planning occurred while he was in the United States – as a visitor (he was frequently invited to speak at American planning conferences), as a government consultant, and, later, as director of planning for what was called the "Regional Plan for New York and Its Environs." It is Adams' views on, and activities in, regional planning that we focus on in the remainder of this section.

Views on Regional Planning

Adams first became interested in regional planning while working in the early 1900s in England's Black Country (including Birmingham and Wolverhampton). He tried unsuccessfully to convince the "powers that be" of the need for an organization that would rationalize local government and its services in the entire region and launch a coordinated attack on its environmental problems. This was probably the earliest attempt at regional planning in Britain, and, from this experience, Adams derived a belief in metropolitan regions and spent much of the rest of his career urging regional planning within such settings (Simpson 1985, 45).

In several addresses Adams gave to the annual meetings of the National City Planning Conference[11] in the United States in the early 1900s, he introduced the concept of regional planning. In Cleveland in 1916 he proposed that the state outline plans into which regional and detailed local plans would dovetail; in short, he elaborated upon the structure he had for many years proposed for London. Adams even startled the American planning world at the Cleveland meeting by telling them that "the first thing ... is not to plan Cleveland but to plan Ohio [the state]," then to prepare a plan for the region and see that the city planning fits in with it (Simpson 1985, 124-5). (As we shall note in a later section, Adams abandoned this position in later years.)

The passage of time only strengthened Adams' conviction that city and countryside were interdependent. In 1919, he delivered a paper at a national conference on city planning held at Niagara Falls, Ontario, and Buffalo, New York, where he gave impetus to the idea of establishing a regional planning program in this area. Many people on both sides of the Niagara Peninsula were impressed by the idea of a joint effort to promote economic development of the cross-border region. In his paper he argued that it is necessary to direct and control growth taking place within the rural and semi-rural districts where new industries are locating and, thus, making the boundaries of cities more and more meaningless. A city planning scheme, therefore, must be prepared with due regard to the regional development surrounding the city. Adams repeated his earlier advice that the skeleton plan of the region should come first, followed by a series of city-town planning schemes, but that a regional survey must precede both (see Adams 1919, 77 and 88; cited in Scott 1971, 178-9).

Adams' views were several decades ahead of the views of his audiences. State planning came about in the United States only during the New Deal of the 1930s, and then to only a modest extent. He also gained the distinction of articulating the idea of genuine regional planning (as opposed to merely metropolitan planning) before anyone else in the United States (Simpson 1985, 125). Moreover, he was at least three decades ahead of his Canadian counterparts, who would not formally begin provincial and regional planning until the early 1940s.

In 1920, at the annual National City Planning Conference, Adams declared that to broaden city planning to take in regional planning seemed to him not only desirable, but also inevitable – because, in an industrialized society, the municipal boundary was no longer the proper boundary for planning purposes (Adams 1920, 128, cited in Scott 1971, 192). He also repeated his advice of the previous year: begin with the region and then the city plan, the village plan, and the plan for the rural areas will all follow logically. Then, he advised, formulate the various elements of each plan (for industry, for housing) and, in due course, turn to zoning. To begin with zoning, as he suspected most planners generally do, would be to start at the "other end," the "wrong end" of the planning problem.

In the meantime, Adams, in his job as advisor to the Commission of Conservation,[12] began prodding it by making a series of strong and innovative recommendations for town planning in Canada. One of the puzzling aspects of Adams' work for the commission, and of the recommendations of the commission itself, is that, as far as we can determine, the commission did not make any proposals for regional planning. This is strange for two reasons: first, because, historically, resource conservation has been one of the strongest arguments advanced for regional planning (see earlier discussion and Chapter 7); and, second, because Adams had such strong feelings on the subject.

It is true that while in Canada Adams did write and talk about regional planning *outside* the confines of the commission. For example, in 1922, he wrote that regional planning was necessary for Canada because of the interdependence of urban and rural society. Adams concluded that "we hear much of city planning and something of country planning, but what is most wanted is the planning of the town-country which is comprised in the region" (Adams 1922, 251).

Adams also elaborated on his methods for regional planning. He proposed, much as Geddes had, that the regional plan be undertaken in stages: survey, analysis, plan and strategy formulation, and implementation (Adams 1921, 9, 10, 49). These stages are familiar to those that most planners use in the rational planning process, but his special contribution was to apply them to the regional planning process.

When the Commission on Conservation was disbanded in 1921, Adams' position came to an end. He was the ideal candidate (in 1923) to head up the planning team responsible for the Regional Plan for New York and Its Environs, sponsored by the Regional Plan Association (RPA).[13] At the time, he was arguably one of the leading planners in the world, and became known as the "planner's planner." Perhaps equally important, as it turned out, the New York plan was to be a "businessman's plan," to use Hall's term (1988, 156), and its main sponsors were former Chicago business leaders, the key one being Charles Dyer Norton (former chair of the Chicago Commercial Club). Norton selected Adams in his capacity as chair of the RPA's advisory committee on the New York regional plan.

Besides being a "businessman's planner," in Simpson's (1985, 135) view, Adams was also a "meliorist," another term used by Simpson to describe Adams. One of Adams' hallmarks was that he felt that regional plans must represent the art of the possible. The New York regional plan was not a revolutionary prescription but, rather, a set of mild controls on market abuses that would aid efficiency plus provide some non-controversial benefits such as new roads, parks, and beaches (Simpson 1985, 135). While this philosophy clearly appealed to his advisory committee, it was in sharp conflict with the idealists of the then fledgling Regional Planning Association of America, whom Simpson (1985, 133) referred to as the "insurgents" in the planning movement at the time.

Regional Planning Association of America: The Planning "Insurgents" [14]

Not really an organization – more like a "club" – the Regional Planning Association of America (RPAA) was a small, brilliant, diverse, and remarkable group of visionary, urban, issue-oriented New York City intellectuals who were housing and urban reformers. Formally established in 1923, the RPAA was organized and led by Clarence Stein (an architect-planner-housing reformer)[15] and met in New York City regularly in the early 1920s to discuss urban problems. Its core members included Henry Wright (architect, landscape architect, and site planner), Benton MacKaye (forester and conservationist), Alexander Bing (developer-builder), and Lewis Mumford.[16]

Mumford's Ideas and Influence

Mumford was probably the intellectual force behind the group, and later he was to achieve international fame as an urbanist, historian, and social critic. Mumford described the group's intellectual foundations as "the civic ideas of Geddes and Howard, the economic analyses of Thorstein Veblen, the sociology of Charles Horton Cooley, and the educational philosophy of John Dewey, to say nothing of the new ideas in conservation, ecology, and geotechnics" (Stein 1957, 14) – all of which had a part in transforming the cut-and-dried procedures of the earlier planners. At other times the sociologists, Comte and Le Play; the cultural regionalists of France, Vidal and Reclus; the anarchists, Proudhon and Kropotkin; various geographers and naturalists such as George Marsh and Henry Thoreau (who spearheaded the early conservation movement in the United States); the English Fabians (who, in the nineteenth century, worked towards gradually replacing capitalism with a more humane and communal order); and, ironically, as it would soon turn out, Thomas Adams, were also counted as being among the intellectual preceptors of the RPAA (MacKaye and Mumford 1929).

Geddes, in particular, was a major influence on Mumford's thinking. Mumford discovered some of the obscure pamphlets written by Geddes in 1915 and that began a correspondence between the two men that lasted about eight years. During this time Mumford referred to Geddes as "master" and named his son after him. Unfortunately, this relationship ended on a sour note. Mumford, longing to meet Geddes, finally persuaded him to meet him in New York in 1923; but when Geddes, then seventy years old, wanted to turn the twenty-eight-year-old rising star into his assistant (to help him promote civics and regionalism), and Mumford demurred, they seldom corresponded again (Mumford 1982, 322). Despite this estrangement, Mumford continued to be the main spokesman, and a most articulate one at that, for the gospel of Geddes. Indeed, Mumford could make his thoughts coherent in a way his "master" never could.

Mumford passed on this philosophy to his colleagues in the RPAA. The work of Mumford and the RPAA also inspired Howard Odum, who, in 1938, wrote *American Regionalism,* which remains the single best summary of North American regionalist expression at that time and, for some people, the only comprehensive book written on regional planning theory. Mumford's influence extended well into the twentieth century, and he often received letters of inquiry and admiration from twentieth-century ecology and regional planning activists such as Kirkpatrick Sale, Ian McHarg, Theodore Rozak, Paolo Soleri, and Abraham Maslow, to name but a few. All of these people were drawn to Mumford's critique of the machine age and the holistic/organic alternative he envisioned to take its place.

To Mumford, "regionalism" was a principle that united three ideas (Luccarelli 1995, 22):

1 *neotechnics:* the adaptation of new technologies for the purpose of restoring the natural environment
2 *organicism:* the restoration of nature's influence on culture through literature, architecture, and the built environment
3 *community:* the recovery of human-scaled, civic-minded social order.

The political and social aspects of regionalism also engaged Mumford. He viewed regionalism as a social theory that builds on Enlightenment principles of democracy and self-government but that goes beyond parliamentary liberalism to the restoration of civic democracy. Further, he associated regionalism and civic-mindedness with cultural diversity and challenged the growing hegemony of an international metropolitan culture. His political idea of regionalism involved the creation or re-creation of a civic culture as well as a politics based on compact and closely integrated communities.

Regional Planning Association of America's Criticisms of the New York Regional Plan

Early on, Thomas Adams was greatly admired by members of the RPAA for the ideas he put forth while in Canada because, in those days, he stressed the importance of linking the urban centre with the rural areas, controlling the use of natural resources, preventing speculation, and meeting social needs. Little did they realize that they would soon find themselves at odds with him. Adams' New York regional plan provoked a bitter response from the RPAA, for the members believed the kind of metropolitan-regional planning that he espoused and practised was at variance with his own earlier statements about planning in general and regional planning in particular, and which had been more in accord with RPAA's views. Their basic quarrel was over his then current belief that, in practice, the form of the region was fixed; only incremental, marginal changes were possible. The RPAA believed that Adams ignored planning's potential to influence the region's development.

Also, the RPAA felt that Adams' views conflicted with and contradicted the regionalism and regional planning concepts of the New York State Commission on Housing and Regional Planning. Its 1926 report (co-authored by RPAA members, Clarence Stein and Henry Wright) embraced views to which the association subscribed and outlined a schematic plan for the state of New York (NY State 1926) – a concept Adams at one time would have endorsed.

Regional Planning Association of America and Survey Graphic

In 1923 the group was provided with a unique opportunity to widely publicize its views. *Survey Graphic,* a magazine with a wide circulation among liberal intellectuals, invited the RPAA to produce a special number on "regional planning" for the New York Meeting of the International Town Planning and Garden Cities Association. Conceived by MacKaye, commissioned and edited by

Mumford, it included articles by MacKaye and Mumford and other key members of the RPAA. Out of print for half a century, until reprinted by Carl Sussman in *Planning the Fourth Migration,* these articles constitute a summary of the group's definitive manifesto. And, according to Hall (1988, 150), this remains "one of the most important documents of this history."

Following the publication of Volume 2 of the Regional Plan for New York and Its Environs, entitled the "Building of the City" (1931), Mumford published a two-part critique in *The New Republic* in June 1932. Representing the views of the association, he condemned the plan in almost every aspect, expanding on some of the criticisms it advanced in the *Survey Graphic.*[17]

The RPAA was not just critical of the New York regional plan. In the special issue of *Survey Graphic,* it laid out its basic ideas for checking the spread of urban-industrialization and achieving internal regional balance through an environmental mix of wilderness and rural and urban habitats. Each of the articles had as its underlying theme the need for regional planning. The goals were:

- to capitalize on what Mumford called the "fourth migration" (the ability of the new technologies to permit dispersal of population and industry into self-contained new towns)
- to direct people and industry into smaller centres because the "dinosaur cities" (such as New York, Chicago, Philadelphia, and Boston) were breaking down under the weight of congestion, inefficiency, escalating social costs, and, ultimately, physical collapse
- to develop garden cities and new towns, the economic basis of which would be dispersed industry. This would be made possible by the use of electric power, which would allow the spread of industrial employment to the farm and also ease the physical burden of rural life
- to make the national economy more economic and efficient through the regional planning of communities and a national plan for the distribution of industry, energy, and population
- to achieve the New Conservation and "ecological regionalism." Here the conservation of human values goes hand in hand with natural resources, including the preservation of permanent agriculture, permanent forestry, and permanent human communities.

In short, according to the RPAA, the ideas of Kropotkin and Veblen – decentralization joined to modern technology – would play leading roles in creating a regional environment in which farm and factory, regional centre and garden city, wilderness and industry would form an intricate mosaic. Highways, of course, would contribute to the same end, connecting city to countryside in such a way that the historical contradictions between them would be laid to rest. As Friedmann and Weaver (1979, 35) noted, the RPAA's faith in such measures, although it never had the power to implement them, was truly heroic. It is no wonder that, when the Tennessee Valley Authority was created in 1933, the RPAA hailed it as a first step towards a new civilization, for it embodied many of its principles (Chase 1936).

Regional Planning Association of America's Contributions

Throughout the 1920s the RPAA collaborated to formulate, build, and write about a vision of future urban communities and regions, and its influence continues to infuse Western city and regional planning thought (Parsons 1994, 462). The RPAA's underlying philosophy was "that we should replace [our] centralized and profit-oriented metropolitan society with a decentralized and more specialized one made up of environmentally balanced regions" (Sussman 1976, 2). Its goal was the ecological reconstruction of the physical environment to promote high cultural development and a "biotechnical economy." Its planning strategies were based on regional development, decentralization, and resource conservation through technological improvements, highway construction, rural electrification, and new towns.

Although the RPAA was a small group, and disbanded in 1933, its ideas were increasingly seen as major sources of Western thought (and often action) relating to city and regional planning. These ideas included city building policies, regional settlement frameworks, open space preservation strategies, large-scale community design and building prototypes, and sustainable development. RPAA members were individually and collectively involved in a wide range of projects, from the conception and initiation of a 4,860-kilometre-interstate regional system of foot trails to early proposals for housing tax incentives and mortgage guarantees for families of moderate means. Their ideas about urban and regional planning issues ranged from the policies for regional river basin planning to the administration of state planning as well as to revolutionary concepts for community housing design production. Elements of their vision were reflected in the activism of the New Deal of the 1930s, the new towns proposals (in the United States, Britain, and elsewhere), and the metropolitan greenbelt and "new urbanism" movements of the 1980s and 1990s. Specifically, the RPAA's contributions can be summarized as follows:[18]

- MacKaye's "backbone open way" – the Appalachian Trail (which was meant to be a "continuous wilderness path from Maine to Georgia") – was a precursor of many metropolitan regional trail systems, now sometimes called "greenways."
- The "regional city" – which Mumford (1938, 489-93) argued "would replace the mono-nucleated city ... with a new type of poly-nucleated city, in which a cluster of communities, adequately spaced and whose environment and resources were adequately planned would have all the benefits of a metropolis that held one million people without its ponderous disabilities" –

has, indeed, emerged in many metropolitan areas and is often a goal of metropolitan-regional plans (see our discussion in Chapter 9).

• Stein and Wright's "Radburn plan" not only gave birth to the two experimental communities at Sunnyside Gardens in New York City and at Radburn in New Jersey, but it also proved to be the ancestor of cluster zoning, planned unit development, and large-scale community building.

• Some European and Third World capitals used RPAA concepts in post-Second World War metropolitan-regional plans and community layouts. The clearest metropolitan embodiment of the RPAA's "regional city" idea is perhaps Stockholm (Sweden) with its new town, Vallenby, and its thirty well-defined rail-connected suburban satellite communities. Also, most of these clustered Stockholm communities' layouts made consistent use of modified Radburn plans (Parsons 1994, 463), as did many of the British new towns. The Radburn plan model also influenced the design of many American new towns (e.g., Reston and Columbia) and a score of planned unit developments all over the country.

• Mumford (1938) elaborated on the new town concept, paying special tribute to the early formulations of Owen and Fourier. The theoretical foundations of the RPAA's new town proposals rested on Howard's Garden City concept. Unfortunately, the "new towns" designed by RPAA members Henry Wright and Clarence Stein, and those actually built (such as Sunnyside Gardens and Radburn) turned out to be "garden suburbs," with no independent economic base.[19]

Finally, it was the role of the RPAA as propagandists that proved to be their most important contribution. Its concepts and proposals, expressed through Mumford's powerful writings and fused with Ebenezer Howard's closely related ideas, spread out across the United States, Canada, and the world, exercising enormous influence. An example of the RPAA's attempt to popularize its ideas is the 1938 film, *The City*, which was shown at the 1939 Chicago World's Fair and featured the ideas of Lewis Mumford and others. Many elements of the story showcased in the film have, indeed, been realized – the automobile has become a dominant means of transportation, the United States' housing stock has been upgraded significantly, and many open spaces have been protected. According to Jacobs (1989, 11), "the mid-1920s work of the RPAA, the 1925 special issue of *Survey Graphic,* the 1926 plan developed for New York State by members of the RPAA, and Mumford's chapters on regionalism in *The Culture of Cities* (1938) represent the clearest early expression in the United States of the decentralist theory of development."

Despite these initiatives and accomplishments, most twentieth-century policy makers and planners ignored the RPAA's broader vision for building and rebuilding American cities and metropolitan regions, and for preserving rural and wilderness areas. Indeed, many of the concerns first raised in the 1920s remain largely unresolved: the impact of suburban sprawl on cities and country-sides, how to reconcile the automobile and highways with the design of livable communities and regions, and the need for high-quality affordable housing. As Peter Hall (1988, 137) ironically noted, despite their accomplishments, "the true radical quality of the message got muffled or distorted and more than half lost; nowhere on the ground today do we see the true and remarkable vision of the RPAA, distilled via Geddes from Proudhon, Bakunin, Reclus and Kropotkin."

The Southern Regionalists and the Natural Region

Another group that advanced the cause of regional planning in the years between the two world wars and that viewed regional planning from the perspective of "regionalism," consisted of a number of sociologists teaching at southern US universities (particularly the University of North Carolina) and led by Howard W. Odum. Called the "Southern Regionalists," they were members of the so-called "new south" movement, which was a more general movement and constituted a reaction against what they saw as the exploitation and underdevelopment of the southeastern states. They were cultural regionalists, and, not surprisingly, Odum and his followers were directly influenced by Charles-Brun and the French regionalist movement. Odum's approach to what he called "regional-national social planning" was strikingly similar to that presented in the platform of the Fédération régionaliste française. The Southern Regionalists proposed to reverse the trends towards political disenfranchisement and economic underdevelopment in the South and to restore a higher degree of equality among different parts of the United States. They wanted to achieve what has since come to be a widely accepted goal of regionalists – "regional balance" (Odum 1935; Vance 1935; Odum and Jocher 1945).

While they share certain basic attitudes and philosophies, and are sometimes treated as one group, it is important to distinguish between the arguments of the Southern Regionalists (as represented by Odum, Rupert Vance, and other social scientists) and those of the Nashville-based group of writers and humanists known as the Southern Agrarians (Entrikin 1991, 76-8).

The Southern Agrarians focused their attacks on the process of cultural levelling and homogenization that threatened to make the South indistinguishable from the rest of the nation. The Twelve Southerners' manifesto, *I'll Take My Stand* (1930), expressed the same concerns about regional homogenization and the lack of regional identity as did Odum; however, they viewed "progressive" regionalists such as Odum as co-conspirators with the industrialists who were destroying the Southern way of life. They thought that the social sciences and a belief in scientific rationality was dangerous, while Odum thought that they were the best means for both preserving the distinctiveness of Southern culture and improving living conditions in the region. Odum viewed regionalism as being akin to an applied social science in that it provided a way of applying a scientific perspective to a region's problems. For the Southern Agrarians, however, social science was the creation of a cosmopolitan cultural outlook that would necessarily override traditional rural ways of life.

The Southern Regionalists stressed that economic betterment in the South could be accomplished only by overall planning, and Roosevelt's New Deal (which we discuss in a later section) provided the impetus for such planning. Furthermore, they believed that the homogeneous, natural region seemed to be ideally suited to the comprehensive planning approach, especially in the South. As Friedmann (1956) notes, it is interesting that no one seemed to be especially surprised by this strange wedding between Southern rural conservatism, with its focus on the natural region, and Northern progressivism, with its emphasis on planning.

The Southern Regionalists and the RPAA shared many planning concepts and strategies. Like the RPAA, the Southern Regionalists conceived of regions as the primary building blocks of human culture and social life. New England, the South, and the Pacific Northwest were real historical places, each sharing a common history, social institutions, and patterns of human and environmental relationships. According to Friedmann and Weaver (1979, 5), Odum understood the threat that industrialism posed for territorially integrated regional societies, and he hoped to contain and move this force through what he called "regional-national social planning." The aim of such planning would be to shape an *organic territorial* structure in which history, natural resources, climate, and cultural traditions combined to form the varied landscapes of the United States. Indeed, one of the most important concepts the RPAA and Southern Regionalists shared was their belief in the territorial approach to regional delimitation and to regional planning – a markedly different concept from the regional definition used by "functional" planners during the 1960s and since (Friedmann and Weaver 1979; see also Chapter 2 in this book).

Both the RPAA and the Southern Regionalists also emphasized mixing town and countryside through the decentralization of industry. This was to be achieved by applying new technologies and reforming regional education and politics. The Southern Regionalists also endorsed the new towns idea, especially when it appeared later in New Deal programs such as the Tennessee Valley Authority and the Federal Resettlement Administration.

The Southern Regionalists published several important books and articles, perhaps the most notable being Odum's *American Regionalism* (undertaken with Harry E. Moore in 1938), which is generally acknowledged to be the classic exposition of American regionalism.[20] Even though their writings on regional planning began to appear somewhat later than the RPAA's, the Southern Regionalists had an immediate impact on the deliberations of the newly elected (1933) Roosevelt administration. In the now-classic National Resources Committee publication, *Regional Factors in National Planning* (1935) – a report based primarily on the early doctrine of regional planning and one that probably used the term "regional scientist" for the first time (see our later discussion of regional scientists) – Odum was the first authoritative source to be cited in the preface.

In retrospect, Odum was no more successful than was Mumford in preventing the growth of the metropolis in the United States (Friedmann and Weaver 1979, 192). And, as we shall see in Part 3, neither Odum's nor Mumford's ideas have succeeded in preventing the growth of the metropolis in Canada.

Beginning of the Focus on City and Metropolitan Regions

In its regional factors study, the National Resources Committee tried to avoid some of the pitfalls of the ideological approach taken by the Southern proponents of regional planning. However, this ideology was pervasive and permeated the committee's thinking, if only unconsciously: the committee rejected the concept of the region based on metropolitan influence, arguing that regions should be based on resources, economic patterns, and regional interests rather than on a single factor such as the city (NRC 1935). That was in 1935. In 1938, Mumford published his *Culture of Cities,* in which his descriptions of regions and regional life could well have been written by Vidal and were generally sympathetic to the Southern exponents of regional planning. He, like his Southern brothers-in-arms, recognized the region as a natural area.

As noted earlier, Mumford describes a region as a territorial community with a unique character – a harmonious synthesis of the attributes of the physical environment and the people who settle it. Certainly, these remarks are reminiscent of Geddes' "valley plan of civilization." Nevertheless, Mumford would not and could not escape the fact that it was the city that gave a region its critical vitality. He saw the city as analogous to the heart of the body: a controlling mechanism that pumps the lifeblood of energy, people, and commerce to all parts of the regional organism.

Moreover, by 1942, there were signs that the city was beginning to make an impression on the consciousness of the nation. Undoubtedly, this stemmed in part from the sudden and remarkable rejuvenation of the US economy during the Second World War, much of which was occurring in major cities across the nation to meet the needs of the war effort. Also, in a challenging paper presented at a conference of professional planners in 1942, Louis Wirth (a renowned University of Chicago urban sociologist) proposed the metropolitan region as the logical planning unit. As though he felt obliged to counter the pervasive influence of the Southern Regionalists, with their focus on the natural region, Wirth very clearly spelled out the basic features of a metropolitan region and principles of metropolitan planning. He argued that the metropolitan region should be the area of daily intimate and vital interrelation between the city, the suburbs, and the periphery; and he argued further that the region should be a unit that "takes account of the city and its surrounding area's place in the national and world economy" (Wirth 1942, 150).

Towards the end of the war, the death knell for the natural region as the proper region for regional planning seemed to have finally tolled. In a sharply critical article the economist Walter Kollmorgen (1945) attacked the rural traditionalist bias of the Southern Regionalists' "brand" of regionalism on the grounds that it failed to take into account the facts of the technological revolution that was then in the early stages of remaking the United States. Urbanism, according to Kollmorgen, was the "wave of the future."

These ideas marked the beginning of the movement for making the metropolitan region the basic regional planning unit. Nevertheless, the rural values the regionalists propounded would not die easily. Two years after Kollmorgen's article and well into the postwar era, a group of Yale University social scientists and planners resurrected the imagery of the natural region, with its foundation in folk culture (Yale University 1947). They spoke of "geographic unities, homogeneous desires, attitudes and wants" and suggested a forceful analogy between the region and individual living organisms. However, the Yale report was probably the last outburst of regionalist ideology in the United States – at least one based on the concept of the "natural region" – until the rise of the "bioregionalism" movement in the 1980s.

The New Deal "Ideologues" and Comprehensive Regional Resource Development

One of Franklin Delano Roosevelt's first moves on assuming the US presidency in 1932 was to step up the flow of public works projects. These construction jobs were meant to provide stop-gap employment for some of the millions of people out of work during the Depression. To coordinate this operation, Roosevelt created the National Planning Board, which soon defined for itself a greatly expanded role. The National Planning Board's successor, the National Resources Planning Board (NRPB), was dismantled in 1943. It had offered much of the United States some experience of regional planning, including organizing regional planning commissions, preparing resource surveys, dam building, and comprehensive regional-resource development schemes. Most important for the present discussion were the river basin development projects, especially the Tennessee Valley Authority (TVA).

As noted earlier, in 1935 the National Resources Committee released its path-breaking report entitled *The Regional Factors in National Planning*. The study accepted many of the tenets of regional planning theory as proposed by the Southern Regionalists in particular. The idea of balanced regional resource development within the context of historically defined cultural areas was adopted as the explicit goal of planning. However, in its attempt to provide a set of criteria for defining planning regions, the National Resources Committee's Technical Committee fell back on the physical watershed or river basin as the desirable regional planning unit. This, it should be noted, was largely a realistic concession to the territorial division of powers within the US federal system and partly the recognition of a number of ongoing small river basin development schemes that the Roosevelt administration had already initiated.

Tennessee Valley Authority: A Model for Many

Most of the regional factors report was devoted to a discussion of four major river basin development projects and their associated regional planning organizations: the Connecticut River watershed and the New England Regional Commission; the Colorado River Basin Compact; the Pacific Northwest regional planning commission and the Columbia Basin study; and, finally, the TVA. The Colorado and Pacific Northwest efforts led to the construction of the Boulder, Bonneville, and Grand Coulee Dams. The dams were all pure and simple federal water control and power generation projects, with no broader regional development objectives.

It was only in the Tennessee Valley that comprehensive river basin development proved truly successful. It is of interest to note that, according to Friedmann and Weaver (1979, 73), formation of the TVA was almost a chance occurrence – the product of several disparate events and attitudes unique to the American scene of the period.[21] This region, based on the Tennessee River in the southwestern United States and comprising seven states, encompassed several hundred thousand square kilometres. For many decades it had been subject to major floods, owing to inordinate cutting of its forests and debilitating agricultural practices that rendered the soils incapable of holding water.

President Roosevelt proposed, and the Congress enacted, the Tennessee Valley Authority Act in May 1933. It gave the president power to plan and develop the entire river basin region for multiple uses and to enact legislation to realize a wide range of purposes in the valley, including flood control, navigation, generation of electric power, and proper use of marginal lands. These objectives were to be realized through the construction of dams, electric power generation, reforestation, promotion of improved agricultural methods, irrigation, and the building of new towns – all for the purpose of improving "the economic and social well-being of the people."

The law also created a public development corporation, the TVA, and a three-person board to oversee its actual operations. This broad mandate was based on similar principles underlying the natural region espoused by Geddes (Hodge 1998, 313-14). Regional planners with quite divergent viewpoints hailed the TVA as pointing the way to a new civilization, although some of their hopes and expectations proved to be unrealistic.

The TVA seemed to symbolize all the regional ideals discussed previously. To Mumford, his RPAA colleagues, the Southern Regionalists, and other admirers of the TVA, it not only proved to be a demonstration of Geddes' original ideas, but it also heralded a new tool for economic and social progress. RPAA members Benton MacKaye and Tracy Augur helped the authority with conservation projects and new town building. One of Odum's colleagues praised the authority's plans in the pages of *Social Forces,* a journal influential among intellectuals. The National Resources Committee held up the TVA as a model for further experimentation in regional development and planning. Proposals were made for a number of river basin authorities that would cover almost the entire country. President Roosevelt himself promised "seven more TVAs" in his 1936 re-election campaign.

Did the TVA in fact realize the hopes and expectations of many people? In its early years, the answer is clearly yes. The authority built dams, sold electricity, produced fertilizer, and greatly improved navigation and flood control on the Tennessee River and its tributaries. It developed a "grassroots" agriculture program that worked through traditional land grant colleges and state agricultural extension offices. Reforestation began through a centralized approach, and new towns were built.

On two matters, however, the verdict on the TVA's accomplishments is mixed. First, the regional planning function of the authority, directly under the wing of the board's first chair, Arthur Morgan, was originally conceived as an all-encompassing social objective. However, significantly, and to the chagrin and disappointment of regional planning advocates, the regional planning division of the TVA was never activated. The chair was enthusiastic about supporting the regional planning function, but his fellow board members felt that the authority's main functions were to generate electricity and produce fertilizer. For them, only activities that directly supported these functions should be encouraged, and, therefore, planning on a regional scale was thought to be impractical and inappropriate.

In 1938, when the chair's term expired and President Roosevelt did not reappoint him, the board's only advocate of "regional planning" was replaced. In a subsequent realignment of the authority's internal organization, the regional planning unit was eliminated altogether, and there was a new, stronger emphasis on power generation and industrialization.

Moreover, as Weaver (1984, 70) points out, it was never Washington's intention that the TVA be a mechanism for regional control and planning of the valley's water and electrical power resources for the residents of the valley; this would have been condemned as too radical. After all, in President Roosevelt's speech on the TVA's potential, he called for "*national* planning for a complete river watershed [our emphasis]," *not* regional control of regional resources. And this is exactly what happened. Also, as Tugwell and Banfield (1950, 50) pointed out, "from 1936 on, the TVA should have been called the Tennessee Valley Power Production and Flood Control Corporation." They were merely reflecting a generally accepted view that the TVA was *not* an example of regional planning but, rather, of enviable construction and development.

The second matter that has disappointed most of the original supporters of the TVA is that, starting in the late 1930s and early 1940s, the authority demonstrated its potential for promoting extensive urban-industrial expansion. By charging lower electricity rates to bulk users than to domestic consumers, it soon became the cheapest source of industrial power in the country. As a corollary to this rapid industrial growth, people moved to the valley's metropolitan areas. So, as Friedmann and Weaver (1979, 78) observe, "far from ushering in Mumford's biotechnical civilization, the TVA had proven itself to be a powerful instrument of urban-industrial expansion and, rather than being a model for comprehensive river basin development, it would be a model that funnelled resources and people into the metropolis."

Most important, by the late 1970s, the TVA had not only grown into the largest electric power producer and coal consumer in the United States, it was also an avid advocate of economic growth and one of the country's strongest supporters of building nuclear generating stations. All of this was to the consternation and disappointment of many of its original supporters both in the valley and in Washington, DC. In essence, the TVA's situation was almost the reverse of what it was in the mid-1930s when, despite the cries of "socialist" and "Yankee," it tried to help the poor people in the valley build more prosperous lives. By the 1970s, the TVA's friends were the establishment: business, labour, and the state government; and its foes were the "socially handicapped": the poor, the anti-establishment advocates of public interests, and environmentalists (see Shapley 1976).

Later Efforts

In 1942 two renowned scholars made an effort to revive interest in the river basin as the major planning unit for comprehensive development. In a little-publicized pamphlet (published by the National Planning Association), the Harvard economist Alvin Hansen and economist-regional planner and educator Harvey Perloff called for the comprehensive development of the nation's natural resources on a regional basis, and they used the TVA as a model. Concerned with laying the basis for economic expansion in the post-Second World War period, the authors argued that, first, "the nation had not yet fully grasped the tremendous potentialities inherent in the comprehensive development and wise use of our water, land, and mineral resources" (Hansen and Perloff, 1942, 3); second, that a program aimed at such development and use should be based on the river valley as the basic development area throughout the United States; and third, that a single autonomous agency (such as the TVA), with specific planning, research, and operating responsibilities, should be located at the site of operation within each of the regions (30).

Hansen and Perloff (1942, 2) stressed that a comprehensive program of regional development would stimulate private enterprise and enable business to plan its investments on a more secure basis. While they dealt with all the topics that had come to be associated with river basin planning during the 1930s (e.g., parks and recreational development, fish and wildlife protection, land-use management, infrastructure location), their primary emphasis was on resource development as a means of economic expansion. This was, indeed, a far cry from the goals that had inspired regional planning a decade earlier, but it did accurately reflect the realities of the TVA's historical evolution.

President Truman's Water Resources Policy Commission tried to reintroduce some of the broader aspects of comprehensive river basin development in 1950, but by then the objective of economic growth was already becoming the focus of development planning. And, for the following three decades, regional planning doctrine would be wedded firmly to the *functional* notion of urban-industrial growth. It was not until the 1990s that regional planning would rediscover the concept of *territorial* regionalism.

The Conservers and the Conservation Movement

The early 1900s saw the Canadian movement for the conservation of natural resources substantially influenced by events in the United States. In the US, the pressure of population growth on natural resources, especially the forests and water, was threatening future supply, leading to the demand for legislation and other measures aimed at more prudent management of these resources. One of the measures adopted was the formation of the United States Inland Waterways Commission, a body that advised President Theodore Roosevelt on various aspects of water use. Its formation led, in turn, to the establishment of the International Waterways Commission of the United States and Canada, a six-person body, with equal representation from each country, that advised the two national governments on the best uses of the waterways common to both countries. The commission exists to this day, as the International Joint Commission, and it is considered by many to be a model of how two countries can cooperate over the use of a common natural resource.

The members of the Inland Waterways Commission were the first to propose to President Roosevelt that he call a conference in 1908, whose purpose, in the words of Roosevelt several months later, was "to consider the amount and condition of natural resources and the most effective means of conserving them" (Thorpe 1961, 2). Its main result was the appointment of the National Conservation Commission and state conservation commissions throughout the United States. A few months later, in 1908, a second conference was held, which, among other things, considered an inventory of natural resources that had been prepared by the National Conservation Commission. This second conference emphasized that the resources in question were not limited by international boundaries. As a result, the US president asked Canada and Mexico to designate representatives to attend a conference in February 1909 in Washington, DC. This conference was to consider the mutual interests of countries concerned with the conservation of resources and to deliberate on the practicality of preparing a general plan that could be applied throughout the whole continent.

Gifford Pinchot, who was then chief of the United States Forest Service and chair of the United States National Conservation Commission (and who later became known as the "father" of the conservation movement in that country), was the bearer of the letter of invitation from President Roosevelt to the Canadian governor general. Canada did, indeed, accept the invitation and sent three official representatives to the North American Conservation Conference. The conference came to an agreement on a declaration of principles that covered a wide variety of subjects. Perhaps its most important recommendation was that each participating country should have a commission of conservation similar to those set up in the United States. Thus was born the Canadian Commission of Conservation.

Commission of Conservation

The groundwork for Canadian acceptance of the North American Conservation Conference's declaration of principles had already been laid in the previous years as a result of a major conference of its own. This was the 1906 First Canadian Forestry Convention, at which many of the ideas then being implemented in the United States were discussed. This national conference was presided over by the prime minister, Sir Wilfrid Laurier.[22] The conference led to regular annual meetings of the Canadian Forestry Association, the establishment of schools of forestry at the University of Toronto in 1907 and the University of New Brunswick in 1908, and the establishment of provincial government forest services. It was also broad enough to encourage a general interest in resource conservation and development throughout Canada.

In May 1909 the Cabinet approved the principle of establishing a Commission of Conservation as a body that would have representatives from the federal and provincial governments and the universities. Clifford Sifton, a former federal minister of the interior and one of the three Canadian representatives at the North American Conservation Conference, was appointed chair.

In the twelve years of its existence (1909-21), the commission's work was considerable and ranged over a wide variety of subjects. It had six main committees – forestry, lands, fish and wildlife, water, minerals and fuels, and public health. A unique aspect of the commission's work is the fact that it linked water and air pollution to public health considerations; and it linked public health with town planning. To a large extent, this was no doubt due to the influence of Dr. Charles Hodgetts, the commission's medical officer, who strongly believed that town and rural planning were related to land use as well as to public health. (See Chapter 7 for a further discussion of the work and accomplishments of the commission. See also Armstrong 1959; Smith and Witty 1972; Simpson 1985; Stein 1994a; Gunton 1981, 97-133; and Hodge 1998.)

The commission's achievements were many, and for this reason its demise in 1921 was generally lamented. Effective liaison among the many agencies working in resources died with it (Dakin 1968, 120). Indeed, the hope was that the commission would result in the preparation of an integrated resource management policy for the development of the country's natural resources. However, to this day, eighty years since the commission was disbanded, this expectation has not been realized, in large part because no comparable agency at the federal level has ever been established. Moreover, as Stein (1994a, 55) has noted: "It should be chastening to consider that many of the problems the commission set out to deal with in 1909 are still with us and, indeed, have become more acute."

The early flourishing of the conservation movement did not last long after the dissolution of the commission in 1921. It seems that the social and economic conditions of the 1920s and 1930s were not favourable to "idealistic" concepts such as resource conservation and prudent planning (Richardson 1994, 56). One notable exception was the Prairie Farm Rehabilitation Act (PFRA), 1935, which was the federal government's response to the agricultural devastation of the dust-bowl years in the Canadian Prairies (see Chapter 6). Thorpe (1961, 11) noted that, "although the PFRA was not a concept of complete integration of resources, in answering an economic need it moved well in that direction."

Later Conservation Initiatives in Canada

The state of Canada's natural resources was not examined on the same scale as it had been under the Commission of Conservation until the Dominion-Provincial Reconstruction Conference was convened in August 1945. In 1942, three years before the end of the Second World War, the federal government set up the Advisory Committee on Reconstruction to make a thorough assessment of all aspects of the economic-social life of Canada and to make a blueprint of the society that was to be established after the end of the war.[23] The key subcommittees dealt with natural resources and agriculture (see Chapter 6).

Another tangible influence on the development of conservation awareness in Canada was the 1942 Guelph Conference on the Conservation of the Natural Resources of Ontario. Largely a response to the dust-bowl conditions created by destructive logging and farming practices in vast parts of Ontario, the conference is generally credited with being responsible for the passage of that province's Conservation Authorities Act in 1946. This act provides for government-funded intermunicipal watershed agencies and – on paper at least – a strong mandate for renewable resource conservation. Unfortunately, in practice the authorities were kept on a tight rein both by the province and by the municipal councils who, not unexpectedly, were jealous of the newly established powers given to the various conservation authorities established throughout the province. As a consequence, many of the problems that gave rise to the conservation authorities' legislation in the first place are still with us, as are newer, more complicated problems.

Resources for Tomorrow Conference

In the late 1950s all levels of government in Canada, the private sector, and the public at large began to evince great concern for the country's natural resources. No up-to-date inventory on the supply of the country's resources was available. The notion of unlimited renewable resources was being threatened by the realization that no systematic approaches to, or public policies for, the conservation and development of Canada's natural resources were in place. Also, Canada was feeling the effects of increasing competition from many other countries in the area of resources production.

These circumstances, which, in 1961, led to the call for a national conference on the present and future status of our resources, were not new. As will be recalled, a concern for conservation had been voiced at the turn of the twentieth century through the Commission of Conservation. However, the approach taken at the Resources for Tomorrow Conference, which was held in Montreal in October 1961, differed from previous approaches in terms of its intention to establish goals, processes, priorities, and guidelines for action. To this point, no conference of this type had ever provided the opportunity for the exchange of so many ideas and viewpoints on the fate of the country's renewable resources.

Planning for this conference involved three years of preparation, during which time leading experts in resource conservation and development (from the government, academic, and private sectors) were invited to prepare papers. These papers served as background material for conference participants and as reference documents for current and future public use. In total, eighty research papers were submitted and assembled in two volumes (see Resources for Tomorrow 1961 and 1962). In addition to the sectoral topics the conference covered (e.g., agriculture, forestry, water), a large number of sessions were devoted to regional planning and development. Fourteen background papers were presented on the general subject, five of which dealt with specific aspects of the subject and another nine of which presented regional case studies. In addition, six workshops were devoted to the subject matter of the background papers on regional planning and development.

Everyone left the Montreal conference full of optimism. Unfortunately, the results and follow-up actions have not lived up to the conference's promises. As far as we know, only one follow-up resources minister's conference was held. Nevertheless, one significant result of the conference is that regional planning was certainly given the "push" it needed to promote itself on a large scale. Throughout the 1960s and 1970s there was a huge increase in regional planning activity, and this may well have been a consequence of the conference.

In the area of resource conservation and development, the Montreal conference had some indirect positive consequences. For example, the widespread laissez-faire policies of the past, based on the principle of short-run profit maximization, which usually entailed wholesale forest clear-cutting and a

variety of ecologically destructive practices, were attacked. Also, in the following decades, provincial departments concerned with resource development,
conservation, and the environment gradually adopted new ideas, such as long-
term planning, public consultation, sustainability, and multiple uses of resources (Richardson 1989a, 1994). British Columbia, Alberta, and other
provinces put in place systems of integrated resource planning and management. More recently, there has been a growing concern over "sustainable development," and this has led to an increased interest in reviving regional
planning (see Chapter 7).

Advent of Regional Science and Regional Scientists[24]

After the Second World War, regional theory, though not regional practice,
took a technocratic turn. The concern for regions and places that was such an
important element in the philosophies of Mumford, Odum, and others was
replaced by the "nomothetic" logic of scientific planning (Entrikin 1991, 81)
known as the "regional science" movement. This movement was the brain-
child of Walter Isard, a distinguished economist who was trained at Harvard
and was, for many years, professor of regional science at the University of
Pennsylvania.

The movement was officially launched in 1954 with the formation of the
Regional Science Association, which was under Isard's aegis. Its membership
has grown from sixty people at the initial gathering to more than 3,000 in the
mid-1990s. The purpose of the association, according to Isserman (1995, 250),
was to "foster exchange of ideas and to promote studies focusing on the region
and using tools, methods and theoretical frameworks specifically designed for
regional analysis, as well as concepts, procedures and analytical techniques of
the various social and other sciences." The association would be an "objective, scientific organization without political, social, financial, or nationalistic
bias," and it would advance "the field of regional science."

For Isard, the primary concern of the regional scientist was practical problem solving through the application of scientific theories (although, as it turned
out, this goal was far from realized). Isard also wished to identify a "true set"
of regions for administration and policy implementation. He recognized that
this could only be approximated, not achieved, through the development of
general theory. His mode of study emphasized structure and functions, and,
as is the case with spatial analysis in general, he saw mathematical modelling
and theory as synonymous (see Isard et al. 1960 and Figure 7). Regions were
modelled as complex systems consisting of natural, economic, social, and psy-
chological subsystems, thus leaving little room for the normative significance
of "place." Also ignored, according to Entrikin (1991, 82), was the subjective
reality of specific places rooted in culture and community – a phenomenon
that had been so important to both the early regionalists and to the previous
generation of planners.

At the fourth Regional Science Association meeting in 1958, Lyle Crane put forward one of the clearest explanations of the relationship among regional planners, regional scientists, and regional analysts (Regional Science Association 1958, 18-22). According to Crane, pure regional scientists seek to discover laws of wide applicability, or "regional universals"; and regional analysts study regional problems or aspects of a particular region. Regional planners, who are concerned with values and goals, use the findings of the regional scientists and regional analysts to determine the "proper" structure and spatial relations between structural units of the regional environment.

Although regional science did not create a quantitative revolution in geography, it did make great advances in quantitative analysis through the works of William Garrison and Brian Berry, among others.[25] Perhaps most important, the regional science movement provided crucial impetus, encouragement, ideas, forums, and publication outlets for a number of different disciplines. To urban and regional planning, regional science contributed quantitative tools for economic and demographic analysis: economic base analysis, input-output analysis, market area analysis, and population projections that remain standard features of planning education and widely used tools in planning practice. The scholarly achievements of regional scientists also had a significant impact on urban and regional economics, quantitative and theoretical geography, and agricultural economics. The methods of regional analysis are now firmly ensconced in numerous government agencies.

The advances in quantitative analysis of regional settings coincided, in the 1960s, with the change occurring in public policy pertaining to the issue of economic growth in Canada. Not least, Canadian federal and provincial governments saw great promise in these methods, which they hoped would enable them both to better diagnose problems of regional disparities and to prescribe solutions. The seeming objectivity that regional scientists could bring to these normative issues was utilized by many studies to identify, for example, "growth poles" in Eastern Ontario and Prince Edward Island (Hodge 1966, 1967), industrial complexes in Nova Scotia (Czamanski 1971), and industrial location indices for the Toronto region (Hodge 1970). Indeed, it can be said that the dependence of governments and their advisors on regional science techniques was both a strength of the period of regional economic development planning (described in Chapter 6) and its ultimate weakness, because it had little place for the human and cultural attributes of each region.

Planning educators embraced regional science early on. One of them, Louis Wetmore (of the City Planning Department at the University of Illinois) noted that, by synthesizing "the many separate contributions of the social sciences for the understanding of the region, the regional scientist promises significant contributions in the field of planning" (quoted in Isserman 1995, 263). Another planning educator, John Friedmann, argued that regional planning "derives its basic orientation from regional science" (Friedmann and Alonso 1964).

Today, most leading planning departments in North America have regional scientists on their faculties.

Despite the many contributions of regional science, in recent years regional scientists themselves (especially those working in the planning and policy-making fields) have offered a number of critical evaluations of it (see, for example, Isserman 1993, 1995; Bailey and Coffey 1994; and a number of papers in IJSR 1995). These various critics generally agreed that regional science is too theoretical and methods-oriented; that it is aloof from, or irrelevant to, planning practice, problems, and policy issues; and that it ignores human and cultural factors. Markusen (1994, 1) notes that regional science failed to meet "the demand for political relevance and contributions to the quality of regional life which have continually been pressed since the 1960s." Anselm and Madden (1990, 7) lament "the lack of diffusion of the advances in regional analysis to the practice of policy and planning," and they cite "the overwhelming emphasis on the analysis of data," much of which they believe was not of great quality.

Notable critiques have been put forward by two well-known Canadian regional scientists. Larry Bourne of the University of Toronto deplores the fact that regional science has done little to address some of the dominant issues of current social, economic, and political concern in Canada (Bourne 1995b); while Mark Rosenberg (1993), of Queen's University, argues that regional science has done little to deal with the problems of regional inequality in Canada. Both Bourne and Rosenberg point out that there are major differences in attitudes, approach, and decision-making criteria between the world of practical planning and policy making and the world of academic regional science. Nevertheless, they persuasively argue that both groups truly "need" each other, and they conclude with some advice as to how this cooperation can occur.

Reflections

Having examined the roots of regional planning, what can we say that will be of help to present-day regional planning and its future? For one thing, the idea of regional planning has persisted for almost 200 years. Although it varied in form, the need for taking a larger view of human settlements and for harmonizing the relationship between people and nature has been sustained in the ethos of regional planning. For another, there is the enduring dichotomy of views as to the underlying purposes of regional planning; these views, in turn, are reflected in different ideas regarding the appropriate region for planning.

The various philosophers whose ideas have had a major influence on the theory and practice of regional planning in the late nineteenth and early to mid-twentieth centuries can be broken down into two groups. One group held that regional planning was a means of developing the *physical* resources of a region, especially its water resources, in order to better the social and economic well-being of people in the region. For this group the proper planning region was the *natural* region or *resource* region. The second group believed that it was the city that gave a region its cultural and economic vitality; in addition to being the focus of the flow of energy, information, goods, and people in a region, the city organized these flows for the rest of the region and thereby controlled its development. For this group, the logical planning unit for regional planning was the *city-centred* or *metropolitan* region.

Today, the same dichotomy is reflected in the approach of bioregionalists versus city-region advocates, as we shall see in Chapters 8 and 9. So, while sharing the same overall goals, regional planners have always proposed two different routes for attaining them. As we shall see in Chapter 2, these basic differences influenced regional planning doctrine and practice, and they would continue to divide academics, professionals, and public officials right up to the present day (Part 2 and 3). Nevertheless, despite their opposing views, the aforementioned philosophers had a great deal in common – most obviously a belief in the need for a regional perspective in planning.

It is also worth noting that both the natural region view and the city-centred region view derive from an enlightened, or "modern," approach to ideas and activities. Although neither is really wrong, some (Wight 1998a) would question whether, in a "postmodern" world such as ours, either of them is adequate as a base for contemporary regional planning. Thus, even though these and other early ideas are necessary building blocks, they may not provide a sufficient foundation for regional planning today. Just as the ideas about regional planning evolved in the past, so must they continue to evolve in concert with contemporary conditions.[26] As we shall note below, the development of regional planning, therefore, is as much about the development of ideas as it is about the activities and other outcomes associated with its practice.

Having said that, we must agree with Richardson (1994, 69), who notes that what is most fascinating about these earlier periods (and professional planners are just now rediscovering this), is the prescience shown by people such as Thomas Adams, and, we would add, the RPAA. After many decades of quiescence, several key ideas promulgated by some of these people are being rediscovered and revived today. For example:

- The concept of regionalism itself, having been explicated by the regional geographers, Mumford, and the Southern Regionalists, is coming to the fore once again in the form of bioregionalism.
- Related to the concept of regionalism is the Commission of Conservation's warning (which anticipated the now famous Brundtland report [UN 1987] by more than seventy years) that "each generation is entitled to the interest on the natural capital, but the principal should be handed on unimpaired."
- The RPAA adopted a doctrine for regional planning based on a harmonious relationship between people and nature, and grounded in a bio-ethics that respected the limits of human intervention in natural processes (Friedmann

and Weaver 1979, 4-5). This concept was diametrically opposed to the prevailing ethic of the time, which emphasized the ability of technology to overcome the resistance of natural processes to the forces of economic development, and which, regardless of environmental damage, captured the resources needed to fuel urbanization and economic growth. This early RPAA doctrine also presaged an interest in "sustainable development" some sixty or seventy years before its current popularity.

- The RPAA experience provides us with another significant lesson from the past – the relevance of collaboration, which is a characteristic of most regional planning tasks. Parsons (1994), who calls the RPAA a "collaborative genius," notes that the ten-year experience of that association teaches us that effective, long-term technical collaboration can occur when the process involves assembling relevant professionals and those with strong leadership abilities within a framework of shared purpose.

- Another example comes from Thomas Adams, who understood very well the *relationships between the human and natural environment*; in particular, he understood that planning, housing, sanitation, and other improvements to cities and towns, together with ecological and environmental protection in rural areas (all undertaken within a regional context) need to be seen as interrelated components of a "healthy environment." Today, professional planners are rediscovering this concept under such rubrics as "sustainable development" and "healthy communities," and the Canadian Institute of Planners has taken an active interest in both (see Chapter 7).

- Finally, among the principles being advanced for achieving sustainable development is the need for a "balanced approach" – one that ensures that the desire to achieve environmental sustainability is balanced against other economic and social objectives. This takes the regional planner back to the 1920s and, once again, to the ideas of the RPAA. As one researcher has noted, the new paradigm "has more in common with the views which were expressed by the RPAA more than half a century ago than it has with the 'slash and burn' regional growth philosophy that has dominated much of the past 40 years" (Roberts 1994, 782).[27]

Another way to view the evolution of regional planning is to see it as a progression from ideas regarding social change to the promulgation of public policy to the formation of institutions with a mandate to carry out regional planning. In short, the precursors of regional planning can be viewed as constituting episodes in the development of this discipline, each episode being a necessary step towards turning social concepts into useful currency: from ideas (Fourier), to experiments (Owen), to demonstrations (Howard), to more ideas (Geddes), to more demonstrations (the RPAA), to more experiments (the TVA) and, finally, to government acceptance (the conservation authorities in Ontario).

In Chapters 5 to 9 we will offer further examples of new ideas of regional planning that are coming forth and vying for public sanction.

The precursors of regional planning have much to teach us about public policy development both in the past and in the future. Interestingly, a large number of planners from Britain, western Europe, and the United States – many of whom studied or were actually trained under some of these early seers – came to Canada right after the Second World War, having been recruited by, or attracted to, planning agencies and the then emerging planning schools in Canadian universities. This further reinforced some of the earlier ideas about regional planning in the immediate post Second World War period, which happens to have been the heyday for regional planning practice in Canada. In conclusion, the ideas of the major precursors of regional planning not only provide an understanding of the roots of Canadian regional planning but, just as important, also help to inform approaches taken by Canadian planners today.

Key Features of Regional Planning

Out of the diversity of ideas, movements, and personalities involved in the early evolution of regional planning there emerged a distinct discipline. This is not to imply that the viewpoints of the precursors of regional planning were completely resolved; indeed, regional planning concepts continue to be debated and refined. But we are able to discern the key features of regional planning, which, in turn, can be used to objectively measure the field of public planning. We can use these relatively unchanging key features to derive a general matrix, or "base map," of any regional planning endeavour. This is an essential first step in objectively comparing different regional planning efforts.

However, upon this base map there exists a subjective, or qualitative, dimension of regional planning practice that reflects its prevailing theoretical base and political ideology. This dimension can and does change. Looking at this aspect of regional planning is like placing different overlays over the base map in order to see the quality of regional planning practice in a particular period. The model of regional planning practice Friedmann and Weaver propounded two decades ago (i.e., in 1979) will give a more complete picture of regional planning in Canada, including where it has come from, where it has gone, and where it might be headed.

The Dual Nature of Regional Planning

How might the basic features of regional planning be discerned from the panoply of its past? Was the RPAA involved in the same activity as were the Tennessee Valley Authority and Patrick Geddes? What did they have in common with each other and with the other precursors? And how do their regional planning experiences compare with ours in, for example, the Toronto-Centred Region, Manitoba's Interlake, the Vancouver region, and the Gaspé?

One of the best places to start is with Harvey Perloff's seminal 1968 article on regional planning. He states at the outset that regional planning deals with two dimensions: *regions* and *planning*. For Perloff, this amounts to something more than stating the obvious. He is alerting us to a basic dichotomy between the two – they are quite different from, but closely related to, one another and are ever-present in regional planning and other forms of territorial planning. One dimension concerns *space* and the other concerns a *social* (i.e., *political*) *process*. We need to understand both, as well as the significance of their combination, to grasp the nature of the activity called regional planning and to dissect past and present experiences. Let us look briefly at each dimension.

The Region Dimension

Regional planners need regions: they are the arena, the turf, the space within which regional planning practice happens. They are what regional planners plan for and with (as we shall more fully discuss in the next chapter). But city, municipal, provincial, and national planners also deal with space in their endeavours, so how does regional planning differ?

Looking at the spatial criteria used by three distinguished regional planners can help with this question. First, Perloff (1968, 153) defines regional planning as occurring in a space "greater than a single community and less than a nation." Second, John Friedmann (1963, 169) maintains that the minimum boundary is "supra-urban space," or "any area which is larger than a single city." He provides no maximum size. Third, Canadian planner Len Gertler's planning region "has its focus on an urban centre but its limits are not clearcut" (1972b, 17). At a minimum, he would also include within his planning region "the surrounding country, towns, and villages." According to these definitions, regional planning regions exclude the single city and the entire nation. A complete province could be considered a planning region if the planning objectives required such a space for their attainment. But even Canada's smallest province, Prince Edward Island, is usually seen as comprising at least three regions: western, central, and eastern.

These earlier observers tell us that one of the basic characteristics of planning regions is that they are relatively large pieces of territory. Again, in the most recent regional planning thrust – bioregionalism – large-scale planning areas are still evident. Even the smallest bioregions, known as "vitaregions," usually consist of several thousand square kilometres (Sale 1984). This size variable, as we shall see in later chapters, repeatedly shows up when defining regions for planning purposes. Yet this seemingly self-evident characteristic of planning regions (i.e., their large scale) contains important implications for regional planning with regard to both substance and strategy. When concerned with large pieces of territory the regional planner will almost always need to deal with a much wider array of factors than does the city planner. For example, economic development, natural resource use, and environmental conditions will be included, and land-use problems will pertain to both rural and urban land. Unlike the city planner, the strategic issues for the regional planner tend to be involved with the *location in space* of facilities and activities rather than with the *allocation of space for them*.

There is another important facet of the regional dimension that needs to be considered, one that is concomitant with a region's size. Planners seek out regions because both the nature of certain planning problems and their solutions encompass more than single municipalities or individual communities can be expected to cope with. Individual communities usually have neither the resources nor the authority to make plans and seek solutions on their own with regard to, for example, establishing a regional airport or waste disposal system (much less conserving a river basin). Thus, almost by definition, planning regions encompass several local areas with the aim of achieving a perspective on the planning problem (and its solution) that is "whole," or complete. This means that planning regions are *holistic* in both the space they encompass and in the range of issues they present. It means that they transcend the capabilities (and authority) of the local areas. Planning regions, indeed all regions, are what Koestler (1976), and later Wilber (1997b), call "holons" – entities that are whole and encompass parts (i.e., the local communities and municipalities). However, holons are also entities that themselves are "parts" of some larger whole, just as planning regions are parts of provinces, which, in turn, are parts of the nation. For regional planners, the implication of this arrangement is that they need to ensure that the constituent parts (including the local territories below as well as the provinces above) collaborate and cooperate in making and implementing plans.[1] As we shall see in later chapters, achieving collaboration and cooperation among the wholes and the parts presents a persistent social and political challenge within regional planning. Thus, the regional dimension has a social component that links it inextricably to the planning dimension, to which we now turn.

The Planning Dimension

Clearly, regions are the "necessary" ingredients of regional planning; however, to use the traditional logical paradigm, they are not "sufficient" to account for the activity. It is the planning dimension that plays that particular role. This dimension deals with a much less objective set of factors than does the regional dimension. Furthermore, it is a set of factors that is continually in flux as residents, the economy, and values and preferences change. Planning for regions is a process that is deliberative, normative, and evaluative, and it focuses on clarifying objectives (as do all planning activities). In short, regional planning is a *value-laden* process. Hence, regional planning practice involves two basic questions: (1) Who makes the decision? and (2) How is that decision made? Consequently, regional planning has both a *political* side and a *technical* side, and, while the professional planner is more closely associated with the technical side, planning practice obliges involvement with both.

We may still say that we carry out regional planning in order to achieve desired outcomes and that planners deal with objectives, preferences, priorities, and trade-offs. However, today both the substance and quality of this activity differ significantly from earlier times. All planning practice varies with the social context of the time and the degree of understanding we possess about both the nature of regions and their development as well as about the effectiveness of procedures for achieving planning objectives. Over the past decade or so, significant changes have been occurring within these planning milieux. For one thing, the context for planning has been becoming more complex and diverse so that, for example, today we deal with "multiple publics," to use Sandercock's (1999) term. Today's regional planners need to recognize and include the diversity of culture, gender, and economic position that exists among people in any given region (Tully 1995). For another, there is the need to recognize that the environment is not just something to be conserved, protected, or managed. We do not stand outside the ecology for which we plan; therefore, planners cannot modify it without affecting human as well as environmental well-being (Bateson 1987; Eisenberg 1998).

Add to this the fact that public planning processes can no longer be seen as synoptic rational processes of identifying goals, analyzing alternative outcomes, and selecting appropriate courses of action that are conducted largely within the technical realm. More and more often, observers urge regional planning to become increasingly interactive and inclusive of people, the economy, and the environment (Christensen 1993; Beatley and Manning 1997; Sandercock 1999). And evidence of this shift towards broader-based regional planning is already evident in Canada in the Alberta Capital Region Alliance in metropolitan Edmonton (Chapter 8) and in the community forest programs in Ontario (Chapter 5).

Although, ultimately, regional planning decisions are made by elected or other political entities, professional planners perform important parts of the planning process. It is the planner's task to understand, and to help others understand, the region and its resources, population, and economic trends. Slocombe (1995) identifies four complementary activities for developing an understanding of a region, from the beginning to the end of the planning process: description, interpretation, perception, and intention. Each of these would be applicable whether we were attempting to understand the region's population, its economy, or its environment. Then there is understanding how they fit together. Thus, an inherent characteristic of regional planning is *integrative* practice, a challenging task in itself.

However, new levels of understanding are posing even greater challenges in this regard, both in terms of process and substance. For example, planning practice now places the planner within a web of relationships that involve the public, in all its multiple forms, as well as politicians. Referring to his own experience in metropolitan-regional planning in Vancouver, Lash (1976) called this a "six-sided triangle" of relationships – a mutual system of relationships within which each of the participants could affect the path of planning. In substantive terms, the planner faces new challenges in her/his attempt to find a balance among economic growth, environmental protection, and social justice. Campbell (1996) suggests that these three goals can also be seen as three points on a triangle, each point linked to the other, thereby generating inherent conflicts within any attempt to attain them. In sum, the fairly straightforward planning dimension identified by Perloff is now more elaborate and demanding than ever. These current challenges and their implications for future planning practice are discussed more fully in Chapters 10 and 11.

The Legacies of the Precursors

What can we learn about the key features of regional planning from the concepts and experiences of its precursors? Are the dual dimensions of region and planning evident in their versions of regional planning? And do other features emerge that might characterize regional planning? To be fair, many of the precursors were engaged in contemplative, speculative activities regarding regional planning. They were generally working with ideas, indeed ideals, rather than with real regions and institutions (although Robert Owen and Ebenezer Howard did see their ideas come to partial fruition). Nevertheless, in the legacy of their ideas we find clear indications as to how regional planning would materialize.

Size of Regions

Let us look first at the spatial dimensions of regional planning as it was envisioned by its early proponents. Throughout the writings of the anarchists, for example, we see ideas concerning linking urban and rural activities, decentralizing industry, and focusing on small-scale markets. While it is difficult to determine the exact scale of such regions, they clearly encompassed large amounts of rural areas and their settlements along with moderately sized cities. In turn, the utopian socialists believed that the solution to Industrial Revolution urban woes lay in creating new small communities in the countryside outside large cities. Ebenezer Howard went the furthest and proposed a complex of new towns surrounding a central city, which, although he did not state its size, would have encompassed at least 6,000 square kilometres (see Figure 4). Patrick Geddes also saw the need to establish large planning areas around big urban centres in order to better plan for emerging conurbations. And the famous Tennessee Valley Authority planning region covered all or part of seven states in the United States in order to encompass the Tennessee River Basin.

Similarly large in area, the regional plan proposed by Stein and Wright (of the RPAA) covered the entire state of New York, an area of about 128,000 square kilometres, while the regional plan proposed by the Southern Regionalists covered the entire US South. By comparison, Thomas Adams's metropolitan Regional Plan for New York and Its Environs covered only about 15,000 square kilometres, but this was still more than twenty times the size of the City of New York.

The "Natural" Region

The planning regions of the precursors of today's region planning were not only large, but they also encompassed a complex of rural and urban elements, all their interconnections, and the land and other natural resources located therein. Indeed, the evolution of regional planning thought and practice reveals another key feature: a belief in the close relationship between human activities and natural resources; that is, a belief in what would come to be called the "natural" region. Beginning with Patrick Geddes, Paul Vidal de la Blache, and Frédéric Le Play, and echoed by Lewis Mumford, there developed the idea of achieving a balance between the human and natural facets of a region. Geddes' "valley section" encapsulated this ideal, and the river basin it connoted came to be a cornerstone for defining the boundaries of planning regions (see Figure 5). It is most evident in the Tennessee Valley Authority, but latterly it is also evident in the conservation authorities in Ontario, the Fraser Basin Management Program in British Columbia, and bioregionalism.

Planning Processes

Now, let us review the institutional settings and processes envisioned by the precursors of regional planning. Given the largely hypothetical nature of the earliest regional planning, we do not see much concreteness in planning processes, either politically or technically, until the 1920s and 1930s. The anarchists had talked about forming federations and "social republics" based on cooperation at different regional levels. And Ebenezer Howard's Garden City concept was realized through a private development company. Presumably, the state government would implement the plan for New York State prepared by members of the RPAA.

The metropolitan Regional Plan for New York and Its Environs, begun in 1922, created the first regional planning institution – the Committee on the Regional Plan for New York and Its Environs. It was a private body that assumed the political role of determining the content of the plan and guiding and receiving input from its staff of technical planners (headed by Thomas Adams). After publication of the regional plan, the committee was superseded by the Regional Plan Association, whose role was primarily to educate and persuade local governments about the plan, develop local planning boards, and monitor progress in carrying out the larger plan. This is echoed in the first decades of the twentieth century, when civic interest groups in many cities (including Toronto) sponsored city plans (Hodge 1998).

The second regional planning institution was the Tennessee Valley Authority, which was established in 1933. This was the first occurrence of a full-blown *public* regional planning process. The authority's board was responsible to the US Congress and the president for its policies, and it had an extensive staff of planners and engineers. The region's issues were complex and covered several jurisdictions. It soon became evident that blending political and technical viewpoints was a difficult process (see Selznick 1966). This model of a semi-independent planning and development body with its own technical staff would, however, come to be used around the world and would leave its mark on Canada in the form of the conservation authorities of Ontario.

The Legacy

From the various regional planning precursors we can discern a number of features that remain with us today:

- Regional planning involves a concern with both a *region dimension* and a *planning process dimension.*
- Regional planning is concerned with *harmonizing* human use and natural resource development, with achieving a *regional balance.*
- The *natural* region is the proper delimitation of a planning region.
- Planning regions are *large in size.*
- Planning regions comprise *several public jurisdictions.*

Perhaps the most problematic of these features is the primacy of the so-called "natural" region. As regional planning evolved, especially through the 1930s and 1940s, the city-centred metropolitan region came to contend with the natural region. This created a tension in planning practice, and we shall discuss this further in Chapter 3. This tension is also evident in recent regional planning experience in Canada.

Key Features in the Canadian Experience

Another way of looking for the key features of regional planning is to review several instances of regional planning in Canada over the past few decades. Four cases suggest themselves as representative of different types of regional planning. The Mactaquac Regional Development Plan in New Brunswick is an example of river-basin planning; the Lower Mainland Regional Planning Board in British Columbia is an example of metropolitan planning; the Eastern Ontario Development Region is an example of economic development planning; and the Regional Resources Project No. 1 in Alberta is an example of rural planning.

Size of Region

If we look at the planning regions for these four cases, we find that each of them involve large areas. The Mactaquac region's planning extended more than eighty kilometres along the river valley and covered more than 4,000 square kilometres of commercial forests and farms (Gertler 1972b, 86). The metropolitan planning region for Vancouver, the Lower Mainland region, covered about 3,500 square kilometres of both city and countryside as well as mountains, rivers, and oceanfronts. The Eastern Ontario Development Region also covered a large area – more than 25,000 square kilometres of rural and urban lands, factories, and farms, from the Ottawa Valley to the St. Lawrence Valley. The rural planning in south-central Alberta's Regional Resources Project No. 1 extended over more than ten municipalities, including small towns and wheat-growing areas, and covering 9,000 square kilometres (Bodmer 1980). Thus, both large-scale and complex combinations of natural resources, human land uses, and activities characterize these planning regions. The same would be found if we were to look at other Canadian regional planning situations.

Planning Processes

What about the arrangement of planning processes in these sample regions? In the Mactaquac River Valley, planning decisions had to be made for a major hydroelectric power project – farms had to be relocated, a new town had to be built, and a forest had to be managed. These came under the jurisdiction of a special agency, the Community Improvement Corporation, which was established by the provincial government and which had its own technical staff. Funding was provided primarily by the federal government through several of its agencies and departments. In addition, some municipal governments were involved, along with a newly formed local Forest Land Development Association, all aiming to create a balance between human use and resource exploitation. Planning decisions for the Vancouver metropolitan region were made through a board composed of representatives of the two dozen constituent municipalities and that had its own technical staff. Concerns ranged from conservation of water resources and agricultural land, to industrial development, to regional transportation facilities, and the distribution of settlements. In the other two examples, eastern Ontario and rural Alberta, we find analogous planning arrangements, with several jurisdictions involved and with a concern over resource use and human activities and facilities.

As did the review of the precursors of regional planning, these brief samples of Canadian experience confirm four features of regional planning: (1) it requires a region and a planning process, (2) it is concerned with harmonizing human use and natural resources, (3) it encompasses a large area, and (4) it involves several public jurisdictions.

Dimensions of Regional Planning

Drawing together the threads of Perloff's views, new challenges to the planning process, inferences from precursors, and the Canadian experiences briefly described above, it is now possible to develop a more elaborate set of dimensions pertaining to regional planning. The starting point, of course, must be the two dimensions of (1) region and (2) planning. However, as our explorations have shown, these two dimensions are too general to account for some important aspects of regional planning, especially some of the more contemporary elements of practice. For example, planning regions differ from one another both in concept and actuality. By the same token, the planning dimension comprises both normative elements and the means of implementing them. Therefore, in order to achieve a more comprehensive means of viewing regional planning experience, we shall need to elaborate upon these two basic dimensions. This will enable us to examine regional planning initiatives in a more objective fashion.

Region Dimension

We need to acknowledge a number of subdimensions within the region dimension. First, however, let us establish two major attributes that remain constant for all planning regions: (1) they always encompass *supra-urban* space (i.e., an area larger than a single community but usually smaller than an entire nation [or province, in Canada's case]); and (2) they always comprise *two or more jurisdictions*. Aside from sharing these two attributes, planning regions tend to differ from one another in several ways:

- *Size*, or scale, of the region affects several aspects of its planning: the extent of planning jurisdiction, the resources to be planned, and the content of planning. In general, the larger the region, the greater the array of elements to be planned for and the greater the number of relationships between elements (human and natural).
- *Type* of region is usually a reflection of the purpose of the planning: *natural* regions such as river basins usually connote an emphasis on natural resources; *functional* regions defined by commuting or economic development tend to be concerned with regional efficiency; other regions may be defined by *governmental* boundaries for jurisdictional reasons; and *bioregions* reflect the need to consider a region's human and natural interconnections.
- *Number of jurisdictions* will affect not only the extent of political cooperation needed within a planning region, but also the range of issues to be taken into account.
- *Relation to the province* is always a consideration, since it is the province (in Canada) that establishes, for its own spatial strategy, a planning region within its bounds. What the province wishes the planning region to accomplish is reflected in the boundaries it allows and the resources it provides for the region.

These subdimensions of the region dimension begin to provide a common nomenclature that we can use to describe regional planning activities and, thereby, distinguish differences between one planning effort and another. Each of these aspects comes into play in the actual definition of, or boundary-setting for, regional planning, as will be seen in Chapter 3.

Planning Dimension

The planning dimension of regional planning reflects the generally normative orientation of the field, but it, too, has an array of different manifestations that need to be identified:

- *Purpose* or *purposes* for which the planning is being done constitutes a central normative feature of regional planning and may encompass such different goals as eliminating regional income disparities, preventing flooding, and protecting agricultural land either singly or in combination.
- A *mandate* is the authorization the province, the federal government, or both levels of government provide in order to conduct regional planning activities. It includes both the legal sanction to proceed with planning and the substantive limitations of any planning action so that regional planners will know what they can plan and what they cannot.
- *Institutional arrangements* define the means for conducting regional planning (i.e., the kind of planning agency). The permission to establish a planning agency is provided by the senior government responsible for the territory. These agencies may range from advisory committees to independent decision-making boards.
- *Technical capacity* refers not just to the staff skills and talents in the agency, but also to the political commitment of the agency and the province to accomplish the mandate. It is required in order for the planning agency to carry out its assigned purpose or purposes.

It can be seen how these four subdimensions of the planning dimension enable us to describe the normative side of regional planning (see Chapter 4). Along with the four subdimensions of the regional dimension, we are now able to describe virtually any regional planning initiative in Canada (and elsewhere) with objective measures. To illustrate how this approach can be used to map regional planning efforts, a selected group of Canadian regional planning initiatives are presented in Table 1.

The Realm of Regional Planning Practice

The key features of regional planning that we have just identified could be considered to be the essential "topography" of a base map of regional planning (calibrated, of course, for the particular planning region). In other words, if we were scanning the terrain of regional planning, these features would be the most visible, just as hills and valleys would be the most visible features of a real landscape. But this landscape is also "populated," so to speak, with planners, policy makers, theorists, and ordinary citizens, all of whom are engaged in the activity – the *practice* – of regional planning. They are also part of the "map" of regional planning. It is here that we can distinguish the elements that characterize its practice and get at its qualitative aspects. Further, as we

Table 1

Key features of regional planning for selected Canadian regional planning initiatives

	National Capital Commission	Peace River Regional Planning Commission	Mactaquac Regional Development Plan
Region			
Region size	4,700 sq. km.	255,000 sq. km.	4,000 sq. km.
Region type	Metropolitan region (nation's capital)	Rural, frontier resource region	Rural, underdeveloped resource region
Number of jurisdictions	Federal, provincial, regional, 25 municipalities	Federal, provincial, 34 municipalities	Federal, provincial, NB Hydro, Community Improvement Corp.
Planning			
Purpose	To create a physical environment appropriate for the nation's capital, including parks, waterways, and transportation	To provide a coherent framework for the activities and facilities of public agencies and private development	To formulate a development strategy for the region affected by the construction and flooding of a major hydro project
Mandate	To prepare and implement a plan for the region, including the acquisition of land for a greenbelt, other parks, and related transport facilities	To prepare an advisory regional plan, approve local plans of subdivision, and provide planning services to local municipalities	To prepare a regional plan that provides for relocated families, renewal of disrupted services, a new town centre, and local economic development capability
Institutional arrangements	Federally appointed commission with executive powers to purchase land	Commission with members from local municipalities and the province	Federal-provincial planning team and local Community Improvement Corporation
Technical and professional capacity	Professional planners on staff	Professional planners on staff	Professional planners on staff

have already seen with its precursors, these qualitative elements of practice are not always the same and may change as they come to reflect prevailing ideologies and knowledge. Thus, in order to complete our map of regional planning, we must know about both the surface "terrain" *and* the "quality" of the development found there. We may think of this as continuing to set "overlays" on top of the basic map in order to reflect the configuration of elements that affect practice at any particular time.

How Regional Planning Practice Develops

The model of regional planning dimensions that Friedmann and Weaver (1979) propounded provides the necessary perspective for our purposes. Looking at the model portrayed graphically in Figure 6, the first thing we should notice is that the *practice* of regional planning is affected by several factors. How regional planners actually conduct their practice is conditioned by both preferred methods of procedure and preferred approaches to the development of regions. What, for example, made it viable for the Mactaquac River Valley planners to relocate farmers in a new town and to create a locally based forest management system? Or, to take another example, what made the planners in British Columbia decide to establish agricultural land reserves that would be overseen by a special commission? Past experience, academic theory, and political ideology all entered into these practice outcomes, as Friedmann and Weaver show.[2]

First, let us establish the main dimensions of Friedmann and Weaver's model and then discuss how their model aids our understanding of regional planning. The model has five basic dimensions:

1 practice
2 doctrine
3 procedural theory
4 substantive theory
5 ideology.

Practice (The Way We Plan)

Regional planning becomes a reality when initiatives are taken to influence, or intervene in, the existing social, economic, political, environmental, and spatial organization of a region, with, for example, plans for water-resource management, metropolitan containment, and/or industrial decentralization.

Doctrine (Why We Plan the Way We Do)

The initiatives taken at the level of practice stem from (1) what the profession knows about the development of regions and (2) what is considered an appropriate concept of development at the time. They can be thought of as reflecting both the need to plan regions and the best approach for doing so (i.e., the style of practice at the time).

Figure 6

Principal dimensions of regional planning practice

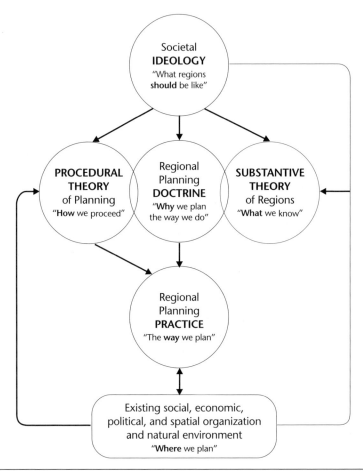

Source: Modified from Friedmann and Weaver (1979).

At any given time, doctrine affects practice, and, in turn, practice affects doctrine; this is an important feedback loop. The doctrine of regional planning draws on substantive theories (i.e., theories and analyses that come from a variety of social and environmental sciences) and links them to prevailing procedural theories (i.e., theories that come from a variety of political and administrative disciplines) (Faludi 1996). Doctrine, therefore, may change over time. For example, the early notions of water-resource development promoted a rational "multi-purpose" approach that is similar to today's "ecosystem" or "bioregional" approach (McTaggart 1993).

Procedural Theory (How We Should Proceed with Planning)

Regional planning practice must be organized and have effective methodologies in order to achieve its ends. Direction tends to be provided by several academic disciplines concerned with organizational development and functioning in the public sphere – among them political science, sociology, economics, public administration, and planning education itself (Robinson 1972). In turn, those working in procedural theory must be cognizant of the problems arising in real world practice – another feedback loop (Slocombe 1995).

Substantive Theory (What We Know about Regions)

A variety of academic disciplines, including geography, economics, environmental science, regional science, and political science, provide knowledge about how regions function and develop (i.e., they provide substance). This knowledge tends to influence the prevailing planning doctrine rather than to directly affect planning practice. An example of this would be the advent of regional location theory in the 1950s (Perroux 1950; Isard 1956a), which, in turn, fed back to major doctrinal changes about the role of cities in regional development (Hodge 1969).

Ideology (What We Should Be Doing about Regions)

Both the content of regional planning and its outcome are affected by prevailing ideological assumptions concerning what society understands with regard to the social relations involved in economic production and the distribution of political power (Friedmann 1992). These assumptions reflect what is thought of as a desirable social outcome and, thereby, legitimize what planning practice can deal with at that time.

Two contrasting examples illustrate the central role of ideology in regional planning. First, the importance of democracy and democratic principles was built into the mandate for the Tennessee Valley Authority when it began its regional planning in the 1930s, and, as Selznick (1949) tells us, it represented both an asset to, and a limitation upon, its planning practice. Second, the seemingly neutral, rational policies for balanced regional economic development that Canada pursued (Brewis 1969) in the 1960s and 1970s were later challenged for their underlying centralist capitalist ideology, which led to regional dependency (Matthews 1983).

The Shifting Perspective of Practice

To repeat, in order to understand why regional planning is practised in a certain way requires us to know what factors influenced it within a particular time period. We need to know about prevailing theories, doctrines, and ideological assumptions. Further, we need to know how they interact with one another as well as how they affect practice.

If we look back at the array of regional planning practices described in Chapter 1, it is evident that regional planning's precursors had differing ideologies: there is Kropotkin's anarchism, Owen's utopian socialism, and the Tennessee Valley Authority's emphasis on democratic participation. Thus, what is considered to be the best way for society to deal with its regional needs and problems obviously changes, affecting what can be planned. And, as we shall see in later chapters, ideological assumptions continue to shift. For example, metropolitan planning, which, in the past, had a strong corporatist-functional ideological basis, is now embracing eco-environmentalist assumptions, as may be seen in recent planning for the Toronto bioregion (see Chapters 7 and 9).

Of course, our substantive and procedural theories also evolved during this same time span. Our knowledge of how regions work grew dramatically from Geddes' rudimentary (albeit sophisticated) folk-work-place trilogy at the turn of the century to the esoteric realms of Walter Isard's space economy network of the 1950s and 1960s (see Figure 7). Our knowledge of how regional planning could be organized also evolved, both theoretically and experientially, thanks to our knowledge of earlier practice. Take, for example, John Friedmann's shift in thinking: he moved from his synoptic, generally top-down view of the planning process of the 1950s to his 1970s bottom-up, agropolitan view (Friedmann 1956; Friedmann and Douglass 1978).

When Regional Planning Doctrine Shifts

At any given time, the various changes in ideology and in substantive and procedural theories are mediated through the prevailing doctrine of regional planning; this, in turn, leads to changes in doctrine and, thus, in practice. Knowing the doctrine of regional planning is, therefore, central to appreciating the kind of practice that is occurring at any particular time. From Friedmann and Weaver's (1979) study, which revealed cyclical shifts (particularly in the United States, between the mid-1920s and 1980), we know something of how doctrine may change over time. Friedmann and Weaver discerned two broad doctrines, which they referred to as "territory" and "function," that, throughout this period, appeared to alternate as the dominant approach to regional planning. Before pursuing these shifts in US doctrine it will be helpful to look at some of the views of European planner Andreas Faludi with regard to planning doctrine. Faludi (1996, 44) notes that, in order for a planning doctrine to be viable, it "must incorporate a spatial organization principle" that conveys both what it is desirable to achieve and what it is possible to achieve. He suggests that this is best expressed by a graphic representation of the desired principle of spatial organization superimposed on the region to be planned. In other words, the planning aims must be able to be communicated easily both to planners and to the public. According to him, it must "stick" in their minds. Thus, in order for doctrine to shift substantially, a new spatial organization

Figure 7

Contrasting views of regional planning doctrines: Geddes versus Isard

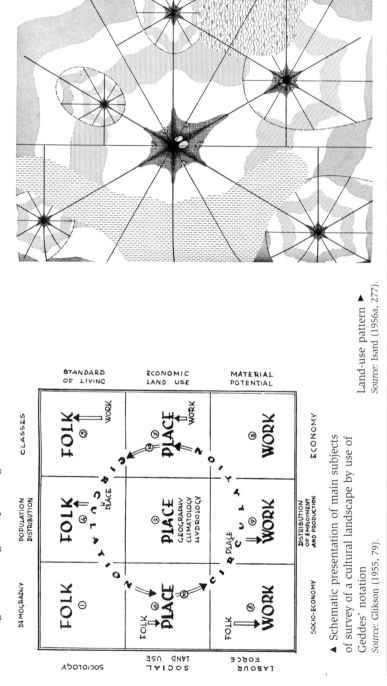

▲ Schematic presentation of main subjects
of survey of a cultural landscape by use of
Geddes' notation
Source: Glikson (1955, 79).

Land-use pattern ▶
Source: Isard (1956a, 277).

principle must be available, and it must be compelling enough to persuade both planners and the public. A striking Canadian example of such a principle is contained in Jacques Greber's 1950 plan for the Ottawa region: the "greenbelt" principle. This principle has now become solidly embedded in Ottawa's regional planning ethos and, in fact, was recently updated (Scott 1996), as will be discussed in Chapter 8.

Two Essential Doctrines

The "territory" doctrine refers to the predisposition in regional planning "to improve the cultural as well as material circumstances of regional communities" (Friedmann and Weaver 1979, 41). It can certainly be seen in the ideas of the RPAA and, at least in the beginning, in the practice of the Tennessee Valley Authority. The physical locale, the people and their history, the social and economic settings – essentially, the region *and* its inhabitants – become the focus of practice under this doctrine. And, to pick up Faludi's notion of a spatial concept, both the RPAA and the Tennessee Valley Authority conveyed strong images of possible regional outcomes. The RPAA published its proposals of a mix of wilderness and urban and rural settlements for New York State in a widely circulated magazine. And the Authority's notion of combining flood control measures with aids to navigation, ways to increase electric power generation, soil erosion control, and reforestation was readily grasped.

In today's parlance, the doctrine of territory is closest to the notions of "place" (see Agnew 1987; Paasi 1991) and of "bioregionalism." Planning regions seen from the point of view of this doctrine are not mere spaces that can be replicated anywhere. Every river basin, as the bioregionalist sees it, is unique: it is a "place." Place has depth as well as surface: it has values, identities, morals, aesthetics, emotions, awareness, memory, and spiritual needs. Place has interior dimensions that encompass personal and individual facets. Communities of humans and of plants and other species contain many attributes and interconnections that we cannot count and, often, cannot see. Friedmann (1988) referred to these regions as "life spaces." Knowing place means looking at the planning region from the inside, from the life of its inhabitants, and making decisions for the region *endogenously.* (We explore these notions further in Chapter 3.)

The "function" doctrine refers to the predisposition to treat any single region as part of a system of regions; that is, to treat it in terms of its functional relationships with other regions. This doctrine was prevalent in the 1960s under such themes as regional redevelopment and erasing regional disparities (e.g., the Canadian DREE program) (Economic Council 1968). It sought, as Friedmann and Weaver (1979, 41) wrote, to influence "the location of manufacturing ... in the belief that 'growth impulses' would eventually spread" from fast-growing regions (generally large urban centres) to slower-growing regions (generally rural regions). Thus, the planning of any particular region hinged primarily on its function in relation to other regions, particularly in relation to economics and transportation.

According to the function doctrine, planning regions were merely spaces and could be replicated according to some spatial organizational principle. For several decades, from the 1950s to the 1970s, this doctrine thrived on the principle of cities as "growth poles," with economic growth radiating outward from them to the rest of the region (Hoover 1971). Over time, the growth pole principle was transformed into the principle of a "system of cities" (Simmons 1977) and, later, into the principle of a system of "world cities" (Hall 1988). Regardless of the prevailing spatial principle, the function doctrine emphasizes economic activities (Friedmann's "economic space") and where they might best be located according to private marketplace needs rather than according to regional needs. Since the 1950s, the location decisions for economic activities within a region began, increasingly, to be made from outside the region; that is, they were made *exogenously,* from the perspective of transnational capital and global corporations (Friedmann and Weaver 1979).

Shifts in Doctrine

Friedmann and Weaver observed that, until the late 1940s, early regional planning in the United States (e.g., the Regional Planning Association of America, the Tennessee Valley Authority, and the Southern Regionalists) followed a *territorial* direction. Then, after the Second World War, when concerns about national economic growth came to the fore, a *function* doctrine provided the guidance for regional planners. For nearly forty years these planners worked on regional policies for industrialization, transportation, and tourism. However, Friedmann and Weaver believed that, as the 1970s were ending, they could see yet another shift in regional planning doctrine – a shift back towards a territory doctrine.

A few pointed questions can help us explore these shifts.

Why Only These Two Doctrinal Orientations?

It makes sense that we are most likely to view regions either from the inside (the territory doctrine) or from the outside (the function doctrine). (It should be noted that it is very difficult to view regions from both perspectives simultaneously.) On the one hand, the territory doctrine (the view from the inside) indicates the need to take into account the special features of particular regions and, in the process, to maintain each region's integrity in social, environmental, and cultural terms. From the territorial perspective a province, for example, would develop a policy *for* and *with* its regions rather than a regional policy *about* them. On the other hand, the function doctrine (the view from the outside) indicates the nation's (or province's) desire to consider the (usually) economic functioning of all parts of its space.

Why Did One Doctrine Fade in Favour of Another?

Doctrine, as we noted above, is influenced by changes in theory (of both substance and method), ideological assumptions, and the outcome of practice. By the early 1950s, there had been significant changes in all these realms. Economic growth and development, rather than rural decay and river basin development, came to be the primary motivation of the nation. Moreover, political pressure mounted in "have-not" regions and nations to redress the evident imbalance in economic well-being. Breakthroughs in regional location theory and urban systems theory reinforced ideas that economic growth is possible in all regions. And methodology and procedures for regional management evolved in a parallel fashion. Regional planners were, thus, coming to know much more about how regions functioned, at least in economic terms, and how urban development figured into this picture (Hodge 1969). This led to a new guiding doctrine for regional planning based on the "functional integration" of regions and urban growth poles (see also Chapter 6).

Why Does Yet Another Shift in Doctrine Seem to Be Occurring?

Since the mid-1970s, shifts in ideology and in substantive and procedural theories eroded the acceptance of the function doctrine. Experience began to show the economic ineffectiveness of, as well as the environmental damage caused by, many regional development policies framed under this doctrine. Theoreticians noted these outcomes and introduced new concepts, while, on the political side, pressures built up to reverse the top-down approach. Together, these changes led to a shift towards the advocacy of more locally based initiatives; greater attention to the environmental consequences of development projects; and, on the part of those whose regions would be affected, active participation in formulating development policies. Two decades later, these changes are still a source of conflict and pose an ongoing challenge to the future of regional planning, as we shall see in Chapters 10 and 11.

Evolving Regional Planning Doctrine in Canada

With this background, it is now appropriate to examine regional planning experience in Canada to see whether we find parallel shifts in doctrine.

Equivocal Beginnings

The kind of regional planning initiatives the United States experienced (first in the 1920s, with the Regional Plan for New York and Its Environs as well as the RPAA's efforts to create a state-wide plan for New York, and then in the 1930s, with the Tennessee Valley Authority) had no counterparts in Canada. It will also be remembered that these early US initiatives adhered to a territory doctrine. It was not until the late 1930s that a similar initiative occurred in Canada, with the proclamation of the Prairie Farm Rehabilitation Act. This was a federal government effort to help farmers in the three Prairie provinces deal with the devastation of the long-lasting drought that coincided with the Great Depression. It featured various kinds of water and soil conservation measures, community pastures, and public education and research programs.

Although the Prairie Farm Rehabilitation Act was aimed at the needs of a particular region, it was not a pure example of the territory doctrine in action. Although the agency that administered it had its headquarters in Regina, it was essentially a federal government agency. It was not aimed at anything other than farming, and its region was huge (more like several regions). Thus, the agency was as much informed by function doctrine as by territory doctrine. The same can be said for a similar initiative begun later in the Maritime provinces under the Maritimes Marshland Reclamation Act. It aimed at facilitating the reclamation of farmland intruded upon by salt water – a major problem of the region.

First Expression of Territory Doctrine

From the mid-1940s through the 1950s, there were several notable instances of regional planning, the foundations of which were formed by the region and its needs. The first instance involved metropolitan planning initiatives in Winnipeg, Vancouver, Edmonton, and Calgary. The conservation authorities in Ontario (scaled-down versions of the Tennessee Valley Authority) soon followed, as did regional agencies in Ottawa and Toronto as well as regional planning commissions for less urbanized regions in Alberta.

Thus, by 1960, upwards of two dozen agencies were engaged in regional planning according to a "territory" doctrine. They drew on two streams of thinking with regard to the need for planning regions. One involved concern over the rapid deterioration of natural resources (described more fully in Chapter 7), the other involved concern over urban sprawl (see Chapters 1 and 8). Both of these concerns generated widespread support and spawned initiatives that built on an ideology that saw regional planning as essential to the public interest. Therefore, it was believed that the agencies that expressed these concerns were deserving of senior government sanction. Although established from the top-down, the new agencies were rooted in their respective regions and were closely connected to their local governments. Many of these agencies continue their regional planning to this day, despite undergoing doctrinal and ideological changes through the years.

The Ascension of Function Doctrine

Another ideological thrust emerged in the late 1950s, as regional economic disparities became severe enough to generate political demands to eliminate them. Some of this was a result of the disparate economic conditions among Canadian regions found by the Rowell-Sirois Royal Commission in the late 1930s, and some was the result of similar concerns found by the Royal Commission on Economic Prospects (headed by Walter Gordon) in the 1950s. This was analogous to concurrent concerns in the United States over economically "depressed areas." Coincidentally, under the umbrella of "regional science," substantive theory on the economic functioning of regions blossomed dramatically in this same period. Canada adopted new theories of economic location, spatial organization, and urban systems as a way of approaching regional disparities.

Therewith arose an array of regional economic development programs (e.g., ARDA, DREE, FRED, ADB) sponsored by the federal government, in concert with the provinces, that would dominate regional planning thinking and practice in Canada for another three decades. The focus of these agencies was primarily "economic" and generally eschewed dealing with the social and environmental aspects of a region's development. Development data for the entire country were arrayed and analyzed, and, in each province, "designated" regions were identified so that they could receive planning and industrial investment funding. There were exceptions, of course – the Gaspé region of Quebec (see Chapters 5 and 6) and the Interlake region of Manitoba – but these were infrequent. The prevailing view was that all regions were to be seen as parts of a national system, and the aim was to provide programs that would generate economic benefits for all parts (or regions) of that system. Further, in economic development matters the federal government could function relatively freely, whereas in social and environmental matters it ran the risk of treading upon provincial areas of responsibility.

The Re-emergence of Territory Doctrine

For a number of reasons, including the lack of success in promoting economic development in many lagging regions as well as changes in national political leadership, by the early 1980s there was little support for the ideology that had driven the federally dominated function doctrine. What began to emerge were a number of distinctively regional, or place-based, initiatives. Several of these derived from rural concerns – "countryside planning" in Ontario and the intercommunity approach of Regional Resources Project No. 1 in Alberta (see Chapter 5). Yet others derived from environmental concerns that would eventuate in country-wide regional round tables on the environment and the economy. Not least, citizens were increasingly seeking to participate in public planning activities, including regional planning. With their involvement came an ideological shift away from seeing regions as having only economic needs towards a more comprehensive view that emphasized that the affected public needed to be a key player in deciding a region's future plans.

From the early 1980s onwards, a "politics of place," as Friedmann (1987) and Kemmis (1990) referred to it, increasingly came to influence the way we approached regional planning in Canada. In other words, regional planning doctrine shifted once again towards the territory doctrine. Three examples of the manifestation of this "new" doctrine confirm this shift. One is the federal government's 1988 shift in its approach to regional economic development: it moved from a centralized program to the locally managed Community Futures program. Approximately 250 regions were identified in non-metropolitan parts of the country, and, in each, organizations (now called "community futures economic development corporations") were formed, each with a board comprised of citizens from the region. Included in these organizations were two dozen or more First Nations Community Futures corporations. These groups were encouraged to prepare regional strategic plans and to administer loan funds for new and expanding businesses. These regional entities cover almost all of southern rural Canada.

The second example of the territory doctrine is found in the Ontario government's 1990 initiative to promote "community resource management partnerships" with forest-based communities in northern parts of the province (Harvey and Usher 1996). The program, which came to be referred to as "community forestry," sought to give people in the regions control over both the harvesting and the management of the lands they were harvesting rather than having them managed by the province's bureaucrats (see also Chapter 5).

The third example of the territory doctrine is found in the Fraser Basin Management Program, which was begun in British Columbia in the early 1990s. The focus of this program was on achieving sustainable development within a single river basin. Not only were the federal and provincial governments involved, but so were all the municipal governments and Aboriginal organizations in the region.

Many other examples of this doctrinal shift towards territory could be cited. It thus seems quite clear that much current Canadian regional planning practice derives from the view that planners must achieve regional integrity. Further, it is clear that a region's citizens have a special understanding of how to achieve this goal and that, as citizens, they have the right to be involved in planning for their region.[3]

Other Dynamics of Practice

Shifting Contexts and Marginality

It needs to be noted that the shifting realms of regional planning practice occur within a social and political context often fraught with tensions and subject to changing priorities. Further, the provincial (or federal) government often invokes regional planning for strategic reasons because the problems that require solving do not fit within normal administrative arrangements. Thus, regional planning practice often tends to operate, to use Wannop's (1995) term, at the "margins" of established levels of government – below that of the Canadian province but above that of the municipality. Add to this the fact that regional planning has no secure constitutional role (see Chapter 4), and we have an activity that seems to have an "ephemeral" quality (to again use a term from Wannop).

As we shall see in later chapters, the forms and intensity of regional planning vary with political and social circumstances. So, while, at a deeper level, the ideology and doctrine of regional planning may change, its immediate context is even more changeable. Consider the implications of what we raised earlier with regard to the number of topics with which regional planning deals as opposed to, say, the number of topics with which city planning deals. Typically, regional planners attempt to influence the investments and actions of a wide range of agencies and interests, most of which are likely not within their direct control (and, of course, there is the long time scale associated with such efforts). This raises questions not just about the permanence of regional initiatives, but also about our expectations of permanence, about whether, in regional planning, being long-lived necessarily means being successful. If regional planning is aimed at addressing regional issues, and if these issues are driven by the flux of politics and, increasingly, by global economics, then stability and permanence may not be achievable.

Enduring Need versus Inconstancy

It is, therefore, something of a paradox that, even though regional planning so frequently manifests itself, its manifestations – as an agency, study, and round table – are often inconstant. In large part, this is due to the almost continual flow of regional issues. Thus, as Wannop (1995) notes, there is an enduring need for regional planning to bridge strategic gaps and to deal with regional issues, even when there may be a lack of support for its desired arrangements. As for regional planning, the ephemeral nature of its context calls for it to be flexible, farsighted, and open to risk and uncertainty – perhaps more so than any other form of planning. In some important respects, as we explore in our final chapters, the emerging milieu of regional planning may be even more subject to this quandary of inconstancy than will be its future milieu.

Reflections

Whenever we examine examples of regional planning there are always two sides to the picture. One is the objective, factual side of what is being planned, by whom, within what regional setting, and through which institutional arrangements. These are common characteristics, or dimensions, by which any regional planning initiative can be described, as we did in Table 1. They allow us to plot the objective "reality" of the regional planning that is taking place in its various facets, to develop a sort of "base map," as we called it, whose form is comparable from one situation to another.

The other side of the picture of regional planning is subjective, or qualitative, and involves the quality and style of practice that occurs within the terrain of the objective base map. Among the several elements that make up practice, it is the particular tack we take in carrying out planning activities (i.e., the doctrine) that is the central guiding factor. Needless to say, doctrine changes with social, intellectual, and political shifts and, thereby, affects the quality and style of regional planning practice. Thus, we need not only acknowledge that any regional planning endeavour has an objective and a qualitative side, but also that the overall planning picture is a reflection of what we know, at that time, about regions and their development.

A map of regional planning in Canada today would be overlaid with a different configuration of practice, doctrine, and ideology than would a map of regional planning in Canada a generation ago. Today's greater concern over people and place reflects a return to the territory doctrine in regional planning. This is dramatically different from the centralist, system-based function of the 1960s and 1970s. It is more like the regional planning perspective of half a century ago, but with the significant addition of public participation. This parallels the US experience with regard to the shifting pattern of regional planning doctrine. Significantly, when it comes to defining regions, planning mandates, and deciding who participates in the planning, such qualitative shifts also have important implications for the objective side of regional planning. More and more, contemporary regional planning efforts tend to define their regions through the use of bioregional principles, set an array of objectives that include social and environmental aims as well as physical ones, and facilitate public participation. Although existing agencies may see no change in boundaries, their planning agenda is likely to be broader and public involvement more explicit.

Another basic characteristic of regional planning doctrine that is partly revealed in this chapter (and that will be discussed further in the next chapter) concerns the stance we take regarding the designation of a planning region. In other words, do we view the region from the "inside," giving primacy to its particular needs and voice (i.e., the territory doctrine), or do we view it from the "outside," giving primacy to the need of the overall system of regions (i.e., the function doctrine)? We must accept the fact that these two doctrines are both logically valid and that they form a dialectic from which a unified position may develop. This, then, accounts for the inherent tension throughout regional planning practice.

Finally, one aspect of contemporary regional planning initiatives that should be emphasized is the prominent role senior governments need to play in this field, even though, in many areas, community (or regional) "self-management" is more and more the guiding principle. This role is rooted in the notion of "holons" and the "holarchy" within which regions have fundamental relations both upwards (to the province) and downwards (to the communities within them). Four perspectives help to clarify this seeming paradox:

1 Authority for the regional territories involved resides, ultimately, with the province within which they lie or, by agreement, with the federal government (as with Community Futures). Thus, there is an inherent constitutional role

for senior governments when control is shifted to regional agencies (see also Chapter 4).

2 Regional planning agencies require the endorsement, or collaboration, of senior governments. In order to have credibility, acceptance, and the resources with which to take action, the agencies need access to "social power," and this is held by the province. As Friedmann (1992, 35) says with regard to analogous local self-management initiatives abroad: "Local empowering action requires a strong state."

3 Presumably, recent joint initiatives and partnerships reflect a preferred way of sharing social power. As such, they are also an indication that the prevailing ideology informing regional planning doctrine today has shifted towards the territory doctrine.

4 Planning regions seeking to express the ideals of the territory doctrine relative to their province must also acknowledge that their own constituent communities may also want to express the same ideals. Thus, a key feature of regional planning is the imperative of achieving a balance between the regional agency and the levels of governance both above and below it.

3

The Regional Boundary Imperative

Defining a planning region is one of the key tasks of the regional planner. Although it has been called a "categorical imperative" (Wirth 1942), it is never easily achieved, for it is neither a neutral task (as natural scientists would lead us to believe) nor a politically pragmatic one (as regional planners would lead us to believe). In large part, defining the planning region is a difficult task because of the uniqueness of every territory and the many interests involved in selecting regional boundaries. So, perennially, the same issues are evoked whenever boundaries need to be set.

Setting spatial boundaries for any purpose is as much a matter of value as of fact, as this chapter will show. The literature of geography, public administration, and regional science offers some help in accomplishing this task and is thus worth examining. When setting boundaries regional planners must have an eye to division of powers, policy implementation, and, not least, the social goals and cultural values of those both inside and outside the region in question. This means that, within regional planning, boundary-setting derives from both practice and theory. And since practice is always culturally determined and, therefore, changing, we need to consider regional planning boundaries that suit Canadian tendencies.

The Boundary Imperative

When we plan for human activities and facilities, it is always with reference to some space, and that space is not limitless. Boundaries exist even if they are not explicitly marked: they may be defined by the limits of human travel or the extent to which a facility's service can be delivered, to name just two possibilities. In other words, there is always a *spatial context* for human activities and facilities; they cannot be planned just anywhere. In regional planning we call this bounded territory the "planning region," and, for Canadian planner Len Gertler (1972b), boundaries rank first among those elements one should consider when attempting to define it.

The need for regional planning boundaries was recognized six decades ago when Louis Wirth (1942) used the term "categorical imperative" to refer to the need of regional planners to define the spatial context of their endeavours. Indeed, how could planners properly conduct their analyses of the planning situation if there were no spatial limit on the range of their observations? How could they respond to the impact of development without knowing the spatial ramifications of the factors and forces they seek to control? Not least, how could they design policies, programs, or settlement systems without knowing the areal distribution of legislative powers available to implement them? In other words, as Guttenberg (1977) points out, planners need regions within which to "prescribe" their proposals.

While both city planners and regional planners require a defined spatial context – a bounded area within which to practise – the situation for these two types of spatial planner is quite different. City planners start off with pre-defined boundaries; they have the benefit of having explicit municipal boundaries that mark the spatial context of their practice. It is not that these boundaries always coincide with the city planner's concerns, especially in metropolitan regions; however, they do specify the spatial extent of her/his mandate. And, with those boundaries, go specific municipal powers that determine what can be planned and where.[1]

In contrast, regional planners seldom enjoy the certainty of established boundaries and powers. In Canada, for example, while we often talk about various regions (such as the Maritimes, the Laurentides, or the Eastern Slopes [of the Rockies]), there is no place in the Canadian Constitution that is allotted to "regions." The only subunits of the nation mentioned in the Constitution are the provinces; as for the number of municipalities the latter may choose to create, that is up to them.[2] (The legislative and institutional bases for Canadian regional planning are discussed in detail in Chapter 4.) So, for the regional planner, there remains the unavoidable task of defining the region because, without it, there can be no regional planning. Further, since the planning region does not enjoy inherent constitutional sanction, it will need to have its own integrity. On the one hand, the planner needs to seek a balance between the technical and the normative aspects of regional planning; on the other hand, as some recent observers remind us, she/he needs to have a firm understanding of both the nature and the development of regions (Richardson 1989a; Turner 1988).

From the regional planner's point of view, the planning region requires an area that approximates the full scope of the problem that is being addressed. As well, the area should encompass the scope of legislative and administrative powers the planner expects to exercise. In other words, it requires a best approximation of the optimum planning region. Again, quoting Wirth (1942, 141), "the search for an all-purpose area may be as futile as the search for the Holy Grail." Nevertheless, the search is itself a vital task, if for no other reason than the fact that it gives the planner a greater understanding of the region. John Friedmann (1966b, 39) also noted this advantage: "[It is] essential for regional planners to acquire understanding of the structural form of spatial relationships" – an admonition Slocombe (1995) echoed three decades later.

On Knowing about Regions

It is often said that Canada is a country of "regions," but a brief probing of this truism shows that there is little consistency regarding what the term "regions" means. For example, the provinces and territories are often referred to singly as regions, as are combinations of them (e.g., "the Prairies," "the North"). And, of course, there are those regions that lie within a province (e.g., the Gaspé in Quebec, the Cariboo in British Columbia) and those that straddle provincial boundaries (e.g., the Ottawa Valley). These variations are important in Canada's economic and political life (Robinson and Webster 1985), for regions thus defined are expressions of the need to describe the country's landscape for political and cultural purposes. They represent one set of Canadian regions; however, this is a set that, generally, we do not use for regional planning. As we discuss below, there are various modes of defining boundaries, including those we use when conducting regional planning.

However, before proceeding further, let us acknowledge the educational effect of defining a region. An important aspect of this is the realization of the uniqueness of these spatial units. In regional planning we actually create regions that were not there before; we literally "carve out" a new space from a larger piece of territory. Guttenberg (1988, 374) is quite clear on this: "Regions are not natural objects." Even though we often delimit them according to natural phenomena such as mountains and rivers, regions are, essentially, mental constructs. In one of the seminal works on the meaning of regions, Whittlesey (1954) calls them the outcome of "areal interests"; that is, regions are the product of the thinking of those with an interest in, or need to designate, such entities. So a planning region derives from the planner's (and policy maker's) need to fulfil planning purposes in a particular territory.[3]

The transient quality of regions stimulated much intellectual ferment, especially in geography in the 1980s, leading to such pointed questions as: "Do regions exist?" (see Brookfield 1984; Eliot-Hurst 1985; Gore 1984). Counterarguments suggest that a more holistic view of regions is required – one that corresponds to the planner's approach (see Paasi 1991; Stern 1992). It is not within the scope of this book to pursue these competing viewpoints; however, we can highlight some of the special circumstances that face the planner in her/his attempt to delimit regions. In this brief excursion, two aspects of the learning process will be pointed out: the first concerns the different modes of defining regions, and the second concerns understanding planning and design.

Modes of Defining Regions

Regions represent the *expression of a need* to delineate an area for a particular purpose. For example, an environmental scientist and a regional planner need to express different purposes, and so we can expect their regions to be different in size and boundaries. Broadly, there are four different modes of defining regions according to Guttenberg (1977) (see also Table 2).

1 *Referential mode:* Typically, natural and social scientists define regions in the referential mode because they need to describe or refer to things such as natural and cultural features (e.g., the boreal region, the commutershed of an urban region).
2 *Appraisive mode:* Policy-oriented analysts concerned with identifying areal problems such as pollution and economic disparity use the appraisive mode to evaluate conditions over a large area (e.g., the incidence of rural poverty in the ARDA program and rural soil productivity under the Canada Land Inventory).
3 *Prescriptive mode:* Since planners need to prescribe actions to deal with problems, they use the prescriptive mode to define regions (e.g., the Fraser Basin Management Program, the Greater Toronto Bioregion planning program). This mode is also used to define areas for governing (e.g., counties, municipalities, or regional districts, as in British Columbia). Essentially, it is the planning mode.
4 *Optative mode:* A fourth mode flows from the need or desire to express aspirations for regions. Cascadia in the west and the Windsor-Quebec Corridor in the east are examples of optative regions that are invoked to encourage people to be more expansive in their thinking about regional issues.

As we proceed through this chapter, and as we consider regional planning practice in later chapters, the way in which the prescriptive mode pertains to the tasks faced by the regional planner will become increasingly evident.

Understanding Regions Better

The paradigm set out in Table 2 helps planners to know more about regions, as does Guttenberg's (1988) later refinement of it, which points up how, in the process of generating a region, we actually create a second region. It helps narrow the meaning of "region" and put the planner's behaviour in perspective. This is closely related to Slocombe's (1995) plea for a framework that would enable planners to better understand regions and, thereby, better plan and design them. Slocombe's ideas parallel and expand those of Richardson (1989a) and Turner (1988) who, for example, point out that regional planning practice has become more complex and multi-disciplinary and requires not only a wider range of information on a wider range of topics, but also tools that can link and interpret different kinds of regional data.

According to Slocombe (1995, 174), knowing about, or developing an understanding of, regions is a "complex, recursive, reflexive process." With regard to understanding the development of complex social and natural entities (i.e.,

Table 2

Modes of defining regions, with Canadian examples

Mode	Basis of regional definition	Relevant spatial phenomena	Canadian example
Referential	Disinterested observations	Past, present, and future natural and cultural features	Canadian Shield Atlantic Region
Appraisive	Evaluation of conditions	Territorial quality-of-life indicators (economic, social, environmental) • poverty • conservation areas • natural hazards	DREE "designated areas" Air-quality levels Flood-prone areas
Prescriptive	Special remedial and/ or preventive rules of action	Types of territorial control exercised, proposed, or planned • preservation • reclamation	Fraser Basin Management Program Ontario Conservation Authorities
	General regulations	Governance	Montreal Urban Community
Optative	Aspirations	Types of ideal territorial order envisioned (aesthetic, moral, political)	"Cascadia" (BC, Washington, Oregon)

Source: Modified from Guttenberg (1988).

regions), this perspective reminds one of the seminal ideas of Bateson (Harries-Jones 1995). It means that we must keep revisiting our understanding of a region and that this, in turn, could change how we think about it, including where we think its boundaries ought to be. For example, knowledge of a region's history needs to be included in the planning process (Paasi 1991), as do interpretations that derive from the perceptions, opinions, and values of residents. As knowledge increases, our overall understanding may need to be revised, including our planning goals and strategies for the region.

Regional planners may, thus, need to go beyond descriptive, objective facts in order to achieve the broader understanding required for better planning, especially when this planning consists of designing future patterns of activities and facilities. The path-breaking work in this area was conducted by Lynch (1960), who sought, through the use of personal interviews, to find out how residents of the Boston metropolitan area experienced their region.

More recently, Leung (1992) replicated his method in Canada's Ottawa–Carleton region. Planners are finding that, more and more frequently, citizens are asking to participate in the planning of their cities and regions. What better way to come to know a region than to listen to its residents?

Finding the "Proper" Boundaries

The task of setting regional boundaries is not unique to regional planners. Other disciplines, including several from which regional planning practice derives part of its theoretical base (e.g., geography, sociology, economics, and public administration), have also had to define regions. We may profitably review these approaches to setting regional boundaries with the understanding that, essentially, they represent factual knowledge about regions. There is also a normative side to regional delineation, and this comes to light when the region is to be used for planning purposes (this is explored later).

From the Factual Side

In looking at Friedmann and Weaver's (1979) paradigm, which was presented in Chapter 2, we saw that regional planning practice is linked to substantive theory and procedural theory. Each of these theories contributes to the delimitation of regions.

Drawing on Substantive Theory

Geographers have the most extensive experience in defining regions. Indeed, they have well developed schema of regional types as well as methods for delineating them. One of the first formal renderings of regional types consisted of the *uniform region* and the *nodal region* (Whittlesey 1954), renderings which, in many ways, remain useful.

A *uniform region* is an area within which a certain attribute or combination of attributes occurs, and it stands in contrast to adjacent areas that do not possess the same attribute to the same degree. It could be an area possessing a specific resource, say, high-quality agricultural soils, the area drained by a particular river (i.e., a watershed), or an area with a population that shares distinctive characteristics (e.g., language or income levels). Sometimes these kinds of regions are referred to as *homogeneous regions*. The boundary of such a region is located at the farthest extent of the attribute's occurrence or where it is no longer considered significant.

A *nodal region* is an area characterized by the relationships associated with a particular node of activity, such as a city or town. These relationships may include the flow of goods, commuters, information, and/or traffic. This is the source of the idea of the metropolitan region; that is, an area whose well-being (and problems) is influenced by the presence of a major city (often referred to as the core city). Sociologist Donald Bogue's (1948) work on "metropolitan dominance" is one of the earliest examples of mapping the boundaries of nodal regions. The same regional idea is implied in the concept of small centres that serve a surrounding "trading area." This idea is found in the classic 1930s work of the geographer Christaller and has been amplified by later geographers (see Preston 1991).

Regional planners have sometimes referred to nodal regions as *interdependent regions* because of the interrelatedness of their various attributes (Friedmann 1966b). The boundary of such regions is at the limit of significant influence of the relations associated with the node (e.g., the limit of labour commuting to the central city).

In recognition that homogeneous and interdependent regions may not exhaust all regional types, two contemporary geographers have identified *non-homogeneous regions* as a third regional type (Poiker and Kennedy 1995). These regions are not characterized by any prevailing uniform characteristic or node; rather, they are characterized by the human uses made of them (e.g., First Nations hunting areas). Boundaries for these regions occur where intensity of use declines to below some predetermined level, and they may need to be defined by a buffer zone rather than a precise line.

Geographers have made enormous strides in developing methods to define all kinds of regions. There are elaborate techniques for mapping various phenomena according to a variety of analytical rules. Market areas, urban hierarchies, influential spheres of information, probability surfaces of industrial location, labour sheds, commodity flows, and migration simulations – all these phenomena can be derived with apparent ease and numeric precision.

Drawing on Procedural Theory

From the perspective of procedural theory boundary definition tends to be pragmatic and related to problems that arise in the real world. According to the disciplines that practise procedural theory (e.g., political science, public administration, regional science), such issues as decision-making power as well as the extent and form of governance are connected with boundaries and jurisdiction. Typically, they suggest using existing administrative boundaries to define regions for planning since many powers and decision-making processes are already in place. Indeed, the entire territory of Canada is already divided into a dozen large-scale provincial and territorial "regions." And many of these are further divided into smaller regions, such as counties and regional districts, that are larger than municipalities.

A further advantage of using existing jurisdictions in order to plan regions is that they are usually integrated with the statistical gathering systems that often need to be consulted. Statistics Canada data, often a major information tool in regional planning, are available at the provincial or territorial, county or regional district, and municipal levels. Moreover, these data are related to boundaries that are relatively invariant over time, thereby facilitating the comparison of economic and social conditions. So another variant is to make regional boundaries conform to those of standard statistical gathering units, thereby providing the planner with a ready database and the capacity to monitor change.

From the Normative Side

Patrick Geddes is quoted as saying: "Geography is a descriptive science, it tells what is. [Planning][4] is applied science, *it shows what ought to be*" (Glikson 1955, 73). Following this dialectic, we would expect that a regional planner's boundaries would differ from those of the geographer or other descriptive scientist. The difference, as we shall see, is in the planner's starting point.

For the planner, the starting point for defining a region depends on what is to be planned. "The very definition of region will vary with our purpose," say Friedmann and Alonso (1964, 19). And they continue: "A region defined for water control will be very different from one for the integration of the iron and steel industry or from one for the measurement of the multiplier effect of an investment ... [it] will depend on both the type of interrelations being considered and on the purpose in mind." But, if purpose provides the criterion defining the region, then is a consistent process of delineation possible? Which purpose will take precedence?

A planning approach that emerged in the 1960s posited the notion of a pattern of regions being identified by the kind of problems they pose for national economic development; in other words, it was suggested that it would be a good idea to define a region according to the functional relations it has with the development of the larger territory. We find schema to define such functional regions in, for example, Rodwin (1963), Friedmann (1966b), and Stohr (1967). In Rodwin's view, in every nation or large territory the development planner contends with two types of region: "leading" and "lagging." As the names suggest, some regions have resources, location, and dynamics that "lead" the nation in economic growth and development, while other regions lack these things and so "lag" behind. Rodwin suggested that we define the leading regions first (usually the large urban complexes and their zones of influence) but that we also pay attention to the boundaries of local data-gathering units in order to facilitate analytical opportunities. A Canadian parallel to this is the 1973 DREE (the Department of Regional Economic Expansion) map, which shows the areas it considered to be in need of industrial incentives. These so-called "designated areas" were DREE's way of indicating Canada's lagging regions (see Chapter 6).

Friedmann (1966b) put forward a more elaborate set of what he referred to as "development regions." These consisted of the following types: core regions (large urban areas), resource frontier regions (new settlement areas), upward-transitional regions (high-growth areas), downward-transitional regions (low-growth areas), and special problem regions (areas of peculiar location or special resources). Functional regions such as these are compatible with either the homogeneous region approach or the nodal region approach.

For example, the Mactaquac River Valley plan in 1960s New Brunswick (Gertler 1972a, 1994) involved a downward-transitional area and used the homogeneous region approach to define the planning region. Conversely, in the 1970s the DREE-designated Halifax metropolitan region plan involved a downward-transitional area and used a nodal region approach to define the planning region.

The increasingly popular notion of the "bioregion" also needs to be mentioned in this discussion of normative approaches to boundary definition. One of the leaders in this field, Kirkpatrick Sale (1984, 169), states that "a bioregion is part of the earth's surface whose rough boundaries are determined by natural rather than human dictates." Further, the essential goal of such a definition is "conservation, preservation and sustenance" of a region's ecosystem and economy. Or, as McCloskey (1993, 62) says, a bioregion's boundaries are "reflections of people living in place" based on "articulations of the diversity" of the earth's features. Bioregional planning boundaries are, thus, defined through the use of multiple criteria – physical, human, economic, and political. Aberley (1993a) calls it a "layering process," whereby we overlay all of the regional boundaries derived from each factor on a basic map of the area. Despite this acknowledgment of the importance of other criteria, the boundaries of bioregions are most often defined by watersheds. This holistic approach to establishing planning regions, which eschews political boundaries in favour of natural and cultural boundaries, both harkens back to the ideals of the "natural region" of two generations ago and invokes the more contemporary territory doctrine.

Accepting the Dilemma

If these opposing methods seem to pose a dilemma for the planner with regard to which regional delineation approach to use – the factual or the normative – or which method to use, then let us acknowledge that this situation is normal. It may help to consider that the descriptive sciences show us *how* to delineate a region whereas the practitioners tell us *why* to do so. Consider, too, that regional planning is geographical in focus, and thus we always know, in general terms, *where* the planning is needed. But is this to be planning for a single region or for a set of regions? Are the problems centred in water resource management, economic development, or metropolitan sprawl? We must start by getting answers to these types of questions; then we can move on to deciding which delineation method will work best.

Here we may pose a caution regarding any approach to regionalization (i.e., boundary selection). Whether it is dealing with functional regions or bioregions, every approach involves a "model" of how its proponents would like to see that region organized. In other words, all regionalization methods construct a model that could be used in regional planning, and the planner must be aware of the appropriateness of this model vis-à-vis the particular planning situation involved. The regional planner is always faced with this tenuous aspect of boundary selection. One way to deal with this situation is to recognize the fact that *there need be no symmetry in the design of regions.* Regions "may vary in character, extend over only sections of the country, be non-contiguous and of varying size, and even overlap to a degree" (Friedmann 1966b, 40). However, this does not mean that we have to proceed randomly; it only means that we need to heed Gertler's advice: "Precision in determining boundaries is not to be expected" (1972b, 17).

Effect of Setting Planning Boundaries

Although precision may not be a crucial issue in boundary setting, several other facets of the process are highly significant. Four, in particular, can have profound influences on the nature and quality of planning and require the planner to make critical choices: (1) spatial inclusiveness, (2) substantive focus, (3) value orientation, and (4) the time perspective. All four of these facets are invoked by regional delineation.

Spatial Inclusiveness

A region comes into existence when, at a minimum, we divide a large territory into two parts. By "a large territory," we mean a nation or some large portion of it (e.g., a province). Two important things happen for the planner during the process of territorial division. First, as Guttenberg (1988, 376) says: "the mere act of delineating a region ... gives rise to another region." Both the planning region and the remaining area are ultimately significant in the planning process because where the boundary is drawn between them determines which space and resources are to be *included* in the region and which *excluded.*

Essentially, boundaries establish *differences* between regions. These, in turn, function to constrain *where* (spatial context) and on *what* (regional characteristics) we may practise regional planning; that is, they determine the "scope" of regional planning. Take as an example a traditional subject of regional planning – water resource management. The river basin is the usual regional unit of definition in this field, and any large territory may have several major ones (e.g., British Columbia has the Fraser, Columbia, Peace, and Stikine River basins). When, in 1992, the joint federal-provincial-municipal initiative known as the Fraser Basin Management Program began to promote sustainable development, it limited its scope to the people, physical resources, terrain, and governmental entities that lay just within the Fraser River basin. This decision prohibited the program from using the resources (e.g., water, minerals, settlements) in any of the adjoining river basins. It is inevitable that, in defining a planning region, the planner will face such inexorable choices. Whatever the boundary excludes will not be easily dealt with in the future – for the simple reason that whatever is excluded will be in a different region. So, while a boundary may be used to exclude problems, in doing so it may also exclude needed resources.

Substantive Focus

By its very nature, regional planning involves focusing attention on a particular piece of a large territory. Thus, when we define such a region it is for the purpose of dealing with that region's needs. It is like saying: The planning here should be approached differently than it is in other regions because the problems in this region, and the potential for dealing with them, are distinctive. In this way, as Harvey Perloff (1968) notes, the process of designation involves "highlighting" a region's planning needs.

Regional designation not only distinguishes the planning needs of a region, it also defines the substantive focus of the planning. Just as boundaries require the regional planner to work within a specific spatial context, so they also prescribe the content of the planning. In effect, they demand that the planning be *specialized* for a particular region. This facet of defining regions also presents the regional planner with a choice; however, this time the choice involves substance rather than space. Would we want to limit our planning approach in this way? Do we have the appropriate tools for the kind of planning this regional designation requires? Which regional boundary would provide the best prospects for achieving planning objectives? These sorts of issues come into play when there is a need to decide between defining wholly new boundaries and using some existing jurisdictional boundaries (e.g., provinces or counties). This consideration is in play regardless of whether the focus is functional or bioregional, referential or prescriptive.

Value Orientation

Boundary selection affects the regional planner's value orientation. The substantive focus generated by a region's boundary leads not only to asserting the purposes of the planning but also to aligning the planner with a set of values (Hodge 1975). This is because regional planning practice always encompasses some concept of development that is embodied in the prevailing regional planning doctrine and the ideology that informs it (Friedmann and Weaver 1979). In other words, if a watershed is to be planned, then it is assumed that the planner implicitly accepts the importance of a harmonious relationship between people and nature. Similarly, metropolitan-regional planning assumes the importance of economic efficiency and the merits of city life. And, with regard to bioregional planning, it assumes the importance of an ecological ethic.

Before we go on to look at the effect of time on defining boundaries, two points require further reflection. First, what may seem, initially, to be an objective attempt to marshal appropriate facts in order to delimit the extent of a region carries with it value-laden elements that will determine much about the nature and quality of the regional planning that is practised. Second, the boundary-setting phase of regional planning always combines technical and normative aspects, as Friedmann (1966b) and Perloff (1968) have pointed out. It creates a fundamental tension that is found in all regional planning practice.[5]

Time Perspective

An eternal dilemma for the regional planner is that the boundary of the planning region chosen for today's conditions will usually not fully suit the conditions of the future. Whether the regional planning aims to promote growth,
arrest decline, or simply maintain stability, change will inevitably occur in the
region's resources (human and physical) and in its relations with other regions (see Slocombe 1995; Paasi 1991). Regional planning is intimately concerned with change and with development, and this involves an unfolding of
conditions over time, as many have pointed out (Wirth 1942; Ginsburg 1958;
Friedmann 1966b; Stohr 1967). This dilemma means that boundaries should,
if possible, remain flexible. The National Resources Committee in the United
States in the 1930s actually posited the idea of "elastic boundaries" for planning regions (NRC 1935). But the exigencies of administration and governance
related to regional planning make this no easy task, especially for large urban-
based regions (see Chapters 8 and 9).

Which Region or Whose Region?

Drawing again on Gertler (1972b, 17): "The issue of exactly where to draw the
line has to be determined by administrative decision." What he would have us
recognize is that the planner is not solely responsible for defining boundaries.
And, by "administrative decision," he is referring to more than managerial
judgment. The final setting of boundaries is conducted within a normative,
indeed, within a political, milieu; that is, it is conducted from a particular
point of view. Boundary setting can be viewed from two perspectives. One
poses the question: Of what kind of space should the planning region be comprised? The other poses the question: Who needs the region for planning?
Both questions have long been posed in regional planning; each carries with it
long-standing perspectives; and each is still pivotal when we consider defining a planning region. Thus, the point of view that prevails is not likely to be
selected randomly.

In each of the two foregoing chapters we identified two perspectives, each
of which came in the form of a dichotomy. In Chapter 2, it was natural region/
city-region (i.e., which region?); in Chapter 3 it was territory doctrine/function
doctrine (i.e., whose region?) (Friedmann and Weaver 1979; Friedmann 1988).
It will be quickly grasped that these dichotomies do not pose simple choices;
in fact, each tends to be a dialectic, and it is the planner's job to resolve each
dialectic by achieving some form of synthesis.

It is possible to display these dichotomies in graphic form as a pair of contrasting dimensions that enter the thinking of regional planners when they
attempt to establish a planning region (see Figure 8). The horizontal dimension portrays the natural region/city-region dialectic, or what we may term the
locus-of-the-region dimension. The vertical dimension portrays the territory

Figure 8

Essential dimensions for defining planning regions

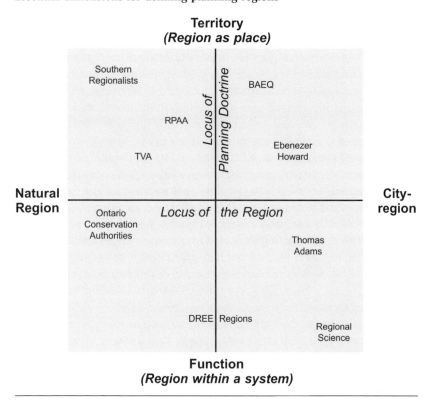

Territory
(Region as place)

Southern
Regionalists

Locus of Planning Doctrine

BAEQ

RPAA

Ebenezer
Howard

TVA

**Natural
Region**

Locus of | the Region

**City-
region**

Ontario
Conservation
Authorities

Thomas
Adams

DREE | Regions

Regional
Science

Function
(Region within a system)

doctrine/function doctrine dialectic, or what we may refer to as the locus-of-the-planner dimension.

Figure 8 provides a means of mapping past, current, and prospective regional delineations. It is important to note that the polar positions of each dimension coexist. There are, for example, always "natural" aspects of city-regions, and, generally, there is some form of human settlement in natural regions. However, it is the dominant position that informs the perspective used. Among the precursors of regional planning, we readily see a number of different stances towards the locus-of-the-region dimension. The Southern Regionalists and the early twentieth-century proponents of conservation could be placed at or near the natural region end of the dimension, whereas Thomas Adams and Louis Wirth (along with latter-day regional scientists) could be placed at the city-region end. However, the stance of other precursors, such as Robert Owen, Patrick Geddes, Lewis Mumford, and the Regional Planning

Association of America, mixed both positions, incorporating both natural elements and human activities and settlements when defining their preferred regions. Today's bioregionalists and those propounding "place" as a basis for regional delimitation would clearly fall towards the natural region end of this dimension.

The locus-of-the-planner dimension poses a different kind of question. Essentially, it asks where the planner stands when viewing a potential planning region – on the inside or on the outside? It "locates" the planner relative to his or her planning region. This question derives from differences in doctrine. When the territory doctrine prevails, the planning region is viewed from the inside – from the point of view of the region's needs, history, culture, landscape, the well-being of all its inhabitants, and its way of life. As Friedmann (1988, x) says, "Territorial space is always particular." In contrast, when the function doctrine prevails, the regional space is seen as part of a system; and, almost always, the system's focus is economic, and its well-being is seen as bound up with exchange relationships with other regions, both national and global. In other words, the region is viewed from the outside, and the planner pays attention to how it fits within a network of nodes, links, and flows.

The crucial element of the function doctrine is the degree of autonomy it affords the region's inhabitants and their planners in deciding about future activities and facilities. From the territory standpoint, decisions are determined endogenously; that is, they are determined inside the region in the region's interest. From the function standpoint, decisions are determined exogenously; that is, they are determined outside the region in the system's interest.

Canadian planner Ian Wight provides a contemporary view of the locus-of-the-planner dilemma within the context of one of the newest regional planning situations – the city-region (see Chapter 9). He poses the dilemma well: "The City and Its Region *or* The Region and Its City?" (Wight 1999). Looked at the first way, we assume that the (core) city is the primary spatial component in the region and that it has the right to control the future of all other (notably suburban) parts of the region. This is, effectively, a functional stance. Looked at in the second way, we assume that all parts of the region, both suburbs and core city, have complementary interests. This is, effectively, a territorial stance. Wight's ultimate concern is how these different stances affect the practice of regional planners in the field and how they view boundaries.

Returning to Gertler's original point: the fact is that *someone* has to make the "administrative decision" of "exactly where to draw the line," and the locus of that decision affects not only what gets planned and who does the planning, but also whose values – those of residents or those of outsiders – will prevail (Hodge 1975). Externally imposed boundaries are often denigrated as "top-down" planning, while locally defined boundaries are often commended as "bottom-up" planning. In practice, both can work well and both may be needed. Possibly more important is the matter of local political support for the planning and for those involved in it. Friedmann and Forest (1988, 128) term this the "politics of place," which emerges as citizens of a region express their "inborn desire to preserve and improve the character" of their region. Place-based politics may emerge in reaction to externally imposed development standards that seem harmful in the eyes of residents. For example, almost all actions by Aboriginal peoples to defend their lands are contemporary instances of the politics of place. Generally, regions defined from the inside (i.e., by residents of the region) can expect to have greater local political support than can regions defined from the outside (depending, of course, on the cohesion among local interests). One of the tenets of bioregionalism is that people in a region should take it upon themselves to articulate their values regarding landscapes, resources, and culture and that they should empower themselves in the process of defining their region's boundaries (Aberley 1993b). This, too, facilitates a politics of place.

Even in situations in which boundaries are established from the outside, local planners may transform the planning to reflect the region's needs. This happened in the Ottawa-designated Gaspé region in Quebec under the DREE program. A locally constituted planning body, the Bureau d'aménagement de l'est du Québec, was established, and it took a very grassroots approach to determining the region's planning needs. This was in contrast to the top-down approach practised in most other DREE regions. In an analogous way, in the early 1980s, the planners and politicians in the Central Kootenay Regional District in British Columbia saw, and pursued, the economic development needs of their region; they did not limit themselves to land-use regulations, as did other regional districts. Thus, a region's boundaries play a symbolic role in initiating and asserting that region's identity in the minds of its citizens (Cohen 1985), and they can then be a significant factor in mobilizing and articulating political action (Friedmann and Forest 1988).

Boundary-Drawing Implications: An Example

Throughout this discussion we have acknowledged the conjunction between the use of facts and the role of values when drawing boundaries for planning regions. To demonstrate this even more forcefully we can draw on an earlier, but still very relevant, example of how these two factors come together. US regional planner Thomas Reiner (1963) posited a hypothetical "nation" made up of eight spatial units, as shown in Figure 9. The larger squares could be considered akin to Canadian provinces, each of which has an urban area (the smaller squares). Reiner also provided basic population and income information for each unit (see Table 3). It can be seen in these data that there are major disparities in per capita income between spatial units – a problem not uncommon in many countries, including Canada.

If this "nation" wishes to pursue a policy of reducing income disparities, as did Canada in the 1960s and 1970s, then it must first delimit the regions with which it wants to work. Reiner suggests that the total area could be divided "geographically" into regions such as north and south or east and west (or some other variant). Or it could follow some "functional" regionalization, such as "urban" and "rural" or "fast-growing" and "slow-growing." Yet another approach, which might be referred to as "political regionalization," would

Figure 9

Subregions in a hypothetical "nation"

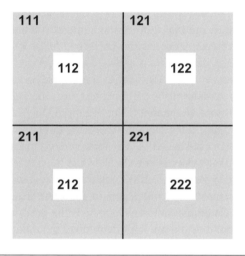

Source: Modified from Reiner (1963).

Table 3

Population and income levels of subregions in Thomas Reiner's hypothetical "nation"

Subregion	Population (000s)	Gross area product ($ millions)	Income per capita ($)
111 (rural)	250	1,000	4,000
112 (urban)	100	100	1,000
121 (rural)	200	800	4,000
122 (urban)	500	2,000	4,000
211 (rural)	500	500	1,000
212 (urban)	200	800	4,000
221 (rural)	50	50	1,000
222 (urban)	50	50	1,000
"Nation" total	1,850	5,300	2,850

Source: Modified from Reiner (1963).

be to designate every province a region. It can be readily seen that any of these regionalizations involves considering the best way to proceed (i.e., it involves making a value judgment): no matter what the choice, it will have political ramifications.

Table 4, using the data in Table 3, displays the income disparities resulting from several possible regional designations. If the four provinces are used as regions, then the income disparity is four to one between the richest and the poorest regions. A north/south partition yields a difference slightly greater than two to one between regions, and an east/west partition yields an even lower disparity between regions. Using urban areas as one region and rural areas as the other, the disparities are in the order of 1.5:1.

One valuable lesson emerges from this exercise: the greater the number of regions, the greater the disparity in regional per capita incomes.[6] But it is more important to consider how, given a particular regional designation, a policy and program whose purpose is to close the gap between the lowest and the highest income regions would be conceived and structured. In other words, not only may the boundaries that are chosen affect the policy solution, they may also affect the difficulty of the task. Further, these observations are not limited to planning problems associated with income disparities. They will also emerge with other policy issues that involve the allocation of resources among regions (e.g., building highways and dams or investing in education). In the end, as Reiner (1963, 72) says, the regional delimitation always "embraces a host of value considerations."

Table 4

Regional income disparities in a hypothetical "nation" resulting from different forms of regionalization

Region	Designation	Comprising subregions				Income per capita ($)
A-1	Rural	111	121	211	221	2,350
A-2	Urban	112	122	212	222	3,500
B-1	North	111	121	112	122	3,700
B-2	South	211	221	212	222	1,750
C-1	East	121	122	221	222	3,600
C-2	West	111	112	211	212	2,300
D-1	Northwest	111	112			3,150
D-2	Northeast	121	122			4,000
D-3	Southwest	211	212			1,850
D-4	Southeast	221	222			1,000

Source: Modified from Reiner (1963).

Whence Canadian Planning Region Boundaries?

There is great variety in the planning regions generated over the decades of regional planning experience in Canada. Although we cannot know the actual process of past boundary drawing, the outcomes can reveal principles as well as dilemmas for planning regions that are relevant both for the present and for the future. Three of the broad regional planning types used in Parts 2 and 3 – resource development and conservation areas, metropolitan areas, and economic development regions – offer a good way of reviewing this experience.

Resource Development and Conservation

When we look at instances of regional water resources planning over the years, the primacy of the natural watershed for defining planning boundaries is clear. We see this in both the oldest and the newest initiatives: the conservation authorities in Ontario and the Fraser Basin initiative in British Columbia. It is also the basis for the boundaries of the South Saskatchewan River Development Project and the James Bay Development Project in Quebec as well as many others. The watershed marks the extent of the water resources to be managed. However, this logic does not usually include the necessary authority to carry out planning and management. So, in all these cases, political structures had to be created in order to provide the necessary authority.

The major issue to be faced concerns melding the natural boundary and its planning needs with existing political boundaries (e.g., municipalities). This is the process Guttenberg (1988) refers to as the "hypostasis" of one region – in this case the watershed "referential" region, which becomes the "prescriptive" planning region. Regarding James Bay, no local governments existed in the region, so the province created one huge unit and assigned the James Bay Development Corporation to govern it. The conservation authorities the province created in southern Ontario in 1947 were superimposed on an existing and long-lived municipal and county system. To provide necessary planning powers, and to accommodate the existing situation, a new regional unit of government, with its own powers, was established, and its membership was drawn from municipalities within the watershed. It is, therefore, typical of regional resource planning efforts to have to create new regional jurisdictions with boundaries that conform to the natural extent of the resource being planned. That there will be competition with existing jurisdictions and, thus, a need for political compromise, is almost guaranteed in these regional planning initiatives. (Further discussion of these area-and-power issues in resource planning is found in Chapter 4.)

Metropolitan-Regional Planning

Boundaries for planning metropolitan regions are almost always defined according to the boundaries of constituent municipalities (as with Toronto and Montreal). Occasionally, as in metropolitan Victoria and Vancouver, unincorporated areas that are of strategic importance for development are also included. It is the province that establishes metropolitan area (and now city-region) planning boundaries, infuses them with the necessary authority, and then superimposes them upon already existing units (i.e., hypostasis). The logic of using municipal units (or, in Nova Scotia, counties) is twofold: first, the municipalities are necessary for the implementation of many metropolitan-region policies, especially regarding land use; and, second, using municipalities (and counties) for boundaries can facilitate the aggregation of planning data.

One of the ongoing dilemmas for metropolitan (and city-region) planning involves determining the outer limits of the planning region. Usually seen as nodal regions, the extent of these areas is defined according to the spread of effects generated by the central city, including commuting to work, water supply, and recreational activities in the surrounding area. Municipal boundaries that have been established for decades, and for more local reasons, are likely to only approximate the area of metropolitan influence. Moreover, as a metropolitan area grows in population, often much of that growth occurs at the periphery, in municipalities that were outside the original planning region. Should the boundaries be shifted outward, and, if so, how far? This has been the case with the eastward expansion of the Greater Vancouver Regional District into the Fraser Valley.

Another tactic for dealing with boundary issues was used when Metropolitan Toronto was created. It consisted of providing the metropolitan government with planning powers over municipalities in a zone beyond its own boundaries. Manitoba took a similar approach in establishing the Metropolitan Corporation of Greater Winnipeg when it gave the corporation planning, zoning, and building controls over an "additional" extraterritorial zone around the metropolis. Ontario's most recent efforts to resolve metropolitan boundary issues involves amalgamating central cities and suburbs into single jurisdictions without addressing the question of the extent of steadily expanding suburbs. Chapters 8 and 9 discuss this perennial problem in greater detail.

Regional Economic Planning

The Canadian experience with regional economic planning, especially under the federal ARDA and DREE programs in the 1960s and 1970s, reflects the use of statistical units to define planning regions. An area was considered qualified for planning if it displayed significant disparities in such criteria as income, education, and unemployment compared with Canadian averages. Statistics Canada data were used to provide nationwide consistency. These regions were, in Guttenberg's (1988) terms, "appraisive" regions rather than "prescriptive," or planning, regions. However, the measures for evaluating regional economic distress were really identifying social conditions and not directly connecting to actual spatial situations. Many of the data-gathering units were municipalities, but many others were not. Further, these were federal initiatives within provincial jurisdictions. Such factors contributed to the difficulty in establishing prescriptive regions. The result was that various bureaucratic arrangements, which can be called "programming regions," came to pass.

Reflections

This brief excursion into the Canadian experience of defining planning regions indicates the serious nature of this part of the regional planning process. Boundary drawing has long-lasting consequences. What begins as a mental construct – an invention, so to speak – often endures as a real region (with its own history and culture) when it is infused with the power to plan. Thus, a paradox arises wherein the inertia of regional identification and support for planning confound the demands for changes in boundaries due to growth and change (thus, in the 1930s, the rationale of the US National Resources Committee's proposal for "elastic" regional boundaries).

For, as Slocombe (1995) emphasizes, both regions and their planning are becoming more complex. Take, for example, the most recent regional planning initiatives across Canada – the various environmental round tables. Their reference point is that regions need to be understood as complexes of biological, physical, social, and economic characteristics. Bioregionalism follows a similar value system, but even more vigorously (Aberley 1993b; McTaggart 1993). Delineating planning boundaries for these new approaches to regional planning will require new understanding and new tools. Thus, we would be wise to continue to heed Louis Wirth's (1942, 151) advice to the planner regarding mapping the planning region: "touch [your] pencil lightly as [you] define its outer rims."

4

Formal Bases of Regional Planning

Even a quick review of the array of agencies that currently practise, or have practised, regional planning in Canada reveals a diversity of organizational formats. Consider, for example, the likes of the regional districts in British Columbia, the regional county municipalities in Quebec, the South Saskatchewan River Development Corporation, the conservation authorities in Ontario, the many metropolitan area planning agencies, and the National Capital Commission. Why the diversity in the ways we conduct regional planning in Canada? That is the overriding question in this chapter.

The answer to this question has two parts: the first part, as we discussed in Chapter 3, concerns the fact that every region is unique and that this is reflected in its choice of boundaries and the array of needs and problems it encompasses. The second part lies in the peculiar status of regions in Canada and in the extent and combination of governmental resources allocated to them for planning and implementation. Regions, by whatever definition, are not part of the nation's normal governing structure. So, when we employ regional entities to accomplish development aims, they literally have to be "invented" for each particular purpose while still being consistent with the formal division of power. The choices made in devising regional planning structures reflect both political pragmatism and the vulnerability of the structure created. In other words, we cannot appreciate regional planning practice without having a good understanding of the formal basis (i.e., the Canadian legislative and institutional setting) within which it exists. This is probably no more aptly illustrated than in the various "inventions" for conducting regional planning in metropolitan areas and city-regions described in Chapters 8 and 9.

Nevertheless, not only is the mandate for regional planning prescribed by constitutional underpinnings, but so is the scope and quality of actual practice. As Perks and Robinson (1979a, 3) have said, "One cannot meaningfully explore substantive or methodological aspects of public planning without reference to the institutional and political correlates that help shade in the outline of how the subject area and practice have evolved." In this chapter we shall first examine the content and processes that have emerged, as well as the diverse formats that have been used, in regional planning. Then we shall reflect on whether or not past formats are adequate for current and future regional planning.

Planning Regions and the Division of Power

A persistent theme throughout this book is that the planners of regions chosen for planning – prescriptive regions, to use Guttenberg's term (1977, 1988) – must have access to governing powers if they wish to implement their goals and objectives. Though the problems being experienced in a region may seem in obvious need of solution – from gridlock in metropolitan areas to water pollution in resource regions – they cannot be tackled unless the region's planners have the capacity to effect solutions. In other words, planners' resources to govern must be commensurate with their planning proposals. This is true, of course, for any spatial entity in Canada, be it a municipality, county, or province, that wishes to attain certain objectives.

How, then, do the planners of a region (or other spatial unit) find the necessary resources to make their planning proposals a reality?[1] Two perspectives can help us to better appreciate this fundamental issue: one is conceptual and the other is constitutional. First, let us examine the larger context of governing. The work of Maass and his associates (1959b) is instructive in this regard, for, as they point out, at any one time a nation has a "total capacity to govern." Yet, as we would expect, to realize the population's basic objectives, especially in a large and diverse nation, this capacity to govern will likely have to be shared.[2] This is referred to as the "division of power," and it can be carried out in two basic ways.

First, power can be divided by apportioning the total capacity to govern among official bodies (or even individual officials) in the capital city; this is what Maass refers to as the "capital division of power." Within the Canadian context we can think of legislative power being divided between the House of Commons and the Cabinet. Second, power can also be distributed by dividing it among areas; this is what Maass refers to as the "areal division of power." This is how power is divided between the federal government and the provincial governments.

Any spatial units that are to be used for governing inside a province (such as a municipality or a county) require the provincial government to make a further areal division of power. Municipal governments, which are often taken for granted, had to be created by provincial legislation in order to enable local communities to exercise power over land use. Indeed, municipalities are sometimes referred to as "creatures" of the province. Therefore, when regions are deemed to be the appropriate spatial mode for planning, they also must be created by the province (as, for example, were the regional districts of British Columbia and the conservation authorities in Ontario). When the required region spans provincial boundaries or involves both the federal government and one or more provinces (as did the St. Lawrence Seaway and the South Saskatchewan River development projects), it has to be created by the legislatures affected.

Any division of power, whether an areal division or a capital division, can also be subdivided in three specific ways: (1) it can be divided according to the process used in governing (e.g., as in federal and provincial courts); (2) it can be divided according to the function being performed (e.g., as in allocating national defence to the federal government and health care to the provinces); (3) or it can be divided in order to represent a constituency (e.g., as in the creation of Nunavut). The division according to function is that which is most familiar to Canadians; it is the basis of our federalism and is at the heart of many constitutional debates. It is also central to the decisions that provincial governments have taken in establishing governing arrangements for metropolitan areas.

Wood (1959) reminds us that such divisions of power in metropolitan areas are usually only for "administering" a particular activity rather than for "governing" the region in a general sense. His point is that any division of power should emphasize the basic values of individuals in the political community, both of the larger territory and of the region. For the sake of argument, let us assume that basic Canadian values are peace, order, and good government, as is so often stated within legislative preambles. With regard to the division of power that brings into existence a metropolitan or other regional planning agency, Wood would have us ask: Are these basic values being served? Or is the purpose of the division of power simply to promote efficiency in government? As was pointed out in Chapter 3, the demarcation of a region for planning purposes is value-laden, not least because it can either promote or erode the basic values of the regional population. When issues of values need to be resolved, this must be done by provincial legislative bodies. Thus, regional planning has inherent political characteristics, and these will be reflected in the criteria used in the areal division of power that pertains to it.

Formal Setting for Regional Planning

Provincial Source of Regional Powers

Formally, a region's planning agency obtains its powers of implementation through areal division of power arrangements based in Canada's Constitution. As we have seen, in Canada there already exists a substantial areal division of power. This is set out, first, in the British North America (BNA) Act, 1867, and, later, in the Constitution Act, 1982. These are the cornerstones of the basic division of power between the federal government and the provinces. Then, section 92 of the BNA Act makes it clear that any further division of power within a province is the sole responsibility of the provincial government in question. The BNA Act makes no specific mention of subsidiary governments such as municipalities, much less regions. However, it is from this act, and this section of this act, that a province receives the power to create separate regions for planning and other purposes. From the regional planning perspective, the primary importance of these constitutional instruments is that they provide a basic "recipe," so to speak, for how to divide power. Being a relatively new public endeavour, regional planning has to accept the extant areal division of power.

Two aspects of this constitutional areal division of power are crucial to the availability and use of power for regional planning. The first is the spatial integrity of the provincial territory: only the provincial government has the power to govern within a province's boundaries. It may, of course, delegate some of its power, which is what it does when it empowers municipalities to engage in land-use planning or to collect property taxes. This is also what it does when it empowers regional planning agencies to establish a region. The second crucial aspect of the areal division of power lies in the substance of the power allocated constitutionally to the provinces. All resources – land, water, forests, minerals – are "owned" by the province in which they occur.[3] Since resource development and land resources are at the heart of most regional planning, we see again the essential role of the province in making such planning possible.

Extraprovincial Planning Regions

Occasionally, there are planning problems that span provincial boundaries and involve other provinces (and/or the federal government). A prime example is the planning system established for building the St. Lawrence Seaway, which involved not only Ontario and Quebec but also, by virtue of its powers concerning waterways that cross international boundaries, the federal government. Each jurisdiction had to agree to share the necessary powers with the others. The formal arrangement that ensued was a regional corporation in which these powers were embodied and in which each jurisdiction had representation. A similar sort of arrangement occurred during the development of the South Saskatchewan River and was concerned with flood control and irrigation in west-central Saskatchewan. The province and the federal government (the river crossed provincial boundaries) formed the South Saskatchewan River Development Corporation, whose purpose was to build dams and related facilities.

Use of extraprovincial planning regions occurred most extensively in the regional economic planning in the 1960s and 1970s under the ARDA and DREE programs (see Chapter 6). These federal programs aimed at eliminating regional economic disparities, and they operated within so-called "designated areas" that federal agencies had identified as being economically underdeveloped. Implementing such programs required the federal government to undertake agreements with each province that wished to participate, with joint ministerial arrangements then being made to administer them. Predating these regional efforts were those made in the 1930s for the federal Prairie Farm Rehabilitation Act (which was to deal with drought in the three-province Prairie region) and in the 1940s for the Maritimes Marshland Rehabilitation Act (which was to deal with saltwater intrusion into the coastal zones of the three Maritime provinces).

Region-Local Relations

Planning regions are relative latecomers in the governing arrangements of Canada;[4] the earliest is probably the Prairie Farm Rehabilitation Agency of the mid-1930s. However, more than a century before this, some provinces had begun to divide their powers in order to establish municipal and county units and school boards to deal with local issues. Early in the nineteenth century, this areal division of power was enshrined in provincial legislation such as municipal acts and school acts.[5] Thus, whenever regions are deemed the appropriate planning (and governing) vehicle, it must be remembered that they are always preceded (if not actually, at least potentially) by municipal or other local governing entities. In other words, planning regions are almost always superimposed upon already established local areal division of power arrangements. It is this situation that underlies the assertion in Chapter 2 that a key feature of regional planning is its involvement with two or more jurisdictions, both below and above. This situation, as we shall see numerous times when regional planning practice is described in the following chapters, creates tensions between the regional agency and its constituent municipalities as well as between the regional agency and its provincial "parent."

Even more important than the spatial juxtaposition of the region and the local units within it are the nature and quality of relations between the two. Planning regions constitute a new form of government – one that transcends that of, say, municipalities. They have usually been set up because planning problems have exceeded the boundaries, and often the resources, of local units. The regional agency usually has functional and spatial powers unavailable to the local units, but these powers tend to be supplementary to, rather than a substitute for, local powers. Thus, the region and the local unit or units must work together in order to be effective in their respective planning and development. But what seems functionally logical (e.g., regional planning for water supply, transportation, air pollution) is often difficult to achieve on the ground. Municipalities are often long-lived and have their own modes of operation, political culture, and sources of revenue, not to mention the inherent values of local autonomy and self-determination. To this, we need to add the inertia of the legislatively entrenched provincial-municipal relationship. The region, by necessity, intervenes in this picture, seeking a new set of allegiances and a sharing of resources for both local units below and the province above.

The various issues raised in these and other regional and local situations should be considered not only by the regional and the local unit or units but also, and not least, by the province that makes the areal division of power. The areal division of power for regional planning cannot be seen simply in functional terms; it must consider the effects (in the long and short term) of intervening in an ongoing social system of political structures and relationships. This constitutes one of regional planning's inherent tensions, a tension that has been added to in recent decades with demands for greater citizen participation. What is emerging is a public milieu for regional planning, and this is challenging the status quo.

Providing Governing Capacity for Regional Planning

In Canada, it is necessary but not sufficient to know the basic recipe for the areal division of power (along with the province's resource mandate) when establishing planning regions. We must also know the "capacity" of the region to carry out planning and implementing activities. This capacity, which must come from the province and/or the federal government, is made up of the powers that the province is prepared to delegate to the regional planning agency. These powers may also be thought of as the agency's "resources" for governing (Rhodes 1986; Elander 1991; Khakee and Low 1996).

Array of Resources

Five such resources[6] will affect the region's planning and its ability to implement plans for development: regulatory resources, financial resources, political resources, professional resources, and planning resources. These are listed below along with some illustrative questions that may help us to grasp their importance for regional planning:

1 *Regulatory resources* regulate private- and public-sector activities and may vary in both scope and strength. (Can the planning agency make environmental regulations to control air pollution?)
2 *Financial resources* receive funds to conduct activities through taxes, borrowing, grants, or any combination of the three. (Can the planning agency raise taxes directly to carry out projects to implement its plans?)
3 *Political resources* make decisions and legitimize the decision-making activities of the planning agency. (Are the region's decision makers elected directly by local voters?)
4 *Professional resources* carry out its planning activities by virtue of the competencies and skills available to it. (Does the agency have its own regional planning staff?)
5 *Planning resources* develop a long-term policy agenda for the region. (Is the region's plan able to "override" local planning decisions?)

These resources cover both of the major activities of a regional planning agency – making plans and implementing those plans. There is, of course, a degree of overlap among all these resources. However, in general, we can say that the planning and professional resources apply mainly to the plan-making side of the agency's work, while the regulatory and financial resources apply mainly to the plan-implementation side. The political resources tend to lie in a pivotal position, being needed in decisions pertaining both to making plans and to getting them implemented.

To expand on these points: in order to make plans, the agency must have a mandate from the province; that is, it must have *planning resources* that specify the area over which its plans will apply, the issues over which it has jurisdiction, and the extent to which it can control a plan's outcome. The *professional resources* make possible the formulation of plans that are technically sound. At the other end of the spectrum, *regulatory resources* and *financial resources* make it possible for the agency to achieve, or implement, its planning goals. *Regulatory resources* provide the agency with the capacity to regulate or control land use and other activities (e.g., by either maintaining and promoting salutary ones or restricting non-desirable ones). *Financial resources* make the agency capable of deciding when and where it wants future regional facilities by funding the size, quality, and location of transportation and other major infrastructure projects. *Political resources* are a necessary ingredient for both planning and implementation because they legitimize the agency's decisions; that is, they establish the degree of accountability the agency has to the citizens of the region. For example, a regional board elected directly by regional residents is more directly accountable to the citizenry than is one whose membership consists of appointed municipal councillors.

It is readily apparent that the extent to which any of these governmental resources is available to a region can vary depending on the willingness of the province to provide them. Indeed, probably most of the differences between the formal arrangements for regional planning in Canada are due to the varying amounts of governmental resources the provincial governments provide to the regions and the planning agencies they create.

One still has to ask: Why the variation in the resources provided? Why, for example, were the regional planning commissions in Alberta primarily advisory in nature? And why is the James Bay Development Corporation able to plan *and* build dams in northern Quebec? In brief, Alberta provided generally fewer resources to the regional planning commissions than did Quebec to the James Bay Development Corporation. The three broad reasons for such differences are:

1 There could be differing political cultures among provinces that define both the expectations of citizens and the response of the provincial government to such expectations.

2 There may be a pre-existing areal division of power within the province (such as a municipal government).
3 There could be different views on the degree to which government or the market should provide services (Khakee and Low 1996).

These various reasons might be referred to as "contextual factors" that affect the extent of allocated resources. In other words, the allocation of governmental resources will depend upon the factors prevailing in the particular province in question.

Bundle of Governmental Resources

As well as the total amounts of governmental resources provided to regional planning bodies, we also need to consider their *composition*. The province provides what could be called a "bundle" of five governmental resources. The composition of this resource bundle, which will be provided to a particular region, may vary depending on the willingness of the province to allocate to it one or the other of the five resources. A provincial government may see the need to plan a region and to provide considerable planning power but, at the same time, not be willing to provide the financial resources necessary for implementation. This was the case with the regional planning commissions in Alberta. They were allowed to prepare regional plans to which local plans were required to conform, but they had no financial resources and few regulatory resources. Their political resources were also weak because their regional planning commission members were appointed from local councils and, for a time, also included representatives of provincial government ministries. The James Bay Development Corporation, in contrast, was allocated considerable amounts of each resource: it was made an arm of Quebec Hydro, with all its professional and financial resources, and a special regional municipality was created for it to manage. It should, of course, not be assumed that this is the approach that either Alberta or Quebec take to all their respective regional initiatives. Each region, as we said, is a new invention, a new areal division of power, for which the province will make a decision regarding the bundle of resources that is appropriate to it.

As we can now see, it is possible to distinguish between regional planning efforts on the basis of their "institutional and political correlates," as Perks and Robinson (1979a) refer to them. We could readily establish a "profile" of the bundle of resources that have been allocated to a regional body and compare it with profiles of those of other regional bodies. We shall employ such profiles in the next section, when we more fully discuss some Canadian examples of regional planning.

Before doing this, however, there is another aspect of these resource bundles that needs to be noted. This concerns their susceptibility to *change over time.* Given the changeable nature of political situations, we should not expect the bundles of governmental resources to be immutable. Governments change hands, and an incoming party may decide that there are better ways to accomplish any given regional planning task. Parties do not so much differ on basic goals (say, the need for regional planning), as on the means of achieving them. The bundle of resources is the means of achieving regional goals, and it thus reflects political (i.e., value) choices. A particularly graphic example of such a political change occurred in the early 1980s in the regional districts in British Columbia when the provincial government removed their planning resources. They were ordered to stop making regional plans, and their previous plans were no longer binding on municipalities. The Province of Alberta made a similarly drastic move in 1993 by removing the financial resources from the bundle provided to its regional planning commissions and, a few years later, by eliminating those commissions entirely.

Yet another source of change may be the result of changed circumstances (e.g., demographic or economic shifts, or even simply having reached a new stage in the planning process). These changes may occasion the need for more resources or for a different combination of resources. Experience shows, however, that it is not easy to obtain more resources from government; in fact, government may just as well summarily withdraw existing resources as grant new ones.

Profiling the Formal Bases of Regional Planning

If planning regions and agencies must be invented each time they are deemed necessary, then what kind of inventions have been devised for regional planning in Canada? Do they have common attributes from which we can learn about both the establishment of agencies and the type of practice that follows? One can systematically view their similarities and differences by comparing the bundles of governmental resources allocated to regional planning endeavours; that is, by preparing a profile of each agency. In this section, a representative group of Canadian regional planning efforts is subjected to this kind of analysis.

The five governmental resources we are concerned with are: regulatory, financial, political, professional, and planning. When a province allocates these resources it can, within its discretion, allocate the amount of each resource it deems appropriate – small amounts in some cases and large amounts in others – depending on the political culture and the prevailing political will. The particular combination of resources that is provided thus defines the scope of the regional planning that the agency is expected, and able, to carry out. To show how this works, we begin by examining the resources allocated to three particular agencies by three particular provinces. These agencies and provinces are as follows:

1 the Lower Mainland Regional Planning Board in British Columbia
2 the James Bay Development Corporation in Quebec
3 the Peace River Regional Planning Commission in Alberta.

Because resource bundles may change, we look at each of these cases relative
to a particular time in their history.

Three Examples

Lower Mainland Regional Planning Board

The Lower Mainland Regional Planning Board (LMRPB) was one of the first
regional planning agencies established in Canada. When it was formed in
1949 its purpose was to provide a regional context for the planning of the
metropolitan area of Vancouver, especially the region's scarce rural agricultural lands. The province's Town Planning Act, 1948, authorized such agencies and mandated each to prepare an official regional plan. The board's
planning region encompassed approximately 3,500 square kilometres and
twenty-eight municipalities of various sizes. (See Chapter 9 for a more complete history and description of the LMRPB's planning activities.) In 1960 the
bundle of governmental resources available to the LMRPB consisted of the
following:

- *Regulatory Resources:* The official regional plan was to be binding on member municipalities once approved by the board (i.e., municipal plans had
  to conform to the official regional plan).
- *Financial Resources:* The board was authorized to raise funds for its planning operations from levies on member municipalities.
- *Political Resources:* The board was composed of elected members of the
  municipal councils that chose to participate in its activities, but its planning outputs were only advisory.
- *Professional Resources:* Provision was made for the board to have a staff of
  professional planners in order to prepare a regional plan and to offer planning services to member and non-member municipalities.
- *Planning Resources:* The province authorized the board to prepare a general plan for land use. This plan covered a defined region of the province,
  subject to the approval of the provincial government. The board was also
  authorized to provide other planning services to constituent municipalities.

The bundle of governmental resources available to the LMRPB in 1960 could
literally be described as having limited regulatory and financial resources. The
regional plan affected local planning by requiring that local plans conform to
its proposals, but it could not compel member municipalities to carry out
planning actions by establishing land-use regulations and constructing capital

works. The board also had assured access to operating funds, but it had no funds for implementing its plans. Politically, the LMRPB was linked to existing political units, which helped validate its plan; nevertheless, these local political units were under no obligation to fulfil the plan. The board had access to ample professional resources with regard to planning and research. Its planning resources were also substantial, both in that they enabled it to make a binding plan and in that it was mandated to deal with the most important region of the province. However, its planning resources were limited to land-use planning, and it had to seek the province's approval when it came to regional planning.

The LMRPB's bundle of resources may be summed up by saying that its allocations of regulatory, financial, and political resources were *modest*, while its allocations of professional and planning resources were *moderate*. What we have offered is a *verbal profile* of this early metropolitan planning agency. We chose the terms "modest" and "moderate" in order to reflect the different degrees to which governmental resources were made available to the LMRPB. Had resources allocated to the board exceeded these levels, then we would have used the term "plentiful." For example, the LMRPB's regulatory resources would have been "moderate" if it had also been delegated, say, zoning authority; and its planning resources allocation would have been "plentiful" if it had also been mandated to deal with economic and social planning issues. Now, using the same kind of scale, we briefly look at two other regional agencies, one in Quebec and one in Alberta.

James Bay Development Corporation

The James Bay Development Corporation (JBDC) was established in 1971 to build several large hydroelectric dams in an approximately 350,000-square-kilometre region of northern Quebec. It was made a subsidiary of Quebec Hydro, and it had access to that corporation's extensive financial and professional resources. Further, it had full governing power through its own board of directors, which had jurisdiction over a special regional municipality established for the project. Thus, by 1975, the verbal profile of the JBDC would be as follows: regulatory resources = plentiful; financial resources = plentiful; political resources = plentiful; professional resources = plentiful; and planning resources = plentiful.

Peace River Regional Planning Commission

The Peace River Regional Planning Commission (PRRPC) was established in 1958 and, at the time, was one of seven regional planning commissions in Alberta. Its region covered 255,000 square kilometres in an agricultural and forest resource region in the northwestern part of the province. As with other regional planning commissions, it had several functions: to prepare an advisory, but binding, regional land-use plan; to approve land subdivision applications both inside and outside constituent municipalities; to provide local planning services to local municipalities; and, potentially, to exercise development control and zoning approval powers throughout the region. Financing of the operations of the PRRPC came partly from contributions of municipal members, based on their population and tax base, and partly from the provincial government. Although the commission was composed of representatives of municipal units within the region as well as of members of important provincial government departments (e.g., highways, agriculture, education), most of its planning decisions could only be advisory. It did, however, have several professional planners on staff. The verbal profile of the PRRPC in the late 1970s may, thus, be described as follows: regulatory resources = moderate; financial resources = modest; political resources = modest; professional resources = moderate; and planning resources = moderate.

Comparing Canadian Regional Planning Agencies

The three foregoing examples represent three different types of regional planning endeavours: metropolitan planning, resource planning, and rural planning. Each bundle of governmental resources is noticeably different, but are they typical for these types of planning agencies? Have other provinces provided different bundles of governmental resources to their regional planning agencies? Do agencies of the same type have common resource allocations or are there persistent differences between types? Further, have the resource bundles changed over time? These and other questions can be broached by developing analogous verbal profiles for similar agencies where such information is available. In this way, we can better understand how the formal arrangements made by provincial governments affect the scope and practice of regional planning.

This task could be facilitated by transforming the verbal profiles into numerical and graphical equivalents. Perhaps it is already evident that the verbal profiles used to describe governmental resource allocations can be adapted to form an ordinal, or rating, scale capable of rating such allocations according to whether they are "modest," "moderate," or "plentiful." The scale needs to provide one more category: no allocations (a not infrequent situation among regional planning agencies). We now have a scale capable of comparing, say, the LMRPB resource bundle with those allocated to other metropolitan area and city-region planning agencies or even with those allocated to the same region some years later.

Thus, it seems reasonable to suggest a simple numerical scale ranging from zero resources to plentiful resources with intermediate points as follows:

0 = *none* of the resource has been allocated
1 = a *modest* amount of the resource has been allocated

2 = a *moderate* amount of the resource has been allocated
3 = a *plentiful* amount of the resource has been allocated.

Profiles derived from this scale can also be plotted graphically. Figure 10 shows the profiles for a dozen representative Canadian regional planning agencies over the past half century.

Overview of Regional Planning Resource Bundles
Upon viewing the array of profiles in Figure 10, we can make two general observations. The first is that there appear to be characteristic bundles of governmental resources depending on the type of regional planning the provinces wish to put into effect. Of course, each regional planning agency will have its own special governmental resource profile, depending on the political aims and will prevailing at the time it was established. However, certain resources are strong in some types of agencies and weak or moderate in others; for example, metropolitan agencies are generally stronger in political, professional, and planning resources than are rural planning agencies. Economic regional agencies seem characteristically weak in most resources, while regional resource planning agencies appear quite strong in all resources.

One reason for similarities within a particular type of agency is the knowledge of what has happened elsewhere. For example, the Tennessee Valley Authority (TVA) was the first major river basin planning agency, and it provided a model for subsequent endeavours in Canada (and several other countries), notably in the river conservation authorities in Ontario. Although agencies in Ontario were not allocated the same strong levels of resources as was the TVA, this, also, was probably due to what Ontario had learned from the TVA experience. In its turn, Ontario provided a model to other jurisdictions for metropolitan planning. Such models do not necessarily provide an exact template for the bundle of resources that is allocated, but they may certainly be used to identify what has worked and what has not worked in earlier situations. In this way, they provide basic criteria for designing bundles of resources.

The second observation that, upon reviewing Figure 10, applies to all types of regional planning agencies is that the allocations of regulatory and financial resources are relatively weaker than are the allocations of other resources. The prime exception is the JBDC and, to a lesser extent, other "project"-oriented agencies (e.g., the South Saskatchewan and Mactaquac River development corporations). We shall examine these exceptions further below; however, here we note that these particular governmental resources – regulatory and financial – are central to the task of implementing plans. Regional plans dealing with land use need to be implemented through such land-use regulations as zoning, subdivision approval, and development control. Regional plans proposing new physical facilities (e.g., roads, airports, and bridges)

Figure 10

Governmental resources: profiles for selected Canadian regional planning agencies, 1949-96

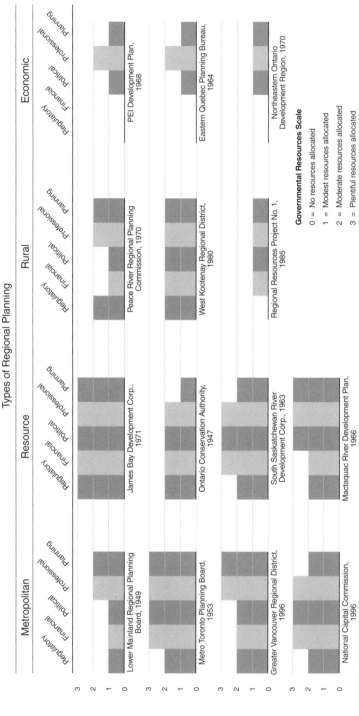

Types of Regional Planning

Governmental Resources Scale

0 = No resources allocated

1 = Modest resources allocated

2 = Moderate resources allocated

3 = Plentiful resources allocated

or the acquisition of park or environmentally sensitive lands need capital. Without resources of the types we have been discussing, regional planning agencies become dependent upon municipal governments, special-purpose bodies, or provincial ministries. In these situations, regional plans are essentially advisory and hortatory.

Resource Bundles for Planning Metropolitan and City-Regions

The examples in Figure 10 suggest that two broadly different resource bundles are allocated to metropolitan and city-region planning agencies, respectively. One is the relatively robust bundle of resources given to the Metropolitan Toronto Planning Board and the Greater Vancouver Regional District. The other is the weaker bundle of resources given to the Lower Mainland Regional Planning Board and, we could add, the likes of the Calgary and Edmonton regional planning commissions. In part, the difference between these two governmental resource bundles lies in the different stage of development and size of the metropolitan area at the time the allocation was made. For example, smaller and less developed metropolitan areas were given weaker resource bundles than were larger metropolitan areas, possibly because, in the eyes of the province, the former's problems were not as urgent or as extensive as were the latter's. Thus plans were implemented in smaller metropolitan areas by the constituent municipalities, while metropolitan plans were simply of an advisory nature. Significantly, different allocations are apparent in the much stronger financial and political resources made available to larger metropolitan agencies. This provides the larger agencies with both the sources of capital and the political clout to follow through on planning decisions. Nevertheless, the generally weaker regulatory resources allocated to all metropolitan agencies is a reflection of the already existing areal division of powers between the province and the municipal units. This existing areal division of power is not readily abridged and usually continues as an underlying political tension.[7] (See also Chapter 8.)

Resource Bundles for Regional Resource Planning

Looking at the four profiles presented in Figure 10, we are struck by the robust bundles of governmental resources provided regional resource planning agencies. What is similar in all these cases is the quite specific mandate to complete a physical project (e.g., dams, power plants, irrigation works, relocation of inhabitants, recreation areas). Further, such projects usually arise out of some strongly felt social need (i.e., stopping flooding, improving power supplies) and thereby generate a strong political commitment to the project. Political commitment is essential since engineering and corporate experience tends to suggest the need for a planning and development agency with the power to carry out a project in its entirety. This raises the need for the provincial government (and the federal government, too, in three of these cases) to share a substantial amount of power if it wants to get the project done. Significantly, the power is usually shared with a regional agency called a "corporation," or "authority," that has its own board of directors, which imbues it with both economic credibility and a sense of political determination. Historically, we should compare the profile of regional resource planning agencies with the TVA, which was also given considerable powers to plan and carry out its plans but only after considerable political debate. That political debate, which continues some sixty-five years later, centres, as much as anything, on whether such strong powers will be returned after the project is completed. Friedmann (1971) has noted this paradox between the need to delegate strong powers if we want to implement a planning project and the difficulty of retrieving such powers from the operating agency once the project is completed.

Two of the examples cited here differ in their resource bundles largely because of their ongoing nature. While physical projects were part of the initial work of Ontario's conservation authorities and of the Mactaquac plan, they had other longer term planning aims and relationships within their regions. In the case of the conservation authorities, they were involved in various public education, conservation, and recreation programs as well as the operation and maintenance of their physical facilities. As a result, their political resources were tempered somewhat by being aligned with local municipal councils, which provided the members of their governing boards. In the Mactaquac region, the long-term objective of the plan was social and economic development, for which several associated agencies were created. Thus, regulatory and financial resources tended to be shared with these other agencies and local governments (see also Chapter 6).

Resource Bundles for Rural-Region Planning

The profiles of rural-region planning agencies generally show that they received fewer governmental resources than did metropolitan and resource agencies. Probably more significant, however, is the variation among them. This reflects, in large measure, the great variety of development in Canada's rural regions as well as the differing government responses to it. Alberta formed its regional planning commissions fifty years ago because, as the government said, "problems refuse to confine themselves to original municipal boundaries" (Alberta 1971, 2). Its perspective was that there was a need to provide extramunicipal planning responses to land-use development issues. This led the province to allocate resources that respected the pre-existing areal division of power to municipalities and that provided supplemental planning, professional, and regulatory resources to deal with cross-boundary issues. The regional planning commissions were intended to be, as their name indicated, strictly "planning" agencies and had advisory powers only. Beyond presenting a persuasive plan, they could do little to compel municipal governments to take action.[8]

British Columbia established a province-wide regional district entity for twenty-six largely rural regions (not including the two urban regional districts abutting metropolitan Vancouver and Victoria). Essentially, it established a form of government that complemented that of the existing municipalities and that provided additional resources that enabled regional districts to perform certain regional functions. Their political resources were enhanced because their board members included appointees from all municipal councils as well as elected members from unincorporated areas. Regional planning was one of several regional district mandated functions, which also included regional hospital administration. Each regional district had its own letters patent specifying the functions it could perform (e.g., water supply, waste disposal, and parks). Thus, moderate amounts of resources were allocated to the regional districts.

Variations of the British Columbia and Alberta rural planning agencies can be found in other provinces – in the district planning commissions in New Brunswick and the regional county municipalities in Quebec. Yet another variety of rural-region planning is that represented by Regional Resources Project No. 1 in southeastern Alberta. There the provincial government allocated very modest resources to a largely voluntary agency arising from the informal co-operation of ten rural and small-town municipalities. Still, the available resources appear to have been appropriate to the planning and development needs of the area. (See Chapter 5 for more on this and other rural planning endeavours.) The basic lesson to be learned with regard to allocating resources for rural planning is the need for pragmatism.

Resource Bundles for Regional Economic Planning

Perhaps it seems peculiar, when looking at the profiles of regional economic planning initiatives, to see that the resource bundles are so meagre. Given the vast amount of money spent upon, and the vast amount of attention paid to, erasing regional economic disparities over nearly two decades, one might expect to see more complete resource bundles (see Chapter 6). However, notice that we refer not to regional planning "agencies" but, rather, to regional planning "initiatives." This is because no formal agencies were established. Intergovernmental agreements (between provincial and federal governments in the Prince Edward Island and Quebec cases) and interministerial arrangements were the means used to effect the sharing of power. During the 1970s, the formal arrangements were minimal for the dozen development regions in Ontario (exemplified here by the one for northeastern Ontario). A regional council was established in each and given the task of formulating a development plan. Although the councils had provincial government backing and, therefore, a modest amount of political resources, they had no actual professional staff and only a limited planning mandate. In neither the federal-provincial nor the intraprovincial cases were regulatory or financial resources made available for implementation.

This seemingly anomalous situation can be explained by the fact that we are here dealing with *economic* planning. On the one hand, unlike land-use planning, economic planning has no traditional format that pertains to metropolitan and rural-region planning. Nor does it have the distinct project orientation of most regional resource planning. On the other hand, economic planning strikes to the heart of governing both the province and the nation. Promoting and achieving economic well-being is considered an essential task of senior governments, for which they have the tools and the responsibility. Not only are such tools diverse and not readily devolved to the regional level, but senior governments tend to hold on firmly to the responsibility and the power that goes with them and are not likely to share this with a region. Within the economic planning approach to regional development, the prevailing principle appears to be that regions may make plans and advise senior governments, but only the senior government may take action.

Formal Foundations: A Summary

The institutional arrangements of regional planning provide, for better or for worse, the formal foundations upon which regional planning is required to function. We will begin by setting out the formal building blocks upon which regional planning endeavours rest in Canada, then we will go on to reflect upon what this country's experience with regional planning arrangements shows us. First, the formal foundations:

- Planning regions have no explicit status within the constitutional arrangements of Canada and must be invented each time one is required.
- Only provinces have the mandate to create regions for planning that occur within their territory (this is referred to as the areal division of power).
- When the federal government wishes to pursue regional planning within a province's territory it must negotiate the content and scope of such planning with the province or provinces in question.

It is vital to appreciate the pre-eminent role of provincial governments in establishing regional planning arrangements (i.e., boundaries, tasks, powers). Formal planning regions can neither be established by the federal government (except in the North) nor emerge spontaneously from local needs. Further, there is neither enabling legislation nor public tradition for establishing planning regions. Regions are either formed for specific purposes (such as planning metropolitan areas or resource projects) or they are given a province-wide mandate (as with the regional districts in British Columbia, the regional county municipalities in Quebec, and the regional planning commissions in Alberta).

Once a province decides that regional planning is necessary and that a separate agency is required in order to carry it out, it must then empower that agency. Thus:

- When provinces create a regional planning agency, they allocate a bundle of governmental resources to enable the plan making and plan implementation to proceed.
- The governmental resource bundles are composed of regulatory, financial, political, professional, and planning resources; the extent of each depends on the province's predisposition to share such powers.
- The allocation of governmental resources from the province to the planning agency may change over time, both in amount and in composition, due to systemic changes, political changes, or both.

Clearly, the allocation of governmental resources to a regional planning agency is always politically charged. For the province it means sharing its power with an agency over which it will never have complete control (short of removing some or all of its powers, as has been done in Alberta and Metro Toronto). For the region it means always having to depend, to some degree, on the province for maintenance of resource levels. As a general observation, the more governmental resources provided, the more *independent* the regional planning agency will be; the fewer governmental resources provided, the more *dependent* it will be.

When we look at the composition of governmental resource bundles provided to various types of regional planning agencies over the past half century, some important regularities appear:

- The characteristics of bundles of governmental resources depend upon the type of regional planning a province wishes to put into effect.
- Generally, regional planning agencies receive relatively weaker allocations of regulatory and financial resources than of political, professional, or planning resources.

Regional agencies engaged in developing resource projects tend to have much more robust bundles of resources for both planning and implementing plans than do those engaged in regional economic planning. Both metropolitan and rural-region planning agencies have resource bundles that reflect their dependency on constituent municipalities and/or special-purpose bodies as well as on provincial ministries, especially with regard to implementation.

These distinctions among resource bundles aside, we must not ignore the other side of the equation: How does the regional agency use the resources it receives from the province? In other words, it should *not* be assumed that the resource bundles the province provides are inadequate for the regional planning task the agencies face. Regional planning agencies, too, are engaged in a political process that requires them to decide how best to use their governmental resources (see Chapter 2). They may decide not to use any or all of their resource bundles, depending upon the perceived political implications of their planning activities. The experience of the TVA in the 1930s and 1940s exemplifies just such a situation (Selznick 1949). The authority chose to limit its broad economic development mandate to resources conservation and electric power generation; and, although it had the power to directly implement its programs, it often chose to delegate this power to various local agencies. Further, the TVA never did prepare the regional plan for which it also had a mandate, and not a few Canadian regional planning agencies also chose not to proceed with making overall regional plans. Among the most notable in this regard were Metro Toronto (see Chapter 8) and many of Alberta's regional planning commissions (see Chapter 7).

Finally, regardless of the resources allocated to them, in almost all instances planning regions have to acknowledge that their territory contains a pre-existing areal division of power (i.e., that between the province and municipalities and/or other local authorities). Local authorities have also been allocated a bundle of resources in order to perform their local functions, many of which could be useful in implementing a regional plan (e.g., land-use regulatory powers), and are thus not available to the planning region's agency. The frequent result of this is inertia with regard to accomplishing regional planning, if not outright conflict between the region's planning agency and the municipalities comprising the region.

Reflections

What are some of the implications for regional planning of its formal foundations? The first arises from the fact that regions, unlike municipalities, neither have a constitutional basis nor seem to exist as part of our political sensibility. Thus, regions and their attendant regional planning agencies have an ephemeral quality, an impermanence, a vulnerability. Even where planning regions have been legislated (as in British Columbia), and especially where they have not, their ultimate dependence on the province cannot be minimized. This poses something of a paradox since, as many have said, regions and their boundaries should be flexible, even "elastic." On the other hand, it is essential that the senior government have a strong and lasting commitment to the region, and this implies the merit of fixed boundaries and resource bundles.

A second implication arises in the relations among the regional planning agency and the municipal and provincial governments. Planning regions exist within a nested hierarchy of planning entities: the province, because of its broad scope and powers, transcends the region, which, in turn, because of its need to take the whole region into account, transcends its municipalities. This logic suggests that a planning region should be given "governing" resources that supersede and encompass those of its constituent municipalities so that it may carry out its holistic functions. But what has happened in almost all regional planning situations is that the province allocated only complementary and parallel resources. Seemingly, this was done to thwart charges that the province was creating "another level of government," a frequent political spectre in most provinces. Nowhere is this more evident than in land-use controls. The legislatively entrenched and generally long-standing land-use planning resources allocated to municipalities have, thus, often undermined regional needs. This means that regional planning agencies are bound to share with municipalities the power to implement any plans pertaining to land use. Similarly, when regional plans impinge upon the realms of resource and economic development, the planners must obtain support and approval from the province. In short, while a regional planning agency may have the appropriate planning resources to *make* a plan, seldom is it in a position to fully *implement* it.

Related to this situation is the division that has occurred between regional planning initiatives that involve land use and those that involve economic and resource development. The implication is that it is difficult to undertake *comprehensive* regional planning. Provinces establish regional planning agencies in characteristic ways and provide them with governmental resources that preclude sanctioning a multifaceted approach to planning problems. Certainly, some agencies established for regional land-use planning broach economic and resource issues (e.g., the Peace River Regional Planning Commission in Alberta in the 1970s and the Central Kootenay Regional District in British Columbia in the 1980s). However, these agencies received little provincial support in implementing their recommendations.

Distinctive exceptions are those regional resource development projects that can be defined in engineering terms. The senior government often sees these as a "business" venture requiring a corporate structure with the power to execute the project. In these cases, the province (and federal government) presumes that it is sharing extensive power for a specific purpose and for a specified period of time. The dilemma for the province lies in the fact that, although it needs to give powers to an outside agency in order to accomplish a given project, once that project has been accomplished, it might not be able to get those powers back. Public corporations quite quickly take on a life of their own and find some reason to continue their activities and retain their powers.

We can only speculate about the implications of the various constraints the provinces might impose for the establishment of, say, a bioregional regional planning agency (see discussion in later chapters). Such a broad-based approach covering ecological, economic, social, and settlement systems will require the relaxing of previous conventions. As regional planning moves towards broad-based environmental planning, it is useful to consider the following question: What bundle of governmental resources would the province provide to planning regions that had such a mandate? Further, regions (and localities) are being pressured to more widely and more effectively involve citizen and citizen-based organizations in managing regional programs. Provinces will need to consider seriously adapting their current perspectives on sharing power not only with regions, but also within regions, in order to keep pace with these trends.

Part 2

Planning Practice in Rural and Non-Metropolitan Regions

5

Planning Rural Regions and Their Communities

Of the different types of regional planning explored in this book, rural-region planning is the one that has been around the longest. Its beginnings can be traced to the Prairie Farm Rehabilitation Act (1935), which established programs to alleviate severe drought conditions on the Prairies. In the ensuing decades, rural-region planning evolved into three broad forms of practice that reflect the diversity of Canadian rural regions and their planning needs:

- practice aimed at maintaining and protecting the countryside and rural communities
- practice aimed at planning resource development, resource conservation, and environmental protection in rural regions
- practice aimed at rejuvenating rural and non-metropolitan economies.

Each of these forms of rural-region planning provides a focus for this and the two following chapters.

Rural-region planning has diverse aims, locations, and substantive foci, as these three forms of practice illustrate. Yet, different though they are, in many respects each form of practice shares some common characteristics with, as well as having some sharp differences from, non-rural types of regional planning. There is even some overlap with the planning in metropolitan regions and the new city-regions, where the majority of the territory is often rural and the disposition of "rural fringe" areas is usually a major issue. An essential starting point in rural-region planning involves the need to recognize how extensively such regions differ from one another. One early observer notes that there is "not *one* rural situation but several on a continuum" (Hahn 1970, 46). Just looking at "the continuously occupied area of Canada," as Russwurm (1987, 185) refers to it, and leaving aside northern and other resource regions, we easily perceive the country's rural diversity: farming regions far from cities as well as those on the edge of cities; rural regions where forestry, mining, and fisheries resource development predominates or where those resources are mixed; and rural regions where scenic resources are important to the development of tourism. Then there are all the variations on these rural types – variations imposed by topography and the relationship of the area in question to the nearest system of cities. Excluding urban areas, these various rural situations make up three-quarters of the continuously occupied area of Canada. Hence the need for planners to grasp the diversity and extent of rural Canada.

Another important characteristic to keep in mind when considering rural planning is its substantive focus. (Indeed, as many have noted, rural planning seems to have several focal points [Qadeer 1979; Hilts and Moull 1988; Dykeman 1988; Bryant and Johnston 1992].) This may be broken down into three parts: (1) a resource focus, (2) an economic development focus, and (3) a community-needs focus. This makes rural planning quite distinct from urban planning, which is concerned with land-use and regulatory allocations that enable one to deal with competing demands for space. Land is not scarce in most rural areas, nor is competition for it a persistent problem. In contrast, rural land-use concerns have more to do with the way various activities are practised in the countryside and, not least, with the impact they have on the rural community's need for stability and survival. However, before focusing on this subject, let us look at the diversity of rural Canada.

Several Rural Canadas

We, like Daniels and Lapping (1996), often think of only two broad types of rural areas – the rural-urban fringe and remote rural areas. However, rural Canada presents itself to the planner in a much broader array of regional forms. Hahn's (1970) notion of a "continuum" of rural situations that vary from the "completely rural" to the "nearly urban" better describes the diversity of rural regions and their differing planning needs. This continuum keeps us from falling into the trap of considering all non-urban areas as rural. Indeed, we need to move away from the impression that rural areas are simply a residuum of urban activities, that they are merely non-cities. We need a more complete perspective on rural regions in order to conduct adequate regional planning. In Canada, part of this perspective comes from our extensive experience in planning rural regions, and part of it comes from identifying different rural situations along a continuum. We must identify a minimum of five broad types of rural regions in order to appreciate the range of rural planning issues and responses in Canada:

- completely rural regions
- Aboriginal rural regions
- rural recreational regions
- the city's countryside
- northern and resource regions.

In this brief review we shall also indicate the planning problems prevailing in each type of rural region (Hodge 1988).

Completely Rural Regions

The most extensive set of Canadian rural regions is that which exists and functions largely on rural terms. We are referring to those regions that have been settled (i.e., occupied) for at least several generations and that have developed the distinctive and widespread use of some natural resource (e.g., agriculture, forestry, fishing, or mining) or a combination of resources. Although the topographical conditions of these rural regions often differ widely, they tend to have the same general characteristics: broad areas of resource use that are often populated by the resource owners and their families who, in turn, are served by small settlements and only occasionally by a small city. We see these rural regions in Newfoundland, the Gaspé, the Prairies, and in every province. Indeed, the majority of each province's territory (or at least the southern portions of those with a northern frontier) is composed of these regions, which take up a little more than two million square kilometres.[1] Canada's rural regions are exceedingly diverse both within and between provinces. A forestry region in New Brunswick is likely to differ from one in northern Ontario or coastal British Columbia. Similarly, we find differences in farming and fishing regions from province to province, but they still display the same general characteristics – a resource-based economy, low population density, and many small settlements. A summary description of the characteristics of these regions follows, with the caveat that accurate and up-to-date data on rural regions are always difficult to obtain.

Despite their diversity, a number of planning problems recur in the completely rural parts of Canada. Some problems tend to be of a domestic nature and affect quality of life – the chronic lack of transportation, health, and education services (e.g., in Prince Edward Island) and few housing choices (e.g., in Manitoba's small towns). We see the rural-region planning approaches to these problems as maintaining and protecting the countryside and communities. Other problems are more developmental in nature – the depletion of resources (e.g., the cutover regions in New Brunswick), limited job opportunities, endemic poverty, and boom-and-bust cycles (e.g., mining regions in Ontario and Quebec). The planning approaches to developmental problems are discussed mainly in Chapters 6 and 7. Of course, the two sets of problems often occur in tandem (e.g., the Newfoundland fishery) and, thus, some discussion of each may be found in all three chapters in Part 2.

Profile

Representative areas: These cover about two million square kilometres in the southern portions of most provinces, including Quebec's Eastern Townships, southwestern Ontario, New Brunswick, the Interior of British Columbia, and the Prairie provinces.

Population characteristics: Approximately 3.9 million people were living in these regions in 1996 (about 14 percent of the country's population). These numbers have been declining for several decades, and the remaining population has been aging (especially in small towns) as younger people leave.

Economic characteristics: Primary activities provide the major source of employment, supplemented by service jobs in small businesses in the towns, villages, and small cities serving them.

Planning problems: The provision of services to low-density settlement, depleted resources, poverty, transportation, meagre housing choice for the elderly and others, small, weak local government, boom-and-bust resource development, excessive exploitation of resources, and degradation of environments and landscapes.

Aboriginal Rural Regions

By far, the bulk of Aboriginal territories and communities are located in "completely rural" surroundings (both inside and outside the North). Some are part of the completely rural regions (e.g., the Mohawk communities in eastern Ontario), while others are located at their margins (e.g., many Aboriginal communities in coastal British Columbia). The general characteristics of rural regions – a distinctive natural resource base, sparse population, and mostly small communities – also apply to Aboriginal regions. And, certainly, Aboriginal regions meet the criterion of having been occupied continuously. However, they are not a simple variant of the completely rural regions we have been describing; they are, for several reasons, a distinctive part of rural Canada. One of these reasons concerns the special relationship between Aboriginal peoples and the land, water, and air – what non-Aboriginal peoples refer to as "natural resources" (Wolfe 1988). Another concerns the severity of their development problems – poverty, poor housing, lack of service, isolation – which are extreme even compared with poorly developed non-Aboriginal rural regions. And yet another concerns the still-to-be-resolved issue of self-government. While the planning problems and geographical settings may appear similar to those in other completely rural regions, special approaches and professional skills are needed to deal with Aboriginal rural regions (Rich et al. 1997).

Profile

Representative areas: These cover about one million square kilometres in both the northern and southern portions of most provinces. Examples include the Queen Charlotte Islands of British Columbia (Haida Gwaii), northwestern Ontario, northern Saskatchewan, and northern New Brunswick.

Population characteristics: Approximately half a million people were living in these regions in 1996 (about half of all Aboriginal peoples). Due to high fertility rates, these numbers have been growing rapidly for several decades.

Economic characteristics: Primary activities, where they exist, provide the major source of employment and are supplemented by service jobs in small villages and towns.

Planning problems: Low levels of service, poverty, isolation, inadequate housing and transportation, depletion of resources, and few job opportunities.

Rural Recreational Regions

Another special type of rural region is that in which the natural resource base is considered desirable for recreational activity on land and/or water. Some of these regions are long-lived (e.g., the Laurentides in Quebec, the Muskokas in Ontario, and Banff National Park in Alberta), while others are of relatively recent origin (e.g., Whistler, British Columbia, and the north shore of Prince Edward Island). Our criteria for defining rural regions – resource base, sparse population, small communities, and long-time settlement – are also applicable for defining rural recreational regions. Typically, most of what are now seen as rural recreational regions were initially settled a century or more ago and developed around the exploitation of some other resource (e.g., fishing in the Bay of Fundy, forestry in the Laurentides, and agriculture and forestry at Whistler). Even the Rocky Mountain national parks are a century old and have well-established settlement patterns emanating from mineral and other economic resources. Today, these regions are the destinations of mainly urban dwellers, and their economic bases are some form of tourism. When the region is located on the edge of a metropolitan urban field,[2] as many are (e.g., the Laurentides, Banff, the Muskokas), the incidence of permanent residences (either year-round or seasonal), along with associated commercial facilities, may be quite prevalent (see Vance 1996). More distant regions (e.g., Jasper, Alberta, New Brunswick's Bay of Fundy, and British Columbia's Tofino–Long Beach area) also draw vast numbers of visitors but do not have as high an incidence of permanent or seasonal residences.

The planning problems of recreational regions stem largely from two sources. One is the often extreme concentration of development and the impact of the large volume of visitors on the environment (Mitchell 1997); the other is the impact of development on more or less indigenous activities and populations. Such impacts include, for example, the pollution of waters previously used for fishing; the escalation of farmland prices; and the escalation of housing prices in nearby communities, which effectively displaces those who are less affluent. Although the problems in these regions have an urban origin, the context within which their solution must be found is distinctly rural (Halseth 1993).

Profile

Representative areas: These cover about 250,000 square kilometres within the southern portions of most provinces, including large destination areas such as Banff National Park, the Laurentides, and New Brunswick's Bay of Fundy as well as more localized recreation destinations such as Prince Edward County in Ontario, Invermere in eastern British Columbia, and Lake Winnipeg's southern shore.

Population characteristics: Approximately half a million people were living in rural recreational regions in 1996, with seasonal populations often triple that; permanent dwellings for seasonal visitors have increased markedly in areas close to large cities.

Economic characteristics: Although primary activities still provide a major source of employment, tourism services often come to dominate both within nearby villages and towns and in the countryside.

Planning problems: Dependence on tourism economy, seasonal employment, housing price differentials and shortages for local people, and social cleavages.

The City's Countryside

Another, and more prevalent, interface between rural and urban populations occurs in the zones surrounding cities. Friedmann and Miller (1964) refer to this zone as the "urban field," while Canadian geographers have (more appropriately) referred to it as the "city's countryside" (Bryant et al. 1982). It may extend as far as 100 kilometres (or one and one-half hour's driving time) from the central city. Although accounting for only 12 percent of the area of rural Canada, the rural regions that surround cities contain more than 40 percent of the farm population and are the most diverse regions with regard to types of activity and forms of settlement. In agriculture alone, as Bryant and Johnston (1992) note, the city's countryside contains a far greater diversity in farm types, farm size, intensity of production, and socioeconomic production arrangements than do any other rural agricultural regions. To this we can add the great array of activities that take place there – from Christmas tree farms to theme parks and art galleries, not to mention the many small manufacturing industries. Along with the traditional independent homesteads and small towns and villages of rural regions, in the city's countryside we also find small suburban-type subdivisions.

The rural-urban interface that occurs in the city's countryside is replete with actual and potential conflict between activities and populations, with predictable social and environmental impacts. Before beginning planning, it is important to know two facts about the city's countryside. The first fact is that the "urban surroundings," as Gertler and Crowley (1977) refer to them, are a *collection of environments.* These environments are used for residence (primary dwellings, cottages, second dwellings), commerce and production (farms, forestry, mineral extraction, water supply), and nature (recreation and wilderness). Moreover, many of these environments have been in place for a long time. Of course, natural environments predate urban development or any other human settlement; however, most activities that occur within rural environments (e.g., farming and forestry) are long-lived compared with the expanded urban activities that are now occurring there. The second important fact about the city's countryside is that, once urbanization occurs, it will be in a state of almost continuous change.

Thus, the spatial patterns of activities in the city's countryside are constantly shifting. One thrust of this change concerns *replacement* (i.e., the way one form of land use is replaced by another, as when a residential subdivision takes over agricultural land or a forestry area is designated a wilderness recreation area). Another thrust concerns *transformation* (i.e., the way in which activities change from one form to another, as in farmland moving to more intensive agricultural uses and seasonal cottages being renovated for year-round use). These changes, and many others, may go on concurrently, for the city's countryside is dynamic. The relation of the countryside to the city is changing and so are country lifestyles, land uses, demographics, and population. And, as with any social system undergoing change, the countryside and its residents and businesses experience stress, which manifests itself in competition and conflict between ideas concerning appropriate land use as well as between "newcomers" and "old-timers" (Walker 1984; Halseth 1996).

Such a dynamic setting generates a great variety of planning problems. Among the primary ones are the loss of agricultural land, the need to extend expensive capital facilities (such as roads and sewerage), the provision of recreation areas, and the maintenance of water supply and sand and gravel sources. Confounding the solution of planning problems in the city's countryside are, on the one hand, the different perspective on land resources among rural dwellers/producers and urban planners/developers and, on the other hand, inadequate governance arrangements. (The issue of governance arrangements is described in some detail in Chapters 8 and 9.)

Profile

Representative areas: Covers about 750,000 square kilometres in zones of 100 kilometres around all metropolitan areas (with smaller zones around other large cities).

Population characteristics: Between four and five million people were living in these regions in 1996 (excluding urban dwellers). These numbers have been growing rapidly for several decades.

Economic characteristics: Primary activities provide employment in intensive agriculture, forestry, and aggregate mining; however, increasingly, manufacturing and the service sector (including recreation) provide most of the employment and income.

Planning problems: Preservation of agricultural and other wilderness lands, water and air pollution, conflicting land uses, upward pressure on land values, transportation, displacement of rural populations, and social cleavages.

Northern and Resource Regions

To the north of the rural regions is a vast frontier of lands that also merits being called "rural." Although we do not deal extensively with regional planning efforts in northern regions, some noteworthy characteristics of this part of rural Canada should be reported (see also Chapter 7). For example, while resource development dominates its economy and settlements are small and widely dispersed, the vast scale of the region affects its spatial character. The North, generally that area north of the sixtieth parallel, covers close to four million square kilometres. When we include the resource regions of Labrador and the northernmost portions of provinces from Quebec west, which cover a further three million square kilometres, we find that the North comprises nearly 72 percent of Canada's territory yet has barely 2 percent of its population. Fewer than 700,000 people live there, including many who are Aboriginal or Inuit.

A few long-lived European settlements in the northern region date back to the late 1900s, but most date from the end of the 1940s and later (Robinson 1962). Many settlements were built as "new towns" in this region for the exploitation of resources such as mining, oil and gas development, and paper milling. Schefferville in Quebec, Leaf Rapids in Manitoba, Frobisher Bay in the Northwest Territories, and Kitimat in British Columbia are examples of this. Many of these new towns pioneered new community designs that were especially appropriate for regions with severe weather conditions (Hodge 1998). Alongside these settlements are a large number of predominantly Aboriginal communities, often located at or near traditional sites for hunting, trapping, and fishing. Much of the northern region is under unextinguished Aboriginal title, hence the Aboriginal interest in its planning and development (Richardson 1989b).

A key feature of these northern regions is that, while physically contiguous to the southern part of Canada, they are not extensively linked to it. Further to this, the few settlements are widely separated from each other, and ground connections between towns (both new and old) are often lacking. The result is not only isolated populations, but also an unintegrated regional economy. Enormous capital costs are a part of any urban or industrial development because of the distances involved, the lack of a secondary industry to produce needed materials (Lotz 1970), and the fact that development may easily damage fragile northern environments. Canada's northern regions also abound in land-use conflicts (Richardson 1989b). These conflicts stem from several factors:

Aboriginal interests in the land, the need to conserve the landscape, and the desire to benefit from the exploitation of non-renewable resources such as oil and minerals. These factors become more acute the farther north we go, and, because of them, regional planning in the North must be more integrated and allow less scope for error than regional planning in the South.

Profile

Representative areas: Covers about seven million square kilometres in the northern portions of most provinces and those lands north of the sixtieth parallel, including Labrador, the James Bay region in Quebec, the Yukon Territory, Nunavut, and the Mackenzie Valley.

Population characteristics: Between 500,000 and 600,000 people lived in these regions in 1996 (including Aboriginal and Inuit peoples). There is some overall growth in the region, but this includes erratic patterns of both growth and decline among communities.

Economic characteristics: Primary activities provide most of the employment (e.g., mining, oil and gas, forestry, trapping) along with activities servicing the primary sector (e.g., transportation) and public-sector activities (e.g., local government, health care, and resource management).

Planning problems: Large distances over which to supply products and services, fragile environments, small, isolated communities, widely varying income distribution, lack of economic integration, Aboriginal land interests, very high capital costs for access and development, and boom-and-bust economies.

Some Essential Principles of Rural-Region Planning

Clearly, rural regions are diverse, and the sets of planning problems affecting them are distinctive, yet some important commonalities need to be taken into account when we proceed with regional planning in any of the types of rural regions just described. These commonalities, which have been commented upon by many observers of rural planning, both in Canada and abroad, provide some principles for considering the Canadian experience in planning rural regions.

Each Rural Region Contains a Continuum of Planning Situations

As we have noted, there are several types of rural regions, and each of these has its own distinctive problems. For example, even in completely rural regions there can be instances of urban overspill, as in the Peace River Region of Alberta. And urban sprawl has been a problem in rural New Brunswick for more than two decades (New Brunswick 1980; Flanagan 1997). Conservation of resources is an issue in all types of rural regions, as is the role and future of small communities. In other words, planners of rural regions of whatever type face not a single planning problem but a whole continuum of them.

Resource Use Is at the Heart of Rural-Region Planning

The life and vitality of rural regions are bound to both the natural resources they possess and to how these resources are used. Whether it be land for farming; forests for logging; fish stocks for fishing; visual assets for recreation; or, for Aboriginal rural dwellers, "the land" as a spiritual and cultural experience, the issue is not *whether* these resources are to be used, but *how*. Many observers have repeatedly emphasized this point (e.g., Hahn 1970; Maclaren 1976; Qadeer 1979; Wolfe 1988). Scarcity of a rural region's resources is not usually an issue, so land-use problems are not normally those that result from competition among users for a certain location or from local externalities. Rural planning problems tend to arise not from *use* of the resource but, rather, from the way that use is *practised* (Davidson and Wibberley 1977). Examples include overfishing in coastal regions, clear-cutting of timber in forestry regions, ribbon development along country roads in farming regions, and mineral development in the North.[3]

Smallness Is a Distinguishing Feature

Although rural regions are large in area – perhaps the largest of the regional types planners encounter – the entities within them tend to be small. Small towns, small producers, and small government institutions are typical of these regions (Hodge and Qadeer 1986). Large installations such as pulp mills, fish plants, resort complexes, and Canadian Forces bases are the exceptions that prove the smallness rule; and even they occur only infrequently. The characteristic of smallness has several implications for regional planning. One is the relatively small scale of resources – human, financial, and governmental – available to carry out planning in a rural region. Populations are small and scattered, and local governments are likely to be small and understaffed. As Qadeer (1979, 118) points out: "Materially and technically, rural communities are heavily dependent on provincial and national resources and advice." Yet another result of smallness is the intricate web of social and economic connections within rural regions. The segmentation between households as consumers and households as producers, between institutions and households, and among business interests, governments, and households is only too evident to urban dwellers. In contrast, roles and functions are much more blurred in rural communities, where interests and memberships overlap. Thus, the impact of change will tend to follow an interconnected path economically, physically, and socially.

Rural Planning: A Process

These characteristics of rural-region development led Gilg (1985) to posit that the three main roles of rural planning are: (1) resource development, (2) conflict resolution, and (3) land management. In other words, rural planning should be viewed as a process of reconciling development needs among resource users, the human community, and the support economy (Qadeer 1979;

Richardson 1989a). And it should be remembered that flexibility is crucial to rural planning, whether in dealing with the use of land or in dealing with the use of other resources (Davidson 1984). With this in mind, we can now turn to some Canadian examples of rural planning.

Planning the Countryside and Communities in Rural Canada

Over the decades, the planning of rural regions in Canada evolved in two general directions. On the one hand, there evolved a *sectoral* approach to planning. This approach focused on a single functional sector, most commonly on agricultural land protection, but also on water resource management and environmental conservation. On the other hand, there also evolved a *land-use planning* approach. This approach focused on rural and regional municipalities, commonly using urban-type regulatory means such as zoning to maintain and enhance rural community development patterns. Despite the complementarity of these two approaches, seldom were they joined in a more comprehensive form of rural planning (Russwurm 1987). Sectoral approaches were also widely used for rural resource planning and for rural-region economic planning (see Chapters 6 and 7).

Agricultural Land Protection: A Sectoral Approach

With the rapid expansion of urban areas following the Second World War, the preservation of farmland became an important issue in several provinces. Often the burgeoning cities were located adjacent to valuable farmland, and provincial governments were urged to protect not only actively used farmland, but also potential farmland (which was often rapidly usurped for urban purposes). Out of the pivotal 1961 Resources for Tomorrow Conference (see Chapter 1) there emerged the Canada Land Inventory. This tool facilitated the planning of rural regions by making it possible to map land capability for agriculture as well as for other rural resource sectors (such as forestry, recreation, and wildlife). Several provinces used the Canada Land Inventory to mount farmland preservation programs in order to reduce or eliminate urban development on good quality farmland (Bryant 1994).

British Columbia was the first province to do this when, with its Agricultural Land Commission Act, 1973, it designated agricultural land reserves that allowed only rural uses. Quebec passed similar legislation in 1978 (Loi sur la protection du territoire agricole). Known as Bill 90, this law also provided for a commission that had the power to designate a "protected zone" within each municipality; within this zone only agricultural land uses were permitted (Reid and Yeates 1991). Also in 1978 Ontario established its Foodland Guidelines, which encouraged municipalities to incorporate the principles of farmland protection into their community plans. Ontario also brought out a companion policy known as UDIRA (urban development in rural areas), which it applied in its role of approving municipal plans. A fourth province, Newfoundland, also enacted legislation to protect its meagre farmland resources and struck a commission to enforce standards.

The farmland protection programs, especially those in British Columbia and Quebec, have undoubtedly helped to conserve agricultural land. Even though both provinces have limited farmland resources along with substantial amounts of farmland occurring around their largest cities, the protection zones have remained relatively stable for more than twenty years. For the most part, non-agricultural uses have been prevented from moving into these protected areas, and land subdivision within protected zones has been reduced. Trade-offs have occurred, of course, especially in dealing with the pressures for urban development around Vancouver and Montreal. In many respects, in both provinces the protection zones and land reserves have been most effective in planning for the city's countryside in and around smaller cities.

The Ontario approach to farmland protection has not been as direct as that of other provinces where commissions were established to oversee and regulate these resources. Ontario has depended on persuading municipal and regional governments to enact their own regulations, based on provincial policies, to protect farmland. The method Ontario has promoted is that of establishing "urban containment boundaries." In some cases this has worked well (e.g., in the Niagara region, with its valuable soft fruit land resources) (Gayler 1994, 1996). The presence of so many cities in Ontario's agricultural heartland, of course, makes the preservation of farmland very difficult. According to a path-breaking study on countryside planning in Huron County, the challenge is: "How do we utilize [rural] resources wisely for the benefit of all people in the Province?" (Maclaren 1975, 4). A recent planning approach that attempts to take pressure off farmlands is rural "cluster zoning," and it works by allowing development on only a small portion of a farm. This plot, in turn, links to similar plots on adjoining farms, thereby forming a cluster of homes and allowing the remaining land to be available for farming (Bowler 1997).

Agricultural land preservation, regardless of its success and its laudable intent, does not constitute rural planning. It is simply a tool that rural planners can use. Valuable though this tool may be, it neither guarantees viable agriculture (Bryant 1994) nor takes into account the social aspects of rural regions (Russwurm 1987). Further, it constitutes a basically defensive policy response aimed at keeping urban or non-farm development out of rural areas. None of the provinces has come to grips with a positive response concerning what should be happening in rural areas. None of them has developed policies for "*rural* development in *rural* areas," as the consultants studying countryside planning in Huron County stressed (Maclaren 1975, 6) [emphasis ours]). Several attempts by rural regions to deal with this dilemma have been significant, as we shall see in the concluding section of this chapter. First, however, it is worth examining the other major approach to rural-region planning.

Rural Land-Use Planning Approaches

Again, some of the earliest land-use planning approaches occurred in the municipalities in and around fast-expanding urban areas. These initiatives, which occurred first around Vancouver and then around Edmonton and Calgary, took the form of professionally staffed regional planning agencies that tended to focus on such planning issues as residential development sprawling into farming areas and ribbon development along rural roads. "Land use" conceived of in this way seldom directly covered the agricultural use of land resources. The approach was largely defensive, and its purpose was to stave off urban encroachment. We shall briefly examine the past occurrences of many instances of this type of rural planning as well as some present-day instances. (See also Chapters 8 and 9 for a review of planning in the rural fringe of metropolitan areas.)

Ontario

Ontario began developing its system of regional municipalities in the period between 1969 and 1974. These municipalities generally corresponded to regions surrounding major urban areas and thus provided a vehicle for dealing with urban intrusions into rural areas. The twelve regional municipalities established in this period were provided with full local governing status, having their own elected councils, taxation powers, and land-use regulatory resources. As Russwurm (1987) notes, governmental arrangements forced the regional municipalities to deal with rural as well as urban needs in their policy deliberations. The instruments they had for doing this were (1) zoning and (2) subdivision control. Regional municipal councils also had responsibility for regional roads, waste management, and recreation facilities. A number of Ontario counties also undertook some rural planning in the 1970s. Several counties hired planners to work with small local governments, most notably Lennox and Addington, Niagara, and Huron counties. Huron County was the locus of a major study, entitled "Countryside Planning," commissioned by the Ontario government to determine land resource management principles (Maclaren 1975; Davidson 1984). Its perspective was distinctive – it began from the needs of the countryside and its communities – and will be explored later in this chapter.

Another distinctive rural planning action in Ontario in the 1970s was the preparation of a plan for the Niagara Escarpment region. In 1973, the Niagara Escarpment Planning and Development Act mandated the preparation of a plan for this almost totally rural area that covers 6,500 square kilometres, stretching more than 700 kilometres along a unique rocky spine extending northward from near Niagara Falls to the tip of the Bruce Peninsula on Lake Huron (Jameson 1978). It is home to several hundred species of birds, mammals, and reptiles as well as to many types of flora and unique geological formations. The heart of the Niagara Escarpment plan is the creation of a continuous special protective zone. Completed in 1978, the plan is administered by a special commission of municipal officials and public appointees. The main instrument of implementation, besides the provincial designation of the area, is "development control," which requires that a permit be issued for development in specified areas within the escarpment zone (Curtin 1994). Although the planning area encompasses several dozen municipalities, counties, and regional governments, the commission's land-use controls have priority.

Quebec

Quebec took a major step when its Regional and City Planning Act, 1980, established a comprehensive framework for regional planning (Quebec 1980). It provided for the creation of ninety-four agencies known as "regional county municipalities," or municipalités régionales de comté. Their main task was to prepare a regional plan that would include proposals for land use; delimitation of areas to become urban; identification of environmentally sensitive, historical, and cultural areas; and the location of intermunicipal facilities and public utilities (Cermakian 1984). This system was never fully completed, although the plans covered the five largest urban communities.

British Columbia

In 1949, this province took the pioneering step of applying land-use planning to the countryside. Its regional planning body – the Lower Mainland Regional Planning Board – was made up of about three dozen municipalities within an estimated 3,500-square-kilometre region extending east from Vancouver (see earlier discussion). Most of the region, along with its municipalities, was rural at the time, and it included some of the most fertile and valuable farmland in the province. The work of the board was dominated by issues concerning the growth and expansion of the metropolis and its suburbs as well as by the resultant industrial land needs, urban sprawl, and transportation. The board and its staff recognized that the latter issues had collateral impacts on nearby farmland, and it provided planning assistance to member and non-member municipalities pertaining to zoning and subdivision control in order to help limit urban development in farming areas. A second, and similar, regional planning board – the Capital Region Planning Board – was established shortly thereafter for the region surrounding the province's second largest city, Victoria.

The next major step in the planning of rural regions in British Columbia occurred in 1965 with the institution of a system of twenty-eight regional districts that covered all but a small northern part of the province. Regional districts differed in composition and mandate from the earlier regional planning boards. Whereas the boards were only advisory and membership was voluntary, the districts required the membership of all municipalities as well as of unincorporated rural areas (called "electoral areas"). Each regional district had taxing power and an array of functions. Planning was one of several regional functions (including water supply, sewage disposal, and hospital planning) that these new agencies could perform. Given that British Columbia is dominantly rural, planning in its regional districts was bound to have a major rural component. Nonetheless, the rural planning approach taken in almost all of these regional districts tended to be defensive; that is, it tended to focus on keeping urban development out of rural areas. This planning was usually accomplished through the regional district's staff, who provided planning services to constituent municipalities and electoral areas. The preparation of regional plans was a rarity,[4] even though, by law, regional plans had power of compliance over local plans. (See Chapter 9 for a discussion of this issue in the Vancouver area.)

Alberta

Alberta had included regional planning in its 1929 Planning Act; however, it did not form its first regional agency until 1950 (for the Edmonton region). It then formed another in 1951 (for the Calgary region). These agencies, and the others that followed, were known as regional planning commissions (RPCs). Five others were formed in the 1950s and, by 1984, there were ten, covering most of the settled area of the province. Other than the two RPCs established for the two major metropolitan regions, the remainder were either centred on small cities (e.g., Red Deer, Lethbridge, Medicine Hat) or covered resource regions (e.g., the Peace River). The RPCs ranged in size from about 15,000 square kilometres (the Battle River) to more than 250,000 square kilometres (the Peace River), but most were about 30,000 square kilometres in area and predominantly rural in development (Alberta 1971). At the outset, commission members consisted of representatives of constituent municipalities and provincial government ministries. Later, in 1977, membership was restricted solely to municipal representatives. Funding for RPCs came mainly from the province, along with a levy on the tax base of member local governments, and each commission retained a small staff of professional planners.

Although the allocation of governmental resources to RPCs was, in many respects, quite extensive, the commissions were limited in the action they could take. Their central function was to prepare a regional plan that would specify land uses and residential densities and propose highways, public services and buildings, schools, and parks and recreation areas. Once the plan was approved, it could restrain (but not stop) municipalities and public authorities from taking actions that were inconsistent with it. The RPCs could not implement their own plans, and the regional plan was strictly advisory. One of the commission's regulatory functions involved approving all subdivision plans within the region. When the Planning Act was recast in 1977, this function was offered to member municipalities if they could show that they had updated plans and related bylaws in place – a condition many could not meet. This made for an even more "ambiguous position" for RPCs (Smith 1994) and led, eventually, to their loss of funding in 1993.

Although most of the RPCs approached the planning of their rural areas by restraining urban development, a more comprehensive rural planning approach did occur in at least two commissions. The Oldman River regional planning commission, in the Lethbridge region, had an extensive planning program related to providing services to its rural residents, including garbage disposal, ambulances, and libraries (Oldman River 1974). And the Peace River Regional Planning Commission, in northwestern Alberta, addressed itself to meeting citizens' desires for growth to occur within a context of small towns and rural areas (Peace River 1973). This is described more fully in Chapter 7.

Other Provinces

Several other provinces also focused on restraining urban land use in rural areas. New Brunswick established district planning commissions in the early 1970s (by 1997 these numbered nine). They covered the eastern one-third of the province and were generally centred on larger towns. Their function was to provide planning services for both municipalities and unincorporated (i.e., rural) areas. Their effectiveness was often reduced because they lacked formal local governments with the taxation resources to implement their plans (Robichaud 1997). In the 1970s, Prince Edward Island established a land-use planning centre to assist its rural municipalities with land-use planning. Manitoba provided similar services through branch offices of the provincial planning department, especially in conjunction with its 1970s "Stay Option" policy, to discourage rural depopulation and to support rural communities. Today, twenty-seven planning districts in rural Manitoba encompass two-thirds of its rural municipalities (Mah 1998).

Rural Planning in Aboriginal Regions

As planning for other rural communities was getting under way in the 1960s, Aboriginal Canadians were increasing pressure on the federal government to allow them more control over the decisions that affected their lives, not the least of which concerned housing and community planning. Planning for these rural communities was conducted by the Department of Indian Affairs and Northern Development, or its consultants, for specific sectors (e.g., the economy) or projects (e.g., schools). Master plans for a community's physical development were introduced in the 1970s, but these were also top-down efforts that made use of non-local planners and that often ignored other initiatives (e.g., in education and housing) (Jones 1985a).

Out of this milieu emerged the concept of integrated community-based planning for Aboriginal communities (Boothroyd 1984). Integrated community-based planning encourages the consideration of "all aspects of life and livelihood and their interrelationships" (Boothroyd 1984, 3) and allows for full community participation. The result is a plan for a "community" in the broadest sense of the term, and it includes the land and water resources that surround and sustain that community. In short, it is a regional plan that recognizes the interrelationship among social, economic, and physical factors. As Wolfe (1988, 216) notes, "for small communities, whose every aspect of life is so closely interwoven and inseparable from every other, integrated planning makes intuitive sense." This planning approach has been used widely in remote parts of the Northwest Territories as well as in less remote regions in Ontario. One of the more recent efforts involving this approach is the building of the new community of Natuashish in Labrador to replace the older community of Davis Inlet (Utshimassits) (Rich et al. 1997). Natuashish is being designed and built by the Mushuau Innu, and this fact emphasizes the respect for Aboriginal values and needs that forms part of an "ecocentric" approach to planning.

Regional Planning in the North

Because of the prominence of Aboriginal interests in the land throughout both the mid- and Far North, many of the planning concerns just described apply there as well. Here there is the need to balance these interests with the imperative of environmental conservation and with the exploitation of rich natural resources from which Aboriginal peoples and other residents enjoy economic benefits. In addition, north of the sixtieth parallel, special governing circumstances involving the federal and territorial governments now also involve the governments of recently formed Inuit territories. Two regional planning efforts, one in the Yukon and one in the Northwest Territories, are worth noting both for their contribution to Northern regional planning and for their contribution to overall Canadian regional planning.

The first of these is the comprehensive planning strategy developed for the entire Yukon Territory (483,000 square kilometres), referred to as "Yukon 2000" by the territorial government (Dector and Kowall 1988). This large-scale vision deals with social, economic, physical, and cultural needs and aspirations and involves extensive public participation. The second is the Lancaster Sound Land Use Plan in the Northwest Territories (originally drafted in 1982), which evolved out of the often contentious Northern Land Use Planning Program (Rees 1982; Fenge 1987). It links land-use considerations, economic development, and conservation into a whole. According to Richardson (1989b, 61), it has a good claim on being "the first serious attempt in Canada, and perhaps in the world," at regional planning for sustainable development.

Towards Rural-Based Regional Planning

The Rural Perspective

Earlier in this chapter, we discussed several essential features of rural-region planning. It involves:

- a continuum of planning situations
- a recognition of the essential role of resources and their use
- the characteristic of smallness.

Numerous observers have cited these features while pointing out that the planning needs of rural areas are different from those of urban areas. One of the earliest noted that "perhaps the most obvious shortcoming of planning which is applied to rural areas is its limited consideration of natural resource elements" (Hahn 1970, 46). Much rural planning has had an "urban bias" in that it has tended to focus on physical development and urbanizing environments. A long-time Canadian observer put it this way: "rural communities are caught in [the] double dilemma [of being] incorporated into the urban milieu and [yet] not [being] full partners in metropolitan opportunities and facilities" (Qadeer 1979, 112). Rural planning is complex, involving land and other resources, the human community and its sociocultural values, and the support economy for both.

In light of these criteria, most planning practice in Canadian rural regions has fallen considerably short of its ideal. As we have seen, rural planning has, for the most part, been practised either in the form of sectoral programs or as a version of urban community planning focusing on land-use controls. The sectoral approach has seldom considered the associated needs of the rural community or other resources. While the land-use approach promised to be comprehensive, more often than not it was oblivious both to resource use and social needs. As Qadeer (1979, 115) says: "whether a community needed a health centre or an industry to employ its youth is a question that cannot even be raised" by this mode of planning. And because rural dwellers, especially landowners, have a much closer relationship to their land and environmental resources than do urban dwellers, they feel as strongly about the process of planning as they do about more substantive issues (Hilts and Moull 1988). Their interest in how land and other resources are used reflects their own roles in resource use. Rural planning "has to be a process and not a statutory procedure ... [it] should not be viewed as merely land use planning ... [but] as development planning which offers solutions to local problems" (Qadeer 1979, 120).

What has been missing, generally, from our rural-region planning has been an integrated approach that recognizes "that the land base and people are a crucially important foundation" for relevant practice (Dykeman 1988, 151).

Such an integrated practice has not been totally absent from Canadian rural-region planning. There are many encouraging examples, some of which we have already mentioned, such as the work of Alberta's Oldman River regional planning commission, the countryside planning approach of Ontario's Huron County, and some recent initiatives among Aboriginal communities. The following four vignettes illustrate both exemplary practice from the past and encouraging new moves towards a more integrated, developmental approach to rural planning.

Four Canadian Examples

Land Use and Economic Planning in Rural British Columbia

One of the most progressive regional planning agencies in Canada in the 1970s and 1980s was the Central Kootenay Regional District.[5] Among perhaps a dozen of this agency's initiatives, all of which went beyond the conventional land-use control approach used by most regional districts in British Columbia, was the Slocan Valley plan, subtitled "A Land Use and Economic Plan for the Slocan Valley" (Central Kootenay 1983). The valley is approximately 100 kilometres long and sixty kilometres wide, and it has an economic base of farming, forestry, mining, and tourism, with settlement occurring in the open countryside and in a set of small towns along its length.

The planning exercise involved a joint process between the regional district and the province, but it also entailed the extensive involvement of the valley's residents. The people identified five broad issues that they wanted planners to pursue: (1) watersheds and water management, (2) integrated resource use, (3) the future of the Valhalla wilderness area, (4) town and village development, and (5) diversification of the economy. Although this plan is, in part, a "land-use" plan, here "land use" refers to the allocation of large blocks of land for particular types of resource extraction and recreation rather than to the establishment of regulatory controls. This is especially important in regions where Crown land is the dominant locus of resource development activities. Allocation of such lands impinges upon the livelihood of regional residents and, hence, upon the viability of their communities. Recognizing these links, and involving residents in decisions, makes for a more relevant form of rural planning (assuming that all government interests "buy into" the process and proposals).[6]

Intercommunity Cooperation in Saskatchewan and Alberta

During the 1980s in Saskatchewan there was a vigorous effort to address the needs of small rural communities. A province-wide committee was formed to promote the development of hundreds of small settlements and their hinterlands. The Saskatchewan Committee on Rural Development recognized that a primary issue for this region of small communities was the ability of its residents to enjoy a level of services that was equitable to that enjoyed by those living in larger centres. Significantly, it was also recognized that this did not mean that there was to be a the proliferation of facilities and activities among all communities, even if that were possible (Baker and Wolfe 1986); rather, it meant promoting cooperation among communities with regard to sharing facilities and activities. The initiative reflected the economic and social interconnectedness among all sizes and types of settlements. Not surprisingly, the array of topics that came up for consideration covered health services, education, libraries, recreation, transportation, and industrial development. Although this initiative did not begin with regional delimitations, it was clear that regional considerations would come to play a major role in determining how, and among which communities, the sharing could occur.

Even earlier, another approach to intercommunity cooperation was taking place in southeastern Alberta. Regional Resources Project No. 1 was established in 1972 and covered a 9,000-square-kilometre region consisting of 13,000 people and about a dozen small towns located just west of the small city of Drumheller. The project resulted when the area's residents realized that they needed to plan together and to cooperate in developing facilities and services rather than to compete for public and private investment. As they worked together, there emerged a spirit of cooperation that, as Bodmer (1980, 84) says, "translates into the attitude that it does not matter so much *where* new developments take place as long as they occur somewhere within the region." Again, the array of concerns goes well beyond those that could be dealt with by conventional community planning methods, and they cover housing, water supply, swimming pools and curling rinks, hardware stores, and restaurants. In other words, they cover needs that are basic to the quality of community life. This project also underscores the need for flexibility in rural planning as well as the need to think "small."

Communities and Natural Resource Management in Ontario

One of the challenges facing rural resource regions everywhere is the separation between the community and the management of the resources upon which they depend. In 1990, the Ontario government launched a community forestry project in order to bridge this gap in the resource-dependent regions in the province's north.

The idea was to forge partnerships with communities and to have them manage forest resources on Crown lands in their regions. "Community" was defined broadly and could include one or a group of municipalities, an Aboriginal community, or a collection of forest interests (Harvey and Usher 1996). Four such partnerships were established for the purpose of evaluating their effectiveness. The results not only showed that this approach could work well, but they also confirmed the need for inclusiveness in decision making, the need to use indigenous administrative and decision-making structures, and the need to achieve community consensus on environmental and resource management objectives (Ontario 1994).

Resource Stewardship in the City's Countryside

Within rapidly urbanizing regions the conservation of resources is in strong competition with city development. A particular instance of this occurs in the Lower Mainland of British Columbia (i.e., the Vancouver city-region), where an innovative program has been developed to create partnerships among government agencies, community groups, and the development sector (Heitkamp 1996) in order to steward vulnerable resource areas. The resource in question is the fish habitats along the region's streams and wetlands. The fish use these habitats for spawning, rearing, and migrating to and from the ocean. The program, Partners in Protecting Aquatic and Riparian Resources, is noteworthy not only because of its success in restoring considerable habitat, but also because of its ability to involve citizens and businesses in the stewardship program. Planners have come to realize that community members care about their environments, and they are prepared to share in decision making and in taking responsibility for a regional ecosystem.

Reflections

These few examples mark a shift in rural planning. Increasingly, we are seeing both a more integrated view of rural resources and a recognition of their importance to the human communities of the region. This has led to directly involving rural citizens in planning issues. This approach to rural planning *begins* within the rural region rather than simply seeing that region as something that supplies the demand of urban residents and businesses for rural resources. In other words, within rural planning, Friedmann and Weaver's (1979) "territorial" perspective is emerging (see Chapter 2). It is also worth noting that most of these examples have come into being without outside assistance; they are the result of the efforts of rural people to be directly involved in the decisions affecting their region's resources. These contemporary efforts within regionalism have a lot in common with what, in other circles, is referred to as civil society (as well as with what Wight [1996] refers to as "eco-regionalism").

This approach to rural planning becomes more and more important as rural regions and their resources face new pressures from the global economy through the restructuring and downsizing of sectors, institutions, and traditional economies (Reid and Fuller 1995). In a parallel manner, the calls for sustainable development also affect rural regions (Fuller et al. 1989) through the potential limits they place on resource development; hence the need to plan in a more integrated way. As Mah (1998, 29) says with regard to Manitoba rural communities, it is becoming necessary to go beyond the traditional, but separate, fields of land-use planning and economic development and to begin linking them through "community facilitation, community economic development and co-management of resources and resource-based economies."

Rural communities may need to be further reconstituted in order to meet these challenges (as is already happening in the form of the increasing mobility of rural residents [Green and Myer 1997]), but they must not be eliminated or further marginalized. Rural communities are a "crucial ingredient" of future sustainable development (Fuller et al. 1989). The responses to integrated rural planning suggest that Russwurm's (1987) belief that rural planning should "maintain rural activities, rural communities and the resource base while coping with trade-offs with varied demands for the land and resource base" may finally be emerging.

6

Regional Economic Development Planning

For nearly twenty-five years, between 1960 and the mid-1980s, much of Canada's regional planning focused on improving the economic well-being of the nation's regions. This was, both in content and practice, in sharp contrast to the regional planning that both preceded and, indeed, followed it. The purpose of this type of planning – economic development – differed from that of other forms of regional planning in that it drew on the newly minted theories of regional science and was led by the federal government. Furthermore, it was a "top-down" form of planning and had little or no connection with the regions within which its projects took place. In other words, it viewed regions "from the outside-in" (see Chapter 3). Also, rarely was any overall plan or strategy produced for public use or debate. In substance, this type of planning began with a rural slant and tended to ignore the urban dimension in regional development. This was largely in response to the attempt to deal with the so-called depressed regions, which were mainly rural and non-metropolitan and had economies that were highly resource-dependent (e.g., many in the Atlantic provinces and in the northern parts of provinces such as Ontario, Alberta, and Manitoba).

Despite the demise of these regional planning efforts, this period is important for regional planning for it taught us many valuable lessons. The economic dimension of a region's development was addressed, and many of the facets of planning pertaining to it were revealed. The role and responsibilities of the federal government in planning for regions within provinces were defined and refined. The provinces, which heretofore had only authorized land-use-type planning in regions, had to consider economic planning. The explicit use of formal theory, especially economic development theory, within regional planning was new and untried. And, not least, regions were compared with one another in regard to their development needs.

Background and Setting

It is important to grasp the context within which regional economic development planning was initiated in Canada and, as we shall see, how that context changed to bring about the demise of this particular form of regional planning. From the early anarchists through Patrick Geddes and the Tennessee Valley Authority, the economic well-being of a region's residents was an important guide for regional planning thinking (see Chapter 1). Yet this economic dimension was pretty much ignored when, in the 1930s and 1940s, the practice of regional planning became a public activity. And this remains the case today. However, in the 1950s in Canada, a convergence of events (following the trend in the United States and Europe) led to extensive national planning for regional economies (Friedmann and Weaver 1979).

The type of regional planning initiated between 1960 and the early 1980s came to be known as regional development planning. Regional development planning is usually defined as an activity undertaken to improve the economic well-being of people living in regions where there is concern about present or future conditions. It distinguishes itself from physical planning through its emphasis on non-physical systems (e.g., economic and/or social activities) and from sectorally defined planning (e.g., employment, health, water resources) through its emphasis on integrated approaches towards a variety of narrowly defined economic systems (Webster 1979, 1984). Thus, although not sectoral in the typical sense, regional development planning was highly focused on a single social dimension – the economy – that had region-wide and nation-wide links to many other sectors. This singular approach to regional planning was dictated largely by constitutional arrangements that gave the provinces power over resources and land. This meant that federal intervention had to be negotiated with the provinces and, thus, that this was easier to achieve if the object of the negotiations was limited.

In Canada, regional development planning is most closely associated with the federal Department of Regional Economic Expansion (DREE) and other related agencies of the 1960s, 1970s, and early 1980s. In addition, most provinces had ministries that undertook regional development planning. In fact, many of the planning programs during this period were undertaken jointly by the federal and provincial governments. Significantly, the direct involvement of senior governments meant that the planning for regions occurred in the national and provincial capitals. In effect, this approach to regional planning constituted a further capital division of power rather than an areal division of power (see Chapter 4). In those instances where metropolitan-regional planning agencies or conservation authorities are established, a distinctive new areal unit was set up and mandated to do its own planning. However, during this period, the economic planning regions were functional regions of the senior governments, which held the planning mandate.

The stimulus for these efforts derived from the fact that, towards the end of the 1950s, Canada's economy entered a new spatial phase. The rapidly growing cities and metropolitan regions were then replacing the rural resource regions in national economic importance. Further, many of the country's primary resource regions, which were based on agriculture, fishing, mining, and/or forestry, were exhibiting signs of economic downturn and underdevelopment. The rapid industrialization that had been occurring fuelled the migration from non-urban, largely resource-based regions to cities and metropolitan areas. The rural regions suffered because they neither shared in the burgeoning industrial development nor held on to the human resources (especially the youth and those who were most skilled) needed for their own development. As a consequence, many signs of underdevelopment – such as high unemployment, low incomes, illiteracy, poor housing, outmoded infrastructure, inefficient technology, and depleted resources – began to show in these mostly rural regions (Canada, Senate 1964). What was becoming apparent, and increasingly politically volatile, was the fact that the country's regions were becoming vastly unequal in terms of development. Simply put, economic growth and prosperity were not evenly distributed across Canada. The rural "have-not" regions and their provincial governments began to demand a "piece of the action"; they wanted to erase "regional disparities" (Economic Council 1968).

Thus in 1960 there began a new and distinctive approach to dealing with economic differences between regions, whereby the federal government would intervene directly in regions in order to stimulate economic growth (with, of course, the cooperation of the provinces). In effect, the federal government acknowledged that neither strong national economic growth nor transfer payments could adequately deal with regional disparities (Cannon 1989).

The considerable alacrity with which these planning efforts were undertaken was, in no small measure, due to the confluence of an emerging political ideology about the need for economic growth and an emerging theoretical framework that supported this notion (Friedmann and Weaver 1979). Academic interest soared with regard to the economics of location, and practical analytical techniques began to be available, including input-output analysis, industrial complex analysis, regional social accounts, growth pole theory, and cost-benefit analysis. A new discipline, known as "regional science," developed around the use of such techniques (see Chapter 1). Thus, the political pressures to eliminate regional disparities could be met, and, according to the emerging substantive theory (see Chapter 2), governments could undertake regional planning with some degree of comfort.

The next two and a half decades was a time of unparalleled regional planning activity in Canada. This activity took many forms, depending on the prevailing theory and political climate. The federal government spent considerable amounts of public money in an effort to mitigate regional economic differences. Figure 11 provides a summary of the main events in Canada's efforts at regional economic development planning. There was little solid experience, either national or international, upon which to draw for this new practice, and the new theories of Perroux (1950), Myrdal (1957), Hirschman (1958), Isard (1960), and Friedmann (1966), although attractive, were untried.

Moreover, it was practice that began within the federal-provincial political arena, with all the volatility of which that bespeaks. It is with these contextual elements in mind that we review these activities and assess their outcomes from 1960 to 1982. We then briefly review the initiatives (and the lack thereof) since the mid-1980s.

Federal Programs for Regional Development from 1960 to 1982

Agricultural Rehabilitation and Development Act: Planning for Depressed Agricultural and Resource Regions

The first major effort by the federal government to counter regional disparities came with the passage of the Agricultural Rehabilitation and Development Act (ARDA), 1961. Through this legislation the federal government undertook to work with provincial governments to rebuild the depressed rural economy in agricultural (and forestry) regions. Much like its predecessor, the Prairie Farm Rehabilitation Act (PFRA), 1935, ARDA provided funding for soil and water conservation projects, land consolidation schemes designed to increase farm productivity, and research into rural problems. But while PFRA programs could be said to be reactive to the drought conditions of the Prairie region (Russwurm 1987), ARDA was much more proactive. The legislation followed the initiatives of at least two major national conferences on resources as well as the deliberations of the Senate Committee on Land Use (see Chapter 7).

ARDA's original aim was to rejuvenate the country's "depressed" rural areas by increasing the output and productivity of farmers, developing soil and water resources, providing assistance for alternative uses of marginal land, and creating other work opportunities. Its overriding goal was "reducing rural poverty" (Savoie 1992), and, in keeping with this goal, areas were designated for assistance through the use of low-income indices among farm families, non-farm families, and male non-farm wage earners obtained from the 1961 census.[1] Indices were applied differently between provinces to account for differences in rural poverty situations. Regions of persistent poverty were identified and designated to receive grants, services, and needed facilities.

During the first few years, programs under the ARDA legislation were largely oriented towards physical projects. A dominant view at the time was that the problem of agricultural poverty was largely caused by poor soil and water management along with small farm size. According to Brewis (1969), this view derived from the considerable influence of geographers and soil scientists with their emphases on the physical properties of land. Several amendments were made to the Act over the next several years, especially as a result of the recommendations of the Senate Committee on Land Use (see Chapter 7), which expanded the program's coverage to include other types of rural regions (e.g., those involved in fisheries and forestry) as well as non-agricultural programs in rural areas designed to absorb surplus farm labour.

Figure 11

Major events in the history of regional economic development planning in Canada

1. Focus on national development and maturing of the Canadian staples economy:
   - 1879   Prime Minister John A. Macdonald's National Policy
   - 1930   Harold Innes presents his staples theory of growth in *The Fur Trade in Canada: An Introduction to Canadian Economic History*

2. Initial awareness of regional and resource disparity issues:
   - 1935   Prairie Farm Rehabilitation Act
   - 1940   *Report of the Royal Commission on Dominion-Provincial Relations* (Rowell-Sirois Commission)
   - 1944   Federal Advisory Committee on Reconstruction
   - 1954   National Conference on Renewable Resources
   - 1958   Senate of Canada Special Committee on Land Use

3. Development planning emphasis (concern with equity):
   - 1961   Resources for Tomorrow Conference
     Agricultural Rehabilitation and Development Act
   - 1962   Atlantic Development Board
   - 1963   Area Development Agency
   - 1965   Mactaquac Regional Development Plan (New Brunswick)
   - 1966   Fund for Rural Economic Development
     Department of Community and Social Development (Newfoundland)
     Bureau d'aménagement de l'est du Québec
     Nova Scotia Voluntary Planning Board
     Community Improvement Corporation (New Brunswick)
     Design for Development Program (Ontario)
     Interlake Region Development Program (Manitoba)
     ARDA expands its functions and changes its name to Agricultural and Rural Development Act
   - 1967   Prince Edward Island Development Plan

4. Formalization of federal regional development function:
   - 1969   Federal Department of Regional Economic Expansion (DREE)
   - 1970   Lesser Slave Lake Program (Alberta)
   - 1973   Major restructuring of DREE
     General Development Agreement–Interim Planning Agreement
   - 1982   DREE eliminated as a separate ministry, with its industry functions transferred to a new ministry, the Department of Regional Industrial Expansion (DRIE)
     Ministry of State for Economic and Regional Development established (MSERD)
   - 1984   MSERD abolished
   - 1984 to late 1990s
     Diminution of federal government involvement with regional development planning
     Creation of the Atlantic Canada Opportunities Agency and the Western Economic Diversification Fund (1987)

Two instances of this broader rural scope are found, first, in the project for the Lesser Slave Lake region of northern Alberta, where forestry was the dominant rural resource activity (see a later discussion of this project), and, second, in the now-discredited Newfoundland Resettlement Program, which was aimed at moving residents from isolated fishing villages and outports to new centres where industrial and commercial jobs and better public facilities were to be created. The latter program was able to relocate about 300 of the more than 600 villages it targeted, but it also caused splits in families and communities that are still evident (Copes 1972). Both these instances reflect a shift in the federal government's regional development focus, which moved away from rejuvenating rural natural resource communities and towards infusing regions with industrial activity in order to promote economic growth (Matthews 1976).

We also need to mention the distinctive experience in the Gaspé region of Quebec under the combined ARDA and FRED programs. This initiative, which was organized under the Bureau d'aménagement de l'est du Québec (BAEQ), had a very strong grassroots orientation. All sectors of the community were involved in what would today be called a bottom-up, or "self management," approach to determining the future of the region (in contrast to the generally top-down approaches used elsewhere). The technique of *animation sociale* was widely used, and with some success, to stimulate participation among citizens, businesspeople, and educators. However, the expectations it raised in the region apparently did not translate into needed political commitments from the province, and the BAEQ was disbanded a few years later.

All in all, forty regional development efforts were sponsored under the ARDA legislation in the 1960s. And, in 1966, ARDA's title was changed to the Agricultural and Rural Development Act and a companion program, the Fund for Rural Economic Development (FRED) was added. The fund was more comprehensive in scope and directed towards diversifying rural resource economies with non-primary resource occupations. It targeted five rural regions experiencing widespread low-income problems and economic adjustment difficulties. Development plans aimed at improving both infrastructure (e.g., roads, schools, municipal utilities) and industrial capability. This new program recognized the interrelation between rural countryside and rural towns and cities (Paris 1967). For example, the FRED plan for the Restigouche region of northeastern New Brunswick, one of the five FRED regions, devoted only 11 percent of its planning budget to agriculture and other resource development. The same broad developmental planning approach was taken in the other four FRED regions: the Gaspé Peninsula in Quebec, the Mactaquac River Valley plan in New Brunswick (see below for discussion), the Interlake region of Manitoba, and all of Prince Edward Island. Attention was paid to improvements in social (e.g., education) and physical (e.g., highways) infrastructure in order to create a strong urban structure that would complement rural resource development and industrial diversification.

Reflecting briefly on these early efforts in rural-region planning under the ARDA legislation, two points become readily apparent. The first concerns the weak link between federal policy initiatives and the regional level, where such policies are actually implemented. Programs were conceived by bureaucrats in Ottawa working within the strictures that govern the expenditure of federal funds as well as under constitutional arrangements with the provinces. Thus they depended on the province in question to facilitate the delivery of the program to the region. Further, while a federal and a provincial ministry of agriculture may be able to agree on a regional program, they have no counterparts within the region to carry them out. At the provincial level, this always raises the issue of whether or not to establish a regional entity to implement the program. In other words, the province must decide on a further areal division of its power. This dilemma led to a variety of arrangements being used throughout the period when the ARDA legislation was in effect.

The second point concerns the limited view of rural regions that the ARDA legislation permitted. One limitation was the constrained focus on one functional sector (such as agriculture or forestry) when the population of a rural region might engage in several resource *and* non-resource activities. Another very serious limitation was the focus on the economic side of life and a failure to account for social structure and social relationships, both of which would be affected by, and necessary for, economic change (Qadeer 1979).

The outport relocation program in Newfoundland showed the worst features of this limited focus, while the BAEQ experience revealed the importance of linking the social and economic within rural-region planning. A worthy exception was the care taken in the Mactaquac River development scheme to involve residents of the valley who would need to be relocated due to flooding for dam construction (Philbrook 1967).

Expanding the Focus with New Programs

Despite the adjustments in programs under ARDA, it is said that some Ottawa decision makers believed that the approach taken in the ARDA legislation still had one serious drawback: it lacked an appropriate geographical focus. Savoie (1992, 28) quotes one federal official as saying that ARDA was "all over the Canadian map."[2] In other words, its programs were responding to specific instances of depressed rural areas all across the country but were giving little consideration to the regional relationships that these areas might have with one another, with nearby urban areas, or even with non-rural locations within the area (Hodge and Paris 1969). Moreover, there was an increasing recognition that complementary programs were needed in order to adequately combat regional disparities. Accordingly, between 1961 and 1968 the government created other alphabetic agencies and programs to deal with depressed urban areas (e.g., the Area Development Agency) and the Atlantic provinces (e.g., the Atlantic Development Board, with its Atlantic Development Fund).

The Area Development Agency (ADA) and the Atlantic Development Board (ADB) marked both geographical and substantive shifts in regional development planning in Canada. ADA and its industrial incentive programs were a response to the fact that not all urban areas were enjoying the fruits of the nation's economic growth, especially in rural and non-metropolitan regions. Instead of the criterion of low income used by ARDA to designate agricultural and other resource regions, ADA used the degree of unemployment among an urban centre's labour force when determining its eligibility for the program. Further, while ARDA sought to improve the productive capacity for farming in a designated area, ADA sought to stimulate manufacturing and other industrial activities and to create jobs in its designated centres. Its primary program tool involved grants provided directly to private firms, which planned to initiate and/or expand industrial enterprises and, thereby, create new jobs. Thus, ARDA worked with regions, while ADA worked with private firms. And, not least, they were run by two separate ministries: ARDA by the federal Department of Agriculture and ADA by the Department of Industry Trade and Commerce.

Altogether, 126 centres across the country were designated as entitled to participate in the ADA program; generally, these were in the same depressed regions to which ARDA programs were also responding. Although the focus was now on specific urban places, the same dispersal of program activities across the nation occurred under ADA as was occurring under ARDA. Little attempt was made to correlate the impacts of the two programs, even when the ADA-designated centres were located in ARDA-designated regions. The emerging knowledge about the role of urban centres in regional development seems to have remained untapped (Hodge 1969).

The ADB represented another shift in direction for regional development planning. In this initiative a specific region was identified for assistance in eliminating regional disparities (albeit a region consisting of four provinces). The ADB was established in 1962 and, initially, was asked to define measures and initiatives for promoting economic growth and development in the Atlantic region. Shortly after its creation the board was given an Atlantic Development Fund (ADF) (totalling $180 million) to administer. By and large, the fund was employed to assist in the provision or improvement of the region's basic physical infrastructure, more than half of which was spent on highway construction and water supply and sewerage. The ADF did not provide direct assistance of any kind to help private industry locate in the region. On this point, the ADB was criticized, notably by the semi-independent Atlantic Provinces Economic Council. It was also criticized for its uncoordinated spending, which was conducted on a project-by-project basis and was often politically inspired (Savoie 1992; Poole 1996). The ADB never did deliver a comprehensive development plan for the Atlantic region, despite its 1963 mandate to do so.

The ADB program for the Atlantic provinces reveals a number of constraints faced by the federal government when it attempted to engage in regional planning within provincial jurisdictions. On the one hand, it could not target, or require the ADB to target, specific projects and areas. At the same time, it could not adequately monitor what was being done in its behalf. Indeed, the provinces in the region resisted federal bureaucrats "meddling" in what they considered to be provincial programs (Careless 1977).

Department of Regional Economic Expansion: Creating the Bigger Picture
By the late 1960s, a kaleidoscope of programs had been created to address different regional development problems independently of one another (Careless 1977; Savoie 1992). There came to be a growing concern that these initiatives, handled by different government departments with different objectives, were far from satisfactory and that what was needed was closer federal-provincial cooperation in regional development matters. The Economic Council of Canada, in its "Fifth Annual Review" (1968, 177), stated candidly that "the stark fact remains that the historical mix of forces and public policy has not resulted in any significant narrowing of regional income disparities." The council urged the government to adopt a new approach, which the newly elected Liberal government of Pierre Elliott Trudeau did by creating a new Cabinet-level post for regional development, the Department of Regional Economic Expansion (DREE). All the alphabetic agencies and their programs were gathered under this new "umbrella" in order to make a sort of "grand push" to erase regional economic disparities. It should be noted that the choice of forming a new ministry for regional development was one of two options considered at the time. The other option was to create a "super ministry" with power to direct the resources of other ministries. Instead, DREE was created as a single ministry among other equal ministries (with their often competing programs) – a decision that was not always to the benefit of DREE and the regions (Lithwick 1986b).

The creation of DREE signalled major shifts in regional policy, shifts that were based much more on the theoretical foundations of economic development than was the case in the past. For one thing, the "worst-first approach," which involved providing assistance first to weak industries in the poorest regions, was discontinued. DREE began to support stronger sectors of the economy in areas with growth potential. DREE also focused on initiatives to industrialize targeted areas and to build urban growth centres, while moving away from strategies targeted to rural poverty. Areas eligible for the industrial incentives program, which began under ADA, were expanded and, by 1971, included 50 percent of the Canadian population (in contrast to the 18 percent who were eligible under the previous policy). Areas such as the Montreal region were now eligible. Also, twenty-three growth centres, or regional "growth poles," were designated for special financial assistance for social and economic infrastructure, workforce training programs, and industrial development.

The concept of growth poles drew its theoretical foundation from the tradition of Perroux (1950), Myrdal (1957), Rodwin (1963), and Friedmann (1966a). This theory holds that *pôles de croissance* in slow-growth regions can become dynamic engines of growth that can engender "spread effects" that move outward to the surrounding regions. Further, it corresponds to the notion that economic growth will occur within the "matrix of urban regions," spreading from higher- to lower-order centres in the urban system and, ultimately, extending across the entire space economy. Thus, resources were deployed to enhance the capacities of the local economies and to make them more attractive to industrial developers, who would be able to receive financial grants and loans if they wished to locate, expand, or modernize within these centres. Projects in such service industries as tourism could also receive grants and loan guarantees.

Between 1969 and 1973, DREE divided Canada into two main types of regional development areas: "designated regions" and "special areas." Designated regions were regions formerly developed but currently undergoing depression or recession ("downward transitional"); they had adequate infrastructure but needed job-creation stimuli in the form of industrial incentives. "Special areas" were regions in remote "resource" (or "frontier") regions and cities; they lacked adequate basic physical infrastructure and social delivery systems, and they required assistance in order to undertake structural adjustments and to achieve economic vitality. For these special areas comprehensive development programs were launched in tandem with employment-creation programs, including investment in physical infrastructure (e.g., industrial parks), education (e.g., basic work skills), housing (e.g., prefabricated housing for Aboriginal migrants in growth centres), and social programs (e.g., credit and family counselling). These special and designated regions and cities were DREE's way of indicating the "lagging" regions of Canada. All the rest, at least those located in the southern parts of Canada, were presumably the "leading" regions (see Chapter 3).

DREE planners increasingly emphasized quantifiable objectives such as numbers of jobs created and determining which objectives were amenable to new management techniques, including cost-effectiveness analysis and the Planning-Programming-Budgeting System (Gunton and Weaver 1982). Furthermore, regional policy had moved away from the comprehensive regional development approach that had been evolving under FRED and towards specific project funding based on efficiency measures such as "jobs created per dollar expended."

General Development Agreements: Decentralization to the Provinces

Decision making under DREE was highly centralized in Ottawa and, not surprisingly, the provinces were critical of this aspect of the program. This, together with other substantive criticisms, caused the government to restructure

DREE in 1973. A review of DREE had concluded that regional disparities were too complex to be dealt with effectively by one federal department. It was further concluded that a federal program working within provinces cannot be effective without the parallel concerted efforts of the provincial governments. Thus, the agency's funding strategy was changed in order to gain more input from, and to give more control to, the provinces (Poole 1996).

As part of this new approach, DREE eliminated the special areas program. In its place, DREE adopted a new, more decentralized approach involving the negotiation of general development agreements (GDAs) between each province and the federal government (DREE 1975). These development agreements were expected to outline a broad development strategy for each province and were complemented by a series of more specific subsidiary agreements (interim planning agreements) that described how the development opportunities identified in the GDAs could be achieved. More than 130 subsidiary agreements were signed between 1974 and 1982, committing $3.3 billion in federal resources and $2.7 billion in provincial funds to joint projects (Savoie 1992). Analysis of these agreements shows that while there was still a strong emphasis on concentrating development in growth centres such as Halifax, Montreal, and Saint John, there was also a return to subsidizing the expansion of staple industries in rural resource regions (Gunton and Weaver 1982).

Provinces would now share costs of programs with the federal government, and the poorer the province, the larger the share the federal government assumed. In contrast with the emphasis of the previous policy, the new thrust was to decentralize regional planning responsibility to the provinces, and DREE established field offices in each province to reinforce this concept. The provinces were responsible for administering the GDAs, thus replacing the direct-action approach of DREE. The GDA program was offered to the provinces with few strings attached.

Provinces could propose almost anything they wanted in terms of regional development planning, which basically meant that Ottawa's only option was to refuse to share in a project's funding. But even this option was limited for DREE because, on most matters, its assistant deputy ministers, who were located in regional centres so that the department could be closer "to the action," could make decisions independently of Ottawa. Not surprisingly, provinces became more proactive, proposing projects to the federal government rather than waiting to react to federal initiatives. The GDAs helped oversee the formation of provincial development agencies and corporations. All in all, with the GDAs, the federal-provincial balance swung emphatically towards the provinces (Poole 1996).

DREE was criticized for devolving too much authority to the provinces as the GDAs reflected provincial priorities that were often at odds with national economic goals (Lithwick 1986a). Furthermore, the GDAs were supposed to coordinate all federal programs bearing on regional development, not only

DREE expenditures; but the DREE regional staff accounted for the only federal officials participating in negotiations with the provinces (Poole 1996). And, because the GDAs included issues beyond DREE's departmental responsibilities, the agreements created tension between DREE and other ministries; consequently, DREE began to lose credibility within the Ottawa "framework" (Savoie 1992). The problem was that the GDA approach was making the provinces too powerful, and it encouraged them to use federal funds to work independently of the federal government. Despite the criticism, the GDAs remained the basic structure for regional economic development planning in Canada until 1982.

Demise of the Department of Regional Economic Expansion

Governmental changes in 1979, albeit short-lived, further eroded DREE's position by supporting the provinces in becoming the senior partners in the GDA arrangement. As a consequence, the department's budget declined precipitously, and the Cabinet began to place constraints on DREE in order to ensure cooperation with other departments and greater consistency between DREE-funded initiatives and national economic policies. In general, regional efforts began to take a more sectoral approach. DREE's lower profile and lesser control spelled its end. This followed on another scathing Economic Council of Canada assessment of regional development policies. The council's 1977 review reached similar conclusions to those reached almost a decade earlier: "Disparities in Canada are surprisingly large; certainly larger than many of us expected and larger than they need to be or ought to be" (Economic Council of Canada 1977, 211). Other analyses and evaluations reinforced the council's findings (Phillips 1978; Webster 1979; Weller 1981). Many critics complained that DREE funding was not addressing regional disparities so much as it was "Balkanizing" the country and contributing to regional divisions such as the growing Quebec secessionist movement (Cannon 1989).

Not only was regional development practice buffeted politically, but the 1981 recession hit the entire country hard, and national economic competitiveness within a global context emerged as the key policy issue for the federal government. Regional disparities could not continue to command strong support in Ottawa. Indeed, the federal Cabinet released a policy document in late 1981 endorsing large-scale natural resource developments – megaprojects – as the national economic focus for the 1980s (Canada 1981). This was a follow-up to earlier evaluations of the increasing importance to the Canadian economy (especially in the West) of energy development and Asian trade and investment. Thus, massive energy projects, such as northeast British Columbia coal and Beaufort Sea gas and oil, were moved to the top of the agenda (Gunton and Weaver 1982).

Although regional approaches to economic development were no longer of major strategic importance in government policy, they did not disappear completely at this time. In 1982, DREE was eliminated as a separate ministry, and most of its functions were combined with the industry side of the Department of Industry, Trade, and Commerce, which was given a new name – the Department of Regional and Industrial Expansion (DRIE). As well, the Ministry of State for Economic Development was given new "regional responsibilities," becoming the Ministry of State for Economic and Regional Development.

Developments since 1982:
From Regional Strategies to Program Strategies

Successive government changes over the ensuing decade, into the mid-1990s, saw the further diminution of federal government activities in regional development planning. The emphasis was no longer on eliminating regional disparities generally across the country but, rather, on programs that took place within regions (such as industrial development and mega-resource projects). In other words, the region became secondary (Gunton and Weaver 1982). When regional considerations did emerge in policy areas, they tended to be in response to provincial criticisms about the lack of federal largesse. Thus, in 1987, the premiers of the Atlantic provinces succeeded in establishing the Atlantic Canada Opportunities Agency as a successor to the ADB. Then, in the same year, the four western premiers joined together to promote their own regional development department, the Western Economic Diversification Fund (Lithwick 1986a). In an apparent show of regional awareness, the headquarters of the two federal agencies were moved from Ottawa to Moncton, New Brunswick (for the Atlantic Canada Opportunities Agency), and Edmonton, Alberta (for the Western Economic Diversification Fund).

In general, since 1994, the regional development programs have been refocused to address the debt and equity capital needs of small- and medium-sized businesses, while the role of the regional agencies have been de-emphasized (Poole 1996). One 1996 observer forecast that the federal government was destined to take Canada in a completely new direction – one based more on a need to reduce spending than on any particular regional priorities (Poole 1996). Poole's forecast certainly proved accurate.

Where Are We Now?

Despite the billions of dollars spent by both the federal and provincial governments since 1966, extreme regional disparities still exist. A 1995 Statistics Canada labour-force survey, for example, provides data for seventy-two economic regions across Canada (Little 1996) and shows the proportion of the working-age population that is working. This is sometimes referred to as "the labour force participation rate."[3] While the average for all these statistical regions was 58.6 percent, there were marked differences among the regions, with rates ranging from below 35 percent to more than 70 percent. In these data we also see two sides of the regional disparity issue: the extreme geographic concentration of both the bottom (the Atlantic provinces and eastern Quebec) and the top (British Columbia and Alberta) regions, and the large disparities within provinces. This was, of course, virtually the same picture that existed in 1960 and to which the federal government and the provinces addressed themselves for more than two decades with, apparently, little success.

So, according to prominent regional planner L.O. Gertler (1994a, 134),[4] who summed up the outcome of the last half century of federal involvement in regional planning, all that remains of the DREE "experiment" is a "pathetically fragmented effort in regional development." Gertler continued: An Atlantic Canada Opportunities Agency, a Western Diversification Fund, a federal office of regional development, and a regionally oriented defence procurement and public works program "do not a regional policy make." What went wrong? And why? The issues are complex; however, at this point we can make three broad observations about the conditions that contributed to DREE's generally unsatisfactory performance:

1 There was no precedent in Canada (and very few elsewhere in the world) for a national government to intervene in regional economies.
2 New theories and concepts that promised planners understanding about the causes of regional disparities and the means to right them were either largely untested or were not given adequate time to be tested.
3 Regional development planning occurred in the volatile arena of federal-provincial relations and was, thus, often subject to abrupt political shifts.

Another contextual hurdle for DREE, and possibly its most challenging one, was its tenuous position in Ottawa (Lithwick 1986b). DREE's mandate to implement the more holistic concept of economic development competed with existing ministries with sectoral mandates (e.g., forestry, fisheries, agriculture). At the regional level, within provinces an analogous competition occurred between DREE and provincial ministries that were used to dealing with their counterparts in Ottawa.

Provincial Programs and Activities

Throughout this period of intense federal activity in the area of regional economic development, provincial governments were also aware of regional economic disparities both between themselves and other provinces and within their own boundaries. All of them took steps to deal with these problems, sometimes using their own resources. While both levels of government accepted some responsibility for improving regional well-being, the fact is that, under the Constitution, the regions in need of assistance (and their natural resources) lie within provincial jurisdictions. This, in turn, often necessitated federal-provincial agreements in order to mobilize the funds available under federal programs (such as DREE) to tackle regional disparities. In this section we discuss the nature and scope of provincial activities in regional development during this period, including several of the joint provincial-federal programs and projects that were undertaken.

Provincial Regional Economic Planning Agencies

It is difficult to define any explicit, solely provincial development policies or strategies that existed during the period under review. Most provinces did have some policies, although it was often difficult to distinguish them from joint federal-provincial policies (when these were operational). Many provinces had development corporations – semi-autonomous agencies that performed a number of different functions (such as lending or granting money to private enterprises, purchasing equity in businesses, acquiring land, or developing industrial infrastructure). Aside from these specific development agencies, provincial development strategies, though often implicit, can be detected in the actions of provincial cabinets. For example, the Ontario provincial Cabinet, an early leader in the development of provincial strategies, formulated a provincial development strategy in the late 1960s. The Department of Treasury, Economics, and Intergovernmental Affairs prepared both a provincial development strategy, known as "Design for Development," and separate regional strategies. (We discuss this program further below.)

Some provinces established regional planning or development agencies specially concerned with economic development. For example, Manitoba established regional development corporations for seven regions in that province; Nova Scotia set up its Voluntary Planning Board; Newfoundland set up its Department of Community and Social Development; and Quebec set up its regional planning agency for eastern Quebec – the BAEQ.

Almost all provinces had (and continue to have) the equivalent of regional planning commissions, agencies, or districts created through their respective planning acts. However, these have limited powers and are essentially advisory. They are usually restrained from commenting on major resource developments, transportation corridors, pipelines, major hydroelectric proposals, and forestry leasing proposals. In short, they are restrained from commenting on all crucial development issues (Robinson and Webster 1985). Also, neither the federal government nor the provincial government give them much information about impending developments. In essence, the regional (land-use) planning agencies undertake adaptive planning; they react to major changes in regional socioeconomic structures, which are essentially determined by private enterprise and provincial-federal governments. In terms of actual power, these agencies are (sometimes) left with subdivision approval roles, prepare regional (actually land-use) plans but have little or no powers to implement them, and give advice on a variety of matters to their constituent municipalities. (See

Chapter 8 for a fuller discussion of the powers of these agencies.) In other words, there is no link between the development planning function of provinces and the resources and powers (limited as they are) of the regional planning commissions.

Provincial Development Planning Goals and Strategies

As expected, provincial goals and strategies differ, as Gertler (1972) observed, and depend on a number of factors. One of these is whether the province shares in the structural economic problems that have stimulated efforts to eliminate disparities, as, for example, was the case in the Atlantic provinces and parts of Quebec. Another factor is the extent to which problems lie with the current pattern of using natural resources (a largely provincial matter). Yet another is the degree of concern a province has with the "quality of life" and environmental resources.

These influences, Gertler noted, do not operate with equal force within each province; and he further argued that the particular mix of influences creates a predilection in each province towards one of two basic approaches to the subject of regional economic development: (1) an integrated, provincially oriented structure and program or (2) a decentralized, regionally oriented structure and program.

The integrated approach, Gertler argued, felt the impact of the first two policy influences – structural and resource-use adjustment – and was therefore preoccupied with overcoming this handicap. While it did not overlook internal regional differences, they were clearly subsidiary to its main thrust. Under this approach, provinces did share a general concern with questions of environment, although the intensity of the interest varied with the size of their growth centres. Also, they had a tendency to use their financial resources to improve infrastructure, diversify and strengthen industrial development, and provide employment. Provinces using an integrated, provincially oriented structure included Quebec, Manitoba, Saskatchewan, New Brunswick, Nova Scotia, and Prince Edward Island.

The decentralized approach was dominant in those provinces that did not feel the major impact of Canada's structural and resource-use adjustment difficulties; within these provinces the main policy motivation was to cope with significant internal regional disparities in economic growth and general well-being. The preoccupation with environmental problems tended to be greater in the second group than in the first group because rapid and large-scale growth created inescapable pressures. The comparative financial buoyancy of the second group allowed it to provide capital grants to municipalities and regions, while tax measures and other fiscal devices were used to encourage the development of lagging areas. This second group of provinces – the regionally oriented – included Ontario, British Columbia, and Alberta. Gertler believed that Ontario epitomized the decentralist approach, and he assigned Newfoundland to a special class, which required separate treatment even though it shared many of the features of the integrated approach.

In the following pages we shall briefly summarize the goals and objectives of some selected provincial policies and strategies, noting, where relevant, the extent to which they subscribed to Gertler's thesis. As Gertler noted, the objectives and content of the various provincial strategies did, indeed, vary considerably.

Atlantic Canada

Historically, the Maritime provinces – New Brunswick, Nova Scotia, Prince Edward Island, and Newfoundland and Labrador – have been a testing ground for economic planning, usually under the auspices of the federal government (with the support of the provinces). As has been mentioned, since the 1960s the federal government has established an alphabet soup of federal agencies – to a large degree for the purpose of stimulating the Atlantic economy. The Atlantic provinces, during this period (and currently, it might be added), had the lowest per capita incomes and highest unemployment rates, and they scored lowest on a host of other socioeconomic indicators. Thus, it is not surprising that regional development programs were of the greatest importance to them. These programs included ADA, ARDA, DREE, the Department of Regional and Industrial Expansion (DRIE), and the Atlantic Canada Opportunities Agency. Particularly during the height of DREE's activity, these initiatives were pursued region-wide, encompassing many economic sectors.

During the 1960s and 1970s, New Brunswick's activities in regional development typify the integrated approach to regional planning. Multiple efforts were launched to improve economic well-being throughout the province. Seven planning regions, covering the entire province, were established and various federally sponsored projects were undertaken. The Restigouche region in the northeast, working with FRED funding, demonstrated an appreciation of the breadth of development needed in the region. In its planning it addressed urban as well as rural, social as well as physical, and industrial as well as resource needs. Perhaps an even better example of a comprehensive planning approach was the Mactaquac development plan, which we will describe later in this section.

Although DREE had enough successes during this period to warrant Maritimers giving it the appellation "Mother DREE," it also had a number of high-profile failures, the most notable being the Bricklin automobile venture in New Brunswick. The DREE program contributed about one-seventh of the total public-sector capital invested in Bricklin, the remainder coming primarily from the New Brunswick government. In addition to attempts at large-scale employment creation, Atlantic Canada also had a tradition of showing concern for small, isolated rural settlements that, for a long time, had exhibited serious economic problems. These concerns were translated into the Newfoundland resettlement programs, which attempted to move people from isolated fishing villages to central areas (Pickette and Wallis 1972.) However, since FRED and the Newfoundland rural resettlement program were amalgamated into DREE in 1969, such approaches tended to take a back seat to large-scale employment-creation projects.

Because the Atlantic provinces all had basic structural problems, the programs emphasized infrastructure and employment creation. Indeed, in Prince Edward Island DREE produced Canada's first provincial-scale comprehensive development plan, based on rural adjustment and innovative approaches to land tenure and management. In the other three Atlantic provinces, development planning centred more on industrial employment creation. Thus, it can be said that the Maritimes clearly fell into Gertler's integrated, province-wide approach to regional development.

An important mid-1980s development in Atlantic Canada is worth noting. There was a move to local economic development based on subprovincial regions (see Heseltine 1998; Greenwood 1997; Clinton 1997). This was exemplified by the formation of regional development authorities in Nova Scotia and regional economic development boards in Newfoundland and Labrador in the 1990s. These agencies focus on coordinating economic development initiatives and capturing benefits from development opportunities. Longer-lived economic development commissions also function in New Brunswick, and a provincial economic development agency (Enterprise PEI) functions in Prince Edward Island.

Alberta

During this period, Alberta's main problems were pockets of poverty in the North, excessively fast provincial growth resulting in labour and material bottlenecks, a dualistic economic structure characterized by a dynamic petroleum sector, a desultory agriculture industry, and an "over-concentration" of its population in its two major metropolitan areas. The Alberta experience represents yet another example of provincial economic development policies. The provincial government tried to diversify the provincial economy, moving it away from a resource-oriented base to a secondary-sector base. The implementation of this policy depended on the actions of the different ministries; for example, agriculture attempted to develop a strong food-processing industry and the Alberta Heritage Fund was established out of oil royalty revenues to provide capital for future industrial diversification. To counter the population concentration in Calgary and Edmonton, the province instituted a population decentralization policy, mainly by trying to attract office and government employees from these urban centres to small towns.

Ontario

Ontario is a good example of the decentralization approach to regional development during this period. It believed that its main regional problem consisted of the negative consequences associated with the extremely rapid growth of the Toronto region and the effect that this might have in other regions of the province. Since Ontario had several second-order urban centres of considerable size (Hamilton, Ottawa, London, Sudbury), it was able to pursue a decentralization policy that did not conflict with the government's economic efficiency-growth objectives. Furthermore, because Ontario then (as now) was the richest of the provinces, it received very little monies from DREE, and the bulk of Ontario's developmental planning efforts were based on provincial initiatives and funds.

The decentralization policy was part of a larger 1966 regional planning initiative known as the Design for Development Program. Ten economic development regions were formed to cover the entire province, each with its own board that was charged with developing its own planning goals, criteria, and plan. Only the Toronto region was slated for a distinctive approach. Some path-breaking planning work was accomplished in some of the regions. For example, regional input-output analyses were completed for the Niagara and Eastern Ontario regions and the Northwestern Ontario region. In Northwestern Ontario, innovative means were developed for citizens to participate in planning the region, which was almost as large as all the other regions put together. Yet the planning frameworks the province had hoped to use for its own regional development planning and policy making failed to emerge from the regions (Macdonald 1984).

In the Toronto region, the province undertook its own planning initiative for a region that fell roughly within an eighty-kilometre arc of the city and that encompassed more than 22,000 square kilometres – the Toronto-Centred Region (TCR). The TCR was slightly larger than the region known today as the Greater Toronto Area (see Chapter 9). The 1970 TCR Concept dealt with future residential, commercial, and recreational areas as well as with basic transportation structure (Ontario 1970). Provincial planners sought to reduce the concentration of population and to provide open space and recreational opportunities for a steadily growing metropolitan population.

Shortly thereafter, under the Design for Development umbrella, several regional governments were established for other urban areas in the province, building on the experience with Metropolitan Toronto. In short, the Ontario approach to regional development dealt with the needs of each of its regions on its own merits. The "design" in Design for Development was essentially organizational. No new programs were announced, and, indeed, its crucial feature was that existing resources devoted to existing programs were of such magnitude as to be effective as instruments of regional development policy. One of the main instruments was to direct government budgetary expenditures to regional needs, thus containing regional development within the broader spectrum of provincial development (Cullingworth 1987).

Three Examples of Joint Provincial-Federal Programs

Many provincial development planning initiatives required federal participation under one of the federal programs we discussed earlier. Here are three examples.

Mactaquac Regional Development Plan

One of the exceptions to the criticism that the federal economic development programs lacked a "planning component" was the Mactaquac Regional Development Plan, which covered a section of the Saint John Valley in New Brunswick (see Gertler 1969, 1972, 1994b). It included many elements missing in other federal regional economic development activities. The plan resulted from the 1964 decision of the New Brunswick Electric Power Commission to further exploit the power potential of the Saint John River by constructing a dam and power-generating station 23 kilometres upstream from Fredericton.

This initial decision to harness the hydro capacity of the Saint John River was controversial. It was a megaproject, involving the construction of a dam with an operating head of 31.5 metres, creating a vast inland lake above the dam. This lake was ninety kilometres long and, on average, one kilometre wide. The project would require the relocation of 300 families, the Canadian National Railways line, the Trans-Canada Highway, and various other roads, bridges, and other facilities. The dam itself would create a barrier to salmon migration. The fact that the regional planning initiative eventually earned a degree of local endorsement reflected the convergence of a number of factors:

1 There were the compelling conditions then prevailing in the region, including extremely depressed economic conditions, low educational levels, and a large amount of idle or non-productive farmland; what appeared at the time to be a crisis turned into an opportunity for improving conditions in an impoverished region.
2 An unexpected breadth of vision was projected by the managers of the New Brunswick Electric Power Commission, who forcefully argued for the "multipurpose" use of the valley and for its sound planning and development (Rowley 1961, 311-23; Gertler 1994b, 40).
3 This vision was reinforced by certain trends in public policy at both the national and provincial levels. At the federal level there were the various regional development programs discussed earlier, in particular the availability of a large capital grant from the Atlantic Development Board. At the same time the province itself, through its Program of Equal Opportunity, was attempting to respond to the economic and social needs of the time.

The Mactaquac initiative went far beyond the usual "impact" issues and, instead, involved a comprehensive study of the region's potential for economic and social development. This led to the preparation and later implementation of a development strategy for the region – the Mactaquac Regional Development Plan. The Mactaquac Regional Development Plan covered an area extending from the confluence of the Saint John River and its tributary, the Mactaquac, to the town of Woodstock, which was 81 kilometres upstream. The plan was a joint effort of the federal government, the Province of New Brunswick, and local municipalities.

Supervising the plan was a committee that linked the power commission, the relevant provincial departments, and the federal-provincial ARDA officials with the planning undertaken by a highly diversified consulting group. The planning period extended from early in 1964 to the spring of 1965. In the end, a comprehensive, multi-sectoral, strategic, action-oriented plan was created, with recommendations for each major resource-based economic sector, land use, parks and recreation, townsite and community development, and the institutional framework for regional planning and development.

The regional plan provided for, among other things, the regrouping of displaced families, businesses, institutions, and industries in the new town of Nackawick (planned by the Canada Mortgage and Housing Corporation) as well as a new provincial park associated with a major tourist attraction, which was created by assembling historic buildings that had been removed from the flooded lands. The Mactaquac Regional Development Plan also provided for the necessary relocation of roads, railway lines, and other structures and physical facilities. Especially significant is the fact that these physical improvements were used as means for the social and economic betterment of the region and were consciously linked to economic development programs. One of the most important of these programs was intended to overcome the impediments to a well-managed and productive use of the forest resource (Richardson 1989a, 21).

A particularly commendable and unusual feature of the planning for the region is that, while the plan preparation work was still under way, the government of New Brunswick established a multi-functional implementing agency – the Community Improvement Corporation. Within a year of formal completion, a federal-provincial agreement was signed (September 1966), committing the two governments to a substantial ten-year investment in the major features of the plan. Much of the plan was, indeed, later translated into action.

Lesser Slave Lake Program

Alberta's two major DREE programs were the Designated Area Program in the southern part of the province and the Lesser Slave Lake Special Area Program in the northeast. It is said that the Lesser Slave Lake Program, which began in 1970, was one of the most comprehensive and successful of the special area programs. Consequently, it deserves further description.

Webster (1979, 45-6) assessed both the pros and cons of the program and the effect of DREE grants. On the positive side, he listed the following:

- As a result of DREE industrial grants and a DREE-sponsored industrial park, industries were attracted to the area. These industries involved first-stage processing of the local wood resource (such as studs and plywood), second-stage activities (modular housing and doors), plus some service activity (a hotel operated by the Native band).
- Extension of the local railway (through a DREE grant) to the industrial park (another DREE grant) ensured both that activities would be spatially centralized near the town of Slave Lake (creating a growth centre) and that the first-stage activities would be developed at the same time (yielding advantages in terms of economies of scale).
- The second-stage activities and the induced service activities would probably not have occurred without DREE grants.
- The range and quality of programs in human resource development (e.g., migration grants for Aboriginal people seeking work and work skills programs) would not have occurred without DREE funding.

On the negative side, Webster listed the following:

- With only one exception, none of the induced firms was linked in terms of input-output relationships. This drawback was typical of Canadian resource regions, where the linkage occurs in further processing or markets located in Canadian or world metropolises rather than within the region. The firms attracted to Lesser Slave Lake were unlikely to attract new firms to use their outputs or to provide inputs to them. In short, the development program did not lead to a restructuring of the regional economy.
- The Lesser Slake Lake Program was not conceived within the context of an overall provincial strategy. Critical workers were being consumed by the induced local industries, while, at the same time, the major provincial initiative of that decade, the Athabasca tar sands development, was competing for the same labour. Moreover, the unemployed of the region either did not want the kinds of jobs that were created or were unable to commute to them.
- It was highly debatable whether the Lesser Slave Lake Program was effective in significantly reducing socioeconomic problems. The gains in wages varied considerably among different socioeconomic groups (e.g., public-sector employees, private-sector induced positions, in-migrants, Aboriginal people, and women). The program benefited some, but not a large percentage, of the hard-core unemployed. As Webster (1979, 46) concluded: "Benefits in terms of wage gains to those employed may [have justified] the expenditures economically, but the program's results represented only a drop in the bucket in terms of the area's problems."

The British Columbia GDA–IPA Developmental Planning Process

As is Ontario, British Columbia was (and still is) a wealthy province; consequently, DREE involvement was minimal. A GDA–IPA (interim planning agreement) between British Columbia and DREE, signed in mid-1974, had two objectives:

1 to improve opportunities in areas or economic sectors of British Columbia that require special measures to realize their development potential
2 to promote balanced development among areas of the province and to encourage equitable distribution of the benefits from such development.

Specifically, the mandate of the agreement was to undertake regional development planning for four regions of British Columbia: the northeast, the mid-coast, the central region, and the Kootenays (the Kootenays having been the target of past intensive development planning and programs).

After the signing of this agreement in 1974, the province embarked on a comprehensive regional development program. The political party then in power (the New Democratic Party) established a developmental planning body, the Environmental and Land Use Secretariat, under the minister of resources. It was given the task of preparing a development strategy for a fifth region, the northwest. It was also given review powers over all initiatives proposed by other ministries, including the Department of Economic Development, which was authorized to prepare most regional development strategies under the GDA–IPA. The late 1970s focused the developmental planning emphasis in British Columbia on the coal deposits of the northern part of the province.

In line with the GDA–IPA process, a team of consultants was employed to identify economic opportunities in the four regions identified in the provincial–DREE agreement (e.g., opportunities for employment, social problems and opportunities, infrastructure bottlenecks, and regional needs). This task was difficult, to say the least, because provincial goals – in the form of an indicative strategy – were lacking (Webster 1979, 46). The consultant team faced some perplexing decisions and trade-offs:

- choosing between policies designed to induce long-run benefits from human resource investments and those promising short-run benefits from employment creation programs
- choosing between policies directly addressing the malaise found in small centres (e.g., declining resource towns) and policies that would aid in decentralizing the province's settlement system and concentrating investments in selected cities with growth potential (e.g., Prince George and Kamloops)
- deciding on interregional investment allocation decisions for the four regions.

The end result was a series of alternative development approaches for each of the four regions. These approaches saw the regions as independent entities rather than as components of a provincial system (Webster 1979, 48). The first two approaches stressed financial incentives to lure new industry into the regions; they also stressed funding various types of needed infrastructure. Webster concluded that the third approach, which stressed focusing on programs that would overcome the human obstacles to industrial development, would not only achieve the same benefits as the first two but would also produce additional benefits. However, he stressed that the problem with selling an approach that produced long-term benefits is that governments require short-term payoffs to stay in power. Furthermore, social programs are typically low profile and, thus, unattractive to all levels of government.

Reflections

This unusually vigorous period of regional development planning in Canada at both the federal and provincial levels, which began in the early 1960s and ended in the mid-1980s, and which, today, may seem something of an aberration, contains many aspects that can be of value for contemporary regional planning. Not least, it recognized the importance of economic factors in regional planning both with regard to their relevance to regions and with regard to the difficulties that seem to surround their planning. What we learn from these two and a half decades concerns the significant differences between traditional land-based approaches to regional planning and the regional economic development approach to planning. Those differences lie in three realms: (1) the primary subject of the planning (i.e., the economy), (2) the venue of the planning, and (3) the nature of the practice. We will now look briefly at each of these realms and draw out the lessons they suggest.

Planning Regional Economies

Some of the hurdles and dilemmas encountered in Canadian regional economic development planning revolved around the complex subject of what constitutes a regional economy and how it might be planned. Regional economics was in its infancy in the 1950s, and prescriptions for ending regional disparities were, at best, rudimentary. Thus, as Lithwick (1986b, 253) would later observe: "Despite clear evidence on the persistence of regional disparities in Canada, and some consensus that public policy should play a role in diminishing those disparities, the fact is that appropriate solutions have been unattainable, largely because the causes of the problem are neither simple nor clearly understood."

As we have seen, a variety of programs and policies was introduced, mostly without full knowledge of the effects to be expected and with little consideration of their relation to one another. Further, they were often discarded before they could be evaluated. The result was only modest insight into root causes of regional disparities and very little progress in terms of their elimination. The outcome was, generally, an unclear sense of direction for the ministry or agency responsible. This was equally true for both federal and provincial participation in regional development.

There was also, throughout this planning period, a general lack of recognition of both social and spatial aspects of regional economic development. The various policies and programs aimed to improve the well-being of the residents of a region, yet non-economic aspects were usually ignored (Webster 1979). As a rule, regional disparities were measured by indicators of low income and high unemployment. Yet, underdevelopment may also reflect, for example, a region's lack of public services and poor housing, a sense of isolation, a lack of access to political decision making, and a deteriorating environment. And all this may be true even though the region may enjoy high incomes and high employment. Of course, the converse may also be the case. The policies and programs of this time did not consider the spatial aspects of planning, such as the interrelation of centres receiving assistance or the true "spread effects" from centres to their regions. While all this was going on, a number of examples of region-sensitive, broad-based regional development were under way in the Interlake, Restigouche, Gaspé, and Mactaquac regions. Oddly, there seemed to exist neither the opportunity nor the desire to learn from these ongoing experiences.

Underdevelopment of regions, indeed of nations, was known, even then, to encompass a range of factors (Berry 1960; Thompson et al. 1962), but it was economic factors that had primacy in Canada's regional development planning. This is understandable, given that we conventionally accord to senior governments the responsibility to promote and manage the economy of the nation and the individual provinces. Dealing with social factors, a disparate array of phenomena at best (e.g., health, education, housing), nominally falls to the provinces. And spatial matters are, constitutionally, a provincial concern. Thus, the federal government had the right, indeed the obligation, to tackle regional economic disparities. To this end, it could, with minimal provincial cooperation, dispense its own funds to private industries and provinces. That the federal government chose to deal with regional disparities in a "planned," systematic way was a politically strategic move that was supported by the theoretical ethos of the time. However, substantively, the federal government agencies could not, on their own, tackle the full scope of regional development (i.e., social and spatial as well as economic). Nor could most of the provinces, with their more meagre resources, do so without extensive federal involvement.

Given the politically charged nature of regional economic development, a broad perspective was difficult to achieve, much less to sustain. As we demonstrated earlier, successful endeavours in individual regions need to be acknowledged. However, their very success seems to emphasize the inability to mount an interregional planning program across the nation or even, in most cases, across provinces. The regional development perspective must be multi-regional: it must view regions as systemically related and dependent upon one another (Friedmann 1965). Although, by definition, regions differ, the solutions to their problems are entwined with those of other regions. While regional distinctiveness was often accorded its due, interregional links were not. Whether this could have been achieved in the circumstances of the time is, of course, mere speculation. Indeed, this issue became, and remains, moot with the increasing globalization of the 1980s.

Decision-Making Terrain for Regional Development

If the subject of regional development planning was tenuous, then the question of *who* ought to do the planning was equally difficult and contentious. Before the economic problems of any region could be tackled there were two venues within which tactics and tools had to be agreed upon. The first was at the ministerial level of the federal government, and the second was at the intergovernmental level (i.e., between the federal and provincial governments).

At the federal level, the initial regional development programs were established within specific ministries (e.g., ARDA [Agriculture] and ADA [Industry]). The decision to create a ministry devoted to *regional* concerns (DREE), but with powers equal to functional ministries, embodied a basic "contradiction" (Lithwick 1986b). The existing ministries functioned within defined sectors – such as labour, industry, welfare, energy, environment, health, and transportation – and, for the most part, there was little overlap. DREE (and its successors), which was trying to work within a spatial context, was bound to overlap with existing ministries where spatial concerns were marginal to their main thrust. The struggle for authority was inevitable and was a constant distraction. This situation stands in contrast to the much more clearly defined situation involved in establishing and mandating a regional development authority to carry out, for example, the South Saskatchewan River and St. Lawrence Seaway projects. Two issues thus present themselves: the first is whether the federal government can maintain a national spatial perspective in its planning or whether it can only attain this perspective in discrete regional situations. (Since provincial governments are also structured this way, the same issue applies to their interregional planning.) The second issue is whether it is possible to mobilize all the resources necessary to tackle multifaceted (economic, social, spatial, environmental) regional development planning on a national, or even regional, scale.

All the federal programs were faced with working directly within the challenging venue of federalism. One of its political realities was the need to include all provinces in the largesse of regional programs. Although not all provinces suffered regional disparities to the same degree, all provinces expected to participate in these programs in a substantial way, and each province had at least one designated region. Another reality emerged when programs were to be implemented in the individual provinces. Although each province demanded to be included in the various programs, the kind and quality of its participation was often circumscribed. In part, this was due to the extent of resources a province was expected to contribute. The results differed; however, in general, the smaller, poorer provinces had little choice but to accept federal funds and federal planning perspectives. There were, as well, the changes in government leadership that were bound to occur over time. These often led to the need to renegotiate agreements and protocols. One of the major "casualties" of this political milieu was the systemic approach to national interregional planning. Satisfying provincial demands came before regional needs.

Paradoxically, the planning successes in this period were in intraregional planning rather than in interregional planning. They occurred in situations that resembled single-region planning endeavours of the traditional land-use type. In the Interlake, northeast New Brunswick, the Mactaquac, and Lesser Slave Lake – each acknowledged successes – we have examples of intraregional planning. Here the planners worked with a clear mandate, and an identifiable planning body had a working connection with the regional population and institutions and even prepared "plans." Why high-level national intergovernmental regional planning either withered or devolved into a simple grants-in-aid program while these latter venues succeeded no doubt holds some lessons about regional economic planning in a federal state.

The Practice of Planning Regional Development

As we have seen, the federal programs (e.g., ARDA, ADA, and DREE) undertook to plan and develop programs for regions that were undefined. They had to contend with a lack of experience, a good deal of uncertainty about what outcomes could be expected, and treacherous political terrain. This yet-to-be-defined and politically uncertain situation was the milieu within which planners had to practise. Since economic considerations dominated the substance of the planning, planners needed the skills of economists, including agricultural economists, and many of them were drawn to these efforts. Beyond this, it was a milieu that featured the delivery of program resources, mostly dollars, in sensitive and complex bureaucratic environments at both the provincial and federal levels.

In many ways, those who came to work as planners within this milieu had to learn "on the job." There were, at the time, few regional planners in Canada and almost none with either the educational or practical background for regional development planning. Most were working in land-use planning situations (e.g., in metropolitan regions or analogous rural settings). Those who came from economics or geography, or from within the bureaucracy, had little experience with planning processes, especially in territorial situations. Further, the "regions" with which they worked were administrative conveniences defined by strategic criteria (e.g., incidence of low incomes, unemployment level) related to the aims of politically driven programs. Planners in DREE and other programs seldom participated directly in a region or with the region's residents. Regions and their needs were considered from "outside" the region, often from as far away as Ottawa. The planners, generally, did not have to wrestle either with setting boundaries and tending them (see Chapter 3) or with the commitment to a regional agency.[5]

There was also something of a contradiction between the way regions were regarded and the planning practice that ensued during the DREE period. The innovative theories of interregional economic growth, of a region's fate being entwined with that of other regions, underlay much of the impetus for improving regional economic balance. Concepts abroad at the time included "dynamic spatial structure," "polarized development," "development corridors," and "spread effects" (see, for example, Perroux 1950; Myrdal 1957; Hirschman 1958; Isard and Schooler 1959; Berry 1960; and Friedmann 1966). Regions were seen, in theory, as part of a system of regions. Yet, in practice, these ideas seem only infrequently to have guided DREE's regional planners. One notable exception was the use of industrial complex analysis (Isard and Schooler 1959) in the formulation of a development strategy for the Saint John, New Brunswick, region. After choosing the city as a growth centre, the development objective became the establishment of a multiple industry complex of firms engaged in non-ferrous metals products (Czamanski 1971; Gertler and Crowley 1977).

However, programs were generally delivered to each region individually, apparently without concern either for their impact upon adjacent regions or their connection to the system of regions as a whole. Even in regions within which planning was considered a success, such as the Mactaquac River Valley, the practice was essentially to see the region, and plan it, from the "outside."

It is difficult to characterize the planning practice in this period of regional development. Was it regional planning at all? Seldom was there a permanent planning staff in a DREE-designated region. There were, instead, federal-provincial task forces, development corporations, consultants, and general funding agreements. Seldom was there a published regional plan against which progress could be measured (Hodge 1994). Perhaps all this should not be unexpected, since economic development problems are complex and require the cooperation of several levels of government and many different program agencies. For the regional planner it meant operating on the front lines of an often rancorous federal-provincial power struggle. At the least, it meant being skilled in understanding and manoeuvring one's way through high-level and complex bureaucracies, both in the provinces and Ottawa, simply to get approval to proceed. Theoretical and analytical precepts about shaping a region's development, even where accepted, were frequently diluted and left the planner to pragmatic, politically acceptable approaches.

Both the character and quality of planning practice in these past decades remain enigmatic. Was it the subject of planning an economy that made governments apprehensive? Was it the many related facets of a region's development, also necessitating planning, that boggled planners' minds? It is true that, as Friedmann and Weaver (1979, 3) observe, "as an activity of the state, actual planning practice is unable to go beyond the structural conditions that give rise to it." And, in this period of regional economic development planning, the structural conditions were ill-defined. Planning doctrine lacked a stable combination of normative, substantive, and procedural dimensions to inform planning practice (see Chapter 2). The ideological commitment to economic equity among regions was fragile at best. Substantive theory about how regions develop was constantly changing. And procedural theory about how to organize the planning of regions was not only untried but, when tried, was undermined by federal-provincial sparring.

A more thorough analysis of regional economic development planning practice awaits. At the national level it is, perhaps, less urgent to know more, given today's understandable preoccupation with the international, rather than with the interregional, situation. However, the provinces cannot avoid addressing regional economic development planning when dealing with regional disparities within their own boundaries, especially between urban and rural regions. These disparities are becoming more insistent and persistent as the new century opens, especially in relation to emerging city-regions (see Chapter 9). Considering both the failures and successes in regional economic development planning from the 1960s to the 1980s will help us to construct appropriate and effective planning approaches to today's and tomorrow's regional disparities.

7

Regional Planning for Resource Conservation and Development and for the Environment

The conservation and development of natural resources has a central position in regional planning. The conservation, use, extraction, and alienation of natural resources is an inherent feature of human social development, and it is characterized by widespread and long-lasting impacts on the region within which the resource is located (and often on adjacent regions as well). Whether it be the soils for farming, forests for lumbering, subsoils for mining and oil extraction, or the rivers and oceans for fishing, the conservation and development of resources affect large areas and their human and non-human residents in social, economic, and biologically important ways. This has been evident to regional planners since the days of Geddes and other precursors (see Chapter 1). Their concerns generated a basic principle for regional planners that persists today: Always seek to establish harmony between human activities and nature.

Natural resource development is predominantly an activity of rural regions. Indeed, as Chapter 5 posits, natural resources and their use are the backbone of economic and social life in rural regions and, thus, of the planning of such regions. Yet most rural resources are urban-bound. Cities, with their productive facilities and large populations, create most of the demand for rural resources and, thereby, establish which resources are required, how much, and at what rate. Rural regions respond with measures that, while intended to be to their advantage, may have unintended negative consequences (e.g., flooding, erosion, exhaustion of the resource, pollution) both for themselves and for urban regions. Thus, there is a high degree of interdependence between urban and rural regions with regard to natural resources, and this becomes very evident in planning for resource conservation and environmental protection.

The importance of natural resources to all regions shows up in Canadian governing structures. From the outset, Canada's Constitution identified natural resources as a central concern. Provincial governments were given rights over natural resources within their territories, while the federal government retained those rights in northern territories as well as specified rights for ocean resources and rivers that cross provincial and national boundaries.[1] The government manifests its concern with natural resources by designating separate ministries to deal with them (e.g., agriculture, fisheries, lands and forests, mining, etc.). These ministries then go on to develop separate programs for managing their resource sector.

Even though the development of resources, including their conservation and protection, occurs within regional settings, much of the planning has been primarily sectoral in nature. Thus a region established to conserve a water resource, for example, may require the protection and management of a large ecologically sensitive area. But such regions often tend to be established for limited functional and administrative purposes (i.e., for managing a resource) rather than for physical, economic, and social planning purposes. The scope of much of this resource planning, as we shall see in this chapter, is as broad as the region but only as deep as the specific sector. This introduces an inherent tension that mirrors the fundamental regional planning dialectic of *territory* versus *function*, which was discussed in Chapter 2. As we shall also see, however, signs point to a greater synthesis in the planning of resources and their regions; that is, the move is towards a territorial approach to planning. There have been manifestations of planned, comprehensive regional resource development projects, all of which cut across a large number of jurisdictions and thus require a special institutional framework.

Figure 12 offers an overview of events in the evolution of Canada's regional resource planning for conservation, development, and the environment.

Planning the Conservation of Regional Resources

Beginnings of Conservation Concerns

The conservation movement, as we have come to know it, began as a reaction to imprudent practices in resource development and was the spawning ground for some of the earliest public regional planning. It was presaged by the transformation of Canada from a rural, agricultural nation to an urban, industrial one, beginning at the end of the nineteenth century. This change led to a realization that the industrial processes that were then driving city economies (and the national economy as well) and, more latterly, our present-day protection of the environment and sustainable development, were consuming natural resources at an alarming rate, often leaving waste and pollution in their wake in both urban and rural areas.

As the nineteenth century came to an end, conservation movements began in both Canada and the United States. Eventually governments were pressed to establish new institutions for natural resources conservation and development, and, by the 1930s, we saw the establishment of the Tennessee Valley Authority in the United States and the Prairie Farm and Rehabilitation Act in Canada (see Chapter 1). Paralleling this awareness of the relationship between human and natural environments was the movement to preserve wilderness areas. Canada's first national park, Banff National Park, was created in 1885, and it was followed in a few years by Algonquin National Park in Ontario and by Laurentides and Mont Tremblant Parks in Quebec. Such interest continues with new variants – protected area networks and wilderness preserves.

Commission of Conservation

The public pressure for conservation of Canada's natural resources led to the creation of the federal Commission of Conservation in 1909. The commission was designed to be a joint federal-provincial effort, and its mission was nothing less than to recommend policies and programs for the best use of Canada's forest, water, and land resources. A notable feature of its work was that it also embraced public health, urban planning, and wise rural land use. In 1917 Thomas Adams (see Chapter 1), who was then the commission's town planning advisor, produced a remarkable report entitled *Rural Planning and Development*. Indeed, according to Richardson (1994), much of the commission's work foreshadowed the ideas on sustainable development contained in the report of the Brundtland Commission, which was written seventy years later.

The Commission of Conservation lasted twelve years, during which time it disseminated information on conservation and resource-related subjects, published papers and longer studies dealing with various resource problems, lobbied all levels of governments about conservation, and awakened Canadians to the need for conservation. Understandably, as Stein (1994, 55) notes, there were regrets about its demise: "It should be chastening to consider that many of the problems the commission set out to deal with in the early 1900s are still with us, and, indeed, have become more acute." Nevertheless, its impact on Canadians has been long-lasting, not least in showing the role that governments need to play in the area of conservation.

Conservation after the Commission

The social and economic conditions of the 1920s and 1930s were not conducive to such idealistic notions as resource conservation. Nevertheless, the years between the two world wars did see one notable conservation achievement: the Prairie Farm Rehabilitation Act, 1935, and its companion Maritimes Marshland Rehabilitation Act, 1946 (see Chapters 5 and 7). The agencies responsible for implementing these acts took a regional approach to their activities, although it was not until 1946 that something close to the classic form of regional planning appeared in Canada.

Even during the Second World War, the growing need for conservation was not completely forgotten; indeed, the vision of a better Canada emerged from the Depression and the effort to stimulate and revive the conservation movement. Before the end of the Second World War, the federal government created the Advisory Committee on Reconstruction (some compared it to England's Beveridge Commission), which produced a report entitled *Conservation and Development of Natural Resources.* While the committee's companion report, entitled *Housing and Community Planning,* received most of the kudos – undoubtedly because it addressed issues that were perceived as being more urgent – the conservation report was, nevertheless, an important harbinger for the future.

The 1942 Guelph Conference on the Conservation of the Natural Resources of Ontario (which, to a large degree, was a response to the dust-bowl conditions created in parts of southern Ontario by destructive logging and farming practices) proved to have more immediate and tangible results. The conference was generally credited with the passage of that province's Conservation Authorities Act, 1946 – one of the landmark launching events in the history of "formal" regional planning in Canada.

Protecting Agricultural Lands

As noted in Chapter 5, British Columbia, Quebec, and Newfoundland enacted legislation designed to preserve their best farming areas. This was a response to concerns about urban sprawl, especially in and around the major cities and metropolitan areas, brought about by the postwar surge of urban growth. The British Columbia Agricultural Land Commission (BCALC) was created in 1973 and given the power to curtail the conversion of good agricultural lands to urban uses. It establishes and administers agricultural zones for the entire province, conducts studies, and makes recommendations concerning conservation and recreational land uses. Using the Canada Land Inventory (discussed later in this chapter), the BCALC established agricultural land reserves (ALRs) – "mini"-regions, as it were – and drew up plans to restrict urban development on areas with soil types that could support agricultural production (usually soil types 1, 2, and 3). The BCALC continues to this day, and, having been given the power of zoning, it has control over the subdivision of lands in zones designated as ALRs inside and outside municipal boundaries. Throughout its history, the commission has been embroiled in controversy. (See Chapter 9 for one example, which led to the demise of regional planning in British Columbia in 1983.)

The Quebec government took a similar action in 1978, when it established "protected areas" under its Commission de protection du territoire agricole (see Chapter 5). Although there has not been a complete halt to the subdivision of agricultural land in either Quebec or British Columbia, there is no question that it has been greatly reduced and that the amount of non-agricultural uses permitted in the protected zones has been considerably lessened. (See, for example, Bryant and Johnston 1992.)

Figure 12

**Major events in the evolution of Canadian regional planning for
conservation, resource development, and the environment**

1885   Banff National Park (Alberta) created, followed in a few years by the
            Algonquin Provincial Park (Ontario) and Quebec's Laurentides and
            Mont-Tremblant Parks.

1870s to 1890s
            Numerous city parks established, e.g., Halifax's Point Pleasant Park,
            Montreal's Mount Royal Park, Toronto's Hyde Park, Vancouver's
            Stanley Park, and London's Victoria Park.

1909   Canadian Commission of Conservation created.

1917   Thomas Adams' *Rural Planning and Development: A Study of Rural
            Conditions and Problems in Canada* published.

1921   Canadian Commission of Conservation disbanded.

1935   Prairie Farm Rehabilitation Act proclaimed.

1942   Guelph Conference on the Conservation of the Natural Resources of
            Ontario held.

1944   Advisory Committee on Reconstruction's Report, *Conservation and
            Development of Natural Resources*, issued.

1945-58   Nearly fifty resource towns planned and built on Canada's resource
            frontier (e.g., Elliot Lake, Manitouwadge, Uranium City, and Kitimat) in
            practically every province and in the northern territories.

1946   Ontario's Conservation Authorities Act passed.

1948   Maritimes Marshland Rehabilitation Act legislated.

1961   Agricultural Rehabilitation and Development Act (ARDA) passed.

            Resources for Tomorrow Conference held in Montreal.

1962   Rachel Carson's *Silent Spring* published.

1963   Canada Land Inventory launched as a federal-provincial program.

1967   Ontario government initiates a series of studies and follow-up actions
            leading to enactment of the Niagara Planning and Development Act in
            1973.

1967-75   Newfoundland Resettlement Program launched.

1970   Canada Water Act proclaimed.

1972   Policy Plan for the Peace River Region (Alberta) published.

1975   BC Agricultural Land Commission established.

            Federal Environmental Assessment and Review Process, and Federal
            Environmental Assessment Review Office legislation passed.

1978   Quebec passes Bill 90 to protect agricultural land.

1979   Saskatchewan creates the Meewasin Valley Authority.

1980   Three international conservation bodies publish the World Conserva-
            tion Strategy (WCS).

▶

◄ Figure 12

1985	Kirkpatrick Sale, arguably the "father" of the bioregionalism movement, publishes *Dwellers in the Land: The Bioregional Vision*.
1987	United Nations World (Brundtland) Commission issues its report, *Our Common Future*. It promotes the notion of "sustainable development" and encourages formation of provincial, territorial, and local round tables on the economy and the environment.
1988	Canadian Environmental Act passed.
1989	Lancaster Sound Regional Land Use Plan released.
	The (Crombie) Royal Commission on the Future of the Toronto Waterfront established. The Commission publishes, *Watershed*, its Interim Report (1990), and *Regeneration*, its Final Report (1992).
1992	BC establishes Commission on Resources and the Environment (CORE).
1992	In BC, federal, provincial, regional, and First Nations' governments form Fraser Basin Management Plan.
1993	BC government announces its "Protected Areas Strategy."
1995	Federal Banff–Bow Valley Task Force reports.
1996	New Greenbelt Plan for National Capital Region (Ottawa) incorporates ecological protection principles.

Ecological Reserves and Protected Areas

Canada had subscribed to the International Biological Program since its inception in 1965.[2] The process of researching and designating sites for conservation was conducted by panels coordinated by the Canadian Council on Ecological Areas. Panel members were drawn from the federal and provincial governments, university researchers, non-governmental organizations, and private citizens. As of 1986, eight of ten provinces had enacted ecological reserves legislation or made some provision for them within existing legislation. British Columbia provided a singularly outstanding example of ecological commitment: it legally designated more than 100 ecosystem reserves. In other provinces, and on federal lands north of latitude sixty, surveys, site research, and interest group lobbying continued, but official designation of sites was slow (Revel 1981). And it continues to be slow.[3] The purpose of designating sites is twofold: (1) to preserve unique natural ecosystems that have demonstrated biological value and (2) to bar human intrusions. In the lands of the arctic and sub-arctic regions, five federal acts bear on this purpose; however, according to Revel, they have serious limitations. In general, it can be said that, as of the early 1980s, Canada did not have a single, all-encompassing piece of federal legislation, or an adequate institution, to advance the objective of securing and preserving ecological sites. In 1984, the federal government created a Crown corporation, Wildlife Habitat, with a mandate to encourage natural habitat preservation and to help prevent its destruction.

Initially, federal funding was two million dollars, with the expectation that private-sector funding would follow.

Several provinces adopted legislation identifying "special places, preserves, and protected areas" and took measures to protect them. While much of the action taken was often too little or too late, there have been some notable exceptions. One such exception is British Columbia's Protected Areas Strategy, which we discuss next.

British Columbia's Protected Areas Strategy

Increasing recognition of the need to protect natural diversity, combined with growing public pressure for more parks, led, in July 1993, to the BC government announcing a new policy: "A Protected Areas Strategy for British Columbia: The Protected Areas Component of BC's Land Use Strategy." This policy established a vision for protected areas in the province and committed the government to double their number, from approximately 6 percent to 12 percent of the land base, by the year 2000; a target, as we note below, that was reached in 2001. This entailed adding approximately 60,000 square kilometres of protected areas over a seven-year period.[4]

Several initiatives already existed for the protection of areas of natural or cultural significance. The protected areas strategy (PAS) was established in order to integrate these initiatives, along with prospective future measures, and to provide a cross-ministry approach to fulfilling new provincial commitment. Within the 12 percent target, the PAS aimed to achieve two goals: (1) to protect viable examples of natural diversity representative of the major terrestrial, marine, and freshwater ecosystems; the characteristic habitats, hydrology, and landforms; and the characteristic backcountry recreational and cultural heritage values of each ecosystem; and (2) to protect the province's natural and cultural heritage as well as its recreational features, including, for example, rare and endangered species and critical habitats. Within these broad goals, the PAS was designed to meet a set of specific objectives, one of which was to reduce jurisdictional complexity and inefficiencies by integrating and coordinating the many protected area programs operating at all levels of government in British Columbia (e.g., provincial and national parks, provincial recreation areas, ecological reserves, forest wilderness areas, wildlife management areas).

The overall intent of the PAS was to provide a provincial framework for determining protected areas. As well, it hoped to provide guidance to the regional negotiating groups convened by the Commission of Resources and the Environment. Once study areas have been approved, recommendations on whether to designate them as protected areas would be made through regional and subregional land-use planning processes, which, using the PAS for guidance, must resolve competing issues and values. The decision as to which study areas are to be designated and managed as protected areas rests with the

Cabinet, which is committed to fully assess any environmental, social, and/or economic implications before it makes its final decisions on proposed protected areas. The PAS was completed in the late spring of 1993, in time for it to be used in the negotiations leading to recommendations for protected areas in each region.

In the nine years between May 1992 (the initiation of the PAS) and January 2001, the number of parks and protected areas has doubled (BC Land Use Coordination Office 2001). As of January 2001, a total of almost 120,000 square kilometres of the province are "protected," representing a little more than 12 percent of British Columbia's land base. This means that British Columbia is the first province in Canada, and arguably one of the first jurisdictions in the world, to meet the United Nations 1992 challenge to protect and preserve 12 percent of one's land base.

Another measure of the ecological integrity of British Columbia's land base is the fact that more than 80 percent of the province has been, or is currently being, planned under comprehensive land-use plans. Half of the administrative regions of the province (four out of eight – Vancouver Island, Cariboo–Chilcotin, Kootenay, and Prince Rupert) have at least 12 percent of their land base dedicated to protected-area status. In addition, the government has set a protected-area target of 13 percent in the Lower Mainland region (see www.luco.gov.bc.ca).

Planning Regional Resource Development

While conservation is concerned with the *preservation* and *protection* of resource regions, for reasons of economic well-being, most regions also have to consider the *use and development* of their resources. Two national conferences, the National Conference on Renewable Resources (1954) and the Resources for Tomorrow Conference (1961) (see Chapter 1), helped to shape a planned approach to resource development that took into account regional settings as well as conservation needs. Manifestations of this approach took many forms in regional planning efforts between the 1960s and 1980s, and even into the 1990s.

Resource and land-use planning projects are not always undertaken within a standardized statutory and administrative framework, as are municipal planning projects or Crown lands management procedures. Particular circumstances call for a special planning project outside the normal institutional system, and this often requires special legislation. Typically, these particular circumstances involve the building of a dam, steel mill, or other major development in a rural area; the need to protect or develop the resources of a river basin or other special natural feature; the need to fashion a provincial land-use strategy; or the need to develop a region's untapped economic potential. Today, this approach to planning is referred to as "planned regional resource development," and, during the last four decades, it took many forms all across Canada.

Here we examine five examples of the special administrative (and some-times legislative) arrangements that are often necessary for regional resource and land-use planning: the Ontario regional conservation authorities, the Meewasin Valley Authority (in Saskatchewan), the Haldimand–Norfolk Study (in Ontario), the Niagara Escarpment (in Ontario), and the British Columbia Commission on Resources and the Environment. In addition, we shall also discuss planning for the Peace River Region (which straddles both northern Alberta and northern British Columbia), where a special administrative arrange-ment is needed to realize the region's potential but has not yet materialized.

Planning for Watersheds and River Basins

Ontario Regional Conservation Authorities

With the work of the Commission on Conservation and the 1942 Guelph Con-ference on Natural Resources as inspiration, Ontario passed its Regional Con-servation Authorities Act, 1946. In this landmark act, the planning of regional watersheds was made possible through government-funded intermunicipal regional watershed conservation agencies. Conservation authorities were es-tablished for a dozen or more river basins in southern Ontario.[5] Each was given a fairly strong mandate to conduct multi-purpose planning and compre-hensive resource development, something along the lines of the Tennessee Valley Authority.

During the more than fifty years that conservation authorities have existed in Ontario, watershed planning has produced numerous positive outcomes, including flood control measures, wetlands preservation, and water-based rec-reation areas. However, despite their strong mandate, the conservation au-thorities have generally been kept on a "short rein" by the province and by the municipal councils, both of which appear to be jealous of their power (Richardson 1994, 56). Despite, or possibly because of, this political constraint, the conservation authorities have kept their role sharply in focus. They know the value of being able to both plan and implement their proposals. The gov-ernmental resources they were allocated appear to have been ample for the planning tasks they were mandated (albeit this was only for a single sector). And the work of the Crombie Commission on the Future of the Toronto Water-front (and its successor, the Waterfront Trust [see Chapter 9]) appears to be taking traditional river basin planning one step further by defining the Greater Toronto Area as a bioregion.

Meewasin Valley in Saskatchewan [6]

Another example of planned resource development based on water resources is the Meewasin Valley Authority (MVA) in Saskatchewan. In the early 1970s, a portion of the South Saskatchewan River's edge was threatened by a pro-posed major residential development. As a result, the City of Saskatoon, the adjacent rural municipality of Corman Park, the provincial government, and the University of Saskatchewan (as the largest landowner) commissioned the South Saskatchewan River Corridor Study. It was completed in 1976 and included a proposal to prepare a 100-year visionary plan. According to a senior planner with the authority, the proposal was "based on the overall conservation concept of achieving 'health' and 'fit' through a balanced use of resources" (Mathur 1989, 44). The study also recommended the creation of an autonomous agency to conserve and develop the valley's natural and heritage resources along the river edges (Tomalty et al. 1994; Gertsmar 1996).

The province of Saskatchewan enacted legislation in 1979, the Meewasin Valley Authority Act, which established the MVA. The authority was composed of the same four partners that initiated the corridor study, and the act gave them jurisdiction over the eighty kilometres of river and extensive adjacent lands as well as far-reaching powers. The MVA had the power to plan the river corridor; to regulate land and water use; to acquire land through purchase, expropriation, and right of first refusal; and to develop, maintain, and regulate the area within its jurisdiction. Implementation of the mandate proved, however, to be difficult. There was opposition from agricultural groups, property owners, the real estate industry, and mortgage lending institutions (Tomalty et al. 1994).

Although the MVA continued to receive strong support from the provincial government and conservation advocacy groups, the municipal and rural councils were reticent, if not hostile. In the end, the Meewasin Valley Authority Act was amended, private lands in the rural municipality were removed, the Meewasin Valley Authority Act's powers of expropriation were repealed, and the rural municipality withdrew as a participating party. This was a severe blow to the MVA, for it significantly reduced its jurisdictional area, restricting its powers to only the river channel in Saskatoon and Corman Park (i.e., primarily to publicly owned lands). Effectively, this meant that the major restructuring needed to protect fragile areas, which were mainly in private hands, could not go ahead.

We need look no further for a more graphic case of the vulnerability of regional planning in divided jurisdictions. In this case the venerable municipal institutions were more than a match for the new agency, despite its strong provincial support.

Fraser River Valley Basin

The Georgia Basin is the British Columbia portion of a larger "Salish Sea" bioregion formed by the watersheds that drain into the Strait of Georgia and the Strait of Juan de Fuca and Puget Sound in the State of Washington. This area, in the British Columbia portion, encompasses the entire Greater Vancouver Regional District (GVRD), extends north to Powell River and east to Hope on the mainland, and includes Victoria and up to Campbell River on Vancouver Island. In 1992, the provincial government asked the British Columbia

Round Table on the Environment and the Economy (now defunct) to develop proposals for addressing growth management in this bioregion, and this resulted in the creation of the Georgia Basin Initiative (GBI). The central goal of the GBI was to promote a sustainable future for the basin through partnership and consultation with other governments, non-governmental organizations, and the private sector. In early 1996, the GBI issued a vision statement, the first of its eight guiding principles being to promote "compact and complete communities" (one of the basic tenets of the Greater Vancouver Livable Region Strategic Plan, as we will see in Chapter 9), which was to be achieved through infill redevelopment. The Ministry of Municipal Affairs and Housing, which now administers the GBI, is still actively promoting the vision statement, and, in recent years, the initiative has been given additional responsibilities. However, our focus here is with the Fraser Valley Basin, the watershed within the Georgia Basin that encompasses the GVRD.

The Fraser River Valley Basin, the area drained by the Fraser River and its tributaries, accounts for more than 25 percent of British Columbia's land mass. It supports more than two-thirds of the province's population and contributes 80 percent of its gross domestic product. The basin is blessed with abundant natural resources, including forests, agricultural lands, fish and wildlife, and mineral resources, which support the basin's economy. The basin provides abundant opportunities for tourism and recreation. It also represents a rich and varied cultural heritage to the indigenous peoples of the region, and this explains the Aboriginal involvement in its membership and funding. The basin is home to more than two million people, and its population is expected to double within twenty-five years. Such growth challenges the integrity of the basin's ecosystems as well as the stability of its social and economic systems. Effectively addressing these emerging issues will require that all those groups with an interest in developing the basin work together towards common goals and objectives. Several government and not-for-profit initiatives have been launched in the past two decades to deal with these challenges.

In 1985 the Fraser River Estuary Management Program (FREMP) was established with the signing of an agreement by five major parties: Environment Canada, the British Columbia Ministry of the Environment, Fisheries and Oceans Canada, the Fraser River Harbour Commission, and the North Fraser Harbour Commission. The goal of the program was to coordinate and build consensus on how to serve both environmental and economic considerations along the Fraser estuary, taking into account the ever-expanding industrial, commercial, recreational, and residential development occurring along its shores. The challenge was to ensure that urbanization and industrialization are considered on a watershed basis and do not take place at the expense of the ecological values of the estuary (Tomalty et al. 1994, 29; Richardson 1989a, 33-4).

For a number of years, faculty at the University of British Columbia had conducted studies on the Fraser River Basin, while, at the same time, mayors from around the Fraser region were lobbying Ottawa for assistance to clean up the river. When funding became available through the Green Plan, the Fraser Basin Management Board (FBMB) was created in 1992, and it had some similarities with the FREMP. The FBMB consisted of a rare combination of stakeholders: three members each from federal, provincial, municipal, and Aboriginal organizations; and six members from non-governmental organizations and/or the public at large. In 1996, the FBMB published a report on the state of the Fraser Basin, which identified urban growth and urban sprawl as the key challenge facing the sustainability of the basin. It recommended, among other things, that a monitoring system be established to assess progress towards urban containment and environmental protection (FBMP 1996).

A three-year study of the Lower Fraser River ecosystem (commissioned by Ottawa), undertaken by twenty departments at the University of British Columbia, concluded that the Fraser River Basin has too many people, almost three times too many to be sustainable (*Globe and Mail*, 24 September 1997, A6). The key conclusion of the study group, according to the principal investigator, is that many of the problems related to sustaining the environment, the economy, and social conditions are linked to population growth, but no one wants to talk about population policies. The group recommended that Ottawa adopt a population policy for Canada that is consistent with the principles of sustainability and that it guide development of policies on immigration, child care, health care, and family planning. And it suggested that the government of British Columbia do the same.

In February 1997, federal, provincial, and local governments, as well as Aboriginal organizations, launched a new not-for-profit society – the Fraser Basin Council – as the successor to the FBMB. The membership of the council consists of representatives from three levels of government; Aboriginal organizations; the four geographic areas of the river system; as well as from social, environmental, and economic sectors of society. The new council's mandate is to promote and monitor the implementation of a charter for sustainability, which the FBMP had developed and which various individuals, organizations, and all levels of government joined together to sign. The charter, which was designed to protect and enhance the sustainability of the Fraser River and its vast basin, will guide social, economic, environmental, and institutional actions. One of the council's first tasks is to produce a five-year action plan to accompany the charter.

Planning for the Impacts of a Major Development

Haldimand–Norfolk Study

The Haldimand–Norfolk Study, a small project group set up by the Ontario Ministry of Municipal Affairs in 1969, is a good example of an ad hoc joint provincial-municipal venture initiated in response to a particular situation (see

Richardson 1989a, 21; Cullingworth 1987, 325-9).[7] The underlying purpose of these studies was to demonstrate cooperation between the provincial and municipal governments involved in developing plans for the areas concerned. As in the case of the Mactaquac Regional Development Plan (see Chapters 1 and 7), the Haldimand–Norfolk Study came about in response to the impending arrival of a major development project in a rural area. In this case, it was the 1969 decision of the Steel Company of Canada (STELCO) to build a large steel-making plant on the shore of Lake Erie southwest of Hamilton, Ontario.

The Haldimand–Norfolk area had shared in the late nineteenth-century industrialization of Ontario but, by the end of the century, was being bypassed; by the mid-twentieth century it had relapsed into rural tranquility. The county of Haldimand was an old, established farming area originally settled by United Empire Loyalists, while to its west the tobacco-growing county of Norfolk was prospering. The village of Port Dover, almost on the county line, was the base of a substantial fishing industry. Given its geographical position, with easy access to mid-west markets in the United States, the region had great potential. In 1967, this seemed to be recognized by Ontario Hydro's construction of a thermal generating station; and, in the same year, STELCO announced plans for the construction of a new integrated steel plant. Later, Texaco announced that it would build a large oil refinery complex adjacent to the hydroelectric power site in the Nanticoke area.

With these impending developments, the future of the region suddenly began to look bright, but also considerably problematic. Clearly, the municipalities were totally unprepared for major industrial developments: their nineteenth-century administrative and political organizations were unequal to the challenge posed by these new industrial initiatives. The provincial government was well aware of this, and, accordingly, in March 1969 the minister of municipal affairs established a special unit – the Haldimand–Norfolk Study – within his department. This unit was to be devoted to the problems, challenges, and opportunities facing the region. The Haldimand–Norfolk Study unit was complemented by the formation of a joint committee of the county councils of Haldimand and Norfolk.

The special Haldimand–Norfolk Study project group quickly identified two basic problems: first, how to accommodate a massive influx of steelworkers and their families; and, second (and most important), how to deal with the environmental effects both of the industrial operations themselves and of rapid population growth.

The potential environmental hazards appeared to be substantial. Atmospheric emissions from all three plants could endanger both human health and crops, which would also undermine the viability of farming by increasing land values. The immediate environmental effects of the industrial operations were addressed by a joint technical committee set up by the province and the industries. The role of the Haldimand–Norfolk Study was to examine the broader interactions among the industries, settlement, and the environment.

For this purpose, the study undertook a comprehensive "environmental appraisal" of a 5,000-square-kilometre area centred on the STELCO site. This appraisal was probably the most complete investigation pertaining to land-use planning carried out in Canada up to that time (Richardson 1989a, 21). It influenced the recommendations the Haldimand–Norfolk Study made for the location of future urban and industrial development; agricultural land use; conservation; and protection of historic, scenic, and recreational resources.

To some extent, the study was anticlimactic, since the expected massive population and employment growth in the region did not materialize. Nevertheless, the environmental appraisal and the land-use recommendations were used as guides by such provincial ministries as natural resources, environment, agriculture and food, and transportation. They were also used by the new regional municipality of Haldimand–Norfolk, the April 1974 creation of which was one of the specific outcomes of the Haldimand–Norfolk Study, in preparing its official regional plan.

Planning for a Special Natural Feature

Niagara Escarpment Plan and Commission

No single dramatic event, such as the advent of a dam or a steel mill, brought about the Niagara Escarpment Plan and Commission; rather, it came about as the result of a continual buildup of multiple land-use conflicts over a unique natural landscape. In view of the nature and location of the escarpment, such conflicts were (and remain) inevitable.

The Niagara Escarpment is a unique natural landscape, stretching nearly 700 kilometres from Queenston Heights near Niagara Falls to Tobermory at the northernmost tip of the Bruce Peninsula. Mostly a great limestone ridge, it runs across the highly productive agricultural lands of the Niagara Peninsula, around the industrialized and urbanized Golden Horseshoe in the Toronto region, and north through long-settled rural areas to Lake Huron. The escarpment has enormous scenic, scientific, and recreational value and is home to a variety of birds, mammals, reptiles and amphibians (many of them rare and endangered), fish species, and special-interest flora, including orchids. It is also home to the Bruce Trail, a remarkable environmental artifact founded solely by volunteers who wished to establish a hiking trail similar to Benton Mackaye's Appalachian Foot Trail in the United States.

In addition, the escarpment's specialized soft-fruit farming and vine-growing areas at the southern end of the Niagara Peninsula are the heart of the Ontario wine industry. Further, it skirts the western edge of a rapidly growing Toronto city-region. These very features made the escarpment worth preserving and, at the same time, made it conducive to urban development. For example, between 1961 and 1971, 23 percent of Niagara district farms, representing 16 percent of the fruit lands, were converted to urban use (Perks 1986, 485).

In 1967 public concern compelled the Ontario government to initiate a study of the Niagara Escarpment; this was followed in 1968 by the appointment of a study team of planners and geographers. As a result, in 1972 the Niagara regional municipality was created and an interministerial task force on the Niagara Escarpment was formed. In 1973, this led to the Niagara Escarpment Planning and Development Act, which created a seventeen-member permanent commission, at arm's length from the government, whose task was to produce an environmental plan "to provide for the maintenance of the Niagara Escarpment and lands in its vicinity substantially as a continuous natural environment and to ensure that only such development occurs as is compatible with the natural environment (Niagara Escarpment 1973)."

Even though by the time the plan received approval in 1980 the fruit belt was only half its original size, the Niagara Escarpment Plan and the various measures adopted to implement it are noteworthy achievements. A special feature of the Niagara Escarpment Plan was that the 2,400-square-kilometre region came under "development control" (which involves obtaining permits before conducting any form of land use) rather than traditional zoning. The jurisdictional milieu of the escarpment region comprises four regional governments, four counties, and thirty-seven municipalities. No development could take place without a development permit being issued by the commission, the membership of which was split equally between municipal appointees and the public. Municipal bylaws were made to conform to the escarpment plan, and a quasi-judicial tribunal was established to hear appeals against the commission's decisions. A public plan review was required every five years. Subsequent years have proved the worth of the plan and its implementing tools. One observer has concluded that, "if only for its mandate and harsh reality, the Escarpment plan must be judged a success ... [it] is making history, thanks to the natural environment. Its mere survival is a success" (Curtin 1994, 67). Moreover, the plan received international recognition when, in 1990, the United Nations seemed to give assent to its underlying philosophy by deeming the Escarpment worthy of being preserved as a UNESCO World Biosphere Reserve.

Planning a Provincial Land-Use Strategy

British Columbia's Commission on Resources and Environment
Although British Columbia is very large – its almost 950,000 square kilometres make it larger than the states of Washington, Oregon, and California combined – the province faces land-use pressures from many sources and interests. These include forestry, mining, oil and gas, agriculture, tourism,

conservation, settlements, and other land uses. In response to these challenges, in 1992 the provincial government established the independent British Columbia Commission on Resources and Environment (CORE) to develop a strategic land-use planning process and provincial land-use strategy. Its mandate emphasized economic, environmental, and social sustainability; public participation; and respect for Aboriginal rights. It was an attempt to resolve what, in some regions, had become bitter land-use conflicts between environmentalists and those who wished to exploit resources. The creation of CORE signalled an important government commitment to move British Columbia towards becoming a sustainable society. According to CORE (1993), the term "sustainable" means "capable of being maintained indefinitely."

Although CORE existed for only three years, having formally wound down on 31 March 1996, during its existence it achieved a number of significant successes with regard to fulfilling its original mandate:

- *a land-use strategy for British Columbia* (mid-1995), consisting of a comprehensive set of recommendations for government, including a provincial land-use charter, strategic land-use goals, a structure for the coordination of regional government programs, and community resource boards to increase local involvement in provincial land-use planning
- *strategic land-use plans* for the four most contentious areas of the province: the Cariboo–Chilcotin, the east Kootenays, the west Kootenays, and Vancouver Island; as well as laying the groundwork for ongoing local and regional land-use planning processes in those regions
- *development of subregional land and resource management plans,* designed to deal with land use and resource management at the subregional level, thus bringing together a diverse cross-section of people and interest groups in smaller regional settings.

Of special interest to regional planning practice is CORE's recognition of the regional and subregional aspects of land-use planning. In one of its publications, the *Strategic Land Use Planning Source Book* (BC CORE 1996), it posits a framework that provides a context and rationale for strategic land-use planning, including advice on the design and delivery of participatory planning processes. The framework is based on the idea that land-use planning takes place along a continuum that ranges from the general to the specific, from the global to the local, and that, in any given jurisdiction, a properly functioning planning system will produce plans at all points along the continuum. The result would be a holarchy[8] of plans; that is, a "nested set" of planning products, including plans, policies, and programs, each one encompassing those below and being encompassed by those above (BC CORE 1996). The land-use planning continuum is, of course, closely linked to the concept of scale, with the province at the top level of planning followed by regional and subregional

Figure 13

CORE's "Continuum of Resource Land Planning Levels"

PLANNING LEVEL	MAP SCALE	EXAMPLE	FEATURES/CHARACTERISTICS
Provincial Principles, goals, policies, and strategies	1:2,000,000	**British Columbia** 95,000 million hectares **East Kootenay region**	*Scope* — province-wide; influenced by national policies and international agreements *Products* — sustainability principles, land-use goals, land/resource laws/policies, sectoral strategies, sustainability indicators, and reports *Process* — provincially assisted; public participation to incorporate public preferences/priorities *Decisions* — Cabinet *BC examples* — Provincial Land Use Charter, Provincial Agricultural Land Reserve, Growth Strategies Act, Environmental Assessment Act, Protected Area Strategy, Forest Sector Strategy
Regional Plans and strategies	1:250,000 - 1:600,000	**East Kootenay region** 4.2 million hectares	*Scope* — region-wide; influenced by provincial laws and policies *Products* — broad land allocation, land/resource laws/policies, implementation/monitoring provisions, socio-economic transition, and mitigation measures *Process* — regionally based public participation, consensus-seeking negotiations *Decisions* — Cabinet *BC examples* — Vancouver Island Regional Land Use Plan, East and West Kootenay Regional Land Use Plans, Cariboo-Chilcotin Regional Land Use Plan, Georgia Basin Initiative

Strategic land use plans: "higher level plans"

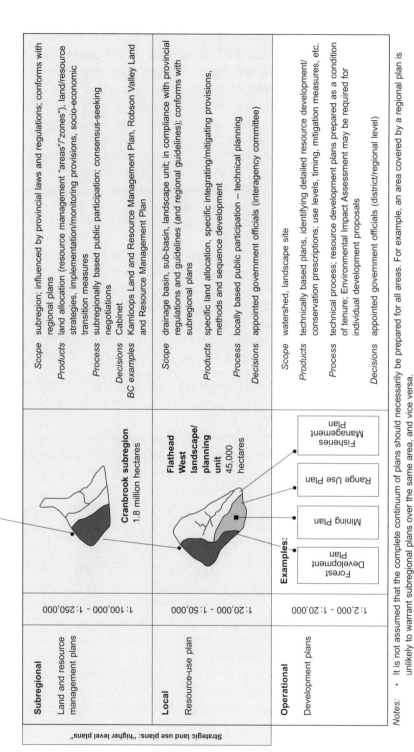

Strategic land use plans: "higher level plans"

Subregional — Land and resource management plans
1:100,000 - 1:250,000

Cranbrook subregion
1.8 million hectares

Scope — subregion; influenced by provincial laws and regulations; conforms with regional plans

Products — land allocation (resource management "areas"/"zones"), land/resource strategies, implementation/monitoring provisions, socio-economic transition measures

Process — subregionally based public participation; consensus-seeking negotiations

Decisions — Cabinet

BC examples — Kamloops Land and Resource Management Plan, Robson Valley Land and Resource Management Plan

Local — Resource-use plan
1:20,000 - 1:50,000

Flathead West landscape/planning unit
45,000 hectares

Scope — drainage basin, sub-basin, landscape unit; in compliance with provincial regulations and guidelines (and regional guidelines); conforms with subregional plans

Products — specific land allocation, specific integrating/mitigating provisions, methods and sequence development

Process — locally based public participation – technical planning

Decisions — appointed government officials (interagency committee)

Operational — Development plans
1:2,000 - 1:20,000

Examples: Forest Development Plan · Mining Plan · Range Use Plan · Fisheries Management Plan

Scope — watershed, landscape site

Products — technically based plans, identifying detailed resource development/ conservation prescriptions; use levels, timing, mitigation measures, etc.

Process — technical process; resource development plans prepared as a condition of tenure; Environmental Impact Assessment may be required for individual development proposals

Decisions — appointed government officials (district/regional level)

Notes:
- It is not assumed that the complete continuum of plans should necessarily be prepared for all areas. For example, an area covered by a regional plan is unlikely to warrant subregional plans over the same area, and vice versa.
- Local resource use plans may or may not, depending on the scope of the planning issues, be considered as "strategic" land-use plans.
- This figure does not identify urban region or community land-use planning, which is conducted primarily for private lands.

Source: Adapted from British Columbia, *Strategic Land Use Planning Source Book* (1996).

levels of planning. CORE's "Continuum of Resource Land Planning Levels" is reproduced in Figure 13. For each of the land planning levels it shows: the map scale to be used, an example taken from each level (including the regional and the subregional), and the main features and characteristics of each level (including the scope, products, process, and where decisions are made).

An integral aspect of British Columbia's land-use strategy involved preparing land and resource use plans for each region of the province. To ensure a balanced, sustainable pattern across the entire landscape, a region must be sufficiently large to accommodate the needs of all legitimate interest groups. According to BC planners and politicians, this objective can only be met fairly and efficiently through a negotiated, shared decision-making process in which all interests are recognized as having equal status, regardless of their authority or power.

In regions of the province where commission-led regional planning had not yet occurred, recommendations on protected area designations would result from land and resource management planning at the subregional level or from special studies. As we shall see below, the land and resource management plan was a public process undertaken by concerned ministries in close coordination with the commission. The ministries were committed to work with the commission to ensure that, when necessary, issues that require regional-level resolution were not compromised by more local-level plans. Recommendations concerning which areas were to be designated and managed as protected areas resulted from these processes and then were presented to Cabinet for approval.

In land-use negotiations in the four key regions, CORE provided an organizational framework based on widely accepted principles of interest-based negotiations. This framework consisted of the following steps: preparation, assessment, process design, agreement building, agreement implementation, and monitoring. (See CORE's 1992-3 *Annual Report*, 21-4, for details.) CORE was also assigned the task of recommending to the provincial Cabinet the location and extent of areas to be included in the protected areas network of the four key regions. In other regions recommendations on protected area designations were expected to result either from planning at the subregional level or from special studies. No timetable was set for land-use plans for the rest of the province.

In 1998, Vancouver Island was the first region in British Columbia for which the government announced that a comprehensive land-use plan would be in effect. The plan was the result of extensive consultation, initiated by CORE, with a wide range of local and regional interests. The plan created a number of protected areas and authorized setting aside a total of 13 percent of the land base for conservation and protection. This land-use decision also led to the establishment of forest land reserves (similar to the agricultural land reserves discussed earlier and in Chapter 5) on 81 percent of the land base composed of

Crown lands and private managed forest lands. The purpose of these reserves is to secure a source of timber in perpetuity for the many Island communities that depend on forestry for their economic livelihood. A set of three zones was established to allow for different degrees of timber extraction, depending on the sensitivity of an area's environment.

Complementing the work of CORE on regional land-use plans, in 1993 the BC government established a planning process for the formulation of land-use plans for subregions of the provincial regions. Known as the "land and resource management plan process," this plan brings together a diverse cross-section of people and interest groups in smaller regional settings. (See Ministry of Municipal Affairs and Housing 1997; and www.luco.gov.bc.ca, the "Muskwa-Kechika" Backgrounder.) The aim of the land and resource management plan is to work to develop land-use plans for Crown land that protect the natural environment while maintaining resource development and creating jobs. The Ministry of Municipal Affairs and Housing's Growth Strategies Office plays a key role in the process by ensuring that it allows for effective and appropriate local government involvement. To help achieve this, in November 1996 the ministry, in close consultation with the Union of BC Municipalities, adopted and published guidelines to assist local governments to participate effectively in the land and resource management plan process in their regions. As of January 2001, fourteen land and resource management plans were completed and six were under way; they cover the entire province.

Planning for Untapped Resource and Economic Potentials

The Peace River Region

North of the fiftieth parallel lies the Peace River region (generally known as the "Peace"), a huge area in northwest Canada that straddles two provinces – Alberta and British Columbia. This region is larger than the State of California (see Figure 14), and it takes its name from a river system that has a drainage basin extending nearly 1,000 kilometres northeast to Great Slave Lake. The total region in both provinces covers an area of more than 300,000 square kilometres and, in 1996, had an estimated population of about 200,000.[9] Its landscape, from the Rockies to the Prairies, is extremely dramatic, deserving to the fullest Alexander Mackenzie's historic characterization of it as "this magnificent theatre of nature" (Gertler and Crowley 1977, 197).

People who live south of the fiftieth probably do not realize that, while the Peace is more than 324 kilometres northwest of Edmonton, most of its agricultural area has a frost-free season (Gertler and Crowley 1977, 195). Indeed, the Peace is unique among northern regions in that it has a large supply of arable land, which has buffered the region's economy from wide fluctuations (as is typical of most other northern regions) and shaped a fairly extensive network of agricultural service centres. In 1996 the largest ones were, on the Alberta

Figure 14

The Peace River Region in the context of western North America

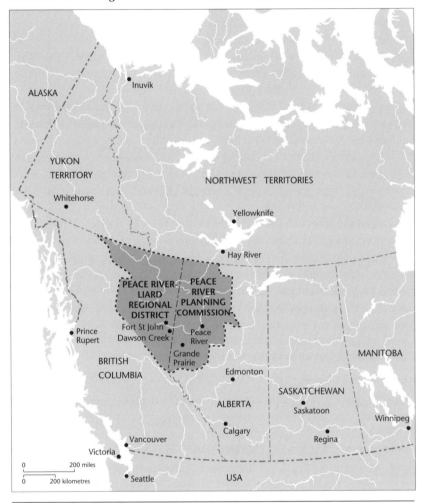

Source: Modified from Peace River–Liard Regional District 1972; Peace River Regional Planning Commission (1973).

side, Grande Prairie (28,371) and Peace River (6,717); and, on the BC side, Dawson Creek (10,981) and Fort St. John (14,156). In addition to its agricultural sector, the region also has the benefit of a diverse array of other resources, including energy, wood, industrial metals, and fresh water. Another factor in the Peace's favour is its strong regional identity: "Its original isolated nature gave its inhabitants a great feeling of attachment, identity and solidarity with the Region" (Peace River Planning Commission 1973, 4).

Interest in the region's planning and resource development goes back at least four decades. In a paper presented at the Resources for Tomorrow Conference, Robinson (1961)[10] concluded that both the Alberta and BC sides of the region should be viewed, planned, and developed comprehensively; that is, they should be treated as a single region. At that time, departments of the respective provincial government shared responsibility for dealing with the problems and challenges of the region; there was no single agency or ministry coordinating government activities in either of the provinces, much less for the region as a whole. Establishment of a special "authority" for the entire region was seen as the most desirable thing to do, even though this would constitute a politically difficult precedent in the Canadian areal division of power. As an alternative, the establishment of a joint Cabinet committee composed of the interested ministers of both provinces, together with their respective provincial planning offices, was proposed (Robinson 1961).

But it was not until a decade later that planning authorities on both the Alberta and BC sides of the region became involved in extensive planning activities, unfortunately independently of each other. A regional district was formed in British Columbia in 1965 – the Peace River–Liard Regional District – with responsibility for regional planning, hospital development and administration, and any other municipal functions delegated to the district. (See Chapter 9 for a description of British Columbia's regional districts.) On the Alberta side, the Peace River Regional Planning Commission was set up in 1958, representing twelve rural units, twenty-three urban municipalities, and four provincial departments.

The approach of Alberta's Peace River Regional Planning Commission's planners was to recognize the region's impressive existing and potential capacity for a wide range of resource and economic developments. They were also aware, thanks to a series of surveys, that residents particularly cherished the region's high environmental quality. Indeed, from the outset, the planners aimed to give voice to the attitudes and preferences of the "People of the Peace" with regard to the future direction of the region's development. Consequently, the challenge facing the region, as articulated in the 1972 preliminary regional policy plan, was to participate in increasingly global economic forces without jeopardizing the quality of the environment and community life. The challenge was how to accommodate resource and economic development within environmental limits at a human scale.[11]

Accordingly, the plan featured a section on environmental quality and policies, drawing attention to the importance of considering watershed, air shed, solid waste disposal, and other environmental conditions when evaluating development proposals. The region's senior planner noted that opportunities to test the plan were limited and that specific developments had received only mixed success (Wight 1980).

The policy plan did not attempt either to forecast growth or to allocate land among competing uses and was, therefore, a major departure from the tradition established by earlier plans (Gertler and Crowley 1977). Instead, it attempted to apply a set of guiding policies and to establish a process that would assist the commission and member municipalities in making key decisions. To assist in the discussion of alternatives and to make the choices clear, the planners developed a number of scenarios for the region. In turn, three development models were prepared, each reflecting a different approach towards the development of resources. The commission preferred a model in which resources development and conservation were balanced.

While generally praising the policy plan, Gertler and Crowley (1977) argued that planning in the Peace River Region had been constrained by two limitations. The first was that the relationship between the Alberta and BC halves of the larger region had not been treated comprehensively (thus concurring with Robinson's 1961 assessment); the second was that the national implications of the region's development had been given scant attention.

Gertler and Crowley argued that, although this "natural region" falls within two provincial jurisdictions, this should not preclude unified resource inventories, economic studies, and joint policy development. They further acknowledged that, by taking a comprehensive view, the potential for development would be enormous. They felt strongly that the full and coordinated development of the south-central portion of the region, including both provincial sides of the Peace, would be the key to releasing the potential of the region. However, at that time, just as was noted a decade and a half earlier, there was no mechanism for that kind of joint provincial regional planning (Harker 1975, 8-9; cited by Gertler and Crowley 1977, 443-4; Robinson 1961).

With regard to the second limitation, Gertler and Crowley noted that the plan generally discusses the prospects for the Peace from the point of view of the region. However, they argued, a region of the size and significance of the Peace should surely have a place in the broad strategy of Canada-wide development. In fact, this point was raised by the Peace River–Liard District (British Columbia) in its 1972 request for designation under the federal Regional Incentives Act (discussed in Chapter 6); it argued that maintaining the vitality of semi-urban and rural areas, such as the Peace, should be viewed as a necessary counterweight to the huge population increases then expected in the country's urban centres (Peace River–Liard Regional District 1972; cited in Gertler and Crowley 1977, 210-11). The national implications of this approach – of fostering development of regions such as the Peace in order to take the heat off areas under urban pressure – had hardly begun to be addressed in urban and regional economic policies at that time. This offers a clear example of one of the fundamental tensions in regional planning – the need to accommodate both local perspectives (i.e., seeing the region from the inside) and national perspectives (i.e., seeing the region from the outside)(see Chapter 3).

New Towns on the Resource Frontier

The bulk of Canada's population (about 90 percent) is concentrated in a narrow belt of land hugging the Canada–US border. Exploitable resources, however – whether underground, on the surface, or in the water – are mainly located north of this populated belt, in an area that lacks settlement and has a consequent shortage of labour at or near most sites of resource development. Thus, in order to exploit these resources, throughout Canada's history it has been necessary to create wholly new townsites – "new towns," as it were – in these isolated areas in order to house workers and their families. These new resource towns, built and usually planned from scratch and dispersed throughout the country's resource hinterland, constitute a unique characteristic of settlement in Canada. They are typically one-industry communities, having come into being by fiat of a single enterprise (usually a private industrial company, although sometimes a government agency) that is engaged in the extraction or primary processing of a non-agricultural resource such as power, oil, gas, metals, fish, or timber. As noted in Chapter 1, many of the earlier towns were sponsored by Canadian industrialists who visited (or had their architect or planner visit) some of the model British new towns planned and built by British businesspeople and philanthropists before or just after 1900.

The most active period of new resource town building was between 1945 and 1958, when nearly fifty such towns came into being, from Kitimat, British Columbia, in the west to Schefferville, Quebec, in the east (Robinson 1962). Although they are located in the resource frontier regions north of the long-settled regions of the south, these towns are not usually connected with one another but, rather, with southern cities. While they are important access points to regions with valuable resources, their dispersed pattern has discouraged more extensive development and settlement of such regions. As for the towns themselves, Robinson (1962) found that one of their key features was economic instability due to their boom-and-bust pattern of growth. Many did not survive the "bust." To deal with this situation, Robinson made two proposals: first, coordinate the development of the several small settlements in a region to permit them, for example, to share certain services and amenities and to moderate the effect of instability in any one town; and, second, establish regional planning agencies for these resource regions so that they can develop their resources for the betterment of the settlements, the region as a whole, and other regions.

Gertler and Crowley (1977) note the complementarity of the frontier resource town and the frontier resource region as well as the national interest in developing "mid-Canada." It is difficult, however, to make this regional strategy a national agenda item because control over resources, and hence over their royalties, is vested in the individual provinces.

Protecting Regional Resource Environments

The sentiments of the long-lived conservation movement were transformed in the 1970s into those of the environmental movement, with its broader concern for the natural environment. No longer was designating specified resource areas for protection seen as sufficient. The publication of Rachel Carson's *Silent Spring* in 1962 had awakened the public to the implications of "chemical agriculture"; and, in its wake, concerns emerged over industrial water and air pollution, unsound waste disposal, destructive logging, and a host of other deleterious environmental practices. The roots of this concern may be traced to those who, in the nineteenth century, espoused the need for clean water and parks. But the imprudent earlier practices in resource development that so upset the conservationists were now more widespread and complex in their impacts. The spatial venue of concern about environmental deterioration was still much the same as before – the region. Since the impacts of resource development are regional in scope, the perspective for environmental protection must also be regional.

The environmental movement of the 1960s spawned so much legislation in Canada during the 1970s that this period has been characterized as the "environmental decade." The legislation was not restricted to the physical and biological environment; it was recognized that there was a need to assess the regional, social, and economic impacts of resource development projects. For example, various inquiries into northern energy development priorities were given mandates to examine social, cultural, and economic as well as environmental concerns. The Berger inquiry (1977) into the practicality and desirability of installing oil and gas pipelines in the Mackenzie River Valley was the most visible and precedent-setting. As a consequence of this inquiry, the National Energy Board now reviews the full spectrum of impacts when deciding whether to issue a certificate of Public Convenience and Necessity for a pipeline. Furthermore, several provinces instituted similar broad reviews for resource development projects (e.g., British Columbia, Alberta, Ontario, Quebec, Manitoba).

The environmental movement was important to regional planning, not least because it heightened awareness among the public, politicians, and government officials, as well as among planners, of the extensive web of relationships affected by resource development. This was precisely what Geddes had posited three-quarters of a century ago (see Chapter 1). In addition, regional planning practice benefited from the wide array of tools, techniques, and institutionalized means that became available with the move to better manage natural resources.

Conservation Strategies

In the late 1970s and early 1980s it became increasingly clear that there was a need for some unifying concept under which to put all of the activities we have been discussing (e.g., resource development, protected areas, environmental protection) – activities whose ultimate objectives were, if not identical, at least very closely linked (Richardson 1994, 64). It took the International Union for the Conservation of Nature and Natural Resources (IUCN), established in 1980, with its World Conservation Strategy (WCS), which was published by three international conservation groups, to provide such a unifying concept. The WCS recognized that environmental protection and resource development can be complementary more often than is usually depicted. In essence, a "conservation strategy" came to mean a comprehensive approach to the conservation of renewable resources, based on the WCS's three goals for sustainable development: (1) maintaining essential ecological processes and life support systems, (2) preserving genetic diversity, and (3) ensuring the sustainable use of species and ecosystems. Later, in Canada, the National Task Force on Environment and Economy proposed a fourth objective: maintaining and improving the quality of life in the urban environment.

To accomplish these goals, the WCS recommended that conservation strategies be developed at the national, subnational, and local levels. Although the WCS focused on the conservation of ecological processes, it recognized that this could not be achieved without a broader set of changes. Thus, it recommended that conservation strategies encompass environmental, social, and economic goals. In Canada, conservation strategies have been developed in many jurisdictions, typically through extensive consultation and collective decision making among a variety of community and governmental organizations. The most effective strategies are those that have:

- incorporated a broad range of social, economic, and environmental factors in the definition of sustainability
- been developed through a "bottom-up" method of consultation
- included recommendations for all public agencies operating within the planning unit (Tomalty et al. 1994, 96).

In these ways, Tomalty et al. argue, conservation strategies and ecosystem planning have many features in common (see later discussion).

Most conservation strategies in Canada have been developed at the provincial or national level, accepting existing jurisdictional boundaries rather than using regional or ecosystem planning units. In contrast, Nelson (1991, 261) has argued that conservation strategies based on regional or ecosystem boundaries should be developed at the local or regional levels, and he argues for the use of the watershed or river basin. In Ontario, Nelson's advice seems to have been followed, for natural boundary conservation strategies have been undertaken for the Grand River, Rideau River, and Maitland River basins. At the provincial level, perhaps the only conservation strategy developed along natural boundary lines so far has been the one for Prince Edward Island – the first and in some ways still the most exemplary provincial effort (for details, see Tomalty et al. 1994, 96-8).

Planning Tools and Techniques for Regional Environments

As environmental awareness increased so, too, did the need for tools and techniques to assess more precisely the characteristics and capacity of natural environments. Fortuitously, major new technical and conceptual tools were appearing at the same time, thus facilitating better measurements of environmental phenomena and better understanding of ecological relations.

Canada Land Inventory

Technically, the Canada Land Inventory (CLI) predated the environmental movement, having been spawned in the early 1960s under the federal Agricultural Rehabilitation and Development Act. At the time, there was no uniform method for rating the quality of land for various types of farm activity, nor was there an inventory of how much of each class of land existed and where it was located, which would be necessary in order to judge development projects brought forth under ARDA provisions. As a consequence, a federal-provincial program was initiated in 1963 to develop such an inventory for the entire country. Within ARDA's statutory framework, an agreement was reached in 1963 to initiate the CLI as a federal-provincial program. (The inventory was later transferred to the Lands Directorate of Environment Canada when that department was established in 1970.)

The CLI was both a comprehensive land capability survey and an "index" for arriving at a measure of the capability of any land area. The overall goal of the inventory was to facilitate adjustments in land use and to improve the basis for regional land-use planning.[12] The goal would be achieved by undertaking surveys and classifying lands according to their inherent productive capability for use in agriculture, forestry, recreation, and wildlife production (ungulates and waterfowl). By mapping the approximate extent and location of each class, and by encouraging their use, regional land use and resource planning would be enhanced. CLI data were used to prepare early regional plans for British Columbia's regional districts and, most notably, in the designation of agricultural land reserves by the province's Agricultural Land Commission.

CLI planners recognized that the program would generate massive amounts of data, and it was thus essential to develop a versatile computerized data storage, processing, and retrieval system. Appropriate technological capabilities and systems designs allowed the Canadian Geographic Information System (CGIS) to become operational in 1972. The CGIS accepted data from both maps and statistical tables and allowed comparisons between sectors or between geographic regions to be displayed. It also allowed planners to correlate socioeconomic with biophysical and other data from secondary sources (Rees 1979, 162).

Other outgrowths of the CLI included a national biophysical land classification program designed to differentiate and classify ecologically significant segments of the land surface both rapidly and at a small scale, to serve as the ecological basis for classification and rating for rural areas, and to help with resource planning in general. In 1971, with the expansion of oil, gas, and mineral exploration in Canada's North, the need for environmental impact studies initiated another program, known as the Northern Land Use Information Program (Perks 1986, 478). This program was joined by the Canada Land Use Monitoring Program, initiated in 1978, to monitor the amount, location, and type of land-use change on national and regional scales. This was done on a five-year period basis in urban regions (including the rural-urban fringes) and on a ten-year period basis in rural and prime resource areas.

Environmental Impact Assessment

Most observers, including its critics, will admit that one of the truly outstanding contributions of the North American environmental movement has been the refinement of environmental impact assessment (EIA) techniques. These techniques have become much more inclusive and sophisticated: they have gradually moved from concentrating on developing inventories of environmental features and identifying specific individual impacts (typically only for biophysical phenomena) to being more explicitly value-laden and systematically emphasizing ecological realities; a concern for valued ecosystem components; and the inclusion of social, economic, and cultural factors as well as biophysical factors. Likewise, the evolution of EIA legislation has moved towards greater openness and empowerment of public participants, broader application and more critical examination of proposals in light of alternatives, and more comprehensive consideration of effects.

EIA, as a distinct formal process, first appeared in Canada in 1973, four years after it appeared in the United States. It was referred to as the "federal environmental assessment and review process," and its objective was to "ensure that the environmental effects of federal projects, programs and activities [were] assessed early in their planning, before any commitments or irrevocable decisions [were] made" (Munn 1979, 107). To implement these objectives, the Federal Environmental Assessment Review Office was established. Reviews of proposed development projects are conducted by panels of experts chaired by the executive chair of the assessment review office or a delegate. A panel issues guidelines to the project proponent, who then presents an environmental impact statement.

Since 1973, every province has adopted some form of assessment procedure, though, in scope and effectiveness, it varies considerably from province to province. In some cases, by dropping the word "impact," certain provinces have broadened the meaning of "environment" and "assessment" – at least in theory – and incorporated them into project planning. The provinces can require impact assessments for projects involving resource development, municipal development, or provincial funding. As a general rule, however, the provinces have required impact assessments mainly for large resource projects. In practice, this dual provincial-federal system of review sometimes results in duplication, confusion, and inefficiency. Nevertheless, there is probably no large mega-construction project carried out in Canada today that has not been evaluated, either provincially and/or federally, for its likely effects on the biophysical environment. It should be noted that environmental impact statements have been the subject of considerable controversy regarding their desirability, their technical competence, their political effectiveness, and even their legality (Munn 1979; Jacobs and Sadler n.d.). This controversy will probably continue for some time, often because EIAs have made the planning process surrounding resource development much more transparent to a wide range of interests.

Cumulative Effects Assessment

A recent extension of the EIA approach is known as cumulative effects assessment (CEA). The Ontario Ministry of Environment and Energy sponsored a cumulative effects monitoring program for the Niagara Escarpment Plan to ensure that incremental changes permitted on the escarpment do not accumulate to produce unacceptable levels of change. Specifically, the monitoring system is designed (1) to monitor the state and functioning of ecosystems along the escarpment, (2) to assess the short- and long-terms effects of Niagara Escarpment plan policies, and (3) to provide the environmental data in a form that can be used to support changes through plan amendments and future plan reviews (Tomalty et al. 1994, 46.)

CEA is well suited to help a community or region choose among possible development scenarios as it is designed to evaluate the environmental impacts of the large number of activities attendant upon any development (Tomalty et al. 1994, 45). Cumulative effects may be measured using a variety of existing techniques, including mapping and overlays, risk assessment, trend analysis and forecasting, weighting and evaluation techniques, cluster impact assessment, and bioregionalism theory. However, despite the technique's great potential, most established environmental assessment processes in Canada are narrowly conceived and applied (Tomalty et al. 1994, 115). Early and open assessment of alternatives is rarely required, and integration into policy making and planning is still rare.

The use and application of EIA or CEA is undoubtedly an important step towards effective protection of regional environments. Richardson (1994, 67) argues that had CEA been integrated into existing land-use planning systems, as has generally been the case in most parts of Europe, it might have avoided a host of jurisdictional and administrative tangles. However, environmental assessment remains separated from the older, municipally based processes on the one hand and from other regional planning activities on the other.[13]

State-of-the-Environment Reporting

A recent technique that emerged from the environmental movement is known as state-of-the-environment reporting. Specifically, it evolved out of the demand for knowledge about environmental conditions and trends. State-of-the-environment reporting tends to take the form of "indicators" that allow the concise and consistent measurement of environmental conditions. They show trends and provide a vehicle for the comprehensive assessment of all aspects of the environment. They also allow public officials (and the public) to monitor progress towards defined environmental goals and offer guidance for policy development and planning.

In 1987, the Province of Ontario produced a state-of-the-environment report. Since then a number of Ontario regional municipalities have followed suit. These reports aggregate pre-existing information on a range of environmental conditions and dangerous situations. They are usually organized around the major elements of the environment (air, water, and land) and are relevant to a broad range of policy issues (water management, wildlife management, pollution control). In 1992, the City of Toronto produced a state-of-the-city report covering an extended range of issues, including socioeconomic and human health factors. British Columbia published a state-of-the-environment report in 1994.

One of the important outcomes of the state-of-the-environment work is the development of a terrestrial ecological framework, involving a nested hierarchy of ecozones, ecoregions, and ecodistricts as the spatial reporting units at the national and provincial levels. Instead of the traditional single-sector approach to reporting and analysis, this framework provides a holistic description of ecosystems that integrates elements such as surface vegetation cover, underlying geology, physiography, hydrology, soil, and climate. The challenge is to collect scientific data using these reporting units and disseminate the interpreted information in such a way that it will be easily accessible and meet the needs of Canadians and policy makers for improving decision making and advancing towards a sustainable environment (Tomalty et al. 1994, 113).

Towards a Synthesis:
In Pursuit of Integrated Regional Resource Development

The environmental movement served to raise awareness in academic and professional circles, leading to the much more sophisticated and sensitive monitoring tools described above. Equally important has been the increased public awareness of environmental matters[14] and the relations between the environment and other social and economic factors, not to mention the call for more inclusive decision-making processes. This forced politicians, at both local and international levels, to acknowledge environmental concerns and to deal with them. The result has been several new assessment processes, such as EIA and CEA. More recently, the approach to environmental planning has been transformed into new and more inclusive concepts and processes. On the conceptual side, bioregionalism, sustainable development, and ecosystems planning are increasingly guiding planning for regional land use and resource development. Using these concepts, several recent, deliberate efforts to join the future of resource use with land-use planning as well as with environmental protection are exemplified by the work of British Columbia's CORE process and by the planning for the Fraser River Basin. More and more, multi-stakeholder settings are being used for decision making. Consequently, these and other new approaches are leading towards a truly integrated approach to regional land use and resource development. We shall conclude this chapter with a discussion of some of these new concepts and approaches.

Round Tables

With the recognition that environmental concerns cut across disciplines and jurisdictions and have multi-disciplinary and multi-jurisdictional qualities came the recognition that many interests would have to be involved in dealing with them. It soon became abundantly clear that the two central interests that must be reconciled were manifested in those who wished to preserve and protect resource environments and those who wished to develop those same resources. Thus, there emerged ways of bringing these interests, and others, to the same table. The term "round table" was used to convey the notion of egalitarian decision making.

Almost all provinces and territories have formed such round tables, following the lead of the federal government and its National Round Table on the Environment and the Economy. In turn, a host of local and regional round tables have been formed. Typically, they are composed of government officials along with representatives of industry, environmental organizations, academia, and the public. Among the most active have been the round tables in British Columbia, including one struck in 1990 for the region surrounding the province's capital city, Victoria, known as the Capital Regional District Round Table on the Environment. This twenty-one-member advisory group provides input to the regional district's board of directors on environmental issues and projects affecting the environment and also recommends solutions to the board.

Since 1994, one of the main projects of the Victoria region round table has been to identify thirteen environmental priorities for the region and a set of forty-one statistical indicators to track the conditions and trends for each priority. In June 1997 it issued a report representing Phase 1 of its work (Westland Resource Group 1997) on conditions and trends in the region covering the following array of topics: settlement patterns, use of infrastructure and resources, land-based habitat, wetlands and water bodies, pollutants in the marine shoreline environment, marine shoreline habitat, marine life, greenhouse gas emissions, stratospheric ozone levels, ground level ozone, smoke that affects visibility and human health, toxic contamination, and drinking water quality. This extensive list is indicative of the perspective through which regional planners now need to be considering the environment and its resources.

The Victoria experience is also instructive of the difficulty to communicate such a broad and complex perspective, for when the regional district issued its own preliminary regional growth strategy, which was used as the basis of public workshops, no reference was made to the round table's report. Thus, the unfortunate separation between those responsible for a region's land-use planning, its environmental planning, and its economic planning continued here as elsewhere.

New Concepts and Approaches

Bioregionalism

Over the past two decades, the principles of bioregionalism have made a strong impact on research and practice in a wide variety of disciplines associated with regional studies and regional planning. Its holistic approach has provided an umbrella for geographers, ecologists, community development practitioners, and regional planners alike. In places as distant from one another as the Toronto waterfront and the Kitimat–Stikine region in northwest British Columbia, its tenets and principles have been invoked (Chapter 1).

Bioregionalism's principles include a belief that natural (as opposed to political or administrative) regions should be the organizing units for human activity; that a land ethic should be applied at regional and local scales; and that regionally (and locally) diverse cultures are the guarantors of environmental adaptation (Alexander 1990). One of the "fathers" of the bioregionalism movement, Kirkpatrick Sale (1985, 43), has given perhaps the most concise definition of a bioregion: "[It is] a place defined by its life forms, its topography and its biota, rather than by human dictates; a region governed by nature, not legislature."

Bioregionalists believe that nation-states and other administrative divisions are artificial constructs, and they advocate "living-in-place," which means "following the necessities and pleasures of life as they are uniquely presented by a particular site, and evolving ways to ensure long-term occupancy of that site" (Berg and Dasmann 1978, 217). It is, in short, a belief system that has a profound effect on contemporary regional affairs. For example, bioregionalism was a major influence on the work of the 1992 Crombie Royal Commission on the Future of the Toronto Waterfront (see Chapter 9). And its popularity led to the use of the term "bioregion" in the context of the Greater Toronto Area (Figure 15 shows the region defined as the Greater Toronto Bioregion). In its uniting of insights from ecology and economics as well as cultural studies, bioregionalism offers practical ways to create a sustainable economy on a regional basis and, at the same time, retain a healthy sense of community and place (Tomalty et al. 1994; see also Chapters 2 and 3).

The most serious obstacle to implementation of the bioregionalism concept is the fact that local and regional economies are increasingly tied to provincial, national, and international markets. Trade agreements and other international initiatives also tend to influence governmental decision making to move further away from the community and regional level. Possibilities for bioregional self-determination are therefore restricted, and bioregional identity is increasingly threatened. Another obstacle to bioregionalism is the fact that a large segment of the public does not understand the concept.

Ecosystems Planning

Ecosystems planning has its origins in the scientific discipline of ecology, and its first application was in resource management and parks planning. The concept has slowly begun to permeate regional and resource planning (as well as urban planning) in Canada and elsewhere. So far, it has not solidified as a recognized specific type of planning or set of planning practices. However, planning initiatives that focus on ecosystem planning concerns are growing and are evident in many different places.

If not the first formal application of ecosystems planning at a regional level in Canada, then certainly one of the most influential, has been that of the Royal Commission on the Future of the Toronto Waterfront (the Crombie Commission). Its 1990 interim report, entitled "Watershed," marked a new stage in the history of ecosystem planning in Canada (see also Chapter 9); until that time, the notion of ecosystem planning was little known outside professional or citizen planning circles. The interim report recognized that what was happening on the waterfront reflected what was happening upstream in the region's watersheds, which empty into Lake Ontario.

In addition to its use by the Crombie Commission, at about the same time a number of regional studies and plans prepared in Ontario used the ecosystem approach (e.g., in the regional municipality of Ottawa–Carleton [see Hostovsky et al. 1995] and the town of Markham on Toronto's fringe), emphasizing restoration of ecological diversity and integrating it with cultural patterns and

Figure 15

Greater Toronto Bioregion

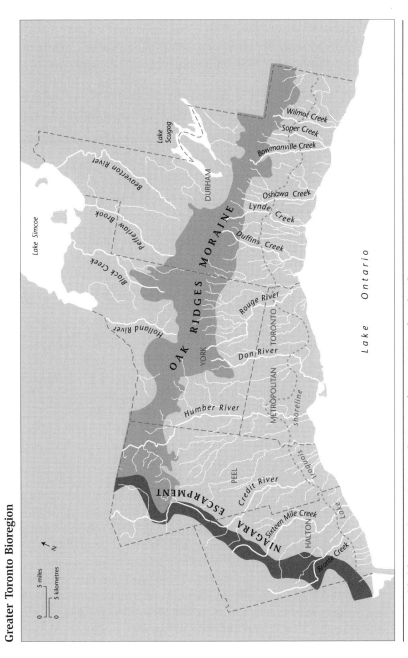

Source: Modified from Royal Commission on the Future of Toronto's Waterfront (1992).

environmental protection (Tamminga 1996). The recent plan for the Greenbelt surrounding Ottawa took a similar approach in its efforts to create a "connected ecological system" (Scott 1996). In a comprehensive report, Tomalty et al. (1994) demonstrate how the ecosystem planning concept can be used to develop a planning framework for managing growth in Canada's urbanized regions.

In its final report, entitled "Regeneration," the Crombie Commission articulated the principles of ecosystems planning as follows. An ecosystem approach:

- includes the whole system, not only parts of it
- focuses on the interrelationships among the elements
- understands that human beings are a part of nature, not separate from it
- recognizes the dynamic nature of the ecosystem, presenting a moving picture rather than a still photograph
- incorporates the concepts of carrying capacity, resilience, and sustainability, implying that there are limits to human activity
- uses a broad definition of human environment – natural, physical, economic, social, and cultural
- accepts the fact that economic health and environmental health are not mutually exclusive but mutually dependent
- encompasses both urban and rural activities
- is based on natural geographic units such as watersheds rather than on political boundaries
- embraces all levels of activity – local, regional, national, and international
- emphasizes the importance of species other than humans and of generations other than the present
- is based on an ethic in which progress is measured by the quality, wellbeing, integrity, and dignity it accords the natural, social, and economic system.

While conventional planning tends to treat human society – its economy and its built forms – as separable from nature, the ecosystem approach to planning sees the human-built world as part of the natural world and recognizes its dependence upon, and responsibility towards, nature. The ecosystem approach gives substance to the words of the famous wildlife biologist Aldo Leopold (1969, 403) who, half a century ago, said that the new land ethic "changes the role of Homo Sapiens from conqueror of the land-community to plain members and citizens of it." A contemporary Canadian planner sees it as a step towards a new form of regionalism that he refers to as "eco-regionalism" (Wight 1996).

A recent development in the environmental and ecology movements has been the realization that decisions about issues affecting the earth are driven as much by practical concerns as by "high-minded" motives. The scientific community is accumulating an increasing body of evidence indicating that biodiversity, for example, is, at every level, as good for our wallets as it is for our spirits. An important contribution to this awareness is a recently published book entitled *The Quest for a Sustainable World* (Raven 2000). In it, a number of authors explore the economic benefits of maintaining diverse natural ecosystems and cite a number of vivid examples demonstrating the "bottom-line" value of biological preservation.

Sustainable Development

The strongest conceptual thrust for regional and other territorial planners at the present time is that of "sustainable development." Since the 1980s, it has become increasingly recognized that squandering our natural capital is neither good business nor sound economics (Daly and Cobb 1989; Jacobs 1991). The cost of restoration is inevitably higher than the cost of prevention. Thus, it came to be realized that environmental protection could not be relied upon as a brake on development or as an "add-on" to secure project approvals. Ultimately, the view that economic growth and environmental quality were mutually exclusive came to be challenged at the international level, leading to the establishment of the World Commission on Environment and Development (i.e., the Brundtland Commission). Sustainable development was the pivotal concept of the Brundtland Commission's 1987 report, entitled *Our Common Future,* which rejected the then dominant argument that economic growth and environmental quality were mutually exclusive. Furthermore, it challenged the prevailing "wisdom" that economic growth could be achieved only in a trade-off with the environment.

In the same year as the Brundtland Commission report, the Canadian National Task Force on the Environment and the Economy issued its report in which it stated: "Our economic system should maintain and increase our resource and environmental base so the generations that follow will be able to live equally well or better" (National Task Force on the Environment 1987, 20). This is often interpreted as "living on the interest without depleting the capital" (Richardson 1994, 65) – a fairly straightforward idea and one with which early twentieth-century conservationists were quite familiar (see Chapter 1).

Sustainable development is a term that has common currency in political and academic discourse as well as in the broader public vocabulary, but is not easily translated into actual policies, plans, programs, and regulations. Moreover, its precise meaning has been the subject of much debate – not least in planning and professional circles. For example, Orr (1992, 23) claims that the World Commission and its definition "politely appeased both sides of the debate" in that the word "sustainable" pacifies environmentalists, while the word "development" pacifies businesspeople and bankers. Moreover, he argues, the phrase "sustainable development" raises as many questions as it answers. It presumes that we know or can discover levels and thresholds of environmental carrying capacity; that is, we can say what is sustainable and what is not. Nevertheless, despite the different visions of a sustainable society and how to achieve it, we cannot deny the power of the basic concept.

In the search for resolution, many see the region as a key element in strategies for sustainable development. Roberts (1994), for one, argues that the region is the most suitable level of spatial organization from which to tackle both ecological and economic problems. Cohen (1993), in considering individual urban areas in less-developed countries, concludes that they are just too small to cope with the trans-municipal incidence of environmental and economic problems. He argues that this implies the need to strengthen regional government. Stohr (1990) agrees and says that, in order to intervene in an effective manner so as to achieve sustainability in any given nation, an integrated policy must be developed at the "meso level," or regional level. As the term "meso level" implies, this policy would be influenced from both above and below. According to Elkin et al. (1991), urban sprawl and the inherent environmental inefficiencies of many spatial forms suggest that individual areas working in isolation from one another are unlikely to generate satisfactory sustainable solutions. An integrated sustainable development policy, they say, requires that:

- the levels of pollution emitted and the demands made on resources be reduced
- the transport required for the distribution of materials, goods, and services be reduced
- waste and pollution resulting from consumption be reduced
- economic development that contributes to environmental sustainability be promoted.

More recently, the terms "sustainable urban development," "urban sustainability," "sustainable cities," and "healthy cities" have emerged as leading concepts in the debate surrounding urban issues, but here, too, views differ concerning the precise meaning of these terms.[15] These have led back to the region, which, again, is being seen as the key level for planning and strategic action. Breheny and Rookwood (1993) argue, for example, that, in dealing with urban sustainability, the basic unit for the development of appropriate environmental strategies and standards should be the whole "interdependent regional complex," or the equivalent of what we have called the "city-region," which, adapting the terminology used by Ebenezer Howard (see Chapter 1), they christen the "Social City Region."

In pursuit of future sustainability, what is needed, they say, is a whole set of distinctive policies attuned to the varying conditions and environmental potential of the different settlement types and parts of the city-region (i.e., their "Social City Region"). At the same time, these policies should be complementary and reinforcing (156). Breheny and Rookwood use a six-part typology – city centres, city inner areas, city suburbs, small towns and new communities, mixed urban-rural areas, and remote rural areas – and discuss the appropriate development strategies for attaining sustainability in these different parts of the region. And, for the city-region, or "Social City Region," as a whole, they discuss the changes required for future sustainability with respect to natural resources, land use and transport, energy, and pollution and waste (158). They also include a "Checklist for Monitoring Progress" towards achieving sustainability. This checklist can be applied in each of the six separate parts of the region as well as in the region as a whole (159-60).

Reflections

Until recently, almost all of the activities, policies, and programs in conservation, resource development, and the environment discussed in this chapter have tended to be pursued independently, generally with little or no coordination. There was often, over the past century, tension between the conservationists (and, later, the environmentalists) on the one hand, and those favouring resource development for economic growth on the other. This should not be unexpected, either in the past or in the future, for major value differences are at its root. Many times resource use and development was undertaken without reference to global or regional environmental capacities. And proponents of environmental protection and conservation often promoted control of resource development, seemingly without paying heed to the role of economic development in meeting human material needs. These tensions are inevitable and, paradoxically, are a product of our greater understanding of both economic development and ecosystems (Eisenberg 1998).

Nonetheless, it is encouraging that the history of this facet of regional planning shows definite signs, if not of reconciliation, at least of acceptance of these contending positions. Greater general awareness of environmental conditions brought with it the need for new descriptive and analytical tools, which, in turn, directed our attention to the complexities faced and the implications of the choices made. The need to confront the tension between the environment and the economy will continue because society's needs for natural resources are not about to disappear.

As well, outstanding differences of opinion over new concepts still need to be resolved, and new concepts arising from new understanding will bring new challenges. For example, even if agreement could be reached on the meaning of "sustainable development," regional planners and other policy makers would still face difficulties administering the various activities associated with conservation, resource development, and the environment, then, in turn, linking those with regional land-use planning and regional economic development planning. Presently, these various planning functions are poorly integrated in terms of institutional structure and process, and they entail jurisdictional and administrative tangles that are still to be solved. And, as we noted earlier, in his survey of twentieth-century planning for conservation and the environment Richardson (1994) concluded that environmental planners might have made even more progress had their work been integrated into existing regional (and local) land-use planning systems, as it had been in most parts of Europe.

Some of this dilemma can be resolved by agreeing on the proper venue from which to address environmental, natural resource development, economic growth, and land-use issues. Thus, it is encouraging that the region will continue to be the spatial unit of choice for planning, for the regional venue is, by definition, an integral part of resource development and environmental activities. However, this would not be the regional planning practice of old; rather, it would have to incorporate new concepts about the environment and ecosystems and new modes of decision making. It would have to take into account, for example, Wallner et al.'s (1996) notion of "islands of sustainability." This notion favours working with parts of a region, the conditions for sustainability for which are easily bounded but allow connectedness to other "islands" and, thence, to the larger region.

In no small measure, current regional planning systems have come into being at the behest of professional planners, and, over the years, they have been tended and shaped by them. Thus, if today's regional planning systems are found wanting, it is because they do not seem to be serving the principles Patrick Geddes set down, or taking up the gauntlet Thomas Adams flung down, nearly a century ago. Adams recognized the essential unity of nature, environmental protection, and economic health, and he was aware of the need to bring urban planning together with public health and housing as well as with rural planning and resource conservation. And he knew that all of this had to be done within a regional perspective.

The planning profession is central to refurbishing the regional perspective. Fortunately, there have been some hopeful signs in recent years in that, under such rubrics as "sustainable development," "healthy communities," and "healthy (regional) environments," the Canadian Institute of Planners is rediscovering Thomas Adams' vision and is taking an active interest in pointing out the integral interrelationships between the natural and the built environments. For example, when the federal government unveiled its Green Plan in 1990, the institute complained that the environmental plan paid scarce attention to developing strategies to create environmentally sustainable cities, towns, villages, and regions (Jewczyk 1994, 122-3). It was the institute's position that a national environmental strategy must recognize the links between our urban and rural settlements. In short, both regional planning practice (for conservation, resource development, and the environment) and professional planners are in a reflexive relationship to one another – each affecting, and affected by, the other.

Part 3

Planning and Governing Practice in Urban-Based Regions

8

Planning and Governing
Metropolitan Areas

Canada is a world leader in metropolitan planning and governance. Almost all of the country's twenty-five census metropolitan areas (CMAs)– the regions encompassing the largest cities – have active metropolitan-regional planning agencies (and many governance mechanisms as well).[1] Canada has the distinction of having had the first metropolitan planning agency in North America as well as the continent's first full-fledged, formal metropolitan government. Recent reviews comparing Canadian and American metropolitan-regional planning experiences conclude that Canadian metropolitan areas generally have more highly developed metropolitan governance and planning systems than do their American counterparts and, hence, better-quality planning and development (Goldberg and Mercer 1986; Rothblatt 1994).

The Canadian experience with metropolitan-regional planning is now more than five decades old, having begun in Winnipeg in 1943, then being followed a decade later (1954) by the Metropolitan Toronto Advisory Planning Board (the planning arm of the Toronto Metropolitan government), and, in subsequent years, by a host of metropolitan-regional planning agencies across the country.

As with all aspects of regional planning, there are great differences among the provinces with respect to the role the provincial government plays in metropolitan-regional planning. This applies not only to statutory provisions, but also to style of operation. The circumstances and planning system in each province differ. Such diversity makes it extremely difficult to summarize or draw definite conclusions about common trends or changes in metropolitan-regional planning. A truly adequate analysis would deal separately with each of the ten provinces. However, within the framework of this book, we have had to adopt two approaches: first, we indicate what we believe are broadly applicable tendencies; second, we supplement this with examples.

Our analysis of the Canadian experience covers the following. First, we deal with the key elements of the metropolitan-regional planning systems,[2] including:

- the geographical area the planning agency covers
- the types of planning agencies or authorities established to undertake metropolitan-regional planning, including the composition of the governing bodies
- the planning and implementation mandates, powers, and tools delegated to the planning agencies
- the administrative procedures the agencies must follow if their decisions are to be legally binding and enforceable.

Second, we review the planning outcomes, the content of plans, and the planned urban spatial patterns (or urban forms) that emerged from the application of these key elements. Finally, we conclude with some reflections on (1) the experience of the metropolitan-regional planning authorities; (2) the future growth of metropolitan regions; and (3) persistent issues that these authorities will continue to face in the future.

However, before discussing the evolution and main features of Canadian metropolitan-regional planning, it will be useful to establish a context for it. This context includes the urbanization forces leading up to the need for metropolitan-regional planning; some key characteristics of Canadian metropolitan areas; and, based on these characteristics, how we can distinguish the "different metros."

Urbanization: The Need for Metropolitan-Regional Planning

Since 1900, Canada has transformed from an essentially agrarian-rural society to one that is almost entirely urban and based on industrial and service occupations. Between Confederation (in 1867) and 1996, the population of Canada multiplied from about 3.4 million to 30 million people. During that same period the urban population grew by a factor of almost thirty-five – from about 615,000 to 22 million (Statistics Canada 1997). Fewer than one in five Canadians resided in a village, town, or city in 1871, but that proportion had increased to one in three by the turn of the century. Then, because of the huge influx of immigrants in the early 1900s, the percentage of Canadians living in urban areas had reached nearly 50 percent in 1921.

During the period between the two world wars, only a modest increase in the proportion of the urban population was recorded. But then, as an accompaniment to the huge population growth following the Second World War, urbanization soared to slightly more than 76 percent in 1971. As of 1996, the urban proportion stood at 78 percent. And, most important, the extensive urban growth during the years following the Second World War created a new type of urban area: *the metropolitan area,* which comprises a central city and its outlying suburbs.

This extensive urban growth created a host of problems for the metropolitan areas' central cities and the surrounding areas within which the new suburbs were being built. The central cities faced an aging physical environment, which had been starved of improvements during the Great Depression and six years of war, as well as a lack of vacant land for new development. As the older residential and industrial areas deteriorated, people and factories moved to the outskirts of these cities, thus creating an urgent need for rehabilitation and redevelopment. All the while, the new suburbs needed a huge increase in new housing units and services. The difficulties encountered by the outlying communities in meeting these needs stemmed from their rapid rates of population growth and the meagre financial resources available to them. On top of this, the rapidly growing metropolitan populations created a need for new facilities to serve the entire metropolitan area – among them hospitals, expressways, regional parks, public transit, airports, new sources of water supply, and sewage treatment plants.

It was out of this complex, large-scale pattern of urban development and its accompanying problems that metropolitan-regional planning originated in Canada immediately after the Second World War. The need for this type of planning grew out of the realization that no single local government could deal with the array of needs and problems appropriate to the metropolitan area as a whole and, at the same time, satisfy the needs of the individual local communities. For example, the location of a new subdivision or shopping centre in one area often generates the need for improved highway access, new schools, and new trunk sewers. The new subdivision or shopping centre is, thus, a matter for local planning, but the repercussions of this are felt beyond the boundaries of the local municipality, and, thus, requires planning at the metropolitan level. Conversely, local development needs often depend on the availability of metropolitan facilities and services. The services are typically quite costly, especially for one community, and it is also very important that they be situated so that they can serve the needs of all communities within the metropolitan area. No single local government can deal with these matters.

Hoping to deal with these problems, in the 1940s and 1950s several provinces established different mechanisms for metropolitan-regional planning.[3] First there was Manitoba's Metropolitan Planning Commission of Greater Winnipeg; this was followed closely by British Columbia's Lower Mainland Regional Planning Board (for Vancouver's urbanizing region) and Victoria's Capital Region Planning Board; a year or so later, the Edmonton and Calgary regional planning commissions (at the beginning they were referred to as "district planning commissions") came into being. Then, in the early 1950s, came the continent's first metropolitan planning agency within a formal metropolitan government – Metropolitan Toronto. And, towards the end of that decade, the National Capital Commission was established in the National Capital Region (Ottawa).

During the 1960s and 1970s the movement to metropolitan-regional planning accelerated throughout the country. In the mid-1960s came the Halifax–

Dartmouth and County Regional Planning Commission in Atlantic Canada, and British Columbia created its new system of regional districts, which covered the entire province, including the Vancouver[4] and Victoria metropolitan areas. In the mid-1970s, metropolitan-regional plans were developed for the Vancouver, Halifax–Dartmouth, and St. John's regions.

Beginning in the early 1980s and continuing up to the early 1990s, metropolitan-regional planning, along with other variants of regional planning noted in earlier chapters, began to change in form, structure, and process. Several of the metropolitan-regional planning agencies were actually disbanded. For example, the regional planning function was taken away from British Columbia's regional districts in 1982 and then reinvigorated under the new provincial Growth Strategies Act, 1995; and the Alberta regional planning commissions were, for all practical purposes, disbanded by 1998. During these years, less official and formal arrangements for achieving intermunicipal cooperation were introduced.

During the past several decades a new trend has become evident: the extensive decentralization of population and economic activity into rural and semi-rural areas, small towns, and villages beyond the boundaries of the largest metropolitan areas. This has resulted in the emergence of a new spatial form – the city-region. Its characteristics differ from those of traditional metropolitan areas, and it constitutes a new set of governance challenges. (See Chapter 9 for a discussion of the Montreal, Toronto, and Vancouver city-regions.)

Selected Characteristics of the Metropolitan Areas

Population Growth

Canada's census metropolitan areas (CMAs) are statistical constructs used by Statistics Canada to measure a city's outreach and influence. Statistics Canada defines a CMA as a very large urban area that shares a degree of economic and social integration with its neighbouring urban and rural areas. Specifically, to qualify as a CMA, a city must have an urban core of at least 100,000 people. In addition to the urban core, a CMA includes surrounding cities and an urban and a rural fringe – areas that are somewhat physically disconnected from the urban core but that are included within CMA boundaries because of a high degree of economic and social integration.[5]

The concept of a census metropolitan area emerged because of the recognition that the reach and influence of the incorporated central city extends well beyond its legal boundaries; in short, the legal entity does not match the economic, geographic, and social phenomenon. A concept was needed to reflect this new urban reality – thus, the census metropolitan area.

As of 1986, Statistics Canada identified twenty-five CMAs. This identification remained constant in both the 1991 and the 1996 census as well as in recent intercensal estimates (see Table 5). Western Canada has seven metropolitan areas; Ontario has ten; Quebec has five; and Atlantic Canada has three. Table 5 includes the 1951, 1961, 1971, 1981, 1991, 1996, and 2000 populations of the twenty-five CMAs, and their average annual growth rates.[6]

In 1941, the Canadian census identified only fifteen metropolitan areas where the population, in total, represented about 40 percent of the national population. By 1961, five more areas had been added, and the metropolitan populations represented 51 percent of the country's total population. In the 1981 census an additional three areas were placed in the metropolitan class; and, as noted above, by 1986 and 1996 a total of twenty-five were so classified. For its 2000 intercensal population estimates of census metropolitan areas, Statistics Canada continued to classify the same 25 metropolitan areas (www.statcan.ca).

As can be seen in Table 5, in 2000 the twenty-five official CMAs varied in size from Toronto, with about 4.75 million inhabitants, to Thunder Bay, with about 126,000. On 1 July 2000, 62.5 percent of Canada's 30.75 million inhabitants, or nearly 19.3 million people, resided in one of the country's twenty-five CMAs.

In the 1901 census, the largest of the present-day CMAs was Montreal, with a population of 392,000. Toronto was ranked second, with 249,000, and it remained in that position until 1976, when it spurted ahead of Montreal. Now it is the largest metropolitan area in Canada. In 1901, the smallest of the twenty-five was Saskatoon, which contained fewer than 500 people.

In 1901, the total population of today's CMAs was 1.3 million, or about one-quarter of Canada's total population at that time. In 1996 their population was 17.9 million, or slightly more than three-fifths of the Canadian population. (If we include the nine agglomerations not officially recognized in 1996, then the total would be 19 million, or 65.7 percent of Canada's population.) Overall, the total population of the twenty-five CMAs increased more than thirteenfold between 1901 and 1996. In 1996, the nine largest metropolitan areas alone accounted for close to half of the total Canadian population of 30 million; and in 2000, one-third of the population was concentrated in the four largest CMAs (Toronto, Montreal, Vancouver, and Ottawa–Hull).

In Canada, metropolitan concentration increased more slowly than it did in the United States. The Canadian population became predominantly urban in the mid-1920s and predominantly metropolitan in the mid-1960s, while, in the United States, this type of shift occurred a decade earlier. No metropolitan areas in Canada had more than one million people before 1930; however, by 1991 there were three, and by 1996 and 2000 there were four.

Hottest Growth Metros since 1991

According to the latest Statistics Canada estimates, the four "hottest growth" metros[7] in the 1991-96 period – Toronto, Vancouver, Calgary, and Ottawa–Hull – continued their growth supremacy through to 2000. Between 1991 and 2000, the national population grew by almost 13 percent (from 30 million to almost

Table 5

Population of census metropolitan areas, 1951-2000, listed according to rank in 2000

CMA [1]	Population (000s) [2]							Average annual growth rate (%) [3]				
	1951	1961	1971	1981	1991	1996	2000	61-71	71-81	81-91	91-96	96-00
Toronto	1,262	1,919	2,628	2,999	3,899	4,264	4,751	4.3	1.5	2.4	1.9	2.9
Montreal	1,539	2,216	2,743	2,828	3,209	3,326	3,480	2.9	0.4	0.9	0.7	1.2
Vancouver	586	827	1,082	1,268	1,603	1,832	2,049	3.7	1.7	2.6	2.9	3.0
Ottawa–Hull	312	457	602	718	942	1,010	1,081	4.4	1.6	2.4	1.5	1.8
Calgary	142	279	403	593	754	822	953	4.4	4.7	2.1	1.0	4.0
Edmonton	194	360	496	657	841	863	944	4.7	3.3	1.4	0.5	2.3
Quebec City	289	379	480	576	646	672	690	3.9	1.5	1.0	0.8	0.7
Winnipeg	356	476	540	585	660	667	681	1.6	0.6	1.0	0.2	0.5
Hamilton	282	401	498	542	600	624	672	2.7	0.8	1.0	0.8	1.9
London	168	227	286	284	381	399	421	3.9	1.2	1.7	0.9	1.4
Kitchener	107	155	227	288	356	383	422	5.4	2.1	2.4	1.5	2.4
St. Catharines–Niagara	189	258	303	304	365	372	390	3.1	0.7	0.7	0.4	1.2
Halifax	138	193	223	278	320	332	356	3.6	1.1	1.6	0.7	1.8
Victoria	115	156	196	233	288	304	317	2.7	1.9	1.9	1.1	1.1
Windsor	183	217	259	246	262	279	304	2.9	-0.1	0.4	1.1	2.2
Oshawa	n.a.	81	120	154	240	269	298	4.8	2.2	2.9	1.3	2.7
Saskatoon	56	96	126	154	211	219	233	3.2	2.8	2.0	2.4	1.7

Regina	73	114	141	164	192	194	200	2.5	1.7	1.1	0.2	0.8
St. John's	81	107	132	155	172	174	175	4.5	1.7	1.1	0.3	0.1
Chicoutimi–Jonquière	91	128	134	135	161	160	160	2.0	1.4	0.2	-0.1	0.0
Sudbury	80	127	155	150	158	160	157	4.2	-0.3	0.1	0.2	-0.1
Sherbrooke	n.a.	84	98	125	141	147	153	1.7	2.0	1.1	0.8	1.0
Trois-Rivières	46	53	56	111	136	140	142	2.0	1.4	0.8	0.5	0.3
Saint John	81	98	107	114	126	126	128	1.2	0.7	0.3	0.0	0.4
Thunder Bay	74	102	112	121	125	126	126	2.5	2.6	0.2	0.1	0.0

1 CMA, as defined in 2000.
2 Population is based on CMA boundary at time of that particular census.
3 Average annual percentage change calculated from population data; based on CMA as defined at the end of each census period.

Sources: (a) 1951-81 (except for Sherbrooke and Oshawa, 1961 and 1971): Colombo (1996, 60); (b) 1961 and 1971 figures for Sherbrooke and Oshawa are taken from Bourne (1995a, Table A2); (c) 1991 and 1996 data taken from Statistics Canada website, www.statcan.ca; (d) 2000 data taken from Statistics Canada website, www.statcan.ca.

34 million). But, in the Vancouver, Toronto, Ottawa–Hull, and Calgary metros, the rates of expansion were much faster – 28 percent in Vancouver, 27 percent in Calgary, 22 percent in Toronto, and 15 percent in Ottawa–Hull.

Sources of Growth

What is perhaps most interesting about these hottest growth metros is the different sources of their growth. Countries have two ways of adding people: natural increase and net international immigration. Provinces have three sources of population growth: natural increase, net international immigration, and net interprovincial migration (i.e., the number of people coming into the province from other provinces minus those leaving for other provinces). Cities and metropolitan areas have the same three sources of population growth as well as net intraprovincial migration (i.e., people coming from and going to other parts of the same province). According to *Annual Demographic Statistics* (Statistics Canada 1998), the four hottest growth metros rely on different sources for new people (Little 1999). International immigration bolstered Vancouver (68 percent of its growth) and Toronto (85 percent), and both lost residents to other parts of their respective provinces. Meanwhile, migration from other provinces helped Calgary in particular (half of its growth) and Vancouver but not Toronto. Natural increase was more important to Calgary (43 percent) and Toronto (45 percent) than it was to Vancouver (only 20 percent).[8]

CMA Growth versus Non-CMA Growth

At this point we might ask two questions. How does CMA growth in Canada compare with non-CMA growth? And how is growth within CMAs distributed? With respect to the first question, growth in the CMA population between 1966 and 1996 has outpaced growth in non-CMA populations by a ratio of five to one. (The percentage increase in the CMA population in those thirty years was 71.2 percent, while it was only 14.6 percent in the non-CMA population [Vander Ploeg et al. 1999, 40-2].) As for the second question, since the 1960s, population distribution within the CMAs has changed considerably as will become clear from our brief discussion that follows on the patterns of growth for each of the four major spatial parts of a CMA – the urban core, surrounding cities, the urban fringe, and the rural fringe (see Table 6).[9]

Spatial Growth within the Metropolitan Areas

Urban Core (or Central City)

As might be expected, the rapid growth of population in the outlying parts of the CMAs resulted in a steady decline in the central city's share of both population and employment. In 1996, in the ten largest metropolitan areas three of the older central cities – Montreal, Toronto, and Quebec City – had

Table 6

Population distribution (%) within components of census metropolitan areas, 1966 and 1996

CMA	Urban core				Urban and rural fringe			
	Anchor city		Surrounding cities		Urban fringe		Rural fringe	
	1966	1996	1966	1996	1966	1996	1966	1996
Vancouver	44.0	28.1	44.3	60.3	4.5	8.0	7.2	3.6
Victoria	32.8	24.2	53.6	67.6	3.5	1.6	10.2	6.7
Calgary	100.0	93.5	0.0	0.0	0.0	3.1	0.0	3.4
Edmonton	89.8	71.4	2.1	11.6	3.5	6.6	4.6	10.4
Regina	99.0	93.2	0.0	0.0	0.0	1.5	1.0	5.3
Saskatoon	100.0	88.4	0.0	0.0	0.0	4.1	0.0	7.5
Winnipeg	50.5	92.7	47.5	0.5	0.3	0.2	1.7	6.6
Hamilton	65.2	51.6	20.5	40.8	7.1	0.3	7.2	7.3
Kitchener	49.1	46.6	16.7	46.8	27.9	3.1	6.2	3.5
London	76.6	81.7	0.0	0.2	11.7	9.3	11.7	9.2
Oshawa	73.3	50.0	19.1	30.0	4.5	11.6	3.0	8.4
Ottawa–Hull	66.5	38.2	24.8	39.8	3.5	10.6	5.2	11.4
St. Catharines–Niagara	34.8	35.2	4.4	44.9	60.9	9.1	0.0	10.8
Sudbury	62.1	57.4	2.6	12.1	22.2	19.5	13.2	11.0
Thunder Bay	96.8	90.5	0.0	4.4	0.0	0.0	3.2	13.9
Toronto	30.5	15.3	60.1	76.6	7.8	3.9	1.7	4.1
Windsor	80.8	70.9	4.7	15.6	5.1	2.4	9.4	11.0
Chicoutimi–Jonquière	24.5	39.3	57.6	30.6	11.6	11.6	6.3	18.5
Montreal	50.3	30.6	42.8	59.6	5.8	6.2	1.0	3.6
Quebec City	43.1	24.9	43.9	65.8	10.4	2.0	2.6	7.3
Sherbrooke	95.0	52.1	5.0	28.8	0.0	0.0	0.0	19.1
Trois-Rivières	60.3	34.6	36.4	50.7	2.3	1.7	1.0	13.0
Halifax	57.6	34.3	30.3	45.6	3.5	1.3	8.7	18.8
Saint John	86.3	57.7	1.3	12.6	5.4	2.9	6.9	26.8
St. John's	68.1	58.6	6.7	12.8	3.7	14.9	21.5	13.7

Note: The figures used for 1966 were the adjusted 1966 census counts based on the CMA boundaries in use as of the 1971 census. The 1971 census provided a more complete look at the four components of the CMA populations. This has not substantially changed the results.
Source: Modified from Vander Ploeg et al. (1999).

experienced an absolute population loss since 1971 (see Table 7). Five of the ten central cities – Toronto, Montreal, Vancouver, Ottawa–Hull, and Quebec City – contained fewer than half of the populations of their census metropolitan areas in 1996.[10]

Central cities have also been experiencing economic restructuring, in particular, declines in manufacturing employment, both in absolute terms and relative to the rest of their CMAs. However, industrial decentralization has affected the cities differently. For example, because Montreal contained a larger proportion of its region's industrial employment in 1975 than did Toronto and Vancouver, it and its immediate suburbs were more severely affected by industrial losses than were the cores of the other two regions. Also, Montreal's losses were more substantial: between 1975 and 1985, Montreal lost fully 25 percent of its manufacturing employment, compared with 17 percent for Toronto and 19 percent for Vancouver (Frisken 1994, 10).

Most analysts forecast that, in the future, central cities will be less able to retain or attract a wide range of activities that benefit from centrality – particularly large corporate headquarters, financial institutions, and major public services together with a broad range of linked services and suppliers. This is because the development of new technologies and information networks makes it possible for firms to move a variety of routine tasks out of the city to less costly office sites in the suburbs or on the urban fringe. In addition, the clustering of major office and commercial complexes in high-density, outer suburban nodes (Garreau [1991] refers to them as "edge cities") provides alternative

Table 7

Central-city populations in Canada's ten largest census metropolitan areas,[*] **1971, 1991, and 1996**

	Population (000s)		
CMA	1971	1991	1996
Toronto	712.8 (27%)	635.4 (16%)	653.7 (15%)
Montreal	1,214.3 (44%)	1,017.7 (33%)	1,016.4 (30%)
Vancouver	426.3 (39%)	471.8 (29%)	514.0 (28%)
Ottawa–Hull	365.3 (68%)	374.7 (41%)	385.6 (38%)
Edmonton	438.1 (88%)	616.6 (73%)	616.3 (71%)
Calgary	403.3 (100%)	710.7 (94%)	768.1 (93%)
Quebec City	186.1 (39%)	167.5 (26%)	167.3 (25%)
Winnipeg	535.2 (99%)	616.8 (95%)	618.5 (93%)
Hamilton	309.2 (73%)	318.5 (53%)	322.3 (52%)
London	223.2 (86%)	303.2 (79%)	325.6 (82%)

* The ten largest CMAs as of 1996
Sources: Populations for 1971 and 1991: Frisken (1994b, Vol. 1, Table 2, 9): populations for 1996: Statistics Canada (1997).

locations for activities that have traditionally benefited from the economies of agglomeration associated with centrality.

Despite these trends, the fact is that all evidence indicates that the future economic health of metropolitan areas, including their suburbs and fringe areas, depends to a large extent on the health of their urban cores.[11] In view of this, it is vital that the metropolitan-regional planners develop approaches and techniques to revitalize deteriorating urban cores.

Growth Outside the Urban Core

Following the trend in most Western countries, recent CMA growth in Canada can be attributed mainly to developments (industrial, commercial, and residential) outside the central cities in the outlying suburban and fringe areas. Table 8 shows that, in 1996, as many as nineteen out of twenty-five CMAs had more than one-quarter of their populations living in the suburbs and fringe areas; and fifteen of these actually had more than 40 percent living on the outskirts of the CMAs.

Surrounding Cities

In most CMAs, the surrounding cities experienced an increased proportion of the population. Between 1991 and 1996 examples of such rapid growth include Kanata, outside Ottawa (28 percent); and Surrey and Port Coquitlam, outside Vancouver (24 percent and 29 percent, respectively). Suburban and fringe communities outside Toronto and Montreal experienced similar growth rates (Statistics Canada 1996). Only seven CMAs did not experience this pattern. Of these, three do not have surrounding cities (Calgary, Saskatoon, and Regina) and four experienced a relative declining population in surrounding cities (Winnipeg, London, Thunder Bay, and Chicoutimi–Jonquière).[12] In 1996, Toronto had the greatest proportion of its population living in surrounding cities (77 percent), followed by Victoria (68 percent).

Urban Fringe

The proportion of population living in the urban fringes increased for most CMAs in western Canada (except for Victoria and Winnipeg.) In the rest of Canada there was a mixture of increases and decreases in the urban fringe proportions.

Rural Fringe

Since 1966, perhaps to the surprise of many people, CMAs across Canada have experienced an increase in the proportion of their population that is rural. The number of rural residents in CMAs increased between 1966 and 1996 by 190 percent, compared with only 58 percent for the urban residents. In 1966, nearly 4 percent of all CMA residents lived in rural areas, but by 1996 this figure had jumped to almost 7 percent. The increase is most noticeable in the Atlantic

Table 8

Selected characteristics of census metropolitan areas, 1996

CMA	Population	Land area (sq. km.)	Population density (per sq. km.)	Population rank Nat.	Population rank Prov.	Number of governments	Suburbs as % of CMA
Calgary	821,628	5,083	162	6	2	9	2.7
Chicoutimi–Jonquière	160,628	1,723	93	21	4	21	29.6
Edmonton	862,597	9,537	90	5	1	36	28.6
Halifax	332,518	2,503	133	13	1	79	65.7
Hamilton	624,360	1,358	460	9	3	8	48.4
Kitchener	382,940	824	465	11	5	5	59.5
London	398,616	2,105	189	10	4	11	18.3
Montreal	3,326,510	4,024	827	2	1	102	67.7
Oshawa	268,773	894	301	16	?	3	50.2
Ottawa–Hull	1,010,498	5,686	178	4	2	27	35.1
Quebec City	671,889	3,150	213	7	2	44	75.2
Regina	193,652	3,422	57	18	2	17	7.2
Saint John	125,705	3,509	36	24	1	22	42.1
Saskatoon	219,056	5,322	41	17	1	24	11.4
Sherbrooke	147,384	980	150	22	5	15	46.9
St. Catharines–Niagara	372,406	1,400	266	12	6	10	44.1
St. Johns	174,051	790	220	19	1	13	41.4
Sudbury	160,488	2,612	61	20	9	7	42.5
Thunder Bay	125,562	2,295	55	25	10	9	9.5
Toronto	4,263,757	5,868	727	1	1	30	34.7
Trois-Rivières	139,956	872	160	23	6	10	65.7
Vancouver	1,831,665	2,821	649	3	1	31	71.9
Victoria	304,287	633	480	14	2	23	89.2
Windsor	278,685	862	323	15	7	11	29.0
Winnipeg	667,209	4,077	164	8	1	11	7.3

Source: Statistics Canada (1997, Tables 3, 8).

CMAs, where almost 20 percent of the CMA populations live in rural parts of the metropolitan areas. The British Columbia CMAs are the least rural (4 percent).

The importance of CMAs to rural life is demonstrated by the fact that 69 percent of all rural growth in Canada actually occurred within CMAs.[13] The existence and growth of rural populations in CMAs have important implications for planning in and for the metropolitan areas. Equally important, as we shall see in Chapter 9, the large proportion of rural populations outside metropolitan area boundaries within Canada's three city-regions pose especially difficult planning challenges (see also Chapter 5).

The largest CMA in land area is Edmonton, with about 9,500 square kilometres. A number of CMAs have between 5,000 and 6,000 square kilometres, and seven have fewer than 1,000 square kilometres (the smallest being Victoria). The largest CMAs (in terms of population) also tend to have the largest land areas as well as the highest population densities (see Table 8). However, some CMAs (e.g., Regina, Saskatoon, Saint John), each with a comparatively small total population, have large land areas and thus very low population densities.

Social Complexity of Metropolitan Areas

Canadian CMAs manifest variations in their social as well as in their economic structure (see Frisken 1994, ch. 6; Vander Ploeg et al. 1999). The populations of CMAs are becoming more differentiated spatially in terms of age, family structure, economic status, employment characteristics, ethnicity, mobility patterns, and housing; but there are also substantial differences in social structure among as well as within metropolitan areas.

Ethnic diversity, which has long been a characteristic of Canadian cities, has become more apparent in some CMAs as a result of substantial increases in the proportion of visible minorities in the immigrant population. The proportion of immigrants from Europe and other parts of North America has declined, while the proportion from Asia, the Caribbean, and, to a lesser degree, South America and Africa has increased.

Toronto is a case in point. The city has one-quarter of Canada's immigrants, with immigration accounting for more than 85 percent of the city's total population growth. Every year, more than 70,000 new immigrants and refugees call the city home. In 1999 alone, they came from over 169 countries and spoke more than 100 languages (the top three foreign languages being Chinese, Italian, and Portuguese). As a consequence, Toronto is now arguably the most multicultural city in the world; or, as Fick and Vincent (2001, 54) put it, "in 2001, Toronto is the world in one city." The continual arrival of so many immigrants has put pressure on the city's already tight rental market, increased the demand for language training and other social services, and contributed to racial tensions and conflict.

This substantial change in the origins of immigrants since 1960 is also a principal reason why ethnic diversity is currently perceived as a social issue in Vancouver.

Political Fragmentation of Metropolitan Areas

While Canadian CMAs are certainly fragmented, it is fortunate that they have not experienced the degree of municipal fragmentation that has occurred in American CMAs. For example, in 1987 the average number of general government units per metropolitan area (excluding special districts and school districts) in the United States was forty-seven (Rothblatt 1994, 512: tbl. 4), while in 1996 the average number of municipalities per individual CMA in Canada was only twenty (see Table 8). (In the United States, fragmentation reached as high as 267 and 205 municipalities in Chicago and Minneapolis–St. Paul, respectively [Rothblatt 1994, 503: tbl. 1].) Until its soon-to-be amalgamation, the Montreal CMA is Canada's most fragmented metropolitan area, with more than fifty municipalities and a total of 110 municipal jurisdictions within its borders. While not as severe as in the Montreal area, fragmentation in the other CMAs was bad enough, and it was this suburban and fringe growth in metropolitan areas following the Second World War – and the difficulties in meeting the need for housing, infrastructure, and transportation in these areas – that led to the establishment of mechanisms for metropolitan planning and metropolitan governance, as we shall see in the following sections.

Different CMAs

Just as we found that there are several different rural Canadas (Chapter 5), so there is no single metropolitan Canada. We can distinguish the various metropolitan areas according to two characteristics: (1) their population (i.e., size, rankings, and differential rates of growth between 1991 and 1996), and (2) their form of metropolitan governance and planning.

Population Criteria

Table 9 shows that, according to population, Canadian metropolitan areas break down into three major groups.

Group 1: The "Big Four"

At the top are the "Big Four": Toronto, Montreal, Vancouver, and Ottawa–Hull, each with at least one million people. (Note that Toronto, Montreal, and Vancouver are each part of a larger city-region, which we discuss in Chapter 9.) This group combined held almost 35 percent of the nation's population in 1996, and in 2000, about one-third. Also, as can be seen in Table 5, the size rankings of the Big Four, with a few exceptions, remained the same between 1951 and 2000. Except for Montreal, the other three of the Big Four also experienced some of the highest growth rates in the period between 1991 and 2000.

Table 9

Population changes among the census metropolitan areas, 1991-2000, listed according to rank in 2000

| CMA | Population (000s) | | | Population change (%) | |
	1991	1996	2000	'91-'96 (average = +6.4%)	'91-'00 (average = +10.2)
Group 1					
Toronto	3,899	4,264	4,751	9.4	21.8
Montreal	3,209	3,326	3,480	3.7	8.4
Vancouver	1,603	1,832	2,049	14.3	27.9
Ottawa–Hull	942	1,010	1,081	7.3	14.8
Group 2					
Calgary	754	822	953	9.0	26.4
Edmonton	841	863	944	2.6	12.2
Quebec City	646	672	690	4.1	6.8
Winnipeg	660	667	681	1.0	3.2
Hamilton	600	624	672	4.1	6.0
Group 3					
Kitchener	356	383	422	7.4	18.5
London	381	399	421	4.5	10.5
St. Catharines–Niagara	365	372	390	2.2	6.8
Halifax	320	332	356	3.7	11.2
Victoria	288	304	317	5.7	10.1
Windsor	262	279	304	6.3	16.0
Oshawa	240	269	298	11.9	24.2
Saskatoon	211	219	233	3.8	10.4
Regina	192	194	200	1.0	4.2
St. John's	172	174	175	1.3	1.7
Chicoutimi–Jonquière	161	160	160	-0.3	-0.6
Sudbury	158	160	157	1.8	-0.6
Sherbrooke	141	147	153	4.7	8.5
Trois-Rivières	136	140	142	2.7	4.4
Saint John	126	125	128	-0.1	1.6
Thunder Bay	125	126	126	0.5	0.8

Sources: 1991 and 1996 data taken from Statistics Canada website, www.statcan.ca; 2000 data taken from Statistics Canada website, www.statcan.ca.

Group 2: "Almost in the Big Time"

Next in line according to size are Calgary, Edmonton, Quebec City, Winnipeg, and Hamilton–Wentworth, with populations ranging between 624,000 and 862,000 in 1996; and 672,000 and 953,000 in 2000. In particular, Edmonton and Calgary are undoubtedly on their way to entering the one-million population class. In the four and a half decades since 1951, both Edmonton and Calgary increased their rankings considerably. Of all the metropolitan areas, Calgary had the highest average annual growth rate between 1996 and 2000.

Group 3: "At the Bottom"

At the bottom are two groups: first, a group of eight metropolitan areas ranging in size from Saskatoon, with a population of 219,000 in 1996 (233,000 in 2000), to London, with a population of 399,000 in 1996 (421,000 in 2000); and, second, a group of eight metropolitan areas, all with populations under 200,000, ranging from Regina, with 194,000 to Thunder Bay, the smallest metropolitan area in Canada, with 126,000. In this group, only Kitchener, Halifax, Windsor, and Saskatoon had growth rates greater than the CMA average for the 1996-2000 period.

Form of Metropolitan Governance and Planning

Today, almost all of Canada's twenty-five CMAs have some form of metropolitan governance and planning mechanism (the exceptions being Saint John and Oshawa). In some instances, these were deliberately created as the provinces realized that metropolitan-regional planning without a commensurate governance mechanism could achieve only limited results. The aim was to create a mechanism that would exercise planning and policy direction, if not actual control, over the entire urbanized area. Thus, we can also differentiate the metropolitan areas, based on their form of planning and governance, according to one of the following four major categories (see Table 10).

One-Tier Forms of Local and Metropolitan Government

The first category includes metropolitan areas with a one-tier form of local government; that is, they have a single municipal government for the entire metropolitan area, covering all or most of the entire urbanized area (including, sometimes, its immediate hinterland). These became consolidated or amalgamated as a result of provincial "encouragement" or "intervention" or through a series of annexations. This group includes Calgary, London, Montreal (following its soon-to-be amalgamation), Regina, Saskatoon, St. John's, Thunder Bay, Windsor, and Winnipeg. Compared with other metropolitan areas, one-tier metropolitan areas have the least population dispersal and least political fragmentation; that is, they have (1) thirty or fewer local government units within their CMA boundaries and (2) fewer than 36 percent of the metropolitan population living in their suburban municipalities (see Table 8).

Two-Tier Forms of Local and Metropolitan Government

The second major category includes metropolitan areas with two-tier forms of local government and planning. Under the two-tier system, each level has its designated functions and responsibilities, which are usually determined by the provincial government, and all the usual powers of municipal government to back them up. Ontario has led the way in the establishment of two-tier forms of municipal government, referring to them as "regional municipalities." Regional municipalities exist not only within the Ontario CMAs (Ottawa–Hull, St. Catharines–Niagara, Sudbury, and Toronto [before the creation of the new City of Toronto]), but also outside them. Quebec also has three two-tier regional municipalities within its CMAs (Chicoutimi–Jonquière, Trois Rivières, and the Quebec part of Ottawa–Hull). In Atlantic Canada the two-tier Halifax regional municipality (which is part of the Halifax Metropolitan Area) was formed in 1996 by the Nova Scotia government as a result of the merging of the Cities of Halifax and Dartmouth, the Town of Bedford, and the County of Halifax.

The Metropolitan Corporation of Toronto (before its recent amalgamation into the new City of Toronto), popularly known as "Metro Toronto," was a classic example of a two-tier form of metropolitan government. Metropolitan Toronto was created in 1954. It took the form of a federation of the thirteen municipalities (later reduced to six) that made up the metropolitan area at the time. There was a fairly clear division of power between the two tiers of government: the metropolitan-wide upper tier, and the lower tier (represented by the twelve local municipalities). The governing principle of the federation (as is true of most other two-tier governments) was that certain services, common to the entire Metropolitan Toronto area, would be the responsibility of the upper-tier metropolitan government (the "Metro Council"), while services of a more local nature would be the responsibility of the individual area municipalities. For shared duties, the degree to which the problem was metropolitan or local in scope determined the division of responsibility. For example, while solid waste disposal was a metropolitan responsibility, garbage collection was the responsibility of the local area municipalities; likewise, while water supply was a metropolitan responsibility, the distribution of water to residents was a local function. This division of responsibilities between Metropolitan Toronto and the local municipalities for roads and utilities established the differences between the metropolitan-regional plans and the local community plans in those fields. This arrangement is fairly typical of the other two-tier municipal governments.

Two-tier governments may be distinguished according to the extent to which the entire metropolitan area is under the planning direction, if not control, of the upper-tier local government. In a later section, we adapt a classification system developed by Sancton (1994) in order to identify two types of two-tier local and metropolitan governments – comprehensive and non-comprehensive – and discuss how we arrived at this distinction. We incorporate this distinction

Table 10

Form of governance in census metropolitan areas, listed according to population criteria

| CMA | Population criteria | | | Form of governance | | | | | |
---	Group 1	Group 2	Group 3	None	One tier	Two tier Comp.	Two tier Non-comp.	Special authority	Voluntary association
Toronto	X					X[1]			
Montreal	X					X			
Vancouver	X							X	
Ottawa–Hull (Ontario)	X					X			
(Quebec)									
Edmonton		X					X		X[2]
Calgary		X						X	
Quebec City		X			X				
Winnipeg		X			X				
Hamilton–Wentworth		X					X		
London			X		X				
Kitchener			X			X			
St. Catharines–Niagara			X			X			
Halifax			X			X			
Victoria			X					X	
Windsor			X		X				
Oshawa			X	X					
Saskatoon			X		X				

Regina	X	X		
St. John's	X	X		
Sudbury	X			X
Chicoutimi–Jonquière	X			X
Sherbrooke	X			X	X
Trois-Rivières	X			X
Saint John	X		X	
Thunder Bay	X	X		

1 As a result of the recent creation of the new City of Toronto; prior to that it had a two-tier, non-comprehensive form of government.
2 Establishment of the Alberta Capital Region Alliance following the demise of the Edmonton Regional Planning Commission.

into Table 10, as our second criterion for determining the different Canadian metros.

Ideally, the upper tier's jurisdictional area of control should correspond closely to the geographic area of the metropolitan area. Where this occurs we call such upper-level local and metropolitan governments "comprehensive." We identified the following in this group: Chicoutimi–Jonquière, Halifax, Kitchener, the Ontario part of Ottawa–Hull, St. Catharines–Niagara, Sudbury, and Trois Rivières. Where this does not occur, we term the upper-level local and metropolitan governments "non-comprehensive." We identified the following in this group: Hamilton–Wentworth, the Quebec part of Ottawa–Hull, Toronto (before creation of the new city of Toronto), and Sherbrooke.

Special-Purpose Authorities

The third major category of governance and planning includes those metros in which upper-level local government is not, in fact, a true level of government and performs only limited functions for the metropolitan area, mainly the preparation of a metropolitan-regional land-use plan. We refer to these as "two-level special-purpose planning authorities" because the upper level is superimposed over a uni-level form of local government. This category includes the Edmonton and Calgary regional planning commissions, the Greater Vancouver Regional District, and the (Victoria) Capital Region District.

These metropolitan areas have a large number of local government units within their boundaries and also have more than 46 percent of their populations living in their suburbs. Despite this population dispersal and political fragmentation, there is no overall, general-purpose, or upper-tier form of government.

Voluntary Associations

A fourth, special category of metropolitan governance and planning, which is usually not initiated by a provincial government, consists of voluntary associations of municipal governments as well as not-for-profit and private-sector interests. These associations are of recent origin in Canada but increasingly popular in the United States. It recently occurred in Alberta, in the form of the Alberta Capital Region Alliance, which came into existence after the demise of the Edmonton Regional Planning Commission.

Table 10 uses these different population and forms of planning and governance criteria to distinguish the different Canadian metros. They are discussed in greater detail later in this chapter.

Metropolitan-Regional Planning Systems

Every province and both territories in Canada have their own individual planning systems (see Chapter 4). These differences are related to the constitutional separation of powers between the Government of Canada and the provinces. Specifically, provincial authority for land-use planning and metropolitan-regional planning derives from section 92(13) of the British North America Act, 1867, as continued by the Constitution Act, 1982, which grants provincial legislatures the exclusive right to make laws relating to matters affecting the use of property.[14]

The fact that the provinces have the right to enact planning legislation has another implication; namely, it is left to the discretion of each provincial government to decide how to structure its planning system, including whether to have any at all. The circumstances and planning system in each province are different, with new and amended planning legislation being made in response to perceived needs and issues, and often reflecting the ideology and background of the people who participated in the review process. Such diversity, as we noted earlier, makes it extremely difficult to arrive at definitive conclusions. Canadian planning systems differ, perhaps not in their broad outlines, but certainly in the detailed powers and procedures that are so vital to local and metropolitan planning practice. For this reason all generalizations should be treated with caution.

Nevertheless, all Canadian planning systems for metropolitan areas are structured around the same relatively few elements. These elements correspond to the basic decisions provincial governments must make when deciding how to structure metropolitan-regional planning (see also Chapter 4).

The four essential elements are: (1) area coverage; (2) planning authorities; (3) planning mandates, powers, and tools; and (4) administrative procedures.

Area Coverage

The issue of appropriate boundaries actually arises when the metropolitan-regional planning agency is first created and the metropolitan-region is defined. If the boundaries extend too far into the countryside, then the metropolitan-region will include rural communities with little in common with the urban residents of the central city. If the boundaries do not extend far enough, then the metropolitan planners would be unable to control developments beyond their boundaries, and this could have adverse consequences for the metropolitan area. Also, once the boundaries have been set, they are generally difficult to change. Finally, it is important that the metropolitan-regional planning agency's area of jurisdiction correspond to the functional boundaries of the metropolitan-region (see Chapter 3).

In Canada's metropolitan areas, there has not always been a correspondence between the area of jurisdiction and its functional boundaries. Take, for example, the boundaries established for Alberta's regional planning commissions, including those for the Calgary and Edmonton metropolitan-regions. The boundaries of the areas allocated to the individual regional planning commissions were based on groupings of existing municipalities. The boundaries of these municipalities had been examined by the Coterminous Boundaries Commission during the early 1950s (Burton 1981, 3). The result was the grouping of municipal and school districts within the multi-purpose county, which represented an attempt to encompass local community areas, areas with similar physical features and a similar agricultural base, and areas with differing income levels. Burton notes that, while the regional planning commissions were further groupings of these municipalities based on a number of criteria, the basic and unquestioned criterion was contiguity.

There was little change in the established boundaries of constituent municipalities during the existence of the regional planning commissions. As municipalities opted to join a commission, their areas were simply added to the geographic area encompassed by the appropriate commission. However, as Burton (1981, 5) points out, the commission regions were, in reality, an aggregation of existing administrative areas selected according to criteria that, while clearly articulated, appear to have been arbitrarily applied. So, except in one instance, the boundaries of the Alberta regional planning commissions remained unaltered.[15]

While the metropolitan-regional planning authority may have appropriate boundaries at the time of its creation, subsequent developments may prove them to be outmoded. For example, if urban development takes place outside the metropolitan area's borders for three or four decades after its initial establishment without any outward adjustment of the boundaries, then the authority is likely to find its planning of the area's overall development ineffective. Unlike CMAs, the boundaries of which Statistics Canada frequently alters in order to meet changing conditions, the boundaries of most Canadian metropolitan planning agencies' planning areas have rarely been altered to accommodate extended growth. This often leads to proposals for annexation, amalgamation, the implementation of two-tier systems of local government, and/or the creation of an overall regional governing mechanism (see Chapter 9).

Several provinces did recognize the boundary problem when they initially established their metropolitan planning agencies, and they assigned them planning and control powers over an extended area beyond their formal administrative boundaries.[16] Two notable cases occurred in Manitoba's Unicity and Ontario's Metro Toronto (before amalgamation).

Winnipeg's Unicity

In the case of Winnipeg, its "additional zone" (formed in 1960) was an area extending eight kilometres from the metropolitan authority's boundaries. Its purpose was to prevent suburban sprawl and to control the urbanization of the immediately surrounding region. It was eliminated from Winnipeg's jurisdiction in the late 1980s.

Metro Toronto

When Metropolitan Toronto was created in 1954, the Municipality of Metropolitan Toronto Act provided for an extended area (more than twice the size of Metropolitan Toronto) to be put under the jurisdiction of the Metropolitan Toronto Planning Board. The total planning area covered about 1,970 square kilometres, of which approximately 620 square kilometres contained the thirteen metropolitan area municipalities. The extended area, which covered about 1,350 square kilometres, took in thirteen fringe-area local jurisdictions.[17] This decision was based on the advice of Lorne Cumming, the Ontario Municipal Board chair and the person responsible for recommending Metropolitan Toronto's original form of government, who argued that metropolitan planning should encompass territory into which the metropolitan area was likely to expand.

In both metropolitan governments, the abandonment of planning control in the extended area resulted in fringe growth and suburban sprawl, with serious consequences for the central city and the surrounding municipalities (on Winnipeg, see Paetkau 1996, Reid 1996, and Brown 1996; on Toronto, see Frisken 1994). Many other metropolitan areas faced similar problems of fringe growth and suburban sprawl, but the metropolitan agencies themselves were likewise unable to contain metropolitan area expansion, and the provincial governments did not come to their aid.

Planning Authorities[18]

Having decided upon the area and boundaries of the metropolitan regions that will undergo planning, the provincial government must then decide to whom it will delegate planning powers and responsibilities for these regions. Three approaches have been used. The first has been to vest the most important planning responsibilities, along with the greatest powers, in the existing institutions of government – in provincial ministries and in general-purpose local governments such as city and county councils. Local governments may be either one- or two-tier, as we discussed earlier. In such cases, certain metropolitan-regional planning responsibilities are usually added to their more general municipal duties.

A second approach involves the creation of ad hoc or special-purpose two-level planning authorities (e.g., boards or commissions of various kinds), each responsible for some or all aspects of planning at the metropolitan-regional level (along, perhaps, with some other area-wide functions, such as transportation). In addition, ad hoc special boards or tribunals with quasi-judicial powers may be created to hear appeals against certain kinds of planning decisions.

A third approach, of recent origin in Canada (and increasingly prevalent in the United States), consists of voluntary associations of municipal governments, together with not-for-profit and private sector representatives. Though they do not necessarily possess any provincially mandated powers and responsibilities, they come together to deal with a specific planning problem or to develop a vision for the region.

One-Tier Planning Authorities

When a one-tier form of local government encompasses a metropolitan area, the planning authority is vested in the responsible elected body of the local government. The planning powers and responsibilities normally assigned to a city would, in this case, apply to the metropolitan area as a whole. In short, the one-tier government would carry out both local and metropolitan-wide planning functions. In one-tier governments, there is usually either a single planning unit (often identified as a department or division of the government) that carries out both the local and metropolitan-wide planning functions or there are two separate units, one concerned only with local planning activities and the other concerned with metropolitan-wide planning issues.

Upper-Level Authorities

Many of Canada's metropolitan areas have established two-tier forms of government. The precise division of powers between the upper and lower levels in these governments is a matter for provincial determination. In practice, the lower tiers are given the responsibility for local planning matters (e.g., local roads and parks, local planning, and zoning bylaws). The upper level is usually given the power to deal with metropolitan-regional planning matters, including preparation of a regional plan, and may also be given responsibility for such other metropolitan-wide functions as major infrastructure (e.g., transportation, water supply, sewage treatment and disposal, solid waste disposal, regional parks).

As we noted previously, the various two-tier metropolitan areas can be differentiated according to whether the entire metropolitan area is under the planning direction, if not the control, of the upper-level local government. We used the statistical relationship between the size of the population of the upper-level municipality and that of the total metropolitan area as a measure of the degree of congruence between them and, most important, as an indication of the extent to which these two-tier governments conform to the planning ideal (see Table 11). Based on this statistical relationship, we identified two types of two-tier local and metropolitan governments – comprehensive and non-comprehensive metropolitan authorities – and incorporated this distinction into our identification of the different Canadian metros (see Table 10).

Comprehensive Upper-Level Authorities

Comprehensive metros, theoretically at least, conform to the ideal, since the central upper-level authority's jurisdictional area of direction and/or control

Table 11

Relationship between the population of selected metropolitan areas and the population of their associated upper-level governments

CMA	Population (1996)[1]		Upper-level government		Population (1996)[1]		Upper-level gov't as % of CMA[2]
Chicoutimi–Jonquière	160,928	('91)	Chicoutimi–Jonquière	(RM)	172,837	('91)	107.4
Halifax	332,518		Halifax	(RM)	342,966		103.1
Hamilton–Wentworth	624,360		Hamilton–Wentworth	(RM)	452,745		72.5
Kitchener	382,940		Waterloo	(RM)	383,319		100.1
Montreal	3,337,200	('95)	Montreal Urban Community		1,799,254	('95)	53.9
Ottawa–Hull	1,010,498						
Ontario	746,179		Ottawa–Carleton[3]	(RM)	692,898		92.8
Quebec	264,319		Outaouais	(RM)	223,332		84.5
St. Catharines–Niagara	372,406		Niagara	(RM)	390,260		104.8
Sherbrooke	140,718	('91)	Sherbrooke	(RM)	127,223	('91)	90.4
Sudbury	160,488		Sudbury	(RM)	164,000		102.2
Toronto	4,283,757		Toronto	(RM)[4]	2,238,487		52.3
Trois-Rivières	136,303	('91)	Trois-Rivières	(RM)	137,393	('91)	100.8
Vancouver	1,831,665		Greater Vancouver	(RD)	1,793,774		97.9
Victoria	304,207		Capital Region	(RD)	312,780		102.8

Abbreviations: RM = Regional Municipality; RD = Regional District.

1 Population data for both CMAs and upper-level governments is 1996, unless otherwise indicated.

2 Some percentages exceed 100 because the boundaries of the relevant upper-tier municipality extend beyond the boundaries of the CMA in which it is located.

3 Before Ottawa–Carleton was amalgamated into a single City of Ottawa.

4 Before amalgamation as the City of Toronto.

Sources: Population data for Ontario regional municipalities was obtained from "Application Services, Ontario Statistics"; data for the other upper-level governments are from their respective websites.

corresponds closely to the geographic area of the metropolis; that is, the population of the upper-level tier is equal to or greater than the population of their metropolitan areas. As can be seen in Table 11 (and as we noted earlier), included in this group are: Chicoutimi–Jonquière, Halifax, Kitchener, Montreal (after amalgamation), the Ontario part of Ottawa–Hull, St. Catharines–Niagara, Sudbury, and Trois Rivières.

Non-Comprehensive Upper-Level Authorities

In contrast to the first type, non-comprehensive metros are presumably *not* able to adequately direct and/or control the metropolitan areas within their jurisdiction because the population of the upper-level municipalities is less than the population of the metropolitan areas. As can be seen in Table 11 (and as noted earlier), this group includes Hamilton–Wentworth, the Quebec part of Ottawa–Hull, Toronto (before creation of the new city of Toronto), and Sherbrooke.

Planning Responsibility

Typically, responsibility for metropolitan-wide planning in both the comprehensive and non-comprehensive two-tier governments resides, as in the case of the one-tier governments, in a metropolitan planning department, or division, established by the upper-level governmental council. Notable examples include those established in the following places.

Greater Winnipeg

Metropolitan planning in the Winnipeg area was handled by the Metropolitan Planning Commission until 1961, when it was disbanded upon the creation of the two-tier Metropolitan Corporation of Greater Winnipeg, which had an upper-level council that established its own planning department. This form of government was superseded in 1972 by the Unicity, which, as noted earlier, has a one-tier planning department that is responsible for both local and metropolitan planning.

Metropolitan Toronto

When the Toronto metropolitan government was first established in 1954, it was provided with an advisory planning board (the Metropolitan Toronto Advisory Planning Board) similar to those in other municipalities in the province. However, what was unique about the Metropolitan Toronto Advisory Planning Board, as discussed earlier, is that it was given planning jurisdiction over a surrounding area that was twice as large as Metro Toronto, with the additional area being composed of thirteen municipalities (amalgamated to six in 1967). The board existed from the original date of formation of Metropolitan Toronto until 1975, when it was abolished (at which time the four regional municipalities surrounding Metropolitan Toronto were created).

Metropolitan planning was transferred to a planning committee of the Metro Council, and the Metropolitan Planning Department was established.

Special-Purpose Two-Level Planning Agencies

The metropolitan-regional planning functions exercised by the special-purpose two-level agencies were delegated to them by the provincial government when it created the board or commission. It should be emphasized that the metro-politan-regional upper level of these special-purpose authorities is not a true level of government. It does not perform general-purpose functions but, rather, is limited to certain functions, usually the preparation (and sometimes administration) of a metropolitan-regional land-use plan. It may also perform other metropolitan-wide functions, as in the case of the Greater Vancouver Regional District (as we describe in Chapter 9).

In Alberta and Atlantic Canada these special-purpose two-level agencies were called regional planning commissions (RPCs). In British Columbia they are called regional districts, and these are described in Chapter 9. The original Alberta district planning commissions (DPCs) (later termed regional planning commissions) were established when it was recognized that the two major cities of Edmonton and Calgary (as well as intermediate urban areas such as Red Deer, Medicine Hat, and Lethbridge) could not independently manage the spatial problems of their urban growth. These problems included speculative fragmentation of land, scattered fringe development, municipal financing problems, loss of easy access to unspoiled countryside, the danger that these cities could become ugly and squalid, and obstacles to economic and attractive industrial and residential expansion (Gertler 1974). The DPCs and RPCs were intentionally created as institutional tools for preventing, or at least minimizing, the occurrence of these evils (Burton 1981, 1).

Demise of the RPCs

The Province of Alberta's commitment to the idea and practice of regional planning began to decline dramatically beginning in the mid-1980s. The resource-based Alberta economy, which had boomed in the 1970s, came to a crashing halt in the summer of 1981, and, in turn, the first cracks in the Alberta planning system appeared. The finances of almost all public agencies and organizations were adversely affected over the next few years, and the RPCs were no exception: planning staffs were cut, and subdivision applications fell off. The economic downturn plus the increasing nation-wide emphasis on local autonomy led Dale and Burton (1984) as well as Smith (1994) to predict (correctly) that the powers of the RPCs were likely to be further eroded and that their influence would continue to decline.

Indeed, even more severe changes began in the 1990s. Previously, funding for Alberta RPCs came from the provincial government as well as from member municipalities. In 1991, with the election of a new Progressive Conservative government that promised to eliminate the provincial deficit and debt, the province began to withdraw its funding. By the end of the 1994-95 fiscal year, provincial funding for the RPCs, some of which had existed since 1950, was completely eliminated.

At the same time, the Alberta government made substantive changes to its planning legislation. One of these changes consisted of abolishing the Planning Act and rolling parts of it into the new Municipal Government Act, 1994. This represented a major departure from tradition as, since 1913, the province's planning legislation had always been "free-standing." The legislation that had created the commissions was totally eliminated. Especially hard hit was the Calgary region, where the Calgary RPC had played a major role in achieving orderly development and avoiding urban sprawl.

Voluntary Associations

The demise of the Alberta RPCs[19] may have given birth to a new form of regional planning: voluntary intermunicipal and inter-organizational planning. This form of planning was exercised through intermunicipal associations and was incorporated into the Municipal Government Act, 1994. There is no legislative constraint on joint planning – in fact, it is encouraged. Through the new legislation, neighbouring municipalities are permitted to become involved in the preparation of municipal development plans and to establish intermunicipal service agencies to provide planning (mainly land-use) services to individual municipalities. But in no way would such an agency be permitted to promote regional planning or problem solving (Dale 1997, 43). These associations are funded locally, and there is no standard method of operation. Seven intermunicipal planning agencies have replaced the RPCs in various areas of the province, with each evolving in a somewhat different way. In the Calgary region, no successor agency has been formed; instead, an interim planning agreement has been negotiated between each of the two surrounding rural municipalities and the City of Calgary.

Alberta Capital Region Alliance

In the Edmonton region in the early 1990s an experimental extension to the intermunicipal agency approach began to take shape. It grew out of the long-lived strains in intermunicipal relations in the Edmonton region. Animosities that had simmered for a long time came to a boil at about the time the government was eliminating the Edmonton Metropolitan RPC, which had superseded the Edmonton RPC (Smith and Bayne 1994; Thomas 1993; Dale 1997). The member municipalities were left with having to determine whether or not some sort of regional entity could be maintained. A renewed interest in "regional thinking," which resulted from a series of round tables and workshops, led to the establishment of a local restructuring committee that sought to sketch out an organization that would not only replace the former commission, but also expand its scope beyond the previous land-use focus. The outcome was the creation of the Alberta Capital Region Forum Ltd. in March 1995. The forum was an association of fourteen municipalities in the region surrounding Edmonton. Together, these municipalities accounted for more than 800,000 people, or 93 percent of the metropolitan area population.

The forum was superseded by the Alberta Capital Region Alliance (ACRA) in 1998, a voluntary association of participating municipalities in the geographic area known as the Capital Region, which corresponds to the boundaries of the Edmonton CMA. ACRA was formed when a number of municipalities within the region came together with common concerns and an interest in cooperating on regional issues. The alliance can now speak with one voice on behalf of the region, with its overall mission being to define, discuss, and explore regional issues. As of late 1998, sixteen of the region's twenty local government units had joined ACRA.

More recently, the provincial government appointed former cabinet minister Lou Hyndman to chair a governance review of the capital region for the purposes of developing a vision for its future, identifying partnerships or initiatives, and establishing a role for the province in attaining that collective vision. The chair works with the chief elected officials in the region, administrators, and the minister of municipal affair. The objective is to develop a broad, comprehensive view of what needs to be done so that Alberta's capital region is ready to meet the challenges of the future. Hyndman submitted his first report to the minister of municipal affairs in March 2000. He recommended a new, formal governance body be created, the Edmonton Capital Regional Council, to develop and implement shared regional priorities and policies (for other recommendations included in the report, see www.capregion.ab.ca).

Composition of Authority Councils/Boards

The planning decisions in one-tier metropolitan governments, such as Calgary and Winnipeg, are made by those people directly elected to their respective governing council. In two-tier governments, metropolitan-wide planning decisions are made by the members of the upper-tier governing councils who, typically, are elected indirectly; that is, they are elected municipal councillors who are appointed to the metropolitan council, usually by their respective mayors. For example, in the case of the Montreal Urban Community, the governing council consisted of the mayor and councillors of the City of Montreal and one delegate from each of the then twenty-nine other municipalities on the island, with voting weighted according to the population represented. The city also had seven of the twelve seats on the executive committee.

When Metropolitan Toronto was first created in 1953, and for thirty-two years thereafter, Metro Council members were chosen by a system of indirect election, with people elected to local councils either selected to serve on the upper-tier body or automatically becoming upper-tier councillors by virtue of winning the larger majority in a two-member ward. In 1985, the City of Toronto began to elect Metro Council members directly, and, in 1988, the provincial government legislated a system of direct elections for the whole of Metro Toronto. Only the six local mayors continued to sit on Metro Council ex officio. This change posed a new set of problems for the new members of the Metro Council, for it took some time for them to develop a sense of identity and purpose that distinguished them from members of local councils (on which many of them had served in the past) (Frisken 1993, 187).

In the case of the special purpose Calgary and Edmonton RPCs, membership was made up of representatives appointed by contiguous municipalities within the designated planning region as well as three members representing the province who were appointed by the Provincial Planning Advisory Board. The minister of municipal affairs is responsible for designating which municipal councils are permitted to appoint members to a commission and for specifying the number of representatives to which each member-municipality is entitled.

Similarly, the boards of British Columbia's regional districts are made up of elected councillors from the constituent municipalities, as are the RPCs in Atlantic Canada. ACRA is governed by a board consisting of the mayors and reeves of the participating municipalities. There is a general assembly that meets several times a year and which representatives from all member municipalities are encouraged to attend. ACRA's day-to-day work is carried out by a small core secretariat, assisted by a management committee consisting of elected and administrative representatives of member municipalities. Task forces, consisting of appointed representatives, are formed to carry out regional initiatives.

Planning Mandates, Powers, and Tools

According to the Alberta Planning Act, 1977, the Alberta RPCs were mandated to carry out the following five functions, which are fairly typical of most provinces:

1 prepare, adopt, and maintain a regional plan to regulate land development within its region
2 prepare other statutory plans, such as general municipal plans, at the request of a member-municipality
3 provide planning advice and assistance to member municipalities, if so requested
4 review and approve subdivision applications within the region, except in cases in which the minister of municipal affairs has granted such authority directly to a municipality
5 promote and encourage public interest and involvement in the planning process.

The Alberta RPCs were considered the primary institutions below the provincial government level for resolving land development and growth management issues in Alberta (Planning in Alberta 1980, 16). Some municipalities, including the cities of Calgary, Edmonton, Lethbridge, and St. Albert, undertook their own planning activities, and the provincial Department of Municipal Affairs provided planning services to communities in the areas of the province not covered by RPCs. The commissions, it was anticipated, would encourage development in those areas where the most beneficial results would be realized. However, as we discuss later on, it is questionable whether the RPCs, especially those in Calgary and Edmonton, achieved this goal.

These mandates, of course, changed over the years, as circumstances, conditions, and, of course, provincial legislation warranted. For example, in 1977 the subdivision approval authority was taken away from the Alberta commissions and granted to municipal councils if they met certain conditions (mainly the adoption of a municipal plan and land-use bylaw). While only a few large municipalities took advantage of this, it was a real blow to the RPCs, as subdivision approval was their only regulatory power and their only direct means of implementing development policies, even though it fell far short of "true regional planning" (Smith 1994, 42). Another case of a change in the planning mandate granted to regional authorities occurred in 1983, when the regional planning function was taken away from British Columbia's regional districts (although it was restored in the early 1990s under the regional growth strategy rubric).

Powers and Tools of Implementation

The planning agencies are mandated to prepare plans; however, for metropolitan-regional planning, perhaps their powers and tools of implementation are most important. To what extent does the metropolitan-regional planning authority have influence or control over the policies and plans of the constituent municipalities? Must the constituent communities conform to the metropolitan-regional plan or strategy, and, if they refuse, can the planning authority force them to conform? These questions are germane to all categories of metropolitan-regional planning authorities.

With regard to Canada's metropolitan planning authorities, the answer to these questions is, in the main, negative. As a generalization, we can say that the metropolitan-regional planning authorities are *not* given the requisite powers to implement their plans. Implementation depends on political will as well as on the actions and decisions of the member municipalities, other local agencies, relevant provincial agencies, and the private sector.

In short, metropolitan-regional plans are not binding upon any municipality or any of these other bodies. This is in contrast to community plans: local planners and planning departments and local councils have a number of tools and techniques, usually embedded in provincial municipal acts or planning acts, that are available to them and that ensure that they are able to implement their plans.[20] The metropolitan-regional planning agencies have no similar powers, thus the plans they produce are purely *advisory* in nature. The underlying reason for this is that the legal authority to plan is vested in the municipalities themselves. Whatever planning powers the metropolitan-regional agencies have are delegated to them from below. And, as a general rule, local municipalities are reluctant to give powers to a higher authority.

It is true that the various provincial planning acts do make it mandatory that any action taken by any local authority should conform to the metropolitan-regional plan for its planning area. Consequently, every statutory plan, replotting scheme, land-use bylaw, or major municipal project has to conform to the plan. Nevertheless, the upper-level council, board, or commission cannot *require* a municipality to undertake any project or program designated in the metropolitan-regional plan. This stipulation parallels the provision in the Municipal Act that requires a municipality's actions to be consistent with its own official community plan, while not committing the municipality to projects specified in it (on the assumption that conditions may change, rendering a project no longer feasible). But with the metropolitan-regional planning agencies having no enforcement powers, for all practical purposes this stipulation leaves outcomes very uncertain.

As a consequence of this situation, relations between the upper-level metropolitan-regional planning agencies and the lower-level constituent municipalities were often strained. The upper levels found it difficult to obtain local support for the development of their metropolitan-regional plan and, most important, for getting the local authorities to carry through with its implementation. For a discussion of the conflicts between the metropolitan-regional agency and its local municipalities in Metro Toronto (before the recent amalgamation), see Frisken (1993); for the Edmonton regional planning commission, see Dale (1997), Smith and Bayne (1994), and Thomas (1993); for the Montreal Urban Community, see Tomalty (1997), Trepanier (1994), and Sancton (1985, 1988); and for the Atlantic Canada regional planning agencies, see Heseltine (1998).

Administrative Procedures

Administrative rules and regulations represent another basic element that all metropolitan-regional planning systems must incorporate. It is through administrative procedures that a planning system has its most immediate and forceful impact on the communities it is designed to serve. The procedural rules and regulations provide a two-way objective: they protect people who administer the system (both elected and appointed officials) by setting clear limits to their legal authority; and, more important, they also protect the people whom planning decisions directly affect. Two main procedures are normally put in place to protect the people affected: (1) opportunities are created for public involvement in the decision-making processes, and (2) procedures guarantee rights of hearing and appeal to those whose interests have been, or may be, harmed by a particular planning decision.

With respect to the opportunities for public involvement, most provinces have some provision in their planning legislation for citizen participation in planning. In most cases, however, this has been more often honoured in the breach than in the observance. One exception is the experience in the Vancouver region, which we discuss in Chapter 9. The public also participates in hearings and appeals; these are handled through quasi-judicial "tribunals," which we discuss below.

Types of Planning Decisions

Another way of understanding how metropolitan-regional planning systems operate is through looking at the variety of decisions they are obliged to make. For descriptive purposes, we group these decisions into three major types: quasi-judicial, technical, and legislative.

Quasi-Judicial Decisions

To ensure that the power of administrative decision is not exercised arbitrarily in those situations in which discretion is permitted, the metropolitan-regional planning system, including urban and rural planning systems, provides quasi-judicial mechanisms that act as checks against possible abuses and unreasonable hardship. Two special situations in which quasi-judicial powers are needed involve disputes: first, between local authorities within the metropolitan area and, second, between a local government or governments and the metropolitan-regional planning agency. The potential for such conflict within a metropolitan area is especially high because actions taken (or not taken) by one municipality may well have detrimental effects (known as "negative externalities") on one or more of its neighbours. Individual municipalities may also find themselves in conflict with their metropolitan-regional planning authority. For example, a suburban municipality desirous of promoting industrial development in order to strengthen its property tax base may want to rezone a block of farmland in order to provide a site for a new industrial park. But the metropolitan-regional plan designates the site as part of a permanent conservation zone, for the protection of prime agricultural land. Suppose neither the metropolitan-regional planning authority nor the neighbouring municipalities are willing to allow the plan to be amended. How is this issue resolved? Whose interests dominate? Similar conflicts occur all the time.

Part of the answer to this sort of situation depends on which agency has the authority to make the final binding decision. In the case of two-tier forms of municipal government, the upper tier usually makes the final decision, and, in this case, it will be arrived at through the normal legislative process. But if the

upper-tier government does not have explicit authority to make binding decisions, or if there is no upper-tier government at all, or if one exists but its
enforcement powers are weak, then the matter is usually referred to some
"independent" person or board (or even to a quasi-judicial tribunal).

It is necessary that the mechanisms established for resolving these disputes be completely outside the influence of the authorities charged with the
responsibility of making the original decision, and this necessitates the establishment of separate authorities. Following British tradition, in Canada this
means vesting the requisite authority in administrative tribunals, which are granted
quasi-judicial powers. They are empowered to act as courts, in the sense that
their decisions are legally binding, and they are the "courts of last resort" on
certain planning matters. Sometimes these agencies are constituted at the provincial level, other times at the municipal level, and sometimes at both levels.
The Ontario Municipal Board is a good example of a quasi-judicial board.

Ontario Municipal Board [21]

The Ontario Municipal Board is an appointed tribunal with broad powers to
decide on matters of municipal administration. Among the most important of
its powers is the authority to hear appeals of municipal (and metropolitan)
planning decisions and to approve municipal capital expenditures. Because
experience indicates that most planning decisions with any substance are appealed, the board's power to decide on the pace and pattern of development in
and around the former Metro Toronto and the newly formed City of Toronto is
considerable. An Ontario Municipal Board decision is final unless the province
has already declared that it has an interest in the matter at issue, in which case
Cabinet could overturn the board's decision. In controversies between the
lower-tier and upper-tier municipal governments, experience has shown that
the Ontario Municipal Board has generally sided with the lower-tier municipalities, making it even more difficult for the metropolitan level of government
to function adequately.

Technical Decisions

Technical decisions are made by professional planners in their capacity as
advisors to the planning authority's governing council. Professional planners
do not initiate the planning process nor do they make the final decisions about
the future development of their regions; but they play a key role in the planning process and planning system. Their decisions are the least visible and
probably the most misunderstood of all planning decisions, and while, in themselves, they do not have legal force, potentially they can exert great influence.
To the extent that their advice is taken and that their proposed plans, policies,
and programs for guiding future physical development of their metropolitan-
regions become the basis for subsequent action, planners must be viewed as
important agents in the planning process and the planning system.

In making their decisions, planners draw upon their own criteria, generally defined as "planning principles." These principles come from several sources: education and training, professional knowledge and experience, and the values and standards of the planning profession. The planners also use a variety of analytical techniques drawn from a number of sources (e.g., economics, sociology, regional science) to arrive at their technical decisions. The planner's knowledge of theory and practice helps him or her bridge the gap between current planning needs and circumstances and the need for preparing viable long-term plans (Hodge 1998, 401).

The metropolitan-regional planning agency depends on the planner to provide the skills, knowledge, and experience necessary to organize and deal with the particular planning task at hand. Thus, it can be said that the professional planner is both a representative of professional mores, doctrine, and standards as well as a member of the metropolitan-regional planning staff. This sometimes places the planner in the awkward position of trying to "balance" his or her role as a neutral technical advisor with the social norms of the profession and his or her own ideological views.

In view of the huge volume of work that the planning systems in metropolitan areas generate, and the often complex technical considerations involved in most planning decisions, no metropolitan-regional planning organization could operate without a professional staff. All the major Canadian metropolitan-regional governments (one-tier and two-tier) and special-purpose agencies have their own staff, as do most suburban municipalities within metropolitan areas. However, if a municipality is too small to warrant having its own permanent planning staff, then it may call on the provincial government or the metropolitan-regional planning staff to provide it with planning services. This has always been an important consideration in the establishment of regional planning agencies in Canada (Hodge 1994). Sometimes, lower-level municipalities within regional governments and the constituent municipalities that make up regional planning commissions prefer to hire private planning consultants, especially if they want to maintain an independent voice and counter what they perceive to be the "regional point of view" that staff planners on metropolitan-regional agencies tend to favour.

The role of the professional planner has been changing in recent years. He or she is no longer viewed as solely a technical advisor at both the city and metropolitan levels (Kiernan 1982). This is because planning is no longer seen as something that only people called "planners" do; rather, it is seen as something that communities do, with the assistance of the professional planner. The kind of help being given is also changing. While the professional planners' primary skills remain in the areas of research, analysis, and design, and they are still considered experts on future urban form, today it is expected that they also possess social skills, which are useful for organizing the planning process that will be followed (including who will participate, when, and to what extent). In the planning process, planners are more and more advocating widespread public participation on the principle that this will make planning more effective.

Increasingly, metropolitan-regional planning is seen as a mechanism for resolving controversial issues – a mechanism that is assumed to be public, open, and democratic. So it is important that professional planners possess the skills of mediators, facilitators, and animateurs. More and more, the planning process is being seen as an exercise in negotiation – as the medium through which community groups, developers, politicians, and professional planners attempt to work out mutually acceptable solutions to urban and metropolitan problems. In these circumstances, the planner's role can be that of "social reformer," "advocate," "referee," and "social learner" (Gunton 1984). This new form of planning is still evolving in Canada, and, as P.J. Smith (1995, 237) notes, it is not yet clear how many of the traditional structures will survive the transition.

Thus, it is through the application of her/his special skills that the planner, in metropolitan areas, serves as an advisor to her/his employers – the planning agencies' councils. It is important to understand the relationship between the planner and her/his employers. The provincial planning enabling legislation rarely, if ever, assigns direct decision-making responsibility to professional planners. On the contrary, it typically goes to great lengths to establish unequivocally that the responsibility rests with the elected bodies, either directly (when they have been elected by the citizens) or indirectly (through their appointed memberships on the upper-level regional governments or the ad hoc special-purpose boards and commissions).

This contradiction places the planner in an awkward and sometimes paradoxical position. A wealth of technical decisions underlies virtually every official action taken by an upper-level municipal government's council and any board of a special-purpose planning commission. However, planners are quick to disclaim any implication that they have power on the grounds that all they do is advise those who have the legal authority to act on behalf of the metropolitan area and the communities they claim to represent. Nevertheless, planners often express frustration over their lack of power, especially when their advice is turned down or the finger of blame is pointed at them for unpopular political decisions.

What planners are really unhappy about, according to Smith (1995, 233), is that they do not have final responsibility for most planning decisions. It is not the planners who are directly responsible to the communities and regions they serve but, rather, the politicians and appointed commission members who employ them. Because of this seemingly incongruous relationship, the planners, as technical advisors, often find themselves in conflict with their employers, who are the final decision makers. Planners tend to feel that their technical advice should prevail over their employers' "politics."

Legislative Decisions

The final kinds of administrative decisions affecting metropolitan-regional planning are those that are the particular responsibility of some legislative body, usually the upper-level council for the regional government and, most important, the provincial legislature. The councils, boards, and commissions are the agencies empowered to adopt planning bylaws; and many planning instruments require bylaws to give them legal effect. The provincial legislatures, in enacting planning legislation, set the rules of the game, specifying the area to be covered by the metropolitan-regional planning agency; the types of agencies to carry out metropolitan-regional planning; and their responsibilities, functions, and duties.

As in other aspects of local government, the councils, boards, and commissions are also expected to be the policy-making bodies in planning matters as well as the ultimate authority on planning policy in any metropolitan area. Professional planners write the actual plan document, incorporating in it their ideas, technical analysis, and decisions. But before the plan becomes official and has legal force, it must be adopted by the one-tier, or upper-level government body, or the board of the special-purpose commission.

The policies postulated in the plan must be embraced by the one-tier and upper-level councils, boards, and commissions as *their* policies and goals. However, neither politicians nor planners are the only people involved in the plan-making process. A principle now generally accepted in Canadian planning practice is that the plan, be it urban or metropolitan-regional in scope, should be the community's plan and not only the planners', or even the politicians', plan. It should capture and reflect the community's real needs and aspirations as expressed by the citizens themselves. It is for this reason that "citizen participation in planning" is now a commonplace principle in the planning process. How this is achieved at the metropolitan-regional level is an issue we take up in Chapters 10 and 11.

Substantive Issues Underlying Planning Decisions

The discussion so far has dealt with the administrative-procedural aspects underlying the resolution of planning decisions in metropolitan-regional planning situations. But administrative procedures alone, no matter how carefully delineated, cannot guarantee that planning decisions will be reasonable and responsible or that no one will be harmed by them. On the contrary, in situations involving trade-offs or conflict – and most planning decisions do entail trade-offs and conflict of some sort – the standard procedures are constructed so as to produce clear winners and losers. The fact is that the crux of any conflict is not procedural but substantive.

On the substance of planning decisions, planning legislation in practically all provinces is virtually silent. If they give any direction at all, it is generally couched in such bland, vague, and nebulous terminology as to be practically useless. For example, the Alberta Planning Act, which went further than the acts in most provinces in stating the purpose of regional planning, refers to "the orderly, economical, and beneficial development and use of land and patterns of human settlement." As fundamental principles these are worthy objectives, but they certainly do not serve as operational criteria to help in the many types of decisions that the planning system is called upon to make. It is up to the respective regional planning authorities, whoever they may be, to determine what these terms mean in particular situations.

In particular, the Alberta planning legislation, like similar legislation in most provinces, was vague about the nature and purpose of the "regional plan." The legislation specified that the regional plan was the "supreme document" in a hierarchy of statutory instruments, all of which had to conform to its provisions – the general plans, area structure and redevelopment plans, and land-use bylaws (Alberta Municipal Affairs 1980). But the legislation was not only silent as to how this conformity was to be accomplished, it was also vague as to what a regional plan was supposed to be. In an effort to clarify this situation, in 1982 the Alberta Planning Board issued a set of revised regional plan guidelines. However, these did not remove all the ambiguities and uncertainties about the province's approval procedure, the purposes of regional planning, or, for that matter, the role of the regional plan.

Similarly, according to Frisken (1993), uncertainty about the nature, role, and requirements of the regional plan, and how it differs from local plans, also plagued the planners and politicians in Metro Toronto and the regional municipalities in the Greater Toronto Area. Neither Ontario provincial planning legislation nor planning guidelines ever succeeded in clarifying this distinction.

While the spirit and intent of the provincial legislation for metropolitan-regional planning and, specifically, the regional plan, was to protect, indeed to provide, greater municipal autonomy, this did not eliminate controversies and conflicts between the planning agency and its constituent municipalities. In our view, the underlying basis for these conflicts is due, to a large extent, to what we have just noted: the lack of clarity over the nature and purpose of the regional plan, which, in turn, is a result of the imprecision in the planning mandate given to the metropolitan-regional planning agencies. This imprecision pertains to what constitutes a matter of regional interest as opposed to a matter of local interest.

It may seem self-evident to say that regional planning is designed to deal with issues and concerns of a regional nature. But what makes an issue regional as opposed to, say, local or provincial? As we noted previously, the establishment of a region for planning and the associated institutions that accompany it represents an intervention in the ongoing activities of an area and its governing arrangements for which there are no constitutional provisions. There is, thus, the important matter of how regional planning is perceived and accepted by citizens and local governments. In other words, we can expect to be asked: Why does this issue need regional planning? This is an elusive question, and it cuts to the heart of the need for regional planning. It requires clarification, and for this reason we address it in some detail in Chapters 10 and 11.

Another way of viewing the issue of representation of the regional interest is to note that the goals and objectives outlined in a metropolitan-regional plan can mean different things to different people. One person's idea of what constitutes order or economical development may be another's idea of what constitutes disorder and economic disaster. As in the example we posited earlier, the underlying question here is: Whose interest should prevail? Other relevant and related questions are: How should the regional interest be reflected in the framework of the planning system? Should some interests be valued above others? Since political and citizen priorities can also change over time, should the recent and growing interest in environmental issues, for example, take precedence over pro-development interests that have long been dominant in Canadian cities? And, in the metropolitan-regional context, a most important question is whether the regional interest should prevail over community interests.

The usual response professional planners give to these sorts of questions is to note that they and the planning system represent the "public interest" in questions involving the urban and metropolitan environment and development. However, because of the difficulties of putting into practice a concept as abstract as the "public interest," even this is not especially helpful. Nor is there agreement that the public interest, however defined, should always come before private interests.

The ambivalence is well illustrated, once again, by the Alberta Planning Act, which states that planning measures must be undertaken "without infringing on the rights of individuals *except* to the extent that is necessary for the *greater public interest*" (our emphasis). If these rights are considered solely in procedural terms, then the Alberta legislation, like all Canadian statutes, can deal with the issues involved. But, as Smith (1995, 236) notes, on substantive grounds the situation is much cloudier if not totally ambiguous. Is it more in the public interest to allow a developer to build high-rise condominium apartments or a "big box" project in a neighbourhood with predominantly single-family homes on the fringe of a central city than it is to insist that the sites continue to be used for recreation or agriculture? On the one hand, it can be pointed out that the new projects will result in the creation of construction jobs; that the influx of new population will benefit the service facilities; that tax revenue will be generated; and that the needs of a special segment of the housing market will be met at a good location. On the other hand, it is clear that the projects will irretrievably alter the established character of the neighbourhoods; that proceeding with the projects probably means ignoring the feelings of the existing nearby residents, who are bound to be overwhelmingly against the proposed project; and that the developments will cause "suburban sprawl," with all its negative consequences. Similar conflicts occur all the time. Where does the public interest lie in such conflicts? And who defines it?

Clearly, there is no easy answer to these questions, nor is there a ready mechanism for defining the public interest. Politicians will argue that citizens, by electing them, have sanctioned their views, whatever they may be. Citizen groups will argue that their grassroots viewpoints reflect the public interest. And planners might argue that their comprehensive, objective view of the region provides the basis for a valid definition of the public interest. We take up this issue in our concluding chapters.

Planning Outcomes

In order to illustrate the nature and scope of the outcomes that emerged when the metropolitan-regional planning agencies applied the planning and implementation mandates delegated to them and followed the appropriate administrative procedures, we shall: (1) briefly describe the planning activities undertaken by Metro Toronto, Ottawa, and Halifax–Dartmouth; (2) offer a brief description of the content of the plans that were developed; and (3) describe the various overall urban-form planning "models" that have been implemented.

Planning Activities

Metro Toronto

The Metropolitan Toronto Advisory Planning Board (MTAPB) was responsible for preparing an official plan encompassing not only Metro Toronto and its thirteen constituent municipalities, but also the thirteen municipalities in the surrounding fringe – the "extended planning area." There was no stipulation, however, that the plan need be adopted by Metro Council or submitted to the minister for approval. Thus, the official Toronto metropolitan-regional plan covering the extended planning area included the municipalities both inside and outside Metro Toronto; these municipalities were required to conform, in their local official plans and planning and public works projects, to the larger area plan prepared by the MTAPB. In 1974, as a consequence of the province's wholesale restructuring of local government that resulted in the creation of four regional municipalities outside Metro Toronto, the Municipality of Metropolitan Toronto Act dissolved the MTAPB and replaced it with a planning committee of council, which established a Metropolitan Planning Department. It also included an amendment requiring the Metro Council to prepare, adopt, and forward to the minister for approval an official plan for the reduced metropolitan regional planning area (i.e., the area now covered only by Metro Toronto), but no time limit was stipulated.

Metropolitan Toronto functioned without an official plan until 1980. However, this does not mean that planning was not an important activity before that time. Quite the contrary: in 1959 initial planning activity resulted in a massive draft official plan that covered in some detail the issues of land use; sanitation, greenbelt, and park areas; and roads and public transportation. Frisken (1993, 180) has argued that, because of the 1959 plan's detailed treatment of these matters, it provided many opportunities for criticism and made little headway politically and, for this reason, was not given official approval. The next draft plan, produced in 1965, was a much briefer and more generally worded document. As with its predecessor, it made no attempt to propose a radical restructuring of the area's development pattern through major forms of government intervention; rather, both documents aimed to accommodate and, indeed, facilitate private-sector decisions, which they depicted as the main determinants of the area's development, by providing for orderly expansion and infrastructure. The documents also incorporated the planning objectives of other metropolitan agencies and local municipalities.

By the end of the 1960s in Metro Toronto, significant changes had occurred in the climate of public opinion, involving the emergence of strong public concerns for social and environmental aspects of the prevailing development trends. Largely as a consequence of these changes, the planning board and Metro Council decided, in 1971-72, to undertake a full-scale review of its 1965 plan. This was accompanied by the initiation, jointly with the provincial government, of the Metropolitan Toronto Transportation Plan Review, which was directed at the comprehensive re-examination of the earlier transportation planning assumptions and proposals and the formulation of major transportation options for the future.

The official plan that Metro Toronto approved in 1980 restated most of the principles of the earlier 1959 and 1965 plans. It differed in that it was what planners call a "structure" plan rather than a "land-use plan." It was concerned with the broad distribution of population, households, and employment activities as well as the major supporting infrastructure elements (utilities, transportation, parks, and social services) for which Metro Toronto was responsible. The plan's overall aim was to realize a "multi-centred urban structure," which would be achieved through the development of new centres along rapid-transit corridors. Specifically, the plan aimed to accommodate and encourage future growth and change, at the same time diminishing the concentration of office employment, services, and amenities in the central area and minimizing the adverse social and environmental impacts inherent in the existing centrally oriented urban structure. The policies that were established and the degree to which they were successful are discussed below.

The 1989 change in membership of the Metro Council (members were now elected directly) seemed to Metro Toronto's planning staff an opportune time to develop a completely new plan that would more clearly specify the nature of metropolitan interests and distinguish them from those of local municipalities. Moreover, the Toronto metropolitan area was facing a new set of urban challenges, comparable in scope and intensity to those the Metropolitan Corporation faced when it was first created in 1954. These included, among others things, the need for economic restructuring.

The work of the planners culminated in a new draft official plan entitled "Toward a Livable Metropolis," which proposed a "re-urbanization strategy" to bring about an increase of 300,000 in Metro Toronto's population by the year 2011. (This plan will be discussed in greater detail later in this chapter.)

Ottawa–Hull

Planning of the nation's capital goes back to 1899, with the federal government's establishment of the Ottawa Improvement Commission. This commission's first priority was to clean up the banks of the Rideau Canal, which were cluttered with warehouses, sheds, lumberyards, and piles of construction material. It also began the park system by taking over the maintenance of Rockcliffe Park from the City of Ottawa, and it envisaged the creation of boulevards and scenic parkways. After the rubble was cleared from along the banks of the canal, part of the present Queen Elizabeth Driveway was constructed as the first of the scenic drives.

In 1903, the Ottawa Improvement Commission employed Frederick G. Todd, a Montreal landscape architect, to outline a general scheme for the enhancement of the city. Todd completed his plan that same year, and, in 1903, two of his major recommendations were the preservation of large natural parks adjacent to the capital and the construction of an impressive boulevard linking Rideau Hall and the Parliament Buildings.

In 1915, the Federal Plan Commission chaired by Herbert Holt prepared another plan for the city and its environs – the Holt Plan – which proposed many of the projects that have since come to pass, including the relocation of the railways out of the downtown area and the creation of the Gatineau Park "greensward" to the north. The Holt Plan also recommended creation of a strong federal district, something that came to pass in 1927, with the new Federal District Commission. Its jurisdiction was expanded to include some parts of Quebec. Among the commission's many accomplishments were expansion of the region's open spaces and extension of the driveways; it also acquired land and began to develop Gatineau Park.

Following the Second World War, a French planner, Jacques Greber, was commissioned to prepare a plan that encompassed a region on both sides of the Ottawa River, including the City of Hull in Quebec. This plan (known as "The Plan for the National Capital"), submitted in 1950, proposed the development of a greenbelt around Ottawa, the expansion of Gatineau Park north of Hull, the development of various urban parks and parkways, the relocation of the railway, and the decentralization of federal government offices. In order to carry out the Greber Plan, in 1959 the federal government reorganized the capital region planning apparatus and created the present National Capital Commission (NCC), a federal Crown corporation with a planning area that extended about 4,660 square kilometres around both Ottawa and Hull.

Unlike other metropolitan regions, the NCC was given special powers to purchase land for its projects in the name of the federal government, which provided substantial funds for this purpose. (The NCC-owned lands cover approximately 10 percent of the National Capital Region.) The ownership of land was a primary planning and development tool of the 1974 plan for the region, which was entitled "Tomorrow's Capital." This was updated in 1988 and entitled "The Plan for Canada's Capital," and it was again updated in 1998. In 1996 a new updated plan for the greenbelt was approved (one of its planners referred to it as "reinventing" the Greber Plan [Scott 1996, 19-21]). (See below for further discussion of the greenbelt plan.) Although the plan for the nation's capital, especially its greenbelt, is exemplary, there have been a few recent criticisms of it.[22]

Regional Municipalities

Since 1970, planning of the Ottawa–Hull metropolitan area was facilitated by the creation of two regional municipal governments: (1) Ottawa–Carleton on the Ontario side of the Ottawa River and (2) Outaouais on the Quebec side. The boundaries of the NCC on the Ontario side are practically identical with those of the Ottawa–Carleton regional municipality. The two regional municipalities are responsible for the planning of all residential and commercial development and roads and parks, which are not part of the NCC's responsibilities. In this endeavour, the regional governments share responsibility with the local municipalities. Each of the regional municipalities produces its own general regional plan, in addition to the overall Ottawa–Hull plan. "The General Plan for Ottawa–Carleton" is considered to be exemplary of a regional plan that takes an ecosystem planning approach to its environment.

The NCC is the lead federal agency in the National Capital Region. It must relate to two provincial governments and twenty-seven municipal governments that provide local services to the various parts of the National Capital Region. These municipal governments represent major urban centres, most notably the cities of Ottawa and Hull, and suburban and rural municipalities on both sides of the river. The NCC also has to relate to the two regional governments.

In January 2000, the Ontario government, through the minister of municipal affairs and housing, announced that the twelve municipalities that currently make up the region of Ottawa–Carleton – the current regional municipality of Ottawa–Carleton, the cities of Ottawa, Gloucester, Cumberland, Nepean, Kanata, Vanier, and Rockcliffe Park, and the townships of West Carleton, Rideau, Goulbourn, and Osgoode – would be amalgamated to create the new City of

Ottawa.[23] The new city became a reality 1 January 2001. It is governed by a twenty-two-member council composed of the mayor (who represents the city as a whole) and twenty-one councillors representing the twenty-one wards that make up the City of Ottawa. The council is the main governing and legislative body for the city. Previously, all levels of government within the Ottawa–Carleton region had employed a total of eighty-four politicians.

Halifax–Dartmouth

Regional land-use planning in Atlantic Canada, including metropolitan-regional planning, was an outgrowth of its urban-centred regional economic development planning initiatives, undertaken with federal assistance, during the 1960s and early 1970s. Since then, regional planning has had a rather uneven history.

While, in 1964, provincial legislation had established a Halifax–Dartmouth and County regional planning commission with limited advisory powers, no regional planning occurred. Some five years later circumstances converged to create the first regional planning commission in the province just as the 1969 Planning Act was being drafted. In that year, Ottawa offered the Halifax region nearly $2 million in DREE (Department of Regional Economic Expansion) funding, provided that it commission a regional development plan. The province hired consultants to draft a plan, and formed the Metropolitan Area Planning Committee (MAPC).

The problem of obtaining cooperation among the member municipalities became apparent immediately. The consultant's regional development plan offered two options, one that Dartmouth liked and the other that satisfied Halifax. The municipalities did not fully implement either version, and public frustration over the apparent secrecy in which the MAPC operated spawned a new opposing citizens' group. Despite all this bickering, the region received and spent the DREE funds on infrastructure development but then, for all practical purposes, shelved the regional plan. The MAPC continued to operate up to the late 1980s but produced no regional plan after the mid-1970s. Municipalities in the region continued to fight each other for industrial and commercial developments. The MAPC managed the transit system, the regional landfill site, and the water system but was relatively inactive in regional planning in general.

Although regional land-use planning never really got far off the ground in Nova Scotia, the Halifax–Dartmouth metropolitan area benefited from the "growth centre" philosophy that guided regional economic development spending during the 1960s and early 1970s (Grant 1989). Halifax–Dartmouth ended up with a strong industrial and service base, and with very good infrastructure. This had the unintended effect of ensuring that regional planning was perceived as intensifying the dominance of the provincial capital at the expense of the rest of the province. In any case, outside of Halifax–Dartmouth, regional planning was seen as a provincial intrusion.

The Nova Scotia Department of Municipal Affairs planners were responsible for the 1975 Halifax–Dartmouth Regional Development Plan, which was adopted under the province's Planning Act. The document established a regional development boundary within which service development was permitted and encouraged. The plan also allocated major areas for commercial, industrial, and institutional development. Many of its policies followed from the broader federal and provincial economic development initiatives of the time (as discussed earlier). Also, the regional development policies provided a framework within which the four municipalities – the Halifax, Dartmouth, Bedford, and Halifax county municipality – could create municipal plans. Until the 1996 formation of the Halifax regional municipality, the region was comprised of these four municipalities.

In the Halifax area itself, the MAPC had limited success in regional land-use planning. The municipalities seemed decidedly ambivalent towards the committee, and the agency did not develop regional plans after the first few years. The province did not give the metropolitan authority any greater powers than the municipalities offered it, so the MAPC's potential was never realized (Grant 1989, 13). Today it falls on the province's shoulders to resolve regional problems such as municipal sewage treatment and the pollution in Halifax Harbour.

By the late 1970s, with the first director of the province's community planning division gone (he had been a strong advocate of regional planning), and following a succession of provincial governments that had lacked the political will to force bureaucrats' visions on constituents, regional planning withered (Grant 1989). In the early 1980s, the province began another review of its Planning Act. This time, "regional development planning" disappeared completely and was replaced by weaker forms of intermunicipal, cooperative "land-use planning" (Grant 1989). At the same time, the Nova Scotia Department of Municipal Affairs began a comprehensive review of the Halifax–Dartmouth Regional Development Plan. However, as with many other regional planning efforts in the early 1980s, it collapsed due to shifting provincial priorities. During this time, as provincial interest in regional planning waned, municipal planning capability increased. So, when the Halifax regional municipality amalgamated in 1996 and the local plans for all the areas of the regional municipality were completed, the regional development plan was made all but irrelevant (Heseltine 1998, 18).

The Halifax–Dartmouth Metropolitan Authority was responsible to a board that consisted of the mayors and one other elected council member from each of the four municipal units in the region and that was chaired by a provincial appointee. Operations of the authority were fraught with disputes over the issue of equitable representation as well as over major philosophical differences.

In his assessment of the prospects for metropolitan-regional planning in Nova Scotia and the other Atlantic provinces, Heseltine (1998) concludes:

1 The two major metropolitan-regional plans – for the Halifax–Dartmouth and St. John's regions – have lasted more than twenty years but without any completed reviews. Although in the past they have been valuable tools with regard to the development of two of Atlanta Canada's major urban regions, their influence today is minor. Without a review, they cannot be effective.
2 Widespread municipal reorganization offers a new environment for regional planning. Plans to attain municipal objectives will now replace the Halifax–Dartmouth Regional Development Plan, and other amalgamated municipalities may also see the virtues of developing municipal-wide plans, which, effectively, will be "regional plans."
3 In the past, the profile and political structure of the regional agencies in the Halifax–Dartmouth region as well as in other areas of Atlantic Canada tended to compromise their effectiveness. As a rule most of them were lightly staffed and were governed by indirectly elected local councillors, thus making them clearly subordinate to the province on the one hand and to the component municipalities on the other.

Content of Plans

The most important function that all the metropolitan-regional planning agencies performed involved the preparation of metropolitan-regional plans. The content of the plans was generally quite similar, with a few minor exceptions. This is perhaps not surprising, since their content is usually dictated by statutory regulation, as set forth in the respective provincial planning acts; moreover, these acts are usually quite similar, having often followed some "standard" planning act. Generally, the content of these plans and the documents incorporating them cover the following:

- the geographical setting and the basis for the plans, including an analysis and forecast of population, economic and social activity, and the physical form of the community
- concepts, objectives, and policies related to the component land uses and parts of the urban structure (e.g., living areas, working areas, recreation areas and parks, transportation system, water disposal system, and other utilities)
- a discussion of the special problems facing the region and a statement of objectives and policies intended to deal with these problems

- a statement of future planning tasks to be undertaken once the plans are adopted, including, for example, fiscal planning, administrative techniques, and development control.

Planning the Urban Form of Metropolitan Regions

The extensive growth Canadian metropolitan areas experienced during the 1950s and 1960s did not automatically produce compact cities, as had been the case in the past; rather, it dispersed new and old populations, businesses, and factories outside the central cities into surrounding suburbs. This created a dilemma, for, as Blumenfeld (1967, 80) notes, "as more and more people moved into ever-widening rings of suburbs, they move farther and farther away from the city and the country moves farther and farther away from them."

Planners on both sides of the Atlantic attempted to deal with this dilemma by proposing new physical patterns of urban development that would be consonant with the new large scale of cities, the need to bring together the amenities of both city and country, and the need to provide a maximum of accessibility among all parts of the metropolitan area. In short, planners were seeking urban forms that would give cohesion and a sense of "community" to the "exploding metropolis."

Four patterns or urban forms gained prominence among planners: (1) the "monocentric," or "concentric" urban form; (2) the "polycentric," multi-nucleated, or "multi-centred" urban form; (3) the "star-shaped," or "finger plan" urban form; and (4) the "linear," or "ribbon" urban form. These urban forms are essentially ideal types, and, in practice, they are modified by the geography of the area, the past history of development, and other considerations. See Hodge (1998) for a description of these different types. Here we shall briefly describe two of them: the polycentric, multi-nucleated or multi-centred concept, and the star-shaped, or finger plan, concept. We will illustrate their use in Metro Toronto plan and in the greenbelt plan for Ottawa.

Polycentric, Multi-Nucleated Urban Form

The concept of polycentric, multi-nucleated urban form derives from Ebenezer Howard's idea of garden cities surrounding a major city. He referred to this idea as the "Social City" (see Chapter 1).[24] Closely associated with this concept is the concept of a "compact city" (Tomalty 1997) – a concept that public planning bodies; academic, architectural, and planning journals; and urban research organizations have advocated for many years. The polycentric, or compact, city concept was embedded in the plans for Metro Toronto and the Montreal Urban Community. Here, we shall briefly describe its use in the planning for Metro Toronto in order to illustrate the impetus for, and the objectives and content of, this concept as well as some issues involved in implementing it.

Metro Toronto Plan

The reurbanization strategy underlying Metro Toronto's 1992 draft official plan, entitled "Toward a Livable Metropolis," was designed to make better use of available service infrastructure; to slow down the rate of suburban expansion; to allow more people to live closer to their jobs; and to reduce the social, economic, and environmental costs associated with central area disinvestment (Gartner 1995).

The cornerstone of the reurbanization strategy involved directing new employment and housing to designated mixed-use centres and corridors. It was hoped that this would result in the redistribution of residential and employment opportunities and the creation of an efficient urban structure – one well-served by transit, arterial roads, and other municipal services and sensitive to such existing metropolitan assets as green spaces, established neighbourhoods, heritage sites, and community service areas (Gartner 1995, 18).

Settlement patterns and growth trends at the time indicated that, because Metro Toronto was already almost completely built up and had a shortage of vacant land, additional population could only be accommodated through a process of redeveloping at higher densities, residential infilling (constructing new housing on vacant or under-used sites), converting large units into smaller units, and developing sub-centres. This challenge would have to be translated into timely, effective investment strategies that would initially focus on municipal service improvements and transit enhancements in the central area and in and around Metro Toronto's designated centres.

Since 1992, Metro Council decisions seemed to indicate a willingness by the councillors to accept this "strategy" and to approve policies that would support it (Frisken 1993, 187). To be sure, as Frisken pointed out, only time would tell how far the City of Toronto and other Metro Toronto municipalities were prepared to go with regard to allowing the substantial changes in residential structure that would enable Metro Toronto to accommodate a significant share of the Greater Toronto Area's future population growth. Most important, it was not clear that the metropolitan government had sufficient resources to carry out the changes required, even before the recent amalgamation, and, with the recent creation of a single City of Toronto, the uncertainty is perhaps even greater.

"Star-Shaped," or "Finger Plan," Urban Form

The essential feature of the star-shaped, or finger plan, urban form – its best known international example being Copenhagen (Denmark) – is that development is confined to radial corridors emanating from the central core, with green areas between each corridor. Major highways and rail transit routes follow the corridors. This interpenetration of green space and urban development increases the distance to the city centre over that found in the concentric form, but it also maximizes the access of city dwellers to the countryside and open space.

Plan for the Nation's Capital and Its Greenbelt

The 1974 plan for the National Capital Region employed the finger plan concept along with a greenbelt. The plan called for a continuous open space system with "the penetration of rural wedges into the urban area" (National Capital Commission 1974, 17). The 1988 plan for Canada's capital also emphasized the Greenbelt, a crescent-shaped mosaic (ranging in width from two to ten kilometres) of farms, forests, and wetlands, complemented by ski and hiking trails, and dotted with federal and private institutions. The Greenbelt encircles the City of Ottawa and parts of the cities of Nepean and Gloucester, and, in 1996, almost half a million people lived within the inner area it surrounds. Its 200 square kilometres virtually equals the area it surrounds (see Figure 16). The Greenbelt is a special and unique feature of the National Capital Region, and there is arguably nothing like it anywhere else in North America.

Figure 16

National Capital Region and Greenbelt

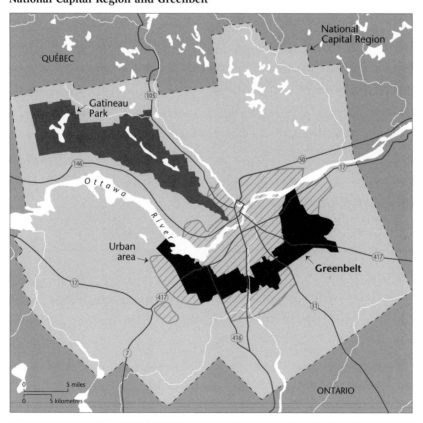

Source: Modified from National Capital Commission (1996).

Its uniqueness stems from, among other things, the fact that it is entirely publicly owned. The Greenbelt is Ottawa's principal rural landscape, offering a breathing space between inner and outer urban areas on the Ontario side of the Ottawa River. Further, the Greenbelt allows visitors to the National Capital Region to experience an important aspect of Canadian geography and society (National Capital Commission 1996).

Comparison of Some Selected Metropolitan Planning Agencies

Having reviewed in great detail the experience of Canada's metropolitan-regional planning authorities, it is now reasonable to ask the following questions: How do the various authorities differ? Most important, have their planning outcomes differed? What might have been responsible for these differences?

To answer these questions we have developed a "scorecard" for six selected metropolitan-regional planning agencies, based on the identification of what we consider to be key variables for understanding how they have operated (Table 12). We have selected one one-tier planning authority (Winnipeg); two two-tier planning authorities (Toronto and Montreal before their amalgamation); two special-purpose two-level planning authorities (Calgary and Halifax–Dartmouth, which preceded the recently amalgamated Halifax regional municipality); and a recently formed voluntary networking association (Edmonton's Alberta Capital Region Alliance). We have assessed each of these agencies in terms of the following factors:

1 the importance of the role of the provincial government, federal government, private-sector, and not-for-profit organizations in the metropolitan-regional planning process
2 whether the boundaries of the agency were appropriate
3 whether the agency has the power to review local plans
4 the benefits of the agency:
    • whether it provides a forum for discussion of regional issues and/or provides planning services to member municipalities
    • whether it develops a regional plan
    • whether it has improved regional development (i.e., the extent to which the agency has successfully guided regional development in terms of efficient and coordinated land use, transportation and services system, and appropriate financing for development needs).

Finally, to partially answer the question about the possible reasons for the differences in the scores of the six agencies chosen for analysis, especially with respect to the benefits of each agency, we have also assessed the nature of the planning and implementation resources (i.e., mandates and powers) the agencies possessed and/or that were delegated to them by either the local, provincial, or federal governments. Our verbal assessment, admittedly quite

Table 12

Scorecard for selected metropolitan-regional planning agencies

	Winnipeg Unicity Planning Department	Metro Toronto Advisory Board[1]	Montreal Urban Planning Department	Calgary Regional Planning Commission	Halifax-Dartmouth Metro Authority[2]	Alberta Capital Region Alliance (Edmonton)
Role in metro planning process						
Provincial government	low	high	high	high	moderate	low
Federal government	none	none	none	none	high	none
Private sector	low	low	moderate	low	low	high[3]
Not-for-profit associations	low	low	moderate	low	low	high[3]
Appropriate boundary	no	no	no	yes	no	yes
Agency review of local plans	mandatory	mandatory	mandatory	voluntary	voluntary	no
Benefits of agency						
Provides forum and planning services	moderate	high	moderate	moderate	moderate	high
Develops regional plan	moderate	high	low/moderate	high	low/moderate	no
Improves regional development	low/moderate	moderate/high	low	moderate/high	moderate	low
Planning and implementation powers	moderate	high	low	moderate	moderate	none

1 This preceded the Metro Toronto Planning Department (1975).
2 This preceded the Amalgamated Halifax Regional Municipality (1996).
3 While it is a key aspect of its concept, so far the Alberta Capital Region Alliance is mainly municipal with little in the way of involvement by the private and not-for-profit sectors.
Sources: Modified from Rothblatt (1994).

crude, uses words and a scale representing high, moderate, and low. It shows, for example, that the Metropolitan Toronto Advisory Planning Board and the later Metropolitan Toronto Planning Department (the planning arm of Metro Toronto) was assessed very highly with respect to the "Benefits Achieved by the Authority," and this was undoubtedly a consequence of its "high" rating with respect to "Planning and Implementation Mandates and Powers."

Future Growth of Metropolitan Areas

Since the 1970s, and especially during the 1990s, cities all across Canada, particularly the metropolitan areas, have played an increasingly important role in the economic, political, and social lives of Canadians. Canada is no longer a nation of rural dwellers, reflecting one of the most important and dramatic demographic changes our country has experienced in the past century. In 2000, almost four out of every five Canadians were living in an urban area, and, perhaps most important, of these, almost 63 percent resided in the twenty-five CMAs.

Emerging Metros

With some demographers predicting that the urban proportion of the population may reach as high as 80 percent by the year 2020, national problems are increasingly becoming the problems of cities and, especially, of metropolitan areas. Moreover, while the focus of attention today may be on what we have called the Big Four (Toronto, Montreal, Vancouver, and Ottawa–Hull), we should not overlook the metropolitan areas we classify as "Almost in the Big Time" (Calgary, Edmonton, Quebec City, Winnipeg, and Hamilton–Wentworth), which, especially in the cases of Calgary and Edmonton, promise to emerge onto the national stage in the next five to ten years. These emerging large metros will likely experience the same planning and governance challenges and problems as do the current Big Four. Thus, they will be informed by the past planning and governance experience of the Big Four, and, most important, by the steps these four CMAs plan to take in the future.

Rural Zones

Planning for the rural parts of CMAs will be a new challenge. In the past, concern about the non-urban parts of the metropolitan-region often did not arise unless there was a need to supply water or recreation space. There were some notable exceptions, including the work of the Lower Mainland Regional Planning Board and the greenbelt planning by the National Capital Commission. Perhaps the most outstanding example of this approach, which recognized the importance of planning the non-urban parts of the metropolitan region, was the Ontario's government's early 1970s initiative for the Toronto Centred Region. This plan recognized and planned two proximate rural zones surrounding the metropolis.

Persistent Issues Still to Be Faced

Of the four forms of regional planning discussed in this volume, metropolitan-regional planning, if not the oldest, has certainly persisted the longest and is still in use today. It has been sustained by provincially mandated agencies for planning and/or regional government, with substantial local input. What was once imposed from above has become almost a routine aspect of local and regional governance, especially in the area of metropolitan-regional planning. (It should be noted, however, that regional economic planning was always an "outsider," not only to the region, but also to the province within which it operated [Hodge 1994].)

Canada, without a doubt, has been a world leader in designing and establishing forms of regional planning and governance for metropolitan regions. Scarcely a metropolitan area in the country does not have some form of regional planning, and many also have a government entity to complement it. We have experimented with metropolitan-regional planning since 1943 (in Winnipeg), and, during this time, five issues have persistently come to the fore:

1 Planning needs a commensurate form of government.
2 Tension between local and metropolitan-regional authorities can be expected.
3 Boundaries can be a problem.
4 Regional representation is in question.
5 A strong and sustained commitment by provincial governments is lacking.

Planning Needs a Commensurate Form of Government

Without a commensurate form of government, metropolitan-regional planning will not be effective. In recognition of this issue, in some metropolitan areas a form of overall governance mechanism has been put in place. Has this really made a difference? Does the presence of these metropolitan "governments" make planning more effective? In particular, does it assist in the implementation of the agencies' plans and planning policies, as has always been assumed? Even more important, has the quality of life improved for residents of the metropolitan areas where a metropolitan government has been established? Metro Montreal and Metro Toronto (before their recent amalgamation) offer two opposite experiences.

Metro Montreal

Beginning in the mid-1960s, and continuing for several decades thereafter, a number of proposals (several emanating from specially appointed commissions such as the Lemay, La Haye, and Brier commissions) advocated rationalizing the local governments within the Montreal metropolis. In 1967, the City of Montreal had gained the blessing of the province to undertake a regional planning exercise, "Montréal Horizon 2000" (Ville de Montréal 1967; see also Guay 1968). The plan covered an area roughly forty kilometres in diameter, radiating out from city hall and covering much of today's Greater Montreal Region. Although it was never implemented (there was no machinery with which to do so), it had a strong symbolic effect, particularly as, throughout these years, then mayor Jean Drapeau had made a strong pitch for "*une île, une ville*" ("one island, one city") (Bédard 1965; cited in Fischler and Wolfe 2000). The only progress Drapeau made in this field involved the annexation of three municipalities that were in financial difficulties – Rivière des Prairies (1963), Saraguay (1964), and Ville St. Michel (1968).

Meanwhile, the provincial government launched a program of amalgamations to reduce the great number of small municipalities, which were considered inefficient. Around the major cities, suburban growth was proceeding apace, and attention was drawn to the scattered nodes of uncoordinated suburban development on Île Jésus. In a surprise move, in 1966 the province forced the fourteen municipalities to amalgamate and, in so doing, created the single municipality of Ville Laval. This demonstrated that the government could act if need be.

At the same time, studies had been proceeding in an attempt to bring the province's administrative districts into line. Until then, each provincial government department had been using its own self-defined regional divisions. In 1966[3], these were standardized. The Région administrative de Montréal was enormous, stretching from the Ontario and US borders to Mont Tremblant. Later it was to be divided into three parts and, still later, into five.

The defeat of the Liberal government in 1966 and the return of the Union Nationale led many observers to fear that the Révolution tranquille was over. However, most of the reforms that had begun in the early 1960s continued. The year of the Expo '67 World Fair saw the creation of the Office de planification et de développement du Québec (OPDQ), which, in collaboration with local Conseils régionaux de développement (regional development councils), was founded to promote economic and social development planning throughout the province. In the region of Montreal, an OPDQ office was established and did much useful data gathering, forecasting, and analysis, but it had no powers of implementation. No regional development council was established for Montreal. In 1970 an attempt was made to set up a Commission de développement de la région de Montréal to handle the special development projects being undertaken in tandem with the new international airport at Mirabel. This commission had a short life, fraught with difficulties and political infighting, and was disbanded in 1972.

By the late 1960s, the Department of Municipal Affairs had become interested in the French model of *communautés urbaines* – upper-tier, indirectly elected governments – as a possible solution to intermunicipal conflicts. In June 1969, plans were tabled for the creation of such communities in Montreal, Quebec City, and Hull, but there were such strong reactions against the idea, especially in the City of Montreal, that the plan was postponed for one year. Then, on 7 October 1969, following months of agitation, a devastating strike by the Montreal police force pushed everyone into action. Only three months later, on 1 January 1970, the urban communities came into being, largely as a way of sharing the costs of demands made by the police force. The Montreal Urban Community (MUC) was assigned responsibilities for police, real estate assessment, water supply and sewerage, garbage, planning, and public transportation – services financed by property taxes that were to be collected by member municipalities. Later, the MUC took on regional parks and some other functions. The police forces on the island were amalgamated by 1972.

In 1969, when the provincial government created the MUC, it seemed to be taking a positive step forward with regard to municipal reorganization. Initially, there was hope that the MUC would become a strong metropolitan government with broad powers to implement a vision for the region. However, in reality, as most observers agree (see, for example, Sancton 1985 and Trepanier 1993), the MUC developed into a weak form of metropolitan government. Several factors can explain this.

First, its territory and powers may have seemed sufficient for the purpose for which it was originally formed, but they proved limited in relation to the problems of the region. There was the overriding issue of population growth and how that growth was distributed. In 1971, the MUC population of two million (essentially the island of Montreal) represented 71 percent of the CMA. By 1991, the MUC population had declined to 1.8 million, or only 57 percent of the 1991 CMA population; and in 1996, it had declined to 54 percent. The implications of these figures are that, first, the metropolitan government (i.e., the MUC) was becoming relatively less important within the entire metropolitan area and that, second, it was not responsible for those areas where "the action is" (i.e., the fringe areas and outer suburbs), a problem we shall deal with in Chapter 10.

Second, according to Sancton (1994) and Trepanier (1993), this situation actually had its roots in the original 1969 delimitation of the boundaries of the MUC. These boundaries were not administratively logical at the time and became even more obsolete as development and population growth accelerated in the outer metropolitan ring. The original boundaries "encapsulated most of the east-west axis of urban development, but were woefully deficient for the north-south" (Trepanier 1993, 77). For this reason alone, Trepanier stresses, the MUC turned out to be a very mild form of metropolitan government because its territory, including its planning area, was small relative to the entire metropolitan area.

Only strong intervention by the provincial government could have changed the MUC from a weak coordinating body into a real regional authority (Sancton 1985). Unfortunately, the 1982 reform did not meet this need; rather, it seemed to function as a neutral mediator between the conflicting parties (Trepanier 1993, 77). It did not force the MUC into new fields of activity but, through the standing commissions and through a reformed planning process, simply provided mechanisms for facilitating better debates between local representatives. The government left open the question of adding similar functions to future intermunicipal agreements. In effect, this meant the province agreed to leave the MUC's future development to the good will of the local municipalities. As a result, the MUC functions, except for police and transit, tended to be limited to non-controversial, technical matters (such as sewage collection or air pollution control) and was little more than an administrative mechanism for delivering a few metropolitan services.

In view of these factors, together with the political tensions between the City of Montreal and the twenty-eight much smaller suburbs on the outskirts, it is not surprising that the MUC was a weak planning and decision-making body and that, consequently, Trepanier (1993, 77) was led to conclude that it was closer to the model represented by the "councils of government" in the United States. With the recent move towards amalgamation and the establishment of a regional mechanism, which we discuss below and in Chapter 9, it appears that the effectiveness of the MUC may be diminished even further.[25]

In December 2000, the Quebec National Assembly approved Bill 170, which would merge Montreal with all its suburbs on the island to take effect on 1 January 2002. The bill would also merge Quebec City with all its suburbs on the north shore of the St-Laurent, and Hull with all its suburbs. In addition to the "mega-city" amalgamation, the government also established the Montreal Metropolitan Community, which encompassed the region (see Chapter 9).

Under this new arrangement the Montreal mega-city would have more than 1.8 million residents and be organized into twenty-six boroughs, with control over a limited range of services, but no powers of taxation or of serious policy making. They will basically be delivering services determined by the mega-city and be funded from budget allotments made by the mega-council. Seventeen boroughs would replace the twenty-six existing suburban municipalities around Montreal (each corresponding to one such municipality or, in the case of the smallest ones, to a merger of two or three of them), and nine boroughs would be located within the existing City of Montreal.

The new city would have a very powerful mayor, who would run it with an executive committee whose members she/he could select and fire at will. The council would have seventy-one members. Boroughs would send between one and six councillors to city hall, depending on population size. As we might have expected, this proposal was met with considerable anger and opposition from citizens and local suburban politicians. Opponents of the proposal (including, most vociferously, the *Montreal Gazette*) called it undemocratic because residents were not consulted. They feared that they would face higher taxes and that local services and community activities would suffer if the mergers went through (*Globe and Mail*, 11 December 2000, A6). Also, some of the suburbs with sizable English-speaking populations argued that they would lose the little political and linguistic clout they had (*Globe and Mail,* 27 November 2000, A4).

The government and supporters of amalgamation, who have long pursued Jean Drapeau's dream of one-island, one-city, argued that the merger is needed for several reasons (Lysiane Gagnon, "Giving Montreal Its Due," *Globe and Mail,* 20 December 2000, A15; *Globe and Mail,* 1 December 2000, A1 and A3). Montreal's crazy-quilt pattern of municipalities produces a situation in which extremely wealthy, completely contained enclaves exist in the middle of the city, only minutes from downtown. These suburbanites, according to mega-city boosters, get all the benefits of living, being entertained, and working in an international city, but they do not pay city taxes and are not involved in Montreal politics. The suburbs can afford high-quality amenities and services, while Montreal must deal with the homeless, subsidized housing, downtown traffic jams, and the flight of middle-class Francophones to suburbs off the island of Montreal. In short, they argued, the merger would bring badly needed fiscal equity to the island.[26]

Only time will tell whether the merger will achieve all the benefits the government and its supporters claim, and, in particular, whether it will have a positive impact on planning and the quality of life of Montrealers.

Metro Toronto

With respect to the first decade of Metro Toronto's existence, it is generally felt that its two-tier system worked very well. Numerous capital works were undertaken, sewerage installed, the water supply improved, new roads and transit lines built, suburban housing developed, and schools constructed – all at a remarkably rapid pace. All around the metropolitan area there were visible signs that the province had made the right move when it established Metro Toronto. As Lionel Feldman, a well-known Toronto authority on housing and urban development, said: "Its first decade was a success because it dealt successfully with that crisis" (Dialogue 1991, 14). Without question, the decision to consolidate twenty-one municipalities into six – and so to create Metro Toronto – did not cause the revolution many local leaders of the day had predicted it would. Municipal taxpayers did not revolt, and the sky did not fall. The province acted decisively and seemed to have won the battle for public opinion. Feldman (1991) further observed that, between 1964 and 1988, Metro Toronto continued to be a success because it was able to make a series of incremental changes without upsetting anyone.

But how about the past decade? The conclusion is the same. There is no doubt that, since the late 1980s, public policies and planning, especially at the metropolitan level, have contributed significantly to the continued economic and social health of the City of Toronto and the six area municipalities. And it has done so by coordinating the provision of physical and social services on a metro-wide basis. Metro Toronto managed to substantially meet the objectives of its 1980s plan: to preserve downtown Toronto as the region's main commercial and cultural centre; to develop secondary centres of commercial activity and high-density housing linked to public transportation; to develop a public transit system whose primary purpose was to carry commuters from Metro Toronto's outer municipalities to downtown Toronto; to locate job sites throughout Metro Toronto's area to enable people to work close to where they live; and to disperse housing of varying densities and income levels (including low-cost public housing) throughout the Metro Toronto area (Nowland and Stewart 1991; Frisken 1994). The public transit system has supported Metro Toronto's plans for high-density nodes of mixed-use development (including residential, commercial, and public-sector activities) at or near several rapid transit stations within Metro Toronto. These nodes were intended, in particular, to help the three largest suburbs within Metro Toronto by attracting some of the office or commercial development that began to become dominant in the region's economy in the 1970s.

Another plus for metropolitan government in Toronto involved the use of pooled tax revenues, which, among other benefits, served to fund social services and public school operations, thus helping to prevent large intermunicipal disparities among individual Metro Toronto municipalities. It also helped poorer municipalities to maintain local services at a quality comparable to that of other Greater Toronto Area municipalities without being charged disproportionately higher taxes (Frisken et al. 1997). These outcomes of tax pooling stand in contrast to the experiences of most of the large US metropolitan areas – which typically have no form of metropolitan governance – where the most disadvantaged residents are concentrated in older (usually central) municipalities and where jobs and other opportunities are declining, while wealthier residents are attracted to suburban, usually newer, municipalities where opportunities are increasing.

Many of Metro Toronto's achievements surely resulted from far-sighted and effective planning and planning policies, which, in turn, could not have happened without the metropolitan form of government. Thus, we concur with Frisken et al.'s analysis of the impact of governance on social well-being in the Greater Toronto Area: "The existence of metropolitan government then was critically important to the way Metropolitan Toronto developed and to the quality of life Metro provided" (1997, 52). At the same time, we must reiterate a point made several times throughout this chapter: Despite all these achievements, Metro Toronto was unable to direct or control the suburban growth that occurred outside its boundaries within the metropolitan area; and, equally important, it was incapable of controlling the extensive growth that has been taking place outside the CMA in the vast outer areas making up the Greater Toronto Area (see Chapter 9). It is also unclear whether the newly amalgamated City of Toronto will have any more success.

Tension between Local and Metropolitan-Regional Authorities

The second, and related, issue in metropolitan-regional planning concerns the uneasy alliance and persistent tension between the metropolitan-regional authorities and their constituent local governments. As contemporary observers continue to note (Heseltine 1998; Wight 1999), this tension sometimes leads to stalemate. When establishing these new planning agencies, the provinces were presumably loathe to deal with a further division of powers and left it to the municipalities to take the advice of their own metropolitan-regional planners (which was to conform to the plan or strategy). Unfortunately, they often did not do so, and that remains the situation today.

This perhaps explains the general paucity of officially approved metropolitan-regional plans produced by the metropolitan-regional planning agencies. Such plans, after all, would remove control of growth and development from local politicians. Most important, this has meant that the majority of metropolitan planning agencies have been merely advisory. They have had little, if any, power either to implement a metropolitan-regional plan or to make the constituent municipalities conform to it. Implementation depended on the political will, actions, and decisions of the member municipalities, other agencies, and the private sector. Plans made by these metropolitan planning authorities could be ignored as they were not binding upon any municipality. This, of course, created continual controversies and conflicts between the planning agencies and their constituent municipalities. This situation was a portent of a deep-seated dilemma – one that continues to bedevil metropolitan-regional planning to this day.

Boundary Problems

The third issue in metropolitan-regional planning involves the fact that, with very few exceptions, in establishing the original boundaries of the planning regions the provinces did not set the boundaries far enough outside the planning agency's official political and governmental boundaries. Nor did they give the planning agency control over this extended area (where future development was likely). Where they did provide such control (e.g., in Toronto and Winnipeg), it was taken away after a decade or so. In addition, even after the original boundaries have been set, unlike Statistics Canada (which frequently alters the boundaries of CMAs in order to meet changing conditions), the provincial government rarely alters the boundaries of the metropolitan planning agency's planning area to accommodate new growth and/or to reflect the true nature of the region. As a result of these inflexible boundaries, sprawl and other extremely low-density developments located on the edges of existing metropolitan areas are leapfrogged into previously undeveloped areas, with serious economic, environmental, and other consequences. The metropolitan planning agency is unable to control these developments.

Who Speaks for the Region?

A fourth issue that has plagued effective metropolitan-regional planning concerns the question: Who represents and speaks for the region and the regional interests? In theory, this question was answered by the creation of special purpose metropolitan-regional planning commissions (or agencies) and of two-tier forms of local government. It was assumed that the special purpose commission and upper-tier council would represent and speak for the region and regional interests. However, in practice, it has not worked out that way. With few exceptions, members sitting on the planning agencies' governing councils tend to be municipal politicians appointed from their lower-tier home municipal councils as representatives to the regional unit. Many observers have voiced concerns over the difficulties of effectively promoting, let alone debating, region-wide issues and proposals under these arrangements.

Among the concerns is the tendency for indirectly elected regional councillors, due to their electoral power base, to take a parochial view rather than to support the regional interest. As we have seen, this was Heseltine's (1998) conclusion in his survey and analysis of regional planning in Atlantic Canada. Smith and Bayne (1994, 733) echo the same conclusion when they note, in the case of the Edmonton regional planning commission, that it was a rare regional planning commissioner who was able to put the metropolitan-regional interest first, especially when it conflicted with the interests of his or her home municipality. In short, there were no directly elected politically responsible people speaking on behalf of the regional interest. This observation could have been directed at most of the upper-tier metropolitan planning agencies as well.

Another problem concerns the double membership on both a local and regional council, as this imposes an undue workload on councillors and tends to result in regional interests receiving less attention than local interests. Possibly most important is the fact that indirectly elected councillors are not accountable to those members of the public who are concerned with regional issues.

As a consequence, the regional perspective is frequently represented more forcibly and consistently by the regional planning agency's technical and administrative staff. This can create tensions between regional planners and regional councillors – a tension that will usually be at its greatest during preparation of the regional plan or strategy. (See Smith and Bayne [1994] for a description of these tensions during the preparation of the Edmonton regional plan.) Another unelected source of support for regional interests often consists of local media who "speak" for the region.

Within this regional milieu many observers argue that the situation could be improved immeasurably if members of the region's governing body were elected directly by the citizens of the region. If this were the case, then the regional body would be composed of people who could genuinely claim to speak for the region and who could be accountable for their positions and actions. There are only a few instances in which members of the upper-tier metropolitan governing councils have been directly elected by the citizens of the region. (This was the case in the Municipal Corporation of Winnipeg up until 1972 and in Metro Toronto after 1985.)[27]

While, admittedly, the proposal for direct elections to the regional body has much merit, there still remains the question: How can valid local concerns and experience also be brought into the deliberations of the metropolitan-regional body?

Lack of Provincial Commitment

The fifth, and perhaps the most critical, issue that metropolitan-regional planning agencies faced – and will continue to face in the future – has been the lack of strong and sustained commitment by provincial governments. This was most noticeable in the following areas of concern. First, given the conflicts between metropolitan and local planning interests noted here, we would have expected the provincial governments to step in on the side of metropolitan interests. After all, why would they have established these planning agencies if not for the express purpose of developing and implementing a metropolitan-regional vision for the region as a whole? And, of course, provincial governments have virtually unlimited legal power to require local compliance with government-stated priorities and metropolitan-regional plans. However, the provinces seldom used that authority to override local planning preferences. Indeed, they were often ready to modify their policies in order to accommodate local objections and local priorities whenever it seemed politically expedient to do so (Frisken 1994). The provinces were reluctant either to force local authorities to take the planning advice of the metropolitan-regional agency or to impose solutions on them. Rather than promoting the metropolitan-regional interests the provinces tended to work out compromises among competing local interests. And sometimes they made decisions directly favouring local plans.

Second, although the provinces established the regional planning authorities, they have been consistently committed to the belief in strong local autonomy – a commitment that has stood in the way of effective regional planning. Indeed, Thomas (1993, 266) claims that the Alberta government's commitment to regional planning seemed to be motivated by a desire to temper or forestall any moves towards the creation of a unicity or two-tiered system of government for the Edmonton metropolitan area. The reluctance of nearly every Alberta provincial government to opt for either of these alternatives was likely due to their fear of having a politically powerful regional government in their own backyard. Whatever efficiencies in urban services and infrastructure development may have been gained through some sort of regional administration was, from the province's standpoint, outweighed by a strong commitment to local autonomy. Repeatedly emphasizing its commitment to the local autonomy of the communities within the regional planning commissions' planning regions, the Alberta government was quite willing to accept the inefficiencies and redundancies that followed from this policy (Thomas 1994; Smith and Bayne 1993).

A third example of the provincial governments' apparent reluctance to take a strong stand on behalf of the metropolitan-regional planning agencies' objectives and interests was their unwillingness to link their own provincial (ministerial) actions with metropolitan-regional plans. Provinces control most of the key elements that affect metropolitan-regional development patterns (e.g., infrastructure such as water supply, sewage disposal, housing subsidy programs, roads, and transit systems). However, as a rule, they have been unwilling to plan and coordinate their programs and projects regarding these elements so that they dovetail with metropolitan-regional plans.

Fourth, with few exceptions, metropolitan planning agencies have not had the power to formulate, coordinate, and implement policy. Most provinces have shown little interest in creating an effective metropolitan planning agency with the power to govern metropolitan regions.[28] For example, although more than half of the population of Quebec lives in the Montreal region, the province has clearly been reluctant to create a metropolitan administrative superstructure that would rival its own influence. Instead, it continues to act as the only public entity capable of mediating conflict among local interests and acting on a metropolitan scale.

A fifth example of the provincial lack of commitment to regional planning and governance concerns the provincial government's resistance to altering political boundaries, as discussed earlier. Many Canadian metropolitan areas have suffered from fringe growth and would have benefited by either having their boundaries expanded or at least being given planning and development powers over an extended area on their outskirts. The metropolitan agencies themselves were unable to contain metropolitan area expansion, and the provincial governments rarely came to their aid.

A final example of the provinces' apparent unwillingness to make regional planning and governance more effective involves the inadequate resources they have delegated to the metropolitan-regional planning agencies.

In summary, it is to the credit of the provinces that they have taken steps to create metropolitan-regions and planning authorities; however, they have failed to pay sufficient attention to the fact that, through development, these regions are subject to change. The provincial governments have not been diligent in supporting and guiding the regions they have created, and they have not dealt with the issues we described above. They have done little to mediate the conflicts between local and metro-regional authorities – conflicts that have often obstructed the realization of programs and projects essential to regional development. And, finally, it has often been difficult to obtain the active participation of provincial ministries and agencies in the realization of a region's plan. And, when this participation has been obtained, it has sometimes been at the expense of the plan's objectives. In short, provincial governments have failed to keep up with new and emerging developments in their metropolitan areas.

Frisken (1994, I: 22), in her review of metropolitan changes and the challenges to public policy, summarizes this situation best:

Provincial governments have shown little willingness to exercise firm or consistent management of the pace and pattern of metropolitan expansion, despite their extensive powers both to administer municipal affairs and to regulate the use of private property ... [T]hey have initiated an impressive variety of institutional arrangements for planning or administering metropolitan areas, [but] they have seldom been willing to provide the support needed to make those arrangements effective ... provincial interest in managing metropolitan area development has been declining as metropolitan areas continue to expand.

9

Planning and Governing City-Regions

Fly over one of Canada's largest metropolitan areas – Montreal, Toronto, or Vancouver – and what strikes you immediately is the spaciousness of the development. It is as if an immense carpet of houses, office buildings, shopping malls, warehouses, manufacturing plants, golf courses, and farm buildings – all crisscrossed by highways – has been unrolled across the entire area in every direction, extending as far as the eye can see and beyond.[1] This new spatial phenomenon, or form of human settlement, is a product of the late twentieth century (Geddes 1997; Senior 1966). Neither "city" nor "metropolitan area" is the right word to describe it. More appropriate terms would be, for example, "citistate" (Peirce et al. 1993), "mega-urban region" (McGee and Robinson 1995), "new city" (Fishman 1990), "regional city" (Gertler 1996; Calthorpe and Fulton 2000), "urban field" (Friedmann and Miller 1964), and/ or "urban-" or "city-region" (Jacobs 1984; Senior 1966). We prefer the term "city-region" and will use it throughout this chapter. Canada has three city-regions – Montreal, Toronto, and Vancouver (sometimes referred to as "Greater Montreal," "Greater Toronto," and "Greater Vancouver").

The city-region is where people live mainly in houses, not apartments, where urban functions are spread out, and where the means of travel are chiefly individual rather than communal. It is an area that does not attract tourists or conventions, nor is it the subject of tourist postcards and slick brochures. It is, rather, the destination of job seekers, industrialists, and entrepreneurs desirous of starting up new businesses; young families wanting to buy their first homes; and corporations interested in establishing their offices (even their headquarters). This new urban form, which is composed of the old central city, its surrounding metropolitan suburbs, and outlying semi-rural and rural developments, is already twice as populated as is the old core city. And it is growing.

Most of us are familiar with the features of these city-regions, but few of us recognize how radically different they are from both the cities of old and the post-Second World War metropolitan areas that were the focus of Chapter 8.

The basic unit of the city-region is not the streets measured in blocks, or even large subdivisions (as in the suburbs), but, rather, the "transportation corridor" that can stretch from sixty to 160 kilometres. Within such city-regions, each element is enlarged many times over. For example, "planned unit developments" of cluster housing are as large as townships; office and industrial parks are set amid several square kilometres of landscaped grounds; and shopping malls dwarf the downtown shopping areas they have replaced. While their populations are large, the most striking feature of these regions is their scale and geographic extent. Their population growth is outpaced by their geographic growth, with the area of built-up, urbanized land sometimes growing at a rate eight to ten times greater than that of the population (Geddes 1997, 1). Where the leading metropolitan areas of the early and mid-twentieth century – places such as New York, London, and Paris – covered perhaps 300 square kilometres, today's city-regions may encompass as much as 8,500 to 10,000 square kilometres.

These sprawling regions should not be judged by the standards of the centralized metropolis, where urban patterns tend to be concentric in form, with the areas surrounding the central city resembling the growth rings of a tree. Not urban, not rural, not suburban, but possessing elements of all three, the city-region eludes all the conventional terminology and criteria of the urban and regional planner and the historian. It lacks definable borders, even a definable centre or periphery, or the clear distinctions between residential, commercial, and industrial zones that shaped the old cities and metropolitan areas. The city-region tends to be amorphous and amoeba-like in spatial form, with no set boundaries or geographic extent. Geddes (1997), for example, describes the current form of the New York region as resembling a flower with petals radiating into five subregions in three states.[2]

The emergence of urban functions in an environment never designed for them produces the anomaly of urban-style crowding and congestion in a decentralized, rural-type setting. These developments are scattered cheek to jowl with subdivisions, apartment complexes, condominiums, golf courses, and, here and there, with farms and green fields. A subdivision of very high-price, single-family homes outside Toronto may sit next to a technological research-and-production complex; or a new mall filled with boutiques once found only in the great shopping areas of Europe rises amid fruit-growing farms and echinacea-producing fields on the outskirts of Greater Vancouver. It is understandable why many urban planners and social scientists trained and brought up on the clear functional logic of the centralized metropolis can, at best, see only disorder and disarray in these "nonplace urban realms" (to use a well-known term popularized in the 1970s). At worst, they see urban sprawl. The city-regions were not planned this way; rather, they were built up piecemeal, the product of untold numbers of uncoordinated decisions made by housing developers, shopping mall operators, corporate executives, highway engineers, and thousands of Canadians who bought single-family homes in an expanding exurbia.

The deficiencies of the new city-regions are perhaps more obvious than the promises and opportunities. Sprawl *is* an issue here. Environmental (as well as financial and social) costs and problems are attached to this low-density, sprawling pattern of development. Horrendous traffic congestion, commutes that take hours instead of minutes, serious air pollution, loss of greenbelts and open space, the obliteration of community life (including the separation of people by class and race) – these are some of the problems created by this pattern. Currently, Vancouver and Toronto rank very high on an international basis in terms of quality of life.[3] If care is not taken, however, the very things that created this high quality of life, and that inspired the emergence of these city-regions in the first place, could be destroyed. The immense speed and scale of development across their territories threaten to annihilate their natural environments, leaving the tranquility and natural beauty that Canadians seek when they move to city-regions perpetually retreating. There is a danger that the regions may degenerate into an urban form that is too congested to be efficient, too chaotic to be beautiful, and too dispersed to possess the diversity and vitality of a great city.[4] These dangers pose real challenges for regional planners, for those in the associated disciplines of urban planning and architecture, and for local and provincial policy makers.

Today there is increasing global recognition that metropolitan areas, and especially city-regions, are the most logical, viable, and competitive economic units (Peirce et al. 1993; Ohmae 1995; Dodge 1996; Kanter 1995). National and domestic regional economies greatly depend on the economies of a nation's major cities. Among the major issues facing city-regions today, perhaps the most important is the lack of coherent governance – either formal or informal – for the regions as a whole. The result is that basic public decisions are usually reached in piecemeal, often haphazard, fashion – or, worse still, are never made at all. It is generally believed that those city-regions with effective region-wide planning and governance systems will compete successfully within the global economy (Foster 1997; Peirce et al. 1993; Downs 1994; Yaro and Bliss 1996). As well, other observers point out that such governance systems will have to achieve ecological sustainability in these regions (World Commission 1987). And this, of course, also applies to Canadian city-regions (Royal Commission on the Future of the Toronto Waterfront 1992; BC Round Table 1992a; Artibise and Hill 1993; Rowe 1999; Avana Capital Corporation 2000).

In view of the significant role city-regions currently play in Canada and will continue to play in the future (as centres of economic development, innovation, knowledge, and technology), this chapter's review of their planning and governance experience – including the various policies and mechanisms they have adopted or are contemplating adopting – takes on added importance.

The review may serve to inform future Canadian efforts as well as those in other countries, where there appears to be a revival of the movement towards more effective city-region (and metropolitan) guidance and governance systems (see, for example, Glasson 1994; Rothblatt 1994).

This chapter is organized as follows. First, as background, we describe the reasons for the emergence of city-regions and their special features and characteristics, and then we present an overview of the three Canadian examples. Second, we examine the nature and extent of the "governmental resources" delegated to each of the Canadian city-regions by their respective provinces. Third, we review the planning and growth management policies, initiatives, and outcomes that resulted from using the resources made available. Fourth, we examine the recent governance proposals for change in each of the three examples and offer some reflections on the future prospects for region-wide planning and governance. Finally, we conclude with a discussion of the common issues that the three city-regions will face in the new century and expand upon one of the most critical – future governance arrangements.

Emergence of City-Regions

In recent decades, change has become as important as growth to the development of many cities in industrialized, industrializing, and post-industrial societies (Hutton 1998, 1). By change, we refer not only to increased population, employment, economic activity, and the familiar ups and downs associated with economic cycles, but also a more fundamental restructuring of the economy. Economic restructuring is marked by dramatic shifts in the industrial mix of metropolitan areas; these shifts generally involve the rising dominance of services and technology-intensive production over traditional manufacturing. Such economic restructuring also brings with it interrelated occupational, social, cultural, spatial, and physical changes. The eminent geographer Jean Gottman (1982, 7) describes these changes as, together, constituting a "metamorphosis of the modern metropolis," by which he means we are dealing with rapid and far-reaching change rather than with gradual evolution.

Since the 1960s, studies of restructuring have tended to focus on the experiences of the largest metropolitan areas – the so-called "world cities," or "global cities" (see Friedmann and Wolff 1982; Sassen 1991). There are logical reasons for this emphasis: world cities with populations of five to ten million or more represent giant markets and centres of production and account for significant proportions of gross domestic product, both nationally and globally. Such world cities exist in the developing as well as in the developed world, and they have attracted the headquarters of many corporations, information- and knowledge-based companies, leading banks and financial institutions, and advanced business-service firms. They also have increasing significance as centres of innovation, creativity, information and knowledge, and technology – what Castells and Hall (1994) refer to as "urban technopoles."

More recently, attention has focused on the growth processes and restructuring processes being experienced by medium-sized, second- and third-tier city-regions, with populations ranging between one and five million.[5] There are now more than three hundred city-regions around the world with populations of more than one million (Scott 2000). Many of these city-regions are subject to the same economic forces working on the world cities, and they possess many of the same characteristics. Our three Canadian city-regions fall into this category, having populations ranging between almost two million (Vancouver) to more than three million (Montreal), and to over five million (Toronto) (Tables 13 and 14).[6] A distinguishing feature of the medium-sized, second- and third-tier city-regions, like their global cousins, is that their spatial impact extends far beyond the boundaries of the central city: indeed, the decentralization of people and jobs occurs beyond the metropolitan area boundaries in outlying suburban, exurban, and rural areas, resulting in a dynamically evolving mixture of town and country activities. These developments often induce severe planning problems – such as congestion, pollution (air and water), and housing shortages – problems for which effective governance arrangements are lacking.

Defining the City-Region

There is no single, universally accepted definition of a city-region. Suburban growth now extends so far beyond central cities and metropolitan area boundaries that economists, sociologists, planners, statisticians, geographers, and urbanologists have widely differing definitions of what constitutes a city-region. The following is a sample of some of these.

The urban region:

> is not simply an overspill of the city, or territorial unit, but a population living in an organically interrelated group of people whose jobs, economic activities, social institutions, leisure time, and mobility are working together in an integrated fashion ... [and] represents more than an enlarged scale of city or town, and more even than an amalgam of cities. It involves no less than a fundamental reorganization of social and economic life so that most of such life is centered on the metropolis. (Senior 1966, 9, 11)

> is defined as a large urban area with a population of 100,000 or more, with adjacent urban and rural areas which have a high degree of economic and social integration with that urban area. (Sancton 1994)

> [is a] key transmission point in the global economy ... [it is] home to skilled labor, extensive communications and transportation networks, and the most supple and innovative of firms. (Editor, *Policy Options*, May 1994, 4)

may be regarded as the key node, "relay point" or "gateway" of national economic space, assuring the connections between national and global economies, and between national economies and the regions. (Coffey 1994, 7)

[is] the places where capital, workers, institutions and infrastructure (both hard and soft) come together to provide the foundations for successful economic activity. (Gertler 1996; Ohmae 1995; Gardner 1992; Seelig and Artibise 1991)

occurs in the hinterlands of some cities – beginning just beyond their suburbs – [where] rural, industrial and commercial workplaces are all mixed up together ... [it is] unique, being the richest, densest and most intricate of all types of economies except the cities themselves ... [the city-region is] not defined by natural boundaries, because [it is] wholly the artifact of the cities at their nuclei; the boundaries move outward – or halt – only as city economic energy dictates. (Jacobs 1984)

Special Features and Characteristics of City-Regions

The three Canadian city-regions represent a new spatial phenomenon and are distinct from the Canadian metropolitan areas discussed in Chapter 8, as well as from all other urban areas, because of (1) the special forces impinging upon their growth and development, and (2) their unique features and characteristics. They warrant special treatment, and throughout this chapter we shall demonstrate how these special features have influenced the nature of the problems, challenges, and opportunities these city-regions face. We will also look at the approaches to planning and goverance (both current and proposed) for dealing with city-regions.

Briefly, the special characteristics of city-regions include the following:

1 Since the early 1970s metropolitan areas in Canada have all experienced a decentralization of population not only to their own suburbs, but also, and more important, to outside their boundaries and beyond (see Chapter 8). As a consequence, the central core cities have declined relative to the total population of the metropolitan areas and the city-regions. In short, the dominant growth in city-regions is occurring in their outlying parts.

2 Each city-region is composed of a central core city, both inner and outer suburbs, exurban and semi-rural municipalities, and a rural hinterland, all of which are closely interconnected by geography, environment, and workforce as well as by a shared economic and social future (Peirce et al. 1993).

3 Each of the municipalities in the city-regions has its own local governance arrangement, resulting in extreme jurisdictional fragmentation throughout

each city-region (more so than its comparable census metropolitan area). This fragmentation, among other things, tends to:

- pit suburban and exurban municipalities against those of the urban core on issues such as transportation policy, taxation, waste disposal, growth management, and provincial funding mechanisms
- exacerbate suburban and exurban resistance to region-wide planning and governance proposals, especially when governance proposals involve tax pooling (or other forms of fiscal transfer to the service-burdened central core city) or entail a significant reduction in their own employment or population growth potential
- increase the electoral influence of the suburbs, which have become very powerful in the provincial legislature as the balance of population has shifted outside the core cities (Tomalty 1997, 184). This has created a cautious political atmosphere in which the provincial governments are reluctant to impose regional planning and governance structures without first building a consensus among their suburban constituencies.
- create special problems for the central core cities because of their declining populations (relatively), their continued "central" function for the entire region, and their higher service needs
- make governance more complex due to the large number of independent municipalities and different levels of municipal government as well as to the numerous provincial ministries operating in the city-region.

4	The scale change from a metropolitan area to a city-region is enormous (the latter is often four times or more greater in area than the former), with the geographic size ranging from 3,000 square kilometres in the Vancouver region to 7,200 square kilometres in the Toronto region, and with the urbanized portions of comparable size. This results in:

- dispersal of population and diverse activities, which, in turn, results in extensive urban sprawl. The urbanized area of each region increases at a much higher rate than does its population, e.g., the Greater Toronto Area, which has a total area of about 7,200 square kilometres, increased in urbanized area from 482 square kilometres in 1967 to 1,737 square kilometres in 1999; that is, the urbanized portion of the Greater Toronto Area increased by 3.6 times, from 7 percent to 24 percent of the total in thirty-two years (see Stevenson and Gilbert 2000b, 13).
- a repetition of nearly equal urban realms throughout the city-region
- large infrastructure requirements due to the dispersal of population and economic activity over a large area
- serious environmental problems due to the cumulative impacts of urbanization and the absence of environmental controls in the outlying parts of the regions
- many more things can go wrong, there are more places to pollute, and there is more diversity; hence, more control points are required.

5 Social conditions, including services for new immigrants, high levels of crime, housing affordability, and equality of access to services, are all special issues in the three city-regions.

6 Since each of the three city-regions includes a large portion of the provincial population, their problems are of concern to provincial governments, which are responsible for creating them in the first place.

7 Each of the three city-regions is vital to the economic health of its province as well as to the country as a whole. For example, Greater Montreal represents about 45 percent of Quebec's population and almost 60 percent of its economic activity; Greater Vancouver represents a little more than half of British Columbia's population and a slightly higher proportion of its economy; the Greater Toronto Area has about 42 percent of Ontario's population and about half of its economy. Tom Courchene, then director of the School of Policy Studies at Queen's University, was one of the first Canadians to point out the increasing role of Canada's three city-regions in a globalized, knowledge-based economy. At a conference at the University of Toronto in September 1990 he wrote: "International cities are the institutional vehicles via which the globe is integrating ... these international cities [Toronto, Montreal, and Vancouver] are the critical nodes in the global communications and trading networks ... [they] have become not only growth poles but the essential connectors outward to the Londons and Tokyos and inward to their regional hinterlands."

8 The three city-regions are all experiencing similar pressures to engage in spatial restructuring due to the broad forces of economic change in the continental and global economy over the past twenty-five years. These include the decline in manufacturing employment (especially in the metropolitan cores), the shift in employment to the service sector, and the spread of high-order information and communication technology. The economic changes have been accompanied by, and interact with, major changes in population distribution within each of the three city-regions. And they combine to produce the new spatial phenomenon known as the city-region.

An Overview of Three Canadian City-Regions

In this section we present an overview of the three Canadian city-regions relative to their boundaries, geography, component parts, population growth, and their respective growth issues. Table 13 compares Toronto, Montreal, and Vancouver with respect to these phenomena as well as other factors.

Boundaries, Geography, and Components

Montreal City-Region

For the purposes of this book, the Montreal city-region is composed of the twenty-nine municipalities on the island of Montreal, including the City of Montreal, along with the 107 South and North Shore municipalities adjacent

Table 13

Overview of the three Canadian city-regions: Montreal, Toronto, and Vancouver

	Montreal	Toronto	Vancouver
Population (2000)	3,480,000	5,164,450	2,011,035
Area (sq. km.)	3,500	7,200	2,910
Regional concerns/ issues	municipal finance economic development decline of central city urban sprawl	infrastructure development municipal finance economic development integration of provincial and regional government policies	infrastructure development environment affordable housing
Regional planning agencies	Metro Transportation Agency Montreal Urban Community Regional county municipalities	Metro Toronto[1] Office of the Greater Toronto Area GO Transit	Greater Vancouver Regional District Greater Vancouver Transit Authority
Provincial policies	agricultural land policies preferred option	urban sprawl urban structure models guidelines reform	agricultural land policies self-contained communities regional growth strategies alternative transportation choices
Governance	localism (autonomy)	provincialism (control)	regionalism (consensus)

	Montreal Metropolitan Community	Greater Toronto Services Board	Greater Vancouver Regional District
Provincial support for regional planning	low	medium	high
Suburban support for regional planning	low	low	medium
Overall regional agency	Montreal Metropolitan Community	Greater Toronto Services Board	Greater Vancouver Regional District
Composition of regional agency	28 members[2]	40 members[3]	35 directors[4]

1 Metropolitan Corporation of Toronto (before its recent amalgamation into the new City of Toronto).

2 Comprising 14 elected officials from Montreal Island (7 Montreal, 7 suburbs) and 14 elected representatives from Laval, the North Shore, and the South Shore (Fischler 1999). There will also be an eight-member executive committee.

3 Comprising a chair; the 26 mayors of all Greater Toronto Area municipalities; one additional member from the City of Mississauga; 10 councillors from the City of Toronto; the chair of Hamilton–Wentworth region; and one additional member from Hamilton–Wentworth, appointed to vote only on matters relating to GO Transit (Tonks 1999).

4 Comprising representatives from the 22 communities (including the two unincorporated electoral areas) in the Greater Vancouver Regional District. Directors representing the 20 municipalities are appointed from their local councils, usually by the mayor, for a one-year term, while in the case of the two electoral areas, directors are elected directly for three-year terms. Because of its voting procedure, each director has one vote for every 20,000 of population, and no director may have more than 5 votes. The municipalities of Vancouver, Surrey, Burnaby, and Richmond each have one board director. So, in total, there are 35 directors on the governing board.

Source: Modified from Fischler (1999).

to the island. This area corresponds roughly to the Montreal census metropolitan area, and we refer to it as the "Montreal Metropolitan Region" (see Figure 17), which is the term also adopted by the Pichette Commission and recently used in legislation establishing the Montreal Metropolitan Community. (Under the new legislation, the boundaries of the city-region will remain the same; only the internal organization and relationships will change.) In 2000, the region had a total land area of 3,500 square kilometres, housing a total population of 3.5 million, of which around 1.8 million live on the island of Montreal, about one-third of a million on Île Jésus (a single municipality, Ville Laval), about two-thirds on the so-called South Shore, and the rest on the North Shore and in Vaudreuil–Soulanges county to the west of the archipelago. The City of Montreal occupies the centre and the northern tip of the island and had a population in 2000 of a little over one million (see Table 13 and Figure 17).

Currently, the 136 municipalities belong to seventeen different regional bodies, sixteen regional county municipalities (municipalités régionales de comté), and one urban community (communauté urbaine). In the centre of the region is the Montreal Urban Community (MUC) (briefly discussed in Chapter 8), which is located on the island of Montreal between the St. Lawrence and des Prairies Rivers. The MUC is linked by bridges to the suburban communities of the South Shore and to the island of Laval to the north. Laval, in turn, is linked by bridges to the suburban communities on the North Shore. The spread-out nature of the outlying communities and their small size – in part a function of the region's geography and the need for bridges to connect the communities with one another – creates special planning and governance challenges.

Toronto City-Region

The term "Metropolitan Toronto" refers to the jurisdictional entity established in 1954 comprising the City of Toronto and the twelve (later reduced to five) suburban municipalities surrounding it (see Chapter 8). However, this entity did not (and the new City of Toronto does not now) signify the extent of Toronto-related urban development. Even the Toronto CMA, as defined by Statistics Canada, fails to serve that purpose. Since the 1970s, growth has been occurring in nearby suburban municipalities and rural areas outside "old" Metro Toronto boundaries, and, as a consequence, planners and policy makers came around to viewing this urban growth within its larger regional context.

In viewing this larger regional context, both the provincial and Metro Toronto planners drew the boundaries of the Toronto metropolis to encompass most of the Oshawa CMA on the east and part of the Hamilton CMA on the west. This larger area (before the soon-to-be amalgamation) was composed of five upper-tier municipal governments – one metropolitan municipality (Metropolitan Toronto) and four two-tier regional municipalities (Durham, York,

Figure 17

Montreal Metropolitan Community

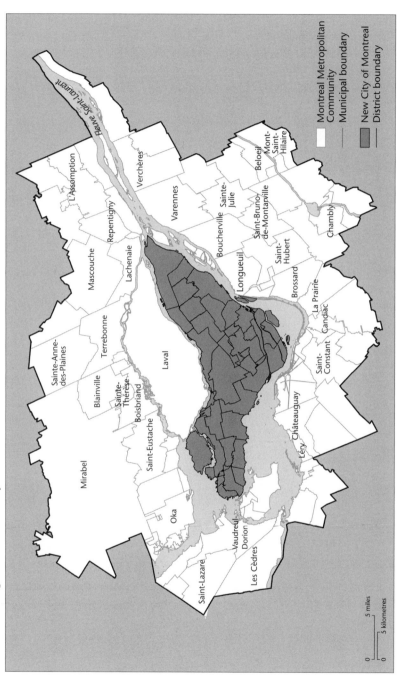

Legend:
- ☐ Montreal Metropolitan Community
- — Municipal boundary
- ▓ New City of Montreal
- — District boundary

Source: Modified from map on Communauté urbaine de Montréal website (www.cum.qc.ca/cum-an/visiteur/cartvisa.htm).

Peel, and Halton) – plus thirty lower-tier municipal governments. Six of the lower-tier municipalities were in "old" Metropolitan Toronto; the other twenty-four were distributed among the four two-tier regional municipalities.

Metropolitan Toronto planners refer to this larger entity as the "Toronto region"; provincial officials referred to it as the "Greater Toronto Area" (GTA). Because the four regional municipalities outside Metro Toronto are also often called "regions," throughout this chapter we shall refer to the Toronto city-region as the Greater Toronto Area (GTA). (See Figure 18 for the components of the GTA prior to the 1998 amalgamation.)

Geographically, the GTA occupies a gently tilting plain roughly defined by the Niagara Escarpment on the west (a steep rock face formed by an abrupt termination of strata [see Chapter 7]) and, to the north by the Oak Ridges Moraine (a unique formation of sand and gravel deposits created some 15,000 years ago by retreating glaciers), which has served as a groundwater recharge and discharge area for thousands of years. North of the moraine, the slope reverses and the water flows north to Lake Simcoe and Georgian Bay (GTA Task Force 1996, 25). The escarpment and moraine are constantly threatened by development pressures, with wildlife habitat and species diversity being at risk from increased urbanization. The landscape is carved by meandering waterways, both large and small, which, together, have created a distinctive network of ravines. These deep, wooded ravines and their valleys help to provide the special geographical feeling and sense of community shared by many GTA communities.[7]

In the late 1990s, throughout Ontario the provincial government enacted far-reaching changes to the entire structure of municipal government, financial arrangements, and provincial-municipal relations. One of the most important set of changes occurred in the GTA. Metropolitan Toronto was abolished, and, in its place, Toronto plus its surrounding five area municipalities (Etobicoke, North York, Scarborough, York, and the Borough of East York), which had constituted "old" Metropolitan Toronto, were amalgamated into one "mega-city" – the City of Toronto. This change took place (on 1 January 1998) despite considerable opposition from citizens and many local politicians (see, for example, Greenberg 1996; *Globe and Mail*, 3 February 1997 and 21 February 1997). According to Anne Golden (who had chaired a special task force on the GTA in 1996), "the fight over Megacity generated a sense of public outrage and galvanized a citizens' opposition movement unlike anything Toronto had experienced since the battle to stop the Spadina Expressway in the late 1960s" (Plan Canada 1998). In addition to the new City of Toronto, the government – in response to widespread citizen, professional, and political clamour for some sort of institution to deal with planning and governing the GTA as a whole – created the Greater Toronto Services Board (discussed below).

As a result of the amalgamation, the GTA is now composed of twenty-nine municipalities, including the new City of Toronto (estimated 2000 population:

Figure 18

Greater Toronto Area prior to January 1998 amalgamation

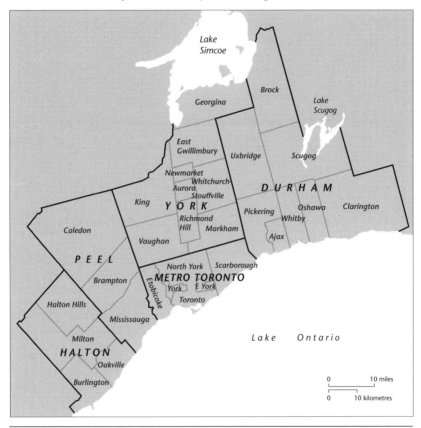

Source: Modified from Greater Toronto Area Task Force (1996).

2,552,290); the regional municipalities of Durham (512,710), Halton (371,950), Peel (1,015,390), and York (712,110); and twenty-four local area municipalities. The 2000 population of the GTA was estimated to be 5.2 million and comprises about 44 percent of Ontario's population, making it the largest urban concentration in Canada (population statistics from www.gov.on.ca)

Vancouver City-Region

With a population of slightly more than four million citizens (as of 2000), British Columbia is Canada's third most populous province (ranking behind Ontario and Quebec) and represents approximately 13 percent of the total Canadian population. A population increase of 13.5 percent between 1991 and 1996 made it the fastest growing province or territory in Canada; it more than doubled the 5.7 percent increase in the overall Canadian population during the same period. Its percentage increase between 1996 and 2000 decreased somewhat (4.7 percent), as did Canada as a whole (3.6 percent) during that period. Outranked only by the Northwest Territories, British Columbia is also Canada's largest province in area (almost 926,000 square kilometres, slightly larger than the combined area of Washington, Oregon, and California).

Yet, despite its physical size, more than half of the provincial population resides in the extreme southwest corner of the province, known as the Lower Mainland. This area experienced the strongest population growth among the regions in the province in the period between 1991 and 1996, with a 15 percent growth rate. The Lower Mainland extends about forty kilometres north of, and runs roughly parallel to, the United States boundary. It extends from the Pacific Ocean at Vancouver about 162 kilometres inland to the village of Hope at the foot of the Fraser Canyon. The Lower Mainland is composed of two regional districts that extend along the Fraser Valley adjacent to Vancouver – the Fraser Valley Regional District and the Greater Vancouver Regional District.[8] These were created as a consequence of 1965 "regional district" legislation that will be described later.

The Vancouver city-region – which we equate with the Greater Vancouver Regional District (GVRD) – lies at the mouth of the Fraser River, where it meets the Strait of Georgia. The GVRD has a land area of 2,910 square kilometres, and is organized into twenty-one municipalities (including eleven cities, six district municipalities, three villages, and one island municipality) plus one unincorporated area (see Figure 19).[9] Langley city and district, Matsqui, Maple Ridge, and Bowen Island were added in the late 1990s.[10] The addition of these municipalities now makes the population of the GVRD and the Vancouver census metropolitan area essentially coterminous (compare Tables 13 and 14). So, in this regard, unlike the two-tier metropolitan and regional governments in Quebec and Ontario, the GVRD has, through the inclusion of these peripheral municipalities, actually expanded its boundaries since its inception. In 2000, the GVRD's population of a little more than two million resides on only 4 percent of the province's land area, yet constitutes a little more than half of the provincial population. Moreover, it contains a majority of the largest (population greater than 50,000) local authorities in the province. There is a great range in population among its 22 constituent communities: the smallest being Belcarra (712 people), Anmore (1,306), Lions Bay (1,478), and Bowen Island (3,167); and the largest, Surrey (340,094) and Vancouver (565,905) (population statistics from www.gvrd.bc.ca).

The importance of the GVRD's geographic location – especially its location relative to the Fraser River – cannot be overestimated.[11] As we shall see throughout this chapter, the protection of the Fraser River has been a major objective of regional planning in the Lower Mainland. The geography of the Lower Mainland is not only scenically beautiful, but in combination with its historical development has produced a decentralized and multi-nodal settlement

Figure 19

Greater Vancouver Regional District as of August 2000

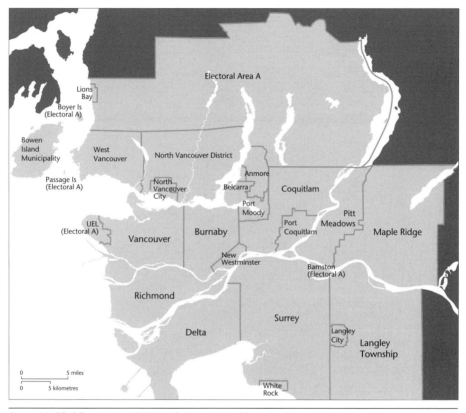

Source: Modified from map on GVRD website, www.gvrd.bc.ca/services.

pattern, which tends to inhibit urban growth. The large urban agglomeration that is the GVRD is literally squeezed onto the lower slopes of the coastal mountains and the delta lands of the Fraser River, stretching 170 kilometres eastward and even spilling over into the Gulf Islands and the Sunshine Coast. Much of the land is too mountainous to be suitable for urban development (Wynn and Oke 1992, 148), and transportation in the Lower Mainland is dominated by bridges (as many as fifteen) and one tunnel. The approaches to these bridges and tunnel are, not surprisingly, the location of major congestion.

Regions of Geographical Affinity

The fact that the territory of the GVRD is almost congruent with that of the census metropolitan area has not stopped some observers from arguing that it is still far too small. They point out that Vancouver and the GVRD are part of wider regions of "geographical affinity," to use McGee's term (1999, 116). Seelig and Artibise (1991), for example, argue that "a realistic definition of our region should cover a true economic unit," which they refer to as the "Pacific Fraser Region."[12] This region encompasses most of the area that was originally under the jurisdiction of the Lower Mainland Regional Planning Board, which functioned between 1949 and 1968 (and is discussed below).

The University of British Columbia's Sustainable Development Research Institute (SDRI) uses the Lower Fraser Basin as its area of analysis, an area extending from Hope to the coast and from the North Shore mountains to the US border. In 2000 the institute increased its area of concern to encompass the entire Georgia Basin, which covers all of the Lower Mainland and stretches across the Georgia Strait to southeastern Vancouver Island, where it includes the provincial capital, Victoria, and a string of towns along the Island Highway as far north as 162 kilometres.[13] McGee (1999, 117-18) refers to this area as the Vancouver Extended Metropolitan Region. Other reseachers, propose the use of the even larger Georgia Basin for planning and policy-making purposes.

The largest region of geographical affinity, termed Cascadia, crosses state, provincial, and international boundaries and is variously defined as comprising British Columbia, the Yukon, and the US states of Washington, Oregon, Idaho, Montana, and Alaska. The more common definition, however, limits its area to Washington, Oregon, and British Columbia.[14] The name "Cascadia" is taken from the Cascade Mountains that parallel the Pacific coastline. Cascadia's core is an urban corridor, a "Main Street" (Geddes 1997), which stretches from the Eugene and Portland (Oregon) metropolitan areas, through the Seattle–Tacoma metropolitan area (Washington), on to Greater Vancouver, and up to the ski resort of Whistler (Artibise 1996; Edgington 1995; Pivo 1996). Along this corridor are four of the world's largest multinational companies: Boeing and Microsoft in Seattle, and Nike and Hewlett-Packard in Portland; and Vancouver is now popularly known as "Hollywood North" because it is the second-largest film-producing city in North America (McGee 1999, 116-17). It is no coincidence that the industries represented by these companies are on the leading edge of post-industrial entertainment and leisure, transportation, and information. The urban corridor's strong Asia Pacific economic link is reinforced by the movement of new immigrants from that part of the world, most markedly to the core neighbourhoods of Greater Vancouver.

Population Growth

The population of each of the Canadian city-regions (including their component parts) in 1986, 1991, and 1996, respectively, as well as their size (in land area), are summarized in Table 14.[15] The Greater Toronto Area's current estimated population (2000) of 5.2 million now makes it the fifth largest urban

Table 14

Population of Canada's three city-regions and their component parts, 1986-96

City-region	Area (sq. km.)	Population (millions) and as % of total region		
		1986	1991	1996
Montreal	3,500	2.92 (100.0%)	3.13 (100.0%)	3.33 (100.0%)
CMA	3,500	2.92 (100.0%)	3.13 (100.0%)	3.33 (100.0%)
Core	500	1.75 (59.9%)	1.78 (56.9%)	1.80 (54.4%)
Fringe	3,000	1.17 (40.1%)	1.35 (43.1%)	1.53 (45.6%)
Toronto	7,200	3.65 (100.0%)	4.13 (100.0%)	4.50 (100.0%)
CMA	5,868	3.43 (94.0%)	3.90 (94.4%)	4.26 (94.7%)
Core	630	2.19 (60.0%)	2.00 (55.2%)	2.38 (52.9%)
Fringe	6,570	1.46 (40.0%)	2.13 (44.8%)	2.12 (47.1%)
Vancouver	2,910	1.38 (100.0%)	1.60 (100.0%)	1.83 (100.0%)
CMA	2,821	1.38 (100.0%)	1.60 (100.0%)	1.83 (100.0%)
Core	113	0.43 (31.2%)	0.47 (29.4%)	0.51 (27.9%)
Fringe	2,797	0.95 (68.8%)	1.13 (70.6%)	1.32 (72.1%)
Canada		26.2	28.11	30.0
Total (3 city-regions)		7.95	8.86	9.66
% of Canada		30.3%	31.5%	32.2%

Sources: CMA and core: Statistics Canada (1997, cat. No. 93-357-xPB, Tables 8, 10); fringe and region totals for Toronto and Vancouver calculated from Bryant and Lemire (1993, Table B-1); region totals for Vancouver, www.gvrd.bc.ca/services.

region in North America and puts it ahead of Montreal as the number one city-region of Canada, in terms of population. While the GTA occupies only 0.3 percent of Ontario's land area, its five million-plus people constitute 44 percent of the province's population, up from 41.6 percent in 1991 (see www.gov.on.ca). By 2021, the GTA is expected to have 6.9 million residents and a workforce of 3.9 million (GTA Task Force 1996).

Whether one uses the census metropolitan area or the city-region as the spatial unit of comparison (see Tables 13 and 14), Vancouver's rate of growth between 1991 and 1996 exceeded that of all other Canadian urban centres by a considerable margin; and between 1996 and 2000 its growth rate was exceeded only by Toronto's. Immigration, both from abroad and elsewhere in Canada, buttressed this growth. The vast majority of Vancouver's immigrants come from South and Southeast Asia. In the early 1990s, it was projected that the population of the GVRD would increase to 1.8 million by 2000, and to 2.5 million by 2040. However, the GVRD has already passed the two million-plus mark in 2000, reflecting the fact that the region has been growing even faster than the more optimistic forecasters predicted. The provincial statistics agency recently added another 277,000 people to its forecast for the Lower Mainland region for the year 2021, bringing the projected total at that time to 3.3 million. Other forecasts have projected even more substantial population growth for this region – 3.5 million by the year 2011, according to *BC Business* magazine.[16]

Growth in the Montreal region has been much slower in recent decades than it has in our other two city-regions, with the growth rate between 1971 and 1991 averaging about 0.7 percent per year; and the growth rate between 1991 and 1996 increasing somewhat to 1.3 percent; and then between 1996 and 2000, increased only slightly to less than 1 percent. In the mid-1990s it was estimated that the region's 1991 population of 3.2 million people would grow to about 3.8 million by the year 2023. This assumed that the growth rate would diminish from 19,600 per year between 1971 and 1996 to about 18,500 per year between 1996 and 2023.

These three city-regions should also be seen within a North American context: Toronto and Vancouver have been among the continent's fastest-growing city-regions (along with several in the US sunbelt); their population growth has been fuelled by high rates of immigration in the last decade, primarily from Asia. Montreal has also been a centre for immigration, but its population increase has been largely offset by the loss of much of the Anglophone population during the past twenty years. Also, according to recent UN estimates (see *World Urbanization Prospects 1995*), Toronto is North America's fifth largest city-region, after Mexico City, New York, Los Angeles, and Chicago. Greater Vancouver has been growing at a rate similar to its neighbours in the United States Pacific Northwest; its current population of slightly more than two million is a little less than the population of Greater Seattle. Greater Montreal is now slightly larger than Greater Houston.

Spatial Distribution of Population: Growth Outside Metropolitan Boundaries

As in city-regions in other developed countries, the pattern of urban development in Canada's three city-regions has, in recent decades, been increasingly dispersed and marked by extreme manifestations of urban sprawl (see, for example, Charbonneau et al. 1994, 459-95). This dispersed growth has been ignited not only by global economic forces, but also by the emergence of what Manuel Castells (1989) calls the "informational city" – the spread and restructuring of urban activities in space due to our increasing capacity to substitute the communication of information for the transportation of goods and people. The pressure for decentralization is further reinforced by the large number of baby boomers who are still entering the low-density, single-family housing market (Dowall 1984; Moore 1991). These housing preferences are generally satisfied these days only in areas outside the large central cities; that is, in small communities where it is easier to control socially sensitive public services such as schools and police (Rothblatt 1982; Hughes 1991). In addition to these factors, there is a tendency for inlying local governments to try to capture the more fiscally desirable, less service-demanding commercial and industrial activity and to push service-demanding residential development to the periphery of metropolitan areas.

Within the regions, the extent to which growth has been occurring outside metropolitan area boundaries between 1986 and 1996 can be seen in Table 14. In all three city-regions, the population of the suburbs and fringe areas has reached almost half of the total regional population, the highest being the GTA, where, by 1996, 47.1 percent of the total population were living in the suburbs. While data for the years since 1996 are not available (see note 15), we feel certain that when the 2000 census data do become available, they will show that the trend towards suburban and fringe growth has continued. The following discussion briefly summarizes the spatial distribution of population within each of the city-regions.

Montreal City-Region

There have been major changes in the distribution of population within the region, beginning in the 1970s. The central part of the Montreal city-region has been experiencing an exodus of households, while a new residential ring is developing at the periphery; employment has also been decentralizing, especially in the manufacturing sector and in consumer services. In 1971, 44 percent of the regional population lived in the central city (Montreal), but this declined to 33 percent in 1991 and to 30 percent in 1996. In 1996 more than one million of Montreal city-region's population of 3.3 million lived within the City of Montreal itself. The remainder were found either in (1) the twenty-eight other municipalities located on the island of Montreal (about 800,000 residents), which, along with the city, make up the metropolitan political-administrative structure known as the Montreal Urban Community, or (2) in the seventy-two municipalities that make up the northern and southern suburban rings of the urban area (about 1.53 million inhabitants). In this period, the Montreal Urban Community declined from more than two-thirds of the regional population to only about half. In the suburban areas, the opposite trend was occurring: on the South and North Shores, the population had grown from a combined 23 percent of the regional population to more than 37 percent in 1996 (Tomalty 1997, 141).

These percentages hide the real changes in population distribution occurring in the Montreal city-region. The central areas during these years actually experienced a significant population loss in absolute numbers: in both the City of Montreal and the rest of the island's population absolute numbers declined by about 200,000 people. In contrast, suburban municipalities on the South and North Shores experienced nearly a doubling of their populations.

Laval's share of the regional population remained almost constant as migration into the area from the island of Montreal was balanced by out-migration to suburban communities farther north.

Toronto City-Region

In 1996, nearly 92 percent of the GTA's population lived in Metro Toronto and in eleven nearby municipalities, which made up less than 40 percent of the total land area. However, while considerable undeveloped land is still available for new settlement within the boundaries of Metro Toronto, the region's population has become increasingly decentralized. Until 1971, Metropolitan Toronto absorbed the bulk of the GTA's new population growth at a rate of about 50,000 people per year; however, since then its growth rate has dropped off sharply. The GTA has continued to absorb more than 70,000 people per year since 1971, but most of this growth has taken place outside Metropolitan Toronto. As a result Metro Toronto's share of the region's population fell from 77 percent in 1961 to 54 percent in 1994.

Projections based on these current trends indicate that the population of the entity defined earlier as Metro Toronto, or the new City of Toronto (which is currently about 2.4 million), would grow little and might even decline by the year 2011, while the GTA would continue to grow. Nevertheless, Metro Toronto's planners had set a population target of 2.5 million for the year 2011 – a figure that assumes that Metro Toronto will be able to encourage a substantially higher increase in in-migration than was projected and, more important, that it would produce the requisite new housing. The provincial government has accepted this population target. However, according to most forecasters, even if Metropolitan Toronto were to succeed in achieving this goal, more than half the region's population would reside outside of Metro Toronto by the year 2011.

Interestingly, the change in Metro Toronto's relative position in the GTA has paralleled the change that occurred in the relationship between the City of Toronto and the rest of Metropolitan Toronto in the mid-1950s. Fortunately, the recent declines in the relative positions of both Metro Toronto and the City of Toronto in terms of population have not been associated with the signs of economic decline that have affected most large US cities, whose populations have also been overtaken or surpassed by their suburbs. In fact, just the opposite is the case: patterns and trends regarding the location of GTA employment indicate that both "old" Metropolitan Toronto and its core city are leading participants in the healthy development of the GTA economy and are likely to remain so for the foreseeable future. For example, while the City of Toronto has only 15 percent of the GTA's population, its workforce accounts for some 30 percent of the region's economy (as measured by labour output) (GTA Task Force 1996, 28).

Vancouver City-Region

The Vancouver city-region's population increase between 1991 and 1996 (about 230,000) was not evenly distributed throughout the region (see Table 14). The municipalities in the regional core, including the suburban areas north of the Fraser River – the City of Vancouver, Burnaby, New Westminster, the Districts of West and North Vancouver, and the City of North Vancouver – have seen fairly modest rates of population growth (within the range of 5 percent to 9 percent), except for Burnaby and New Westminster, each of which had a 13 percent increase. Outside the regional core, and up the Fraser Valley – in Maple Ridge, Pitt Meadows, Surrey, Langley, Coquitlam, and Port Coquitlam – growth rates have been much higher, ranging from 14 percent to 17 percent for the same five-year period. In the 1996-2000 period similar trends are seen: the core municipalities, except for Vancouver (10.1 percent) and New Westminster (11.2 percent), experienced percentage growth rates of less than 10 percent. The communities outside the core, up the Fraser Valley, experienced percentage growth rates of more than 10 percent, except for Delta (6.3 percent) and Langley City (7.8 percent)(see www.gvrd.bc.ca).

It is safe to predict that the fastest-growing areas in the Vancouver region will continue to be the Fraser Valley suburbs within and beyond the eastern boundaries of the GVRD. The fastest-growing suburb between 1992 and 1996 was Port Coquitlam (it grew by 22 percent), and Surrey grew from 300,000 in 1996 to 340,000 in 2000. By 2015, the GVRD's own projections indicate that the population of Surrey will pass the 500,000 mark, at which time the central city of Vancouver should increase to only 645,000 people (see www.gvrd.bc.ca). Also, the adjacent outer suburbs of Mission, Abbotsford, and Chilliwack, which are outside the GVRD, are among the fastest-growing areas in the province and are projected to continue to be so; this will have implications for the future boundaries of the GVRD.

Growth-Related Issues

In this section we review the issues the three city-regions faced as a result of their total and spatial population growth. We will differentiate between those issues that are common to all three regions and those that are unique to each.

Common Issues

All three city-regions were concerned with growth management and issues related to growth. Overall, transportation, the environment, and controlling urban sprawl were the most frequent issues addressed in plans and policy statements. The priority given to transportation reflects the ongoing stresses (both social and physical) associated with the increasing separation of home and place of work within a complex urban milieu. (On Toronto, see Tomalty 1997; Urban Development Institute 1989; IBI 1990. On Vancouver, see *Globe and Mail,* 24 September and 20 October 1997.) The high priority accorded the environment reflects the growing environmental awareness among citizens, politicians, and planners as well as the dangers posed by changing settlement systems.

All three city-regions were concerned with economic and fiscal issues related to growth management and controlling sprawl. In Montreal these issues were paramount because of the slow growth the city has been experiencing. (On the economic and fiscal issues in the Toronto city-region, see the Boston Consulting Group 1995; Bourne and Olvet 1995; Gertler 1996; GTA Task Force 1996. In the Montreal city-region, see Coffey 1994; Carboneau et al. 1994; Québec, ministère de la Métropole 1996. In the Vancouver city-region, see Hutton 1998; Tomalty 1997.)

In all three city-regions social issues resulted, to a large extent, from the growth-related issues described above. For example, environmental problems reduce the quality of the living environment and add to the personal stress of city life; traffic congestion increases the amount of time wasted in cars; and decentralization of industrial employment leaves some neighbourhoods in the central areas with extremely high rates of unemployment, poverty, and social decay. Social issues also involved housing choice and affordability, the mismatch between housing needs and housing supply, the general aging of the population, and other demographic changes. (On Toronto, see Frisken et al. 1997; on Montreal and Vancouver, see Tomalty 1997.) In the case of Vancouver, its multicultural harmony is being marred by recent racial and ethnic tensions, and its reputation for civility is belied by a rate of violent crime that is higher than that of many other Canadian cities.

The Montreal city-region lacks an overall region-wide planning, or governance, mechanism, and, until the early 1990s, no serious consideration had been given to establishing one. For a long time this was also true of the Toronto city-region. For example, the 1970s Toronto-Centred Region Concept was prepared by provincial planners, but there was no regional authority, and no resources were allocated to implement the plan. Also, an office for Greater Toronto was established in 1988, but it lacked any legislative basis for preparing or implementing a regional plan.

Montreal's and Toronto's region-wide governance problems reached such a bad state in the late 1980s and early 1990s that their respective provincial governments appointed special commissions to investigate them and to propose new governance structures (these proposals are discussed later in this chapter). During the period that these commissions were doing their work, no formal studies of governance were undertaken with regard to the Vancouver city-region. The existing region-wide planning and governance mechanism, the GVRD (which was formed in 1967), has features akin to those found within a separate level of government. During the years the other two city-regions were undergoing intensive governance studies, the GVRD was engaged in a major participatory planning process and was seeking final approval for its Livable Region Strategic Plan. Nonetheless, some have suggested changing the existing regional district format (see discussion later in this chapter).

Specific Concerns

Beyond the common issues faced in all three city-regions, they each had specific concerns. For example, Vancouver and Toronto were concerned about rapid growth, while Montreal was concerned with slow growth. And, in the Vancouver region, GVRD residents gave highest priority to environmental concerns such as air pollution and energy use, encroachment of urban development upon agricultural lands, and maintenance of a high quality of life (see Seelig and Artibise 1991; *Globe and Mail*, 24 September and 20 October 1997). Indeed, Sancton (1994, 68) goes so far as to claim that, more so than in any other large urban area in Canada, planners in Vancouver are "obsessed" with protecting the physical natural environment and maintaining a "livable region."

In the Toronto region in the 1980s the growth-related issues concerned housing supply and affordability as well as the environment. (On environmental issues in the Toronto region, see the Crombie Commission report on the Greater Toronto bioregion; Tomalty 1997; and the Commission on Planning and Development Reform 1992.) However, by the 1990s, economic development, apportionment of the fiscal burden, decline in the core, and the need to integrate provincial and regional policies in the larger GTA were in the ascendancy.

Another way of viewing the differences among the three city-regions with regard to their priority issues involves looking at interest group attitudes towards the issue of growth. With regard to the "political landscape," we can discern two distinct interest groups. While both groups tended to agree that provincial action was required in order to direct growth and to set priorities for infrastructure investment, their approach to realizing these objectives differed. The first group advocated growth as an end in itself and sought greater coordination of public investment and provincial transfer payments in order to remove barriers to conventional growth patterns; in short, this group favoured "development." The second group stressed management of growth in order to achieve collective goals and to minimize negative externalities associated with growth. This group wanted to redirect traditional growth patterns in order to prevent deterioration in quality of life, the polarization of classes, and environmental degradation; in short, this group advocated managed growth, or sustainable development.

These competing views existed in all regions, and one or the other came to prominence depending on its political currency among politicians, planners, and the public. In Montreal, for example, the attitude of the first group was prominent in tackling regional issues and was best represented by the Montreal Board of Trade. In Vancouver, the second group is ascendant. Its view –

the need for growth management – is clearly epitomized by the regional district's Livable Region Strategic Plan, which assumes the need to control and, if necessary, oppose growth in order to maintain the region's environment and quality of life. In Toronto, growth management advocates were quite vocal, if not dominant, in the 1970s and early 1980s, but, since the early 1990s, the call has been for regional economic development and for less concern for negative externalities and the unintended consequences of unmanaged growth.

Those interested in growth management typically consist of a professional cadre of provincial officials, municipal and private planners, academics, architects, and some journalists. In terms of the larger public, the need to plan on a regional basis and to manage growth was widely recognized in Vancouver (as we shall point out later on), less recognized in Toronto, and almost not recognized at all in Montreal (where the link between regional economic development and land use, including urban sprawl, was rarely made).

Governmental Resources Delegated to City-Regions

Planning regions have no explicit status within the Canada's constitutional arrangements and so must be "invented" each time such a region is required. Only provinces have the mandate to create planning regions within their territory (see Chapter 4). Once the province decides to do this, it then specifies the name and type of the regional planning agency (e.g., authority, commission, board, committee), the geographic area over which its plans will apply, and the issues over which it will have jurisdiction. Once these initial decisions have been made, the province then specifies the type and extent of powers and responsibilities – we refer to these as "governmental resources," or "capacities" – it is willing to delegate to the new agency to enable it to plan and govern. Five sets of such resources affect the region's planning and its ability to develop and implement plans: planning resources, regulatory resources, financial resources, political resources, and professional resources (see Chapter 4).

To these five resources we have added, appropriate to our city-regions, two others, and we treat them separately. The first is *citizen participation.* Since we define planning as "planning *with* rather than *for* citizens," we consider the nature and extent of citizen participation an important political resource in both plan making and plan implementation. Citizen participation is not provincially mandated but, rather, develops locally (although the provinces may perform an encouraging or facilitating role). The second resource is *provincial coordination.* Because of the key role of provincial ministries in influencing the growth and development of city-regions, we believe that provincial coordination must be identified as a separate resource.

In assessing the resources allocated to, or proposed for, the three city-regions, we have adopted (as in Chapter 4) a simple numerical ordinal scale ranging from zero resources to plentiful resources, with intermediate points as follows:

0 = none of the resource has been allocated
1 = a modest amount has been allocated
2 = a moderate amount has been allocated
3 = a plentiful amount has been allocated.

Table 15 summarizes the results of this assessment. Discussion of our key findings follows.

General Traits

As expected, the resources allocated to the three city-regions varied considerably, both within the resource bundles themselves as well as within the same region over time. Overall, planning resources were the strongest (though they were generally restricted to land-use planning), while implementation resources (in terms of finances and regulations) were the weakest. For example, in contrast to the ample planning resources delegated to the Lower Mainland Regional Planning Board and the GVRD, the government felt inclined to delegate only limited regulatory and financial resources for implementing their plans. Without the requisite financial and regulatory resources, the regional planning agencies become dependent upon such authorities as local municipalities, special purpose bodies, and/or provincial ministries to implement their plans. As a consequence, their plans are essentially advisory and hortatory.

True, legislation requires local plans to conform to the city-region plan or strategy, but it does not compel member municipalities to carry out planning actions with regard to regulating land use and constructing capital works. Nor can the planning agency veto a local plan.

None of the three city-regions had or will have funds of its own with which to directly finance infrastructure or to implement its regional plans, although the Golden Task Force recommendations (discussed later in this chapter) for the Toronto region come close to achieving this objective. They each, however, had different arrangements for raising funds to finance their regional plans and other operating functions.

The differences in resource allocations over time in the same city-region is well illustrated in the cases of the Lower Mainland Regional Planning Board and the GVRD. In general, over a ten-year period, the GVRD was delegated much more generous powers than was the Lower Mainland Regional Planning Board. It received more plentiful planning resources plus the additional region-wide "developmental" functions; it benefited from the existence of regional context statements under the Growth Strategies Act (see later discussion); and it benefited from citizen participation. With respect to the latter, we found that this resource was especially noteworthy when comparing the Vancouver city-region to the Toronto city-region. In fact, it was probably the single most important factor in the success of the GVRD's planning activities (see later discussion in this chapter).

Also, provincial governments, especially newly elected ones, may decide to withdraw some or all of the resources previously delegated. A graphic example occurred in British Columbia in the early 1980s, when the re-elected government withdrew the power to make new regional plans and determined that previous plans were no longer binding upon municipalities. (Later, these resources were restored under the Growth Strategies Act.) The Province of Alberta made a similarly drastic move in 1993 when it removed the financial resources from the bundle provided to the regional planning commissions and later took away the planning resources themselves.

Provincial coordination has two aspects: (1) coordinating ministerial decisions that affect city-regions, especially those areas that fall outside municipal boundaries, and (2) coordinating provincial actions and decisions with the goals and plans of the regional agencies. In the past, all three provincial governments too often did not use the policy instruments available to them to the benefit of their city-regions. Provincial actions have been uneven with regard to growth management in the regions, largely due to a lack of coordination among the policies and decisions of the various provincial ministries. Too frequently this resulted in actions that were opposed to regional and, indeed, provincial goals. A few examples from British Columbia will illustrate this point.

In 1980, the provincial government proposed a new Land Use Act that would have provided a basis for coordinating the activities of various provincial ministries with regard to land use. However, in 1993, the legislation was quietly dropped, and, since then, there has been no formal mechanism to coordinate government actions in the area of land use.

Some provincial actions have openly violated the Greater Vancouver Livable Region Strategic Plan. For example, the agricultural land reserves were allowed to erode throughout the 1980s, in some instances causing outright conflict between the GVRD and the province. According to Tomalty (1997, 70), although the recently dethroned NDP government demonstrated that it was concerned with preserving agricultural land, the "grandfather" provisions of the new regulations permitted the erosion of the land reserves to continue.

Transportation is another feature of provincial policy that has tended to undermine the regional growth management goals of the GVRD. Since the mid-1960s the province has provided major subsidies to automobile use through its highway-funding program; in some cases, funding decisions directly contradicted the GVRD's growth management goals. However, a bright spot concerns the agreement recently worked out in 1999 between the provincial government and the GVRD. This agreement made the GVRD responsible for all rapid transit and most road expansion throughout the rapidly growing city-region. A new Greater Vancouver Transportation Authority was established under the aegis of the GVRD. Critics of government inaction welcomed this

Table 15

Extent of government resources allocated to the three Canadian city-regions

City-region	Planning			Financial	Political			Provincial coordination
	The plan	Other planning activities	Regulatory		Representation	Participation	Professional	
Montreal								
Pichette Task Force	3	2-3	n.a.	n.a.	1	n.a.	n.a.	n.a.
Enactment of Montreal Development Commission	3	2-3	n.a.	n.a.	1	n.a.	n.a.	n.a.
Montreal Metropolitan Community	2	2-3	1	2	1	n.a.	n.a.	n.a.
Toronto								
Design of Development/ Toronto-Centred Region	2	0	0	0	0	0	3	0
Office of the Greater Toronto Area	1	0	0	0	0	0	1	1-2
Golden Task Force	3	2	2	2-3	1	n.a.	n.a.	2
Greater Toronto Area Services Board	1	1	0	0	1	n.a.	n.a.	2
Vancouver								
Lower Mainland Regional Planning Board	3	0	0	0	1	0	3	0
Greater Vancouver Regional District	3	3	1	2	1-2	3	3	1-2

new agreement, under which the BC government will absorb the huge debts on the existing transit line and commuter train, plus pay more than half of the construction costs of a new transit line (by 2008) and transfer several revenue sources to the new local transit authority. More important, this arrangement means that transportation can become a more integral part of the Livable Region Strategic Plan and, thus, provide the GVRD with an important tool for implementing its strategy.

In light of this promising new agreement, it is difficult to understand why, in June 1998, the provincial government announced a twenty-kilometre extension of Vancouver's SkyTrain system without consulting the GVRD or its member municipalities (Howard and Gibbon 1998). To add further to this apparent contradiction in provincial policy, shortly thereafter it was announced that the government was considering legislation that would exempt the SkyTrain extension and any future urban transit projects from its own existing environmental legislation (the Environmental Assessment Act), which requires that the SkyTrain extension and any urban transit project must be reviewed for a host of environmental, social, cultural, and economic impacts. To compound the province's ambivalence even further, it was reported that, because of financial difficulties, the provincial government appears to be backing away from extending the SkyTrain to Coquitlam Town Centre.

Specific City-Regions

In the Montreal city-region, the Pichette Task Force's proposal, the 1997 legislation that would have established the Montreal Development Commission, and the recent (2000) legislation creating the Montreal Metropolitan Community would all result in a "moderate" to "plentiful" allocation of planning resources; however, as for other resources, the allocation was "none" or "modest."

In the Toronto city-region, if the Toronto-Centred Region Concept had been implemented in the 1970s, then its mandate would have defined its area of jurisdiction as covering a section of southern Ontario almost three times the size of the GTA. And its main function would have been to relieve a number of problems associated with the pattern and rapid rate of growth in and around Metro Toronto. A unique feature of this plan was that it recognized and planned for the integrity of each of two proximate rural zones surrounding the Toronto metropolis. However, no planning agency was recommended and, thus, no specific resources were delegated. If the Golden Task Force recommendations had been implemented, then there would have been plenty of planning resources for the Toronto city-region; however, that was not the situation with the Office for the Greater Toronto Area or the recently created Greater Toronto Area Services Board (see discussion later in this chapter).

All in all, the GVRD had the most robust resource bundle – especially for planning resources and for the citizen participation component of political resources. However, as noted, the GVRD was weak in terms of regulatory, financial, and provincial coordination resources. On the other hand, without doubt, a unique feature of planning and governance in the Vancouver city-region has been the impressive involvement of citizens in the planning process. Starting with the livable region plan in the early 1970s, the idea that citizens should be intimately involved in the policy-making process was cultivated and has since become part of the accepted dialogue around planning.[17] The goal of achieving livability and preserving green space has remained a constant theme; indeed, it is a collective vision that has guided and influenced the discussions and debates among politicians, planners, and citizens for almost fifty years. And, as Reid (1996, 19) notes, "this has affected the culture of planning in Vancouver." Reid goes on to conclude that, unlike Vancouver, Toronto has no such shared regional vision to anchor and mobilize the various stakeholders involved in regional governance, and it has no tradition of public participation. Therefore, it is not surprising that regional planning and regional government in Toronto have been vulnerable to the ebb and flow of the political climate of the day.

Region-Wide Planning and Growth Management: Actions and Outcomes

This section reviews and compares the actions, initiatives, and outcomes in each of the three city-regions with regard to region-wide planning and growth management. We shall also show to what extent these actions and initiatives pertained to the concerns the city-regions faced as well as to what extent they took into account the special features and characteristics of these regions. We follow this with a section that discusses various proposals for changing governance arrangements and then a section in which we speculate on the consequent prospects for effective regional planning.

Montreal City-Region

In the past, the provincial government took certain legislative and policy steps to manage growth and to reduce sprawl in the city-region. These included the creation of the Montreal Urban Community (see Chapter 8); the enactment of environmental and housing policies (see Tomalty 1997, 148-9); the Protection of Agricultural Land Act (see Chapters 5 and 7); the introduction of the "preferred development option for the region of Montreal" (option préférable d'aménagement pour la région de Montréal); and the creation of regional municipalities. The latter two are described next.

Preferred Development Option

By the late 1970s, the provincial government could no longer ignore the problems presented by the patterns of growth in the Montreal region. Studies undertaken by its Office de planification et de développement du Québec indicated that the creation of the Montreal Urban Community in 1969 had not resolved regional issues, that the agricultural economy was under intense pressure, that infrastructure costs needed to be brought under control, and that provincial action was badly needed to better coordinate provincial policies and the planning activities of municipal governments (Tomalty 1997, 152).

Within this context, in 1978 the Parti Québécois government introduced the "preferred development option for the region of Montreal." The preferred option was based on three principles:

1 consolidate the urban fabric within the presently built-up area of the region
2 give priority to redeveloping the island of Montreal
3 pay special attention to improving the quality of life on the island of Montreal.

In general, the preferred option was an attempt (1) to guide such strategic decisions as the location of government facilities and infrastructure investments, and (2) to curb sprawl. The latter objective was to be realized by a moratorium on bridges and freeways connecting the central city to its suburbs (which served as the basis for the 1979 transportation plan) and by preventing the urbanization of farmland in the outer reaches of the region (as expressed in the Loi sur la protection des terres agricoles [Protection of Agricultural Land Act]). The preferred option was also meant to provide guidance to the newly formed regional county municipalities with regard to adopting their first strategic plans.

The preferred option plan was not well received by suburban municipalities, who resented the constraints it put on their growth. As a result, not only did the government compromise on certain of the plan's goals, but, more important, the fact that it did not delegate any enforcement mechanisms meant that the objective was effective neither in coordinating provincial decisions nor in influencing the decisions of local governments. Thus, the preferred option plan soon came to be viewed merely as a statement of the government's good intentions, having limited impact on the nature and form of growth in the region (Quesnel 1990).

After 1982, urban sprawl was somewhat contained by the recession and the oil crisis; and, in 1984, the province reiterated its commitment to the preferred option plan. After 1987, however, the tendencies towards sprawl resumed. This was, in part, due to the region's improving economic circumstances (which always create conditions ripe for sprawl), but which was also due to policy changes: in 1985 a new government lifted the moratorium on highway construction, began to invest in new highways in the outer suburbs, froze public transport funding, and adopted policies that weakened the Protection of Agricultural Land Act (Tomalty 1997, 153).

Creation of Regional County Municipalities

In 1979 the new planning law, the Loi sur l'aménagement et l'urbanisme (Land Use Planning and Development Act), was adopted, which created municipalités régionales de comté (regional county municipalities). These are groupings of several municipalities whose function is to prepare plans d'aménagement (development plans). The Montreal metropolitan area contains twelve regional county municipalities plus the Montreal Urban Community (Communauté urbaine de Montréal). Ostensibly, these upper-tier municipal jurisdictions were introduced on the North and South Shores to help coordinate services at a wider level and to encourage more effective regional land-use planning. The regional county municipalities each produce a master plan; however, the various plans are not coordinated with each other and most do not support a coherent policy of growth management (Fischler 1999).

As stated in the preferred option plan, the Ministry of Municipal Affairs was supposed to ensure the compatibility of the various development plans, both with each other and with government policy. This, however, did not occur, and, according to Fischler (1999), the only benefit of the regional county municipalities has been the better coordination of planning between groups of municipalities – but *not* at the metropolitan level. Moreover, most observers agree (see, for example, Trepanier 1993; Sancton 1994; Fischler 1999) that, as regional planning authorities, the regional county municipalities are relatively weak compared, for example, to the upper-tier regional municipalities in Ontario. On top of all this, the province has not until recently authorized any region-wide planning authority; consequently, no planning or regulatory resources were delegated to carry out region-wide planning.

One positive development has been the creation of the Agence métropolitaine de transport (Metropolitan Transportation Agency), which took over from the Conseil métropolitain de transport en commun. This agency has a larger territory (the entire metropolitan area) than did the council, and it has independent funding. The Metropolitan Transportation Agency was to prepare a regional strategic plan for public transit within the policy framework defined by the Quebec Ministry of Transport. Otherwise, however, there is currently no comprehensive planning going on in the Montreal city-region and no arrangement for coordinating its extremely large number of municipal governments. To be sure, under the MUC, metropolitan-regional planning does occur to some extent; however, except for the areas of police, transportation, and parks, it is limited in scope and impact. The most effective land-use planning powers reside with the lower-tier municipalities. This failing is directly related to the absence of region-wide governance, which we discuss later in this chapter.

Toronto City-Region

The region-wide planning activities and initiatives undertaken in the Toronto city-region can be broken down into two periods: (1) the early efforts between 1965 and 1982, and (2) the developments since the 1980s.

Early Efforts, 1965 to 1982

The years 1966 to 1975 mark what has been called the "golden age of planning" in the Province of Ontario. Some say it was the most comprehensive planning program undertaken by a senior government anywhere in Canada (a few would say in all of the developed world) (Richardson 1984). The golden age began in early 1965 when the province co-hosted two major international conferences on regional disparities, regional development, and economic change. The meetings attracted wide interest throughout the province, promoting a climate of opinion that favoured government action in the area of regional planning and regional development and recognition that such activity required special administrative machinery.

These conferences, plus some other events at the time, provided the impetus for the provincial government to initiate a comprehensive effort in the area of regional planning and regional development that lasted until the early 1980s. Mounted with much fanfare in 1966, Design for Development was a multifaceted program comprising a series of major regional planning efforts. The primary aim of the program was to stimulate economic growth in the less favoured regions and to produce regional development plans for the ten economic regions of the province, including the Toronto-Centred Region (see Chapter 6).[18]

Toronto-Centred Region Concept

The Toronto-Centred Region (TCR) Concept came out of the earlier work of the provincially sponsored Metropolitan Toronto and Region Transportation Study that had been launched in early 1963. The purpose of that study was to devise a transportation plan for an area, including Toronto and its region, roughly a ninety-seven-kilometre radius, incorporating the commutershed, stretching from Hamilton and Guelph, east to Bowmanville, and north to Lake Simcoe – an area slightly larger than the Greater Toronto Area, as currently defined by the provincial government. The study found that it was impossible to plan a transportation system without some knowledge of how the area was going to develop. Consequently, it devoted most of its final report, entitled "Choices for a Growing Region" (1968), to a discussion of alternative land-use scenarios, beginning with a discussion of a so-called "trends plan," which was based on an extrapolation of existing municipal plans and policies. As alternatives to the trends plan, it outlined four "goals plans" for the region, each having features that would circumvent future problems implied by existing trends. Provincial planners incorporated elements of these plans into the Toronto-Centred Region Concept that was finally developed.

The TCR proposal took in a section of southern Ontario almost three times the size of the GTA, encompassing Kitchener–Waterloo, Brantford, Midland, Peterborough, and recreation districts to the north (see Figure 20). It had a population of 3.6 million in 1966, which was expected to increase to about eight million by the end of the century. Indeed, this forecast came very close to being on target. The TCR proposal was a development concept aimed at relieving a number of problems identified with the pattern and rapid rate of growth in and around Metro Toronto – the increasing tendency of Ontario's population to concentrate in the large urban areas in the central and southwestern portion of the province (at the expense of rural places and of the north and east); the tendency towards unstructured sprawl; and the trend towards careless and unwise use of the physical environment (e.g., waste of prime farmland,

Figure 20

Toronto-Centred Region Concept

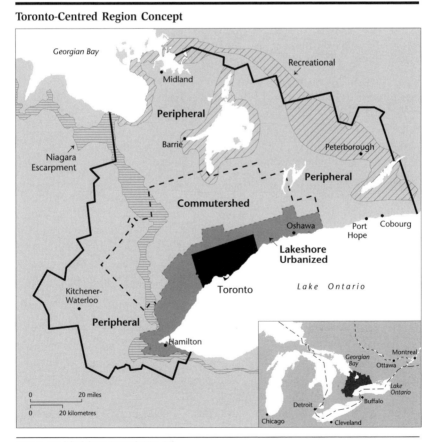

Source: Modified from Perry (1974, 33).

open-pit mining, air and water pollution). The TCR Concept sought to counter these conditions through a number of measures and actions, including, among others, dividing the region into three zones and confining growth to only two of them.

The report, "Design for Development: The Toronto-Centred Region," prepared by the provincial planners was released in May 1970. Its objectives were to change the emphasis of new growth from west to east of Metro Toronto. In popular terms, this came to be known as the "go-east" policy: to structure the growth of the urbanizing lakeshore area; to encourage concentrated urban growth in selected communities beyond commuting range of Toronto, especially to the north and east; and to set down basic guidelines for land use within the region.

The go-east policy appeared promising, with the prospect of a second international airport and an associated new town (at Pickering) becoming more plausible; however, unfortunately, nothing happened, except for some continuing large-scale land acquisitions that generated controversy until the mid-1980s. The failure of these developments to materialize showed, among other things, that the development pressures to the west of the region were stronger than could be contained (Macdonald 1984, 97). This contributed to the prevalent feeling among provincial officials that the TCR Concept was too general to be translated into programs: it lacked a plan for implementation. In 1973 the province decided to set up the Central Ontario Lakeshore Urban Complex Task Force for the purpose of refining the TCR Concept so as to overcome this problem (see Cullingworth 1987, ch. 8).

The task force was hard-hitting and realistic in its criticisms of previous government actions and programs, and it emphasized the need for firm government commitment. These strong words apparently did not sit well with those powerful political forces who preferred generalized, non-specific "motherhood" statements (Cullingworth 1987). The government allowed the TCR Concept to languish and the Central Ontario Lakeshore Urban Complex to disband. And in 1975 it announced that it would no longer finance roads or other services to the new airport site, forcing the federal government to shelve the project. Later the province abandoned the plan for a new town on Metropolitan Toronto's eastern boundary.

The epitaph for the Design for Development and the TCR Concept was anticipated by the Bureau of Municipal Research in 1977, when it noted that "a significant swing in provincial policy with respect to regional planning is under way. The notion of a 'grand plan' for all of Ontario has apparently been abandoned" (cited in Cullingworth 1987, 301).

The Design for Development program officially died in 1982 and, along with it, the TCR Concept. Several reasons have been put forward for their demise. Richardson (1981, 568), for example, emphasizes the inadequacy of central planning, the program's lack of a power base, and its consequent undue reliance on a small group of individuals; in short, the program was never "bedded down" in the governmental system.

Yet another "insider" referred to provincial planning in Ontario as "a not-so-great planning fiasco," arguing that what went wrong was nothing more than "old-fashioned failure in implementation," and that it took the planners four years after the government proudly proclaimed its plans to "figure out what it would take to make them work, [but] when they told the politicians, the plans died; the planning process dried up" (Comay 1984, 163). Likewise, a "high-level" participant in the process sadly concluded that the difficulties of implementation, particularly the political difficulties, were too great to be overcome (Macdonald 1984).

Smith (1998) offers a different explanation for the failure of the TCR Concept: with the exception of the Municipality of Metropolitan Toronto, he argues, it was not well received at the municipal level. The many municipalities in the region were not consulted during preparation of the plan and thus had no stake in its outcome; many, in fact, were downright hostile due to its implications for their communities.

There were (and are) only three remnants from the province's incursion into regional planning during that period. First, there are the segments of the parkway belt in the Peel and York regions; second there is the Niagara Escarpment Plan, which partially protects lands for agricultural and recreational use in the GTA's rapidly growing western portion (see Chapter 7); and third, there are the almost 2,600 square kilometres of undeveloped land in the Durham region, upon which the government had planned to build a model community (Seaton). (However, the economic slowdown and a sharp drop in housing prices in the early 1990s once again made the future of Seaton uncertain.)

According to one government official who was intimately associated with the Design for Development program, the TCR plan was by far the boldest attempt at that time at planning the overall form of a metropolitan region (MacDonald 1984). And, to one scholar, Frances Frisken (1982, cited in Smith 1998), its demise represented the beginning of the "retreat from regional planning" in Canada.

Developments since the 1980s

The best evidence that the TCR Concept had failed in its objectives to manage growth in the region was the continuation, indeed the acceleration, of dispersed, unplanned growth trends in the outer parts of the region. The pattern of settlement in the GTA in the 1980s and early 1990s was more in line with the Metropolitan Toronto and Region Transportation Study than with the TCR Concept or with its 1974 update. Consequently, beginning in the early 1980s, planners and policy makers came around to viewing urban growth within its broader regional context. Indeed, the advent of the concept of the GTA was an expression of that new perspective. However, regional planning still faced considerable difficulties with regard to policy coordination for the area as a whole.

Office for the Greater Toronto Area

In an effort to deal with this matter, in 1988 the Ontario provincial Liberal government created the Office for the Greater Toronto Area (OGTA), headed by a deputy minister. This was perhaps the most important action taken by the province during this period. At the same time, the province also created the Greater Toronto Coordinating Committee (GTCC), which was made up of the chief executive officers of Metropolitan Toronto, the four regions, the City of Toronto, and seven local municipalities bordering on Metro Toronto.

The government established the OGTA as a means of promoting discussion, coordination, and, if possible, cooperation among the large number of local municipalities and provincial agencies with an interest in how the area develops. The TCR experience had convinced the government that it could not plan the region in a "top-down" fashion. Therefore, it did not give the OGTA any formal legislative basis for its responsibilities. It gave it no formal mandate to plan, to prepare a plan, or to provide (let alone to coordinate) area-wide services; nor did it allocate resources among competing functional requirements and local jurisdictions. The OGTA was to depend on the willingness of other governments to implement its recommendations.[19]

There is no question about some of the OGTA's accomplishments: it played an important role in enunciating the principles of a more compact urban form, and it gradually built support for region-wide solutions to region-wide problems. And, through its efforts behind the scenes (e.g., with regional and municipal governments), it also contributed to the learning process that resulted in a greater acceptance of the need to manage growth (Tomalty 1997, 131).

When the OGTA and the GTCC were created, many observers felt that the Ontario provincial government was finally recognizing the need to deal with regional urban growth in the GTA and that it was even expressing a serious interest in rethinking the role of regional planning (and regional governance) in Canada's largest city-region. However, as it turned out, most observers believe that these bodies have been ineffectual. After nine years, it was patently clear that the OGTA was no substitute for a full-fledged regional planning institution. It played only a minor role in coordinating the land-use plans of the separate municipalities of the region (it could only comment upon them to the Ministry of Municipal Affairs). It had little public profile and had lost its deputy minister.

Treating the Greater Toronto Area as a Bioregion

Quite a different view of the Toronto region and its planning and management – and probably the greatest boost to making politicians and citizens aware of the region as a single ecological entity – came from the work of the Royal Commission on the Future of the Toronto Waterfront, chaired by David Crombie (see Chapter 7). Established in 1988 to examine issues related to the health of Toronto's waterfront, the Crombie Commission soon extended the geographical scope of its mandate to take in the Toronto ecological region – what it termed the Greater Toronto Bioregion (GTB). It comprised the major basin formed by the Niagara Escarpment on the west, the Oak Ridges Moraine to the north and east, and the Lake Ontario shoreline. In other words, it was defined on the basis of natural boundaries rather than on the basis of political jurisdictions (see Figure 15 in Chapter 7). The GTB is a much larger regional area than is the GTA: it is a region covering a shoreline of some 250 kilometres, seventeen local municipalities, six conservation authorities, four regional municipalities, and four counties on the waterfront. To the north, approximately two-thirds of the GTA is included in the GTB.

The commission chose to use an ecosystem planning approach in analyzing the waterfront, the watershed, and the bioregion. This approach, which emphasizes the attempt to achieve a balance between human society and nature, stands in contrast to "conventional" planning approaches that tend to treat human society (along with its economy and built forms) as separable from nature. (Chapters 1 and 7 describe other features of the Crombie Commission's and similar approaches.)

Because the ecosystem approach highlighted interactions among ecological, social, economic, and political systems in the GTB, it enabled the Crombie Commission to recognize that, working singly, the various GTA governments could not hope to solve the environmental problems facing the region. It was clear that, because the environment does not correspond to political boundaries, actions in one jurisdiction may well affect the environmental health of others. Accordingly, the commission stressed the importance of developing new administrative mechanisms that would bring jurisdictions together and enable them to solve problems cooperatively. Existing institutional arrangements in the GTB are often part of the problem, for its bureaucratic systems are generally rigid and its jurisdictions are fragmented. Unfortunately, the commission made no recommendation with regard to an appropriate institutional arrangement, and it would take several years before the provincial government would do something about the governance problem in the GTA (see further discussion below).

In summary, the Crombie Commission tried to demonstrate how the environmental regeneration of the GTB could be achieved at no increased economic costs and could, perhaps, even result in the region's economic advantage. It expressed confidence that it was possible to develop a strategy for the GTB that would allow a clean, green environment to co-exist with a healthy, growing economy and self-sustaining communities.

The government never adopted the concept of the Greater Toronto Bioregion as appropriate to regional planning pertaining to the GTA. Nor was it given any legislative base or regulatory powers. However, publication of the commission's interim and final reports marked a new stage in the history of ecosystems planning in Canada. They very soon spawned other planning reports, which were based on the ecosystems concept and were undertaken by the old City of Toronto, Metro Toronto, and the provincial government.

Moreover, in 1992 the Ontario legislature established the Waterfront Regeneration Trust as a successor to the royal commission. It had the authority to carry out specific projects (based on the ecosystem approach); to coordinate programs and policies of the Ontario government and its agencies relating to waterfront lands; to advise the province on any matters concerning the use, disposition, conservation, protection, and regeneration of waterfront lands; and to serve as a resource centre and information clearinghouse for policies about waterfront lands (Tomalty et al. 1994, 53).

In the early 1990s, as GTA-wide planning problems became more intense and their negative impacts were increasingly acknowledged, and as the deficiencies of the OGTA were recognized, questions about decision making, implementation, and regional governance became more important. Pressure began to mount from municipal leaders, bureaucrats, business representatives, and citizens to reform governance in the GTA to reflect the new realities. There was a growing recognition that individual municipalities could not deal effectively with a large number of current and emerging issues in the GTA and that some sort of coordinating planning mechanism (and perhaps an overall governance authority as well) was needed.

Vancouver City-Region

Region-wide planning in the Vancouver city-region can be broken into two periods: (1) between 1949 and 1968, when the Lower Mainland Regional Planning Board was operating, and (2) between 1967 and the present, when the GVRD is operating.[20]

Lower Mainland Regional Planning Board

The first step towards formalized regional planning in the Vancouver region was taken in mid-1948, when the provincial Town Planning Act was revised to allow "for contiguous authorities in a metropolitan area to develop a joint land use planning function, for the purpose of achieving a coordinated regional approach to development problems."[21] As with most of the other Canadian metropolitan areas following the Second World War, governments in the Lower Mainland had to address the immense suburban boom and demand for municipal services resulting from converting to a peace-time economy. And it had to develop housing to accommodate returning soldiers and their families. In the Lower Mainland, there was an additional factor: the threat of urban encroachment on valuable agricultural land. On top of these factors, the Fraser River flood of 1948 made it clear that building housing on the Fraser River Delta had inherent risks.

It was in order to meet these challenges that, in 1949, the provincial government designated the entire Lower Mainland area – from the western part of Greater Vancouver to the narrowing of the Fraser River 162 kilometres to the east – as a planning region and established the Lower Mainland Regional Planning Board (LMRPB) as the decision-making body.[22] The board was composed of representatives from each of the twenty-eight cities, towns, and district municipalities in the region (assuming they chose to participate, and most did).

Under the province's Town Planning Act, 1948, the LMRPB was empowered to conduct planning studies, to provide planning services to constituent municipalities (whether or not they were members of the board), and to prepare an official regional plan covering the Lower Mainland region. An official regional plan, which was subject to the approval of the provincial government, was defined as "a general scheme without detail for the projected use of land within the planning district" (British Columbia Municipal Act). This plan would establish broad principles that were to be applied to the allocation of land use as well as to determining the location of new communities, highways, roads, utilities, and regional facilities. For these purposes the LMRPB could collect a per capita levy from the member municipalities to help it meet its annual budget.

The LMRPB's proposed regional plan of 1963, entitled *Chance and Challenge*, covered both the Vancouver metropolitan area and the Fraser Valley, and was based on the vision that "the region is a unity, but a unity of many diverse parts." In August 1966, following three years of staff research and consultation with member municipalities and the general public, the LMRPB's Official Regional Plan had gained the necessary approval of two-thirds of the Lower Mainland municipalities. It called for "a series of cities in a sea of green – a valley of separate cities surrounded by a productive countryside and linked by a regional freeway network"; and its objectives were "the orderly, staged and diversified development of the region, its communities and its resources."

The LMRPB's plan established a logical framework for regional and local land-use development in the region. However, the plan, and some of the board's activities, had caused friction and jealousy among the local bureaucracies as well as conflicts with the provincial government – indeed, it had begun to threaten provincial authority (Oberlander and Smith 1993, 358-9). During the period between 1965 and 1968, some LMRPB board and staff members publicly criticized the provincial government over a number of provincial land-use decisions that were at variance with their newly adopted official regional plan. In addition, the LMRPB was critical of the ministry's program for creating regional districts all over the province, which had begun in 1965.

As a consequence of such intergovernmental friction, in 1968 the government dissolved the LMRPB without much warning, fanfare, or public debate. Probably the most successful of British Columbia's special regional authorities (and the province had a long history of such authorities), ironically, the board's success probably led to its demise. Nevertheless, the legacy of the LMRPB ensured that regional land-use planning remained central to governance in metropolitan Vancouver and the rest of the Lower Mainland, and it left a solid foundation upon which its successor, the GVRD, could build.

Regional Districts

In the late 1950s and early 1960s, throughout British Columbia a large number of special-purpose districts were established (in addition to the normal local government units – municipalities). Despite the multiplicity of jurisdictions, the bulk of the province's territory remained without formal local government organization. More important, from the provincial government's perspective, rapid urbanization was threatening to outstrip the capacity of existing municipal institutions to cope with it. In particular, it was felt that, in the two metropolitan regions (Vancouver and Victoria), the informal, voluntary method of resolving common problems among adjacent municipalities was both too slow and too uncertain.

It was believed that larger, more sophisticated units of government were needed in order to supply services to a growing population and to engage in regional planning. Additional special-purpose agencies were proposed here and there to deal with these problems. But, as a 1971 review committee noted, there was a danger that the number of special-purpose agencies would proliferate to the point where they would be providing services in a completely uncoordinated, unprioritized, and random fashion.

It was out of this background that, in 1965, the provincial government scrapped the informal, advisory, intermunicipal planning approach and introduced a new concept – regional districts (RDs)[23] through a process and procedure Tennant and Zirnhelt (1973) refer to as "gentle imposition." For example, the district in the Vancouver area originally did not even include the word "Vancouver." It was called regional district of Fraser–Burrard – a tactic the authors claim was used to obscure the creation of a Vancouver-centred regional district; in 1968, the name was changed to Greater Vancouver Regional District. Tennant and Zirnhelt (1973) also have suggested that, ironically, the success of the LMRPB in fulfilling its mandate – plus the success of the various other single-purpose authorities (e.g., hospital boards, water, sewerage, and drainage districts) – undoubtedly made a lasting impression on provincial policy makers. According to them, this was a key factor in the government's decision to establish regional districts.

The government wanted the machinery of regional districts to be equally applicable to urban, rural, and unincorporated areas in the province. More specifically, it had two purposes in mind. First, it wanted to provide the rural areas of the province with some semblance of local government. Until the creation of regional districts in 1965, about 99 percent of the province's territory remained municipally unorganized. If citizens in non-municipal areas desired special services, then they had to look to special districts, direct provincial provision, or municipal incorporation. With the creation of regional districts, however, a flexible form of general government became available; and, indeed, since that time regional districts have been used to perform a variety of functions for citizens living outside municipal boundaries. Second, the government wanted a way of organizing the most highly urbanized and urbanizing areas, which were fragmented politically and awash in a sea of multiple jurisdictions. In short, the provincial regionalization policy was perceived as an alternative to metropolitan government and special-purpose authorities; it was not viewed as another level of government (however, see later discussion in this chapter).

The province was divided into twenty-eight regional district areas, corresponding to informally recognized economic regions, or "trading areas," all of which, with the exception of the Stikine in the northwest corner of the province (as of 1995), have "incorporated" to form regional district "governments" under letters patent issued by the lieutenant-governor. As do municipalities, regional districts play a dual role. The first role involves undertaking activities and functions mandated by the provincial government; the second involves performing purely local functions decided on by locally elected officials and authorized by letters patent. When regional districts were first created in 1965, the provincial government mandated them with only one major activity – general planning for the development of the region. All regional boards were required to supervise plan preparation and to approve general regional plans and settlement plans for areas outside municipal boundaries. Municipalities, as they had been doing before the new legislation, would continue to prepare their own official community plans for their municipal areas; however, the municipal plans and development policies were now required to be consistent with the general regional district plan.

Technically, regional districts are *not* regional governments; thus they are not higher than municipalities but, rather, constitute parallel local governments. Regional districts provide cooperative services by agreement among the members. Board members, rather than being elected by the voters, are appointed by the participating municipal councils. Voting by board members was weighted according to their municipalities' voting strength; this provision gave municipalities, with their larger populations, a major voice in most regions.

The districts do not have any taxing powers and receive their revenues as levies from the municipalities and grants from the province. They were conceived as functional rather than as political units. Their functions were not enshrined in legislation but, rather, depended upon being approved by two-thirds of the municipalities; however, some functions, such as hospital capital financing and planning were directly imposed upon the regional districts (Magnusson and Sancton 1983).

Greater Vancouver Regional District

In 1968, the LMRPB's territorial responsibilities were divided among four newly created regional districts – one of them being the GVRD. In the two decades between 1951 and 1971, the Vancouver metropolitan area had experienced a very high rate of population growth (averaging about 4 percent annually), and, in the process , the population grew to more than one million. The expectation was that growth would continue for the foreseeable future.

Spurred by these population data, the debates on the future of the area in the late 1960s and early 1970s produced a political party in the city of Vancouver – The Electors' Action Movement (TEAM). TEAM members argued eloquently that Vancouver was different from US cities, that it was developing its own direction, and that it needed made-in-Vancouver plans. They sought to make the city more livable for a population engaged in management and service activities, producer services, finance, tourism, and the information industries. And they wanted it to be less dependent on traditional port-related and primary industries. They also focused on universities, colleges, and science parks, recognizing that higher education, research, and development were important components of this new vision of the future.

A key aspect of their argument was the desire to protect Vancouver's unique natural physical environment and to create a high-quality public environment with safe, attractive, and accessible neighbourhoods. This vision clearly had the support of the majority of city officials and, in fact, provided the basis for a broad political consensus that would last for at least three decades. This vision would provide the foundations upon which the GVRD would develop its plans.

Livable Region Plan

In the late 1960s and early 1970s, the GVRD board decided to undertake its own process of developing a planning strategy distinct from the one prepared by the LMRPB. Partly motivated by a desire to get around what they saw as difficulties associated with the traditional hierarchical formal planning mandate, GVRD planners developed a completely new plan, one "more populist and policy-focused" (in the words of the current GVRD's manager of strategic planning, Ken Cameron [1996]). They called it the "Livable Region Plan," and it was to serve as a companion to the official regional plan. In 1975 the GVRD and its constituent municipalities approved the 1976-86 plan, but it was never formally adopted as board policy. The plan laid down a set of "proposals to manage the growth of Greater Vancouver," including the need to channel new growth "so as to maintain or enhance the livability of the Region" (GVRD 1975, 5, 8, 18). The plan attempted to bring order to development that was now sprawling south and southeast.

One of the important differences between the LMRPB's official regional plan and the GVRD's Livable Region Plan (LRP) is that the latter was intended to be pro-active and dynamic enough to respond to change. The GVRD's first director of planning, and the initiator of the LRP, Harry Lash, depicted the plan as flowing from "a new process, a different kind of planning," involving the interaction of public, planners, and politicians (Lash 1976). The plan comprised a set of strategies and principles for dealing with regional growth (GVRD 1975).

The Greater Vancouver LRP was probably one of the first plans (it was certainly the first at the metropolitan and city-region scale) to have been developed out of an extensive citizen participation process (Lash 1976). Although virtually no agreed-upon methods of implementation were specified, the strategies and principles used would continue to be dominant themes in the revisions to the LRP that took place in the following two decades. And they would continue to influence public debate about the way the region should develop.

In the meantime, the four regional districts that were created for the Lower Mainland in 1968 decided to cooperate and update the 1966 regional plan. They adopted it as the 1980 plan for the Lower Mainland of British Columbia. Each district was now responsible for maintaining its portion of the official regional plan for its own jurisdiction. The GVRD's 1980 official regional plan was concerned with the entire Lower Mainland, not only with the metropolitan area. Further, it differed from the earlier LRP in that it focused mainly on land use rather than on the coordination of growth and change in jobs, population, housing, and transportation. It also differed from the LMRPB's 1966 vision of "a series of cities in a sea of green" in that cities would be smaller in size and fewer in number to reflect a lower population growth than had originally been anticipated. Also, there would be no freeway network (GVRD July 1994 [revised]).

Changing Provincial Commitment

Following the May 1983 re-election of the Social Credit government, all regional districts in British Columbia were stripped of their planning and zoning authority. The Municipal Amendment Act declared null and void all regional plans and removed the right of a regional district to plan for its region as a whole. The regional planning system, for all practicalities, was gutted. While the minister tried to use some technical justification for the legislation (the stated reason was to free municipalities from the regulatory authority of regional districts), some analysts attribute the change to a "hidden political agenda" involving the agricultural land reserve system established in 1973 by the NDP government of the day (see Chapters 5 and 7; also see Oberlander and Smith 1993; Magnusson et al. 1984; Allen and Rosenbluth 1986).

The truth of the matter is that, during the late 1970s and early 1980s, continuing differences between the GVRD and the provincial government arose over land-use issues involving the agricultural land reserves. These differences came to a head in the early 1980s when the provincial Cabinet upheld a proposal by a Social Credit supporter and agricultural land owner to exclude a substantial farm area (known as the Spetifore Lands) from an agricultural land reserve (located in the Vancouver metropolitan suburb of Delta) in order to allow the building of an extensive housing development. According to the chair of the GVRD planning committee, the province's decision to remove the board's statutory regional planning function was "a move of retribution over the Spetifore Lands issue" (which the regional board had opposed) (Oberlander and Smith 1993, 363).

Although regional planning authority had been taken away from all regional districts in 1983, this did not mean the end of regional planning – at least not as far as the GVRD was concerned. Almost alone among the districts, the GVRD continued a regional planning service after 1983, falling back on the province's tradition of voluntary municipal support. Fourteen of the fifteen municipalities in the Greater Vancouver region participated voluntarily. This voluntary arrangement was strengthened and made "official" when, in 1989, legislation restored regional planning on a cooperative, voluntary basis, thus enabling regional districts to provide coordination, research, and analytical and non-regulatory "development services" to constituent municipal and non-municipal areas. The very fact that, under these circumstances, all but one of the municipalities in the GVRD continued to participate in this activity supports Oberlander and Smith's (1993) view that regional planning is and will continue to be an ongoing function in the Lower Mainland.

Livable Region Strategic Plan

By the end of 1989, the GVRD board had concluded that, due to the changes that had occurred in the region, a major update of the LRP was needed. Increasing numbers of people were moving to the Lower Mainland, creating severe growth pressures on Greater Vancouver. GVRD planners launched what they called the "Creating Our Future" program and, in March 1989, a report entitled "The Livable Region: A Strategy for the 1990s" was published, building on the earlier LRP and the principles of the former official regional plan. The program aimed to stimulate a broad discussion of the challenges facing Greater Vancouver. In 1989-90, the board approved seven broad livability goals in order to begin the formal consultative process, which was called "Choosing Our Future" (GVRD 1989a). The process involved an open, inclusive, and honest search for solutions that all residents of the region could widely support.

The "Choosing Our Future" program was designed to be informative and to involve a wide cross-section of the community; it consisted of seminars, public attitude surveys, children's educational programs, public forums and meetings, and a television program and public phone-in. Thousands of people were involved in the process, and they submitted hundreds of ideas. What resulted was an ambitious statement about the vision of the region's future:

Greater Vancouver can become the first urban region in the world to combine in one place the things to which humanity aspires on a global basis: a place where human activities enhance rather than degrade the natural environment, where the quality of the built environment approaches that of the natural setting, where the diversity of origins and religions is a source of social strength rather than strife, where people control the destiny of their community, and where the basics of food, clothing, shelter, security and useful activity are accessible to all. (GVRD 1990a)

Some of the most critical choices participants identified involved land use and transportation. Therefore, a growth management planning process, together with a provincial and regional joint transportation planning process, took most of the attention of the planners between 1991 and 1993. The key question they tried to answer was: How, in terms of physical development, will the region be able to accommodate one million more residents over the next twenty-five years, while sustaining high levels of livability and environmental quality?

In 1993, the GVRD issued its proposed plan (GVRD 1993), which entailed four key features:

1 It placed environmental values before the pressures for urban development.
2 For the first time, the planning of regional land use and transportation took place with the full involvement of the implementing authorities.
3 The plan covered the entire Lower Mainland, including the Vancouver census metropolitan area and extending 125 kilometres from the City of Vancouver in the west to Chilliwack in the east (with an overall population of 1.78 million).
4 Planning and implementation was to be accomplished through partnerships among regional, provincial, and local governments rather than through a hierarchy of plans and regulations.

In January 1996, the Livable Region Strategic Plan (LRSP) (see Figure 21), after thousands of hours of research, reflection, political debate, and citizen participation, was finally adopted by the GVRD board and the twenty constituent municipalities and three unorganized areas. (Another unorganized area had been added since the original establishment of the GVRD, and, as noted earlier, since then one municipality has been added, and two unorganized areas eliminated.) The plan built on those strategies and principles first set down in the 1975 plan. The LRSP, buttressed by the provincial Growth Strategies Act, was based on the premise that high-quality and high-value economic development and employment depends on a livable and efficient city-region and on business and government partnerships at the local, regional, and provincial levels. Specifically, the LRSP includes four basic strategies:

Figure 21

Greater Vancouver Livable Region Strategic Plan

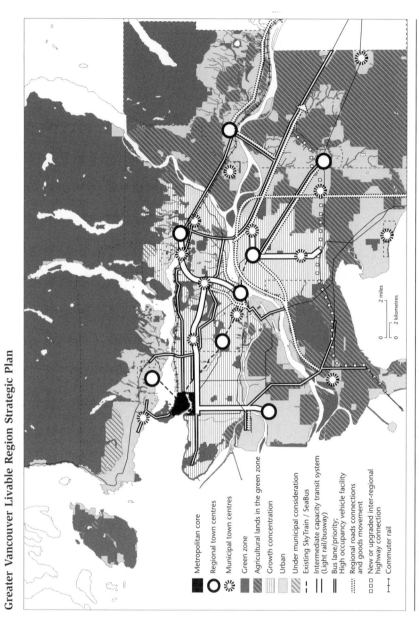

Metropolitan core

Regional town centres

Municipal town centres

Green zone

Agricultural lands in the green zone

Growth concentration

Urban

Under municipal consideration

Existing SkyTrain / SeaBus

Intermediate capacity transit system
(Light rail/busway)

Bus lane/priority;
High occupancy vehicle facility

Regional roads connections
and goods movement

New or upgraded inter-regional
highway connection

Commuter rail

0   2 miles

0   2 kilometres

Source: Modified from map on GVRD website, www.gvrd.bc.ca/services.

1 Protect the green zone surrounding the region. This is an extension of the Livable Region Plan open space conservancy concept. The green zone is designed to protect areas with great economic, environmental, recreational, and ecological value. The green zone also includes the farmland in the agricultural land reserves. Long-term protection of these lands will depend on the coordinated action of a large number of government agencies.

2 Build complete communities, each focused on a town centre, with a wide mix of day-to-day activity destinations located close by that enable people to live, work, and shop with a minimum of commuting.[24] The LRSP carries forward the LRP notion of a hierarchy of centres, including municipal town centres, regional town centres, and the metropolitan core in downtown Vancouver. The plan envisions such communities in the urbanized portion of the region as well as in the existing valley towns and at their edges.

3 Achieve a compact metropolitan region, enabling residents to live closer to job centres and to enjoy other benefits. The LRSP also tries to achieve a balance among housing affordability, urban containment, and environmental sustainability by seeking to ensure that a sufficient variety of housing types are constructed in the different communities of the region.

4 Increase transportation choices, encourage use of public transit, and reduce reliance on single-occupancy vehicles.

Since the growth management strategic planning and joint transportation planning processes were developed in the absence of provincial enabling legislation, the GVRD board and its member municipalities established the rules for completing and adopting the strategic plan on a consensual basis. These rules actually formed part of the basis for the Growth Strategies Statutes Amendments Act, which was adopted in 1995 to provide a provincial legislative context for growth management planning throughout the province. In February 1996 the minister of municipal affairs signed an order recognizing the GVRD's LRSP as a regional growth strategy under the terms of the new legislation (described below).[25]

Implementing the Livable Region Strategic Plan

Implementing the LRSP has required that the GVRD and local jurisdictions not only coordinate plans, but also work together to calculate the current estimated growth capacity in each municipality; identify regional town centres that would serve as a focus for new development; and set aside upwards of two-thirds of the regional land base for inclusion in the green zone outlined in the regional plan. The GVRD is also implementing the LRSP through its plans for managing sewage, solid waste, air quality, drinking water, health services, and major parks throughout the region. In addition, it is developing demand-side management programs designed to reduce the need for many of these services rather than merely increasing service capacity.

To gauge its progress in implementing the LRSP, the GVRD currently monitors a variety of regional indicators, including, for example, the location of housing starts, where new jobs are created, how many people are car-pooling, and how many are riding public transit. The GVRD prepares an annual report regarding its progress towards realizing the LRSP.

Most important in the implementation of the LRSP are two special techniques: (1) regional context statements, and (2) implementation agreements.

Regional Context Statements

Under the Growth Strategies Act, each community within the region must prepare a regional context statement indicating how its community plan relates to the LRSP and what it intends to do to adjust its plan to conform to the regional growth strategy. The statement must be submitted to the GVRD board for approval, and, if the board decides not to approve the community's statement, then a dispute resolution process is triggered. When finally approved, a regional context statement can be altered only by formally changing the community plan and the regional growth strategy.

Under provincial planning legislation, a local jurisdiction's zoning must conform to its community plan, thereby linking planning efforts to local implementation mechanisms. In this way, the regional growth strategy is meant to be carried out, in part, through local community plans and zoning bylaws that are consistent with it.

Implementation Agreements

The Growth Strategies Act recognizes that regional districts will not be able to implement their regional growth strategy on their own and will require the cooperation and assistance of provincial ministries and agencies (adjoining regional districts or other local bodies such as airport or port authorities) and their member municipalities. Accordingly, section 942.3 of the act gives regional districts authority to enter into an implementation agreement with these various bodies and to formalize these partnerships for sewer or highway construction, regional parks development, and the like. This provision has similarities with the waterfront agreements proposed by the Royal Commission on the Future of the Toronto Waterfront (briefly mentioned in Chapter 7).

Related Region-Wide Planning Initiatives and Supports

Region-wide planning in the Vancouver city-region in general, and the Livable Region Strategic Plan in particular, have benefited from the existence of a number of strong, related "outside" initiatives and supports, including stakeholders, the public, and formal programs – all of them contributing to an awareness of region-wide problems and the need for growth management. Perhaps the most important of these is the provincial Growth Strategies Act.

Growth Strategies Act

In 1983, as noted earlier, the provincial government deprived the regional districts of their regional planning function. During the remainder of the 1980s there was much public discussion of the need to develop a comprehensive provincial plan or land use act that leaned towards a stronger and more central role for provincial planning in the regions. While such ideas received little support from local governments, in 1989 the provincial government did update the regional district legislation. However, this legislation only solidified and streamlined the servicing role of regional districts while including amendments that allowed them more autonomy and flexibility: it did not address the subject of regional planning as such.

Nevertheless, in the late 1980s, the government was faced with continued population growth (especially in the Lower Mainland, along the east coast of Vancouver Island, and in the Okanagan) as well as with public concern about the effects of uncoordinated rapid urban growth and the demand from a number of interest groups to return to some form of regional planning. In response, in 1992 the government began to pursue the idea of reintroducing regional planning into British Columbia's planning system. The province began to lay the groundwork for this, which, it hoped, would strengthen regional planning institutions in British Columbia. An extensive consultation process was conducted throughout the province during 1992 and 1993, culminating in a 1994 discussion paper, "Growth Strategies for the 1990s and Beyond: Interactive, Inclusive, Flexible: Updating British Columbia's Planning System." The report set out a number of basic guiding principles that would help to shape what was referred to as an "updated planning system" for the province as well as the details of the subsequent legislation.

The Growth Strategies Act became law on 8 June 1995 and was folded into the existing Municipal Act through the creation of a new part. The Growth Strategies Act provides authority for regional districts to develop regional growth management strategies, and it makes possible the creation and adoption of such strategies with a high degree of support among member municipalities and other non-governmental organizations (e.g., Aboriginal organizations). The act also makes it more likely that municipal plans will be consistent with regional strategies – a persistent problem everywhere in Canada – by requiring each member municipality to show how its official community plan is (or will be) consistent with the regional strategy.

The act contains three new interrelated regional planning tools to which we have already referred: (1) a regional growth strategy, (2) regional context statements, and (3) implementation agreements (for details see BC Ministry of Municipal Affairs 1995).

Other Supports

In addition to the Growth Strategies Act, several other government and not-for-profit initiatives and programs have been (and are) promoting an awareness of region-wide problems as well as the need for growth management based on ecological and sustainability concepts, objectives, and principles in planning for the Vancouver city-region. Moreover, these initiatives and programs advocate the use of a larger geographic area as the appropriate planning region – either the Lower Fraser Basin or the Georgia Basin. Most of them were initiated in the early 1990s (and a few of them still exist). They include the Georgia Basin Initiative; the Fraser River Estuary Management Program; the Fraser Basin Management Board and its successor, the Fraser Basin Council; and the Lower Fraser River Ecosystem Study (see Chapter 7).

These government and non-governmental initiatives also provide a vehicle by which public interest groups and citizen organizations can involve themselves in issues related to regional growth management. The growing awareness in these groups of the links between urbanization and sustainability represent a shift in the traditional focus of environmental groups. Whereas at one time these groups focused their attention solely on environmental protection (e.g., of the region's forests and agriculture), they have now come to realize that the extent and nature of a region's urban growth, and its land-use patterns, have extremely serious impacts on its sustainability (see Chapter 7 for further discussion of this issue).

In summary, we have seen that, in addition to the GVRD, a number of regional organizations (both governmental and non-governmental) in the Vancouver city-region favour regional planning and growth management. However, this should not lead us to think that there is an established coalition of interests collectively promoting these policies, as there is in some US urban regions (for example, Portland, Oregon). We return to this issue in the last two chapters.

Region-Wide Governance Arrangements: Proposals and Prospects

As noted earlier, proposals have been made for changing the governance arrangements in the three city-regions. In this section, we discuss these proposals and their prospects for establishing effective region-wide planning and governance arrangements in each of the regions.

Of the three examples, Vancouver, for more than five decades, has had the most continuous and advanced region-wide planning and growth management activities, beginning with the LMRPB and culminating with the "quasi-regional government" known as the GVRD. Despite its comparative success, however, in recent years there have been proposals to make the GVRD even more effective (discussed later in this chapter).

The situation in the other two city-regions has been different: the Toronto city-region has also had a long history of region-wide planning, going back to 1965 and continuing to 1975, but this so-called "golden age of planning" was short-lived; and the initiative during the early 1990s – the OGTA – was devoid of any planning or implementation powers, as is the Greater Toronto Services Board (GTSB) established by the provincial government in 1999. Metropolitan-regional planning does occur in the Montreal region (under the Montreal Urban Community), but, except for the areas of police, transportation, and park systems, it is limited in scope and impact; the most effective land-use planning powers reside with the lower-tier municipalities.

In both the Montreal and Toronto city-regions, as we noted earlier, during the past decade the provincial governments initiated special commissions to study and recommend changes in their structures. These proposals will be described next.

Montreal City-Region

Currently, the Montreal city-region was Canada's most fragmented municipal jurisdiction, containing 110 municipalities, fourteen regional county munici-palities, one urban community, the Montreal Urban Community (MUC), five regional development councils, five regional health and social services boards, thirty-one school boards, and some twenty public transportation authorities. (This will change with the new legislative changes – see below.) The dominant MUC, focused on the island of Montreal, represents 60 percent of the area's population. It has mandates in the areas of public transit, policing, sewage disposal, regional parks, and planning. The other thirteen regional municipali-ties have only a statutory planning mandate.

By creating the upper-tier regional county municipalities in the early 1980s, the Quebec government appeared to be rejecting the option of extending the boundaries of the MUC. At the time there was no overwhelming pressure to extend the boundaries in order to attain more efficient service delivery. How-ever, a case could have been made for establishing boundaries that would enable the MUC to carry out metropolitan-wide regional planning (Sancton 1994). Ever since 1977, the provincial government had carried out this func-tion. The MUC and regional county municipalities were themselves unable to create any kind of plan for the whole of metropolitan Montreal. It was not until 1987 that the MUC approved its first development plan for its territory (see Communauté urbaine de Montréal, 1986 and 1987). This is not to say that the provincial government had a common policy for metropolitan Mon-treal – far from it – many provincial policies were in conflict with one another (Sancton 1994).

Indeed, this extreme municipal fragmentation extended to provincial minis-tries as well, when, in 1988, the province split the census metropolitan area into five administrative regions. Consequently, the decision-making process was fragmented, making it difficult, if not impossible, for the province to coor-dinate interventions through its various ministries while still, when necessary, being able to adopt measures on behalf of the entire city-region. The legiti-macy and accountability of the chief decision makers in the region depended primarily on their defence of local or sectoral interests (Québec, ministère de la Métropole 1996, 6). As we note below, while over the years there have been a number of proposals to rationalize decision making, as of the early 1990s there was still no overall regional planning body or coordinating governance mechanism that encompassed the entire region.

Proposals for the Montreal City-Region

The desirability of a metropolitan-wide agency for the Montreal region has been debated at least since the turn of the century, when settlement began to flow out of the city, and indeed off the island, as the major railroads were built. One of the earliest proponents of regional governance was George Nantel, once provincial minister of public works, who advocated the creation of a general council for the whole island to resolve problems of service delivery and road planning (Fischler and Wolfe 2000, 9). The League for Civic Improvement, made up of business and professional leaders, was equally insistent in the early 1900s. Perhaps the first government effort to create a regional governance occurred when it stepped in to impose a government structure, the Montreal Metropolitan Commission, on the island, in response to the city of Montreal's decision to annex four near-bankrupt suburban municipalities. The commission was made responsible for fiscal management, namely, the control of borrowing by suburban municipalities and the servicing of debt; other duties included the planning of major infrastructure, especially main roads.

The enormous suburban growth following the Second World War renewed interest in metropolitan problems. During the 1950s and 1960s a number of special commissions were created to study the problems and recommend solutions: the Paquette Commission, the Croteau Commission, the Blier Commission, and the Sylvestre Commission. All of them recommended creation of a regional governance authority in one form or another but, despite all their recommendations, the governments of the day took no decisive action.

By the early 1990s, continued growth of the outer suburbs, coupled with the declining economic and fiscal conditions in Montreal, brought the issue of governance and planning in the Montreal region to a head. In December 1991, the Quebec Cabinet's Standing Committee on the Development of Greater Montreal, composed of MLAs from the Montreal region, published a strategic plan for sustainable economic recovery in order to promote better coordination of governmental actions regarding economic development in the region. Entitled "Change Today for Tomorrow," the report targeted the two critical issues facing the region: the absence of a regional vision and the decline of the regional core (Québec, ministère du Conseil exécutif [1991], summarized in Tomalty [1997, 162]). In a word, the regional question was back on the public agenda.

As a result, the minister of municipal affairs in April 1992 announced the creation of a twelve-person "Task Force on Montreal and Its Region," which, among other things, was to recommend possible changes in the municipal organization of the territory covered by the ministerial committee (Trepanier 1993, 89). The task force was headed by Judge Claude Pichette; none of its members was a municipal politician.

Pichette Commission

The main recommendation in the Pichette Commission's final report, issued in December 1993, was a call for the province to create a Montreal Metropolitan Region (MMR). The MMR was to have a Metropolitan Regional Council that would be responsible for region-wide issues in a territory that would correspond exactly with that of the Montreal census metropolitan area and that would automatically be adjusted to match future census metropolitan area boundary changes. The MMR would be a federated rather than a unicity form of regional government, and it would consist of the twenty-nine municipalities on the island of Montreal along with the 107 municipalities adjacent to the island (Task Force on Greater Montreal December 1993).

The proposed regional council would have the power to levy taxes and user fees and to coordinate regional planning, land use, economic development, transportation, waste disposal, environmental protection, arts and culture, and public safety. The commission proposed that the MMR be administered by a twenty-one member metropolitan council with a seven-member executive committee, which would constitute a major change from the seventy-nine-seat MUC. It also proposed abolishing the regional county municipalities created only a decade earlier, reinstating one single administrative region, and creating Organismes intermunicipaux de services (Intermunicipal Service Agencies) for actual service delivery (one for the Island of Montreal and three for the outer suburbs, with Laval retaining its own municipal service system).

The Intermunicipal Service Agency of Montreal would be responsible for MUC functions not assigned to the region. Its governing body would be made up of the twenty-nine mayors and nine additional representatives from the City of Montreal. Votes would be weighed in accordance with population, and the "double-majority" system currently used within the MUC to protect suburban interests would be retained.

At that time the province made no significant move to implement the Pichette recommendations, which came just before an election year (when bold changes were not likely). Moreover, the Pichette Commission gave the metropolitan region and the regional council more autonomy than the Quebec government was prepared to allow, for it feared that this might serve as a political platform for those opposed to the policies of the Parti Québécois (Reid 1996, 15). In general, it can be said that, in dealing with the issue of region-wide planning and governance, political concerns heavily influenced the government of Quebec. Neither it nor the Pichette Commission was able to tackle the thorny political question of rationalizing the highly fragmented system of government in the region. The Pichette Commission proposed what amounted to a three-level local government system and avoided any recommendations that aimed to rationalize the large numbers of small municipalities, which have vigorously resisted any attempts at their abolition. As a consequence, there continued to be more than 100 local municipalities as well as fourteen regional municipalities, including the MUC. This fragmentation continued to reinforce fiscal inequities among municipalities and old-style competition for new business investment.

Ministry of Metropolitan Affairs

The Pichette Commission's failure to induce government action proved to be only partial. Three years after the Pichette Commission report was issued, the problems it identified in 1990 – urban sprawl, a crumbling tax base, and uncoordinated public transit – not only remained but had grown worse. Consequently, in 1996, the Parti Québécois government of Lucien Bouchard created a new ministry, the ministère de la Métropole (Ministry of Metropolitan Affairs), whose primary responsibility was to coordinate government action in the Montreal region and to foster regional planning. In February 1997 the ministers of metropolitan affairs and municipal affairs announced that the government wanted to stop the urban sprawl that had slowly drained Montreal's population towards the island's suburbs. In the coming years, they said, development plans would aim to consolidate the Montreal core, with public funds being spent to overhaul Montreal's infrastructure rather than building more schools and roads on the periphery.

Despite considerable opposition, in June 1997 the minister of metropolitan affairs succeeded in getting a law passed creating a regional planning body for the whole region of Montreal – the Commission de développement de la métropole – and it was to begin its work in September. However, due to lack of political support, the commission was never formally constituted: there was a lack of agreement on its mandate and composition, along with strong opposition from the outer suburbs (Fischler 1999, 5). Moreover, no specific implementation powers appear to have been assigned to the commission. Then, in 1999, the ministry was more or less abolished, being fused with the Ministry of Municipal Affairs.

All is not completely negative: a few positive developments should be noted. For one, there appears to be solid support in the City of Montreal, the MUC, and the provincial government for the principle that economic development will increasingly depend upon quality of life factors, including a revitalization of the core of the region (Gilbert and Stevenson 1997, 14). Indeed, an economic promotion agency for Greater Montreal, Société Montréal internationale, has been established, and at the time it hoped to build a $10 billion fund to attract foreign investment. Arrangements have yet to be worked out to relate its work to that of the Greater Montreal Development Commission. In addition, a Metropolitan Transportation Agency was established in 1996 to plan and coordinate transit operations in the metropolitan area and to operate commuter rail lines. So far it is unclear what its relationship will be to the development commission and the Ministry of Transportation. This reflects a perennial problem to which we have alluded many times – the difference, and often conflict, between territorial (comprehensive) and functional (sectoral) planning approaches.

Reasons for Failure

While, as we have noted, there have been a number of attempts to "rationalize" the region-wide planning and governance arrangement, they have failed repeatedly. The main reasons for this can be attributed to a number of conflicts (see Fischler 1999; Ducas 1998; Ducas and Trepanier 1998; Gilbert and Stevenson 1997; Trepanier 1993) between:

- the City of Montreal and island suburbs
- island and off-island municipalities
- Montreal and the provincial government.

Achieving better regional collaboration in Greater Montreal was difficult. Most people agree that a more consistent and inclusive dialogue was necessary in order to find solutions to city-region development problems, but this is where the consensus ends (Ducas 1998, 356). And the efforts of the ministry to achieve more consensus about the proposed metropolitan development commission in the existing fractious climate was neither easy nor rapid (Ducas and Trepanier 1998). The new minister of metropolitan affairs probably recognized this when he decided, in February 1998, to postpone establishing the proposed development commission while considering possible revisions to its format.

Gilbert and Stevenson (1997, 12) were not so pessimistic. They believed that the Montreal Development Commission could, in the long run, turn into a de facto city-region government. The commission members (and the provincial government) could be pushed by representatives of the core city to promote a regional vision, to share resources across the region, and to plan a more rational approach to infrastructure. However, they do admit that the uncertainty and complexity represented by the existing maze of subregional and local governments would most likely continue to hinder this. Moreover, according to Sancton (1994), the Pichette Commission's proposed three-tier structure is not the most effective with regard to simplicity and accountability.

Finally, in view of the conflicts in the Montreal region, one of the conditions that was considered essential for effective metropolitan-regional planning was strong provincial support. However, this required that the government be convinced of this need and, further, that it be willing to impose this view upon citizens and local governments who might think otherwise. Equally important, the province had to be willing to delegate enough resources, especially implementation resources, to establish the Montreal Metropolitan Region on solid footing. Gilbert and Stevenson themselves, despite their apparent optimism at the time, warned that it remained to be seen whether or not there would be the political will to carry the restructuring arrangements beyond the promising steps of 1997.

Several observers at this time did not believe that this would happen. Polese (1996, 33), for one, said that the idea of regional government is a "non-starter and will remain so until the constitutional question is resolved." He also argued that "Premier Bouchard's option of creating a centrally controlled ministère de la Métropole is a shrewd compromise, allowing him to cater to Montrealers' sense of distinctiveness but without actually devolving powers to the region."

And Fischler (1999, 12) warned that, given the demographic and political map of the region, the inconsistency of the provincial government's own policies (e.g., regionalization versus a single region), and the province's current feeling that a body with strong regional planning powers would be a threat to it, we should not expect rapid progress in the creation of strong regional planning powers in the Greater Montreal area.

Recent Developments

In light of subsequent events, these varying viewpoints regarding Montreal's future seem to have proved prescient.[26] On 15 June 2000, the Quebec Assembly's Bill 134 created the Montreal Metropolitan Community (MMC). The MMC will cover the area defined as the Montreal census metropolitan area, the same area recommended by the Pichette Commission. An administrative body, and not in itself a new level of government, the MMC is to be in charge of land-use planning (aménagement du territoire), economic development, social housing, metropolitan infrastructure and facilities, public transit, and solid waste management. It will be financed by contributions from the member municipalities (it may also impose user fees as well as borrow and issue bonds), and it will establish a tax-sharing program with the member municipalities. This tax program is designed to lessen competition for new construction and to endow a development fund for metropolitan infrastructure and facilities. However, no specific plan-implementation powers appear to have been delegated to the MMC.

The MMC will be supervised by a twenty-eight-member council (with fourteen elected officials from the island of Montreal and fourteen from Laval, the North Shore, and the South Shore), with the mayor of Montreal holding the deciding vote. In typical Montreal fashion, it will be run by an eight-member executive committee that meets behind closed doors (Fischler 2000). Despite its powers, the MMC will remain under the firm control of the provincial government. In its first meeting to nominate committee heads, the MMC's council, according to Fischler (2000), has already shown the tension that exists between central municipalities (on the island of Montreal) and peripheral communities.

As discussed in Chapter 8, in addition to the creation of the MMC the provincial government enacted legislation in December 2000, merging Montreal with all its suburbs on the island (and Quebec City with all its suburbs on the north shore of the St-Laurent, and Hull with all its suburbs). Also, in the Montreal region eight South Shore suburbs were to be merged into one large city (to be named after the most important one in the group, Longueuil), with a population of close to 400,000 people.

The idea of "one-island, one-city" will indeed become a reality on 1 January 2002. In this regard, the provincial government has kept its word with regard to effecting real change in municipal structures. However, with a highly centralized central city, small municipalities in the outer suburbs, and a weak Montreal Metropolitan Community, it is far from certain that suburban sprawl will slow down and that the region as a whole will learn to speak with one voice.

Toronto City-Region

As noted previously, in the early 1980s the GTA was composed of five two-tier regional municipal governments plus thirty lower-tier municipalities, whose planning and servicing decisions often affected the municipalities as well as the region as a whole. For example, the existence of regional-municipal government in the four regions surrounding Metro Toronto, with their mandated regional planning function (weak as it was), did little to reduce the influence of local governments on the area's physical development. The regional development pattern was determined largely by the land-use policies of the local municipalities and, to a much lesser extent, by the regional municipalities. In addition, a number of provincial ministries were involved in GTA planning and servicing issues and, thus, exerted tremendous influence over the region's development. These ministerial actions were rarely coordinated. So, despite the array of governments operating in the GTA, there was no single coordinating agency or mechanism for the region as a whole.

Without such a coordinating mechanism, planning and the provision of services within the GTA was, in the words of the Golden Task Force (GTA Task Force 1996, 118), "fragmented, compartmentalized and complex." As a consequence, cooperative and collaborative efforts in the GTA depended on unanimity and often either degenerated into lowest-common-denominator results or were blocked by one or two recalcitrant municipalities. Indeed, without a governmental authority with a GTA-wide mandate, lack of unanimous support for bold action sometimes resulted in the province taking over responsibility for region-wide functions, and this did not sit well with most local municipalities.

As GTA-wide planning problems became more intense, as their negative impacts became increasingly acknowledged, and as the shortcomings of the

OGTA became quite apparent, questions of decision making and implementation at the regional level became increasingly important. In the early 1990s, pressure began to mount from municipal leaders, bureaucrats, business representatives, and citizens to reform governance in the GTA to reflect these new realities. There was growing recognition that a large number of current and emerging issues in the GTA could not be dealt with effectively by individual municipalities within the region and that some sort of coordinating planning mechanism (and perhaps an overall governance authority) was needed. While the need for better region-wide planning and coordination had been generally accepted, there was no consensus about how much coordination was needed or what form a coordinating body should take.

In 1954, the reason for creating the metropolitan level of government, which reached out beyond the urbanized area, was precisely to provide the same kind of coordination as was required in the early 1990s in those areas currently beyond Metro Toronto. The question on many peoples' minds was whether the provincial government would face up to the new situation and circumstances just as had the 1954 government. A number of proposals were made by private and government groups for improving the situation. In addition, the province itself finally came around to realizing that some sort of coordinating mechanism for the GTA as a whole was needed. We now briefly discuss the major proposals.

Proposals

Golden Task Force

In 1995, in order to break the impasse over regional planning and governance for the GTA, the province convened a task force to recommend a new and more effective approach to managing the city-region. The five-person task force was headed by Dr. Anne Golden, president of the United Way of Greater Toronto and formerly research director of the Bureau of Municipal Research. The task force presented its report (GTA Task Force 1996) in January 1996. The task force accepted the definition of the GTA as comprising Metropolitan Toronto and its four surrounding regional municipalities (thus containing a total of thirty municipalities).

The report's main finding and conclusion was that the continued health and prosperity of the GTA are critically important because Greater Toronto is the economic heartland of the province and the nation as well as a major source of tax revenues for all levels of government. The task force recognized the GTA as a city-region, composed of a central core city, inner and outer suburbs, exurbs, and a rural hinterland, all of which are closely interconnected in terms of geography, environment, and workforce. It called for a number of radical changes in regional government, with respect to delivery of services, taxation, reform of the property tax assessment system, economic development, governance structure, and regional planning. It is governance structure and regional planning that are of most concern to us in the remainder of this section.

The Golden Task Force came to the "inescapable" conclusion that nearly all the problems and issues facing the GTA were due to a fundamental lack of coordination. Greater Toronto's five regional governments lacked the collective sense of purpose and momentum to address issues that could be handled more effectively on a region-wide basis (Task Force Report 1996, 13). Examples of fragmentation abound: disputes among the regions over water, roads, sewers, and garbage disposal erupted frequently as municipalities resorted to infighting and competition; and competition over taxes and self-serving economic development activities were both common and destructive to the city-region's interests.

Therefore, the task force concluded, a new governance model was needed – one that could coordinate decision making at the regional level, promote investment on behalf of the whole region, reduce the number of decision loops, provide for integrated resource management, and also recognize the key role of local municipalities in delivering local services. To simplify local government within the city-region, the task force recommended abolishing the upper-tier metropolitan government and the four surrounding regional governments, and reducing the number of local municipalities. They would be replaced by a new single super-entity, to be known as the "Greater Toronto Council (GTC)," which would have clear responsibility for planning and coordination with regard to matters of region-wide interest.

Before arriving at its recommendation the task force examined and rejected four other ways of coordinating services in the region: the so-called consensual model (as exemplified by the GVRD); the supercity model proposed by Metro Toronto; intermunicipal agreements; and strong provincial leadership. Finally, the task force recommended that the province establish a Greater Toronto Implementation Commission to refine and carry forward its recommendations.

Responses to the task force's recommendations were generally negative. Tomalty (1996, 24) suggests that this was due, in part, to the fact that the Ontario provincial NDP government originally gave the task force eighteen months to deliver its report, but its timeline was cut in half by the newly elected Progressive Conservatives. Among other things, this meant that public consultation and research programs had to be drastically curtailed. Public consultation took place only with organized interest groups, not with the broader public. Thus, Tomalty felt, it amounted to a "top-down" exercise with little opportunity to build a "regional consensus."

The basis of the controversy that followed the release of the Golden Task Force report lay in the differences over which institution was most appropriate to deliver regional planning. Most politicians and citizens seemed to agree on the need for infrastructure planning to support population and employment growth in the region. However, beyond this, consensus broke down. Because of the intense controversy surrounding some of the task force's proposals, the province set up a review panel to gauge public opinion on its most important recommendations. As further evidence of the negative or, at best, ambivalent attitudes towards regional planning and regional government, the panel found little support for regional government anywhere in the GTA.

Other Similar Proposals

Several other studies and reports also recommended the establishment of some form of coordinating governance mechanism for the GTA. These included the review panel on the Golden Task Force report and the "who-does-what" panel (chaired by David Crombie), which emphasized the need for a way of knitting together the Toronto core and the municipalities in the GTA. During 1997 and part of 1998, debate over the government's proposal to create a Toronto "mega-city" (now called the "City of Toronto") included many voices arguing against the government's primary focus on the proposal for an amalgamated Toronto. It was felt that this would create a weak regional structure in the rest of the GTA, where most of the recent growth has been taking place. Therefore, many people wanted greater attention to be paid to some sort of region-wide coordinating mechanism for the GTA as a whole.

Changes in the Province of Ontario

As noted earlier, in 1997, the Ontario government enacted far-reaching changes to the entire structure of local government, financial arrangements, and provincial-municipal relations in Greater Toronto. It merged the old City of Toronto and the surrounding five area municipalities to form the new City of Toronto (colloquially called the Toronto mega-city), and it shifted the financing of social service costs across the entire metropolitan region. As for the Greater Toronto Area, the government ignored most of the existing proposals and, instead, enacted legislation (in mid-1998) that resulted in the creation of the GTSB in January 1999.

In announcing the new legislation, the minister of municipal affairs indicated that, although the government does not consider the GTSB to be a level of government, it could evolve into such a body over the course of the coming decade.

The objectives of this board are to promote and facilitate coordinated decision making among the municipalities in the GTA. The government hoped that this action would promote better coordination and integration of interregional services within the GTA, leading to better service delivery at lower cost to taxpayers. The act also established the Greater Toronto Transit Authority (GT Transit), which takes over operational responsibility for the GO Transit regional transit system from the Toronto Area Transit Operating Authority.

Another potentially positive development is that, as in Montreal, a public-private partnership, the Greater Toronto Marketing Alliance, has been established to promote the urban region as a place to invest. It is just getting off the ground; however, according to Anne Golden (1998), it is a far weaker economic promotion agency than was envisaged by her Greater Toronto task force.

Making the Toronto City-Region a Province

A completely different and radical proposal is to detach the Toronto city-region from the Province of Ontario and make it a separate province. This idea has a rather long history, going back to proposals by historian Arthur Lower in 1948, political scientist Donald Rowat in 1962, and Paul Godfrey (then chair of Metro Toronto) in 1975. It surfaced in early 1999 when the mayor of the new City of Toronto made a similar proposal. Later, a *Globe and Mail* article by Richard Gilbert (26 November 1999), once a member of the Toronto and Metro Toronto councils and former president of the Federation of Canadian Municipalities, made a strong case for the GTA becoming a separate province.

Gilbert's article presaged the thinking and ideas of a group of some thirty people, including academics, urbanists, writers, activists, civil servants, and three former mayors of the City of Toronto, that met throughout 1999 and early 2000 to discuss the issue of self-government for the Toronto region. The meetings came about as the result of a radical idea proposed by Jane Jacobs at a special conference held in Toronto in 1997. This conference was dedicated to her work in, and contributions to, urban ideas and urban development. At the conference Jacobs suggested that perhaps Toronto and its surrounding region should become a separate province and no longer be a "creature of the province." The group, recognizing that Toronto has become a region of global significance, concluded that a new form of self-government is now required to cope with the economic, financial, social, environmental, social, and physical challenges and problems the city will face in the coming years. The idea of it becoming a separate province was widely discussed, and, although no consensus was reached, it received considerable agreement.

Out of these discussions there emerged a book entitled *Toronto: Considering Self-Government,* edited by Mary Rowe (2000). This book consisted of a collection of papers by many of the same persons who had met throughout 1999 and early 2000 (including, among others, Jane Jacobs, David Crombie, John Sewell, and Richard Gilbert). They addressed three basic questions: (1) Can Toronto take greater control of its destiny? (2) What types of governance might we consider? And (3) What are the political paths by which Toronto could gain greater autonomy? More important, a proposed "charter" for the Toronto region was developed, which included ten basic principles to guide governance in the region (see www.torontocharter.com).

Future Prospects

In the Toronto city-region, with the recent amalgamation creating the new City of Toronto, the GTA will comprise a single core-city surrounded by twenty-four area municipalities and four regional municipalities. However, there will be no effective governance mechanism for the region as a whole. The government's focus on its proposal for an amalgamated Toronto has had the effect of creating a weak regional structure in the rest of the GTA, where most of the recent growth has been taking place. As the urban affairs columnist for the *Toronto Star*, David Lewis Stein (1996, 19), said at the time, amalgamation is a "side dish to the main course of expanding the geographic scope of a regional authority" and should not be undertaken without a commensurate governmental structure established for the outlying areas. It is difficult to know whether or not the Greater Toronto Area Services Board will be equal to the task.

In a 1997 paper on governance and social well-being in the Toronto city-region, three prominent Toronto academics concluded that actions and initiatives taken by the provincial government of the day in the early 1950s (specifically, creating Metro Toronto) were critically important to the development of policies pertaining to tax sharing, social housing, and public transportation, all of which have contributed to Toronto's well-deserved reputation for success and for being a "city that works" (Frisken et al. 1997). They further add that the extent of foresight and imagination that the current provincial government shows in responding to the needs of the new spatial urban form – the Toronto city-region – will be equally critical to the ability of the various governments in the GTA to deal effectively with the many challenges they now face. But, so far, Frisken et al. caution, the provincial government has not risen to the challenge. It has not consolidated the municipalities in the area of the GTA that lies outside the new City of Toronto, nor did it accept the main recommendations of the Golden Task Force. Instead, it established a weak GTSB.

As a consequence, a multiple two-tier system remains in that part of the region, and the GTSB does not appear to be a great improvement over the Office for Greater Toronto. The GTA will undoubtedly be weaker at its perimeter (Gilbert and Stevenson 1997); it has few mandatory functions, and no authority to undertake regional planning or to pool tax revenues to fund regional services – a most successful tool under the old Metropolitan Toronto. Above all, the GTSB was not delegated the requisite planning, regulatory, and financial resources to make it an effective coordinating mechanism. In short, as Anne Golden (1988) points out, it has no real power whatsoever, only the power to "recommend" various actions to its member municipalities. In Mendelson's (2000, 75) words, "it is a shadowy body ... with no direct elections, no clear mandate, no taxing powers, no democratic accountability, and no independent power ... [It] is purpose-built for impotence."

It is true, as Gilbert and Stevenson (1997) suggest, that the GTA governance arrangements are in a period of transition, and it will probably take some time before the structures are sorted out and the impact of the changes fully assessed. Nevertheless, the system of government that seems to be emerging is likely to be both uneven and fragmented. It will likely be made up of a mosaic of government units with diverse needs and responsibilities, and with few institutional or legal requirements to cooperate with each other. Indeed, in view of this situation, the idea of making the region a separate province makes a lot of sense.

Vancouver City-Region

The Vancouver city-region is quite different from Montreal and Toronto. The GVRD already covers the vast bulk of the population in Greater Vancouver and has, in fact, expanded its boundaries since its creation in 1967. It also has a long successful history of planning and governance. Vancouver's formal planning powers are as extensive as those proposed for Greater Toronto (by the Golden Task Force) and those for the soon-to-be-established Montreal Metropolitan Community, though much weaker than those of the original Metropolitan Toronto. Moreover, in addition to carrying out strategic planning, the GVRD also has responsibility for a number of other region-wide functions (e.g., regional parks, air quality management).

Sancton (1994) argues that the GVRD's planning activity has been more influential than has comparable activity in Montreal and Toronto both because its territory covers almost the entire Vancouver city-region and because there appears to be (and has been for three decades) a greater sense of urgency about the necessity of managing urban development in order to protect the environment.

A combination of efforts by the provincial government, the business and academic communities, the media, non-governmental groups, local governments, and broad-based citizens groups has produced a remarkable degree of consensus on a vision of the city-region as a dynamic gateway to the Pacific (see *Maclean's,* 29 September 1997). Increasingly, the Vancouver city-region has taken on a more international and Pacific-centred orientation. There is little doubt that the existence of the GVRD has been of great assistance in promoting this regional vision and, in particular, in trying to balance the area's environmental and social quality of life and its economic development.

More than in Greater Toronto or a Greater Montreal, there is a public and local government awareness of the issues the Vancouver city-region is facing and a greater consensus on a strategic vision for the future. This has been achieved even though the GVRD is not a separate level of government and has no formal statutory planning powers over its member municipalities. For this reason, it has depended on trust and cooperation among member municipalities (and, in turn, between them and the regional district) for any significant action. Indeed, it has succeeded in building a level of trust and cooperation that is unknown in Greater Toronto and Greater Montreal or, indeed, any major metropolitan areas where urban, suburban, and rural conflicts are intense (Tomalty 1997, 71). This level of trust and cooperation may be attributable to the long-held consensus in the region that the environment needs to be protected. Not least in importance were the strongly held views of the citizens of the region, which were incorporated into the LRSP (see earlier discussion).

Based on the interviews he conducted for his report, "The Compact Metropolis," Tomalty (1997, 57) concluded that there is widespread agreement that the current structure of regional planning in the Vancouver city-region, which relies on a partnership between municipal governments and the regional district, has served the region fairly well, in particular with regard to building support for the vision of the region and for the need for growth management. However, in view of recalcitrant municipalities and neighbourhood groups that are trying to preserve existing conditions, and in view of its lack of legislative implementation powers, there is serious doubt about the GVRD's ability to implement this vision.

In an analysis of the provincial Growth Strategies Act, a consultant with extensive experience at all three government levels (most recently as director of planning in Vancouver's largest suburb) pointed out that "without the province establishing structures of government capable of making the tough decisions concerning public infrastructure, population distribution, and environmental protection, it is difficult to see how 'interactive, inclusive and flexible' approaches [the aims of the Growth Strategies Act] will address the deteriorating built and natural environment" (Murchie 1995, 10). Moreover, Murchie noted that the similarities of these proposals (the Regional Growth Strategies Act provisions) to what is in place in the States of Oregon and Washington are striking, but with the important difference that municipal funding in those jurisdictions is tied to participation in an agreed and approved regional plan.

Future Prospects and Proposals

The success of the current GVRD approach to regional planning will receive its true test in the coming years, when implementation of the regional growth strategy is to take place. The twenty-two constituent communities making up the GVRD have had their regional context statements – which specify what changes, if any, they would make to their official community plans to conform to the Regional Growth Strategies Act – accepted and approved by the GVRD board. But, as exemplary an accomplishment as this was, there is still one outstanding issue: the twenty-two communities do not, either singly or together, have any legal obligation to do the things they said they would do. In short, the GVRD has no leverage over member municipalities to induce them to implement the Livable Region Strategic Plan. This dilemma was best expressed by the administrator for the policy and planning development division in the GVRD (i.e., the person responsible for overseeing the regional context statements), who admitted that "the question now is whether the municipalities will follow through with the commitments" (Kellas 1998). Broad objectives are one thing, but increasing densities in established areas is another (and is extremely politically dangerous). Only time will tell the outcome of this situation.

Perhaps the key long-term problem facing the Vancouver city-region involves deciding the most appropriate form of governance for a new century. Should the GVRD be converted into some form of metropolitan or regional government, as Artibise (1996, 1997, 1998) argues, or should all of the communities in the GVRD planning area be amalgamated into a single "city," such as recently occurred in Toronto, as Christie and Ferry (1998) propose? Or should the concept of "regional governance," which is what Oberlander and Smith (1993) and Smith (1996) claim is currently being represented by the GVRD, be extended to emphasize the need for "networking" among a wide variety of "stakeholders," including special interest groups, citizens, and public agencies? Or is there still another approach? This issue is addressed next, in our concluding section.

Conclusions

We recognize that the Montreal, Toronto, and Vancouver city-regions have developed slightly differently, in light of their unique geography, political structure, and culture, and that they may evolve somewhat differently in the future. Nevertheless, in trying to cope with their similar special features and characteristics, these city-regions will face a number of common issues and needs, including the need to:

- integrate the various parts of the city-region
- remain economically competitive
- balance economic and other objectives
- integrate transportation planning with land-use and urban-structure planning.

More important, in order for the city-regions to realize their true potential, to adequately deal with their common issues and needs, and to guide development in desirable directions, the provinces will have to deal with some key challenges, including the challenge to:

- set appropriate regional boundaries initially, and allow for their change in order to cope with new developments and pressures
- delegate to the city-regions the appropriate type and amount of governmental resources so that they can plan and implement their plans as well as cope with their common issues and needs
- coordinate their own ministerial decisions and actions at the provincial level and mesh these with the planning goals and proposed actions of the city-regions themselves
- create for their city-regions appropriate region-wide governance mechanisms.

Integration of the Parts of the Region

As we have pointed out, each of the three city-regions comprises a centre core city, inner and outer suburbs, and a rural hinterland, all of which are closely interconnected by geography, environment, and workforce as well as by a shared economic and social future. Each is evolving into a highly interdependent region, the whole of which will be greater than the sum of its parts and the health of which will depend on the prosperity of the constituent parts (see Peirce et al. 1993 on the interdependence of the various parts of city-regions). Within this ascendant urban spatial form the old, central core city will continue to play a key role as the region's heart, and its continued health is of critical importance to that of the entire region (see note 11, Chapter 8).

However, in the evolving city-region, the core city will be only one (albeit the most important) among several centres (see Rybczynski 1998; Wight 1999). Many of the older suburbs have already matured to the point of now having shopping and work opportunities as well as institutions such as hospitals, colleges, and recreation and sports facilities, and they are serving as core centres for a large tributary population. Almost all the major land uses and activities can be found in these mature suburbs, or what have also been referred to as "urban realms" (Vance 1990) or "urban communes" (Friedmann 1982); this maturation will undoubtedly continue among other centres in the city-region. Wight (1999) argues that these evolving developments – he refers to them as "territorial autonomies" and "functional interdependencies" – *may* replace the traditional "centre-periphery" relationships. And, as Gertler (2000, 35) notes, the Boston Consulting Group (in its study undertaken for the Golden Task Force) conclusively showed that "city and suburb in the region remain locked in a symbiotic economic embrace. Even though the nature and type of economic relations between them may have changed in recent years, the degree of functional integration remains strong."

The first common issue, then, facing each of the three city-regions is how to achieve the integration of their various parts (including the core cities, surrounding cities, and fringe areas) – the urban realms, urban communes, territorial autonomies, and functional interdependencies – and ensure that all of them are healthy and strong. At a minimum, this will clearly require the integration of urban and rural planning throughout the city-region. This issue is especially relevant in light of (1) the need for the city-regions to become economically competitive, and (2) the need for appropriate governance arrangements.

Economic Competitiveness

Globalization of the economy is the primary force behind the emergence of Canada's city-regions. It will continue to affect the planning of these areas and to pose challenges for planners and local and provincial policy makers. The economic success of the Montreal, Toronto, and Vancouver city-regions is critical to the well-being of their respective provinces and, equally important, of the nation as a whole. Together these three city-regions account for more than one-third of Canada's population and almost 40 percent of its gross domestic product. The Toronto region alone accounts for more than 20 percent of Canada's gross domestic product. These three Canadian city-regions can truly be considered the prime "engines of growth" that drive the economies of their provinces and, by extension, that of the nation.

At the same time, they are engaged in high stakes economic competition with other large city-regions, particularly those in the United States – Boston, Philadelphia, Chicago, and Seattle (Tonks 1999a, 1). The trade ties, economic flows, and competitive pressures are increasingly found not to the east and west but, rather, to the south. In short, the Canadian economy largely depends on the competitiveness of these major city-regions and will continue to do so in the future. These three city-regions are currently the key spatial units within their respective provinces and the nation. As will city-regions the world over, they will continue to be the most logical, viable, and competitive economic and spatial units, and they will be the lead players on the world economic stage (see Peirce et al. 1993; Ohmae 1995; Dodge 1996; Kanter 1995).

It is therefore vital that Canadian city-region planners and local and provincial policy makers make a huge commitment to reinvest in the urban infrastructure of these city-regions. Infrastructure provides the foundations of these economies, and it needs to be renewed if they are to face the economic challenges of the future. Since it is mainly provincial governments that provide these facilities, the provinces must provide the city-regions and their planners with the means to make their regions competitive. Thus retaining, indeed enhancing, their economic competitiveness is another common issue faced by all three city-regions.

This focus on the economic competitiveness of the city-region must not be undertaken without considering the economic needs of the smaller towns and rural areas within the region. Also, the emergence of Canada's global city-regions affects the planning of all other regions in Canada. Until recently, regional planners the world over typically developed their initiatives on the assumption that national economies would progressively come to be spatially more integrated and that economic and social disparities between regions would disappear, as Myrdal (1956), Friedmann (1966), and others had forecast decades ago. However, the globalization of large urban areas sharpens the differences between them and non-metropolitan/rural regions. The expectations of "spread effects" and "backward links" from the growth and development of an urban core region to surrounding peripheral regions can no longer be counted on to stimulate growth on the periphery. Thus, in a globalized world, both the city-regions and the non-urban regions will be forced to consider their own futures independently, thereby reducing the options of regional planners for interregional strategies – yet another common issue faced by all city-regions.

Balance Economic with Other Objectives

Although globalization forces the city-regions to try to be as economically competitive as possible, economic competitiveness must not be pursued at the expense of other objectives. While city-region planners pursue their economic objectives, they need to balance them with the region's goals pertaining to social well-being, environmental protection, and ecological sustainability. This is one more common issue faced by city-regions.

Integration of Transportation Planning with Land-Use and Urban-Structure Planning

Vancouver and Toronto planners attempted to achieve growth management via land-use and urban-structure planning supported by transportation planning. The most serious threat to transit effectiveness and efficiency involved the land-use decisions of suburban and exurban municipalities that persisted in approving plans for low-density segregated development. None of the three city-regions managed to bring into being the necessary link between regional land-use/urban-structure planning and transportation planning. In both the Montreal and Toronto city-regions, no metropolitan-wide transit planning authority existed until recently. In the case of Montreal, it is not clear how the newly established Metropolitan Transportation Agency will relate to the proposed region-wide planning and servicing arrangements that we described earlier. In the Vancouver city-region, the metropolitan transit authority has, until recently, had only advisory status vis-à-vis the provincial government; however, the recent agreement to establish an independent authority as part of the GVRD bodes well for relating land-use planning and transportation planning in the future.[27]

Given the need to integrate transportation planning with land-use and urban-structure planning, it is fortunate that all three city-regions are in the process of developing regional transportation plans and that all three are using a consultative provincial-municipal framework. Since the provinces are responsible for infrastructure development and the municipalities for land-use planning, this development holds great promise for linking the two planning processes.

Key Role of the Provinces

To say that the provinces play a key role in the health and well-being of our current three city-regions and their constituent municipalities, and that they will continue to do so in the future, is to state the obvious. The provinces not only designate the regions for planning and the decision-making agency, they also allocate the resources for plan preparation and implementation; moreover, the degree and extent to which they coordinate their ministerial actions largely determine whether the city-regions can fulfil their responsibilities and meet their future challenges. Thus, another common issue facing the city-regions is the extent to which their respective provinces will rise to the challenges they will face in the future. Four specific issues in which the provincial role will be critical are as follows:

1 setting the boundaries of the planning region
2 delegating resources
3 provincially coordinating decisions and actions
4 creating an appropriate region-wide governance mechanism.

Setting the Boundaries of the Planning Region

Setting the boundaries of the planning region, which is a concern in metropolitan areas (see Chapter 8), is even more of a concern in city-regions. Two issues are relevant here. The first issue concerns the fact that, whenever feasible, the initial boundaries of new planning regions should be based on natural boundaries and processes and bioregional considerations rather than on political and administrative jurisdictions. The second issue concerns how to respond to the fact that, very likely, city-regions will continue to develop and grow larger. For example, should the BC government keep expanding the GVRD's boundaries into the Fraser Valley (going as far as Chilliwack), or to the Lower Fraser Basin, or even to the Georgia Pacific Basin, as a number of researchers have proposed?

Allocating Resources

As we saw earlier, the resources allocated, or proposed to be allocated by the Quebec, Ontario, and British Columbia provincial governments to their respective city-regions varied in the bundles themselves, as well as within the bundles, and sometimes within the same region over time. These variations certainly go a long way to explain the different planning initiatives and outcomes we described earlier (as well as the potentially different outcomes should the proposed changes in governance structures be made).

Overall, the allocation of resources (including the proposals for change) were strongest in the area of planning resources, although they were confined to land-use planning. The weakest were the regulatory and financial resources, which, of course, are crucial for implementing plans and planning policies. Implementation of regional land-use plans is difficult, if not impossible, without the necessary regulations (e.g., zoning, subdivision approval, and development control); and regional plans that propose physical infrastructure facilities (such as airports or roads) or the acquisition of parks or environmentally sensitive areas require capital in order to achieve these objectives.

In the future, if the provinces want the three city-regions to successfully meet their goals and the challenges and opportunities of the new century, then they must provide them with the appropriate resources. This will probably mean expanding and broadening the current scope of planning resources, regulatory resources, and financial resources. For example, making the city-regions more economically competitive, while at the same time achieving the goal of sustainability, will require more and different planning and regulatory resources than have hitherto been delegated. Indeed, the situation of city-regions is such that we are only now coming to appreciate the resource bundles that are needed, and, since these regions will continue to grow and to develop in unforeseen ways, future needs are difficult to anticipate. We can, however, assume that the resource bundles will have to be more and more robust.

Provincial Coordination

Not only do the provinces provide city-regions with the requisite resources, but they also affect their development through providing and controlling physical infrastructure, water supply distribution, sewage treatment, and transportation. How these are handled at the provincial level can help or thwart the realization of the region's goals. It is important that the provinces coordinate their decisions and actions at the provincial level and also that they mesh these with the goals and proposed actions of the city-regions. This, too, is another common issue that city-regions will face in the future.

Creating an Appropriate Region-Wide Governance Mechanism

The final key issue facing the three provinces involves creating a governing mechanism that will be appropriate and effective in enabling their city-regions to meet the challenges of the twenty-first century. As we have argued throughout this book, in order to be effective, accountable, and democratic, planning must be tied to an appropriate governing mechanism – one that will make it possible both to make a plan and to implement it. At the beginning of the twenty-first century our three city-regions have grown so large and complex that their present form of government is unmanageable. This, of course, is not surprising, as it was devised at a time when their current size, scale, complexity, and economic importance were unimaginable.

Most observers argue that, if city-regions are to be successful and to realize their potential, they must adopt region-wide governance mechanisms that are appropriate to their special features. However, thus far the relevant provinces, especially Quebec and Ontario, have been unwilling to establish such a mechanism. But what is the best governance model? As we have seen in the previous section, the approaches of the three provinces to the governance arrangements for their city-regions differ greatly. Is there a single approach appropriate to all three Canadian city-regions? Or should each province, due to individual political, cultural, governmental, and economic differences, pursue its own direction? More important, is there some new approach that would be more appropriate? We think that there is, and, because of its critical importance to the future health and stability of the city-regions and their component parts, we conclude this chapter with a discussion of it.

An Inclusive, Networking Approach to Region-Wide Governance

More and more, the idea is being advanced that we need to focus on governance rather than government, and we need to emphasize process, inclusiveness, and flexibility as much as structure. Such an approach to region-wide governance relies on a network of interrelationships rather than on a constraining institutional mechanism. It depends upon voluntary, cooperative agreements among all private as well as all public "stakeholders." Until recently, such approaches would have been considered "too weak," but they now form a key component of the current school of thought pressing for regional "governance," which advocates the need for networking among public agencies, municipalities, and special interest groups (Dodge 1996; Sancton 1994; Wallis 1994; Wight 1996, 1998a).

Under these arrangements, two or more communities come together, either voluntarily or with the encouragement of the provincial government, and form a sort of alliance in order to address a specific issue (such as watershed protection or the supply of a needed service). These arrangements would not only provide a forum for discussing issues of regional concern, but they would also possess the resources to prepare a regional plan or regional strategy.

Somewhat similar contemporary examples of this approach in Canada include the Winnipeg Capital Region Committee (Manitoba 1998),[28] the OGTA, Edmonton's Alberta Capital Region Alliance, and British Columbia's CORE initiative. The latter, while not an institutional arrangement as such, did involve local stakeholders in regional decisions about resources and the environment. Another, more recent, example is the South Island Sustainable Communities Network, which covers Greater Victoria (South Island Sustainable Communities Network 1998). Formed in 1997, this network links community organizations, concerned individuals, the University of Victoria, and other groups for the purpose of seeking innovative growth management approaches to the region and to aid in developing a regional growth strategy.

In short, this new governance approach advocates the need for an all-inclusive regional organization that can inform and facilitate governmental decision making; broaden the array and support for new ideas regarding development, growth management, environmental protection, and other pressing issues; and counter not-in-my-backyard parochialism (Wray 1997).

As the Canadian examples suggest, most of the cases in which this approach has been used apply to metropolitan regions. We know of no examples of its use in city-regions. Nevertheless, we would argue that this new approach to regional governance would be ideal for the city-region. This is because of the city-region's spatial form, which is characterized by dispersed population, activities, and functions as well as by a scattered array of urban, rural, and exurban municipalities, each of which treasures its independence and local autonomy. In addition, these city-regions are in a dynamic state of change and evolution: existing activities, functions, and boundaries may (and probably will) change over time. Under these conditions, doesn't it make more sense to establish a flexible regional governance process and system?

Clearly, given the dynamism of the existing city-regions, the concept of gov-ern*ance* rather than govern*ment,* and the idea of networking with public, pri-vate, and citizen groups, seems to have much merit. In order to be effective, this approach to region-wide governance should have at least three features:

1 There should be separate inclusive governance organizations or subregional units within each city-region, each with broad representation and each reflecting logical economic and social boundaries; however, at the same time, each should be flexible enough to change as circumstances warrant.

2 There should be an overall regional governance body (with a certain number of members elected region-wide) that would be concerned with regional issues and concerns (e.g., it would develop a vision for its city-region, cov-ering such items as the preferred regional development pattern).

3 The regional vision must ultimately be translated into action – through plans, policies, programs, projects, and bylaws – through public infrastructure investments and land-use regulations. Thus, the public sector and govern-ment must continue to play a key role in region-wide planning and govern-ance, both as stakeholders and as implementers. How this can be done is discussed in Chapter 11.

Part 4

The Future of Regional Planning in Canada

The Continuing Need for Regional Planning

The evolution of regional planning in Canada over the past six decades has been somewhat tumultuous. There have been periods of intense activity, during which considerable advances were made, and there have been periods lacking vitality. There have also been significant shifts in doctrine and, consequently, in practice. These changes have all contributed to the development of regional planning as a field of public policy implementation. Undoubtedly, regional planning in the future will have new cultural and political ingredients and, possibly, a new style, but it will continue to unfold from its past. Regional planning in the future will still address issues of spatial development (such as sprawl, congestion, unequal development, pollution, and conservation) as well as other issues that we can now, at best, only partly perceive. Whatever formal governing arrangements are devised, they will never be able to encompass all the spatial implications of human economic and social development that will unfold. This has been, and will continue to be, our experience. Nonetheless, we will continue to need regions to accomplish many social purposes. Thus, in order to consider the shape of regional planning in the twenty-first century, a good place to begin is with our past experience. This will enable us to identify important foundation blocks for future regional planning, regardless of the form it might take.

Summing Up Canadian Regional Planning

First, let us briefly remind ourselves of how the general form of this field has evolved, then consider questions such as the following: What do the events and activities say, for example, about senior governments' commitment to regional planning? What do the different approaches, with their different mandates (from metropolitan to rural to economic development and resources planning), reveal about the nature of regional planning and its strengths and vulnerabilities? How has practice in regional planning evolved during this period? We shall return to these and other questions later.

Sixty Years in Retrospect

In the vital, if variable, period of region-scale public planning in Canada since the 1940s, both successes and setbacks can teach us important lessons.

Important Precedents

Although Canada's formal experience with regional planning goes back to nearly 1940, some earlier roots provided the necessary context for its formal development. Among these was the developing concern for the conservation of natural resources (including parks), rural planning, and the environment; this concern led the federal government to create the Commission of Conservation in 1909. Although lasting only twelve years, it and its planning advisor, Thomas Adams, opened for public scrutiny a wide range of regional issues, many of which continue to trouble us today. Adams also developed his own concepts of regional planning (see Chapter 1). Another significant precedent in Canadian regional planning was the institution, in the mid-1930s, of the Prairie Farm Rehabilitation Act in response to severe drought conditions in the Prairie provinces. This act established an active role for the federal government in planning Canada's regions – a role it would again pursue in the 1960s regarding economic disparities.

The 1940s: First Steps

To the provinces, given their constitutional responsibility for land and other resources, fell the task of establishing the land-use type of regional planning agencies to which we have become accustomed. The first of these was Winnipeg's 1943 metropolitan planning agency, and then, a few years later, British Columbia and Alberta took steps to establish metropolitan regional planning agencies. Ontario continued this trend soon after with its first full-fledged metropolitan government for Toronto. Indeed, concern about burgeoning metropolitan regions occupied most provinces during the 1950s as they sought ways to deal with spatial needs and problems to which single municipalities could not respond. New areal divisions of power were required. While the metropolitan-regional planning agencies set up at this time, and in the following two decades, have generally proved viable, the tension between them and their constituent municipalities remains (see Chapter 8). One federal metropolitan planning effort during this time involved the Greenbelt Plan for the Ottawa region and the subsequent establishment of the National Capital Commission. Non-urban regions also received attention during this period. Ontario established the set of now long-lived conservation authorities for river basin planning in the southern part of the province. Alberta took a major step in developing an almost province-wide system of regional planning commissions for its non-metropolitan and metropolitan regions.

The 1950s and 1960s: Federal Involvement

Canada's economy entered a new spatial phase in the 1950s, and rapidly growing urban and metropolitan regions began displacing rural regions in economic importance. Rural regions were also showing signs of extensive economic under-development, which would lead them to apply political pressure for a larger share of the nation's prosperity. Over the next twenty-five years, the federal government responded with numerous programs whose purpose was to elimi-nate "regional disparities." These programs focused primarily on rural and non-metropolitan regions. The first was the Agricultural Rehabilitation and Development Act, 1961 (see Chapter 6). A host of other federal programs for regional economic development followed and, in 1969, the Cabinet-level agency, the Department of Regional Economic Expansion (DREE), was formed to co-ordinate such efforts.

The DREE approach to regional development included, in addition to job creation and financial incentives to industries, resources for housing, munici-pal infrastructure, education, and transportation. It also attempted to relocate regional populations, as in the ill-starred Newfoundland Resettlement Pro-gram. Over time, DREE's highly central, Ottawa-based regional planning stance devolved to general development agreements implemented by the provinces. Other federal activity in regional planning included a number of megaprojects, notably, the St. Lawrence Seaway and the South Saskatchewan River Develop-ment Project. The South Saskatchewan project was facilitated by the Canada Water Act, 1970, which allowed for joint federal and provincial river-basin planning. Another federal initiative during this period, the Canada Land In-ventory, also proved to be a major tool for regional planners throughout the country. In addition, the federal Ministry of the Environment developed envi-ronmental impact assessment procedures and state-of-the-environment report-ing. Some of these approaches were emulated by provincial and territorial governments and proved valuable tools for regional planning.

The 1970s: New Provincial Initiatives

The 1960s to the 1970s also proved to be a fecund period for regional planning at the provincial level. British Columbia established its regional districts and, soon after, its Agricultural Land Commission (Quebec followed suit in the late 1970s); New Brunswick's Mactaquac Regional Development Plan was formu-lated and implementation mechanisms were set in place. In Ontario, the prov-ince-wide regional development program, Design for Development, was instituted; the plans for the Niagara Escarpment and Toronto-Centred Region were published; Huron County's "countryside planning" project was under-taken; and regional governments were created outside Metro Toronto. The Meewasin Valley Authority was established for the Saskatoon region, and regional plans were completed for Vancouver and Saint John as well as for the Northwest Territories' Cumberland Sound. Meanwhile, with its integrated social, economic, and environmental approach, the Mackenzie Valley pipeline study set standards for more sensitive regional planning.

The 1980s to the Present

The decades since the early 1980s have been transitional for Canadian regional planning. Some significant regional planning activities folded: Ontario's Design for Development and the Toronto-Centred Region Concept (in 1982), DREE (in 1982), British Columbia's regional districts (in 1983), and Alberta's regional planning commissions (in the early 1990s). Despite these reverses, regional planning was not dead. Many long-lived agencies continued (e.g., the Office de planification et de développement du Québec, the conservation authorities in Ontario, and metropolitan planning agencies from Halifax to Victoria). Further, British Columbia's regional districts were reinvigorated with the new Growth Strategies Act, and, throughout the country, regional round tables on the environment and economy flourished, as did intermunicipal arrangements for delivering services. A number of notable regional planning initiatives emerged during this period, including the tri-level Fraser River Basin Management Program, an updated Greenbelt Plan for Ottawa, the federal Banff–Bow Valley Task Force Plan, the country-wide Community Futures Program for rural and Aboriginal regions, and the Alberta Capital Region Alliance (a new regional forum for metropolitan Edmonton). Not least was the emergence of Canada's first city-regions – Toronto, Montreal, and Vancouver – and the efforts to find viable approaches to the planning and governance of these massive and extensive urban entities (see Chapter 9).

The Patterns of Past Practice

This is a venerable history, one worthy of full consideration for the guidance it can provide for future endeavours in regional planning. Of the several ways in which we might consider past experience, looking at the general patterns and functional characteristics of Canadian regional planning practice holds the most promise.

General Patterns

Out of the flux of the history of Canadian regional planning there emerge at least four general characteristics:

Persisting Need

Since the institution of regional planning in metropolitan Winnipeg and in Ontario river basins in the 1940s, it has remained on Canada's public agenda. Even though it has broached a variety of problems and taken many forms, the idea of large-scale, extramunicipal, spatial planning continues to have currency. This implies that a regional approach to regional planning is crucial to the task of fulfilling various public policy goals. For example, although it does so in quite different ways, the current Community Futures Program tackles much the same problems as did the Agricultural Rehabilitation and Development Act and the Fund for Rural Economic Development in the 1960s. So part of the persistence of the regional planning format lies in the spatial nature of policy problems: they extend into a space that exceeds a single municipality and at the same time are functionally associated with the needs of larger areas.

Evolving Doctrine

The changeability of regional planning approaches reflects shifts in basic doctrine concerning the best way to achieve regional goals. In other words, as our knowledge of regions has expanded and as our beliefs about the best way to tackle problems has shifted, so too has regional planning practice (see also Chapter 2). The top-down approach of the conservation authorities in Ontario in the 1940s contrasts with the bottom-up approach used in the Fraser Basin Management Program in the 1990s. Today's doctrine appears to be becoming much more "place-based." Thus, the Canadian experience shows us that regional planning will continue to change to meet evolving social and ecological perspectives and needs.

Recurring Policy Areas

The Canadian experience clearly identifies four realms of public policy for which regional planning has proved to be valid: (1) natural resource development, conservation, and the environment; (2) metropolitan area and city-region development; (3) economic development; and (4) rural area development. Each of these realms tends to be extramunicipal in spatial extent and each, as well, is inherently linked with several sectors. Consequently, both of these attributes demand a regional approach to planning in order to engage cross-sectoral and trans-jurisdictional situations. We can expect these and similar realms to continue to require attention in the future.

Enduring Political Tensions

By definition, regional problems cut across jurisdictional and sectoral lines. When they are tackled, tensions emerge between different levels of government, as has been evident with regard to the attempts of provincial and federal governments and ministries to execute programs for reducing economic disparities (see Chapter 6). Probably more insistent is the tension experienced between metropolitan and city-region agencies and their constituent local municipalities (see Chapters 8 and 9). These tensions arise out of the inertia of constitutions and/or political customs that attend the areal division of power. These tensions could not have been eliminated through boundary and structural modifications, for, invariably, social and economic change would have rendered them obsolete. So another reason for the persistence of regional planning lies in the need to respond to emergent problems that exceed conventional modes of government and administration (preferably without disturbing the status quo) (Wight 1999).

Functional Characteristics

Several aspects of the actual conduct of regional planning help to define its practice more precisely than do the general characteristics listed above. These concern how Canada's constitutional arrangements have affected practice, how the arrangements for planning and governing metropolitan regions have been constrained, and how a persistent separation between economic and land-use planning issues has shaped regional planning approaches.

Federal and Provincial Roles

From the outset, both the federal government and the individual provinces have taken significant initiatives in regional planning, as may be witnessed in the Prairie Farm Rehabilitation Act as well as in the establishment of metropolitan regional planning agencies. Yet, as the decades unfolded, each seems to have pursued distinctive roles. The federal government has primarily limited its participation to economic development through program funding, income transfers, and megaprojects (a point Gunton and Weaver [1984] perceived some time ago) as well as, more recently, to environmental matters. Provincial governments, in contrast, have limited themselves to regional planning that is linked to land use through municipal and other local institutions – metropolitan region planning and service agencies, environmental planning agencies, and so on. It should not surprise us that the reason this occurred has to do with the constitutional areal division of power between the federal and provincial governments (see Chapter 5). More surprising is how little effort is ever made to bridge this gap. Both the regional round tables on the environment and economy and the Healthy Communities initiatives, which promised such bridging, have delivered little. This is evidence of an enduring intractability that Canadian regional planners need to recognize.

Metropolitan Governance

Canada has been a world leader in devising and establishing forms of regional planning and governance for metropolitan regions. There is scarcely a metropolitan area in this country that does not have some form of regional planning, and many also have a governmental entity to complement it. As Canadians have experimented with metropolitan planning, two issues have persistently come to the fore. First, the planning of metropolitan areas requires a commensurate form of government to be effective. The truth of this has continually assailed metropolitan planners as well as citizens living in these areas. The second, and related, issue concerns the persistent tension between the metropolitan agency and its constituent local governments (Heseltine 1998; Wight 1999).[1] When establishing these new governing agencies, the provinces were loathe to deal with this division of power and left it to the municipalities to take the advice of their own metropolitan planners. Unfortunately, planners were often ignored, and this remains the case today (see Chapter 8). Both these issues still need to be resolved, and they are of such importance that we devote a special section to them later in this chapter.

Economic versus Environmental versus Land-Use Planning

Throughout the history of regional planning in Canada, despite extensive activity in all three planning realms (i.e., economic planning, environmental planning, and land-use planning), seldom have these areas come together in a joint effort at regional development. As noted above, in part the reason for this has to do with the constitutional division of labour, which permits the federal government to become involved in economic planning but not in land-use planning. And, although provincial governments have the power to be involved in all three realms of regional planning, there are few instances of them combining these realms in their regional planning endeavours. Three examples of the provincial separation of regional, economic, and land-use planning are as follows: (1) the separation of agricultural development from agricultural land preservation in British Columbia, (2) the parallel structures of regional development commissions (economic) and district planning commissions (land use) in New Brunswick, and (3) the continuing separation of the regional development authorities in Nova Scotia. While it is obvious that these three areas of planning are interdependent (see Chapter 6), they have been, and continue to be, seen as separate from one another. Perhaps this is due to the ministerial separation of these areas at both the federal and provincial levels as well as to the lack of economic and environmental planning powers available to municipalities. Further, the professionals involved in each of these fields tend to belong to separate professional associations, to write for and read different journals, to have different philosophies and objectives, and to work within different institutional settings. All this makes for difficulty in coordinating and integrating efforts among regional, economic, and land-use planning activities.

Overall Picture

Regardless of the form regional planning takes in the future, the characteristics identified above will be part of it. Beyond this, the overall picture provides some other indications of what will be important in the future. The first involves what, in his analysis of British, European, and American activity, Wannop (1995) referred to as regional planning's "mercurial" quality. And, indeed, the Canadian experience in regional planning is certainly variable. It follows the same shifts in doctrine that Friedmann and Weaver (1979) observed in the

United States and that Glasson (1992) would later note in Britain and elsewhere. But surely this is to be expected.

Regional planning is, after all, an interloper in the conventional areal division of power. Whenever regional planning is deemed a strategic tool for public policy, a place must be found for it among long-established instruments of government (see Chapter 4). This is a reflection of both its longevity and its necessity. Planning regions are vulnerable, on the one hand, to the aims of other governments (both the provincial government above and municipal governments below) and, on the other hand, to the need for a regional planning strategy that may well be time-limited (e.g., resource development projects). Add to this the evolution of ideology and doctrine as well as of social consciousness and theoretical appropriateness, which guides how and when regional planning gets carried out (see Chapter 2). For example, the Fraser Basin Management Program of the 1990s was approached much differently than was the Mactaquac's regional planning project of the 1960s. Thus, regional planning's inconstancy needs to be seen less as a flaw than as an inherent characteristic. Not that there have not been failures in Canadian regional planning; however, these have often been the result of the lack of an adequate governing structure or of an agency not being allocated the appropriate resources for implementing its plans (see Chapters 8 and 9 regarding the metropolitan and city-region situation). The demise of numerous advisory regional planning agencies testifies to yet another characteristic of regional planning: the difficulty experienced by local and provincial governments, as well as by citizens, in sustaining their commitment to a regional plan.

Despite these characteristics, which give it an ephemeral quality, regional planning has persisted both as a concrete form (e.g., as manifested in Ontario's conservation authorities) and as a strategic approach (e.g., as embodied in Newfoundland and Labrador's regional economic development boards). The fact that, over the past sixty years, regional planning has arisen in different places, in different forms, and with varying intensity shows its endurance as a strategy for meeting many public policy needs. This does not mean there are not some chronic problems within regional planning (such as the seeming incompatibility of economic and land-use planning or the tensions between local and metropolitan levels of government). But even if these were to be resolved, regional planning would not necessarily have a uniform future. Regional issues change with regional boundaries and with the efficacy of administrative and governing arrangements. The need for regional planning will continue and will undoubtedly require new organizational approaches. Consider, for example, the area of metropolitan and city-region planning, to which we now turn.

Planning Metropolitan Areas and City-Regions

The extensive Canadian experience with planning metropolitan areas and, more recently, with city-regions allows us to identify some key planning issues. In general, rapid growth, and its attendant physical development, was the biggest problem facing all large urban regions. This, in turn, generated economic, fiscal, environmental, social, and governance concerns. Planners differed significantly regarding which issues they considered most important. This is illustrated in the planning approaches to two of our three largest urban regions (e.g., agricultural land encroachment issues were considered most important in the Vancouver city-region, while urban sprawl was considered most important in the Montreal city-region). Planners also differed regarding how best to manage growth.

Some of the attitudinal differences towards growth management reflect, among other things, different physical environments and their perceived effect on the spread of development. Also influential are differing ideas concerning the roles of the three major spatial components of the metropolitan area or city-region – core areas, suburbs, and fringe areas (Bryant and Lemire 1993). Choices concerning where growth (and, therefore, investment) should take place have been debated against the backdrop of such issues as equity of tax burden, access to open space, waste management, and the match between labour supply and demand. Canadian metropolitan regions learned that accommodating or attracting new population growth and investment was not a simple matter of finding the space. Location of development, always a key aspect of regional planning, made a great deal of difference, and public and political attitudes about location influenced the decisions to be taken. It must be remembered that all decisions regarding regional location fall within a particular municipality, thereby, in the eyes of other local units, conferring upon it an actual or presumed advantage. Further, all municipalities feel that such decisions leave them with less power, thus fuelling an inherent local-regional tension.

Pursuing the "Compact Metropolis"

A central theme underlying most metropolitan and city-region plans and/or policy statements has been the need to develop a "compact city." This concept is evident in the plans for the Montreal Urban Community, the Greater Vancouver Regional District, the earlier plans for Metropolitan Toronto, and the later plans for the Greater Toronto Area. The associated goal of developing regional centres – nodes of fairly high residential densities along with associated commercial and other job-creating activities – was part of several plans. Metro Toronto's Toward a Livable Metropolis plan was termed a "reurbanization strategy." The Livable Region Strategic Plan for Greater Vancouver promoted a hierarchy of sub-centres throughout the suburbs, some of which have come to fruition. In Montreal, the decentralization approach has been limited by the need to support the core area.

Most provinces supported policies that would create more compact urban forms, especially those that control sprawl, but their interest and involvement varied. Ontario intervened directly in metropolitan planning decisions affecting transportation and sewage treatment, and it attempted to change the institutional arrangements for planning (as when it created the Office for the Greater Toronto Area). In Quebec, provincial policies were much less forceful, but the province did make key decisions pertaining to highway and transit planning, and, of course, it controls agricultural land resources. The BC government retained control over certain key functions affecting the shape of urban development – notably, highways, agricultural land protection, and, until 1999, regional transit – but has been little involved in promoting higher densities. In the Atlantic region, the two metropolitan region plans were prepared by provinces: Newfoundland prepared the one for St. John's, and Nova Scotia prepared the one for Halifax–Dartmouth (Heseltine 1998).

At the metropolitan or city-region level, planning authorities attempted to achieve the goal of a compact city through urban structure planning, allocating growth to different areas, and coordinating region structure planning with transportation planning. In regions where they have control over public investments in water supply and sewerage, housing, parks, and waste disposal, urban-structure planning tools (such as zoning and development control) are also used. However, overall, there has been only modest success in changing actual growth patterns. The main barriers have been threefold: (1) the lack of coordination of strategic infrastructure decisions at the provincial level, (2) the reluctance of individual municipalities to conform to the regional targets, and (3) the lack of integrated transportation and land-use planning. The lesson in all this is that we need to establish links among the provincial, metropolitan, and local levels of government as well as among environmental, economic, and land-use planning (Tomalty 1997). Current efforts to develop regional transportation plans for the Vancouver city-region using a consultative process seem to hold promise for establishing such links.

Regional Strategic Planning Frameworks

Over the years, two essential features of growth management at the regional level came to be recognized by Canadian metropolitan planning authorities. The first is that, in order to manage urban growth effectively, one must develop policies and strategies for both the urban area and the surrounding municipalities and countryside (including smaller unincorporated settlements). This, of course, reflects the symbiotic relationship between urban areas and the surrounding countryside, which provides living space for commuters, open space and recreational opportunities for core area residents, and room for agricultural production and water supply. The second feature of growth management is that, because transportation has such a strong influence upon urban structure at the regional level, it is essential to combine planning for transportation infrastructure with planning for land use. Unfortunately, this is frequently difficult because transportation is controlled more by the provincial government than by metropolitan authorities.

Recognition of the need to develop region-wide policies and strategies – to develop a strategic plan for the region – has become evident in the three city-regions. Indeed, the 1996 plan for the Vancouver region is subtitled "a strategic plan" (see Chapter 9). Planning for the Greater Toronto Area is moving in this direction, as is planning for Montreal. Strategic planning provides the region with a coherent frame of reference against which individual municipal plans can be measured, along with the host of infrastructure interventions made by local governments. It can also be seen as promoting more effective regional communication between municipalities without imposing a regional form of government.

One overriding issue affecting city-region planning that is yet to be resolved concerns the proper role of the province. So far, the provinces have not provided desirable leadership with regard to city-regions. Given the size of these regions, their jurisdictional complexity, and their economic importance, this is lamentable. Some people have speculated that the provinces are reluctant to create the governmental entities necessary to do the job because they would be in potential competition with them (Tomalty 1997). In any case, such "incipient citistates," as Wight (1998a) calls them, would still require provincial cooperation in order to maintain economic, social, and physical links with population and markets in the surrounding territory.

Planning and Governance Approaches

Canadian metropolitan areas and city-regions have employed a number of approaches to regional planning and governance. These have ranged from making use of agencies with no resources or authority to develop a plan to those able to both make plans and implement them. A recent American classification system pertaining to US regional institutions is useful. It posits a continuum of varying levels of governing and planning capability vested in the regional agency (Greater Triangle Regional Council 1998). The four positions on this continuum range from the ad hoc approach (in which the regional agency has the least governing and planning capability) to the advisory approach, to the supervisory approach, to the authoritative decision-making approach (in which the regional agency has the most capability).[2] To these we have added the category of "strength of planning and implementation powers."

Ad Hoc Approach

The ad hoc approach to regional planning involves two or more communities coming together, either voluntarily or with the encouragement of the provincial government, to form a committee, board, or commission to address a specific issue (such as watershed protection) or to supply a needed service.

These arrangements provide a forum for discussing issues of regional concern, but they do not provide the resources necessary to preparing a regional plan, let alone implementing it. In Canada, the Capital Region Committee for Winnipeg, the Office for the Greater Toronto Area, and the Alberta Capital Region Alliance for Edmonton exemplify this approach. The ad hoc approach relies on a network of interrelationships rather than on formal institutional arrangements, and it is characterized by voluntary agreements among public and private stakeholders. Under this approach, there is seldom a regional plan in place to address the future physical development of the region as a whole. Somewhat paradoxically, the ad hoc approach to regional planning is now looming large thanks to its potential for planning and governing city-regions (see Chapters 9 and 11).

Advisory Approach

Some metropolitan and city-region agencies have been allocated sufficient governmental resources to draft a regional plan but not to implement it. In other words, they are essentially advisory. In the 1950s and 1960s, this was the first approach that provinces took to metropolitan area planning. As it became apparent that regional problems and needs could only be met by agencies that had greater powers, some of them were transformed. However, the advisory approach to regional planning continues to be prevalent in small metropolitan areas.

Supervisory Approach

Regional bodies with supervisory powers are able to administer a metropolitan regional growth strategy that has been developed as part of the regional body's planning function. However, responsibility for implementing most, if not all, of the planning strategy lies with local municipalities, while the regional body oversees compliance with certain aspects of the plan and tracks progress towards realizing its goals. This supervisory approach to regional planning succeeded the advisory approach in many metropolitan regions. The best examples of the supervisory approach is found in the Greater Vancouver and Greater Victoria regional districts in British Columbia. Other supervisory agencies across the country include most regional governments in Ontario. Recent proposals for an overall coordinating mechanism for both the Greater Toronto Area and the Montreal Metropolitan Region contain supervisory provisions.

Authoritative Decision Making

The authoritative decision-making approach to regional planning may be found in those agencies that have the statutory authority both to develop a growth plan and to oversee its implementation. Such agencies also have the governmental resources to make budgetary choices, and they may also have authority over a variety of sectors (such as roads, parks, the environment, and economic development). Moreover, they can require changes in the plans and development bylaws of constituent municipalities in order to ensure their consistency with the regional plan. Two systems of governance possess these "authoritative" characteristics: the two-tier system and the one-tier system.

The two-tier system was used in governing Metro Toronto (until 1997), the Montreal Urban Community, and the regional municipality of Sudbury.[3] This system is often used when member municipalities resist overall amalgamation.

Theoretically, single, or one-tier, metropolitan cities encompass the entire urbanized region, have a single government with all the powers of a municipality, and have an overview of the region's needs. Winnipeg's Unicity, Toronto's megacity, and the Halifax–Dartmouth regional municipality are examples. Under the one-tier system of regional planning the single municipality is responsible for both planning and governing the area within its boundaries. However, these boundaries often fall short of including the entire metropolitan region, as we see with the new City of Toronto and the much larger Greater Toronto Area.

A Blending of Approaches

In retrospect, the pioneering efforts to establish metropolitan and city-region planning and government agencies in Canada have proved durable, and there is nothing to suggest they will not continue in the future. Part of their durability lies in their ability to change, albeit in an often unsystematic manner. Indeed, no apparent set of steps has been followed either in establishing or in refining planning and governance structures in metropolitan areas and city-regions. They did not always move from, say, lesser to greater degrees of power being accorded to regional bodies. While Metro Toronto moved from a two-tier authoritative system to a one-tier system, the Edmonton region moved from a one-tier system to an ad hoc approach to regional planning. The logic for creating a regional entity in a metropolitan area or city-region must always contend with the logic already extant in the current arrangements between provinces and local governments. Deciding which logic will prevail is a matter of value and political will. The same challenge occurs during each subsequent attempt to "update" a regional entity.

This, of course, does not justify remaining with the status quo vis-à-vis our metropolitan and city-region arrangements. We must appraise the arguments for shifts in how we plan and govern our metropolitan areas and city-regions. Our urban regions are not static: they constantly reflect ongoing social and economic realities. For example, the ad hoc approach to regional planning – which works through a network of public agencies, municipalities, and special interest groups and has long been maligned as "too weak" – is now considered to be an appropriate vehicle for regional governance in the Edmonton and Winnipeg metropolitan regions. Others argue that we need to view urban regions as distinct "citistates" (Wight 1998a). (These and other ideas are addressed in Chapter 11.) In any case, few would argue that we should discard our metropolitan and city-region instrumentalities, for, as noted in Chapter 8, the stronger the form of governmental and planning structure, the greater the impact on social well-being (Frisken 1996).

Lessons from Canadian Regional Planning

Many lessons can be learned from looking at the history of regional planning in Canada. The most important of these lessons are presented below.

Lesson 1:
Setting regional boundaries is as much a matter of values as it is of fact.

The unavoidable task of setting regional boundaries is confounding, paradoxical, and far from the neutral task it is often thought to be. Gertler (1972b) ranks the creation of the planning region as first among the elements of regional planning. It is a decision that affects both our planning solution and the difficulty of the planning task itself. Although we often delimit regions according to natural physical phenomena, they are essentially mental constructs. Planning regions are constructed by those who have a need to fulfil some planning purpose, whether it be managing urban overspill or reducing regional disparities. The seemingly "natural" logic of today's bioregion is no less a rationalization than is Walter Isard's space economy, Patrick Geddes' valley section, or the Ontario government's decision to use the county to define regional governments (see Chapters 1, 2, and 3).

Every planning region is unique. It embodies a choice about which resources (human, physical, economic, and settlement) will be included in the region, remembering that what is excluded cannot be readily included in the future. The very nature of regional planning is to focus attention on a particular piece of space; however, by doing so we also choose a particular substantive focus to pursue and particular tools to use. For example, a regional planner will plan a river basin differently, and with different tools, from what she/he would use to plan a trading area of the same size in the same locale. As well, we can be quite certain that today's boundary will not fully serve tomorrow's economic and social conditions, much less its political leanings. Few regions are not driven by political factors and/or economic forces; in other words, today's boundaries will seldom suffice in the long run. This has become very evident in the type of planning needed in metropolitan areas from Victoria to St. John's (see Chapter 8). Future boundary-setting needs to allow for this dynamic aspect, especially for metropolitan and city-regions.

Closely associated with defining a region's planning boundaries is the matter of equipping it to effectively perform its mandate. This brings us to Lesson 2.

Lesson 2: Regional planning initiatives depend for their effectiveness on the bundle of governmental resources they receive from the province.

No regional planning can take place without the approval of the province within which it is to occur or without a planning agency that has been granted the capacity to carry out its mandate. Establishing a planning region involves an areal division of the power to govern, a right reserved to each province. However, planning regions only become effective planning entities to the extent that the provinces allocate them "governmental resources" (Khakee and Low 1996) (see Chapter 4). These resources pertain to making regulations, raising funds, having political autonomy, obtaining professional staff, and providing a planning mandate. They are provided in a bundle that may vary in both the amount and mix of resources, depending on the disposition of the province. Hence, they are politically highly charged.

The bundles of governmental resources provided to Canadian regional planning agencies over the past half century show several regularities. One of these is that the amount and mix of resources vary according to the type of regional planning being sanctioned. For example:

- Agencies engaged in resource development (e.g., the James Bay Development Corporation) tend to have robust bundles that enable them to carry out both planning and implementation.
- Those engaged in regional economic planning (e.g., the now defunct Ontario economic development regions) tend to be provided few resources, especially those needed for implementing plans.
- Metropolitan, city-region, and rural planning agencies have bundles that do not contain many regulatory resources (e.g., most metropolitan planning agencies and the former regional planning commissions in Alberta), hence their dependence on municipalities and other bodies for implementing their plans.

Overall, regional planning agencies have weaker regulatory and financial resources than planning, political, and professional resources. A related lesson follows.

Lesson 3: Regional plans concerned with land use can seldom be fully implemented by the regional planning agency.

Planning regions are always superimposed on a pre-existing areal division of power that was instituted by the province when it established municipalities and counties. Moreover, municipalities, by convention, are allotted regulatory resources for land use, and these are not easily abridged. Thus, regional proposals are fraught with an underlying political tension. This is as evident in rural-region planning (e.g., British Columbia's regional districts) as it is in metropolitan-region planning (e.g., Metro Toronto and the Halifax–Dartmouth Metropolitan Authority). Somewhat paradoxically, regional agencies are frequently allotted functional powers that are greater than those of its constituent municipalities (e.g., hospitals, sewage treatment, highways). But the region's powers are usually meant to supplement local powers rather than to substitute for them.

Lesson 4: Effective planning of rural regions requires that land and other natural resources not be considered commodities.

The planning of wholly rural regions and the rural portions of other regions has almost always laboured under planning provisions conceived for urban areas. Rural planning has been seen as a land-use problem rather than as a resource-use problem. When seen as a land-use problem, land is a commodity that is limited in supply and must be allocated among competing uses. But land and other natural resources are seldom in short supply in rural regions, where the problem is more likely to centre around the location of the resource use within the region and the kind or quality of its use. In a forested region, the problem is usually not whether logging should occur, but where it should occur and of what it should consist. And the same may be said for agricultural, fishing, and other resource regions because the resource base is central to the economic base of the region. Thus, while zoning can be very precisely applied in urban areas – down to the individual parcel of land – in rural areas, even where its use is appropriate, zoning must remain general. Add to this the often close connection between rural residents and ownership of the resources being planned (i.e., ownership of the economic base), and we have a very different mix of basic ingredients and participants in rural planning than we do in urban planning (see Chapter 5).

Lesson 5: It is difficult to sustain the commitment of provincial governments to regional planning over the long term.

With few exceptions, provincial commitment to regional planning has been more honoured in the breach than in the observance. Probably the most dramatic instance of this was the 1982 demise of the previously much-heralded Toronto-Centred Region Plan. In 1970, at the time of its inception, many observers regarded this plan as the boldest attempt ever made to plan the overall form of a metropolitan region. It failed because, it seems, the political difficulties were too great to overcome. The situation as continued under the new rubric of the Greater Toronto Area, with development being determined largely on the basis of local land-use policies. Thus, while the Ontario government has virtually unlimited authority to bring regional plans into effect, it has seldom used that authority to override local planning preferences.[4] Ontario is not alone in this failing; other provinces, too, have often chosen to work out compromises among competing local interests rather than to promote regional interests. Heseltine (1998, 18), reviewing Atlantic Canada's experience, notes the lack of compatibility between the 1975 Halifax–Dartmouth Regional Development Plan and the situation in 1998, when "more than 20 land use plans govern[ed] development." A provincial effort to review the regional development plan "collapsed owing to shifting provincial priorities," and "the story of the St. John's urban region plan is similar."

In so many of these situations it seems incongruous that the province, which took the initiative to establish a regional planning agency in the first place, is unable to sustain its support over the long run. Given social and economic changes, there may, of course, be good reasons for the province to revise the basis of its commitment. It may need to change boundaries or the governing structure, or it may need to amend the bundle of resources it makes available to the region. Indeed, it is in the province's interest to regularly review the viability of the planning regions it establishes as they are bound to change. (See note 1 regarding Victoria's recent experience.)

Lesson 6: Metropolitan growth soon spills over the political boundaries created to contain it.

This is one of the few certainties about the nature and pace of metropolitan development in market-driven economies such as Canada's. Every Canadian metropolitan area we examined has exhibited substantial decentralization of population, economic activity, and political activity, beyond the boundaries of the metropolitan-regional planning agency that had been created earlier. Even Metro Toronto, the agency with the most advanced form of governance, was unable to contain and control its increasing growth. The global and other forces pushing for dispersion and deconcentration seem to be leading to what Castells (1989, 1996) refers to as the "informational city," wherein urban activities are not only further spread out, but also become spatially restructured due to our increasing capacity to substitute communication of information for transportation of people and goods. This decentralization will be reinforced by the large numbers of people in the "baby boom" and "echo" generations who are still to enter the single-family housing market, which can only be easily done outside central cities and older suburbs. We can expect new challenges and problems for planning and governance from this emerging metropolitan expansion (see Chapters 8 and 9).

Canada's "mega" metropolitan areas, or city-regions, are currently key spatial units both in their respective provinces and in the nation as a whole. They produce between 40 percent and 50 percent of their province's gross domestic product and, thus, can truly be considered the prime "engines of growth" that drive their provincial economies – and, to a great extent, that of the nation as a whole. Thus, Canada's city-regions will continue to be important, viable, and competitive economic and political units, and they will continue to be key players on the world economic stage. Indeed, some observers (Peirce et al. 1993) foresee the breakdown of the traditional nation-states and their replacement by "citistates" and "region states." At a minimum, the means by which these regions are currently planned and governed will need to be reviewed.

Two subsidiary lessons assert themselves in light of these trends.

Lesson 6a: An organ of governance at the metropolitan level is needed to ensure that planning is holistic, integrated, and considers the entire region.

Among others, Gardner Church (1996), a Toronto urbanist, indicates that we need a single focal point of governance that has statutory responsibility for planning the entire metropolitan region. Canadian experience vis-à-vis governing our metropolitan areas and city-regions provides much evidence to support this. Most metropolitan-regional planning agencies in Canada have never possessed the powers they need to be effective agents of large-scale urban growth management. The inevitable tensions between local autonomy and regional needs and interests are at the heart of this problem of governance. Experience and recent thinking suggest a further lesson.

Lesson 6b: Successful metropolitan-regional planning must be linked to a process of governing that is both more inclusive and that possesses the requisite powers to act in order to meet regional needs and goals.

Since metropolitan-region planning began in Canada, it has been clear that it is difficult to establish any form of authority over the entire metropolitan area or city-region because the constituent municipalities believe that this diminishes their autonomy. The two-tier system of governance (e.g., the municipal corporation of Winnipeg between 1961 and 1972, Metro Toronto until 1997, and the Greater Vancouver Regional District) was designed to rectify this problem. However, local planning goals and aspirations usually take precedence over regional interests. This has meant that planning for metropolitan areas and city-regions in Canada has remained advisory.

Even the usual requirement that community plans must "conform" with the regional plan has little teeth in it. In a few cases, things have worked out well (e.g., during the first decade of Metro Toronto's existence, when numerous regional capital works were undertaken, new roads and transit lines built, and suburban housing developed). However, generally, there has always been much tension between local autonomy and region-wide authority. And this tension seems to have been aggravated in recent decades, with public opinion undergoing a pronounced shift towards favouring local initiative and local control. This new thinking will have to be reconciled with the need for a form of regional governance that has the capacity to implement a comprehensive long-term vision of where the region should be going.

The Continuing Need for Regional Planning

The Regional Imperative

Regional planning will continue to play a vital role in twenty-first-century Canada. Indeed, as our communities become more entwined with social and economic systems both here and abroad, there is little likelihood that the need for regional planning will diminish. Air and water pollution do not stop at community boundaries, and few communities are able to supply their own water or dispose of their own wastes. And the ongoing need for urban high-ways and transit will likely continue to be in the vanguard of our regional planning efforts. And then there are issues as crime, ethnic and racial integra-tion, uncertain economic competitiveness stemming from various forces of globalization, intercommunity inequities, and participation in major league sports activities. Regional thinking is vital for environmental planning, if only to force us to recognize the spatial extent of human use of the earth, or our "ecological footprint" (Wackernagel and Rees 1995). Cooperation among com-munities will be needed in order to provide the spatial extent necessary for eco-systems planning (Wight 1996). Urban and rural environments will con-tinue to remain distinctive, but their futures will be even more closely inter-connected through the need to supply resources to industry and "playgrounds" to urban dwellers. Moreover, the next generation of regional problems could be even more demanding, as the number of people and their vehicles expand and, thereby, press regions into new and perhaps unfamiliar phases and levels of development.

This perspective confirms that, as Wannop (1995, 48) has said, "there is an irrepressible regional imperative" in our modern lives. This imperative stems from two general factors. On the one hand, daily economic and social activi-ties are played out over extensive areas that seldom correspond to local politi-cal and administrative boundaries. Yet these human activity areas are not limitless; they have practical and cultural limits with which people and their institutions identify and to which they ascribe meaning. Even though regions are increasingly linked to one another on a functional basis, frequently, on a global level, human experience is related to actual locales, to *places* (Castells 1996). This leads to the other general factor related to the regional imperative – the environment. Obviously, natural as well as cultural forces are involved in creating a region's identity; indeed, as Hough (1990, 19) contends, "the native landscape ... is the primary determinant of regional identity." He also invokes the term "regional imperative" and calls attention to the need to re-spect the principles of energy and the nutrient flows of natural systems with a regional context. In other words, regions exist both objectively and subjec-tively and, regardless of political and administrative caveats, will assert them-selves as we attempt to meet our social needs and aspirations. Therefore, we need a "sense of a region" (Lynch 1976) as well as functional criteria when attempting to define and plan regions.

The Need for Planning Regions

The planning region used to be thought of as a geographic unit with boundaries that were fixed for planning, administrative, and political purposes; however, this thinking is changing. A common thread running through current thinking is that a region needs to be able to transcend political borders and to encompass somewhat amorphous social, economic, and environmental interdependencies.

This thinking recognizes what has always been known about regions: they are inconstant. Thus, while we will continue to need regions for planning and governance, no single model is likely to fit all circumstances. The new flexibility called for with regard to regional boundaries also calls for the involvement of a great number of actors in the planning process as well as recognizing that a variety of functions (not only land use and physical development) contribute to the desired outcomes of regional plans.

There is mounting evidence that the economic and social well-being of communities rises or falls with that of their region. While they may differ about its precise meaning and boundaries, many academics and planners – going back as far as Patrick Geddes, the Regional Planning Association of America, and Lewis Mumford – view a region as a special kind of spatial phenomenon that possesses an intrinsic unity. This is a view echoed by Canadian planner Len Gertler (1998). Paradoxically, in an era of multinational corporations imbued with the ideology of globalism, regions have, if anything, become more important than ever for an area's economic well-being (Castells 1996; Storper 1997). A study by the German Marshall Fund of the United States (1992) concludes that regions in which communities work together effectively perform better in global economic situations than do regions in which they do not. In particular, the urban region is increasingly being seen as a real organic phenomenon that is comprised of the central city, suburbs, and nearby rural areas; that is, it is being seen as a city-region (Jacobs 1984; Ledebur and Barnes 1993). Further, in a time of limited financial resources and intense competition among city-regions, key infrastructure and development investments must be coordinated to ensure that decisions are cost-effective. Such coordination demands a regional perspective in order to ensure the achievement of area-wide objectives for urban structure, transportation, economic competitiveness, and environmental quality.

City-Regions as Citistates

According to the 1996 census, more than 60 percent of Canadians live in our city-regions, and each produces as much as half of their respective province's gross domestic product. As such, they hold sway over considerable areas, and some liken city-regions to modern-day "citistates" (Peirce et al. 1993; Wight 1998a). Under the press of globalization the future role of the city-region will be even greater than it is now. This important spatial unit will be of critical importance for understanding and addressing economic issues, from infrastructure needs and workforce training to international competitiveness and affordable housing and living-wage jobs (Dodge 1996; Kanter 1995; Foster 1997). City-regions will need to adopt deliberate economic infrastructure and cultural strategies in order to capitalize on the emerging information technologies, socio-political shifts, and fiscal realities of the twenty-first century. While there will be a need to develop policies and programs in realms well beyond those of land use and related physical infrastructure, it is the latter that will suffer if this tack is not taken (Downs 1994).

Rural Regions within a Global Setting

In sharp contrast to the pressure of population growth and investment expected to be experienced in metropolitan areas and city-regions is the situation faced in most of the regions that make up the other 90 percent of the nation. Rural Canada, with its agricultural and other natural resource regions, will also be under pressures, both external and internal, that will generate a continuing need for regional planning. Externally, rural regions, including the small- and medium-sized cities within them, will be affected by globalization in that there will be increased demands for natural resources products, a tendency towards sectoral downsizing, and pressure towards greater regional specialization. This, in turn, will affect local labour markets and job opportunities and will necessitate more intercommunity cooperation (Fuller et al. 1989). And then there is the rising acceptance of "sustainable development," which is now an essential criterion for evaluating development proposals (World Commission 1987). This is already being taken into account in rural-region planning in Manitoba (Mah 1998).

Probably nowhere will sustainable development cause more of an impact than in rural and resource regions, where development of resources immediately affects natural environments. Any reduction in environmental impacts through regulation and conservation, as we see with both the West Coast and East Coast fisheries will have both economic and social consequences at both the community and regional levels. The interlocking nature of communities will become even more evident as we seek sustainable solutions to development. Increased international tourism is another part of globalization, and this, too, will affect rural and resource regions and demand forms of regional planning that will take into consideration the protection of natural environments (Reid and Fuller 1995).

Internally, one demographic feature of rural communities is the exceptionally high number elderly people. In 1996, people sixty-five years and older made up about 30 percent of the rural population as compared to about 12 percent of the national population. Given the small size of communities in rural regions, we need to establish shared facilities and services (Hodge 1993). A trend already being seen in rural Manitoba involves a shift to a "community self-help posture" that has resulted in eighty-two community round tables on future development (Mah 1998). Not only is there a demand for more participation, but also for planning skills and more understanding of rural regions.

In sum, regional planning will continue to be needed in both rural and urban regions of Canada. But how will it be structured to meet both the foreseen and unforeseen needs of the twenty-first century? This is the subject of Chapter 11.

The Future Shape of Regional Planning

Perhaps it is presumptuous to suggest what the future of regional planning will or should be. It will, undoubtedly, unfold from its past, with the addition of new cultural and political ingredients. Some of those new ingredients are already evident – globalization, sustainable development, bifurcated provincial economies, community-based economic initiatives, and an appreciation of ecological diversity. Regional planning will need to continue to adapt to these phenomena. This should not be surprising, for the history of regional planning is one of adaptation to changing ideas, professional capacity, and political will, as the foregoing chapters have demonstrated. The past, therefore, should not be seen as constituting only fitful progress among setbacks and "retreats" (Douglas 1997). Regional planning in the future will, undoubtedly, continue to be equally changeable.

There will be new challenges for regional planners and governments seeking strategic ways to respond to new spatial realities that may, at times, seem contradictory. Two trends exemplify what can be considered an underlying dialectic in regional planning's future. On the one hand, the demands for local autonomy and civil society will tend to draw us inward, towards a regional planning that nurtures the micro level, the region, the place. And, on the other hand, the increasing growth of the metropolis – of the "cosmopolis" as some would say (Sandercock 1998b) – and economic globalization will draw us outward. Central to resolving this dialectic is the need to move away from our current structures of government towards structures of governance – towards a governing process that is inclusive and that promotes collaboration and partnerships (Healey 1997). And then there is the need to increase provincial (i.e., political) commitments and to respond to emerging city-regions and the effects they have on non-metropolitan regions. And, not least, there is the need to respect and respond to ecological challenges. All of this suggests that planning practice will require a new paradigm for the twenty-first century.

This chapter describes the direction such a new paradigm is likely to take. It examines the concept of the "region" itself as well as possible sources of a revised concept that includes bioregionalism, sustainable development, ecosystems diversity, and community economic development. What we can be most certain about in preparing for the future is that our past experience enables us to employ valuable lessons. Still, several knotty issues will remain, not the least of which is the "plan-versus-process" issue. In other words, should the primary concern of regional planners be to prepare a plan or should it be to focus on the process by which plans get made, approved, and implemented. Previous chapters have already made it evident that we think both are necessary for effective regional planning. While the most admirable side of regional planning is its predisposition to envision what *might* be, the future well-being of a region's people, resources, and environment obliges us to also consider what *can* be and to provide the institutions and arrangements to bring it into being.

Current and Emerging Trends and Forces

The planning region has always been subject to forces that "push" it towards resolution with the larger entity from which it has been carved (e.g., the province or nation) and forces that "pull" it back towards the place – the complex of historical, cultural, and environmental elements – from which it was derived. In other words, planning regions can never be considered permanent either in terms of policy direction or boundary. And, since they are a strategic instrument for achieving particular social and economic needs at a particular time, they must be able to adapt to changing needs in order to continue to be relevant. As well as responding to new substantive needs, planning regions, their planners, and their agencies must respond to the changing processes of participation and decision making.

Which forces will affect the shape of regional planning in the next few decades? Which will push them outward? Which will pull them inward? First, we shall examine those forces that push a region's perspective outward (e.g., globalization and sustainable development); then we shall examine those that pull a region's perspective inward (e.g., bioregionalism and community economic development); finally, we shall review the net effects of both.

Pushing Regions Outward

Three broad tendencies will continue to push regions well beyond national and provincial boundaries. The advent of global corporations and economies, the concomitant emergence of large-scale city-regions throughout the world, and the concern about world environments are already changing both the role and concept of planning regions.

Global Economies

It is self-evident that activities in today's global marketplace transcend national economies. But what is their effect on regions within nations such as Canada? Our national economy, like those of most nations, is made up of a combination of regional economies that differ from one another in their products and circumstances. In the past, there was a mutual interdependence between regional (often provincial) economies and national economic policy, especially in the realm of exports. Indeed, the economic health of regional economies was a matter of national policy and led to considerable regional planning under the Agricultural Rehabilitation and Development Act and Department of Regional Economic Expansion programs of the 1960s and 1970s (see Chapter 6). Through incentives to manufacturing and resource industries, earlier regional planning evolved to include social and infrastructure concerns as well as economic development. Today, international ("free trade") economic arrangements tend to work against national (and provincial) economic initiatives that could be interpreted as subsidies to a particular industry or resource sector. This, in turn, directly affects the regions in which these economic activities are located. Trade disputes in the past decade, which affected regional economies from dairy producers in southern Quebec to grain producers on the Prairies and softwood timber producers in coastal British Columbia, show how severely limited the scope of policy intervention on the part of both federal and provincial governments has become. Within the global economy, even resource conservation is constrained (witness Canadian dilemmas over protecting fish stocks on both the east and west coasts).

The global economy is affecting regional planning in two major ways. On the one hand, economic prospects need to be seen in an international perspective that both opens opportunities for a region's products and resources and reduces any protection that the federal government might have provided them. Whether or not regional economies will prosper seems, to a large degree, to depend on the investment strategies and decisions of global corporations – strategies and decisions that are determined well beyond regional and Canadian boundaries. On the other hand, the global perspective, while broadening their economic scope, is eroding the ability of regional planners to link economic objectives with social and environmental needs. Thus, in the future, when a region seeks such goals of social well-being and environmental protection, these will have to compete with economic goals not only within the planning agency, but also often within distant corporate headquarters.

Another effect of the globalization of economic activities is the spatial reorganization that has been occurring worldwide. Large cities, which have always attracted corporate headquarters and ancillary financial and investment activities, are, with the tremendous expansion in capital and information flows that has occurred over the past two decades, becoming even more dominant. Large cities around the world, especially in the Third World, have become even larger, thereby creating problems of governance and infrastructure (McGee and Robinson 1997). And rural regions have been affected by multinational companies and their resource industry consolidations, transnational trading blocs, and reductions in the need for skilled labour in resource industries.

City-Regions

As is the case in most developed countries, a significant shift is occurring in the spatial structure of Canada's economic and urban development. This involves the emergence of a new spatial form, which, in earlier chapters, we have referred to as the "dispersed metropolis" or the "city-urban region" (see also Bunting and Filion 2000). Indeed, these new, very large-scale, heavily populated dynamic places are a product of current globalization tendencies that manifest themselves in increasingly mobile and affluent populations, electronically fostered capital and investment flows, and international economic competition. Evidence of such city-regions is already found in Montreal, Toronto, and Vancouver (see Chapter 9).

This new spatial form has two broad implications for regional planning: the first involves planning for the city-region itself, and the second involves the impact of the city-region on planning for other regions. Latter-day city-regions will pose major challenges for planners and policy makers who will have to make them work effectively and keep them globally competitive. The conventional notions of physical planning pertaining to a large "city," or even a "metropolitan area," are not sufficient to encompass the economic and social realities with which the planners of city-regions will have to contend. Among the crucial questions that will face these planners are the following:

1 What structural and financial strategies are likely to prove most suitable and practical with regard to keeping city-regions globally competitive while still meeting their specific social and environmental needs as they continue to grow and evolve?
2 What is to be the role of the various parts of the city-regions – the old central city, old and new suburbs, fringe communities, small rural towns – and how might they best be integrated so that they are healthy and strong?
3 What arrangements will provinces have to provide for the effective planning and governance of city-regions, including the setting of boundaries and the allocation of governmental resources?

Planners of city-regions will have little choice but to seek a balance between global considerations and the region's distinctive social and environmental needs and concerns.

The advent of city-regions also affects the planning of all other regions. Until recently, regional planners fashioned their initiatives on the assumption that national economies would progressively come to be spatially more integrated with the result that economic and social disparities between regions would disappear (Myrdal 1957; Friedmann 1966). However, the globalization of large urban areas sharpens the differences between them and non-metropolitan and rural regions. The expectations of "spread effects" and "backward links" from the growth and development of an urban core region to surrounding peripheral regions can no longer be counted on to stimulate growth at the periphery. In a globalized world within which very large, interconnected cities are the norm, both urban and non-urban regions will be pushed to consider their own futures independently, thereby reducing the options of regional planners to employ interregional strategies.

Sustainable Development

Probably no other regional planning concept has been embraced so universally and so quickly as has that of sustainable development, proclaimed by the World Commission on the Environment and Development (the Brundtland Commission) in 1987. Its importance lies in its insistence that environmental policy and economic policy be considered together (Jacobs 1991). Further, sustainable development inescapably incorporates concerns about both the future and social equity. It is not simply about the creation of wealth and the conservation of resources; it also includes a commitment to distribute them fairly, both now and in the future. Interpretations of what is meant by the "fair distribution" of resources differ, but sustainable development clearly demands a radical departure from the economic policy of most corporations and governments (something already evident in current business practice) (Coopers and Lybrand 1992).

There is, of course, a familiar echo to this call for integrating environmental concerns and economic development initiatives. It recalls, for example, the work of Patrick Geddes and the Regional Planning Association of America (see Chapter 1), which aimed to promote harmony between resource use and human needs (Roberts 1994). The difference is that it now seems attainable as both the business community and governments begin to address environmental issues when making economic decisions (Frankel 1998). Possibly more important, the regional level, all but ignored in past discussions about sustainable development, also has a key role to play. It can deal both with environmental problems that extend beyond a single region as well as mediate provincial policies (e.g., pollution control and distribution of wastes) and local concerns (e.g., restrictions on land use) (Stohr 1990; Wallner et al. 1996; Wight 1998b).

While it may seem as though the focus is on the individual region, we should not forget that the standards for sustainable development are being set globally by international agencies, multilateral agreements, and corporations. The decisions corporations make have profound implications for regions: quality of life and social equity may be enhanced when corporations are willing and able to comply with sustainable principles, but the converse may hold true when they do not. Regions that currently have degraded environments may face the prospect of becoming "environmental sinks," or waste repositories, for environmentally advanced regions. Some in Europe have already referred to this as a new form of regional "specialization" (Commission 1989). In considering sustainable development, it is also necessary to determine whether there can be economic development *without* growth (Daly 1996). Thus, regional planners need to recognize that, on the one hand, it is important to incorporate principles of sustainable development into their plans and policies and, on the other hand, that the future economic role of their regions will often be determined elsewhere. Although the long-standing ideal of "harmony of human and resource use" may be within sight, it will only be attained at the expense of increased uncertainty about its social consequences. This will be as true for metropolitan areas and city-regions as it is for rural resource regions.

Pulling Regions Inward

Countering the tendencies that will induce regional planners to favour external forces are some concurrent and equally insistent ones that will demand they focus inward on the region and its internal relations. In no small part these "pulls" to consider the region first are a reaction to the external forces discussed above and other tendencies in the modern world that seem to threaten human and place identities (witness the debates in European countries over joining a common currency union). Though this inward pull has always been part of regional planning, in the past two decades significant social initiatives have arisen that push us to view regional planning from the inside. Bioregionalism and community economic development are two such initiatives, and they have been joined by the pragmatic need to protect local ecosystems and to deliver regional services.

Bioregionalism

Drawing on roots not dissimilar to those of many of the precursors of regional planning (e.g., Geddes, Le Play, and Mackaye) (see Chapter 1), the bioregionalism movement enjoins planners to focus on the intertwined needs of human beings and the natural ecosystem when determining a region's future. Bioregionalism, while centred on the local bioregion, also sees the region as part of a system of nested natural regions. The boundaries of each region are determined by "natural rather than human dictates" so as to reinforce the notion that human communities arise from within natural confines (Sale 1985; McGinnis 1999). This perspective is implicit in the numerous round tables on the environment and economy that have been held over the past decade or so, and it is explicit in the planning for the Toronto watershed and for the Kitimat–Stikine Regional District in British Columbia (Chapters 5 and 7).

The bioregionalism approach has a strong appeal because it recognizes the connections between the natural environment and the impact of human activities (something that corporations and governments seem to forget), and it also offers empowerment through inviting people to define the boundaries of their own region (Aberley 1993a). One of the touchstones in bioregional boundary drawing is the watershed, a readily grasped holistic concept that owes much to Patrick Geddes. Through this and other tools (such as the "cognitive mapping" of cultural space), bioregional planning regions can be expected to diverge from the functional regions of economics, urban systems, and political administrative regions. It will not be easy for future regional planning practice to avoid being influenced by bioregional ideas. They will affect the establishment of new or expanded boundaries of, for example, city-regions and regions created for environmental protection; and they will also determine who gets to set the boundaries and what gets on the planning agenda. Bioregionalism is more than a heuristic notion: it has a regional methodology that other natural systems-based planning initiatives currently lack, and it will be hard to resist (McTaggart 1993).

Environmental Perspectives and Ecosystems Planning

Closely related to bioregionalism, but more general in approach, is the broad concern with the environmental consequences of excessive economic and physical development. A loss of faith in economic progress and expert advice, coupled with a rise in environmentalism, has shifted the focus of many people towards the protection and stewardship of local and regional environments. As the adverse consequences of many projects have come to light, demands for the assessment of the effects of development proposals on the environment have become commonplace. There is, once again, a strong conservation ethic among the public, who want to see a reversal of environmental damage and the creation of sustainable natural habitats (see Chapters 7 and 9).

There are already many instances of planners recognizing and responding to this public concern. For example, Wackernagel and Rees (1995), with their "ecological footprint," have identified useful parameters for determining environmental impacts. Planners on the fringe of Metro Toronto are aggressively using ecological principles to restore biodiversity to landscapes in that urbanizing region (Tamminga 1996). This is the case in a number of cities and regions across the country, whose plans also embody a strong tendency towards conservation, environmental protection, sustainability, and ecosystem diversity (see Chapter 7). In the Vancouver region, for example, agencies and community groups are working in partnership to protect and enhance fish habitats and ecosystems (Heitkamp 1996).

These various efforts signal three important things to regional planners. The first is that there is a strong public commitment to having planning incorporate ecological principles. This, in turn, demands that planners consider the ecosystems that underpin the region. Second, ecosystem planning moves the focus of regional planning from the city towards achieving ecological balance for an area in which the city is no longer the centrepoint (Tomalty et al. 1994). And, third, community members want to be involved in regional planning and, in many cases, are taking the lead (Bernard and Young 1997). Thus, in the coming decades, planners will be pressed to play a role in organizing effective collaboration for environmental planning and sustainability. Perhaps, as Wight (1996) hopes, this will lead to a "new eco-regionalism." That this is a realizable goal is shown in the work of Tomalty et al. (1994), who have developed ecosystems concepts and methods for planning Canadian urban regions.

Dual Provincial Economies

During the last quarter century, one of the hallmarks of regional economies in Canada has been the increasing disparities within provinces as opposed to the disparities between them. All provinces now have spatially bifurcated economies consisting of a more or less vibrant urban region and less well developed (and often economically tepid) hinterlands. Not surprisingly, the hinterlands make up the bulk of the province, are mostly rural (with many towns and villages and some small- and medium-sized cities), and depend upon natural resources for their economic base. We need only think of Newfoundland outside of St. John's, Quebec outside of Montreal and Quebec City, Cape Breton, northern Ontario, and the north coast of British Columbia (see Chapter 7).

Geographically, this economic split is not dissimilar to that identified under the ARDA and DREE programs in the 1950s and 1960s, which fought to reduce regional disparities (Chapter 6). However, the situation has become more pronounced, and the dynamics under which it is occurring are different and more difficult to plan. This is because this set of regional disparities is largely the reverse side of the success of cities and city-regions in the global marketplace. Up until the last decade or so, cities played their expected role: they were the provinces' "engines of economic growth" as well as the link between the rural/non-metropolitan economies and the urban economy. However, in this era of global markets and city-regions, the links between the major provincial cities and the rest of the province have been upstaged by links with other city-regions. Thus, while city-regions look outward, other regions are looking inward. This will not only affect planning for non-urban regions, but it will also affect planning the relationships between them and urban regions.

Community Economic Development

Community economic development is a spatial counterpart of global economics, and it is most certainly its ideological competitor. Community economic development has roots that extend to the beginnings of the cooperative movement in Canada and the values of community self-reliance evident in other local endeavours. Its contemporary form emerged in the wake of the many unsuccessful top-down regional economic initiatives in the 1970s and with the rise of global corporations. In many ways, community economic development can be characterized as a form of "alternative development," the phrase used in the Third World to denote efforts to secure basic needs and local autonomy

(Friedmann 1992). It seeks to achieve economic development by means that are not wholly dependent upon either the market or the state (Bruyn and Meehan 1987). It starts with goals espoused by the community, which also encompass social and environmental objectives and are delivered through community institutions and businesses.

The ethos of community economic development has become widespread in Canada in both non-urban and urban regions, and the result has been the development of many stable, vigorous community enterprises from coast to coast (Perry and Lewis 1994). Much support has been provided by the federal government's Community Futures Program, which is a regional program whose purpose is to assist non-metropolitan regions in promoting their own forms of economic development. More than 250 such regions exist, including several dozen representing Aboriginal territories. These same Community Futures regions also correspond to the languishing provincial regions, thereby reinforcing the inward pull on the planning perspective of those regions located outside the city-regions. We need to add that, where it exists, the community economic development perspective will bring a more holistic approach to the regional planning agenda. It will include not only linking social and environmental objectives with those of economic development, but also linking the achievement of these objectives to increased well-being in all spheres.

Public Participation and Civil Society

The community approach to economic development that we have just described is a variant of a much broader concern – the concern of individuals, families, and communities over their lack of power to deal with economic, social, and environmental problems. Over the past few decades, trust in government to solve the problems of environmental degradation, unemployment, economic restructuring, crime, and racism has waned considerably. In reaction, citizens have sought various ways, individually and in groups, to become empowered and to assume a significant role in decision making. The term "civil society" denotes today's movement to re-establish a greater sense of control and responsibility for social choices on the part of those affected by them, that is, the citizens. This is reminiscent of what, a third of a century ago, was known as "participatory democracy" (Dahrendorf 1995; Shils 1991).

There have been, and continue to be, a variety of manifestations of the desire of people to express their citizenship. As we noted, community economic development is one such example, but so are local and regional round tables on the environment and economy, community schools, local currency systems, and a host of citizen protest movements. For regional planners, these sentiments have often manifested themselves in the recalcitrant positions taken by municipal governments vis-à-vis the proposals of regional agencies. Municipal reluctance regarding regional proposals is often the result of people using one of the very few direct avenues they have to protect the interests of their communities.

Although this inward-looking tendency of the municipalities within a region has always been part of regional planning, it may prove to be an even bigger challenge in the future, with many global factors buffeting a region's citizens with issues seemingly beyond their control and understanding. In this situation, regions and their agencies could take on a mediating role between the local and the global arenas of decision making. Indeed, there is some evidence that the regional level is appropriate for promoting civil society (Foster 1997; Wight 1998b). The interests of civic organizations, universities, religious groups, private corporations, and citizen groups often transcend local boundaries and reach to the extent of the region that naturally encompasses their activities. Regional planning and governance will have to take this into consideration with regard to policy design and implementation.

Balancing the Competing Factors

The forces of change will affect the planning for any two regions in different ways, just as those two regions will develop in different ways. Some will be drawn to give maximum consideration to their internal development, while others will feel the need to cater to external demands. And still others, perhaps the majority, will find themselves seeking to balance both perspectives. City-regions, for example, are naturally drawn outward, but they, too, will have to contend with demands to protect local ecosystems and local jobs as well as to provide for more local autonomy and participation. And rural regions, which have an inherent tendency to protect local interests, will find global interests determining the markets for their resources.

These factors will provide the context for regional planning in the twenty-first century and will constrain and condition any planning that is attempted, but they will do so much more forcefully than they have in the past. The push-and-pull tendencies we have described are now more powerful and insistent as well as more likely to compete with one another. They could militate against a provincial government's attempt to coordinate interregional planning. Even planning between adjoining regions could prove difficult if one region is pulling inward while another is pushing outward. Within any region, the integration of goals could be problematic. In other words, attempts at more comprehensive planning approaches will not be easy within this context of competing factors.

This also raises the question of the future role of regions with regard to planning within an economic and social milieu that seems dominated by global and/or local tendencies. Here the prospects appear encouraging, for, as a number of observers point out, the region has the advantage of being more human in scale than the abstract global networks of information and finance

(Castells 1996; Storper 1997; Korten 1999). Moreover, regions are the places where people live and relate to one another, where their culture and their institutions are rooted, and where they derive meaning. In an increasingly connected world, regions are "building blocks" (Storper 1997) and could act as "cultural and physical bridges" (Castells 1996) between the global and the local. Indeed, with nation states increasingly unable to act in a world of global corporations and finance, and with local areas being too small to cope with problems that transcend their boundaries, regions may be the only reasonable spatial venue left. We seem to need an intermediate scale – a "meso-level," as Stohr (1990) would say – to provide a setting within which these competing but related forces and tendencies can be mediated. Regions could play this role and, in so doing, promote an ecosystems view of an interconnected world (Vasishth 1996; Wight 1998b). Or, to modify the current rallying cry of "think globally, act locally," we would add: "and plan regionally."

Learning from the Past

Having sketched out the contextual elements with which twenty-first-century regional planning will find itself contending, let us now consider those elements of past practice that will require attention lest they unduly constrain future efforts. In this regard, the lessons from the first sixty years of Canadian regional planning point to several areas of chronic concern. One of these revolves around the role of provincial governments in establishing and supporting regional planning efforts. Another relates to the special needs of planning and governing city-regions. And a third bears on substantive gaps between land use, the economy, and the environment in regional planning practice. It is important to consider each of these if we are to learn from our past and not repeat its shortcomings.

Provincial Commitment to Regional Planning

An essential player in the field of Canadian regional planning is the provincial government, from whose territory and jurisdiction a planning region is carved. Creating a planning region involves a further areal division of power (beyond that already provided for creating spatial units for local governance), and only the province can undertake it. As a general rule, provinces create planning regions in order to achieve certain strategic ends. As previous chapters have shown, regions are created when a province wishes to satisfy the desire to gain local control of the delivery of services and management of spatial resources (as in metropolitan and city-regions) and/or to achieve more equitable economic development (as with conservation authorities and regional economic development commissions). Further, beyond making the crucial decision to establish a planning region, a province must also provide adequate governmental resources to enable the region to play the strategic role intended for it (as described in Chapter 4).

One aspect of creating planning regions that has commonly received insufficient attention from the provinces is that such regions evolve after they have been created. Indeed, regions are initially established in order to achieve change, to help transform the regional economic, social, and environmental situation. So it is not surprising that their needs for governmental resources and boundaries may also change. To their credit, Canadian provinces have taken steps to create planning regions for a wide variety of purposes, but they have been less than assiduous in supporting and guiding these regions. For example, metropolitan boundaries have not been easy to change, even though urban development has inexorably spread beyond them (see Chapters 5, 8, and 9). And provinces still tend to offer bundles of governmental resources that are not adequate to implementing rural-region plans (see Chapter 5). Conflicts between local and regional authorities, arising from the province's areal division of power, have often thwarted the realization of projects essential to a region's development (see Chapters 7 to 9). And it has often been difficult to get provincial agencies to participate in the realization of a region's plan. Some would add that, as a result, regional planning agencies have been able to do little more than engage in "local land use planning writ large" (Robinson and Webster 1985).

The central point to be learned from this aspect of the Canadian experience is that a strong and sustained provincial presence is crucial to effective regional planning, especially during the implementation phase. Friedman (1971) made a comparable point three decades ago when he contended that regional planning had to be "joined to effective power" in order to successfully achieve its plans. As we have seen, planning advice that comes in the form of advisory plans accomplishes little. The province has the power to make regional planning effective. However, if a province intends to use its regions strategically, then it needs to ensure not only that it provides them with the necessary instruments of action, but also that it knows when they are needed. Successful future regional planning will require the province to maintain a continuous and healthy tension with its planning regions – a tension that will be to the mutual benefit of both. This could involve a number of innovative arrangements, such as a ministry dedicated to metropolitan affairs and committed to facilitating the delivery of provincial services and programs. Or a province might offer incentives (such as tax sharing) in return for greater collaboration among municipal units.[1] The political commitment implied in such initiatives should not, of course, be underestimated.

The Need for Substantive Integration

From the earliest days of regional planning there came an ethos of holism – an ethos devoted to the importance of linking physical, social, economic, and environmental factors when planning a region (see Chapter 1). As regional planning became accepted and institutionalized significant gaps appeared in this projected integration. The substance of regional planning practice became limited to one or two factors. Thus, regional planning agencies pursued either a single factor (such as water resource management or economic development) or two (such as metropolitan land use and transportation); but seldom did they pursue all factors. The reasons for this are several and include bureaucratic and political rigidities between levels of government, professional separation, and differing disciplinary knowledge bases.

Over the first sixty years of Canadian regional planning, three disjunctures were notable: (1) the disjuncture between land use and the economic aspects of a region's planning, (2) the disjuncture between land use and environmental factors, and (3) the disjuncture in rural planning situations in seeing land as a commodity rather than as a resource. This trio of shortcomings have been described previously (in Chapters 5 to 9) and need little further elaboration. Suffice it to say that the substantive differentiation that occurred sometimes tended to result in an almost permanent dissociation between seemingly complementary fields.

For example, in the 1970s, instead of seeing the integration of environmental and regional land-use planning, we saw the development of a whole new field (environmental impact assessment) devoted to evaluating the environmental consequences of regional plans and projects (Lawrence 1992; Richardson 1994). A watchdog agency was established, thereby creating yet another player, another stakeholder. In an analogous way, the regional economic planning that characterized much of the 1960s and 1970s had little place for land-use concerns, even though land and its location are of strategic importance to economic development. We see this division perpetuated in the separate planning entities in New Brunswick: regional development councils for economic planning and district planning commissions for land-use planning. During the 1980s and 1990s, the formation of national, provincial, and local round tables spoke to the attempt to blend the mutual interests of the environment and economic development. However, these initiatives had weak political support and never got beyond the advisory stage. Many have since been abandoned. Similarly, the importance of rural needs with regard to guiding the quality of land and resource use have not been met because agricultural land protection measures and rural zoning have mainly been concerned with the amount of land in use.

The separation of these substantive areas, which continues to this day, impairs regional planning's effectiveness, if not its credibility. Each area is mandated by different legislation, each is governed by different ministries, and each is tended by different professions with different mind-sets and doctrines. All of this makes coordination difficult. A major step towards addressing this problem could be taken if federal and provincial governments would be willing to make regional planning mandates more inclusive and to remove the barriers between substantive areas within their own administrative structures.

Of course, regional planners, too, will have to be attentive to the interconnectedness of these substantive factors. This will not be simply a matter of recognizing links with other professionals; it must also include citizens' organizations in all planning processes. The emerging planning milieu will require that networks of various types of participants be established in order to enable planners to comprehend the situation more fully and, hence, to plan more adequately.

Planning and Governing Metropolitan and City-Regions

Several broad lessons have emerged about Canadian experience with planning for metropolitan areas and city-regions (see Chapter 10). There is almost no doubt that metropolitan growth will continue, and probably accelerate, in coming decades, and this should urge us to consider those lessons carefully. First, among the regions encountered in regional planning, the type most likely to require progressively larger boundaries is the metropolitan area. This has a number of major implications, from the content of the planning to the planning mandate.

From one perspective, both the scale and the spatial configuration of planning needs (e.g., the shifting location of the fringe) keep changing and affecting the planning agenda. From another, the ability to expand boundaries does not lie with the metropolitan agency but, rather, with the provincial government. Thus, the naturally occurring forces that generate metropolitan expansion demand institutional, professional, and political responses that must, themselves, be planned for. When establishing metropolitan or city-region planning regions provincial governments should be committed to conducting a regular review of boundaries and powers.

A second lesson involves the recognition of the need to join planning capacity with governing capacity. This need stems as much from the unfortunate experience of those metropolitan planning agencies that could only offer advice as it does from the practical need to guide the efforts of agencies and authorities to implement regional plans. In the instance of further metropolitan expansion, we can only expect the need for a single governmental focal point to become more insistent as this is really the only way to ensure integrated planning. The need for regional coordination of services and planning actions will, thus, become even more crucial.

The third lesson involves the style and quality of governing metropolitan areas and city-regions. Two factors will be crucial in revising current approaches. One concerns resolving the inherent tension between metropolitan authorities and constituent municipalities so that regional needs and goals can be met and local interests protected. The lack of such a balance has plagued metropolitan planning from the outset and remains unresolved. To this perennial problem of metropolitan and regional governance we now add the growing demand for more participatory arrangements of governing, for processes that are more inclusive of the interests in metropolitan areas and city-regions.

Thus, as the future unfolds, those involved in regional planning will still have to contend with a number of unresolved problems. In all of these, the need for greater provincial involvement is crucial. As we can see from past practice, we must allow for evolving boundaries, unite substantive areas, and provide for more effective metropolitan and regional governance. As new trends and forces begin to impinge on regional planning, it is crucial that we deal with its past shortcomings. Even this will not be enough. Several other underlying issues need to be confronted before we can achieve a more effective paradigm for the future. We turn now to a discussion of several of these.

Key Questions Still to Be Considered

As regional planning has evolved, a number of questions have persisted that go to the essential nature of this field. These are less functional than are the issues of, for example, linking metropolitan planning and governance or uniting land and environmental planning. They are also not like the contextual trends we discussed at the beginning of this chapter. These questions are inherent within the ethos of regional planning and, perhaps because of this, never get fully answered; they have to be asked again with each new era of regional planning. It is appropriate, therefore, that we explore them briefly, if only to ensure that we are aware of them when we begin to describe the shape of future regional planning, as we do in the final section of this chapter.

What Makes an Issue "Regional"?

It may seem self-evident to say that regional planning is designed to deal with issues and concerns of a regional nature. However, what makes an issue "regional" as opposed to, say, local or provincial? Is an issue regional because it transcends the administrative boundaries of a single municipality? Or is an issue regional because the management of its impact and the handling of its costs fall between two levels of government? Or is it regional because the decisions relative to the costs and benefits of the proposed action can only be made in an interjurisdictional manner? These are elusive questions: they cut to the heart of the need for regional planning, and they require clarification. The establishment of a region for planning, and the associated institutions that accompany it, represents an intervention in the ongoing activities of an area and its governing arrangements for which there are no constitutional provisions. There is, thus, the important matter of how citizens and local governments perceive and accept regional planning. In other words, we can expect them to ask: Why does this issue require regional planning?

Further, if we turn to regional planning legislation, where we would expect to find an answer to our questions, there is no response. As Frisken (1993) notes in the case of the Greater Toronto Area, a major restraint on regional planning involved the uncertainty about the nature and requirements of regional plans as distinct from local plans, and this issue was not resolved by provincial planning legislation. Likewise, the otherwise commendable British Columbia Growth Strategies Act, which makes much of the need for a regional growth strategy, does not provide an operational definition of this concept. The story is the same in all provinces regarding definitions of the content and purposes of a regional plan.

It is possible, however, to approach this question from several sources: one involves the "subsidiarity" principle used in framing federal systems of government, another involves the criteria and principles developed in assessing regional government options in Canada and California, and a third involves the array of functions metropolitan and city-region authorities actually carry out. Before advancing our own criteria for defining "regional," we offer a brief review of these sources.

First, the subsidiarity principle used in considering national federations has relevance for regional governing arrangements, which, for the most part, are also federations. It states that decisions should be made at the level closest to the community that has the breadth of vision and the competence to make that decision (Healey 1997). Since some spatial or functional specialization and division of tasks is necessary in an urban or any other region (due to the scale of the area and the spread of development), coordination problems inevitably arise. Thus, the decision to locate a major airport or principal health care facility would fall to the agency whose working perspective takes in the entire region. Such decisions always directly affect some (but not all) localities; those affected would, under this principle, be able to be part of the decision-making process.

Second, principles that identify the roles of an agency for regional planning and governance have emerged in a number of reviews. A survey of citizens and city planning directors in California (Baldassare 1996) as well as reviews of two regional governments in Ontario – Metro Toronto (Tonks 1996) and Ottawa–Carleton (Bartlett 1988; Kirby 1992) – provide some clear direction for establishing regional roles. For example, from the California survey we can derive the following principle:

- The regional government role should be one of "system-maintenance," that is, maintaining functions that affect the entire regional "system," such as public transit, solid waste disposal, water supply and distribution, environmental protection, and open space preservation (Baldassare 1996).

This principle also emerges in reviews of Metro Toronto and Ottawa–Carleton regional governments:

- A regional government has a role when it is necessary to coordinate a service or a function over the whole region to ensure the service is provided effectively in all parts of the region.

The Ontario reviews offer three additional principles for invoking a role for a regional government:

- when there are cost savings and when quality is improved by having large-scale operations (i.e., when economies of scale can be achieved)
- when it is important that all residents throughout the region have access to a common standard of service
- when matters affect the long-term well-being of the region.

Further, it was pointed out that, unless there are good reasons to the contrary, each resident of the region should be able to participate in the decisions of both the local government and the regional government (Bartlett 1988; Kirby 1992).

While these principles help narrow the search for an answer to the question of what constitutes a regional issue, they do not provide a clear picture of what this might look like in practice. So we look at actual practice in three Canadian metropolitan regions – Metro Toronto (before the recent amalgamation), the Greater Vancouver Regional District, and the recently formed commission for Metropolitan Montreal – and examine the responsibilities of each agency:

- *Metro Toronto:* Debenture borrowing for capital works in all its constituent municipalities, police protection, transportation for the disabled, the environment (including water purification, trunk sewers, garbage disposal, and recycling), ambulance services, hospital grants, welfare assistance, metropolitan parks and libraries, and planning and development services (including approval of local plans, subdivision approval, and condominium approval).
- *Greater Vancouver Regional District:* Regional water supply and sewerage, solid and liquid waste management, hospital planning, air quality, public housing, regional parks, regional strategic planning, and transportation planning (through the Greater Vancouver Transportation Authority).
- *Montreal Development Commission:* Expected responsibilities include the power to levy taxes and charge user fees; prepare an economic development plan; and coordinate land use, economic development, transportation, waste disposal, environmental protection, arts and culture, and some policing.

These lists of functions are markedly similar despite some obvious differences due to each metropolitan region's geographical and political contexts.

Further, they appear to fit with the principles (noted above) pertaining to regional scope, scale economies, and common standards of service. Complete uniformity should not be expected, however, because regions differ, as do the political values that ultimately inform the process of formulating such lists. One final note: some functions, for example, parks and libraries, have both a regional and a local level.

The larger question of what makes an issue regional can now be broached more solidly. We suggest that "regional issues" are those that arise when:

1 a problem (issue, policy, program) is important throughout all or a large part of a region
2 it is essential to apply uniform planning, policy, and practice across the entire region
3 a problem (issue, policy, program) affects the well-being of the region as a whole
4 the management of the impact of an action or decision, including its costs (by the private sector and/or higher levels of government) falls between two levels of government
5 it is necessary to maintain functions that are vital to the entire region's system of activities.

The foregoing criteria will never completely resolve the larger question, for that question reflects an inherent characteristic of all regional planning situations. A planning region encompasses all the "parts" of a large area (the local communities and municipalities) but is itself "part" of some larger whole (a province, which, in turn, is part of the nation). A region is a "holon," to use Koestler (1978) and Wilber's (1997b) term, but so, too, are the municipalities below and the province above; each level has roles to play in making and implementing plans. Although resolving the question of what makes an issue regional seems only to involve the division of tasks between the local and regional levels, it also involves divisions of tasks between regional and provincial levels. The implication of this arrangement for regional planners lies in the need to seek the cooperation of the constituent parts. This is as true for non-metropolitan regions as it is for metropolitan regions. We turn now to another facet of this tension within regional planning.

Who Speaks for the Region?
The establishment of a planning region identifies functions, situations, and qualities that are neither local nor provincial and to which regional agencies must pay particular attention. Initially, these special aspects of the region are manifested through informal processes and pressures (from both political bodies and citizens) to create some form of regional body that can speak to these interests. The question posed here concerns both the form and the effectiveness of

the formal arrangements that are intended to "speak for the region." The experience in metropolitan and city-region planning is the most illuminating, but the issue is often equally insistent within rural and other regional planning settings.

The members of a metropolitan or other regional planning body are, typically, municipal politicians who have been appointed by their municipal councils to represent the regional unit. There is a modest exception in British Columbia's regional district system (and those modelled after it), where non-municipal areas have directly elected representatives who serve on the regional body. In both cases, local interests rather than region-wide interests determine who serves on the regional body. In addition to the political participants, it should be noted that most regional bodies employ a staff of planners and other officials whose major obligation is to the regional unit. Many observers voiced concern about the difficulties, under these arrangements, of effectively promoting, if not debating, region-wide issues and proposals affecting the region.

Among the concerns is the tendency for indirectly elected regional councillors to take a parochial (i.e., municipal) viewpoint because of where their electoral power base is located. Another is double membership on both a local and regional council, which imposes an undue workload on councillors and tends to result in regional interests receiving less attention. Possibly most important is the lack of accountability to the public. A recent commentator (Kellas 1998, 3) has said of Vancouver's regional arrangements: "Since the public is not directly involved in establishing the GVRD Board ... no one runs for office on regional issues and there is a tendency to address regional public concerns – such as growth management, transportation and the environment – through a local perspective." Despite such concerns, one of the newest metropolitan bodies, the Commission de développement de la métropole (Metropolitan Development Commission in Montreal) was created with an indirectly elected governing body.

As a consequence, we often find the regional perspective being represented more forcibly and consistently by the region's technical and administrative staff than by its councillors. This can create a tension between, say, the regional planners and the regional councillors – a tension that will usually be at its greatest in the preparation of the regional plan and in its implementation (Smith and Bayne 1994). Another unelected source of both support for, and criticism of, regional interests is often the local media who allegedly "speak" for the region. Within this regional milieu, most observers agree that the situation could be improved immeasurably if citizens of the region directly elected members of the region's governing body. If this were to occur, then the regional body would be composed of people who could genuinely claim to speak for the region and could be accountable for the positions they took. Regardless, there remains the question: How can valid local concerns and experience be incorporated into the deliberations of the regional body?

How Can We Build Regional Understanding among Citizens?

The question of building regional understanding among citizens is closely related to those questions already discussed. The citizens of a region are a central fact of the region itself: it is with them that regional issues arise and it is both for them and to them that regional representatives speak. Citizens are the focal point of the tension between regional and local authorities, both of whom claim to speak for citizens of the region. Thus, the role of citizens can never be underestimated. Yet there is mounting evidence of a lack of a popular constituency for regional planning and other regional concerns. Therefore, while regional planning may be eminently logical to regional planners, the concepts used by regional planners and other advocates for regional services and administration may be too complex for most citizens (and many politicians).

The average citizen tends to view regional policies from the perspective of his or her community rather than from the perspective of the region. BC planners found that, when addressing development issues in connection with the new regional growth strategy provisions, few people supported the concept of the region (Harasym 1996). In other words, the validity of dealing with things regional was denied. A similar response was found in a study of citizen understanding with regard to the Greater Toronto Area (Tomalty 1997). There was much lower interest in area-wide planning issues than there was in those concerning specific neighbourhoods. Moreover, many were unaware of what the designation "Greater Toronto Area" actually meant. None of this bodes well for garnering support for regional issues. It also reinforces any tendency of local political leaders to oppose regional programs and projects, and, thus, it increases the tension between the regional and the local levels.

In Canada, the mere mention of regional planning and regional government often seems to conjure up images of centralization and provincial interference. This reaction emanates from the tradition of governance out of which spatial planning developed – a tradition that disliked the strong centralism of Britain as well as the unfettered localism of the United States, preferring a hybrid position between the two (Hodge 1985). This tradition is an important element when considering regional planning and governance because it affects what structural arrangements can be put in place (Healey et al. 1996). For example, strongly hierarchical structures do not garner widespread citizen support, while top-down provincial initiatives do (as we have seen with environmental issues). Healey (1997) points out that environmental issues often arise out of citizen interests that are not local (or even regional) in origin, much less governmental in character. And this raises the issue of how regional governance processes are to accommodate all who have a stake in a region's future. Increasingly, we find that, with regard to many public issues, leadership resides in interest groups that exist outside of formal structures. If these interests are seen to be ignored or excluded in regional deliberations, citizen support of regional initiatives will be hard to attain. Hence, regional authorities face the crucial task of achieving a balance between localism and centralism while, at the same time, being sufficiently inclusionary in their governance.

The promised benefits of regional planning and regional cooperation (such as increased global competitiveness for city-regions) tend to be rather abstract and distant, while the costs of, say, improved transit or waste disposal are immediate. As Katz (1997) points out, typical regional planning goals (such as providing more affordable housing or promoting more compact patterns) are viewed as increasing "density" and reducing the quality of life. Thus, motivating citizens to better understand regions and to support regional planning is not easy. Seemingly, we should be able to link the negative impacts of, say, urban sprawl and traffic congestion to the need for regional planning. However, in most people's eyes, this is an engineering question that is to be answered by providing more highway lanes or building rapid transit. At the same time, planners tend to discuss such problems in terms of "land use" and "transportation links" and the "need to maintain the balance between housing and jobs" – terminology many citizens find difficult to understand.

If the indications about the need for greater participation of citizens in regional affairs are correct, and if, conversely, there is a desire for a more enhanced civil society, then we need to deal with these discrepancies. Wray (1997, 15) suggests that we need to "nurture a regional consciousness among citizens and policy makers" and that we can do this by bringing various regional interests together to work on common goals, by forming regional civic associations, and by training leaders. Katz (1997) urges us to use visual imaging techniques to make clear the connection between what is done at the regional level and its importance to neighbourhoods.

Others cite European experiences that involve using a spatial organizing concept that can be expressed in graphic terms in order to build consensus among citizens, their organizations, and their local governments (Faludi 1996; Healey 1997). The aim is to convey both what is desirable and possible within regional planning: the Ottawa Greenbelt is a striking example of this approach (see Chapter 8). In other words, planning goals must be easily communicated to the public so that the benefits of regional planning are not only evident, but also encourage broad participation.

Can There Be Effective Regional Planning alongside Local Autonomy?

Regardless of how regional councillors are elected, there remains the dichotomy of regional and local interests, thus the question posed in the subheading. The answer to this question is relatively easy if the area is consolidated under the jurisdiction of a single planning and governing body (such as Winnipeg's Unicity). However, where a region is composed of a number of independent municipalities (which is the most common situation), the answer is more difficult. The establishment of a two-tier planning system, with both regional and local units, has been the customary way of reconciling these two perspectives: first, there is the need for some kind of regional authority to address area-wide needs and problems and to overcome interjurisdictional conflict; second, there is the belief that land-use planning and planning that affects land use is properly the responsibility of local communities (Jacobs 1989). Supposedly, the first need is satisfied by the upper tier and the second need by the lower tier; however, in practice, this reconciliation has always proved difficult.

The act of a province creating a regional planning organization – metropolitan, city-regional, or rural – entails a restructuring of powers that has large political ramifications for the existing municipalities, the regional body, and the province. It involves, at the outset, trade-offs between those aspects under regional control and those under local control as well as, later, an appropriate balance between the two. The experience in Canada is that regional planning organizations have seldom had sufficient powers to be effective agents in managing regional problems. This has been especially irksome in metropolitan and city-regions. Much of the real power over the planning of Canadian metropolitan regions is vested in municipal governments, as is governance over land and physical development. This is equally true when an ad hoc regional planning body is superimposed over existing rural municipalities, as occurred with Alberta's regional planning commissions, British Columbia's regional districts, and regional planning commissions in several Atlantic provinces. Moreover, the usual legislative requirement that local plans must "conform" to the regional plan turns out to be weak, with no powers of compliance being allocated to the regional authority.

Further, from the point of view of the community and its local government, a regional authority often tends to be seen as representing a form of "centralization" and as the local agent of the province. In other words, as Magnusson (1985) notes, it represents one of the instruments by which provincial policies are "imposed" on the municipalities. Thus, because of this inherent conflict, regional planning operates within an ambiguous environment, thereby creating profound uncertainty and elusiveness about its role and powers (Perloff 1957).

It is also worth noting that traditional regional planning theory tends either to gloss over, give short shrift to, or completely ignore the basic conflict between local autonomy and the need for area-wide planning. For example, even in classic works on regional planning by people such as Hall (1974), McDowell (1986), and Branch (1988), there is barely a mention of this conflict. There seem to be three assumptions underlying traditional regional planning theory: (1) there is a functional logic of metropolitan and regional integration, (2) the benefits of a regional approach will be so apparent that local governments and their citizens will willingly trade off some degree of autonomy, and (3) regional planning represents a way of dealing with regional problems and needs on their own merits rather than having them subjected to parochial interests.

Of course, the real world of regional planning is far different from that which these assumptions portray. Regional planning is a thoroughly political process beginning with the act of defining a planning region and creating a regional planning organization. These acts harbour an eternal paradox within the realm of regional affairs – one that has counterparts in many other areas of human endeavour. To reiterate, planning is a normative process that involves making difficult value-based judgments, and it deals with a basic dialectic between facts and values. It is relatively easy for planners to determine *which* needs are to be addressed (e.g., the need for a metropolitan expressway or a regional park). But translating this into *whose* needs are to be served – the needs of those who live in the municipality or the needs of those who live in the larger region – is much more problematic. In the realm of city planning, the counterpart to the local/regional dichotomy is to be found in the neighbourhood/city dichotomy (Hodge 1998). The new spatial forms we see emerging in our city-regions bring home the need to achieve a better understanding of such dichotomies and to try to determine the structural and other strategies that are most likely to be suitable to meeting their evolving economic, social, and physical needs. Beyond these realities are those that embody the vast, complex webs of cultural relationships (e.g., social concerns, business concerns, environmental concerns, and so on) that exist within regions and that, at an informal level, act to mediate many regional issues.

In view of the above, there is a need for more research concerning the types of regional decision-making arrangements that work within the fragmented governing systems found in planning regions, especially in metropolitan and city-regions. Even with years of experience we still do not know how best to achieve effective regional growth management. Porter (1989) provides suggested directions for the requisite research in this area:

1 identify areas in which smaller units of government can effectively solve problems
2 identify issues that have impacts beyond the boundaries of existing local governments, and propose new structures for dealing with them
3 provide models of regional and provincial decision making (and service provision) in which decisions are currently made by many fragmented governments.

And there are recent indications that these leads are being followed with some success (Pastor et al. 2000; Calthorpe and Fulton 2000). To these we would add the necessity of examining ways in which institutional capacity can be structured so as to accommodate the input of both formal governments and the wider society, allowing both to become more inclusionary and collaborative (Healey 1997).

How Best to Govern Regions?

The need for further research on appropriate regional governance systems is given added weight when we recognize the future importance of city-regions in the economic life of Canada. But this need goes beyond economic values to social values, as is seen in the work of many American and Canadian observers (Dodge 1996; Sancton 1994; Wallis 1992, 1993, 1994; Wight 1998a). More and more, we hear that a fresh approach to governing is required – one that focuses on *governance* rather than on *government* and that emphasizes process and inclusiveness as much as structure. In part, this is a reflection of the concerns about civil society to which we referred earlier, and, in part, it is a reflection of the idea that governing at all levels needs to involve a wider array of stakeholders. And, not least, it is a reflection of the recognition of the complex web of social relations, both inside and outside of formal government, through which public policies are aired, debated, mediated, and resolved. New partnerships are argued for, within which the roles of participants would be transformed: the state (the province or regional authority) moves from being sole guardian and rule-maker to being initiator and facilitator; business moves from being supplier to being in partnership with governments and citizens; and citizens move from being mere consumers to being actors, stewards, and decision makers.

The concept of involving stakeholders in decision making is coming increasingly into practice throughout North America (Innes 1996; Susskind and Cruikshank 1987). "Stakeholder groups," "advisory councils," "negotiated rule-making groups," "round tables," and "citizens' commissions" are some of the terms used to describe the entities involved in this process. Edmonton's Alberta Capital Region Alliance and British Columbia's Commission on Resources and Environment initiative, both of which involve local residents in regional resource and environment decisions, are two notable Canadian examples. Another is the South Island Sustainable Communities Network (for the Victoria metropolitan region), which links community organizations, concerned individuals, and other groups that are seeking innovative growth management approaches for their region (SISC 1998). Typically, membership in these new regional initiatives includes representatives of business groups, neighbourhood organizations, Aboriginal peoples, environmental groups, religious institutions, universities, and individuals. Indeed, Canada's record of establishing multi-stakeholder round tables is widely respected as a means of allowing all sectors to conciliate differences, create preventative strategies, and cooperatively influence governmental planning (Stark 1990).

In essence, this pluralistic approach to governing regions emphasizes the need for inclusive regional organizations both to facilitate public decision making and to broaden the array and support for new ideas about development, growth management, and environmental protection (as well as to counter not-in-my-back-yard parochialism) (Wray 1997). Governance of regions, however, is not simply a case of making government more open and accountable, of seeing that it receives advice from a wider array of participants; rather, it involves making sure that all stakeholders collaborate in decision making, sharing power, and in strengthening support for regional policy. And it is built on a base of both "hard infrastructure" (for making formal decisions and carrying out regulations) and "soft infrastructure" (for facilitating and sustaining relations among stakeholders) (Healey 1997). Both top-down and bottom-up approaches coexist within such arrangements because they are each natural social processes and are mutually supportive with regard to sustaining stability and growth over the long term. The final form that this will take within any given region will need to be "invented," and it must take into account that region's history and geography (Healey 1997).

Of course, the connection between a pluralist vision of a region's future and how to implement that vision is tenuous (Helling 1998). The identification of the preferred regional development pattern must be translated into action and, not least, into public infrastructure investments and land-use regulations. Herein lies the major challenge: Do we design and maintain institutional arrangements for regional planning and governance? Or do we, as in the past, let public policy be decided largely by the market and the state? In short, this issue reflects the delicate nature of the relationships that will be involved in future regional planning processes; that is, relationships that are open and inclusive and that, concomitantly, unsettle established structures without destroying them. Nor is this a matter of isolating the region or severing it from the territory of which it is a part. Paradoxically, as Friedmann (1992) has pointed out, local and regional action can only be effective within a strong state.

Towards a New Paradigm for Regional Planning

In the manner of a stage play, the topics in the preceding sections provide a backdrop, settings, and stage instructions for the further unfolding of the character of regional planning in the twenty-first century. And, as with a stage play, the future of regional planning will unfold according to the players and their interpretation of the play within which they have been placed. Thus, we can be fairly certain of the direction regional planning will be taking even if we cannot predict its precise route or destination. Nevertheless, it seems certain that there will be a further transformation of regional planning in coming decades, just as there has been during the past six.

One approach to regional planning may be highly sensible and rational; however, it is becoming clear that, in the future, no single "map," or theory, will suffice. It is not that earlier maps – such as Geddes' valley section, or Friedmann's development regions, or the Tennessee Valley Authority – are wrong; it is simply that the world has reached a new stage of development. For example, large city-regions are now part of urbanization, and this has resulted in the transformation of some non-urban regions. These spatial transformations have been accompanied by social and intellectual transformations occasioned by a host of factors, including environmental awareness, civil society concerns, international inequities, postmodern critiques, and gender and multicultural realities. In combination, these spatial and social factors portend a new, communicative, more inclusive, and relational view of regional planning – one that encompasses our previous understanding and doctrine but that goes beyond it to cover emerging spatial, economic, social, and environmental dimensions as well as new approaches to regional governance. In other words, we are moving towards a new paradigm.

This new paradigm represents a further evolution of the mix of ideas, methodology, and social relations that have occurred in regional planning since its beginnings (Kuhn 1970). It will enfold our accumulated experience and theory – our previous paradigms – and will probably reorder parts of them, moving on to frame the most appropriate approach to future regional planning. The evidence shows us that we are moving to a new level of development in the field of regional planning and that significant shifts are occurring in how we practise and in the context in which this practice occurs. As with most paradigm shifts, the change is not instantaneous but, rather, is the result of an accumulation of factors. Thus, the direction of these shifts is already fairly well known, as we have seen in the trends and lessons discussed in foregoing chapters.

Let us now set out the most likely future direction of regional planning practice in terms of its content and focus, its methods, its administration, and its participants. Here we note the prominent shifts likely to occur *from* its late twentieth-century orientation *to* its twenty-first-century orientation:

1 shifts in content and focus
2 shifts in methods and procedures
3 shifts in administration and governance
4 shifts in participation.

Shifts in Content and Focus

The content of regional planning (i.e., what regional plans are about) and the practice of regional planners (i.e., how planners plan) are being affected by current and emerging trends and forces. The general tendency will be a shift from fixed perspectives to those that accommodate a variety of regional situations and that allow for a variety of outcomes:

- *from* a "function" regional planning doctrine *to* one in which "territory" is the dominant, but not exclusive, doctrine

- *from* four distinctive kinds of regional planning (resource, metropolitan, economic, rural) *to* a greater variety of forms that arise and are configured as needed (including, among others, the city-region)
- *from* dissociated land use, economic, and environmental planning *to* integrated land use, economic, and ecosystems planning
- *from* central city and periphery dichotomies *to* inclusive, open city-regions
- *from* "producing" services *to* "arranging" services through growing interdependencies.

Shifts in Methods and Procedures

Central to any paradigm shift are changes in methodology. In regional planning we can expect a shift that is at once more focused on achieving plans and more integrated in concept:

- *from* comprehensive planning *to* strategic planning
- *from* physical planning methods *to* sustainability planning and ecosystems planning
- *from* the use of regulations, coercion, and direct controls on the market *to* consensus building, volunteerism, and indirect incentives
- *from* relatively low-level relationships (such as communication, coordination, and cooperation) *to* higher degrees of interaction and collaboration through relational links that cross organizational divisions, cultural barriers, and disjunctures in the division of power (Healey 1997).

Shifts in Administration and Governance

The workings of regional planning agencies will need to shift, as many already have, to broader based organizations that are able to accommodate more interests and to respond to a greater variety of stimuli, from globalization to bioregionalism. Not least will be the need for commensurate shifts in commitments and relations both with and within provincial governments and their ministries with regard to their dealings with regional planning agencies of whatever form:

- *from* government structures *to* institutions of governance that have the capacity to build consensus regarding comprehensive long-term visions for the region
- *from* exclusively hard infrastructure *to* the inclusion of soft infrastructure for decision making (so that governments can develop and sustain informal relations among non-government stakeholders)
- *from* centralization *to* decentralization in organizational structure
- *from* hierarchical "commanding" *to* horizontal "networking"

- *from* governmental resource bundles that restrain regional planning implementation *to* bundles that expand the implementation capacity of regional
agencies
- *from* nation-state and province building *to* subprovincial and city-state
building.

Shifts in Participation

Paradigm shifts also involve the changing social relations of participants. In
our case, we are concerned with who gets involved in regional planning. Following upon the other shifts, there will be an expansion of the number and
types of participants:

- *from* bureaucracies and institutions *to* a much broader involvement of interest groups
- *from* predominantly government actions and decisions *to* coalitions and
networks, including private, not-for-profit, and volunteer sectors.

The precise shape of this paradigm must be left to the interaction of future
forces and players; however, we can be fairly certain of three things: (1) regional planning will be multifaceted (i.e., no single ideology will guide it); (2)
it will be more focused on realizing its plans (i.e., being "advisory" will not be
enough); and (3) it will be obliged to be more holistic (i.e., it will link inherent substantive areas in both word and deed. Remarkably, many of these shifts
were presaged by Eric Trist (1970) three decades ago in a paper he delivered to
the 1968 Canadian Institute of Planners conference.

There can be little doubt that this new paradigm will emerge in regional
planning. As Wannop (1995) has noted, regional tendencies endure. Although
various events and political pressures seem to have overtaken many regional
planning efforts in Canada, the need for a regional perspective in many recent
initiatives, especially regarding the environment and economic development,
attest to the truth of Wannop's observation. Regional round tables and forums, regional visioning exercises, and regional programs for sustainable development (which, today, seem almost commonplace) reassert the necessity
of planning at the regional level. These new initiatives join long-lived regional
planning efforts in our metropolitan areas and in the realm of conservation.

Regional planning activities, whether today's or tomorrow's, may seem
unfocused, but that is the nature of this particular social undertaking. Few
planning regions are as stable as is the traditional river basin, and few regional
planning issues fit permanently into administrative structures. As we have
discerned from six decades of experience with Canadian regional planning,
the field has evolved: it has had to respond to new situations, and it has had to

discard inappropriate methods. Regional planning is not a field in decline but, rather, a field that is currently undergoing a significant period of change. There is, as Wannop (1995, 364) so wisely says, "an irrepressible regional imperative" that guarantees a future for regional planning.

Notes

Introduction: Regional Planning in Perspective

1 For this distinction between regional planning activities in nation-building and province-building phases we are indebted to Ian Wight.

2 The establishment of the large regional "municipality" in northern Quebec to facilitate activities of the James Bay Development Corporation, where no local government previously existed, is a rare exception.

Chapter 1: Roots of Regional Planning

1 By a "precursor" we mean a person, idea, event, or movement that goes further than before: a forerunner, antecedent, harbinger, or predecessor.

2 See also Hall 1974, 1988; Weaver 1984; and Aberley 1994.

3 Similarly, in the United States, the railroad engineer George Mortimer Pullman (who invented the Pullman railroad car) built a model town named after himself, outside Chicago, in 1910. A similar "copycat" new-town building activity took place in Canada in the 1910s and 1920s when industrialists built a number of new planned "resource towns" to house their workers in remote areas. These industrialists themselves, or their architects, visited some of the British model towns to learn about them (see Robinson 1962; Hodge 1998).

4 Originally entitled *To-morrow: A Peaceful Path to Real Reform* and published in London in 1898 by Swan-Sonneschein. It was re-issued four years later under its current title, *Garden Cites of To-morrow*. In 1946 it was republished (in London by Faber & Faber) with the same title (with a preface by F.J. Osborne and an introduction by Lewis Mumford); and a paperback edition came out in 1965. It was reprinted again in 1970 and 1974.

5 According to Hall and Ward (1998), the exact original title of Howard's book is *To-Morrow! A Peaceful Path to Real Reform*. Note the use of the hyphen and exclamation mark. This would seem to reinforce Luccarelli's (1995, n. 2: 76) point that, given the original title of his book, Howard favoured less radical and less utopian formulations and, specifically, must have thought of the garden city as an alternative to a socialist revolution, which was, indeed, a popular idea during his time.

6 The "regional" content of Howard's work is detailed in Hall and Ward (1998, ch. 10: 171-90). For those interested in Howard's legacy, the Hall and Ward (1998) book is a significant contribution; its first part focuses on Howard's influence over the last hundred years.

7 Much of this discussion on the "anarchists" is drawn from Weaver (1984).

8 These contacts ranged from Reclus and Kropotkin to John Dewey, Thorstein Veblen, Jane Adams, and Lewis Mumford, to mention but a few. Geddes advised kings, prime ministers, and other rulers around the world about how to run their cities. He also built the famous Outlook Tower ("Camera Obscura"), which still stands in Edinburgh – a local survey centre in which people of all kinds would come to understand the relationship of the human and natural environment.

9 Artur Glikson describes an application of this method to regions in northern Israel and the Netherlands (1955, 78-84).

10 Geddes' young assistant, who had studied with the famous Oxford geographer, H. Mackinder, transformed the concept into environment, function, and organism (Dickinson 1970, 25).

11 These national conferences on city planning led to the formation, in 1919, of the American City Planning Institute, the forerunner of the American Institute of Planners (AIP), so-named in 1938, which is now known as the American Planning Association (APA), with 30,000 members. The American Planning Association actually resulted from a merger on 1 October 1978 between the American Institute of Planners and the American Society of Planning Officials (ASPO). The American Planning Association encompasses its professional institute, known as the American Institute of Certified Planners (AICP), with 13,500 members.

12 The commission had hosted the sixth annual National City Planning Conference in 1914 in Toronto, and this is how Adams came to its attention.

13 Not to be confused with the Regional Planning Association of America (RPAA), which we discuss in the section that follows. The Regional Plan Association (RPA) is a non-governmental organization, which was founded in 1923 and is still active in the thirty-one county New York, New Jersey, and Connecticut metropolitan area. This makes it the oldest and arguably the most influential independent, non-governmental regional planning organization in the United States and probably the entire world.

14 Except for Simpson (1985), we were not aware of the use of the term "insurgent planners" by anyone else until quite recently when we came across two uses of the term but for different circumstances. Leonie Sandercock (1998a) used it in a recent collection of edited papers referring to "insurgent planning histories," which represent alternative traditions of planning, including community-based and community-driven *historiographies.* Also, see the paper by James Holston (1998), "Making the Invisible Visible" in the Sandercock collection. A second recent use of the term, we have discovered, was made by Patrick Mazza (1997) in a review of a recent book by Dorman (1993), which explores the legacy of the American regionalism movement of the 1920s, 1930s, and 1940s. Mazza entitled his review of Dorman's book, "Uncovering the Hidden History of Regionalism: The American Regionalist Insurgency of the 1920s–1940s." The Mazza review can be found on the "Cascadia Planet" website (www.tnews. com/text/regionalist_insurgency.html). Cascadia Planet is an ecological information service based in Portland, Oregon, providing news and views about creating sustainability from the whole-systems perspective.

15 Coincidentally, Stein was to become some thirty years later the chief planner for the consulting team responsible for the master plan for the new town of Kitimat in northwestern British Columbia.

16 Other members who contributed to the group's work and achievements were Catherine Bauer (who was appointed executive director and research assistant to Stein), Frederick Ackerman, Charles Whittaker, Stuart Chase, Albert Mayer, Henry Churchill, Charles Ascher, Robert Bruere, and Robert Kohn.

17 For detailed discussion of these and other RPAA criticisms of Adams' New York regional plan, see Hall 1988; Sussman 1976; Simpson 1985; and Scott 1969, 1971.

18 For the history and contributions of the RPAA, see Lubove 1967; Sussman 1976; Parsons 1994.

19 This limitation was to plague new towns the world over, including the post Second World War British new towns program, even today.

20 Howard Odum never achieved the reputation or acclaim that he deserved. His important contributions were all but passed over. For example, The *Encyclopedia of Urban Planning* (Whittick 1974) discusses the work of MacKaye, Mumford, Stein, Bauer, and Wright (all members of the RPAA, it will be recalled), but does not mention Odum. Mel Scott in his history of *American City Planning* (1969, 1971) refers to Odum on five different occasions but never hints at his major ideas or impact on regional planning.

21 The Tennessee Valley experiment actually had begun with construction of a large dam and two munitions plants on the Tennessee River at Muscle Shoals, Alabama, during the First World War. After the war, these facilities proved to be a political "hot potato" because of the ideological implications of government ownership – a number of groups (including the RPAA) and several influential US congressional politicians advocated formation of a public corporation to operate Muscle Shoals. The dispute remained unsolved until President Roosevelt took the matter in hand, at the beginning of the New Deal, when his latitude for implementing a

variety of program proposals was considerable. Drawing on his enthusiasm for planning and rural reform, Roosevelt expanded the Muscle Shoals project into a project of comprehensive river basin development. Accordingly, he proclaimed that "this power development of war days leads logically to national planning for a complete river watershed involving many states and the future lives and welfare of millions" (1938, 122).

22 For a fuller discussion of this conference as well as other events and developments in the early history of the conservation movement in Canada, see Thorpe (1961).

23 This initiative was taken to avoid the same recessionary and unemployment conditions that followed the First World War.

24 Much of the material for this section is drawn from a 1995 special issue of the *International Regional Science Review*, which focused on the history, status, and future of regional science since its beginnings in 1954, especially the introductory article by Andrew Isserman.

25 See the papers in various issues of the *Papers and Proceedings of the Regional Science Association*; see also Friedmann and Alonso (1964).

26 For example, Robert Owen's concepts might be compared with the more mature versions of those of Benton MacKaye and Lewis Mumford, as could those of Ebenezer Howard's "Social City" and Thomas Adams' New York regional plan.

27 However, it should be noted that the participants in a round table convened in New York in April 2000 (in conjunction with the annual meeting of the American Planning Association) to explore the extent to which the RPAA shaped the vision of twentieth-century regionalism and how that vision is still relevant today, raised some caveats. Doubts were expressed as to whether the social problems of today could be "solved" by manipulating physical form (as RPAA essentially assumed), especially since the agendas of sixty years ago and today are not the same. Sixty years ago, there was also a naivety about the role of markets and a limited vision of the regional problem as it exists today. Regional planning today also has to contend with more diverse and complex social and economic issues than was the situation in the 1920s (see Seltzer 2000).

Chapter 2: Key Features of Regional Planning

1 Wilber (1997b) elaborates these arrangements of wholes and parts for which there are analogous and cogent issues for regional planning. As he notes, holons depend on both being the "agency" of action and achieving the willingness of parts to share in "communion" with other component parts. There is an inherent tension in this arrangement for all holons, including planning regions, which we shall see affecting regional planning in fundamental ways in Chapters 5 and 6 and later case studies.

2 Although Friedmann and Weaver do not mention it, this model seems equally applicable to a range of professional activities involved in the public domain, including city planning, social work, and public education.

3 Those familiar with international affairs will know that these instances parallel the trend to regional "self-management" (Williams 1983) occurring in many other countries.

Chapter 3: The Regional Boundary Imperative

1 The regional districts that cover almost all of British Columbia are not fully functioning regional municipalities although they are specified in the province's Municipal Act, now the Local Government Act.

2 These derive from what Arthur Maass (1959a) terms the "areal division of powers," which in Canada we find in the national Constitution and in provincial legislation. See Chapter 4 for a detailed discussion.

3 A further question that is usually begged is whether or not the planning region still exists when the planning purposes have been attained.

4 "Geotechnics" is the word used in the original quotation, which was reported by Benton Mackaye from a conversation in which Geddes insisted on a more comprehensive term that included planning and conservation but also conveyed the scientific nature of "making the earth more habitable," as *Webster's* dictionary at the time defined geotechnics.

5 Although city planners face this same tension of the technical and normative aspects of planning, the predetermined boundaries of municipalities are not an essential cause of it. An

interesting variation on the regional planner's boundary dilemma is often encountered when city planners wish to establish boundaries for neighbourhood planning. See, for example, Gerald Hodge (1998).

6 Reiner also points to the broader statistical issue of using averages. Such measures may encompass a variety of distributions. For example, two regions may have the same average per capita income (or education level and housing quality), but the distribution within each may be quite different. That is, one may have many poor and few rich residents while the other has few poor, few rich, and many middle-income residents, resulting in the same average. Reiner urges care in the use of averages.

Chapter 4: Formal Bases of Regional Planning

1 Even an agency that has prepared a regional plan meant only to be advisory will have had to acquire some powers just to be able to undertake the task.

2 Highly centralized states such as dictatorships usually represent the least amount of power distribution. But even here some sharing is required, especially if the territory is large.

3 The major exceptions to this principle are the inherent powers over resources held under treaty by some Aboriginal peoples.

4 Of course, the earliest regional delimitations would be the initial division of the territory of Canada into Upper and Lower Canada, Rupert's Land, the three Maritime provinces, and the (later) Northwest Territories.

5 Ontario's Baldwin Act of 1849 was the first comprehensive provincial areal division of power covering municipal government, although a few cities and towns in other provinces had self-governing status before this time, notably Saint John, New Brunswick, in 1785. The first provincial legislation allocating power to local school boards was Ontario's Public School Act in 1816.

6 Rhodes (1986) actually lists an initial governmental resource – constitutional-legal – which is equivalent to the basic areal division of power discussed above. And Khakee and Low (1996) offer a sixth resource – planning – which we include here. In addition, a regional agency may be given responsibility, or what might be called "development resources," to supervise or even provide specified public services that are regional in nature, including parks and hospitals. The latter are a specific attribute of financial resources.

7 A major aim of the recent amalgamation of Metro Toronto's municipalities into the so-called "mega-city" was, according the provincial government, to eliminate this very tension and clarify responsibilities for planning and development. New community councils will only be advisory to the metropolitan government, thereby effectively reversing the areal division of power.

8 Actual practice in regional planning may sometimes exceed the planning resources that have, or seem to have, been allocated. The Central Kootenay Regional District in British Columbia is a case in point in which it saw the need to broach economic development questions in its planning (see Chapter 5). The Peace River Regional Planning Commission's practice also exceeded its nominal planning resources, at least until the early 1980s.

Chapter 5: Planning Rural Regions and Their Communities

1 Much of the data and the rural framework in this section derive from Hodge (1988).

2 The outer edge of the urban field is approximately 150 kilometres or two hours' driving time, according to Friedmann and Miller (1964).

3 There are special cases in which land use competition is salient in rural regions such as the Niagara Escarpment and the Niagara fruit lands and, of course, in the immediate fringe areas of other metropolitan regions.

4 Even the Lower Mainland Regional Planning Board did not prepare a region-wide plan until fifteen years after its inception.

5 It is not surprising that this agency should have taken this approach since Floyd Dykeman, a strong advocate for integrated rural planning, was its director at the time. See Dykeman (1988).

6 In the early 1990s, the province authorized the development of a Slocan Valley land planning exercise under its CORE initiative (see Chapter 6), which achieved a high degree of consensus among region residents and interests, only to have the province make forestry land allocations contrary to it.

Chapter 6: Regional Economic Development Planning

1 The index the ARDA program used to define regions that would receive assistance was based on a predetermined percentage of the population with "low" income levels within census subdivisions (e.g., municipalities, townships, parishes). It was flawed not only in its inability to distinguish between rural areas with different structural features (e.g., farm versus non-farm activities) but in other ways as well (see Paris 1967).

2 This is a reflection of the convention of regional "equity" practised in developing federal programs, which tries to ensure that more than one region or province benefits from the expenditures of federal funds (see Gunton and Weaver 1982).

3 Unemployment rates can be misleading, because a person has to be seeking work to count as unemployed. When people stop looking for work because so few jobs are available, their numbers will not be included in the unemployment rate. Thus, the participation rate may be a better indicator to compare job availability among regions. Regions with the lowest participation rates include Newfoundland's south coast, from Port-aux-Basques to Placentia Bay (the lowest, with 32.9 percent); Newfoundland's west coast and Labrador (36.4 percent); Quebec's Gaspésie and Magdalen Islands (37 percent); Newfoundland's northeast coast (41.9 percent); and Nova Scotia's Cape Breton Island (42 percent). These are followed by northeast New Brunswick; Nova Scotia's south shore down to Yarmouth; the northern counties of Nova Scotia; the Saguenay–Lac Saint Jean area of Quebec; and Newfoundland's Avalon Peninsula, which takes in St. John's. Canada's top regions, with participation rates as high as 70 percent, are found in Alberta and British Columbia. Further, the picture provided by these seventy-two regions is more specific than using gross provincial rates and shows up intraprovincial differences in regional economic well-being (see Little 1996).

4 Gertler was a prominent member of the regional planning teams that developed regional plans for the Mactaquac River Valley and Prince Edward Island.

5 As noted earlier in the text, there were some prominent exceptions to this, notably, in the Mactaquac, BAEQ, Lesser Slave Lake, and Interlake regions.

Chapter 7: Regional Planning for Resource Conservation and Development and for the Environment

1 A major exception concerns the extent of the inherent powers over natural resources held by Aboriginal peoples, which is a central concern of Aboriginal land claims negotiations.

2 The IBP officially ended in 1974. The task of completing its work in Canada was taken on by the federal government, first through the Associate Committee for Ecological Reserves and subsequently the Advisory Committee on Canadian Ecosystem Conservation.

3 Revel (1981) includes a list and description of proposed northern ecological sites. Some 150 sites had been identified and documented at the time Revel published his work, but as of 1986 the federal government had designated only one.

4 For a detailed discussion of the protected areas study, including their characteristics, a provincial overview of the key gaps, priorities, and remaining opportunities, and the philosophy underlying the strategy, see British Columbia Land Use Coordination Office (1997).

5 Some conservation authority regions comprised two or more river basins.

6 "Meewasin" is the Cree word for "beautiful."

7 The Ontario government initiated several other joint provincial-municipal studies at the same time (see Cullingworth 1987, ch. 8).

8 "Holarchy" is the term coined by Koestler (1976) and used later by Wilber (1997b) to capture the notion that each level in a nested set (or level of a plan in this case) is complete and whole in itself (although encompassed by plans for levels above) and in turn encompasses those plans in levels below.

9 On the Alberta side, the estimated population in 1996 was 140,000; on the British Columbia side, 60,000.

10 It will be recalled from Chapter 1 that a number of case-study papers on resource-development regions throughout Canada were presented at the Resources for Tomorrow Conference held in Montreal in 1961.

11 According to the commission's senior regional planner responsible for developing the plan, its final version, which had been considerably modified from a more environmentally oriented draft, lacks teeth and consistency but generally retains a respect for the environment

(Wight 1980). Policies to preserve good farmland and minimize environmental consequences of resource development are well stated, though not adequately backed up. The rural land-use policy in the plan is environmentally oriented in a more immediately workable way, according to Wight. The plan also features a section on environmental quality and policies, which draws attention to the importance of watershed, air shed, and solid waste disposal considerations when evaluating development proposals, and refers to avoiding noise and safety hazards around airports as well as protecting the region's lakeshore and landscape (river valley) corridors.

12 See Rees (1979) for a brief description of the Canada Land Inventory program, including specific objectives, evaluation criteria, land-use capability classifications, and mapping program. See also the Canada Land Inventory Report Series (various dates), available from Environment Canada.

13 Robinson and Webster (1985) make the same point relative to the situation prevalent in the mid-1980s. Lawrence (1992), discussing the "shared characteristics" of the planning and environmental impact assessment movements (their principal differences and interconnections), points out the potential contributions of each to the other, and makes a strong case for greater integration between the two movements.

14 Canadians place a very high personal priority on environmental quality and are prepared to make sacrifices to protect it. This has been made clear in numerous public opinion polls throughout the 1980s and 1990s, both at times when the economy has been healthy and when it has been weak (see Sadler 1985, vi).

15 See Richardson (1996) for a discussion of the various definitions and meanings of these terms, including his own.

Chapter 8: Planning and Governing Metropolitan Areas

1 We consider metropolitan planning as a subset of "regional planning," and therefore throughout this chapter we use the term "metropolitan-regional planning"; further, we use the term "metropolitan-region" as the equivalent of metropolitan area. Also, throughout this chapter we use the term "agencies" or "authorities" to apply to formally established metropolitan-regional planning commissions, boards, and service districts, as well as departments or divisions of metropolitan governments that are concerned with metropolitan-regional planning.

2 For the purposes of our analysis, we have adopted P.J. Smith's definition of a planning system as a system of public administration that is created to deliver land use planning services to "metropolitan areas." Further, we have adapted his definition of the essential "elements" around which most Canadian planning systems for metropolitan areas are structured (see Smith 1995, 217).

3 For details on the specific circumstances, conditions, and problems the various metropolitan areas faced, leading to the establishment of metropolitan-regional planning agencies, see, for Montreal, Sancton (1985), Trepanier (1993), Charbonneau et al. (1993); for Toronto, BMR (1945), Toronto Civic Advisory Council, Committee on Metropolitan Problems (1949); for Winnipeg, Levin (1993); for Edmonton and Calgary, Gertler (1972), Royal Commission on Metropolitan Development of Calgary and Edmonton (1956).

4 While we refer to the Vancouver Metropolitan Area in this chapter, we discuss its planning agency, the Greater Vancouver Regional District, only in Chapter 9. This is because we consider the Vancouver region a "city-region," the focus of Chapter 9.

5 While the designation of a census metropolitan area requires an urban core of 100,000 people, there apparently is some latitude in its application. For example, while the city of Victoria had a population (in 1996) of only 73,504, it is placed in the 100,000-plus category because its surrounding areas form part of the urban core. This method allows Statistics Canada to control for the problem of different incorporation practices throughout the country. It is also of interest to note that in 1991 five urban aggregations that satisfied this size criterion were *not* classed as CMAs: Moncton, Cape Breton, Kingston, Abbottsford, and Kelowna. In 1996, Barrie, Brantford, Guelph, and Peterborough joined these five urban areas as exceptions. Each of these nine urban areas has a larger population than the smallest official CMA, Thunder Bay. No explanation is given for these exceptions.

6 It should be noted that our assessment of the growth of CMAs – for 1996 and earlier years – is, with a few exceptions, based on Statistics Canada CMA boundary definitions that existed at the time of the particular census. As a city grows and expands its reach, its borders expand, the surrounding parts are attached to its urban core, and the CMA is adjusted accordingly. Since each CMA's boundaries have expanded over the years to include more of the outlying areas, it is clear that we are not measuring the same entities over time. This has the effect of perhaps inflating our growth figures and, consequently, growth rates must be viewed with the redefinitions of the CMAs in mind.

7 This term has been borrowed from Little (1999).

8 Note that the four sources of growth do not always add up to the grand total because of the residual deviation.

9 Much of these data are taken from Vander Ploeg (1999).

10 Statistics Canada has not published nor made available their intercensal estimates for population of central cities.

11 All the evidence points to the following two observations. First, the healthiest suburbs are those that surround healthy core cities; and the converse is also true – unhealthy suburbs surround unhealthy core cities. In short, the better the core city, the better the suburbs, and, thus, the better the metropolitan area as whole. Second, metropolitan areas with the largest income differentials between centre city and suburbs are the least healthy and suffer the most in a recession. (See, for example, Rusk 1993; Savitch and Vogel 1996.)

12 It should be noted that the Winnipeg population change reflects the 1971 amalgamation and unification rather than true population shifts.

13 The increased size of rural populations in the census metropolitan areas has been due, in part, to changing boundaries during this period, as well as outright population growth in rural parts of the census metropolitan areas.

14 It may seem strange that the entire apparatus of Canadian planning systems rests on this one sub-clause and the authority it gives provincial governments to make laws for the use of property.

15 Effective 1 January 1982, the Edmonton Regional Planning Commission became the Edmonton Metropolitan Regional Planning Commission. The area of jurisdiction was also reduced by almost half, with the western halves placed in a newly created regional planning commission. The purpose of this change, according to the government, was to give the Edmonton region the opportunity to concentrate on the management of urban growth in the area most influenced by expansion of the city of Edmonton. Subsequent work on the metropolitan-regional plan focused on the "metropolitan part" of its plan.

16 This is similar to the European-style "greenbelt."

17 Cullingworth (1987, 303) feels that the decision to give the Metro Toronto Planning Board planning authority over an area more than twice the size of Metro Toronto was itself even more extraordinary than the two-tiered structure of Metro Toronto itself, since the thirteen municipalities in the wider area had no representation on the metropolitan council.

18 Following P.J. Smith (1995), the term "planning authorities" is used to encompass the planning agencies, boards, and commissions, as well as the departments or divisions of planning that have been established in one- or two-tier forms of government.

19 We are indebted to Scott McAlpine of Grande Prairie Regional College for the following clarification and viewpoint as to the current situation vis-à-vis the demise of the Alberta regional planning commissions and emergence of the intermunicipal arrangements. The provincial Municipal Government Act, as well as the Planning Act, still seem to reference the notion of planning in general as well as the notion of regional planning commissions more specifically. However, the reality is that for most of the non-metropolitan areas (Edmonton and Calgary excepted), land-use planning has become more of a local function with a decreasing emphasis on conformity to established joint municipal plans. The bottom line is that the planning function has become much more related to development and zoning (engineering and technical functions). This utilitarian focus has, on the one hand, increased local autonomy and, on the other, decreased the coherence of planning in Alberta. The reinvention of some regional planning commissions as intermunicipal service agencies is similarly limited by funding and by political vision.

20 The means for implementing a community plan include zoning, land subdivision control, development control bylaws, and, in some places, the program for capital improvements is required to conform to the community plan. There are, in addition, detailed plans for development that a council is occasionally called on to approve; these may include plans for downtown revitalization, neighbourhoods, street and highway improvements, and parkland acquisition and development (see Hodge 1998, 236-7).

21 In late October 2000, the provincial government transferred the Ontario Municipal Board from the Ministry of Municipal Affairs and Housing to the Ministry of the Attorney-General.

22 For one, the urban historian Witold Rybczynski (1998) has criticized the National Capital Commission's report, entitled "A Capital for Future Generations," which aims to create a more vital city centre. Rybczynski argues that the proposals for revitalizing the downtown will not realize its objectives. What is needed, he says, is not a "grand plan," but more housing, careful architectural guidelines, and smaller scale, mixed-use developments – along the lines of certain foreign capitals such as Oslo and the Hague, rather than the "pomp" of Washington or Paris. There has also been some controversy about the National Capital Commission's plan to widen the interprovincial Champlain Bridge, which connects the Ontario and Quebec sides of the metropolitan area (*Globe and Mail,* 22 October 1997).

23 Similar restructuring initiatives are taking place in Hamilton, Halidmand–Norfolk, and Sudbury. The Ontario Municipal Affairs Minister has said that the goal of these amalgamations is to reduce the number of politicians, save costs, introduce efficiencies, and lower taxes in each of these regions and in general make local government simpler, more efficient, and more accountable (regional municipality of Ottawa–Carleton website).

24 Perhaps the best example of application of this concept was the Patrick Abercrombie (1944) plan to guide the growth of London after the Second World War. A greenbelt of parks, agriculture, and exurban development was established to limit the physical expansion of the central city about sixteen kilometres from the centre. Beyond the greenbelt, at a distance of between thirty and forty kilometres, a dozen or more new "satellite" towns were planned to surround London and absorb its new growth, as well as decant some industrial activities from the central city. The towns would not be large, ranging from 30,000 to 60,000 in population, and would afford residents quick access to the countryside. Also, they would be self-sufficient, and it was expected that this feature, together with a high-speed transportation system connecting the new towns to the centre of London, would minimize the need for commuting. Parts of the Abercrombie plan for London have been implemented. Stockholm's regional plan is another example of this concept.

25 Much of the up-to-date information concerning the Montreal situation has been kindly provided by Raphael Fischler of McGill University through personal correspondence and from his and Jeanne Wolfe's article in the *Canadian Journal of Regional Science,* a copy of which he kindly provided.

26 For a critical evaluation of all this reforming and restructuring, consult the following op-ed articles written by Raphael Fischler and Jeanne Wolfe: *La Presse,* 23 January 2000, B3; *La Presse,* 12 February 2000, B3; *The Gazette,* 19 February 2000, B7; *La Presse,* 27 April 2000, B3; *Le Devoir,* 22 August 2000, A7; *The Gazette,* 17 October 2000, B3; *La Presse,* 13 October 2000, A13; *La Presse,* 18 November 2000, A19.

27 There is a modest exception in British Columbia's regional district system (and those modelled after it in other provinces) in which the representatives of non-municipal areas are elected directly to serve on the regional unit.

28 This occurs in the Portland (Oregon), metropolitan government district, considered by many as the "model" governance arrangement for dealing with the sorts of problems Canadian metropolitan areas face, as discussed in this chapter.

Chapter 9: Planning and Governing City-Regions

1 The theme of this introduction to Chapter 9 draws on Witold Rybczynski's perceptive essay on the millennium, "Urban All over the World," *Maclean's,* 14 September 1998, 48-52. A more extensive version of the same material is found in his 1995 book, where, among other things, he has an interesting discussion of the meaning of "metropolitan" as connoting a "mother-city" dominant situation.

2 Two urban historians (Fishman 1990; Rybczynski 1995) see similarities between this new urban form and Frank Lloyd Wright's "Broadacre City."

3 A recent international survey of 213 world cities ranked Vancouver tied for first place with Zurich, Switzerland; Toronto and Montreal were tied at nineteenth (*Vancouver Sun*, 30 June 2001, H3). Vancouver has been repeatedly ranked as the place to be: in its 1999 edition of *The World in Figures*, the *Economist* magazine picked Vancouver as the number one city in the world in a quality-of-life index; and the North American Travel Journalists' Association picked Vancouver as the best international destination in 1998 (*Globe and Mail*, 13 January 2000, A3).

4 For example, a 1998 CBC-TV National Magazine program on the Vancouver region situation, was entitled "Paradise Lost?"

5 While the concept of a "city-region" became commonly accepted beginning in the 1980s, it is not altogether new. As long ago as 1964, an Anglo-American seminar sponsored by the Ditchley Foundation was held in Oxfordshire, England, at which leaders in the field of urban design and planning from both sides of the Atlantic came together to examine the structure and functioning of the urban region. The seminar was based on the assumption that "the urban region represents a new form of civilization, with its own distinctive possibilities and problems" (Senior 1966, 1).

6 "City-regions" are not recognized by Statistics Canada as special statistical units and thus they do not publish data on them. We have developed our data for Table 14 from a variety of sources, which are credited in the notes to the table. Moreover, some researchers (e.g., Sancton 1994; Hutton 1998) analyze the development and significance of Canadian "city-regions" but use Canada's twenty-five metropolitan areas as the statistical basis for their analysis.

7 Robert Fulford (1995) has written that "the ravines are to Toronto what canals are to Venice and hills to San Francisco – understanding Toronto requires an understanding of the ravines."

8 The Lower Mainland was originally composed of four regional districts: the Greater Vancouver Regional District (GVRD), Central Fraser Valley, Dewdney–Alouette, and Fraser–Cheam. The Fraser Valley District (FVRD) was formed in 1995 as a result of the amalgamation of two of the latter three regional districts plus part of the third.

9 Unorganized areas are administered by regional districts on behalf of the government of British Columbia.

10 Before that, these municipalities belonged to the GVRD for specific service functions but were not full members.

11 See Patterson (1998, 4-5) for a discussion of the role and significance of the Fraser River.

12 This larger region includes the area encompassed by the GVRD, the rest of the Lower Mainland, British Columbia's adjacent Sunshine Coast, and the area north-northwest of Vancouver, including the destination tourist resort of Whistler. The region includes all or part of four different regional districts. Its maximum east-west dimension is 170 kilometres and its maximum north-south dimension is 130 kilometres – a total of 5,250 square kilometres.

13 Personal correspondence with the SDRI's project manager.

14 The premise underlying this regional concept is that the national and state borders that cross the land between the Arctic Ocean and Oregon are simply political artifacts hiding a harmony of interest and opportunities that makes Cascadia as meaningful an economic entity as California. As borders come down with free trade the prospects for Cascadia are as endless as its magnificent shorelines on two great oceans, and its folding mountains stretching from the Pacific to the plains (see Artibise 1996).

15 Since the 2000 census results were not available at the time of this writing, we are unable to update the detailed data in Table 14. From other sources we did obtain the estimated 2000 total population for each of our city-regions as a whole.

16 The slowdown during the late 1990s in the British Columbia economy might be expected to dampen all previous population forecasts, including those cited in this chapter.

17 The dominant role of citizen participation in planning the Vancouver city-region continued through the British Columbia Growth Strategies Act of 1995. The act requires that a broad-based consultation comprising local citizens, First Nations organizations, and interested groups, as well as key ministries, must be included in the process for developing a regional growth strategy, and a public hearing on the regional growth strategy proposal is required. Also an intergovernmental advisory committee "to advise ... [and to] help coordinate provincial and local government involvement" must be established.

18 For a detailed description and analysis of the Design for Development program and the To-
    ronto-Centred Region Concept, see Cullingworth 1987, ch. 8) and MacDonald (1984).
19 This viewpoint had nothing to do with political party affiliation or ideology, since it was the
    view of both the Liberal and NDP governments in Ontario in the late 1980s and early 1990s,
    which followed the Progressive Conservative Party into power. The sad fate of the Design for
    Development program, the Toronto-Centred Region Concept, and other elements of local gov-
    ernment reform probably helps to explain the cautious approach the Liberal and NDP govern-
    ments took when devising policies for the Greater Toronto Area.
20 A recent publication, prepared by Christopherson (2000) and commissioned by the Planning
    Institute of BC and the BC Ministry of Municipal Affairs and Housing to celebrate fifty years of
    regional planning in British Columbia, includes a comprehensive bibliography on regional
    planning activities in British Columbia and a complete chronology of regional planning in the
    province with particular reference to the Lower Mainland (see also BC Ministry of Municipal
    Affairs 1999).
21 Metropolitan-regional land-use planning for the Lower Mainland actually began in 1937 when
    six municipalities (Vancouver, Burnaby, Coquitlam, Port Moody, and North and West Vancou-
    ver) created a voluntary planning association for the Lower Mainland, but it had no statutory
    authority.
22 Between 1949 and 1964, five additional regional planning boards were formed covering a
    number of regions in the province. In each case, the boards created were designed to deal
    with intermunicipal concerns.
23 For a more detailed description of the history, background, objectives, and structure of the
    regional districts, see Bish (1990).
24 For a fuller description of the town centre strategy, see Gertler and Crowley (1977, 174-83)
    and Davis and Perkins (1992).
25 As of July 2001, in addition to the GVRD, other regional districts have had their growth
    strategies approved (Nanaimo, Thompson–Nicola, Central Okanagan), which are in various
    stages of implementation. Two regional districts (the Capital [Victoria] Region and the Fraser
    Valley) are in the draft strategy stage, and the remaining five regional districts are in discus-
    sion with the Growth Strategies Office of the Ministry of Housing as to the appropriateness of
    them preparing such a strategy. Seventy-four percent of the population in BC lives in an area
    where there is either an adopted regional growth strategy or one under way. In the fastest
    growing regions of the province (i.e., the Lower Mainland, Southeast Vancouver Island, and
    the Okanagan), 91 percent of the population lives in an area with either an adopted regional
    growth strategy or one under way.
26 As noted in Chapter 8 (see note 25), much of the up-to-date information concerning the
    Montreal situation has been kindly provided by Raphael Fischler of McGill University through
    personal correspondence and from his and Jeanne Wolfe's article in the *Canadian Journal of
    Regional Science*, a draft copy of which he kindly provided.
27 In 1999, the Greater Vancouver Transportation Authority, authorized under the Greater Van-
    couver Transportation Authority Act of 1998, took over transit services from BC Transit on 1
    April 1999 and was renamed "TransLink." Its goals were to improve the quality and availabil-
    ity of public transit services and transportation demand management in order to increase
    transportation choices and reduce the reliance on single-occupant vehicles; support a major
    road network to improve the movement of people and goods throughout the region; and
    provide transportation infrastructure and services to support the region's growth strategy,
    economic development, and air quality objectives.
28 The Winnipeg Region Committee evolved into the Capital Region Committee for most of the
    1990s, when the Filmon government was in power. The Capital Region Committee was par-
    ticularly active in helping to come up with the Capital Region Strategy, which developed in
    May 1996 in partnership with the public, the region's sixteen municipalities, and the Mani-
    toba Round Table on the Environment and the Economy. The new NDP government's "Next
    Steps" document (which came out in January 2001) speaks of capital region planning and
    forming an advisory committee (Manitoba Intergovernmental Affairs 2001). As Ian Wight, a
    keen observer of the Winnipeg planning scene, has noted (personal correspondence, April
    2000): "It will be interesting to see if this new committee will involve any departures from the

previous approach – which primarily featured municipal government participation, with limited participation of other levels of government, and with no participation of non-government sectors." It is too early to tell, he continues, if it will come anywhere close to warrant inclusion as a "new, inclusive governance approach" similar to what we propose in Chapter 9. Wight argues that the past and current Winnipeg/Capital Region approach is best characterized as one of a series of comparatively ad hoc and/or piecemeal, periodic efforts at "regional planning by committee," with City of Winnipeg representation being treated equally with the other municipalities in the region.

Chapter 10: The Continuing Need for Regional Planning

1 An example of this tension surfaced in the Capital Region District for the Victoria metropolitan region just as this book was going to press. The region's growth strategy, which has been under discussion for five years, is now being rejected by several municipal councils and, apparently, by the newly elected provincial governemnt (Victoria *Times-Colonist*, 17 July 2001, 1-2).
2 Somewhat similar classification systems are also found in Savitch and Vogel (1996) and Rothblatt and Sancton (1993).
3 The authoritative regional decision-making approach is also found in development authorities that are entrusted with special powers to plan and implement resource development projects such as the Meewasin Valley Authority in Saskatoon, the James Bay Development Corporation in northern Quebec, and, of course, Ontario's conservation authorities.
4 Incongruously, the ill-starred amalgamation of the metropolitan Toronto municipalities is a notable exception.

Chapter 11: The Future Shape of Regional Planning

1 We are indebted to Ian Wight for these suggestions.

Regional Planning Resources
on the Internet:
A Selective Directory

The following list of websites is indicative of the increasingly rich resources available online for regional planning practice and research. Users are encouraged to explore links to other sites. Web addresses are current as of the year of publication, but because they often change, we have provided sufficient information to identify the source and allow readers to locate a changed address, if necessary.

Nodal Sites

These sites provide a central node with the capability of linking to many relevant regional planning sites in Canada, the United States, and abroad:

American Planning Association
www.planning.org

Canadian Institute of Planners
www.cip-icu.ca

Royal Australian Planning Institute
www.rapi.com.au

Sprawl Resource Guide
www.plannersweb.com/sprawl/sprawl6.html

University of British Columbia School of Community and Regional Planning
www.scarp.ubc.ca

University of Buffalo Cyburbia Resource Directory Database
www.cyburbia.org

University of California Environmental Design Library
www.lib.berkeley.edu/ENVI

Virginia Commonwealth University Urban Studies and Planning
www.vcu.edu/hasweb/usp/ ~ links

Canadian Regional Sites

Many Canadian regional agencies engaged in planning and governance and other activities have websites that allow users to observe similarities and differences in practice in regions across the country:

Alberta
Alberta Capital Region Alliance
www.capregion.ab.ca

Alberta Capital Region Governance Review
www.acrgr.org

British Columbia
British Columbia Land Use Coordination Office
www.luco.gov.bc.ca

British Columbia Ministry of Municipal Affairs Growth Strategies Office
www.marh.gov.bc.ca/GROWTH

Environment Canada Georgia Basin Ecosystem Initiative
www.pyr.ec.gc.ca/GeorgiaBasin

Georgia Strait Alliance
www.georgiastrait.org

Greater Vancouver Regional District Livable Region Strategic Plan
www.gvrd.bc.ca/services/growth/lrsp/lrsp_toc.html

Greater Victoria Economic Development Commission
www.bizvic.com

Victoria Capital Region District Regional Planning Services
www.crd.bc.ca/regplan

Manitoba
Manitoba Capital Region Review
www.susdev.gov.mb.ca/ia/capreg

New Brunswick
New Brunswick Regional Development Corporation
www.gov.nb.ca/rdc/

Newfoundland
Department of Industry, Trade, and Rural Development
www.gov.nf.ca/drr

Nova Scotia
Greater Halifax Partnership
www.greaterhalifax.com

Halifax Regional Municipality
www.region.halifax.ns.ca

Regional Development Authorities
www.gov.ns.ca/ecor/ced/rdas.htm

Strait–Highlands Regional Development Agency
www.strait-highlands.ns.ca

Ontario
Greater Toronto Charter
www.torontocharter.com

National Capital Commission (Ottawa)
www.capcan.ca

New City of Ottawa
www.city.ottawa.on.ca/index_en.html

New City of Toronto Amalgamation
www.city.toronto.on.ca/council/amal_report1.htm

Regional Municipality of Halton
www.region.halton.on.ca/ppw/planinfo

Regional Municipality of Hamilton–Wentworth
www.hamilton-went.on.ca

Regional Municipality of Niagara
www.regional.niagara.on.ca

Regional Municipality of Waterloo
www.region.waterloo.on.ca

Prince Edward Island
Ministry of Community and Cultural Affairs Provincial Planning Branch
www.gov.pe.ca/commcul/pais-info

Quebec
Ministry of Municipal Affairs
www.mam.gouv.qc.ca

Montreal Urban Community
www.cum.qc.ca

Ordre des urbanistes du Québec
www.ouq.qc.ca

Saskatchewan
Meewasin Valley Authority
www.meewasin.com

Regina Regional Economic Development Authority
www.rreda.com

Saskatoon Regional Economic Development Authority
www.sreda.com

Other Canadian Sites Relevant to Regional Planning
A number of other sites in Canada also provide resources for those concerned with regional planning practice and research:

Canada West Foundation Cities @ 2000 Project
www.cwf.ca

Canadian Urban Institute
www.canurb.com

Centre for Human Settlements, University of British Columbia
www.chs.ubc.ca

Community Futures Development Corporations of Western Canada
www.communityfutures.ca

Intergovernmental Committee on Urban and Regional Research
www.icurr.org

National Roundtable on the Environment and the Economy
www.nrtee-trnee.ca

University of British Columbia Sustainable Development Research Institute QUEST Project
www.sdri.ubc.ca

Sites for United States and Other Regions

Below is a small selection of websites in the United States and other countries that are relevant to regional planning practice:

California Association of Bay Area Governments
www.abag.ca.gov

Citistates Research
www.citistates.com

Edge City Planning
www.ssc.msu.edu/~patmcgov/jper.html

Minneapolis–St. Paul Metropolitan Council
www.metrocouncil.org

New Zealand Bay of Plenty Regional Council
envbop.govt.nz

People for Puget Sound, Washington
www.pugetsound.org

Puget Sound Water Quality Action Team, Washington
www.wa.gov/puget_sound

Regional Plan Association of New York
www.rpa.org

Southern California Association of Governments
www.scag.ca.gov

University of Buffalo Institute for Local Governance and Regional Growth
www.regional-institute.buffalo.edu

Urban Land Institute
www.uli.org

References

Abercrombie, Patrick. 1944. *Greater London Plan*. London: HMSO.

Aberley, Douglas C. 1985. Bioregionalism: A Territorial Approach to Governance and Development of Northwest British Columbia. Master's thesis, University of British Columbia.

–. 1993a. How to Map Your Bioregion: A Primer for Community Activists. In *Boundaries of Home: Mapping for Local Empowerment*, edited by Douglas C. Aberley, 71-129. Gabriola Island, BC: New Society Publishers.

–, ed. 1993b. *Boundaries of Home: Mapping for Local Empowerment*. Gabriola Island, BC: New Society Publishers.

–, ed. 1994. *Futures by Design: The Practice of Ecological Planning*. The New Catalyst Bioregional Series. Gabriola Island, BC, and Philadelphia, PA: New Society Publishers.

–. 1999. Interpreting Bioregionalism. Ph.D. diss., Heriot-Watt University, Edinburgh, Scotland.

Adams, Thomas. 1917. *Rural Planning and Development: A Study of Rural Conditions and Problems in Canada*. Ottawa: Commission of Conservation, Canada.

–. 1919. Regional and Town Planning. Paper presented at the Eleventh National Conference on City Planning, May.

–. 1920. Remarks. Proceedings of the Twelfth National Conference on City Planning.

–. 1921. Town and Regional Planning in Relation to Industrial Growth. *Plan Canada* 1, 1:9, 10, 49.

–. 1922. Modern City Planning: Its Meanings and Methods. *National Municipal Review* 11, 6: 157-76. Reprinted in *Saving the Canadian City*, edited by P. Rutherford, 247-75. Toronto: University of Toronto Press.

Agnew, J.A. 1987. *Place and Politics: The Geographical Mediation of State and Society*. Winchester, MA: Allen and Unwin.

Alberta, Municipal Affairs. 1980. *Planning in Alberta: A Guide and Directory*. Edmonton: Inter-Agency Planning Branch, Planning Services Division.

–. n.d. *A Guide to Land Use Planning in Alberta*. Edmonton: Alberta Municipal Affairs.

Alberta, Task Force on Urbanization and the Future. 1971. *The Role of Regional Planning*. Edmonton: Alberta Task Force on Urbanization and the Future.

Alberta Planning Board. 1982. *Revised Guidelines for Regional Plan Preparation and Review*. Edmonton: Alberta Planning Board.

Alexander, Don. 1990. Bioregionalism: Science or Sensibility? *Environmental Ethics* 12, 2: 161-73.

Allen, Robert, and G. Rosenbluth. 1986. *Restraining the Economy: Social Credit Policies in BC in the 80s*. Vancouver: New Star.

Alonso, W. 1970. Spontaneous Growth Centres in Twentieth-Century American Urbanization. *Working Paper No. 11*. Berkeley: University of California Institute of Urban and Regional Development.

–. 1971. Problems, Purposes and Implicit Policies for a National Strategy of Urbanization. *Working Paper No. 158*. Berkeley: University of California Institute of Urban and Regional Development.

Anselm, Luc, and Moss Madden, eds. 1990. *New Directions in Regional Analysis: Integrated and Multi-Regional Approaches*. London: Belhaven Press.

Armstrong, Alan. [1959] 1968. Thomas Adams and the Commission of Conservation. *Plan Canada* 1, 1: 14-32. Reprinted in *Planning the Canadian Environment*, edited by Leonard Gertler, 17-35. Montreal: Harvest House.

Artibise, Alan. 1996. Redefining BC's Place in Canada: The Emergence of Cascadia as a Strategic Alliance. *Policy Options* (September): 27-30.

–. 1997. Regional Governance without Regional Government: The Strengths and Weaknesses of the Greater Vancouver Regional District. Unpublished background report prepared for the Regional Municipality of Ottawa–Carleton. Vancouver: University of British Columbia School of Community and Regional Planning. April.

Artibise, Alan, and Jessie Hill. 1993. Governance and Sustainability in the Georgia Basin. Paper presented at the British Columbia Round Table on the Environment and the Economy. Victoria: Queen's Printer for British Columbia. April.

Avana Capital Corporation. 2000. Towards a Greater Toronto Charter. www.torontocharter.com.

Bailey, A.S., and W.J. Coffey. 1994. Regional Science in Crisis: A Plea for a More Relevant Approach. *Papers in Regional Science* 73: 3-14.

Baker, Harold, and Bertram Wolfe, eds. 1986. Inter-Community Cooperation: An Opportunity for Rural Development. Proceedings of a provincial conference held in Saskatoon, 19-21 June 1986.

Baldassare, Mark, Joshua Hassol, William Hoffman, and Abbey Kanarek. 1996. Possible Planning Roles for Regional Government: A Survey of City Planning Directors in California. *Journal of the American Planning Association* 62, 1: 17-29.

Barnes, W.R., and Larry C. Ledebur. 1998. *The New Regional Economies: The US Common Market and the Global Economy*. Beverly Hills, CA: Sage Publications.

Barrett, Tom. 1998. Victoria Seeks Way to Avoid Review for SkyTrain Route. *Vancouver Sun*, 12 September, 1-2.

Bateson, Gregory. 1987. *Steps to an Ecology of Mind*. 2nd ed. Northdale, NJ: Jason Aronson.

Baxter, David. 1964. The BC Land Commission Act: A Review. *Urban Land Economics Report No. 8*. Vancouver: University of British Columbia Faculty of Commerce and Business Administration.

Beatley, Timothy, and Kristy Manning. 1997. *The Ecology of Place*. Washington, DC: Island Press.

Beaudet, Gerard. 1999. Metropolitan Planning in Montreal, 1960-1998. *Plan Canada* 39, 1: 10-15.

Bédard, R.J. 1965. *La bataille des annexions: la petite municipalité, institution démocratique par excellence, est-elle vouée à la disparition?* Montréal: Éditions du jour.

Bellamy, Edward. [1884] 1959. *Looking Backwards*. New York: Harper.

Berg, Peter, and Raymond Dasmann. 1978. Reinhabiting California. In *Reinhabiting a Separate Country: A Bioregional Anthology of Northern California*, edited by Peter Berg, 217-20. San Francisco: Planet Drum Books.

Berger, Thomas R. 1977. *Northern Frontier, Northern Homeland: The Report of the Mackenzie Valley Pipeline Inquiry*. Ottawa: Printing and Publishing Supply and Services Canada.

Bernard, Ted, and Jora Young. 1997. *The Ecology of Hope: Communities Collaborate for Sustainability*. Gabriola Island, BC, and Philadelphia, PA: New Society Publishers.

Berry, Brian J.L. 1960. An Inductive Approach to the Regionalization of Economic Development. In *Essays on Geography and Economic Development*, edited by Norton Ginsburg. Chicago: University of Chicago Department of Geography.

Bish, Robert L. 1990. *Local Government in British Columbia*. 2nd ed. Richmond, BC: Union of British Columbia Municipalities.

Blumenfeld, Hans. 1967. Metropolitan Area Planning. In *The Modern Metropolis*, edited by Paul D. Spreiregen, 79-83. Montreal: Harvest House.

Bodmer, Hugh G. 1980. Regional Resources Project No. 1: An Innovative Approach to Economic and Social Development. *Plan Canada* 20, 2: 81-90.

Bogue, Donald J. 1948. *The Structure of the Metropolitan Community: A Study of Dominance and Subdominance*. Ann Arbor: University of Michigan.

Boothroyd, Peter. 1984. *To Set Their Own Course: Indian Band Planning and Indian Affairs.* Paper prepared for BC Region, Indian and Inuit Affairs Canada.

Boston Consulting Group. 1995. *The Fourth Era: The Economic Challenges Facing the GTA.* Study prepared for the Greater Toronto Area Task Force. December.

Bourne, Larry S. 1984. Planning for the Toronto Region: By Whom and For Whom. *Plan Canada* 24, 3/4: 137–9.

–. 1995a. *Urban Growth and Population Redistribution in North America: A Diverse and Unequal Landscape.* Major report 32. Toronto, ON: University of Toronto Centre for Urban and Community Studies. May.

–. 1995b. Living on the Periphery: Regional Science and the Future of the Canadian Experiment. *Canadian Journal of Regional Science* 18, 1: 21–37.

Bourne, Larry S., and Antony E. Olvet. 1995. *New Urban and Regional Geographies in Canada: 1986–91 and Beyond.* Major report 33. Toronto, ON: Centre for Urban and Community Studies, University of Toronto. July.

Bowler, Christi. 1997. Farmland Preservation and the Cluster Zoning Model. *Journal of the American Planning Association* 63, 1: 127–8.

Branch, Melville. 1988. *Regional Planning: Introduction and Explanation.* New York: Praeger.

Breheny, Michael, and Ralph Rookwood. 1993. Planning the Sustainable City Region. In *Planning the Sustainable Environment*, edited by Andrew Blowers, 150–89. London: Earthscan Publications.

Brewis, Thomas. 1969. *Regional Economic Policies in Canada.* Toronto: Macmillan.

British Columbia. 1995. Growth Strategies Statutes Amendment Act, 1995. S.B.C. 1995, c. 9. In force 8 June 1995.

British Columbia, Integrated Resource Planning Committee. 1993. *Land and Resource Management Planning: A Statement of Principles and Process.* Victoria: Province of British Columbia.

British Columbia, Land Use Coordination Office. 1993. *A Protected Areas Strategy for British Columbia: The Protected Areas Component of the BC's Land Use Strategy.* Victoria: Land Use Coordination Office.

–. 1997. *Report Overviews and Invitation to Comment on Planning Framework Statements and Resource Management Zones.* Victoria: Province of British Columbia. December.

–. 2001. *Land Use Planning in BC, BC's Parks and Protected Areas: Doubling the Legacy.* Victoria: Province of British Columbia.

British Columbia, Ministry of Finance and Corporate Relations, Department of Municipal Affairs. 1972. *Regional Districts in BC, 1971.* Victoria: Queen's Printer for British Columbia.

British Columbia, Ministry of Municipal Affairs. 1995. *An Explanatory Guide to BC's Growth Strategies Act.* Victoria: Ministry of Municipal Affairs. October.

–. 1997. LRMPs Provide Communities with Keys to the Future. In *Taking Action: Growth Strategies in BC*, 1. Victoria: Ministry of Municipal Affairs. October

–. 1999. A Look at 50 years of Regional Planning in BC. In *Taking Action: Growth Strategies in BC.* Victoria: Ministry of Municipal Affairs. March.

British Columbia, Ministry of Municipal Affairs and Housing. 1998. News Release, 25 June.

British Columbia, Office of the Premier. 1997. Decision on North-East Land Use Plans Protect an Area the Size of Nova Scotia. News release. Victoria: Media Relations, Communications Branch, Ministry of Environment, Lands and Parks. 8 October.

British Columbia Commission on Resources and Environment. 1993. *1992-93 Annual Report to the British Columbia Legislative Assembly*, 7, footnote 1. Victoria: Commission on Resources and Environment. June.

–. 1996. *Strategic Land Use Planning Source Book.* Prepared by Daryl W. Brown. Victoria: Commission on Resources and Environment. March.

British Columbia Round Table on the Environment and the Economy. 1992. *Towards a Strategy for Sustainability.* Victoria: BC Round Table.

–. 1993. *Georgia Basin Initiative.* Victoria: BC Round Table. May.

–. 1994. *Local Roundtables: Realizing Their Full Potential.* Victoria: BC Round Table.

Brookfield, H. 1984. Experiences of an Outside Man. In *Recollections of a Revolution*, edited by M. Billings et al., 27–38. London: Macmillan.

Brown, Victoria. 1996. Future Scenarios for the Winnipeg Region. *New City Magazine* 17 (Special Issue): 48-53.

Brunhes, Jean. 1910. *La géographie humaine*. Paris: Armand Colin.

Bruyn, Severyn, and James Meehan, eds. 1987. *Beyond the Market and the State*. Philadephia, PA: Temple University Press.

Bryant, Christopher. 1994. Preserving Canada's Agricultural Land. *Plan Canada* 34, 4 (July): 49–51. Special edition.

Bryant, Christopher, and Thomas Johnston. 1992. *Agriculture in the City's Countryside*. Toronto: University of Toronto Press.

Bryant, Christopher E., and Daniel Lemire. 1993. *Population Distribution and the Management of Urban Growth in Six Selected Urban Regions in Canada*. Toronto: Intergovernmental Committee on Urban and Regional Research (ICURR). March.

Bryant, Christopher E., L.H. Russwurm, and A.G. McClellan. 1982. *The City's Countryside*. New York: Longman.

Buckley, Helen, and Eva Tihanyi. 1967. *Canadian Policies for Rural Adjustment: A Study of the Economic Impact of ARDA, PFRA, and MMRA*. Special Study No. 7. Ottawa: Economic Council of Canada.

Bunce, Michael, and Michael Troughton, eds. 1984. *The Pressures of Change in Rural Canada*. Geographical Monograph No. 14. Toronto: York University Department of Geography.

Bunting, Trudi, and Pierre Filion, eds. 2000. *Canadian Cities in Transition: The Twenty-first Century*. 2nd ed. Don Mills: Oxford University Press.

Bureau of Municipal Research. 1945. *Where Are Toronto and Its Metropolitan Area Heading?* White Paper No. 305. Toronto: Bureau of Municipal Research.

–. 1977. *Design for Development Where Are You?* Toronto: Bureau of Municipal Research.

Burton, Thomas L. 1981. *The Roles and Relevance of Alberta's Regional Planning Commissions*. Edmonton: University of Alberta Department of Recreation Administration.

Calthorpe, Peter, and William Fulton. 2000. *The Regional City*. Washington, DC: Island Press.

Campbell, Scott. 1996. Green Cites, Growing Cities, Just Cities? Urban Planning and the Contradictions of Sustainable Development. *Journal of the American Planning Association* 62, 3: 296-312.

Cameron, Ken. 1996. Regional Districts in British Columbia. *Plan Canada* 36, 5: 16–17.

Canada. 1961. Agricultural Rehabilitation and Development Act, S.C. 1960–61, c. 30, secs. 9–10. Elizabeth II.

Canada, Ad Hoc Committee of the Federal Government. 1981. *Economic Development for Canada in the 1980s*. Ottawa: Supply and Services Canada.

Canada, Department of Regional Economic Expansion (DREE). 1975. *The New Approach*. Ottawa: Supply and Services Canada.

Canada, Senate. 1964. *Report of the Special Committee on Land Use in Canada*. Ottawa: Queen's Printer.

Canadian Institute of Planners. 1984. Ontario Planned? *Plan Canada* 24, 3/4 (December). A Special Issue on the Golden Age of Planning in Ontario, 1966–1975.

Canadian Urban Institute. 1992a. *72 Questions about Issues in the Greater Toronto Area*. Urban Focus Series. Toronto: Canadian Urban Institute. September.

–. 1992b. *Dialogue on Urban Issues: A Series of Discussions with Prominent Speakers on Current Urban Issues II*. Toronto: Canadian Urban Institute.

–. 1993. *Dialogue on the Future of the Greater Toronto Area: Leaders Debate the Issues*. Toronto: Canadian Urban Institute.

Cannon, James B. 1989. Directions in Canadian Regional Geography. *Canadian Geographer* 33, 3: 230–9.

Careless, A.G.S. 1977. *Initiative and Response: The Adaptation of Canadian Federalism to Regional Economic Development*. Montreal: McGill-Queen's University Press.

Carpenter, Miles. 1930. The Nature and Origins of the French Regionalist Movement. *Studies in Quantitative and Cultural Sociology*. Papers presented at the Twenty-Fourth Annual Meeting of the American Sociological Society. Chicago, IL: University of Chicago.

Castells, Manuel. 1989. *The Informational City: Information Technology. Economic Restructuring, and the Urban-Regional Process*. Oxford: Blackwell Publishers.

–. 1996. *The Rise of Network Society.* Cambridge, MA: Blackwell.

Castells, Manuel, and P. Hall. 1994. *Technopoles of the World: The Making of 21st Century Industrial Complexes.* London: Routledge.

Central Kootenay Regional District. 1983. *Slocan Valley Plan (Draft).* Nelson, BC.

Central Ontario Lakeshore Urban Complex Task Force. 1974. *Report.* Ontario: Government Publications.

Cermakian, Jean. 1984. Geographic Research and the Regional Planning Process in Quebec: A New Challenge. *Proceedings of the New England St. Lawrence Valley Geographical Society.*

Charbonneau, François, Pierre Hamel, and Michel Barcelo. 1994. Urban Sprawl in the Montreal Area: Policies and Trends. In *The Changing Canadian Metropolis: A Public Policy Perspective,* edited by F. Frisken, 459–97. Berkeley: University of California Institute of Governmental Studies; Kingston: Queen's University Institute of Intergovernmental Relations.

Charles-Brun, Jean. 1911. *La régionalisme.* Paris: Blout.

Chase, Stuart. 1936. *Rich Land, Poor Land.* New York: Whittlesey House.

Cherry, Gordon E. 1974. *The Evolution of British Town Planning.* London: Leonard Hill Books.

Creese, Walter. 1966. *The Search for Environment: The Garden City Before and After.* New Haven and London: Yale University Press.

Christensen, K.S. 1993. Teaching Savvy. *Journal of Planning Education and Research* 12:202-12.

Christopherson, Frances. 2000. *Bibliography and Chronology of Regional Planning in British Columbia.* Richmond: Planning Institute of British Columbia.

Church, Gardner. 1996. The North American Failure: The Governance of Regional Cities. In *Local Places in the Age of the Global City,* edited by Roger Kell et al. Montreal: Black Rose.

Clinton, Stan. 1997. Changing Times: Newfoundland's Municipal Planning and Implementation System. *Plan Canada* 37, 2: 18–20.

Coffey, William J. 1994. *The Evolution of Canada's Metropolitan Economies.* Montreal: Institute for Research on Public Policy.

Cohen, Anthony. 1985. *The Symbolic Construction of Community.* New York: Tavistock Publications.

Cohen, M. 1993. Megacities and the Environment. *Finance and Development* 30: 40-7.

Cohn, Theodore H., et al. 1989. North American Cities in an Interdependent World: Vancouver and Seattle as International Cities. In *The New International Cities Era: The Global Activities of North American Municipal Governments,* edited by Earl Fry et al., 73–117. Provo, UT: Brigham Young University.

Colombo, John Robert, ed. 1996. *Canadian Global Almanac.* Toronto: Macmillan.

Comay, Eli. 1964. A Brief to the Royal Commission on Metropolitan Toronto. Unpublished manuscript.

–. 1984. Provincial Planning in Ontario: A Not-so-great Planning Fiasco. *Plan Canada* 24, 3/4: 163-4.

Commission of the European Communities. 1989. *Report of the Task Force on the Environment and the Internal Market.* Brussels: Commission of the European Communities.

Commission on Planning and Development Reform in Ontario. 1992. *Draft Report on Planning and Development Reform in Ontario.* December. Toronto: Commission on Planning and Development Reform in Ontario.

Committee for Economic Development. 1970. *Reshaping Government in Metropolitan Areas.* New York: Committee for Economic Development.

Communauté urbaine de Montréal. 1986. *Service de la planification du territoire, Development Plan.* August.

–. 1987. *Development Plan, Modifications.* August 1987, December 1987, coming into force, 31 December 1987.

Coopers and Lybrand. 1992. *Protecting and Enhancing the Physical Environment: The New Challenge.* London: Coopers and Lybrand.

Copes, Parzival. 1972. *The Resettlement of Fishing Communities in Newfoundland.* Ottawa: Canadian Council on Rural Development.

Courchene, Tom. 1990. Global Competitiveness and the Canadian Federation. Paper presented at the University of Toronto Conference on Global Competition and Canadian Federalism, September.

Cullingworth, J. Barry. 1987. *Urban and Regional Planning in Canada.* New Brunswick, NJ: Transaction Books.

Curtin, J.A. 1994. A Light in the Forest: The Niagara Escarpment Plan. *Plan Canada* 34, 4 (July): 66–7. Special edition 4.

Czamanski, Stan. 1971. Some Empirical Evidence of the Strengths of Linkages Between Groups of Related Industries in Urban-Regional Complexes. *Papers of the Regional Science Association* 27: 137–50.

Dahrendorf, Rolf. 1995. A Precarious Balance: Economic Opportunity, Civil Society and Political Liberty. *The Responsive Community: Rights and Responsibility* 5, 3: 13–39.

Dakin, John. 1968. Resources for Tomorrow: The Background Papers. In *Planning the Canadian Environment*, edited by Leonard O. Gertler, 119–36. Montreal: Harvest House.

Dale, Lynne. 1997. The Alberta Capital Region Forum: An Experiment in Regional Cooperation. *The Regionalist* 2/3: 41–51.

Dale, Lynne, and T.L. Burton. 1984. Regional Planning in Alberta: Performance and Prospects. *Alberta Journal of Planning Practice* 3: 17–41.

Daly, Herman E. 1996. *Beyond Economic Growth: The Economics of Sustainable Development.* Boston: Beacon Press and Cambridge, MA: Lincoln Institute of Land Policy.

Daly, Herman E., and John B. Cobb, Jr. 1989. *For the Common Good: Redirecting the Economy Toward Community, the Environment, and a Sustainable Future.* Boston: Beacon Press.

Daniels, Thomas L., and Mark B. Lapping. 1996. The Two Rural Americas Need More Not Less Planning. *Journal of the American Planning Association* 62, 3: 285–8.

Davidson, Gary. 1984. Current Issues in Rural Planning Policy. In *The Pressures of Change in Rural Canada*, edited by Michael Bunce and Michael Troughton, 328–48. Geographical Monograph No. 14. Toronto: York University Department of Geography.

Davidson, J., and G. Wibberley. 1977. *Planning and Rural Environments.* New York: Praeger.

Davis, H. Craig, and Ralph A. Perkins. 1992. The Promotion of Metropolitan Multinucleation: Lessons to Be Learned from the Vancouver and Melbourne Experiences. *Canadian Journal of Urban Research* 1, 1: 16–37.

Dector, Michael, and Jeffrey A. Kowall. 1988. *Yukon 2000: Comprehensive Planning for Diversification.* Local Development Series Paper No. 13. Ottawa: Economic Council of Canada.

Dickinson, Robert. 1970. *Regional Ecology: The Study of Man's Environment.* New York: John Wiley and Sons.

Diermenjian, S., and M. Jones. 1983. *Planning for Communities in the North: A Preliminary Evaluation of an Innovative Approach in the Northwest Territories.* Occasional Paper No. 10. Toronto: Ryerson Polytechnical Institute Department of Urban and regional Planning.

Dodge, William R. 1996. *Regional Excellence: Governing Together to Compete Globally and Flourish Locally.* Washington, DC: National League of Cities.

Dorman, Robert J. 1993. *Revolt of the Provinces: The Regionalist Movement in America, 1920–45.* Chapel Hill, NC: University of North Carolina Press.

Douglas, David. 1997. The Return of Regional Planning: New Directions? Paper presented at the Canadian Institute of Planners National Conference held in St. John's, NF, July.

Downs, Anthony. 1994. *New Visions for Metropolitan America,* Washington, DC: The Brookings Institute.

Ducas, Sylvain. 1998. Greater Montreal, *Plan Canada* 38, 3: 34–5.

Ducas, Sylvain, and Marie-Odile Trepanier. 1998. Les difficultés d'un consensus régional. *Plan Canada* 38, 3: 25–8.

Dykeman, Floyd W. 1988. A Return to the Past for a Rural Community-Based Planning and Action Programme for the Future: A Challenge for Planners. In *Integrated Rural Planning and Development*, edited by F. Dykeman, 147–66. Sackville, NB: Mount Allison University Small Town and Rural Research Program.

Economic Council of Canada. 1968. *The Challenge of Growth and Change.* Fifth Annual Review. Ottawa: Queen's Printer.

–. 1977. *Living Together: A Study of Regional Disparities.* Ottawa: Supply and Services Canada.

Eisenberg, Evan. 1998. *The Ecology of Eden.* Toronto: Random House Canada.

Elander, I. 1991. Analyzing Central-Local Relations in Different Systems: A Conceptual Framework and Some Empirical Illustrations. *Scandinavian Political Studies* 14, 1: 31-58.

Eliot-Hurst, M. 1985. Geography Has Neither Existence Nor Future. In *The Future of Geography*, edited by R.J. Johnston, 59–91. Andover, Hampshire, UK: Methuen.

Elkin, T., D. McLaren, and M. Hillman. 1991. *Reviving the City*. London: Friends of the Earth.

Entrikin, J. Nickolas. 1991. *The Betweenness of Place: Towards a Geography of Modernity*. Baltimore: Johns Hopkins Press.

Faludi, Andreas. 1996. European Planning Doctrine: A Bridge Too Far? *Journal of Planning Education and Research* 16, 1: 41–50.

Feldman, Lionel. 1991. Discussions With Prominent Speakers on Current Urban Issues. In *Dialogue on Urban Issues III*. Toronto: Canadian Urban Institute.

Fenge, Terry. 1987. Land Use Planning in Canada's North: A Wind of Change or a Bag of Wind? In *Hinterland or Homeland? Land Use Planning in Northern Canada*, edited by T. Fenge and W.E. Rees. Ottawa: Canadian Arctic Resources Committee.

Ferry, Jon. 1998. United We Plan. *BC Business* (July): 30–1.

Fick, Steven and Mary Vincent. 2001. Toronto, a Global Village. *Canadian Geographic* (January/February): 54-5.

Fischler, Raphael. 1999. Regional Planning in Canada. A paper presented at the Joint Conference of the CIP/ICU and the OUQ held in Montreal, 7 June 1999.

–. 2000. Personal correspondence.

Fischler, Raphael, and Jeanne Wolfe. 2000. Regional Restructuring in Montreal: An Historical Analysis. *Canadian Journal of Regional Science* 23 (Spring): 89-114.

Fishman, Robert. 1988. *Urban Utopias in the Twentieth Century*. Cambridge: MIT Press.

–. 1990. America's New City: Megalopolis Unbound. *Current* (October): 10–8.

Flanagan, Frank. 1997. The Choice is CLURE. *Plan Canada* 37, 5: 8–11.

Foster, Kathryn. 1997. The Civilization of Regionalism. *The Regionalist* 1, 4: 1–12.

Fourier, Charles. [1808] 1841. *Théorie des quatre mouvements*. 2nd ed. Paris: Librairie societaire.

Frankel, Carl. 1998. *In Earth's Company: Business, Environment and the Challenge of Sustainability*. Gabriola Island, BC, and Philadelphia, PA: New Society Publishers.

Fraser Basin Management Program. 1996. *State of the Fraser Basin: Assessing Progress towards Sustainability*. Burnaby, BC: Fraser Basin Management Program.

Friedmann, John. [1956] 1964. The Concept of a Planning Region: The Evolution of an Idea in the United States. *Land Economics* 32, 1: 1–13. Reprinted in *Regional Development and Planning: A Reader*, edited by John Friedmann and William Alonso, 502–18. Cambridge, MA: MIT Press.

–. 1963. Regional Planning as a Field of Study. *Journal of the American Institute of Planners* 29, 3: 168–75.

–. 1966a. *Regional Development Policy: A Case Study of Venezuela*. Cambridge, MA: MIT Press.

–. 1966b. The Problem of Regional Boundaries. In *Regional Development Policy: A Case Study of Venezuela*. Cambridge, MA: MIT Press, 39–44.

–. 1971. *The Implementation of Urban-Regional Development Policies: Lessons of Experience*. Los Angeles: University of California, Los Angeles School of Architecture and Urban Planning.

–. 1972. A General Theory of Polarized Development. In *Growth Centres in Regional Economic Development*, edited by Niles M. Hansen, 82–107. New York: Free Press.

–. 1975. Regional Development Planning: The Progress of a Decade. In *Regional Policy: Readings in Theory and Applications*, edited by John Friedmann and William Alonso, 791–808. Cambridge, MA: MIT Press.

–. 1982. Urban Communes, Self-Management and the Reconstruction of the Local State. *Journal of Planning Education and Research* 2, 1: 37–53

–. 1987. *Planning in the Public Domain: From Knowledge to Action*. Princeton, NJ: Princeton University Press.

–. 1988. *Life Space and Economic Space: Essays in Third World Planning*. New Brunswick, NJ: Transaction Books.

–. 1992. *Empowerment: The Politics of Alternative Development*. Cambridge, MA: Blackwell.

–, ed. 1999. *Urban and Regional Governance in the Asia Pacific*. Vancouver: Institute of Asian Research, University of British Columbia.

Friedmann, John, and William Alonso eds. 1964. *Regional Development and Planning: A Reader*. Cambridge, MA: MIT Press.

Friedmann, John, and Robin Bloch. 1990. American Exceptionalism in Regional Planning, 1933–2000. *International Journal of Urban and Regional Research* 14, 4: 576–601.

Friedmann, John, and M. Douglass. 1978. Agropolitan Development: Towards a New Strategy for Regional Development in Asia. In *Growth Pole Strategy and Regional Development*, edited by F. Lo and K. Salih. Oxford: Pergamon Press.

Friedmann, John, and Yvon Forest. 1988. The Politics of Place: Toward a Political Economy of Territorial Planning. In *Regional Economic Development: Essays in Honour of Francois Perroux*, edited by Benjamin Higgins and Donald J. Savoie. Boston: Unwin Hyman.

Friedmann, John, and John Miller. 1964. The Urban Field. *Journal of the American Institute of Planners* 31: 312–20.

Friedmann, John, and Clyde Weaver. 1979. *Territory and Function: The Evolution of Regional Planning*. Berkeley: University of California Press.

Friedmann, John, and G. Wolff. 1982. World City Formation: An Agenda for Research and Action. *International Journal of Urban and Regional Research* 6, 3: 309–44.

Friedrich, Carl J., ed. 1962. *The Public Interest*. Nomos 5: Yearbook of the American Society for Political and Legal Philosophy. New York: Atherton Press.

Frisken, Frances. 1993. Planning and Servicing the Greater Toronto Area: The Interplay of Provincial and Municipal Interests. In *Metropolitan Governance: American/Canadian Intergovernmental Perspectives*, edited by D.R. and A. Sancton, 153–204. Berkeley: University of California Institute of Governmental Studies; Kingston, ON: Queen's University Institute of Intergovernmental Relations.

–. 1994a. Provincial Transit Policy-Making for the Toronto, Montreal and Vancouver Regions. In *The Changing Canadian Metropolis: A Public Policy Perspective*, edited by F. Frisken, Vol. 1, 497–540. Berkeley: University of California Institute of Governmental Studies; Toronto: The Canadian Urban Institute.

–. 1994b. Introduction: Metropolitan Change and the Challenge to Public Policy. In *The Changing Canadian Metropolis: A Public Policy Perspective*, edited by F. Frisken, Vol. 1, 1-25. Berkeley: University of California Institute of Governmental Studies; Toronto: The Canadian Urban Institute.

–, ed. 1994c. *The Changing Canadian Metropolis: A Public Policy Perspective*. Vol. 1. Berkeley: University of California Institute of Governmental Studies; Toronto: The Canadian Urban Institute.

Frisken, Frances, L.S. Bourne, Gunter Gad, and Robert A. Murdie. 1997. *Governance and Social Well-Being in the Toronto Area: Past Achievements and Future Challenges*, 12–29. Research Paper No. 193. Toronto: University of Toronto Centre for Urban and Community Studies.

Fulford, Robert. 1995. *Accidental City*. Toronto: McFarlane, Walters and Ross.

Fuller, Tony, Philip Ehrensaft, and Michael Gertler. 1989. *Sustainable Rural Communities in Canada*. Canadian Agricultural and Rural Restructuring Group, First Rural Policy Seminar, Saskatoon, SK.

Gardner, James N. 1992. Global Regionalism. *New Perspectives Quarterly* 9: 58–9.

Garreau, Joel. 1991. *Edge City*. New York: Doubleday.

Gartner, John. 1995. Toward a Livable Metropolis. *Plan Canada* 35, 2 (March): 16–20.

Gayler, Hugh. 1994. Urban Development and Planning in Niagara. In *Niagara's Changing Landscape*, edited by Hugh Gayler, 241–77. Ottawa: Carleton University Press.

–. 1996. Planning Reform in Ontario and its Implications for Urban Containment and Agricultural Land Use. *Small Town* 26, 4: 4–13.

Geddes, Patrick. [1915] 1968. *Cities in Evolution: An Introduction to the Town Planning Movement and to the Study of Civics*. 3rd ed. London: Ernest Benn.

–. 1925. The Valley Plan of Civilization. *Survey* 54:288-90, 322-5.

Geddes, Robert. 1997. Metropolis Unbound: The Sprawling American City and the Search for Alternatives. *The American Prospect* 8, 35 (November–December).

Gendron, François. 1984. *Option d'aménagement de la région métropolitaine de Montréal*. Québec: Secrétariat à l'aménagement et à la décentralisation.

George, Roy E. 1970. *A Leader and a Laggard: Manufacturing Industry in Nova Scotia, Quebec and Ontario*. Toronto: University of Toronto Press.

Gerecke, Kent. 1988. Patrick Geddes: A Message for Today. *City Magazine* 10, 3: 27–35.

German Marshall Fund of the United States. 1992. *Divided Cities in a Global Economy: The 1992 European-North American State-of-the-Cities Report.* Washington, DC.

Gerstmar, John. 1996. Beautiful Meewasin, *Plan Canada* 36, 3: 11–13.

Gertler, Leonard O. 1972a. Observations on the Mactaquac Regional Development Plan. In *Regional Planning in Canada: A Planner's Testament* (Montreal: Harvest House). First published in Plan Canada 10, 2 (1969): 47-56.

–. 1972b. *Regional Planning in Canada: A Planner's Testament.* Montreal: Harvest House.

–. 1994a. The Federal Role: A Rich Heritage or Severe Discontinuity? *Plan Canada* 34, 4 (July): 131–6. Special edition.

–. 1994b. The Mactaquac Regional Development Plan. *Plan Canada* 34, 4 (July): 40–1. Special edition.

–. 1996. The Regional City of the 21st Century: Looking Back to Look Forward. *Plan Canada* 36, 1 (January): 10–4.

Gertler, Leonard O., and Ron W. Crowley. 1977. *Changing Canadian Cities: The Next 25 Years.* Toronto: McClelland and Stewart.

Gertler, Meric S. 1996. Urban Regions in a Global Context: Directions for the Greater Toronto Area. Proceedings of a conference, University of Toronto, 18-20 October, 1995, 124-8. Toronto: Centre for Urban and Community Studies and Program Planning, University of Toronto.

–. 2000. Self-Determination for Toronto: What Are the Economic Conditions and Do They Exist? In *Toronto: Considering Self-Government*, edited by Mary W. Rowe. Owen Sound, ON: Ginger Press.

Gibson, Robert, and Ray Tomalty. 1995. Ecosystems Planning for Regions. *Colloqui* 10: 1–10.

Gilbert, Richard. 1999. Make Toronto the 11th Province. *Globe and Mail*, 26 November, A13.

Gilbert, Richard, and Don Stevenson 1997. Governance and Economic Performance: The Montreal, Toronto, and Vancouver Regions. December. Unpublished.

Gilg, A. 1985. *An Introduction to Rural Geography.* London: Edward Arnold.

Ginsburg, Norton. 1958. The Regional Concept and Planning Regions. Proceedings of a seminar on regional planning, 31–45. Tokyo: United Nations.

Glasson, John. 1992. The Fall and Rise of Regional Planning in Economically Advanced Nations. *Urban Studies* 29, 3/4: 505–31.

Glikson, Artur. 1955. *Regional Planning and Development.* Leiden: A.W. Sitjhoff's Uitgeversmaatschappij N.V.

Globe and Mail. 1966. The Middle Kingdom: Best and Worst Areas for Jobs in Canada, 17 June, A7.

–. 1996. Editorial, 11 December, A18

–. 1997a. Office Leasing Explodes in Toronto, 4 March, B4.

–. 1997b. Politicians Will Try to Fill in the Doughnut, 25 February, A2.

–. 1997c. Population Controls Needed to Protect B.C., Study Says, 24 September, A6.

–. 1997d. Why a Hot Spot Has Growing Concerns, 20 October, A2.

Goldberg, Michael, and John Mercer. 1986. *The Myth of the North American City.* Vancouver: University of British Columbia Press.

Golden, Anne. 1998. The Ecstasy and the Agony. *Plan Canada* 38, 6: 22–5.

Goodwin, B. 1978. *Social Science and Utopia: Nineteenth Century Models of Social Harmony.* Sussex: Harvester Press.

Gordon, Peter, H.W. Richardson, and H.L. Wong. 1986. The Distribution of Population and Employment in a Polycentric City: The Case of Los Angeles. *Environment and Planning* A, 18: 161–73.

Gore, Charles. 1984. *Regions in Question.* London: Methuen.

Gottman, Jean. 1961. *Megalopolis: The Urbanized Northeastern Seaboard of the United States.* New York: Twentieth Century Fund.

–. 1976. Megalopolitan Systems Around the World. *Ekistics* 41, 243: 109–13.

–. 1982. The Metamorphosis of the Modern Metropolis. *Ekistics* 292: 7–11.

Governing Greater Vancouver: A Region of Communities. 1992. *City Magazine* 13, 3/4. Special issue.

Graham, Katherine A. 1992. Capital Planning, Capital Budgeting: The Future of Canada's Capital. In *How Ottawa Spends: The Politics of Competitiveness, 1992–93*, edited by Frances Abele, 125–50. Ottawa: Carleton University Press.

Grant, J. 1989. Hard Luck: The Failure of Regional Planning in Nova Scotia. *Canadian Journal of Regional Science* 12, 2: 273–84.

Greater Toronto Area Task Force. 1996. *Greater Toronto: Report of the GTA Task Force.* Toronto: Queen's Printer

Greater Triangle Regional Council. 1998. *Regional Case Study Series. Regional Development Choices Project.* Research Triangle Park, NC: Triangle Council of Governments.

Greater Vancouver Regional District, Planning Department. 1975. *The Livable Region, 1976–1986 (LRP): Proposals to Manage the Growth of Greater Vancouver: The Greater Vancouver Regional District.* Burnaby: Greater Vancouver Regional District (GVRD).

–. 1980. *The Livable Region from the 70s and the 80s.* September.

–. 1989a. *Livability Goals for Greater Vancouver.* Burnaby: GVRD.

–. 1989b. *Who Are We? What Do We Do?*

–. 1990a. *Creating Our Future: Steps to a More Livable Region.* September.

–. 1990b. *Choosing Our Future: Regional Challenge Seminar Reports.* April.

–. 1993a. *Creating Our Future 1993: Steps to a More Livable Region.* February.

–. 1993b. *Livable Region Strategic Plan Growth Management: A Compact Metropolitan Vancouver Region Option.*

–. 1994 (revised). *Creating Our Future: The History, Status, and Prospects of Regional Planning in Greater Vancouver.* July.

–. 1996. *Livable Region Strategic Plan.* April.

Green, Milford B., and Stephen P. Meyer. 1997. An Overview of Commuting in Canada With Special Emphasis on Rural Commuting and Employment. *Journal of Rural Studies* 13, 2: 163–75.

Greenberg, Ken. 1996. Toward a Supercity That Works. *Globe and Mail*, Focus section, 23 November, D1.

Greenwood, Rob. 1997. Righting a Capsized Economy. *Plan Canada* 37, 2: 21–6.

Guay, Jean-Paul. 1968. Montréal: Horizon 2000. Note retrospective. *Plan Canada* 9, 3: 94–107.

Gunton, Thomas. 1981. The Evolution of Urban and Regional Planning in Canada, 1900–1960. Ph.D. diss., University of British Columbia.

–. 1984. The Role of the Professional Planner. *Canadian Public Administration* 27, 3: 399–417.

Gunton, Thomas, and Clyde Weaver. 1982. From Drought Assistance to Mega Projects: Fifty Years of Regional Theory and Practice in Canada. *Canadian Journal of Regional Science* 5, 1: 5–37.

Guttenberg, Albert Z. 1977. Classifying Regions: A Conceptual Approach. *International Regional Science Review* 2, 3 (Fall): 1-13.

–. 1988. Regionalization as a Symbolic Process. *Canadian Journal of Regional Science* 11, 3: 373–92.

–. 1995. Whence "Regional" Science? *International Regional Science Review* 17, 3: 307–10.

Hahn, Alan J. 1970. Planning in Rural Areas. *Journal of the American Institute of Planners* 36 (January): 44–49.

Hall, Peter. 1974. *Urban and Regional Planning.* Hammondsworth Middlesex, England: Penguin Books.

–. 1988. *Cities of Tomorrow: An Intellectual History of Urban Planning and Design in the Twentieth Century.* Oxford, UK: Basil Blackwell. Updated 1996.

–. 1993. Forces Shaping Urban Europe. *Urban Studies* 30, 6: 883–98.

–. 1997. Modelling the Post-Industrial City. *Futures* 29, 4/5: 311–22.

Hall, Peter, and Colin Ward. 1998. *Sociable Cities: The Legacy of Ebenezer Howard.* New York, Toronto, and Chichester: John Wiley and Sons.

Halseth, Greg. 1993. Communities Within Communities: Changing "Residential" Areas at Cultus Lake, British Columbia. *Journal of Rural Studies* 9, 2: 175–87.

–. 1996. Community and Land-Use Planning Debate: An Example from Rural British Columbia. *Environment and Planning* A, 28: 1279–98.

Hansen, Alvin, and Harvey S. Perloff. 1942. *Regional Resource Development*. Washington, DC: National Planning Association.

Harasym, Don. 1996. Chapter Event: Interior "Growth Strategies." *Planning Institute of British Columbia News* 38, 5: 8-9.

Hardin, Garret. 1977. *The Tragedy of the Commons*. San Francisco: W.H. Freeman and Sons.

Harker, Harry. 1975. *The Peace River Region*. Briefing paper. Waterloo: University of Waterloo School of Urban and Regional Planning.

Harries-Jones, Peter. 1995. *Recursive Vision: Ecological Understanding and Gregory Bateson*. Toronto: University of Toronto Press.

Harvey, Stephen, and Anthony Usher. 1996. Communities and Natural Resource Management: Bridging the Gap. *Plan Canada* 36, 6: 34-8.

Healey, Patsy. 1997. *Collaborative Planning: Shaping Places in Fragmented Societies*. Vancouver: UBC Press.

Healey, Patsy, A. Khakee, A. Motte, and B. Needham. 1996. *Making Strategic Spatial Plans*. London: UCL Press.

Heitkamp, Fern. 1996. Using Stewardship as a Guide for Planning. *Plan Canada* 36, 4: 28-32.

Helling, Amy. 1998. Collaborative Visioning: Proceed With Caution! Results from Evaluating Atlanta's Vision 2020 Project. *Journal of the American Planning Association* 64, 2: 335-49.

Heseltine, John. 1998. Grow East, Young Plan. *Plan Canada* 38, 3: 16-23.

Higgins, Benjamin. 1981. The Task Ahead: The Search for a New Local and Regional Development Strategy in the 1980s. United Nation Centre for Regional Development. Nagoya, Japan, November.

Higgins, Donald J.H. 1986. *Local and Urban Politics in Canada*. Toronto: Gage Educational Publishing.

Hilts, Stewart, and Tom Moull. 1988. Toward a Theory of Rural Planning. In *Integrated Rural Planning and Development*, edited by F. Dykeman, 105-12. Sackville, NB: Mount Allison University Small Town and Rural Research Program.

Hirschman, Albert O. 1958. *The Strategy of Economic Development*. New Haven, CT: Yale University Press.

Hodge, Gerald. 1966. T*he Identification of "Growth Poles" in Eastern Ontario*. Toronto: Ontario Department of Economics and Development.

-. 1967. *Development Capability of Rural and Urban Areas in Prince Edward Island*. A Report to the Province of Prince Edward Island. Toronto: Acres Research and Planning.

-. 1969. *Urbanization in Regional Development: A Research Agenda*. Ottawa: Canadian Council on Urban and Regional Research.

-. 1970. *Parameters and Patterns of Industrial Location in the Toronto Urban Field*. Research Paper No. 31. Toronto: University of Toronto Centre for Urban and Community Studies.

-. 1975. Regional Planning: Where It's At. *Plan Canada* 15, 2: 87-94.

-. 1985. The Roots of Canadian Planning. *Journal of the American Planning Association* 51, 1: 8-22.

-. 1988. Canada. In *Policies and Plans for Rural People*, edited by Paul Cloke, 166-91. London: Unwin Hyman.

-. 1993. *Canada's Aging Rural Population: The Role and Response of Local Government*. Toronto: ICURR Press.

-. 1994. Regional Planning: The Cinderella Discipline. *Plan Canada* 34, 4: 35-49. Special edition.

-. 1998. *Planning Canadian Communities: An Introduction to the Principles, Practice and Participants*. 3rd ed. Toronto and New York: International Thomson Nelson.

Hodge, Gerald, and Jacques D. Paris. 1969. *Identifying Parameters of Rural Non-Farm Poverty in Canada*. A Report to the Canada Department of Health and Welfare, Toronto.

Hodge, Gerald, and Mohammad A. Qadeer. 1986. *Towns and Villages in Canada: The Importance of Being Unimportant*. Toronto: Butterworths.

Hollo, William S. 1989. Enforcing Regional Priorities Through Regional Official Plans. Paper presented at a session entitled Working with Regional Government: Development Issues. 13 February. Toronto: Insight.

Holston, James. 1998. Making the Invisible Visible. In *Making the Visible Invisible: A Multicultural History of Planning*, edited by Leonie Sandercock. Los Angeles: University of California Press.

Hoover, Edgar M. 1971. *An Introduction to Regional Economics*. New York: Alfred A. Knopf.

Hostovsky, Chuck, David Miller, and Cathy Keddy. 1995. The Natural Environment Systems Strategy: Protecting Ottawa-Carleton's Ecological Areas. *Plan Canada* 35, 6 (November): 26-32.

Hough, Michael. 1990. *Out of Place: Restoring Identity to the Regional Landscape*. New Haven, CT: Yale University Press.

Howard, E. [1902] 1946, 1965. *Garden Cities of Tomorrow*. Republished with the same title in 1946 (with Preface by Frederic J. Osborne and Introduction by Lewis Mumford) London: Faber and Faber; paperback edition 1965. Reprinted in 1970 and 1974. Originally published as *To-Morrow! A Peaceful Path to Real Reform*. London: Swan-Sonnenschein, 1898.

Howard, Ross. 1997. Why a Hot Spot Has Growing Concerns. *Globe and Mail*, 20 October, A2.

Howard, Ross, and Ann Gibbon. 1998. SkyTrain Expensive Ride, Municipal Leaders Fear, *Globe and Mail*, 25 June, A9.

Hutton, Thomas A. 1998. *The Transformation of Canada's Pacific Metropolis: A Study of Vancouver*. Montreal: Institute for Research on Public Policy (IRPP).

IBI Group and Associates. 1990. *Greater Toronto Area Urban Structure Concepts Study, Summary Report*. Toronto: Greater Toronto Coordinating Committee.

Innes, Judith E. 1995. Planning Theory's Emerging Paradigm: Communicative Action and Interactive Practice. *Journal of Planning Education and Research* 14, 3: 183-90.

–. 1996. Planning Through Consensus-Building. *Journal of the American Planning Association* 62, 4: 460-72.

Innis, Harold A. 1957. *Essays in Canadian Economic History*. Toronto: University of Toronto Press.

International Union for the Conservation of Nature and Natural Resources (IUCN). 1980. *World Conservation Strategy*. Gland, Switzerland: IUCN.

Isard, Walter. 1956a. *Location and Space Economy: A General Theory Relating to Industrial Location, Market Areas, Land Use, Trade and Urban Structure*. Boston: MIT Press/John Wiley and Sons.

–. 1956b. Regional Science, the Concept of Region, and Regional Structure. *Papers and Proceedings of the Regional Science Association* 2: 13-26.

Isard, Walter, et al. 1960. *Methods of Regional Analysis: An Introduction to Regional Science*. New York: John Wiley and Son.

Isard, Walter, and Eugene W. Schooler. 1959. Industrial Complex Analysis, Agglomeration Economies and Regional Development. *Journal of Regional Science* 1, 2 (Spring): 19-34.

Isserman, Andrew. 1993. Lost in Space? On the History, Status, and Future of Regional Science. *Review of Regional Studies* 23: 1-50.

–. 1995. The History, Status, and Future of Regional Science: An Historical Perspective. *International Regional Science Review* 17, 3: 249-96.

Jacobs, Harvey M. 1989. Localism and Land Use Planning. *Journal of Architectural and Planning Research* 6, 1: 1-18.

Jacobs, Jane. 1984. *Cities and the Wealth of Nations*. New York: Vintage Books.

Jacobs, Michael. 1991. *The Green Economy: Environment, Sustainable Development and the Politics of the Future*. London: Pluto Press and Vancouver: UBC Press.

Jacobs, Peter, and Barry Sadler, eds. n.d. *Sustainable Development and Environmental Assessment*. A background paper prepared for the Canadian Environmental Assessment Research Council.

Jameson, Carolyn. 1978. The Niagara Escarpment: A Unique Approach to Planning. *Ontario Housing* 21, 4: 6-8.

Jewczk, Stephen. 1994. Towards a Sustainable Society: CIP's Agenda for the Millennium. *Plan Canada* 34, 4 (July): 122-3. Special edition.

Jones, Margaret. 1985. *The Community is Quite Capable*. Guelph, ON: University of Guelph School of Rural Planning and Development.

Kanter, Rosabeth Moss. 1995. *World Class: Thriving Locally in the Global Economy.* New York: Simon and Schuster.

Katz, Peter. 1997. A New Urbanist Perspective on Regionalism. *The Regionalist* 2, 4: 50-5.

Kellas, Hugh. 1997. Six Degrees of Interaction. *Plan Canada* 37, 6: 10-1.

–. 1998. Panel Discussion on Regional Planning. *Plan Canada* 38, 3: 3.

–. 1998. Personal correspondence, 25 October.

Kemmis, Daniel. 1990. *Community and the Politics of Place.* University of Oklahoma Press: Norman, Oklahoma and London.

Khakee, Abdul, and Nicholas Low. 1996. Central-Local Relations in Sweden and Australia: Power, Responsibility and Territorial Equity in Comparative Equity. *International Planning Studies* 1, 3: 331-56.

Kiernan, Matthew J. 1982. Ideology and the Precarious Future of the Canadian Planning Profession. *Plan Canada* 22, 1 (March): 14-22.

Kirby, Graham. 1992. *Final Report of the Ottawa–Carleton Regional Review Commission.* November.

Koestler, Arthur. [1967] 1976. *The Ghost in the Machine.* Danube edition. London: Hutchinson. Reprinted New York: Random House.

Kollmorgen, Walter M. 1945. Crucial Deficiencies in Regionalism. Papers and proceedings. *American Economic Review* (May): 374-89.

Korten, David. 1999. *The Post-Corporate World: Life After Capitalism.* San Francisco: Berrett-Koehler; West Hartford, CT: Kumarian Press.

Kropotkin, Peter. 1899. *Fields, Factories and Workshops; Or Industry Combined with Agriculture, and Brain Work Combined with Manual Work.* London: Hutchinson.

–. [1902] 1955. *Mutual Aid: A Factor of Evolution.* London. Boston: Extending Horizons Books.

Kruger, John. 1995. A Bold New Look. *Plan Canada* 35, 2: 12-3.

Kuhn, Thomas S. 1971. *The Structure of Scientific Revolutions.* 2nd ed. Chicago: University of Chicago Press.

Lash, Harry. 1976. *Planning in a Human Way.* Ottawa: Ministry of State for Urban Affairs and Macmillan Canada.

Lawrence, David. 1992. Planning and Environmental Assessment: Never the Twain Shall Meet? *Plan Canada* 32, 3: 22-6.

LeBlanc, Janice M. 1988. New Brunswick Regional Development Commissions: An Integrated Approach to Local Area Planning and Development. In *Integrated Rural Planning and Development*, edited by F. Dykeman, 197-211. Sackville, NB: Mount Allison University Small Town and Rural Research Program.

Ledebur, Larry D., and William Barnes. 1993. *All in It Together: Cities, Suburbs, Local Economic Regions.* A Research Report of the National League of Cities. Washington: National League of Cities.

Léonard, Jacques. 1978. Rencontre avec les maires de la région de Montréal (Option préférable d'aménagement pour la région de Montréal). Québec: Ministère du Conseil exécutif.

Leopold, Aldo. 1969. The Land Ethic. In *The Subversive Science: Essays toward an Ecology of Man*, edited by Paul Shepard and Daniel McKinley. Boston: Houghton Mifflin.

Leung Hok-Lin. 1992. *City Images: An Internal View.* Kingston, ON: Ronald P. Frye.

Levin, Earl. 1977. Lessons from Regional Government: Winnipeg. Seminar on Lessons from Regional Government, School of Business Administration, University of Western Ontario, London, Ontario, 23 September.

–. 1978. Planning in the Context of Alternative Forms of Government, *Seminar on Alternative Forms of Government*, Edmonton, Alberta, 13 September.

–. 1993. City History and City Planning. In *Winnipeg*, vol. 2, chap. 2. Ph.D. diss., University of Manitoba.

Lithwick, N.H. 1976. *Regional Economic Policy: The Canadian Experience.* Toronto: McGraw-Hill Ryerson.

–. 1986a. Federal Government Regional Economic Development Policies: An Evaluative Survey. In *Disparities and Interregional Adjustment*, edited by Kenneth Norrie, 109-57. Toronto: University of Toronto Press.

–. 1986b. Regional Policy: The Embodiment of Contradictions. In *The Canadian Economy: A Regional Perspective*, edited by Donald J. Savoie, 252-68. Toronto: Methuen.

Little, Bruce. 1999. Tale of Three Canadian Cities: What Makes Them Grow So Big? *Globe and Mail*, 20 September, 2.

Lotz, Jim. 1970. *Northern Realities*. Toronto: New Press.

Lower Mainland Regional Planning Board. 1963. *Chance and Challenge*. New Westminster.

–. 1966. *Official Regional Plan for the Lower Mainland Planning Area*. New Westminster.

Lubove, Roy. 1967. *The Urban Community: Housing and Planning in the Progressive Era*. Englewood Cliffs, NJ: Prentice Hall.

Luccarelli, Marc. 1995. *Lewis Mumford and the Ecological Region: The Politics of Planning*. New York and London: Guilford Press.

Lynch, Kevin. 1960. *The Image of the City*. Cambridge, MA: MIT Press.

–. 1976. *Managing the Sense of a Region*. Cambridge, MA: MIT Press.

Maass, Arthur. 1959a. Division of Powers: An Areal Analysis. In *Area and Power: A Theory of Local Government*, edited by Arthur Maass, 9-26. Glencoe, IL: Free Press.

–, ed. 1959b. *Area and Power: A Theory of Local Government*. Glencoe, IL: Free Press.

Macdonald, H. Ian. 1984. A Retrospective View from the Top. *Plan Canada* 24, 3/4: 92-9.

Mackaye, Benton. 1921. An Appalachian Trail: A Project in Regional Planning. *Journal of the AIA* 9(October): 325-30.

–. [1928] 1962. *The New Exploration: A Philosophy of Regional Planning*. Urbana: University of Illinois Press. Originally published in New York: Harcourt, Brace.

Mackaye, Benton, and Lewis Mumford. 1929. Regional Planning. In *Encyclopedia Britannica*, 14th ed. 19: 71-2.

Maclaren, James F. Ltd. 1975. *Countryside Planning: A Methodology and Policies for Huron County and the Province of Ontario*. Toronto: Ontario Ministry of Housing.

Magnusson, Warren. 1985. The Local State in Canada: Theoretical Perspectives. *Canadian Public Administration* 28 (Winter): 575-99.

Magnusson, Warren, and Andrew Sancton, eds. 1983. *City Politics in Canada*. Toronto: University of Toronto Press.

Magnusson, Warren, et al., eds. 1984. *The New Reality: The Politics of Restraint in BC*. Vancouver: New Star.

Mah, Peter. 1998. Changing the Dynamics of Rural Planning: A Rural Manitoba Planning Perspective. *Plan Canada* 38, 2: 25-9.

Manitoba, Committee of Review, City of Winnipeg Act. 1976. Taraska Report. *Report and Recommendations*. Winnipeg.

Manitoba Intergovernmental Affairs. 2001. *Planning Manitoba's Capital Region: Next Steps*. Winnipeg: Manitoba Intergovernmental Affairs. January.

Manning, E.W. 1990. Presidential Address: Sustainable Development: The Challenge. *The Canadian Geographer* 34, 4: 290-303.

Manuel, Frank E., and Fritzie P. Manuel. 1979. *Utopian Thought in the Western World*. Cambridge, MA: Belknap Press of Harvard University Press.

Markusen, Ann. 1994. *Growing Pains: Thoughts on Theory, Method, and Politics for a Regional Science of the Future*. Working Paper No. 81. Piscataway, NJ: Center for Urban Policy Research.

Masson, Jack. 1985. *Alberta's Local Governments and Their Politics*. Edmonton: Pica Pica Press.

Mathias, Philip. 1971. *Forced Growth*. Toronto: James Lewis and Samuel.

Matthews, Ralph. 1976. *There's No Better Place Than Here: Social Change in Three Newfoundland Communities*. Toronto: Peter Martin.

–. 1983. *The Creation of Regional Dependency*. Toronto: University of Toronto Press.

Mathur, Brijesh. 1989. Conserving the Urban River Corridor: Experience from Saskatoon. *Plan Canada* 29, 5: 43-9.

Mazza, Patrick. 1997. Uncovering the Hidden History of Regionalism: The American Regionalist Insurgency of the 1920s-1940s. Cascadia Planet website (www.tnews.com/text/regionalist_insurgency.html).

McCloskey, David. 1993. On Ecoregional Boundaries. In *Boundaries of Home: Mapping for Local Empowerment*, edited by Doug Aberley, 60-3. Gabriola Island, BC: New Society Publishers.

McDowell, B.D. 1986. Regional Planning Today. In *The Practice of State and Regional Planning*, edited by F.S. So, L. Hand, and B.D. McDowell, 133–65. Chicago: American Planning Association.

McGee, Terry. 1999. Governing Mega-Urban Regions: The Case of Vancouver. In *Urban and Regional Governance in the Asia Pacific*, edited by John Friedmann. 115–26. Vancouver: UBC Institute of Asian Research.

McGee, Terry, and Ira M. Robinson, eds. 1997. *The Mega-Urban Regions of Southeast Asia.* Vancouver: UBC Press.

McGinnis, Michael Vincent. 1999. *Bioregionalism.* London: Routledge.

McMahon, Fred. 1996. *Looking the Gift Horse in the Mouth: The Impact of Federal Transfers on Atlantic Canada.* Halifax: Institute for Market Studies.

McTaggart, W. Donald. 1993. Bioregionalism and Regional Geography: Place, People and Networks. *The Canadian Geographer* 37, 4: 307–19.

Meller, Helen. 1990. Some Reflections on the Concept of Megalopolis and Its Use by Patrick Geddes and Lewis Mumford. In *Megalopolis: The Giant City in History*, edited by Theo Barker and Anthony Sutcliffe, 116–29. London: St. Martin's Press.

Mellon, Hugh. 1993. Reforming the Electoral System of Metropolitan Toronto: Doing away with Dual Representation. *Canadian Public Administration* 36, 1: 38–56.

Mendelson, Michael. 2000. The Emancipation of Cities. In *Toronto: Considering Self-Government*, 73–7. Owen Sound, ON: Ginger Press.

Meyerson, Martin, and Edward C. Banfield. 1955. *Politics, Planning and the Public Interest: The Case of Public Housing in Chicago.* New York: Free Press.

Mitchell, Alanna. 1997. World Watches as Banff Debates Its Future. *Globe and Mail*, 30 May, A2.

Momsen, Jane. 1984. Urbanization of the Countryside in Alberta. In *The Pressures of Change in Rural Canada*, edited by Michael Bunce and Michael Troughton, 160–80. Geographical Monograph No. 14. Toronto: York University Department of Geography.

Montréal, Ville de. 1967. *Montréal: Horizon 2000.* Montréal: Ville de Montréal.

Mumford, Lewis. 1929. *Encyclopedia Britannica*, 14th ed., s.v. "regional planning."

–. 1932. The Plan of New York. New Republic 71, (15 June): 121-6; (19 June): 146-154

–. 1938. *The Culture of Cities.* New York: Harcourt Brace and Company.

–. 1982. *Sketches from Life: The Autobiography of Lewis Mumford: The Early Years.* New York: Dial Press.

Munn, R.E., ed. 1979. *Environmental Impact Assessment: Principles and Procedures. Scope 5.* Toronto: John Wiley and Sons. Published on behalf of the Scientific Committee on Problems of the Environment (Scope) of the International Council of Scientific Unions (ICSU).

Murchie, Graham. 1995. Looking Beyond Vancouver's Picture Postcard Beauty. *Plan Canada* 35, 3 (May): 9–10.

Myrdal, Gunnar. 1957. *Economic Theory and Underdeveloped Regions.* London: Duckworth.

Nader, George. 1976. *Cities of Canada.* Vol. I. New York: Macmillan.

National Capital Commission. 1974. *Tomorrow's Capital.* Ottawa: National Capital Commission.

–. 1991. *A Capital in the Making: Reflections of the Past and Visions of the Future.* Unpublished. Ottawa: National Capital Commission Planning Branch. April.

–. 1996. *Greenbelt Master Plan Summary.* Ottawa: National Capital Commission.

National Task Force on Environment and Economy. 1987. *Report.* Ottawa: Canadian Council of Resource and Environment Ministers.

Nelson, J.G. 1991. Sustainable Development, Conservation Strategies and Heritage. In *Resource Management and Development*, edited by B. Mitchell, 245–67. Toronto: Oxford University Press.

New Brunswick, Department of Municipal Affairs. 1980. *A Study of Sprawl in New Brunswick.* Fredericton.

New York State, Commission of Housing and Regional Planning. 1926. *Report to Governor Alfred E. Smith.* Albany: Commission of Housing and Regional Planning.

Newman, Monroe. 1997. Living in Two Worlds: Regional Scientists and Policymakers. *International Regional Science Review* 19, 3: 247–51.

Niagara Escarpment Planning and Development Act, 1973. Toronto: Queen's Printer.

Nowlan, David, and Greg Stewart. 1991. Downtown Population Growth and Commuting Trips: Recent Experience in Toronto. *Journal of the American Planning Association* 52, 2 (Spring): 165–82.

Oberlander, H. Peter, and Patrick J. Smith. 1993. Governing Metropolitan Vancouver: Regional Intergovernmental Relations in British Columbia. In *Metropolitan Governance: American/Canadian Intergovernmental Perspectives*, edited by D.R. Rothblatt and A. Sancton, vol. I: 329–73. Berkeley: University of California Institute of Governmental Studies; Kingston, ON: Queen's University Institute of Intergovernmental Relations.

Odum, Howard. 1935. *The Regional Approach to National Social Planning.* New York: Foreign Policy Association.

Odum, Howard, and Harry E. Moore. 1938. *American Regionalism: A Cultural-Historical Approach to National Integration.* New York: Henry Holt.

Odum, Howard and K. Jocher, eds. 1945. *In Search of the Regional Balance of America.* Chapel Hill: University of North Carolina Press.

Ohmae, Kenichi. 1990. *The Borderless World: Power and Strategy in the Interlinked World Economy.* New York: Harper Bros.

Oldman River Regional Planning Commission. 1974. *Intermunicipal Services: Libraries.* Lethbridge, AB.

Ontario, Department of Municipal Affairs. 1967. *Choices for a Growing Region: A Report of the Metropolitan Toronto and Region Transportation Study.* Toronto: MTRTS.

Ontario, Ministry of Housing. 1976. *Countryside Planning: A Pilot Study of Huron County.* Toronto: Queen's Printer. A report prepared by James F. MacLaren Ltd.

Ontario, Ministry of Municipal Affairs. 1970. *Design for Development: The Toronto-Centred Region.* Toronto: Queen's Printer.

Ontario Design for Development. 1966. Statement by the Prime Minister of the Province of Ontario on Regional Development Policy, 5 April.

–. 1968. *Design for Development, Phase 2:* Statement by the Honourable W. Darcy McKeough to the Legislature of Ontario, 2 December.

–. 1972. *Design for Development, Phase Three:* Statements by the Honourable William Davis, Premier of Ontario, and the Honourable D. McKeough, Treasurer of Ontario, June.

Ontario, Ministry of Natural Resources. 1994. *Partnerships for Community Involvement in Forestry.* Toronto: Queen's Printer.

Ontario Round Table on Environment and Economy (ORTEE). 1992. *Restructuring for Sustainability.* September. Toronto: ORTEE.

Orr, David W. 1992. *Ecological Literacy: Education and the Transition to a Postmodern World.* Albany: State University of New York Press.

Osborne, Frederick J. 1946. Preface. In *Garden Cities of Tomorrow* by Ebenezer Howard. London: Faber and Faber.

–, ed. 1965. *Garden Cities of Tomorrow.* Introduction by Lewis Mumford. Cambridge, MA: MIT Press.

Ottawa-Carleton Regional Review Commission (David Bartlett, Commissioner). 1988. *Report, Phase II.* Ottawa-Carleton: The Commission.

Owen, Robert. 1913. *A New View of Society, or Essays on the Principle of the Formation of the Human Character.* London: Cadell and Davies.

Paasi, A. 1991. Deconstructing Regions: Notes on the Scale of Spatial Life. *Environment and Planning* 23: 239–56.

Paetkau, Wesley D.P. 1996. Form versus Function: A Critique of Manitoba's Capital Region Initiative, 1989 to 1996. Master's thesis, University of Manitoba.

Paris, Jacques. 1967. Policy Development for Redevelopment in Depressed Rural Areas. Master's thesis, University of Toronto.

Parks, R.B., and R.J. Oakerson. 1989. Metropolitan Organization and Governance: A Local Public Economy Approach. *Urban Affairs Quarterly* 15, 1: 18–29.

Parr, Anthony. 1998. Editor's Foreword to a special issue on planning. *Plan Canada* 38, 3: 3–5.

Parsons, Kermit C. 1994. Collaborative Genius: The Regional Planning Association of America. *Journal of the American Planning Association* 60, 4: 462–82.

Pastor, Manuel Jr., Peter Dreier, J. Eugene Grigsby III, and Marta Lopez-Garza. 2000. *Regions That Work: How Cities and Suburbs Can Grow Together.* St. Paul: University of Minnesota Press.

Patterson, Jeffrey. 1998. Greater Vancouver: Testing the Partnership Model of Growth Management. Final draft of a paper presented at an International Symposium on Emerging Land Use Law. *Pacific Rim Law and Policy Journal* 7, 3 (June): 721-63.

Peace River-Liard Regional District. 1972. *Economic Incentives for the Peace River-Liard Region.* Dawson Creek, BC.

Peace River Regional Planning Commission. 1972. *The People of the Peace: Their Goals and Objectives.* Grande Prairie, AB.

-. 1973. *The Preliminary Regional Plan.* Grande Prairie, AB.

Peirce, Neal R., Curtis W. Johnson, and John Stuart Hall. 1993. *Citistates: How Urban America Can Prosper in a Competitive World.* Washington, DC: Seven Oaks Press.

Perks, William T. 1965. Planning in the Province of Quebec: Towards a Regional Development Policy. *Town Planning Review* (October): 197-210.

-. 1986. Canada. In *International Handbook on Land Use Planning*, edited by Nicholas N. Patricios, 447-98. New York and London: Greenwood Press.

Perks, William T., and Ira M. Robinson, eds. 1979. *Urban and Regional Planning in a Federal State.* Stroudsberg, PA: Dowden, Hutchinson and Ross; Toronto: McGraw-Hill.

Perloff, Harvey S. 1957. *Education for City, State, and Regional Planning.* Baltimore: Johns Hopkins University Press.

-. 1968. Key Features of Regional Planning. *Journal of the American Institute of Planners* 34, 3: 153-9.

Perroux, F. 1950. Economic Space: Theory and Applications. *Quarterly Journal of Economics* 64: 90-97.

Perry, John. 1974. *Inventory of Regional Planning Administration in Canada.* Staff Paper No. 1. Toronto: Intergovernmental Committee on Urban and Regional Research. June.

Perry, Stewart E., and Mike Lewis. 1994. *Reinventing the Local Economy.* Vernon, BC: Centre for Community Enterprise.

Philbrook, Tom. 1967. Regional Development and Social Change. *Canadian Journal of Agricultural Economics* 15: 80-9.

Phillips, P. 1978. *Regional Disparities.* Toronto: James Lorimer.

Picard, André. 1996. Boosters Cheer as City Perilously Declines. *Globe and Mail*, 14 May, A2.

Pickett, S.H., and B.E. Wallis. 1972. The Evolution of Regional Planning in Newfoundland. *Plan Canada* 2: 3.

Planning Institute of BC. 1996. Chapter Event: Interior Growth Strategies. *PIBC News* 38, 5: 8.

Poiker, Tom, and Michael Kennedy. 1995. Dynamic Spatial Objects. Proceedings of an ESRI conference.

Polese, Mario. 1996. Montreal: A City in Search of a Country. *Policy Options* (September): 31-4.

Poole, Kenneth. 1996. Federal Regional Development Initiatives in Canada and the United States: Lessons from History. *The Regionalist* 1, 4: 21-40.

Porter, Douglas R. 1989. Significant Research Needs in the Policy and Practice of Growth Management. In *Understanding Growth Management: Critical Issues and a Research Agenda*, edited by D.J. Brower, D.R. Godschalk, and D.R. Porter, 181. Washington, DC: Urban Institute.

Preston, Richard E. 1991. Central Place Theory and the Canadian Urban System. In *Canadian Cities in Transition*, edited by Trudi Bunting and Pierre Filion, 148-69. Toronto: Oxford University Press.

Proudhon, P.-J. [1840] 1966. Qu'est ce-que la propriete? Or Recherche sur la principe du droit et du gouvernment. Paris: Garnier-Flammarion.

Qadeer, Mohammad A. 1979. Issues and Approaches of Rural Community Planning in Canada. *Plan Canada* 10, 2: 106-21.

Québec, Gouvernement du. 1980. *Guide explicatif de la loi sur l'aménagement et l'urbanisme.* Québec: Ministère des Affaires municipales.

Québec, Ministère du Conseil exécutif, Comité ministériel permanent de développement du Grand Montréal. 1991. *Pour un redressement durable: plan stratégique du Grand Montréal.* Québec: Gouvernement du Québec.

Québec, Ministère de la Métropole. 1996. Toward a Greater Montreal Development Commission, Consultation Document. Greater Montreal Fostering Prosperity. Montreal: Ministère de la Métropole.

Quesnel, Louise. 1990. Political Control over Planning in Quebec. *International Journal of Urban and Regional Research* 14, 1: 25-48.

Raven, Peter, ed. 2000. *The Quest for a Sustainable World.* Washington, DC: US National Research Council.

Rawson, Mary. 1976. *Ill Fares the Land - Land Use Management at the Urban, Rural, Resources Edges: The British Columbia Land Commission.* Ottawa: Minister of State for Urban Affairs.

Rees, William E. 1979. The Canada Land Inventory and Its Impact on Regional Planning. In *Urban and Regional Planning in a Federal State: The Canadian Experience,* edited by W.T. Perks and I.M. Robinson, 159-71. Stroudsberg, PA: Dowden Hutchinson and Ross.

-. 1982. Planning Our Arctic Frontier. *Plan Canada* 21, 4.

Regional Planning Association of America. 1925. *Survey Graphic* 7 (May): entire issue.

Regional Science Association. 1955. *Papers and Proceedings* of the First Annual Meeting, held in Detroit, MI, December 1954. Edited by Gerald A.P. Carrothers. Philadelphia: University of Pennsylvania.

-. 1958. *Papers and Proceedings* of the Fourth Annual Meeting held in Philadelphia, PA, December 1957. Edited by Gerald A.P. Carrothers. Philadelphia: University of Pennsylvania.

Reid, Barton. 1995. City Beat, *New City Magazine* 16, 1 (Spring): 6-9.

-. 1996. New Agendas for Regional Government. *New City Magazine* 17. Special Issue.

Reid, Donald G., and Anthony Fuller. 1995. Tourism: Saviour or False Hope of the Rural Economy. *Plan Canada* 35, 2: 22-6.

Reid, Evelyne, and Maurice Yeates. 1991. Bill 90: An Act to Protect Agricultural Land and Assessment of Its Success in LaPrairie County, Quebec. *Urban Geography* 12, 4: 295-309.

Reiner, Thomas. 1963. Organizing Regional Investment Criteria. *Papers and Proceedings of the Regional Science Association,* 11: 63-72.

Resources for Tomorrow. 1961. *Conference Background Papers,* Vols. I and II. For the Resources for Tomorrow Conference, held in Montreal, Quebec, 23-28 October, 1961. Ottawa: Queen's Printer.

-. 1962. *Proceedings of the Conference.* Vol. III. February. Ottawa: Queen's Printer.

Revel, Richard. 1981. Conservation in Northern Canada: International Biological Conservation Sites Revisited. *Biological Conservation* 21: 263-87.

Rhodes, R.A.W. 1986. *The National World of Local Government.* London: Allen and Unwin.

Rich, K., J.M. Rich, P. Wilkinson, and C. Lowe. 1997. Location Vocation, Natuashish: Planning a New Aboriginal Community. *Plan Canada* 37, 6: 16-17.

Richardson, Nigel H. 1981. Insubstantial Pageant: The Rise and Fall of Provincial Planning in Ontario. *Canadian Public Administration* 24: 563-86.

-. 1984. Guest Editor's Foreword. Special Issue on Planning in Ontario, 1966-1975. *Plan Canada* 24, 3/4: 88-91.

-. 1989a. *Land Use Planning and Sustainable Development Planning in Canada.* Ottawa: Canadian Environmental Advisory Council.

-. 1989b. Land Use Planning and Sustainable Development in the Canadian North. *Plan Canada* 29, 2: 56-62.

-. 1994. Canada in the Twentieth Century: Planning for Conservation and the Environment. *Plan Canada* 34, 3 (July): 52-65. Special edition.

-. 1996. What Is a Sustainable City? *Plan Canada* 36, 5: 34-8.

Richardson, Nigel H., John Hitchcock, Barry Mitchell, and Beth Savan. 1991. *Ontario's Future: People, Land and the Environment: A Discussion Paper.* Toronto: University of Toronto, Innis College and the Department of Geography.

Richert, Evan D., Mark B. Lapping et al. 1998. Ebenezer Howard and the Garden City. *Journal of the American Planning Association* 64, 2 (Spring): 125-207.

Roberts, Peter. 1994. Sustainable Regional Planning. *Regional Studies* 28: 781-8.

Robichaud, Armand G. 1997. Rural Planning in New Brunswick (Wake Up and Smell the Coffee). *Plan Canada* 37, 5: 42-4.

Robinson, Ira M. 1961. The Peace River Region. In *Resources for Tomorrow Conference Background Papers*, vol. I: 505-26. Ottawa.

–. 1962. *New Industrial Towns on Canada's Resource Frontier*. Chicago: University of Chicago Program of Education and Research in Planning, Research Paper No. 4; and Department of Geography, Research Paper No. 73.

–. 1972. *Decision-Making in Urban Planning: An Introduction to New Methodologies*. Beverly Hills, CA: Sage Publications.

–. 1979. Trends in Provincial Land Planning, Control and Management. In *Urban and Regional Planning in a Federal State: The Canadian Experience*, edited by W.T. Perks and I.M. Robinson, 204–337. Stroudsburg, PA: Dowden, Hutchinson and Ross.

–. 1995. Emerging Spatial Patterns in ASEAN Mega-Urban Regions: Alternative Strategies. In *The Mega-Urban Regions of Southeast Asia*, edited by T.G. McGee and Ira M. Robinson, 78–107. Vancouver: UBC Press.

Robinson, Ira M., and Douglas R. Webster. 1985. Regional Planning in Canada: History, Practice, Issues and Prospects. *Journal of the American Planning Association* 51, 1: 23–33.

Rodwin, Lloyd. 1963. Choosing Regions for Development. In *Public Policy: A Yearbook of the Harvard University Graduate School of Public Administration*, edited by Carl Friedrich and Seymour Harris, vol. 12: 141–62.

Romanos, M.C. 1978. Energy-Price Effects on Metropolitan Spatial Structure and Form. *Environment and Planning*, vol. A, 10: 93–104.

Roosevelt, Franklin D. 1938. *The Public Papers and Addresses of Franklin D. Roosevelt*. Vol. 1. New York: Random House.

Rose, Albert. 1972. *Governing Metropolitan Toronto: A Social and Political Analysis, 1953-1971*. Berkeley: University of California Press.

Rosenberg, Mark. 1993. Has Regional Policy Failed Canada or Has Regional Science Failed Regional Policy? *Canadian Journal of Regional Science* 16, 1: 107-13.

Rothblatt, Donald N. 1982. *Planning the Metropolis: The Multiple Advocacy Approach*. New York: Praeger.

–. 1994. North American Metropolitan Planning. *Journal of the American Planning Association* 60, 4: 501-20.

Rothblatt, Donald N., and Andrew Sancton, eds. 1993. *Metropolitan Governance: American/Canadian Intergovernmental Perspectives*. Berkeley: University of California Press.

Rowe, Mary W., ed. 2000. *Toronto: Considering Self-Government*. Owen Sound, ON: Ginger Press.

Rowley, H.J. 1961. The St. John River Basin. In *Resources for Tomorrow*. Conference Background Papers, 311-23. Ottawa: Queen's Printer. October.

Royal Commission on Dominion-Provincial Relations (Rowell-Sirois Commission). 1940. *Book 2: Recommendations*. Ottawa: Queen's Printer.

Royal Commission on the Future of Toronto's Waterfront (Crombie Commission). 1990. *Watershed*. Interim Report. Toronto: Queen's Printer.

–. 1992. *Regeneration. Toronto's Waterfront and the Sustainable City: Final Report*. Ottawa and Toronto: Supply and Services Canada and Queen's Printer of Ontario.

Royal Commission on Metropolitan Development of Calgary and Edmonton. 1956. *Report*. Edmonton: Queen's Printer. January.

Royal Commission on Metropolitan Toronto. 1977. *Report*. 2 vols. The Honourable John Robarts, Commissioner. Toronto: Ontario Government Publications.

Rusk, David. 1993. *Cities without Suburbs*. Baltimore: Johns Hopkins University Press.

Russwurm, Lorne H. 1987. Perspectives on Post World War II Rural Planning in Canada. In *International Yearbook of Rural Planning*, edited by A. Gilg, Vol. 2: 185-223. Cambridge, MA: Geo Books Cambridge University Press.

Rust-D'Eye, George H. 1989. *The Planning Act: Is Council in Control?* Toronto: Insight.

Rybczynski, Witold. 1995. *City Life: Urban Expectations in a New World*. New York: Scribner/ Harper Collins Publishers.

–. 1998. Urban All Over the World: Essays on the Millennium. *Maclean's*, 14 September: 48-52.

Sadler, Barry, ed. 1985. *Environmental Protection and Resource Development: Convergence for Today*. Publication of Proceedings funded by Canadian Petroleum Association, and

Northern Affairs Program, Department of Indian and Northern Affairs. Calgary, AB: University of Calgary Press.

Sale, Kirkpatrick. 1984. Bioregionalism: A New Way to Treat the Land. *The Ecologist* 14, 4: 167-73.

–. 1985. *Dwellers in the Land: The Bioregional Vision.* Philadelphia, PA, and Gabriola Island, BC: New Society Publishers; San Francisco: Sierra Club.

Sancton, Andrew. 1985. *Governing the Island of Montreal: Language Differences and Metropolitan Politics.* Berkeley: University of California Press.

–. 1988. Montreal's Metropolitan Government. *Quebec Studies* 6: 12-25.

–. 1994. *Governing Canada's City-Regions: Adapting Form to Function.* Montreal: Institute for Research in Public Policy (IRPP).

–. 2000. The Municipal Role in the Governance of Canadian Cities. In *Canadian Cities in Transition*, edited by Trudi Bunting and Pierre Filion. 2nd ed. Toronto and New York: Oxford University Press.

Sandercock, Leonie, ed. 1998a. *Making the Invisible Visible: A Multicultural History of Planning.* Los Angeles: University of California Press.

–. 1998b. *Towards Cosmopolis: Planning for Multicultural Cities.* New York and London: John Wiley and Sons.

–. 1999. Anti-Hero and/or Passionate Pilgrim. *Plan Canada* 39, 3: 12-15.

Sassen, S. 1991. *The Global City: New York, London, Tokyo.* Princeton: Princeton University Press.

Savitch, H.V., and Ronald Vogel, eds. 1996. *Regional Politics: America in a Post-City Age Urban Affairs Annual Reviews.* Thousand Oaks, CA: Sage Publications.

Savoie, Donald J. 1981. *Federal-Provincial Collaboration: The Canada-New Brunswick General Agreement.* Montreal: McGill-Queen's University Press.

–. 1992. *Regional Economic Development: Canada's Search for Solutions.* 2nd ed. Toronto: University of Toronto Press.

Scott, J. Allen, ed. 2000. *Global City Regions: Trends, Theory, Policy.* London: Oxford University Press.

Scott, Mel. 1971. *American City Planning since 1890.* Berkeley, Los Angeles, and London: University of California Press.

Scott, Richard. 1996. Canada's Capital Greenbelt: Reinventing a 1950s Plan. *Plan Canada* 36, 5: 19-21.

Seelig, Michael, and Alan Artibise. 1991. *From Desolation to Hope: The Pacific Fraser Region in 2010.* University of British Columbia, School of Community and Regional Planning. Published in cooperation with the Vancouver Board of Trade.

Seltzer, Ethan. 2000. Regional Planning in America: Updating Earlier Visions. *Land Lines* (Lincoln Institute of Land Policy) (November): 4-6.

Selznick, Philip. 1966. *TVA and the Grass Roots.* Berkeley: University of California Press, 1949. Reprint, New York: Harper and Row.

Senior, Derek, ed. 1966. *The Regional City: An Anglo-American Discussion of Metropolitan Planning.* Chicago: Alden Publishing.

Shapley, Deborah. 1976. TVA Today: Former Reformers in an Era of Expensive Electricity. *Science* 194: 814-18.

Shils, Edward. 1991. The Virtue of Civil Society. *Journal of Government* (Winter): 3-20.

Simmons, James W. 1977. *The Canadian Urban System.* Toronto: University of Toronto Press.

Simpson, Michael. 1985. *Thomas Adams and the Modern Planning Movement: Britain, Canada and the United States, 1900-1940.* London and New York: Mansell Publishing.

Slocombe, D. Scott. 1995. Understanding Regions: A Framework for Description and Analysis. *Canadian Journal of Regional Science* 18, 2: 161-78.

Smith, C., and D.R. Witty. 1970 and 1972. Conservation, Resources and Environment: An Exposition and Critical Evaluation of the Commission of Conservation Canada (2 parts). *Plan Canada* 11, 1 and 3.

Smith, Patrick. 1986. Regional Governance in British Columbia. *Planning and Administration* 13, 2: 7-18.

–. 1992. The Making of a Global City: Fifty Years of Constituent Diplomacy: The Case of Vancouver. *Canadian Journal of Urban Research* 11, 1: 90-112.

–. 1996. Restructuring Metropolitan Governance: Vancouver and B.C. Reforms. *Policy Options* (September): 7-11.

–. 1998. *Municipalities Come Through: GVRD Regional Context Statements Completed.* Victoria: Ministry of Municipal Affairs. September.

Smith, Peter J. 1994. Alberta's Regional Planning System. *Plan Canada* 34, 4 (July): 42-3. Special edition.

–. 1995. Urban Planning Systems in Metropolitan Canada. In *Canadian Metropolitics: Governing Our Cities*, edited by James Lightbody. Toronto: Copp Clark.

–. 1998. An Ambiguous Enterprise: The Short, Unhappy Life of Canadian Regional Planning. In *Twentieth Century Planning Experience*, 848-52. Proceedings of the 8th International Planning History Conference. Sydney, Aus.: University of New South Wales.

Smith, Peter J., and Patricia E. Bayne. 1994. The Issue of Local Autonomy in Edmonton's Regional Plan Process: Metropolitan Planning in a Changing Political Climate. In *The Changing Canadian Metropolis: A Public Policy Perspective*, edited by Frances Frisken, vol. 2: 725-50. Berkeley: University of California Institute of Governmental Studies; Kingston, ON: Queen's University Institute of Intergovernmental Relations.

Snyder, Gary. 1990. *The Practice of the Wild.* San Francisco: Northpoint Press.

So, Frank, and Judith Getzels, eds. 1988. *Environmental Land Use Planning in the Practice of Local Governmental Planning.* 2nd ed. Washington, DC: International City Management Association.

South Island Sustainable Communities Network. 1998. *A Capital Idea: Alternative Approaches to Growth Management for the Capital Regional District.* Victoria, BC: University of Victoria Faculty of Law and School of Environmental Studies.

Stalley, M., ed. 1972. *Patrick Geddes: Spokesman for Man and the Environment.* New Brunswick, NJ: Rutgers University Press.

Stark, Linda. 1990. *Signs of Hope: Working on Our Common Future.* Toronto and London: Oxford University Press.

Statistics Canada. 1997. *A National Overview.* Ottawa: Statistics Canada.

Stein, Clarence. 1957. *Toward New Towns for America.* With an Introduction by Lewis Mumford. Cambridge, MA: MIT Press.

Stein, David Lewis. 1994a. The Commission of Conservation. *Plan Canada* 34, 3 (July): 55-7. Special edition.

–. 1994b. Thomas Adams: 1871-1940. *Plan Canada* 34, 3 (July): 14-5. Special edition.

–. 1997. Al Leach Got It Down Right – Almost, *Toronto Star*, 16 December.

Stern, D.I. 1992. Do Regions Exist? Implications of Synergetics for Regional Geography. *Environment and Planning A,* 24: 1431-48.

Stevenson, Don, and Richard Gilbert. 2000a. *Restructuring Municipal Government in the Greater Toronto Area.* A Report prepared for the City of Montreal, 30 July 1999.

–. 2000b. State of the Region in 2000. Draft.

Stohr, Walter. 1967. The Definition of Regions in Relation to National and Regional Development in Latin America. A paper presented at the Inter-American Seminar on the Definition of Regions for Development Planning held in Toronto.

–. 1990. Introduction to *Global Challenge and Local Response*, edited by Walter Stohr. London: Mansell.

Storper, Michael. 1997. *The Regional World: Territorial Development in a Global Economy.* New York: Guilford Press.

Susskind, Larry, and Jeffrey Cruikshank. 1987. *Breaking the Impasse: Consensus Approaches to Resolving Public Disputes.* New York: Basic Books.

Sussman, C., ed. 1976. *Planning the Fourth Migration: The Neglected Vision of the Regional Planning Association of America.* Cambridge, MA: MIT Press.

Tamminga, Ken. 1996. Restoring Biodiversity in the Urbanizing Region: Toward Pre-emptive Ecosystems Planning. *Plan Canada* 36, 4: 10-15.

Task Force on Greater Montreal (Pichette Task Force). 1993. *Montreal: A City-Region.* Montreal: Task Force on Greater Montreal. December.

Tennant, Paul, and David Zirnhelt. 1973. Metropolitan Government in Vancouver: The Politics of "Gentle Imposition." *Canadian Public Administration* 16 (Spring): 124-38.

Thomas, Ted. 1993. Edmonton: Planning in the Metropolitan Region. In *Metropolitan Governance: American/Canadian Intergovernmental Perspectives*, edited by Donald N. Rothblatt and Andrew Sancton, chapter 6. Berkeley: University of California Institute of Governmental Studies; Kingston, ON: Queen's University Institute of Intergovernmental Relations.

Thompson, John H., et al. 1962. Toward a Geography of Economic Health: The Case of New York State. *Annals of the Association of American Geographers* 52 (March): 1-20.

Thorpe, F.J. 1961. Historical Perspective on the Resources for Tomorrow Conference. In *Resources for Tomorrow Conference Background Papers*, 1: 1-13. Ottawa: Queen's Printer. July.

Tomalty, Ray. 1996. Governance Reform in the GTA: An Overview of Reform Options. *New City Magazine* 17: 21-5. Special issue.

–. 1997. *The Compact Metropolis: Growth Management and Intensification in Vancouver, Toronto and Montreal.* Toronto: Intergovernmental Committee on Urban and Regional Research (ICURR). February.

Tomalty, Ray, Robert B. Gibson, Donald H.M. Alexander, and John Fisher. 1994. *Ecosystem Planning for Canadian Urban Regions.* November. Toronto: ICURR.

Tonks, Alan. 1996. There's No Turning Back: A Proposal for Change. In *Urban Solutions to Global Problems*, edited by Patrick Smith, Peter Oberlander, and Tom Hutton. Vancouver: University of British Columbia Centre for Human Settlements and Simon Fraser University Institute of Governance Studies.

–. 1999. Summary Notes on the Greater Toronto Services Board Act. A talk presented at the Canadian Institute of Planners 1999 Conference, The City and Its Region, held in Montreal, Quebec, 8 June 1999.

Trepanier, Marie-Odile. 1993. Metropolitan Government in the Montreal Area. In *Metropolitan Governance: American/Canadian Intergovernmental Perspectives*, edited by Donald N. Rothblatt and Andrew Sancton, 53-110. Berkeley: University of California Institute of Governmental Studies; Kingston, ON: Queen's University Institute of Intergovernmental Relations.

Trist, Eric. 1970. Urban North America: The Challenge of the Next Thirty Years. *Plan Canada* 10, 3: 3-20.

Tugwell, Rexford G., and Edward Banfield. 1950. Grass Roots Democracy: Myth or Reality? *Public Administration Review* 10: 47-59.

Tully, James. 1995. *Strange Multiplicity: Constitutionalism in an Age of Diversity.* Cambridge, MA: Cambridge University Press.

Turner, R.K., ed. 1988. *Sustainable Environmental Management: Principles and Practice.* Boulder, CO: Westview Press.

Twelve Southerners. 1930. *I'll Take My Stand: The South and the Agrarian Tradition.* New York: Harper and Bros.

United Nations. 1995. *World Urbanization Prospects: The 1994 Revision.* New York: United Nations.

United States, Department of Commerce, Bureau of the Census. 1994. *Statistical Abstract of the United States.* Washington, DC: United States Government Printing Office (USGPO).

United States, National Planning Board. 1934. *Final Report, 1933-34.* Washington, DC: USGPO National Resources Committee. 1935.

United States, National Resources Committee. 1935. *The Regional Factors in National Planning.* Washington, DC: USGPO.

Urban Development Institute, Ontario Region. 1989. *The Greater Toronto Area Outlook – Year 2011.* Toronto: UDI.

Vance, James E., Jr. 1990. *The Continuing City: Urban Morphology in Western Civilization.* Baltimore: Johns Hopkins University Press.

Vance, Mike. 1996. The Resort Municipality of Whistler. *PIBC News*, May: 6-12.

Vance, Rupert, B. 1935. *Regional Reconstruction: A Way Out for the South.* New York: Foreign Policy Association.

Vander Ploeg, Casey G., Loleen Youngman Bordahl, and Roger Gibbins. 1999. *Cities @ 2000 – Canada's Urban Landscape: New Trends, Emerging Issues.* Calgary: Canada West Foundation.

Wackernagel, Mathis. 1994. Toward Eco-Cities. *The New Catalyst* 27 (Spring): 1-12. Gabriola Island: New Society Publishers.

Wackernagel, Mathis, and William Rees. 1995. *Our Ecological Footprint: Reducing Human Impact on Earth.* Philadelphia PA and Gabriola Island, BC: New Society Publishers.

Walker, Gerald. 1984. Networks and Politics in the Fringe. In *The Pressures of Change in Rural Canada*, edited by Michael Bunce and Michael Troughton, 202-14. Geographical Monograph No. 14. Toronto: York University Department of Geography.

Wallis, Allan D. 1992. New Life for Regionalism? Maybe. *National Civic Review* 81, 1 (Winter-Spring): 19-26.

–. 1993. Governance and the Civic Infrastructure of Metropolitan Regions. *National Civic Review* 82, 2 (Spring): 125-39.

–. 1994a. Evolving Structures and Challenges of Metropolitan Regions. *National Civic Review* 83, (Winter-Spring): 40-53 (Part 1).

–. 1994b. Inventing Regionalism: The First Two Waves. *National Civic Review* 83, (Spring-Summer): 159-75 (Part 2).

–. 1994c. The Third Wave: Current Trends in Regional Governance. *National Civic Review* 83, (Summer-Fall): 290-310 (Part 3).

–. 1994d. Inventing Regionalism: A Two-Phase Approach. *National Civic Review* 83, (Fall-Winter): 447-68 (Part 4).

Wallner, H.P., M. Narodoslawsky, and F. Moser. 1996. Islands of Sustainability: A Bottom-up Approach Towards Sustainable Development. *Environment and Planning* A, 28: 1763-78.

Wannop, Urlan. 1995. *The Regional Imperative: Regional Planning and Governance in Britain, Europe and the United States.* London: Jessica Kingsley.

Watkins, M.H. 1963. The Staple Theory of Economic Growth. *Canadian Journal of Economics and Political Science* 79, 2: 141-58.

Weaver, Clyde. 1984. *Regional Development and the Local Community: Planning, Politics and Social Context.* Toronto: John Wiley and Sons.

Weaver, David Bruce. 1997. A Regional Framework for Planning EcoTourism in Saskatchewan. *Canadian Geographer* 41, 3: 281-93.

Webster, D. 1979. Developmental Planning: State of the Art and Prescription. In *Urban and Regional Planning in a Federal State: The Canadian Experience*, edited by W.T. Perks and I.M. Robinson. Stroudsburg, PA: Dowden, Hutchinson and Ross.

–. 1984. *New Canadian Encyclopedia*, s.v. "regional planning." Edmonton: Hurtig Publishers.

Weller, B., ed. 1981. National and Regional Economic Development Strategies: Perspectives on Canada's Problems and Prospects. Occasional Papers No. 5. Ottawa: University of Ottawa Department of Geography.

Westland Resource Group. 1997. *Report on the Environment: Monitoring Trends in the Capital Region District*, Phase 1. Victoria: Capital Region District.

Whittlesey, Derwent. 1954. The Regional Concept and the Regional Method. In *American Geography: Inventory and Prospect*, edited by P.E. James and C.F. Jones. Syracuse, NY: University of Syracuse Press.

Wight, Ian. 1980. A Policy Plan for Alberta's Peace River Region. In *Environmental Resource Handbook*, edited by Reg Lang and Audrey Armour. Case Study No. 87. Montreal: Lands Directorate, Environment Canada.

–. 1996. Framing the New Urbanism with a New Eco-Regionalism. *Plan Canada* 36, 1: 21-3.

–. 1997. Six Degrees of Interaction. *Plan Canada* 37, 6 (November): 10-11.

–. 1998a. Canada's Macro-Metros: Suspect Regions or Incipient Cititstates? *Plan Canada* 38, 3: 29-37.

–. 1998b. Mediating the Global and the Local: A Natural Crossroads for Planning and Planners? *Plan Canada* 38, 6: 37-9.

–. 1999. The City and Its Region or The Region and Its City? *Plan Canada* 39, 1: 23-7.

Wilber, Ken. 1996. *A Brief History of Everything.* Boston and London: Shambhala.

–. 1997. *The Eye of Spirit: An Integral Vision for a World Gone Slightly Mad.* Boston: Shambhala.

Williams, Deborah. 1991. Planning for Our Tomorrows: The Ecosystem Approach and the Greater Toronto Bioregion. *Plan Canada* 31, 5: 25-31.

Williams, Florence. 1997. Do Fence Me In: Farmland Preservation in Colorado? It's a Fact. *Planning*, May: 18-19.

Williams, Raymond. 1983. *Year 2000*. New York: Pantheon.

Wirth, Louis. 1942. The Metropolitan Region as a Planning Unit. Proceedings, National Conference on Planning, held at Indianapolis, Indiana, 25-27 May 1942. 141-51. Chicago: American Society of Planning Officials.

Witty, David. 1994. Healthy Communities: A CIP Initiative. *Plan Canada* 34, 3 (July): 116-17. Special edition.

Wolfe, Jackie. 1985. Comprehensive Community Planning Among Indian Bands in Ontario. Paper presented at the Annual Meeting of the Association of American Geographers held in Detroit.

–. 1988. The Native Canadian Experience with Integrated Community Planning: Promise and Problems. In *Integrated Rural Planning and Development*, edited by F. Dykeman, 213-34. Sackville, NB: Mount Allison University Small Town and Rural Research Program.

Wood, Robert C. 1959. A Division of Powers in Metropolitan Areas. In *Area and Power*, edited by Arthur Maass, 53-69. Glencoe, IL: Free Press.

Woodcock, George. 1962. *Anarchism: A History of Libertarian Ideas and Movements*. New York: New American Library.

World Commission on Environment and Development (Brundtland Commission). 1987. *Our Common Future*. Oxford: Oxford University Press.

Wray, Lyle. 1997a. Building Regional Success on Citizen-Centered Performance Measurement. *The Regionalist* 2, 4: 62-65.

–. 1997b. Regional Civic Organizations: Strengthening Citizenship in Changing Times. *The Regionalist* 2, 2: 13-20.

Wynn, Graeme, and T.R. Oke. 1992. *Vancouver and Its Region*. Vancouver: UBC Press.

Yale University. 1947. *The Case for Regional Planning, with Special Reference to New England*. New Haven: Yale University Press.

Yaro, Robert, and Tony Bliss. 1996. *A Region at Risk: The Third Regional Plan for New York-New Jersey-Connecticut Metropolitan Area*. Washington: Island Press.

Index

Note: Page numbers in *italics* refer to figures or tables.

Set in The Sans and Slimbach by Artegraphica Design Co.

Printed and bound in Canada by Friesens

Cartographer: Eric Leinberger

Index: Annette Lorek